I0050054

Designing the Human Business

Leveraging Design Thinking to craft powerful and innovative business models

Anthony Mills

‹packt›

Designing the Human Business

Copyright © 2024 Anthony Mills and Packt Publishing

All rights reserved. No part of this book may be reproduced, stored in a retrieval system, or transmitted in any form or by any means, without the prior written permission of the publisher, except in the case of brief quotations embedded in critical articles or reviews.

Every effort has been made in the preparation of this book to ensure the accuracy of the information presented. However, the information contained in this book is sold without warranty, either express or implied. Neither the author, nor Packt Publishing or its dealers and distributors, will be held liable for any damages caused or alleged to have been caused directly or indirectly by this book.

Packt Publishing has endeavored to provide trademark information about all of the companies and products mentioned in this book by the appropriate use of capitals. However, Packt Publishing cannot guarantee the accuracy of this information.

Group Product Manager: Aaron Tanna

Associate Publishing Product Manager: Puneet Kaur

Book Project Manager: Prajakta Naik

Senior Editor: Rounak Kulkarni

Technical Editor: Vidhisha Patidar

Copy Editor: Safis Editing

Proofreader: Rounak Kulkarni

Indexer: Subalakshmi Govindhan

Production Designer: Alishon Mendonca

First published: October 2024

Production reference: 2251024

Published by Packt Publishing Ltd.

Grosvenor House

11 St Paul's Square

Birmingham

B3 1RB, UK

ISBN 978-1-83508-494-6

www.packtpub.com

This book I dedicate to my lifelong partner, Susan Mills – my wife and confidante – without whose support I would not be where I am today nor have accomplished all that I have. She has given me a lifetime of encouragement and support, and for that, I am eternally grateful.

Contributors

About the author

Anthony Mills is a leading global authority on strategic business innovation. He spent over 30 years working in industry, where he led innovation efforts for a broad range of organizations, spanning the Fortune 100 to the entrepreneurial. For the past decade, he has consulted all over the world on strategic innovation, while also serving as the executive director of Global Innovation Institute, the world's leading professional certification, business accreditation, and membership organization in the field of innovation. He previously authored or co-authored five other books on innovation. He also serves as an advisor to start-up accelerators in both Europe and the Middle East. Learn more about Anthony at www.anthonymills.com.

In writing this book, I had the wonderful privilege of interviewing a cohort of incredibly insightful business leaders – each of whom I wish to acknowledge here. They are as follows:

- *Dev Patnaik, CEO, Jump Associates*
- *Marc Payne, Co-Founder and CEO, Electric Innovation*
- *Bob Moesta, President and CEO, The ReWired Group*
- *Ericá Eden, Founder and CEO, Citizen Collab*
- *Lisa Rose, Principle in CX Strategy, City Innovations*
- *Larry Faragalli, Co-Founder and CEO, Brightly*
- *Shawn Crowley, Co-CEO, Atomic Object*
- *Kevin Budelmann, President, Peopledesign*
- *Kerry Bodine, CEO, Group of Humans*
- *Vijay Kumar, Charles Owen Endowed Chair in Design, IIT Institute of Design*
- *Cara Antoine, Executive Vice-President and CTO, Capgemini*
- *Dr. Marc Sniukas, Strategy Advisor + Facilitator, Executive Coach, and Keynote Speaker*
- *Ann Asensio, Vice-President of Design Experience, Dassault Systemes*
- *Ryan Anderson, Vice-President of Global Research and Planning, MillerKnoll*
- *Mohammad Musleh, Zone Digital Services and Solutions Leader, GE Healthcare*
- *Ken Milman, Senior Consultant in Digital Transformation, Marriot International*
- *David Dombrowski, Head of R&D Packaging Open Innovation, Haleon*

About the reviewers

Mike Pinder is a cross-industry sustainable business and innovation consultant, trainer, thought leader, author, lecturer, and international keynote speaker with over 15+ years of experience. He's driven by using innovation to leave the world a better place than we found it. He is the founder of consultancy Explorer Labs, co-founder of research center Wicked Acceleration Labs, Honorary Practice Fellow at Imperial College Business School, Member of the Board of Advisors at **Global Innovation Institute (GInI)**, and Exec-Ed course author at Open University. He consults and leads at Fortune 500 organizations using approaches such as Design Thinking, Wicked Problems, Systems Thinking, Lean Start-up, and Business Model Innovation in both B2B and B2C contexts and has trained over 4,500+ executives globally.

Lisa M. Rose, MPA, seamlessly blends classical anthropology with cutting-edge technology, creating innovative solutions across various industries. With a career spanning over two decades, she has made significant contributions as a strategic leader from start-ups to large enterprises, addressing complex challenges in economic, environmental, and social domains. As a respected alumna-in-residence at Grand Valley State University, Lisa has shared her extensive knowledge of public administration and nonprofit management, enriching the academic community. Her work in Design Thinking and customer experience further showcases her versatile skill set, positioning her as a true polymath who bridges diverse fields to promote a deeper understanding of our world and drive progress toward a sustainable future.

Finbar OHanlon is an Imagineer, Inventor, Entrepreneur, and Coach with over 25 years of experience in creating and commercializing innovations in the technology, media, and arts sector. Finbar led one of his inventions all the way from idea to IPO on the Australian Stock Exchange. He has lived and worked in 5 countries, been granted 16 Patents in relation to cutting-edge technologies covering the Music, Video, Blockchain, Cybersecurity, and AI areas. He is a subject matter expert on the Australian Human Capability standards and is a Certified Innovation Professional and Chief Innovation Officer from GInI (Global Innovation Institute), USA.

Table of Contents

3

Going a New Route – What Business Model Innovation Is   35

4

A Matter of Reason – When, Where, and Why Business Model Innovation Is Needed   53

5

The Master Designer – How to Dissect Business Models and Develop New and Better Ones   91

6

The Business Model Toolbox – An Evolution of Tools for Business Model Innovation   **119**

Part 2 – The World of Design Thinking

7

Thinking Like a Designer   **149**

8

Thinking Like a Scientist – Centering Our Design around Humans   171

9

Acting Like a Designer – The Design Thinking Process in Application — 215

10

Working the Problem Space – Up and Down the Mountain — 265

11

Intermission   309

12

Working the Solution Space – Up and Down the Next Mountain   329

13

Design Thinking's Final Act (So Far) – Our New Solution   395

Part 3 – The Worlds Merged

14

Back to Business Model Innovation – à la Design Thinking   409

15

Execution – Bringing Our Business Model to Life   457

16

The Final Outcome – Consistent Ongoing Success   473

Preface

By now, most have heard of Design Thinking and human-centered design… trying to put one's human subject at the very center of their design efforts so as to develop empathy for them and their situation, and then develop solutions that meet their true needs. Many have also heard of business model innovation… innovating one's overall business model so as to unlock massive new value that's not currently being achieved. However, has anyone ever truly explored how to marry these two together, or how to use them as one practice to create powerful and innovative business models that unleash massive new value by being truly human-centered all around? The answer is "no"… not until now.

This book does precisely that. It first explores the world of business models and business model innovation, so that we have the foundation needed to build on. We come out of this knowing when, where, and (most importantly) how to innovate our business model to unleash massive new value. It then explores the world of Design Thinking – including a deep dive into understanding the human psyche and a step-by-step journey through this process via case study. We come out of this knowing what Design Thinking is and how we can use it to develop empathy for, and an empathic understanding of, our subjects – so that we can then develop solutions that address their true needs and the deeper human aspirations and motivations belying them.

The book then marries these two worlds together. It does this by demonstrating how to use Design Thinking, with its processes and methods, to craft each of the functional elements of our business model so that they are human-centered. This results in a coherent business model whose every attribute is centered on our human subjects and their unique needs. That, in turn, results in the greatest possible chance of success for whatever new business venture we're using the business model for.

The book also shows us how to institutionalize this holistic process inside of larger organizations – so that we can scale it broadly to all of our new venture creation efforts. It finishes by looking at what our future holds, which is actually more human businesses. We invite you on this journey with us.

Who this book is for

This book is for any business leader who has responsibility, in whatever form, for launching powerful and innovative new business ventures.

This includes the following:

- *senior executives in corporate settings with responsibility for identifying, developing, launching, and scaling new lines of business for their organization;*

- *other leaders and contributors in business environments who share in some way in the responsibility for defining, developing, launching, and scaling these new lines of business;*

- *corporate intrapreneurs trying to develop new corporate ventures – including spin-outs and spin-out/spin-ins – on behalf of their organization;*

- *entrepreneurs looking to capitalize on new opportunities by launching entirely new business ventures (startups) on their own.*

Each of these roles can, and will, benefit immensely from the knowledge and insights shared in this book.

What this book covers

This book is divided into three parts with sixteen chapters altogether. They are as follows.

Part 1: The World of Business Model Innovation

Chapter 1, The Value Machine – What a Business Model Is, provides an exploration of what the business model is, and the role it plays in empowering organizations to both deliver and capture value from their activities in various markets.

Chapter 2, Cogs in the Machine – What Makes Up a Business Model, gives a detailed structural breakdown of the business model used to help us understand its respective elements and how they each fit and work together to make the business work the way it does.

Chapter 3, Going a New Route – What Business Model Innovation Is, offers an introduction to business model innovation, including its respective aims and some of its historical uses.

Chapter 4, A Matter of Reason – When, Where, and Why Business Model Innovation Is Needed, takes a look at the situational contexts in which business model innovation is warranted, and what exactly it does for those who pursue it.

Chapter 5, The Master Designer – How to Dissect Business Models and Develop New and Better Ones, provides an introduction to, and exploration of, a specific process for dissecting business models, bit by bit. It also studies their attributes in light of newer goals and objectives, so as to reconstruct a new business model (from the different parts and pieces) that best achieves those newer goals and objectives.

Chapter 6, The Business Model Toolbox – An Evolution of Tools for Business Model Innovation, delves into a historical exploration of the different business model and value proposition tools that have come into play over the past quarter century, including where they each fit into the process and therefore get used.

Part 2: The World of Design Thinking

Chapter 7, Thinking Like a Designer, provides an introduction to the world of Design Thinking and human-centered design, exploring what is at the core of each of these, why so, and how, in general, we are to go about pursuing their aims.

Chapter 8, Thinking Like a Scientist – Centering Our Design around Humans, gives a deep exploration of the human psyche – breaking it down into its respective parts so as to understand what makes humans desire what they do, and why, therefore, they often behave in the ways they do – as well as what that means for us as innovators.

Chapter 9, Acting Like a Designer: The Design Thinking Process in Application, provides a careful explanation of the Design Thinking process, revealing its respective stages and steps, as well as the goals, objectives, and processes associated with each of those stages and steps. It also includes an introduction to the Design Methods used to support the process.

Chapter 10, Working the Problem Space – Up and Down the Mountain, takes a vicarious journey with our case study subjects showing us, in detail, how to undertake the first stages of the Design Thinking process so as to 'work our Problem Space' and come away with a properly reframed understanding of our subjects' outcome needs.

Chapter 11, Intermission, takes another vicarious journey with our case study subjects showing us how, at this intermediate point, to articulate our Point of View and thereafter craft a unique set of Design Principles that we'll work toward in our new solution.

Chapter 12, Working the Solution Space – Up and Down the Next Mountain, takes a final vicarious journey with our case study subjects showing us, in detail, how to undertake the latter stages of the Design Thinking process so as to 'work our Solution Space' and thereby come away with an optimal solution that fully meets our subjects' outcome needs.

Chapter 13, Design Thinking's Final Act (So Far) – Our New Solution, provides a closing examination of the resultant solution and the Unique Value Proposition that it supports – including why ensuring that our solution does in fact support a compelling Unique Value Proposition is so important to us.

Part 3: The Worlds Merged

Chapter 14, Back to Business Model Innovation – à la Design Thinking, offers a detailed exploration, via the case study, of how to apply the overall Design Thinking process (and its methods) to our broader business model. It does this by applying it to, in turn, each of the respective functional elements of our business model so that each one is, in fact, human-centered and coherent.

Chapter 15, Execution – Bringing Our Business Model to Life, provides an examination of all the steps we'll have to take in relation to this process to actually execute our new business model and bring it to life – including the many lessons that the real world will hand us that a conceptual process up to this point couldn't, and how to agilely adapt to those lessons.

Chapter 16, The Final Outcome – Consistent Ongoing Success, goes into an exploration of how to turn this process into a consistent and repeatable one inside any organization, thereby institutionalizing it as a core competency in that organization – plus a look at what the future has in store for us in this context.

To get the most out of this book

To get the most out of this book, you'll want to have a strong understanding of business and how businesses operate – including, in general, the value creation and delivery process and the standard workings of revenues, costs, and profits. You'll also benefit from having at least a rudimentary understanding of innovation practices inside organizations, and where and how those practices fit into the broader strategic aims of the organization.

If you feel deficient in any of these areas, you are encouraged to augment this book with other books on innovation, business models, and Design Thinking, as required.

Get in touch

Feedback from our readers is always welcome.

General feedback: If you have questions about any aspect of this book, email us at customercare@packtpub.com and mention the book title in the subject of your message.

Errata: Although we have taken every care to ensure the accuracy of our content, mistakes do happen. If you have found a mistake in this book, we would be grateful if you would report this to us. Please visit www.packtpub.com/support/errata and fill in the form.

Piracy: If you come across any illegal copies of our works in any form on the internet, we would be grateful if you would provide us with the location address or website name. Please contact us at copyright@packt.com with a link to the material.

If you are interested in becoming an author: If there is a topic that you have expertise in and you are interested in either writing or contributing to a book, please visit authors.packtpub.com.

Share Your Thoughts

Once you've read *Designing the Human Business*, we'd love to hear your thoughts! Scan the QR code below to go straight to the Amazon review page for this book and share your feedback.

https://packt.link/r/183508494X

Your review is important to us and the tech community and will help us make sure we're delivering excellent quality content.

Download a free PDF copy of this book

Thanks for purchasing this book!

Do you like to read on the go but are unable to carry your print books everywhere?

Is your eBook purchase not compatible with the device of your choice?

Don't worry, now with every Packt book you get a DRM-free PDF version of that book at no cost.

Read anywhere, any place, on any device. Search, copy, and paste code from your favorite technical books directly into your application.

The perks don't stop there, you can get exclusive access to discounts, newsletters, and great free content in your inbox daily

Follow these simple steps to get the benefits:

1. Scan the QR code or visit the link below

https://packt.link/free-ebook/978-1-83508-494-6

2. Submit your proof of purchase
3. That's it! We'll send your free PDF and other benefits to your email directly

Part 1 –
The World of Business
Model Innovation

Part 1 of this book explores **business models** and **business model innovation** (**BMI**). This includes defining what a business model is, and therefore what makes up a business model. It explores in even more detail what BMI is, and the conditions under which BMI is needed.

This part finishes with an explicit process for dissecting existing business models so as to build out even newer and better ones, complemented by an exploration of the different contemporary business model tools and frameworks used to aid in this process.

Collectively, *Part 1* gives you all of the background and insights you'll need to be able to use an approach like Design Thinking to conceive and define an entirely new business model for your particular business aspirations.

This part contains the following six chapters:

- *Chapter 1, The Value Machine – What a Business Model Is*
- *Chapter 2, Cogs in the Machine – What Makes Up a Business Model*
- *Chapter 3, Going a New Route – What Business Model Innovation Is*
- *Chapter 4, A Matter of Reason – When, Where, and Why Business Model Innovation Is Needed*
- *Chapter 5, The Master Designer – How to Dissect Business Models and Develop New and Better Ones*
- *Chapter 6, The Business Model Toolbox – An Evolution of Tools for Business Model Innovation*

1
The Value Machine – What a Business Model Is

In your hands, you hold a roadmap – a roadmap that has been designed very carefully to guide you toward using and applying human-centered design in the task of uncovering and deploying the most optimal business model for your situation.

As we will soon see, this will prove crucial to ensuring your new venture – whether in a start-up or an established business – achieves its maximum potential in the crowded marketplace of new offerings around us. Applying what you learn here will ensure your business model delivers exactly what your customers want and need, in a way that yields a maximum return on your investment of time, energy, and resources.

This and the first several chapters of this book lay the foundation for our journey together. In this chapter in particular, we'll learn what a business model is, why it's so crucially important for us to get our business model right, and how business models actually get used. These are all points we'll apply directly in later chapters as we, bit by bit, work through the different layers of business model innovation and design.

Specifically, we examine the following topics:

- **What is the purpose of a business?**: A foundational understanding of why businesses exist.

- **What is a business model?**: A foundational understanding of what exactly a business model is.

- **What makes for a viable business model?**: Insight into what makes a business model viable, as it relates to producing sustainable profits and positive impacts.

- **Why is getting our business model right so important?**: The reasons why every business has to get its business model right if it hopes to succeed.

- **How does a business model get used?**: The early prescriptive nature and the later descriptive nature of business models.

- **Our case study – Intensifi**: An introduction to our case study subjects and their contextual situation.

Don't worry if any of this feels overwhelming in the beginning. As we work through the book, we'll be demystifying each part as we go along. In the end, it will all be understandable, manageable, and actionable for you.

What is the purpose of a business?

It is important to start by first laying the groundwork of understanding why one even has a business in the first place – or in other words, "What is the purpose of a business?"

The answer to this is actually quite simple. The purpose of a business is *to create value*. No business ever lasts that does not create, deliver, and somehow profit from *real value*. Value here is defined as something that's important to its recipient because it achieves some specific outcome for them and is therefore desirable to them.

We must also be very clear on whom value is being created for and what their relative priorities are – as this has been a point of serious contention over the past five decades. On September 13, 1970, economist Milton Friedman introduced, via an essay he wrote in the *New York Times*, the *Friedman Doctrine*. This doctrine held that the sole purpose of a business is to improve the value of the common stockholder's equity. From this was born the idea that the sole purpose of a business was to create value *only for its shareholders*. But over the ensuing 50 years, and with very clear evidence of the degree of harm that so many businesses pursuing that philosophy had caused, sentiments in the business world eventually changed.

This change culminated on August 19, 2019, when a consortium of some of the largest business organizations in the US – under the banner of the **Business Roundtable** (BRT) – declared publicly that *Friedman was wrong…* that the purpose of a business is not just to deliver *shareholder value* but rather to deliver long-term value to *all of its stakeholders*. This included – in addition to its shareholders – its customers, employees, suppliers, the communities in which it operates, and even the earth and its environment.

We conclude therefore – in agreement with BRT – that you, the reader, must first understand, at the most fundamental level, that the purpose of your business is to create value for its customers, employees, partners, communities, environment, and – yes – its shareholders too. They all matter – and how you choose to prioritize them will in many ways determine how successful and long-lived your business will ultimately be.

What those five decades of experience and wisdom have taught us is that businesses that have focused solely on shareholder value have ended up pursuing extremely *short-term (usually quarterly) goals* – what has become known as *short-termism*. This in turn has typically produced very poor *long-term value* for those very shareholders, such that in the end, some years later, they were actually *equity poorer* and *not equity wealthier*.

In contrast, those same five decades have shown us that businesses that have pursued a far more balanced perspective – usually placing customers first, employees second, and shareholders last (as Amazon has), or employees first, customers second, and shareholders last (as Virgin has) – have actually, in the end, produced far greater long-term wealth for their shareholders than any former businesses ever did. This is because **customer orientation** forces the business to think far more long term – in terms of preserving customer loyalty over the long run for ongoing repeat purchases over those customers' (and their descendants) lifetimes – thus leading to true long-term wealth creation.

It's important for us to also understand where this evolution in thinking is headed. To date, it has evolved from shareholders to customers to wider communities. But as we continue to move forward into the future, it's going to evolve even further – to encompass broader ecosystems at large and, ultimately, the entire planet. The implication of this is that the world we have to design our new business models for is an increasingly complex one, with increasingly complex challenges – ones that demand we think about our new business model from far more perspectives than we ever have before.

You are encouraged, therefore – before doing anything else – to first consider and decide who it is your business will be creating value for and what you believe needs to be their relative prioritization among each other.

Now that we understand the *purpose* of a business, we'll turn our attention to the next key question, which is namely, *What, exactly, is a business model?*

What is a business model?

Quite simply, a business model is the arrangement and use of different mechanisms and activities that we will deploy in our business to determine and act on the following matters:

- *who* we will serve;
- *why* we will serve them as such;
- *what* we will serve them;
- *how* we will serve them that;
- *how* we will ultimately *capitalize on* this.

As such, our business model allows us to do each of the following successfully:

- **Select our customer**
  - Decide and define *who* we will serve – will it be individuals, families, small businesses, large organizations, governments, or whom? And inside of that, specifically which ones and under what conditions (when and where) will we serve them?
  - Specifically, what markets and market segments do these represent?

- **Define our purpose**

  - Decide and define *why* we intend to serve these parties in the ways we intend to serve them…

    - What is it we are ultimately trying to empower them to do or achieve?

    - Why is that so important to us?

- **Define our value proposition**

  - Decide and define *how* we will serve these customers – through what forms of value…

    - Will it be through products, services, experiences, some combination of those, or via some other form(s) of value?

  - Decide and define – specifically, and on an ongoing basis – exactly what *value* we will serve our customers (today and in the future) – the *specific* products, services, experiences, and so on – and in each case, the relevant features, functions, and attributes that define them.

  - Decide and define the specific *details* behind each of our unique offerings – with respect to their *product categories* (existing and/or new), the *platforms* they employ and any *product ecosystems* that they necessitate, and the specific *technologies* and *service methods* they will each use (both now and in the future).

- **Define our brand**

  - Decide and define what *brand* we intend to create – in terms of the specific *brand experience* we want our customers to have and the unique *brand promise* (value proposition) we will be making to convey that – as well as what this means to the *positioning* of our business and its offerings (which in turn infers certain pricing tiers that must equate to the perceived value our customers receive from our offerings).

- **Define our go-to-market (GTM) strategy**

  - Decide and define how we will *organize* our business and its ecosystem to be able to do everything herein.

  - Decide and define the specific *channels* we will leverage to *market to, sell to, distribute to,* and otherwise *service* our chosen customers.

  - Decide and define how we will *support* our customers, both pre- and post-sales – so as to maintain their ongoing delight and long-term loyalty. This includes how we will *find them* or they will *find us*, how we will *market to them*, how we will *sell to them*, how we will *fulfill their purchases*, and how we will otherwise *support them* throughout and following this process.

- **Operationalize our business**

  - Organize our business and its ecosystem in the intended ways – so as to achieve everything we've decided to do.

  - Utilize specific assets in the conduct of these activities – whether those are our own, those of our ecosystem partners, or some combination of the two.

  - Design, develop, and validate specific forms of value that we've decided to provide.

  - Produce and deliver specific forms of value that we've decided to provide.

  - Activate and employ specific partners, business ecosystems, and other value networks that we need to use to be able to develop, produce, and deliver these forms of value.

  - Create the brand we intend to become – ensuring we communicate a clear brand message using unequivocal brand language that articulates a unique brand promise to our customers.

  - Deliver on our brand promise – so that our customers actually have our intended brand experience and thereby become loyalists and enthusiasts of our brand.

  - Monetize or otherwise capitalize on the aforementioned activities – to generate revenue in excess of our costs of operations, and thereby produce a profit for the business that we can reinvest back into its ongoing health, growth, and positive impact on the world.

That is what a business model is.

Metaphorically, we can think of our business models as a story. Like a good story, a good business model weaves together a narrative about whom we're serving, why we're serving them, what we're serving them, and how we're serving them – as well as how we hope to prosper ourselves from doing so. And like a good story, it has a great ending with an enlightening win-win outcome for all the "good guys" involved!

As can be appreciated from this explanation, business models can be very complex and involved – and there are certainly a large number of options that we can select from for any one of these areas and activities. Given this, it should be quite clear that in any given business situation, the number of permutations this permits can be astronomical – resulting in what can quickly become a bewildering array of questions to answer.

In most cases, we will already have some general sense of the answers to some of these questions – such as *who* we intend to serve and *why* we desire to pursue that particular customer and situation. But many others of these questions may be completely non-obvious to us, leaving us in the dark as to where to turn for optimal answers to them – and thus the purpose of this book. It's also helpful to keep in mind that a business model exists to serve some concept… it's what allows us to bring that concept to life and deliver it in a way that creates new value, but it is not an end in itself, and, therefore, we should never treat it as such.

Now that we understand what a business model is in its basic essence, let us explore the question of what makes for a *viable* business model.

What makes for a viable business model?

As we look at the set of activities noted earlier that our business model will define, it is the last of these – how we *monetize* and/or *capitalize* on the value we deliver (or how we *commercialize* our offerings) – that is ultimately most important to us.

If we do not have a viable means of converting our capital, energy, and material resources into a real financial stream that *exceeds* our costs of capital, energy, and resources – so as to produce a profit – then our business model is *not viable* – and all of its other points are entirely moot and for naught. The same can also be said of its impacts on societal and environmental planetary needs; if it does not produce *positive* impacts, and in so doing avoid *negative* impacts (perhaps in keeping with regulatory legislation), then our business model is once again *not viable* and we need to abandon it for one that *is viable*.

Ultimately, businesses experience one of two outcomes – either they make a *profit* or they make a *loss* – there is no in between (break-even is not considered a robust or reliable state as it will not last forever). If our business makes a loss for long enough, then it will deplete whatever capital reserves it has (which are used to secure its energy and resources). This clearly is unsustainable. If, on the other hand, our business consistently makes a profit, then that profit can be reinvested back into growing our business and its positive impact on the world. The only viable and sustainable option of these two scenarios is to make a profit!

I invite you, if you will, to recall back to the dot-com bubble of 1999. What happened there was that so many investors and entrepreneurs were so utterly enthralled with this new platform called the Internet and the World Wide Web (they were drunk on its technology) that they jumped head-long into new businesses on the platform without ever bothering to try to stop and ask themselves, "Wait… how are we going to make money on this?" They simply assumed that just being on the internet meant that would somehow magically make money and keep going. It wasn't until after being there for some time that they all started to realize, "Wait… we aren't making any money at this… that stinks… how are we going to keep going at this if the investors don't keep propping us up and giving us more runway?" But a runway – even an extended runway – only lasts for so long when one doesn't have a **viable business model**. And so, consequently, it all came crashing down in late 1999 when the dot-com bubble burst.

But the internet itself hasn't been alone in this. There have, in fact, been many other technologies too – *cryptocurrency*, *non-fungible tokens*, and many others – that have had parties just jump in without first having a viable business model in hand. The thinking is usually that their need to act fast and be a first-mover outweighs their need to have a worked-out business model… that if they wait until they have a worked-out business model, they'll miss the first-mover window of opportunity that currently exists and may never have that opportunity again. Sometimes that is, admittedly, true, and sometimes things do, in fact, work out that way, but they are certainly the exception and not the rule (except in very fleeting technologies such as certain electronic hardware).

The problem – and the reality – in these cases is that the markets are just too new and involve too many new unknowns for anyone to really know for sure which business model is going to work best for it. But – as investor Peter Thiel points out repeatedly in his 2014 book *Zero To One* (paraphrasing)

– the business fundamentals still have to be right (inferring that if they're not, investing in it is a fool's errand). Nevertheless, in entirely new markets, someone has to be the guinea pig… the pioneer who jumps in first. The problem is that very few of those businesses survive the first few years in these markets; in most cases, others enter later on and supplant them with better business models.

Indeed, in most cases, first-mover advantages tend to be quite short-lived (not least because the first-movers go in with a wrong business model and burn through their capital inefficiently), while second- and third-movers – having sat back and watched the mistakes the first-movers made and learned from them – come in later on with far better and more viable business models and quite often take most or all of the market share away from the first-movers because they have a far better offering, a far better value proposition, and a far better business model. In most cases, and in the long run, it ends up being those who wait, watch, observe, think, and study – and then eventually come to market with a very well-thought-out strategy and business model – who survive, thrive, and in the end win in those markets over the long run.

So, in any event – whether a new market or an existing, established market – the bottom line is this… a business model has to be viable in order for the business to be able to survive and thrive over the long run. If the business model is *not viable*, then it is only a matter of time before that business runs out of capital reserves and has to cease its operations – as no investors will dump money into a non-viable business forever.

Therefore – as was noted earlier in this chapter – the purpose of a business is to create value for *all* of its stakeholders. A viable business model lets the principals do just that. A non-viable business model fails to do that, and in almost all cases will prove to be unsustainable over the long run. Adding to this complexity can be activist shareholders – whether they be the shareholders of a publicly traded enterprise or the general partners of a venture capital investment firm – who are not aligned with what makes this business model viable. This is something to be guarded closely against, as it can derail even the best-conceived business venture.

Now that we understand what makes for a viable business model, we can address one of the most critical questions before us – namely, *Why is getting our business model right so important?*

Why is getting our business model right so important?

Getting our business model right is critically important because it is what will determine, when all is said and done, whether our business ultimately *succeeds or fails*. Get our business model right, and it succeeds. Get our business model wrong, and it fails. It's really that simple – as we saw earlier when discussing a viable business model.

Of course, that being said, a business model is just a means to an end, not the end in itself. We use it as the mechanism for value creation and value delivery – creating and delivering something that someone, somewhere needs to address a particular challenge, problem, or other situation. It moves us from a point of lesser value to a point of greater value. The end is actually delivering that value and in doing so, succeeding as a business.

Our business model is thus the magic formula, so to speak, by which we'll be able to connect all the different dots in our business – those on the *demand side* in our marketplace, those on the *supply side* behind the scenes in our industry, and those in between, inside our business (making all the calls and decisions) – to be able to conceive, define, design, develop, produce, deliver, and service the customer value that we offer our customers in a way that remains forever viable and therefore profitable to us and that consequently allows us to continue doing what is we do day in and day out indefinitely.

If we get our business model **right**, then we get to keep doing this, and we'll produce value for all (and wealth for some). If we do **not** get our business model right, then we don't get to keep doing this; we will have failed at some point to create adequate value for one or more of our stakeholders. Of course, as we'll see in our next section, "right or wrong" is a moving target that only has meaning at a particular point in time. It actually comes down to us getting our business model right on an *ongoing, continual basis* – as we constantly explore our way in the dark to learn how our business model has to perpetually change and evolve to remain relevant to the world around us, as well as resilient to changes we'll inevitably encounter.

This is why, as noted earlier in this chapter, the **purpose** of a business is to create value for *all* its stakeholders. A **viable business model** allows it to do just that. A **non-viable business model** fails to do that, and in most cases will prove unsustainable over the long run.

It is, therefore, critically important that, above all else – other than perhaps our strategy – we get our **business model** right if we aspire to survive and thrive in our business over the long run. Our partners, customers, and investors will all thank us for doing so.

Moreover, beyond just getting our business model right, properly **documenting** that business model will serve to align all of our stakeholders. That documentation would include – in addition to our business model – our vision, our overall strategy, and our operational GTM plan at this point. Communicating these things to ourselves, our investors, our partners, and our customers ensures that they have each been scrutinized, tested, and (eventually) aligned on, and that will help to set the course for the business moving forward.

Now that we understand why getting our business model right is so important, let's turn our attention to the final critical question, which is, namely, *How does a business model get used?*

How does a business model get used?

As we've seen, one's business model is how they operate their business so that it is profitable and thus viable over the long run. That is ultimately how one's business model gets used.

But we must distinguish – especially when starting out – between what we *intend* our business model to be (and what we thus document on paper) and what our *actual* business model ends up being after we've learned all the realities and details of our market situation. The first is prescriptive in nature… what we intend it to be. This can work in very established and stable business scenarios. The second is descriptive in nature… what actually occurs. In completely new business scenarios, what actually occurs will become far more prevalent for us. This reality reflects the key knowledge gap we have in any new business situation – which is *why* some amount of iterative business model design and testing effort will almost always be necessary.

In fact, business models and strategies both work in the same way in this regard – in that they are both just *plans* at their beginning and must typically evolve over time. Or, as the late Dr. Clayton Christensen pointed out in his 2003 book *The Innovator's Solution*, the emergent strategy tends to be the cumulative effect of day-to-day prioritization and investment decisions made by middle managers, engineers, salespeople, and financial staff – all of which tends to bubble up from inside the organization.

Consequently, in the real world, especially when we're facing very new business situations and environments, "almost" no one ever gets their business model dialed in just right from the get-go, coming out of the gate. In almost every situation, the business will begin with a particular business model, and then, after some time, come to the realization that certain aspects of that business model simply aren't optimal for the situation. All new business scenarios are full of uncertainty, which is *why* we can **never** just "execute" our business model and hope that we got everything right or that nothing changes from when we first defined it; inevitably that will not work!

This is particularly true for new start-ups starting from ground zero with no prior basis or context for their business model, especially when they are introducing an entirely new-to-the-world value proposition or product category – something that no one else has ever done before. In those cases, they are the pioneer – the first ones to blaze this path – and so, they must create the path as they walk it, discovering all of its necessary details as they press forward. This has been compared to jumping off a cliff with all the parts to build an airplane (but no airplane quite yet) and having to build that airplane on the way down – in the hope we will get it built and be able to fly before hitting the ground (at which point it's "game over" and won't matter anymore).

So, almost no one starts with a perfect business model on Day 1 – a model that lasts forever and in the end looks exactly like the theoretical one they defined on paper and started out with at launch. Or as was so well stated by the 19th-century field marshal and war strategist Helmuth von Moltke (paraphrasing), "*No plan ever survives contact with the enemy*" – from which a similar euphemism in business has been extracted, namely that "*No strategy ever survives first contact with the market*" (a statement made popular by start-up expert Steve Blank). The same can usually be said for business models.

Thus, the way the business model gets used in the real world is – yes, to operate the business in the manner noted previously, but also, and just as importantly, to empower our business to be able to iterate and learn as it goes along – tweaking and adjusting each and every element of its business model as it does so – including *who it serves, why it serves them, what it serves them, how it serves them*, and ultimately how it *capitalizes on that*. This is very important, given that most truly impactful "innovation" inside businesses actually occurs at the business model level – rather than as truly disruptive product or service innovations, or even core technologies (R&D).

Now that we understand what a business model is, what makes for a viable business model, why getting our business model right is so important, and how our business model actually gets used in practice, let's introduce ourselves to **Ian**, **Zoe**, and **Watson** – three fictitious entrepreneurs running a fictitious start-up called **Intensifi** – a business we'll be following in this book, as they strive to apply the principles of this book to their quest.

Our case study – Intensifi

Let us introduce you to Ian McAllister, Zoe McPherson, and Watson Afrik, three entrepreneurs aspiring to launch an entirely new type of digital-technology-enabled, AI-powered, business called Intensifi.

Their idea behind Intensifi is to sell a service – augmented by whatever technology and tools are needed – that allows both consumers and businesses (large and small) to track their every activity and asset. The service would moreover let these users examine patterns of usage and then compare those to their stated life aspirations (it would do this in a purely data-oriented way via the data from embedded sensor / transmitter devices). This will ultimately allow them (via AI algorithms) to map out specific life and asset choices and plans that will allow them to attain their stated aspirations. Their platform can do this because it knows all (in effect) about all the available options to them and how to access them. It is able to match these to their aspirations, thus opening them up to new choices and options they may never have been aware of before – including stuff such as the following:

- What city they live in.
- What job they do.
- What company they work for.
- What home they own or apartment they rent.
- What vehicle they drive – or public transportation they take.
- What they wear (and don't wear).
- When, where, and what they eat (and don't eat).
- When, where, and how they exercise.
- What hobbies and avocations they pursue.
- What extracurricular and volunteer activities they engage in.
- Where they shop.
- What they purchase.
- Whom they associate with professionally – and when and where they do so.
- Whom they associate with personally – and when and where they do so.
- Whom they date and ultimately marry.

- How many children they have.

- When, where, and how they vacation.

- And so on.

Ultimately, Intensifi aspires to leverage AI and technology to optimize everything conceivable about these individuals' lives, and in so doing, empower them to structure and live their lives in an optimal way, in accordance with their personal and professional aspirations. The tool would even "re-route" their lives from any "missed turns" they made by not following its prior prescripts, moving them forward from any point or situation they find themselves in for the remainder of their lives.

Of course, all social relationships involved in the platform work best when all parties involved are mutually using the platform – particularly in the case of dating and marriage.

Given this, I invite you to consider who might be Intensifi's *ideal customer* – and what might be its *ideal value proposition* for those customers. Those are questions we'll explore in a lot more detail further on in this book.

As we go forward, we're going to follow Ian, Zoe, and Watson in their journey of defining, developing, and launching Intensifi – to see how they use the methods and practices of this book in a practical way to achieve their aspiration. As you might guess, they've got a long way to go before they have a fully viable business that's ready to launch and can actually do so. They want to ensure they do so with the best possible (in other words, most optimal) business model they can – one that is truly human-centered in its orientation around their potential future customers.

Summary

In this chapter, we've learned what the purpose of a business is, what a business model is, how a business model gets used, what makes for a viable business model, and why getting our business model right is so important to us and the longevity of our business.

Understanding these things creates the right *foundation* for being able to move forward into our next chapter, where we'll be exploring in much greater detail how a business model breaks down into its constituent parts and how those different parts all have to work *together* with each other for the business to be able to operate effectively and viably over the long run.

Further reading

- *Zero To One: Notes on Startups, Or How To Build The Future, Peter Thiel, Blake Masters, Crown Business, New York, 2014.*

- *The Innovator's Solution: Creating and Sustaining Successful Growth, Clayton M. Christensen, Michael E. Raynor, Harvard Business Review Press, Boston, 2003.*

- *Customer Value Foundation, Gautam Mahajan,* www.customervaluefoundation.com.

Cogs in the Machine – What Makes Up a Business Model

In the previous chapter, we learned about what a business model is, how business models get used, and why it is so crucially important to get our business model right.

In this chapter, we're going to explore how business models are structured, and consequently what their constituent parts are and how they all fit together to define a coherent business model that can accomplish its intended objectives. This will give us a clear appreciation for all the moving pieces and parts of a business model, so that later on we can start to use this insight to design our own business model.

We'll also take a brief look at the fact that there are standardized business model typologies in use around the world, examine some examples of those typologies, see where you can learn more about these typologies, and explore how they are characterized.

We will specifically examine the following topics:

- **Understanding the structure of a business model**: Conceptualizing our business model via a useful framework.

- **Breaking our business model down into its constituent parts**: Breaking our business model down into its core elements so that we can address each one as needed.

- **Understanding the interchangeability of the parts and ensuring the congruity of the whole**: Appreciating how the elements of our business model have variants that are interchangeable, yet have to work together.

- **Recognizing and applying standardized business model typologies**: Developing awareness of the standardized typologies that have been identified and codified by several sources.

We'll also check in with our friends at Intensifi to see what they're thinking about in terms of their prospective business model at this point in the process.

Understanding the structure of a business model

In *Chapter 1*, we learned that our business model is what lets our business define the following:

- *who it will serve;*

- *why it will serve them;*

- *what it will serve them;*

- *how it will serve them;*

- ultimately, *how it will capitalize on doing this.*

In this chapter, we want to go deeper into the actual *structure* and *operation* of a business model to understand what makes up a business model and how its elements all get structured together in a way that lets them work together to produce their intended outcomes and results. By doing this, you'll understand what makes up a business model and (eventually) be able to design, prototype, and validate business models far faster and more easily. That in turn will allow you to develop much better business models, including ones suited to addressing exogenous shocks and/or crucial opportunities in your situation.

As we do this, please keep in mind that we're not yet at the actual business model *design process*, as that process will come later on (in *Chapter 5* to be exact). For now, and in the following two chapters, we're simply laying out all the necessary groundwork for being able to go there. So if you're itching to get to that process, then please be patient as you read along, since you'll first need these elements of groundwork to do so.

Similarly, if you find yourself starting to wonder in this breakdown how this all relates to the business's *strategy*, then, once again, don't worry… we address that question in *Chapter 4*. For now, we just need to understand how a business model gets built and operated *structurally*. In *Chapter 3*, we'll explore what it means to *innovate* that business model, and in *Chapter 4* we'll look at a more *functional* framework for the business model – all of which will lead us up to *Chapter 5*, where we'll explore the process for designing, prototyping, and validating business models, as well as *Chapter 6*, where we'll look at different tools and models for doing so.

Introducing the Future Lens Business Model Framework

To achieve our goal here, we introduce the **Future Lens Business Model Framework**, or **FLBMF**, as shown in *Figure 2.1*. This is a *structural framework* for the business model – as opposed to a *functional framework* (which will be explored in *Chapter 4*).

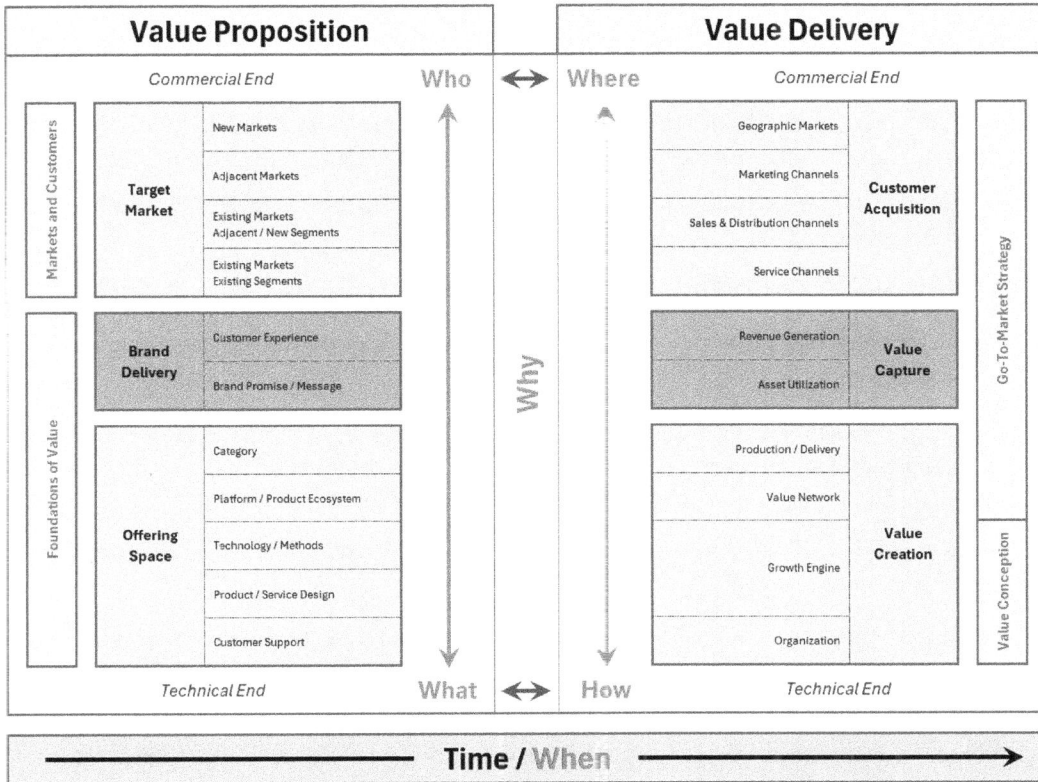

Figure 2.1: The Future Lens Business Model Framework

This framework is a direct reflection of both the elements of a business model and how they all fit together to make that business model work. Understanding this framework allows us to examine different business models to see how they each use these elements to operate the way they do.

We will explore this framework by starting at the topmost level and then working our way down through its structure. As we go about explaining it, we will introduce some specific nomenclature associated with it.

At the framework's *topmost level*, we have the entire (overall) framework, which – holistically – models the business model so that once its respective elements have each been explicitly defined and spelled out, it prescribes exactly *how* that business model works.

At the framework's *second level*, it is divided into two halves – one on its left side and one on its right side:

- On its *left side* we have **Value Proposition**. All of the elements of this side define the business' *unique value proposition* (as its name suggests).

- On its *right side* we have **Value Delivery**. All of the elements of this side define the business' approach to *value delivery* (as its name suggests).

> **Note**
>
> I created this framework in 2016 for the consulting firm Legacy Innovation Group (`www.legacyinnova.com`) and subsequently used a variant of it for Global Innovation Institute (`www.gini.org`) under the name *The Gini Business Model Innovation Framework*, or *BMInF*.

At the framework's *third level*, these two halves (sides) are each further divided into three specific **Domains of Potential**, or **DOPs**:

- The Value Proposition's DOPs are, respectively, **Target Market**, **Offering Space**, and **Brand Delivery**.
- The Value Delivery's DOPs are, respectively, **Customer Acquisition**, **Value Creation**, and **Value Capture**.

At the framework's *fourth level*, each DOP is divided further into a set of **Points of Differentiation**, or **PODs**. Altogether, the framework contains twenty-two different possible PODs so that a given business model ends up being some structured collection of a *subset* of these PODs.

These DOPs are explained in greater detail later in the section entitled *Breaking our business model down into its constituent parts*.

Now that we have this framework and can see its overall structure, we'll dive down into exploring its different elements so as to understand what they each mean. This will allow us to understand the framework at a detailed level, and thereby be able to use it in our work.

We should also mention that, should you already be wondering how this (and other frameworks to be introduced in this book) compare and contrast to some of the very prolific business model tools in use, such as the *Business Model Canvas*, for example, well then never fear. That topic, together a careful survey of all such tools in use (there are many), is explored in detail in *Chapter 6*. By that point, you'll have amassed a much greater insight into designing, building, and validating business models, where such tools will make even more sense to you.

Framing out the key anchor points of our business model

We pause at this point to observe that this framework – as any such framework must – addresses the *six key questions* of our business model:

- **Who** – Who we will serve, and therefore deliver value to (our main customer).
- **What** – What we will serve them (our offering).
- **Where** – Where and how we will find and connect with them (our channels).
- **How** – How we will conceive, create, produce, and deliver this value for them (our value factory).
- **Why** – Why we will do all of this (the unique problem we are trying to solve for them).
- **When** – When we will do all this (which may be now or later; at certain specific times or always) Your business model can be dynamic in this regard, and therefore change and evolve over time.

Associated with this, we see that each of the two sides of the framework shown in *Figure 2 1*, *Value Proposition* and *Value Capture*, reflects a specific spectrum of questions with anchor points at their ends:

- **Value Proposition: WHO ↔ WHAT**

  Offering Space / Brand Delivery / Target Market

- **Value Delivery: WHERE ↔ HOW**

  Value Creation / Value Capture / Customer Acquisition

Centered in between these is the question of *WHY*, which – in keeping with proper human-centered design practice – places customer needs and motivations front and center in the business model, which are crucially important to the entire model!

These five anchor points reflect the first five fundamental questions of our business model.

The last POD introduces the question of *WHEN*… a *sixth anchor point* the business model must answer. This is often a question that has to be addressed in light of the timing of one or more key trends, especially when we are trying to launch a new business endeavor that's intended to intersect a specific *emerging situation* associated with this trend, such as a new type of market need. In such cases, careful *trends analysis* has to be undertaken to define what that proper (most opportune) *intersection point* should be – that point in time when the organization must launch the new business model and its related solution. This is important because quite often we're designing a new business model to be launched two or three years from now, and so this has to address the question of – often in the context of that *trend timing* – when **is** and **is not** the right time to launch that particular business model, because launching it too early or too late can have disastrous effects (too early, and the market is not ready for it yet; too late, and it may have missed a critical window of opportunity).

Sometimes, it will take longer to work out this detail than is required for the rest of the business model. When that is the case, we can proceed with working on the rest of the business model while holding off on answering that question until additional foresight is developed. Doing so should not, however, delay us in working toward our intended solution at that point in time. We will need that solution ready whenever that time does arrive.

If desired, the team designing the business model can leave open a number of different options in the business model, and then select one of them later on as they get closer to launching the new solution to the market, at which point they should have greater clarity on which of those options will prove optimal for the situation as it has emerged.

Yet another feature of this framework is that its two halves – **Value Proposition** and **Value Delivery** – each have a **Commercial End** and a **Technical End**:

- The **Commercial End** involves the **who** and the **where**, both of which deal with monetizing value in the marketplace.

  It is quite likely that those in the business who bring the necessary insights to this area are those involved in the business' commercial operations, such as sales and marketing staff, for example.

- The **Technical End** involves the **what** and the **how**, both of which deal with creating value from inside the business.

  It is quite likely that those in the business who bring the necessary insights to this area are those involved in the business' technical operations, such as engineering, manufacturing, supply chain, and other operational staff.

In between these are **Brand Delivery** and **Value Capture**, both of which serve to bridge their respective ends. It is often that those who are charged with these DOP must be versant in both commercial and technical operations, and thus serve as hubs inside the business. For example, on the Value Proposition side, these may be product management or marketing professionals, while on the Value Delivery side, these may be finance or operations professionals.

Finally, for the sake of greater clarity and better understanding when applying this framework, its two sides are also structured into distinct **aggregated areas of focus** (as seen in its light-yellow-highlighted boxes):

- Its **Value Proposition** side is structured into **Foundation of Value** (Offering Space + Brand Delivery) and markets and customers (**Target Market**).
- Its **Value Delivery** side is structured into **Value Conception** (portions of **Value Creation**) and **Go-To-Market Strategy** (Customer Acquisition, Value Capture, and the remainder of Value Creation).

In both cases, these offer additional clarity to the business model conceptualization and design process so that those designing the business model can be clear about which (overall) area of the model they are focusing on. We'll get into that design process (in detail) in *Chapter 5*, but for now, and for the next two chapters hereafter, we're laying all the groundwork necessary to be able to explore that process.

Breaking our business model down into its constituent parts

Now that we've introduced the preceding structural framework for our business model, our next step is to use it to break down that business model into its constituent parts representing its different possible variations. These constituent parts start with the twenty-two different PODs alluded to earlier.

Don't worry if this exploration (and the next section on interchangeability and congruity) seem a bit abstract to you, because shortly we'll examine some examples from situations we're all familiar with, showing what they look like in practice.

Understanding the points of differentiation

A given business model – as represented in the framework used here – will structurally comprise some subset of variants of the 22 PODs. For each of the six main DOPs, one or more of the PODs will thus be employed.

In some cases – such as with Target Market, for example – the Domain can work with one POD or with multiple PODs, depending on the aspiration at hand. So, in this case, for example, the Target Market may be a single new market, or else a new market plus an adjacent market.

In other cases – such as with Value Creation, for example – the Domain will almost always work with some combination of variants of the PODs. So, in this case, for example, Value Creation will entail some form of organization using some form of growth engine and some form of value network to produce and deliver the value being created.

In this way, each Domain of Potential will consist of the unique POD variants defining it.

Consequently, each of the different PODs offers us the opportunity to differentiate our business and our offering in the marketplace, hence their names – they are distinct prospective PODs that we can use on behalf of our business and its efforts to stand out and succeed in the marketplace.

The PODs are listed in *Figure 2.2* at the third indented level, underneath their respective DOPs:

DOMAIN	INTENTION
VALUE PROPOSITION	**OUR DEFINED VALUE PROPOSITION**
MARKETS & CUSTOMERS	**How we define our intended markets & customers**
Target Market	*Who our targeted markets & customers are*
New Markets	Pursue an entirely new-to-the-business market
Adjacent Markets	Pursue a market that is adjacent to the business' current markets
Existing Markets – Adjacent/New Segments	Pursue a new or adjacent segment of a current market
Existing Markets – Existing Segments	Pursue the business' existing markets & segments
FOUNDATION OF VALUE	**The unique foundations of value we will deliver**
Brand Delivery	*How we will deliver our brand*
Customer Experience	The specific CX we will deliver to our customers
Brand Promise / Message	The specific brand promise we make & brand language we use
Offering Space	*What we will provide to our markets & customers*
Category	The specific category of product or service we will offer
Platform / Product Ecosystem	The specific platform / product ecosystem used for our offering
Technology / Methods	The specific product technology or service method used in our offering
Product / Service Design	The specific product or service we will offer
Customer Support	How exactly we will support our customers in using these offerings
VALUE DELIVERY	**OUR DEFINED APPROACH TO VALUE DELIVERY**
GO-TO-MARKET STRATEGY / VALUE CONCEPTION	**How we will create value & take it to market**
Customer Acquisition	*How we will connect & communicate with our customers*
Geographic Markets	The specific geographic markets we will target
Marketing Channels	The specific marketing channels we will use to reach those customers
Sales & Distribution Channels	The specific sales & distribution channels we will use to sell to them
Service Channels	The specific service channels we will use to service them
Value Capture	*How we will capture value for ourselves (commercialization)*
Revenue Generation	How we will generate revenue from these activities
Asset Utilization	What assets we will utilize and how we will utilize them to deliver this value
Value Creation	*How we will conceive, create, and deliver value to our customers*
Production / Delivery	The specific methods of production and delivery we will leverage
Value Network	The unique value network we will employ (partners and suppliers)
Growth Engine	How we will continue to innovate in the future to continue driving our growth
Organization	How we will organize ourselves to so conceive, create, and deliver this value

Figure 2.2: 21 Points of differentiation inside the six Domains of Potential

Listed here are twenty-one PODs. The twenty-second POD is the question of **when**, or **timing** – which applies equally to all the other elements of our business model.

Applying our points of differentiation

Collectively, these PODs define everything (structurally) about a business model that must be defined for it to be executable and thereby achieve its intended outcomes and results.

For example, we may decide – for various strategic reasons – that we are going to do the following:

- Serve a market that is entirely new to our business – **Target Market / Who**.

- By offering it a new product in an existing product category that uses a new technology comprising a specific product platform that can be extended further in the future – **Offering Space / What**.

- In the process, stating that this new product will transform their lives via its four key attributes (**Brand Promise / Message**) and then actually doing so in a way that absolutely delights them [**Customer Experience (CX)**] – **Brand Delivery**.

- Using direct-to-consumer paid advertising (**marketing channel**), direct-to-consumer sales (**sales & distribution channel**), and contracting service providers (**service channel**) for customers in North America (**geographic market**) – **Customer Acquisition / Where**.

- By having our Advanced Innovation Department (**growth engine**) inside our technical R&D unit (**organization**) develop this product, and having our own captive manufacturing facilities produce and ship it (**production / delivery**), using parts supplied by our network of strategic suppliers (**value network**) – **Value Creation / How**.

- By utilizing both our own assets and those of our suppliers, plus those of our customers (their mobile phones) (**asset utilization**), and having these customers pay us directly through our online e-commerce site – **Value Capture**.

- Starting 12 months from now – **When**.

Taken together, these seven DOPs – made up of its unique PODs – structurally define our unique business model, including who we will deliver value to; how we will conceive, create, and deliver that value; where and how we will connect with those customers; what we will promise and deliver to them; and how we will ultimately capitalize on doing this.

Such is the power of a structural business model framework.

Consequently, when thinking about our business model *structurally*, we can dissect it into precisely such a framework to understand its structural elements and how they each function together to achieve our intended outcomes and results.

Understanding the interchangeability of the parts and ensuring the congruity of the whole

Given this structural framework, a key point to be made here – and an important takeaway for the would-be Business Model Designer – is that business models are structurally modular – meaning that variants of its PODs inside their respective DOPs are, for the most part, interchangeable with each other.

Interchangeability of the parts

As a result of a business model's structural modularity, we can take out one variant of a POD and substitute for it a different variant of that same POD to come up with a slightly different business model.

Likewise, if one substitutes enough of these POD variants, they will end up with a very different business model (structurally).

In this sense, we can see that a business model is structurally not unlike a clothing wardrobe… you have any number of shirts, pants, shoes, belts, ties, sweaters, and scarves that you can mix and match to yield an incredibly high number of outfit combinations Some of them will be formal, others will be casual, others athletic, and on and on the combinations will go. So, structurally, in a business model, we can quite readily remove any POD variant and substitute for it some other POD variant to create a nearly infinite number of business model combinations, each presenting a specific flavor of business designed to achieve a specific type of objective and outcome. Such is the interchangeability of its parts.

Congruity of the whole

There is an important caveat, however. Despite our ability to very easily mix and match different structural elements (PODs) of our business model, in the end, the final business model has to be *internally congruent.*

This means that each of its parts (PODs) must make sense in the context of the other parts, and consequently be able to function coherently as a congruous business model.

For example, it would not make sense to say that we were going to develop and launch an entirely new product category to create an entirely new market inside a geographic region that did not experience any real need for that category, and on whom, as a result, our brand promise would fall on deaf ears. That would not represent an internally coherent business model: its parts would not be congruous with one another. For most experienced Business Designers, their experience and common sense will tell them this.

In contrast, if we were to say that we were going to develop and launch a new product that was an incremental extension of our current product lines, for our existing core markets and segments, using our established sales, marketing, distribution, and service channels, via an existing Innovation Group inside our current organization, using our existing brand messaging and language, and our existing value capture methods and assets, then certainly everything about that would be coherent and internally congruent. It would make full sense.

There are of course many intermediate aspirations that fall somewhere between those two, for which more research has to be undertaken to justify them and ensure they are internally congruous. An example of this might be the intention to develop a new product platform to reach an adjacent market we've never previously operated in, with a new brand promise / message / experience, but that otherwise exists inside our present geographic markets, using new sales and marketing channels to reach that market, but otherwise using our existing organization / growth engine / value network / production and delivery assets / revenue-generation methods to do so. In this scenario, there are certain well-known and well-understood PODs, as well as certain new, less-well-known and less-well-understood PODs involved. This makes the risk level higher than in the fully well-known case, and consequently, more research has to be undertaken to ensure that the business model we will be using for this situation is in fact not only a congruous one, but an optimal one – one with the highest possible chances of success.

Examples of novel business models using this interchangeability and congruity

To further illustrate the interchangeability of the parts to yield a new congruent business model, it is helpful to explore certain business models in which the normal constructs of the prevailing business model of that industry and time were upset by removing certain of the standard PODs and substituting for them quite different PODs that weren't commonly being used in those scenarios.

To this end, the following is a series of examples of business models that – at the time of their entry into the market – were quite novel and unique for their time. By contrasting them – via the Future Lens BM Framework – with the prevailing business models of their industry at that time, we can see what was so unique and novel about them that set them apart from the other players in their industries at the time.

To do this, we will encircle the areas of the Future Lens BM Framework where the business model was uniquely different from the prevailing business model of its industry at that time.

Our first example is that of business models used for the **On Demand / Sharing Economy**, such as those associated with Uber, Airbnb, and ZipCar (see *Figure 2.3*). The following was the scenario here:

- **Offering Space** was new in that it involved a new technology platform for that industry (mobile app-based service with listings and a reservation system).

- **Brand Delivery** was new in that using a mobile app to access the On-Demand Service was an entirely new Customer Experience in that industry that delivered an entirely new brand message / brand promise , all of which was packaged and priced in a manner acceptable to the market.

- **Target Market** was not new. It was pulling from the same market that already existed for traditional taxi and hotel services.

- **Value Creation** was new in that it employed a radically new business ecosystem of private partners (the value network) from which it now created the core value.

- **Value Capture** was new in that it used a radically new approach to asset utilization. These companies owned none of the assets themselves; they were all held by private citizens; the businesses simply accessed them. Their approach to Revenue Generation was not novel, however; just as with traditional services, they charged for using the service.

- **Customer Acquisition** was somewhat new in that it used the free mobile app to access the service, deliver the service, and charge for the service. Thus, to the extent that a mobile app was now the Sales & Distribution channel, as opposed to a direct B2C interaction model, this was a part of the new business model. The balance of this Domain was not new.

As can be seen from this example, delivering the On-Demand Economy business model represented a combination of new variants in five of the six domains. This made for a fairly radical departure from the prevailing business model of these industries, and therefore a substantially impactful new business model (as well as very lucrative businesses). Because this business model was so novel compared to the prevailing business model of these industries, it in some ways disrupted these industries.

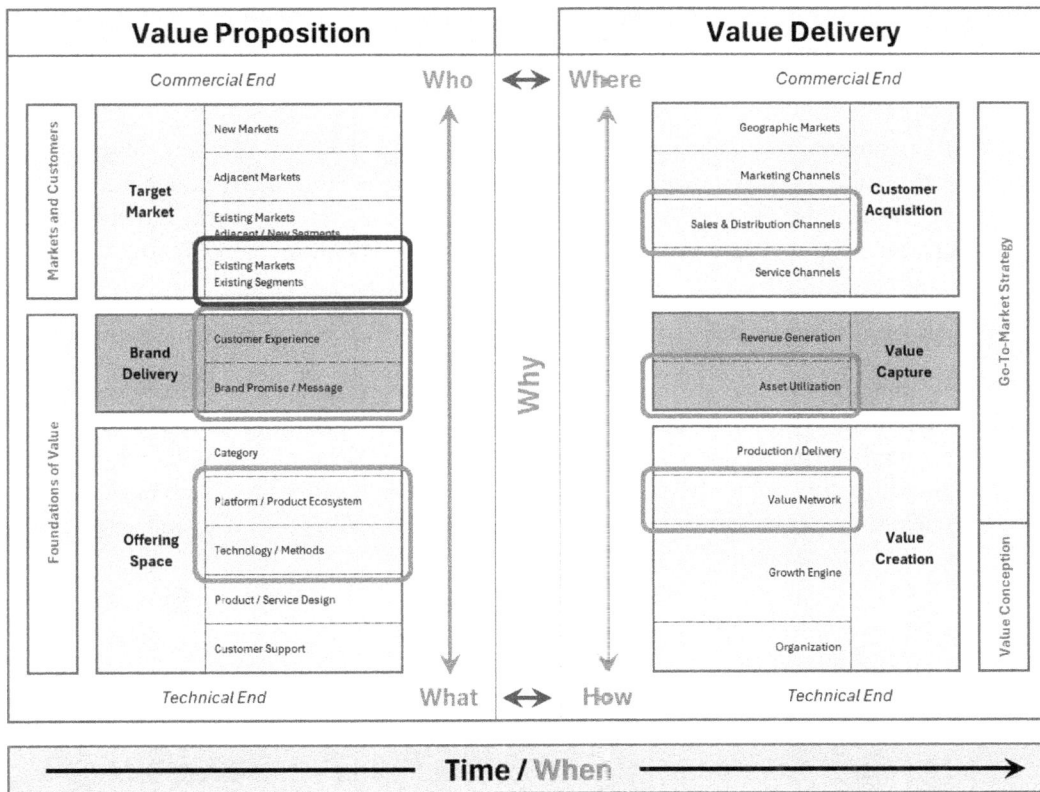

Figure 2.3: The Future Lens BM Framework showing changed PODs
for the On-Demand / Sharing Economy Business Model

Our second example is that of the **Software-As-A-Service**, or **SaaS**, business model, such as those associated with Adobe, Salesforce.com, and Concur (the very first business to employ this business model) (see *Figure 2.4*). The following was the scenario here:

- **Offering Space** was not new. The core product technology being marketed and sold did not fundamentally change when the switch was made to the SaaS business model.

- **Brand Delivery** was new in that the customer experience associated with a more transparent and seamless automated update process and a monthly subscription arrangement was a very different – and in general much more palatable – experience than that of the previous annual upgrade model.

- **Target Market** was, in general, not new. When these businesses made the switch to the SaaS model, they were targeting the same customers as they had with their prior business model. The exception to this was the extent to which the new SaaS model allowed them to attract new customers that they would not have attracted otherwise with their older model – a coincidental benefit.

- **Value Creation** was new to the extent that the manner in which the product was delivered to customers was now new.

- **Value Capture** was new, in that the approach to revenue generation – monthly subscription versus the annual upgrade – was a radical departure from the prior model, and this did three things… it smoothed out the income model for the business, it made payment and upgrading more palatable for the customers, and it brought on select new customers as a result.

- **Customer Acquisition** was not new. Nothing fundamentally changed about the sales, distribution, marketing, and/or service channels these businesses were using, or about their geographic presence.

As can be seen from this example, switching over to the SaaS business model involved a combination of new variants in three of the six domains. This switch represented not a radical departure, but rather a pivot of the prior business model, and therefore a more moderate level of evolution (but one that was very financially beneficial to these businesses). Because this business model has been readily accessible to all businesses in the software industry, it has tended to bolster the overall industry rather than disrupt any one piece of it.

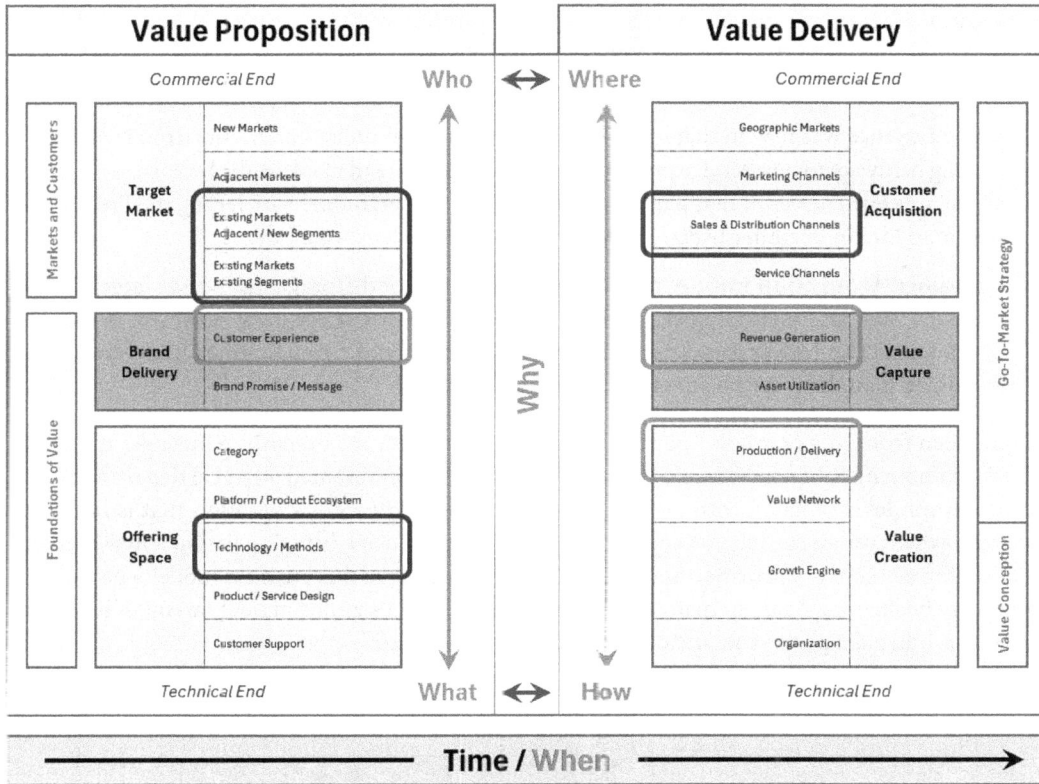

Figure 2.4: The Future Lens BM Framework Showing Changed PODs
for the Software-As-A-Service Business Model

Our third example is that of the **Cloud / Freemium** business model, like that used by Cloud Storage vendors Box, Dropbox, and Google Drive (see *Figure 2.5*). The following was the scenario here:

- **Offering Space** was new in that Cloud Storage solutions, when they were first introduced, represented an entirely new product category that did not previously exist. As such, this category disrupted the market for private on-site storage hardware and support services.

- **Brand Delivery** was new. Because Cloud Storage was sold, delivered, and used in a new and different way, it represented a radically new customer experience together with a completely new brand promise.

- **Target Market** was partially new in that Cloud Storage, first of all, targeted the same customers as were previously using private on-site storage, so the segment did not change, but it also allowed these businesses to go after and secure an entirely new set of customers who previously had no effective backup solution, and thus a far broader overall market.

- **Value Creation** was new in that the method of production was completely new relative to on-site storage, and the approach to delivery was likewise completely new, as it depended on connectivity and cloud infrastructure, which the prior solution did not.

- **Value Capture** was new in that it radically shifted the asset utilization model from customers owning hardware to now service providers holding the assets, and likewise, the revenue generation model was even newer in that it used a monthly subscription model – including the Freemium option to lure in beginner users – rather than a one-time hardware buy.

- **Customer Acquisition** was not new in the sense that Cloud Storage businesses largely used the same sales and marketing channels as hardware vendors. It was new, however, in that its distribution channel was completely different, as was its service channel, which likely saw much less usage than the prior business model's service channel.

As can be seen from this example, Cloud Storage – married with the Freemium business model – involved a combination of new variants in all six domains! This represented a radical departure from the business model associated with private on-site storage hardware – a situation that is not that uncommon whenever an entirely new product category is introduced, bringing with it a new market and disrupting an older one. Furthermore, the Freemium element of this business model – because it allowed these businesses to lure in many new users – represented a significant new variant of business model that produced a positive financial impact for the businesses.

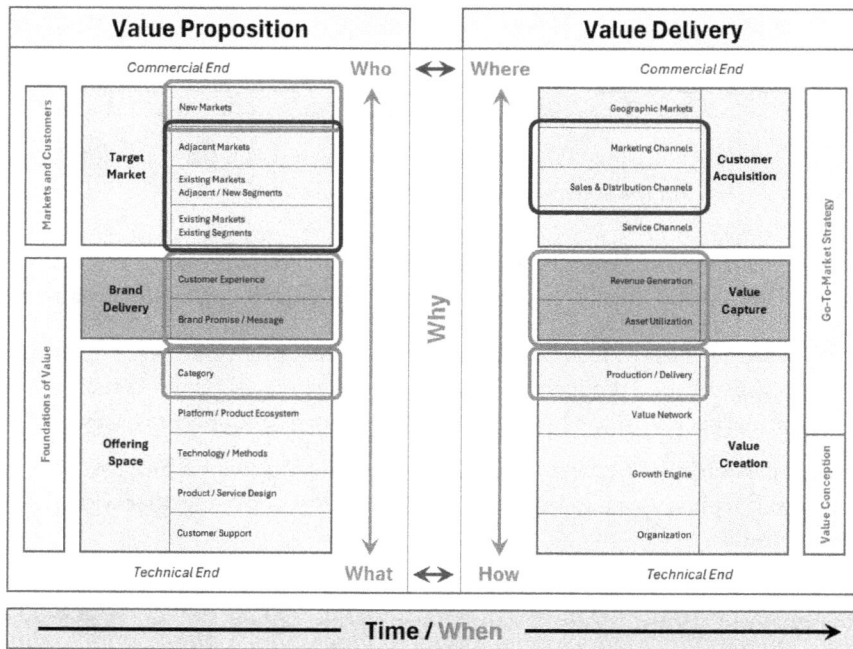

Figure 2.5: The Future Lens BM Framework showing changed
PODs for the Cloud / Freemium business model

Now that we've seen these examples and better understand what's involved in such a structural framework of the business model. spend some time thinking about your own (prospective) business model in this context. What might its constituent elements be and look like? You don't have to necessarily answer those questions right now, as we'll do more of that later on when we're exploring the business model design process, but for now, just spend some time thinking about them in this context.

Now that we understand the interchangeability of the different parts of our business model, and that each of those parts have to work together harmoniously to ensure we have a coherent business model that works effectively – just as we saw in the preceding examples – we can next think about different types of business models and what makes them work the way they do. To this end, we'll explore the topic of standardized business model typologies, including how these typologies have been used throughout modern history to accomplish some very specific types of business outcomes. As we'll see, there are scores of such typologies, some of which may provide inspiration for our own business model.

Recognizing and applying standardized business model typologies

In addition to understanding business models *structurally* – as has been presented thus far in this chapter – the Business Model Designer must also be aware that there have been, and continue to be, good efforts put into characterizing standardized business model typologies as they are applied to certain business scenarios – some existing and some new.

These efforts are especially insightful whenever a new business model arrives on the scene that the world has never seen before, and which a new entrant is using to either create a new market or else disrupt an existing market – or possibly both.

For the most part, most of the business model typologies in use today have been with us for some time now, having evolved out of the emerging needs of the Industrial Revolution and the evolving consumer patterns of the 20th century. Consequently, most business models in use today are anywhere from 40 to 100+ years old. That being said, every once in a while, an entirely new business model typology is conceived and born, and successfully comes to market (but not surprisingly, certain other attempted typologies have ended up being stillborn and unsuccessful in the marketplace, and as a result have largely faded into history now).

The historical evidence would also seem to suggest that new business model typologies arise in clusters and waves, owing to the interactions of different trends in the world. Thus, at any given time, a new wave of three, four, or five new business model typologies might appear on the scene all at the same time, with an intervening lull of many years (or even decades) before such a wave occurs again. Indeed, the three business model typologies profiled previously in this chapter all arrived on the scene at around the same time, in the mid to late 2000s (2004 – 2011 to be exact).

Some common examples of these standardized business models include – but are certainly not limited to – the following:

- Barter
- Cross-selling
- Franchising
- Freemium
- Licensing
- Lock-In
- Long Tail
- Mass Customization
- Open Source
- Razor and Blade
- Subscription
- Trash-to-Cash
- White Label.

Given the existing resources and literature documenting these standardized business model typologies, it is not necessary to repeat them here. Instead, we refer you to two resources that can, and may, prove helpful in this context.

The first such resource is the 2014 book *The Business Model Navigator* by Oliver Gassmann, Karolin Frankenberger, and Michaela Csik. This book briefly explores how to navigate your business model in the context of a changing environment, and thereafter presents characterized profiles of 55 different standardized business model typologies. The book's authors made the claim that – at the time – these 55 different business models were responsible for 90% of the world's most successful companies. Consequently, studying these typologies can help one appreciate how they each work, including what is unique and special about the structure and operation of each one, and why that is so important to them.

The second such resource is the website **Business Model Ideas** (www.businessmodelideas.com) operated by *updoon GmbH* in Germany (the author has no affiliation with this platform nor the business that operates it). This site, which is researched by academic professionals and entrepreneurs, seeks to scout out and analyze the business models of successful companies and start-ups from all over the world. The site purports to publish the details of a new business model every week into its database of 200+ business models. Here are some examples of companies whose business models have been profiled here:

- Alphabet
- Airbnb

- Amazon
- Aldi
- Patagonia
- monday.com
- Tupperware
- SpaceX
- Peloton
- Glassdoor
- Forbes
- Sonos
- Nike
- Dollar Shave Club
- TED
- Pinterest
- Spotify
- Only Fans
- On Running.

This site also contains a very useful section called *Business Model Patterns – Proven Strategies To Design Successful Business Models*. The business model patterns it presents are collections of themes, structures, mechanics, and strategies used to delineate the different business model building blocks. We can use these for inspiration, and as blueprints, whenever we are designing our own business models. We would do this by examining the design theme and then asking ourselves what it might mean for our business. Each design theme includes a short explanation, some key questions we can ask ourselves about it, and links to analyses on the site illustrating that particular design theme in use.

Using this site can potentially expose the Business Model Designer to new business models as they emerge on the scene, further enlightening them on what is working in the context of current trends and their drivers, and why so. The Designer can then use these new insights – as appropriate – when building out their own business model, should there be structural elements involved that are relevant and pertinent to their particular situation. (Note, again. that we'll be exploring the actual Business Model Design process later on, in *Chapter 5* of this book.)

This site and its database – formerly known as *Business Model Gallery* – were originally conceived and curated by Marc Sniukas and Georg Stampfl. Dr Sniukas is the co-author, together with Parker Lee and Matt Morasky, of the book *The Art of Opportunity: How to Build Growth and Ventures Through Strategic Innovation and Visual Thinking* (*Wiley, 2016*). Dr. Sniukas is also the author of the book *Business Model Innovation as a Dynamic Capability: Micro-Foundations and Case Studies* (*Springer Nature, 2020*).

Back to Intensifi – What about its business model?

Back at **Intensifi**, our friends Ian McAllister, Zoe McPherson, and Watson Afrik (remember them from the previous chapter?) are starting to spend more time together thinking about both exactly what type of solution they should offer and what sort of business model they should use to do so.

While they haven't settled yet on the details of either one of these, they are at least now starting to look at different types of business models and think through the structure and operation of each one in an effort to discern which type of business model might work best for their situation, and exactly what structure it should have in light of the options and resources they will likely have available to them.

Consequently, they are kicking around some different ideas for this business model, but at this point, these are all just conceptual in nature. Until they get further down the road – into the thick of their market situation and what sort of solution will prove most optimal for it – they are a long way away from defining the best business model to use for it. But for now, they at least understand what they should be looking at structurally, and how to think about these different parts, and how they each may or may not fit together to accomplish their specific goals and aspirations for the business. Otherwise, they understand that it's a bit too premature to propose a particular business model for their venture, as they don't yet have the insights they need into the solution to do so adequately.

That being said, some of the structural options they are kicking around and considering include the following:

- **Who** – Busy established professionals, young aspiring professionals, well-established seniors.
- **What** – A comprehensive tech solution, a simplistic design-first solution, a subscription service.
- **Where** – In developed markets (North America, Europe), in developing markets (Latin America, and so on).
- **How** – Via VC-backed innovation development, via technology partners, via existing platforms.
- **Why** – To help people optimize their lives given the latest and greatest digital tools available to them.
- **When** – As soon as they can pull together sufficient resources to start market testing different concepts and learning from the market how it responds to each of these; thereafter, as soon as they can assemble all the necessary parts and pieces, to go to market with a properly validated and reliable concept.

Time – and proper human-centered design practice – will (as we will learn bit by bit) bear out which of these options will prove optimal for them. For the time being, however, it would seem that Ian, Zoe, and Watson are at least more or less clear on what their **why** and **when** are. The biggest questions for them will thus be their **who**, **what**, **where**, and **how** – though, of course, the journey of learning about any of these may hold the potential for reshaping their **why** and **when**. Time will tell about this!

Summary

In this chapter, we've learned how to think about business models *structurally*, via their *structural definition* – including what their respective elements are and how those elements must all work together interactively to produce a coherent business model that's capable of achieving our unique aims and aspirations.

We've also learned what the key *anchor points* of our business model are – the *who*, *what*, *where*, *how*, *why*, and *when* that our business model has to answer if it is to succeed – and, likewise, how that certain of these – in particular the *who* and the *where* – are more *commercial* in nature, while others – in particular the *what* and the *how* – are more *technical* in nature, with each being prototypically answered by different parties in our business.

Furthermore, we've learned – and seen examples demonstrating – that *variants* of the business model's different elements can all be interchanged to yield a nearly infinite number of combinations, and that these variants have to produce a *coherent* and *internally consistent* business model if they are to function effectively and achieve the business model's intended outcomes and results.

Finally, we've learned that there are standardized business model *typologies* that we can all learn from and apply whenever defining our own unique business models.

Understanding these different insights offers us much more detail around which to conceive, define, and design our unique business model. It also sets us up for our next chapter, where we'll be exploring the topic of *business model innovation* and what it means to innovate one's business model – including what this has looked like historically.

Further reading

- *The Business Model Navigator: 55 Models That Will Revolutionise Your Business*, Oliver Gassmann, Karolin Frankenberger, Michaela Csik, Pearson, Edinburgh Gate, Harlow, UK, 2014.

- *The Art of Opportunity: How to Build Growth and Ventures Through Strategic Innovation and Visual Thinking*, Marc Sniukas, Parker Lee, Matt Morasky, Wiley, Hoboken, NJ, 2016.

- *Business Model Ideas*, updoon GmbH, www.businessmodelideas.com.

3

Going a New Route – What Business Model Innovation Is

In the previous chapter, we learned how business models are structured, and thus how to think about them structurally. That included an exploration of their constituent parts and how those parts all fit together to create a coherent business model that addresses the fundamental questions of any business – namely, *who*, *what*, *where*, *how*, *why*, and *when*. We also learned about standardized business model typologies that have been applied successfully in numerous cases across countless industries. All of that gave us new key insights we can use when designing our business models.

In this chapter, we're going to explore the topic of **business model innovation** – including what it *means* to "innovate" a business model, what business model innovation has historically looked like over the years, and what some of the approaches and tools that are used for pursuing business model innovation in recent times are. This will enlighten us further on not only *what* business model innovation is, but, more importantly, what's happening in our world today that this *drive* for business model innovation has become so imperative. It will also show us how – in response to that drive – different parties have conceived different methods and approaches for thinking about and pursuing business model innovation.

Specifically, we will explore the following topics:

- **Doing business in a new way**: We'll explore what innovation is, what business model innovation is, and what makes a business model truly innovative.

- **Appreciating the history of business model innovation**: We'll learn a bit about the history of business model innovation and what has changed about it in recent years (and why so).

- **Why does business model innovation matter so much today?**: We'll learn why business model innovation is so important to us today in light of the realities surrounding us.

- **Technology as a key enabler**: Finally, we'll learn about the different ways that technology is playing a critical role in business model innovation.

Understanding these insights will give us a foundation to think about business model innovation in our situation, according to our context. This is a necessary prerequisite for being able to start designing a new business model that at least has the possibility of being innovative.

We'll also check in with our friends at Intensifi to see what they're up to now concerning their new venture and its business model. We'll find out if they're taking the time to be thoughtful about their business model or if they're just jumping headfirst into the market with their best guess.

Doing business in a new way

Our goal here is to take a new route – to do business in a new and novel way. In other words, we're looking to pursue an innovative new business model. But this raises two quite natural questions, namely, "What is business model innovation?" and "What makes a business model truly innovative?" Let's tackle those questions.

What is innovation?

If you've been around the innovation space long enough, you'll know right away that there are *hundreds* of definitions of this word, hence some of the confusion and consternation around the term.

For our purposes, we're interested in **business innovation**. In that context, we define *innovation* as doing something in a new or novel way that creates new value for *both* the recipient and the deliverer.

Recall from *Chapter 1* that we defined **value** as being something important to its recipient because it achieves some specific outcome for them and is therefore desirable to them.

Combining these concepts, we're trying to do something in a new or novel way that – for both the recipient and the deliverer – creates something important to them, because it achieves a specific outcome for them and is therefore desirable to them.

That's our goal with innovation. On a more practical business level, this typically manifests as "the commercialization of an idea" – with commercialization inferring that the "idea" was commercially successful because it unlocked sufficient new value on both sides.

Of course, when we talk about "new and novel" here, these are extremely relative concepts. The "thing" that's involved may not be new to the world; it may only be new to a certain part of the world (a certain market) that previously had no access to it. So, to *them*, it *is* new and novel, and thus an innovation. Similarly, unlike social innovation, where the value tends to be skewed to one side (only the recipient), in the context of *business innovation*, acceptable value must be attained by **both sides** – to make delivering the innovation worthwhile to the business, and paying for it worthwhile for the customer – given that both sides naturally have limited resources and certain outcome-maximization goals to address.

This is reflected in the classic Venn Diagram of **desirability**, **feasibility**, and **viability** shown in *Figure 3.1*, which was first introduced by Dr. Peter M. Drucker over 60 years ago. Here, it's clear that for something to even qualify as an innovation, it has to first be *desirable* to its recipient because it meets a real human outcome need, be *technically feasible* given the capabilities available to us presently, and be *viable* as a business effort, meaning we, as a business, must benefit from it somehow, typically starting with revenues, and then profits, and then finally brand uplift:

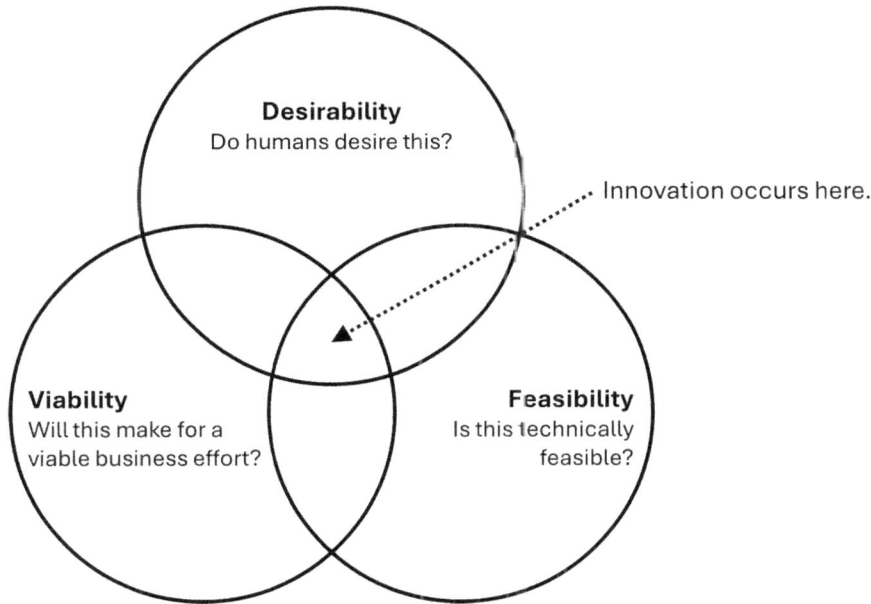

Figure 3.1: The Venn diagram for desirability, feasibility, and viability

Of course, this concept also applies in the *public sector*, to government organizations. It's just that the question of *desirability* focuses more on the broader positive social and economic impacts of a particular territory rather than on the individual wants and needs of a single customer, and the question of *viability* is answered differently given the different funding mechanisms involved.

So, now that we understand what we mean by *innovation*, we need to address the question of "What, exactly, is *business model innovation*?"

What is business model innovation?

Given that the most fundamental purpose of a business model is to enable the transactional *exchange of value* between two or more parties (encompassing numerous *types* of value), **business model innovation** is defined as the use of a new business model in which some *aspect* of that business model is completely **novel** for its context – either for the market being served (on the demand side), or for the business itself (on the supply side).

By *novel*, this means that some key aspect of that business model has never been used in that particular situation or context before – it is entirely foreign to the parties involved. This, as noted previously, can be on either the *demand side* or on the *supply side* – or, more impactfully, on **both sides**, where it is new and foreign to *everyone* involved – the business and those it serves.

So – thinking back to our structural framework – the business model might be novel in terms of *who* is being served, *why* they are being served, *what* they are being served, *where* they are being served, *how* they are being served, or *when* they are being served. But, what we generally find – and this has been borne out by multiple parties' research, including our own – is that the greatest impacts will occur when *multiple* of these structural variables are novel *together* – in combination. In most cases, it is this **combination** of multiple aspects of your business model – not just one aspect – that produces a *truly impactful outcome* for both the business and its market(s).

There are a couple of points that are worth taking note of here. *First*, when we talk about "novel" in this context, that novelty can be very *nuanced*. Sometimes, even a really small change in the business model can be highly effective at unlocking new value, and thus impactful to both the business and its customers – and even possibly disruptive to its industry and markets. Thus, the *scale* of novelty is relative to the situation, and need not always be massive. *Second*, "novel" can sometimes include *pivoting back* to something that worked well in the past, went out of fashion, but is now all of a sudden relevant again. That's why it's important to avoid pursuing innovation – including *business model innovation* – purely for the sake of innovation… purely for the sake of being "new" and/or "novel." Sometimes, that's not always the best course of action – especially when we consider *all* of our stakeholders and understand the *full* consequences of our actions. Sometimes, it's best to consider all of our options – including things that worked well in the past that can be useful again.

What makes a business model truly innovative?

Thinking back to the standardized business model typologies that were introduced in *Chapter 2*, what we find when we study different business models is that what makes them truly *novel and unique* (innovative) tends to lie in the following aspects:

- How they establish and maintain the *customer relationship*.

- How they *position* and *brand* themselves – and the brand message / brand promise / brand language they use to do so.

- How they leverage different *assets* and *partnerships* to deliver their value.

- How they *monetize* the value they deliver.

Everything else tends to be, in most cases, more or less standard and traditional.

The truly important nuance here isn't in these elements in and of themselves, but rather in exactly what the business *does with them* and *how* it uses them to unlock greater value for everyone.

This is because it isn't always enough just to solve a market's problems and deliver on its needs. Instead, *how* a business goes about solving those problems and delivering on those needs is critically important. It must do so in a way that truly *resonates* with these customers' deep-rooted **aspirations**. This will start to become more apparent in *Chapter 4* when we explore a *functional framework* (rather than a *structural framework*) for the business model. But it will become even more apparent (fully apparent) when we move into *Part 2* of this book and start looking at human-centered design practices. As we'll eventually learn, emerging capabilities often open up new areas of our business model, including new products, services, and experiences, and within those, new functionalities and other attributes that let us address human needs in even deeper and better ways.

Appreciating the history of business model innovation

While innovative business models aren't entirely new, what we see happening today is that the conditions surrounding them, and thus the drivers driving them, *are* in many ways new. Today, there are constant and rapid changes happening all around us that are altering the environment surrounding business models, giving an entirely new context to their use. Let's examine this further.

Recognizing the roots of a movement

Business models are not new. Ever since societies chose to engage in peaceful value exchange between one another (as opposed to exploiting each other through war and plundering), business models have been in use – dating back to the Neolithic era.

Likewise, business model *innovation* isn't entirely new either. It has also been occurring throughout history, and in particular ever since the Industrial Revolution, where whole new categories of goods and whole new types of financial transactions emerged on the scene.

What has changed today, however, is the *pace* and *scope* of business model innovation, as well as society's level of *comfort* with it – to the point that it would be fair to say that today, there is a *movement* around business model innovation. But to truly appreciate the historical roots of this movement, we must first look at 20th-century examples of business model innovation.

To start with, and to set a bit of context, if we were to ask people back in the 20th century about *innovation*, what most would immediately think of is **product innovation** – or in some rare cases, **service innovation**. In other words, innovation was generally only thought of back then in terms of *what* was being sold and delivered – not *how* it was being sold and delivered.

It was not at all well understood at the time that some of the most impactful innovations could be had not by changing *what* the business offered, but rather by changing *how* it offered that. In other words – by changing its *business model*.

That being said, it wasn't that innovative business models didn't exist in the 20th century – they did. Purpose-designed business models were used throughout the 20th century. It's just that they were nowhere near as *common* as they are today, nor did they appear as *frequently* as they do today.

To appreciate the roots of this movement, let's take a look at just a few of the innovative business models that arose during the 20th century – some of which have become very iconic now. These include the following:

- **1920s:** *Schick* (razor blades) and *Morton* (iodized salt).

- **1930s:** *Dollar General* (extremely low prices).

- **1940s:** *Dick's Sporting Goods* (focused sporting goods retail).

- **1950s:** *McDonald's* (fast food) and *Toyota* (compact, fuel-efficient sedans).

- **1960s:** *Walmart* (rural superstores and "hypermarkets"), *Domino's* (pizza delivery), and *Southwest Airlines* (no-frills air travel).

- **1970s:** *FedEx* (efficient global parcel delivery), *Costco* (membership-based retail), and *Toys R Us* (focused toy retail).

- **1980s:** *Blockbuster* (movie rentals), *Dell* (fast, efficient, built-to-order computers), *Intel* (captive marketing ("Intel Inside")), and *The Home Depot* (focused DIY retail).

- **1990s:** *Netflix* (streaming video), *Amazon.com* (extensive e-commerce), *Starbucks* (the Italian café experience), and *eBay* (P2P auction retail).

Each of these business models was the product of applying innovative thinking to how new value could be delivered to existing markets – often without ever changing the core product or service being sold.

Given that each of these business models is rooted in *capitalism* (in one form or another), they've all been influenced to a degree by the writings of Adam Smith, such as in *The Wealth of Nations*, and his philosophies surrounding capitalism, free markets, and free market economies.

What's changed now?

So, innovative business models have been around for at least a century now, especially in the service industries such as retail, parcel, and food service. But things have changed – a lot – in recent years regarding business model innovation. What's changed in particular?

What's *changed* in more recent times has been the **pace** at which new business models have been developed and used for breakthrough and disruptive innovation in various industries. That pace has *increased dramatically* since the 1990s when the first *digital* business models began to appear on the scene. This has largely been due to new software technologies that enable *radically different business models* – especially *digital* business models – impacting both the *demand side* and the *supply side* of the business model.

Another thing that has *changed* in more recent times has been the academic **study and understanding** of business models – largely in response to this increased pace. This is reflected in the evolution of academic thinking around business management in general. Up until the 1980s, that focus was on understanding the macro environment and the competitive forces at work in that environment. Then, it became more about understanding and orchestrating the internal dynamics of a business (its knowledge, resources, capabilities, and so on). Today, it is much more about network dynamics and business ecosystems, recognizing the need for businesses to work together to effect a much grander and more holistic value proposition inside their markets. This is having a noticeable impact on the business models we use today.

In many cases, this has led to the "unbundling" of traditional markets and industries – especially in B2B markets – where the value equation has been broken down into increasingly smaller chunks that an increasingly greater number of startups have been addressing in increasingly more focused ways. This is most commonly done through a new technology or technological approach that addresses that particular part of the equation much better, typically through some type of automation. This is seen, for example, in the marketing industry, where *hundreds* of startups with all manner of highly focused niche *marketing automation tools* have entered the market and automated some very specific pieces of the overall marketing effort. This has arisen largely due to the increased democratization of access to the means of production and service delivery, which itself has occurred on account of the digitalization of so much of what's required to operate a business now.

This has resulted in these markets being splintered into hundreds of niche players servicing only a tiny portion of the market with a highly optimized solution. This has meant that customers in these markets have had to put forth additional effort to aggregate the different platforms and tools they need. However, the overall outcome of doing so has, overall, been far better for them. This is one more reason why markets tend to *welcome* this type of business model innovation and why business model innovation is expected to continue indefinitely – disrupting any number of traditional markets and industries along the way.

This is reflective of a much broader economic phenomenon occurring – one known as "the long tail." This is a powerful economic force in which markets have been shifting away from the traditional mass markets of one-size-fits-all mass appeal to an unlimited array of unique offerings suited to every need and taste – the true rise of the niche market. As the cost to reach and service customers has dropped precipitously, the proliferation of such niches has risen commensurately, as witnessed by the nearly infinite array of choices in streaming video entertainment, in online vendors to purchase from (even if through a centralized channel such as Amazon.com or alibaba.com), and in numerous other domains. This can have a massive impact on how we think about our markets – who they are and how we access them – and thus a massive impact on our business model. This phenomenon is well-documented in the 2006 book *The Long Tail: Why the Future of Business is Selling Less of More*, by Chris Anderson.

Business model innovation – as we now know it today – is truly a child of the 21st century!

Why has this changed?

This has changed largely on account of **three things**:

1. **Business model innovation matters a lot more today**: There's a rapidly growing appetite in our world today for new business models (fueled in large part by the next two things).

2. **The embrace of technology as a key enabler**: The ubiquity of automated digital software that enables new business models that previously couldn't have been possible – including ones with a far better overall **user experience (UX)**.

3. **The availability of new methods and tools**: The broad availability of new methods and tools for conceiving, designing, testing, and validating new business models – methods and tools that didn't exist before the 21st century.

We'll explore the first two of these in the next two sections. We'll explore the third later in *Chapter 5*.

Why does business model innovation matter so much today?

Business model innovation matters – and is far more relevant today – than it ever has been before in history!

This is on account of what's happening around us in our world today – and will continue to happen throughout the foreseeable future. Namely, there are three key forces at work shaping this reality:

- the fading allure of product, service, and experience innovation in isolation;
- society's growing comfort with – and to a large degree, expectation of – new business models that unlock greater value for them;
- the pace and scale of technological transformation – especially digitalization.

Let's explore each of these in greater depth.

The fading allure of product, service, and experience innovation in isolation

In writing this book, I interviewed Dev Patnaik and Ryan Baum, CEO and Partner, respectively, of the innovation and strategy firm *Jump Associates*.

A key insight that Dev and Ryan pointed out, and which we discussed at length, was that – inside different markets – there is this rapidly growing appetite today for new, innovative business models.

This is fueled by the perception – an accurate perception I believe – that product innovation, service innovation, and even customer experience innovation – when used alone in isolation – are no longer having the same appeal, allure, and impact that they once did. In most cases, markets just aren't responding to those types of innovation (when used in isolation) like they did 20, 30, 40, or 50 years ago. These types of innovation (when used in isolation) have lost their appeal – *especially in traditional industries*. The more traditional the industry, the more this seems to be the case.

A part of the reason for this is that new technologies (and therefore new products, services, and experiences) are coming at us much faster than they ever did back in those days – causing each one to have *incrementally less allure* to it. Thus, the time we spend being infatuated with each one continues to become increasingly shorter! It is also, however, because in many cases, the fundamental *assumptions* and *orthodoxies* of our industries are being challenged and upset – such that the business model formulas we've historically used simply no longer work so well. A great example of this is the blurring of customer expectations arising out of new cross-industry innovations – such as where food delivery tracking is expected now because it's been made available by Uber on account of having driver tracking built into its platform. This raises all sorts of new requirements for businesses that simply didn't exist previously.

So, what does a business do once their product innovations, service innovations, and experience innovations no longer have the same pizzazz and appeal that they once did (especially since most of them are so incremental)?

At that point, the only thing left to do is to pursue *business model innovation* – to try to find some novel new way of "turning over the apple cart," so to speak, to unlock even more value for everyone. At some point, this becomes the **only way** a business will ever be able to stand out and differentiate again – especially when every other business in that market has, by and large, access to the same technologies and capabilities – almost all of which can be outsourced from outside partners today (except for in very heavy R&D-intensive industries).

Consequently, CEOs – recognizing this, and not wanting to be the CEO under whose watch the business tanked – are naturally looking to business model innovation – often in desperation for answers they don't have otherwise. For clear evidence of this, you need look no further than the 27th Annual Global CEO Survey conducted by the professional services firm PwC (published in January 2024, PwC's 27th Annual Global CEO Survey, PwC, https://www.pwc.com/gx/en/issues/c-suite-insights/ceo-survey.html). In that survey, PwC found that 45% of CEOs didn't believe their organizations would be economically viable in 10 years if they stayed on their current path and didn't reinvent their business model somehow. We've seen recent examples of this, such as when GE failed miserably at trying to capitalize on lean startup concepts, or when 3M over-bureaucratized its innovation process and initiated a long dry spell. The business model has to be right under all circumstances and at all times!

So, CEOs are quite worried and stressed out about what's happening around them; some are even, it would seem, outright terrified of their organization's dismal prospects for the future. So, quite naturally, their attention is turning to finding novel new business models that will unleash massive new value to turn around those prospects and ensure their business is still relevant to a future world. That is the reality we're being faced with today, and consequently, the pressure to reinvent your business model continues to intensify.

Society's growing comfort with – and expectation of – new business models

In writing this book, I interviewed Mark Payne, CEO of the innovation firm *Electric* (and former CEO and founder of *Fahrenheit 212*, a leading innovation firm that was sold to the design agency *Frog*).

One of the key things that Mark pointed out, and which he and I discussed at length, was that because so much business model innovation has occurred over the past 20 years, society has, by and large, become extremely comfortable with it – especially the younger and more digital-native generations. The sort of changes that we witnessed in the 2010s with SaaS, the cloud, and other major business model transformations have acculturated these generations to business model innovation – to the point that they've not only become comfortable with it but rather are starting to expect it – and in some cases demand it.

Consequently – and especially as these digital-native generations grow older and fill out more of the mainstream – the use of business model innovation has, to a large degree, already become second nature to them. They see it as being part and parcel of how business gets done anymore – a key component of competitiveness in any industry and any market. If they can conceive and implement an innovative new business model that undermines some older, preexisting business model – by delivering greater value than that one does – then that is what they're going to do. Of course, by doing so, they typically benefit both themselves and the markets being served – at the expense of the incumbent organizations who choose to not adopt the new business model. With shifting population (age) dynamics, this reality will only continue growing stronger in the future. Indeed, once the majority of consumers in the marketplace are fully digital natives, and no longer just Baby Boomers, these expectations will only increase.

The world is increasingly recognizing the incredible impact that business model innovation is having on industries and markets – and the incredible power it's unleashing for both businesses and their customers!

According to Mark Payne, innovators and entrepreneurs shouldn't squander this moment in time – when the world is so open to, and eager for, new business models that unlock far greater value. We should work hard to capitalize on this moment in history and make the most of it – for all involved!

The pace and scale of technological transformation

The third key force that's shaping this reality is the pace and scale of technological transformation today – which probably comes as no surprise to anyone who's paying attention.

Technology is *the most significant enabler of business model innovation today*. New technological advances are making business models possible that simply weren't possible in the past – given the technologies available at those times.

In particular, there has been an advent of digital technologies and capabilities – and the ensuing digitalization of nearly everything that business organizations do. This – together with the new types of *automation* it has enabled – has been responsible for the vast majority of the business model innovations we've witnessed in the past 20 years. It has made business model practices such as open architectures, cloud computing, electronic commerce, SaaS frameworks, the sharing economy, and much more possible. If it were not for these newer technology-enabled business model practices, our whole business landscape would look *radically different* from how it does today!

Fortunately, at least for those who have arrived at this point, we know how to leverage these technologies to unlock greater value. The **key** to doing so lies in what any digital transformation effort should ideally be trying to do – namely go back to *first principles* and reengineer the value model based on those, by leveraging these new capabilities.

What's meant by "going back to first principles" here is *starting over* with our customers, their situations, and their needs – abandoning whatever previously-held *assumptions* were baked into our prior understanding of these things and our present solutions for them – and starting again from **ground zero** – with the customers, with their situations, and with their needs (their *real needs*… not what we might have perceived them to be in the past, which may or may not even be relevant anymore). Then – given the digital capabilities now available to us – we should ask if there is some **fundamentally better and different way** of addressing that situation to meet their needs. Quite often, this may look *nothing at all* like how our current business addresses that situation and meets that need, and thus nothing at all like our present solutions. It may mean taking an *entirely different approach altogether* – one based on delivering an entirely different type of value using an entirely different set of resources and capabilities. This will often *inherently* change something about our business model – just by going back to these first principles and starting over with an entirely new perspective emboldened by entirely new capabilities. Doing this can unlock tremendously greater value on both sides, in any number of forms – including intangible forms such as speed, convenience, flexibility, transparency, and so on (all of which the customer may value).

And so – with these technological transformations – business model innovation becomes an incredibly important and powerful way of delivering breakthroughs, disruptions, and even transformative innovation!

The implications for business organizations

As a result of the preceding three forces, and the realities they create, business organizations all over the world have started to realize – quite rapidly – that there may be **massive opportunities** in front of them to expand their market presence and leadership through an innovative new business model. Doing so can result in all the benefits noted in *Chapter 2* – greater market share, new-to-the-business markets, new-to-the-world markets, more esteemed positioning, and greater brand equity – all of which typically translate into some type of growth. Fortunately, the nice thing about business model innovation is that it also tends to deliver far greater value to our markets – and ideally to all of the stakeholders we impact, including addressing the many existential challenges we face today.

Of course, business organizations have to be prepared to accept the different *changes* this will require of them – including anything from restructuring their organization, to taking on new partners, to developing new capabilities, to developing new relationships, and so on – *including* the *exclusion* of other things they've done in the past (which inherently means letting go of those things).

Now, on the *other side* of this "opportunity" is the existential **threat** that a competitor – including an upstart that didn't exist previously in someone's industry – becomes the *first* in that industry to introduce an innovative new business model to it. This can portend **disruption** to the incumbent players of that industry. Consequently – and to ward off this threat of disruption – business organizations should be watching diligently for this possibility – and be prepared to alter their business model as needed – either *preemptively* before anyone else can or *responsively* to remain relevant to their markets. In this sense, business model innovation can serve as a type of *insurance* – in which you join or even lead this disruptive movement (and therefore are *a part of the disruption*), rather than sitting around and waiting to be disrupted by it – not what any business organization in its right mind wants to do!

Whether they're pursuing business model innovation preemptively or responsively, either case will require the organization to be "in shape" to do so – including being able to restructure itself agilely as needed, something that doesn't always come easy or natural for large, bureaucratic organizations. This is a warning to be heeded.

This is perhaps an opportune moment for you to pause and reflect on what these forces might mean to your prospective new business model. How will the fading allure of product, service, and experience innovation, society's growing comfort with and expectation of new business models, and the pace and scale of technological transformation affect what you and your business are trying to achieve? These are important questions you need to be considering and pondering as we move ahead.

Embracing technology as a key enabler

It perhaps comes as no surprise that today, technology is playing a significant role in business model innovation. It's doing this in several different ways, each of which we'll take a look at in turn.

Using digital technology as the key enabler for a business model

Technology's first role is as a **key enabler** of innovative new business models.

In particular, it enables *entirely new ways* of doing the following:

- connecting with customers;
- engaging customers;
- communicating our brand to customers;
- producing value for customers;
- delivering that value to customers;

- monetizing the value we deliver;
- addressing the various socioeconomic and environmental challenges we face.

This is largely on account of modern *digital technologies*, such as the following:

- the internet
- local and wide-area networks (including Wi-Fi)
- cellular voice and data
- mobile computing
- cloud computing
- cybersecurity
- biometric identification
- streaming audio and video
- the **Internet of Things (IoT)**
- the **Global positioning systems (GPSs)**
- artificial intelligence and machine learning
- automation/autonomous operation.

When used together, these different technologies enable a nearly infinite number of possibilities for different value propositions that solve different customer problems and make it possible to capture value through different forms of monetization. There's no end to how these technologies can be combined to solve different problems for different customers, and in so doing deliver differentiated value to them. The only limit is our imaginations.

However, one marked difference between *these technologies* and *other technologies* is that these digital technologies make it **far easier** than ever before to unlock massive new value. This is because they empower us to do things in ways that, in and of themselves, unlock massive new value that couldn't be accessed before.

We've seen this in countless situations based on, for example, The Sharing Economy, in which digital-native platforms such as Uber and Airbnb have unlocked massive new value for both their customers and themselves.

As a result, almost every new business today – no matter what solution it's offering, and thus what value proposition it's selling – will make at least some portion of its business model digital. In other words, somewhere in the business, it will leverage one or more of these technologies to facilitate some part of its business model – whether that's on the demand side (such as with customer connection), on the supply side (such as by delivering a digital app that does something special), or on both sides.

Digital technologies like this have now become *a nearly ubiquitous element of all business models*. Almost no modern business model can exist without at least some of these. And in general, the more digital capabilities we can integrate across *both sides of our business model*, the more impact they tend to have.

That being said, and in the interest of balance and full transparency, there is also a growing rebellion against all things digital and always-on connectivity. This is mirrored in such niche interests as 4-day work weeks, tiny houses, mindfulness, and simple retreats. This anti-tech sentiment also represents new opportunities for innovative business models.

The takeaway here is that whenever we're considering designing new business models, we have to think very carefully, creatively, and divergently about all the different ways and areas we can appropriately leverage digital technologies – ideally in very novel ways – to, somewhere in the process, unlock massive new value that doesn't currently exist (either on the customer side or the business side – or ideally on both).

If we can do that – if we can unlock massive new value on both sides of the business model – then we will at least be setting ourselves up for initial success. There will be other important considerations to take into account as we go along, but this is the most important one to start with.

Addressing the evolving UX situation around us

When designing our business model, and when we're trying to scale our business, it's important to not only think about where certain key technologies are today but also where they'll be tomorrow (in the future).

Just like trying to "skate to where the puck is going to be," to use the now-famous Wayne Gretzky quote, we cannot design our business model just for where the technology is currently. Rather, we have to design it with where that technology is going to be in the future in mind – so that our business model is designed to be able to evolve and adapt with the technology as it constantly changes and matures.

In perhaps no other area is this more salient to businesses today than that of UX.

In writing this book, I interviewed Larry Faragalli, CEO of the digital strategy firm *Brightly*. A key insight that Larry shared with me, and which we discussed at length, was that today, we're dealing with a major, radical shift in markets' expectations of the UX. We now have generations – Millennials, Gen Z, and Gen Alpha – who have grown up not with the old clunky computer technology of the 80s and 90s but, rather, with "screens" and "magic bricks" (mobile devices). As a result, these generations have come to **expect** "The Apple Experience" without even really knowing – or caring, for that matter – what's required to achieve this experience.

Consequently, when building our business models, we have to ask ourselves very serious, hard questions about what these changing expectations will mean for our business and its offerings. They may mean that a key element of unlocking new value will lie in a radically different and reimagined UX, among other possible things.

Larry Faragalli and I discussed the fact that almost all solutions today are becoming increasingly personalized to the end user – largely because digital technologies allow us to do so. What this means for the UX might be significant changes in how customers interact with businesses and their offerings. It may even mean that the **user interface (UI)** involved becomes a separate layer belonging to the individual, rather than to the business and its platform. In such a scenario, the UI becomes portable across different platforms, allowing the user to experience a persistent and highly personalized interface no matter where they go. It's certainly feasible that more streamlined Extended Reality devices will make this possible.

Time will tell how this plays out, but the point to be taken here is that whenever we're designing our business models, we'll do well to put a lot of thought into how our customers are going to interact with our business and its offerings, both physically and digitally. In particular – how can we make that interaction as personalized and as persistent as possible? In most cases, we'll do well to use digital technologies to move our business and its offerings in that direction.

Ensuring the ongoing scalability of our business

One of the very important questions that confronts us whenever we design a new business model is how *durable* we need that business model to be. By this, we mean how long we want the business to be around – something we have to consider in light of typical industry life cycles (the so-called "s curve" pattern).

In particular, we have to ask ourselves, is this a business model that will let us scale to the point where we can get to a mature business – or at least to the next major pivot? Does it have the ability to do that? In other words, have we thought far enough ahead about how our business is going to scale once it's launched – and have we thought far enough ahead about what its business model will need to look like to be able to accommodate that growth and scaling?

Of course, this is a question that exists outside of the technology itself, but the reason it is interjected here is that technology will be the primary means by which we facilitate that growth and scaling.

In particular, when designing both the business model and the actual *business*, we need to exercise the discipline to institute **processes** and **systems** that let the business automate different facets of its operations – including using its data in intelligent and automated ways to make customer-centric decisions – so that, as it does scale, it doesn't get bogged down by an inability to keep up with that scale.

According to Larry Faragalli during our conversation, a properly "digitally-transformed" business is one in which its people are empowered to do what they do best while the business itself can grow comfortably at a rate that keeps pace with the demands of its growth. Consequently, those who *haven't* done this – who *haven't* taken a true systems-level view of their entire business and integrated it holistically through digital tools – will inevitably struggle with the **scalability** of that business as it tries to grow. The business won't be able to keep pace with the demands its growth places on it. That, in turn, will hold it back from being able to scale up to the level it should, and thus hamper its overall growth and market valuation.

Therefore, and this being the case, the takeaway here is that whenever you're designing your business model, think very long and hard about how you expect and want this business to scale over its first 10 years. Then, look very hard at the business model and ask yourself, "Will it be suitable for accommodating that level of growth and scale?" Also, ask yourself what it will take for the business to *not* encounter these scalability issues. Will this be a particular tech stack? These technological decisions will have a massive impact on our ability to succeed – or not succeed – here.

It's also important to understand that, no matter what tech stack the business ultimately chooses to use, its **culture** will play a critical role in making that tech stack work or not. So, its culture must be "designed" thoughtfully as well – a consideration that we often don't give much thought to when we're designing new business models (since this culture tends to exist outside of the business model, though it will certainly influence how well that business model succeeds) – but should. On top of this, the cultural expectations we face as businesses will continue changing and evolving as older generations shift out of, and newer generations shift into, our business. That too is a consideration we must keep in mind.

Never lose sight of the human experience – it's what makes or breaks the technology

Amid all the hype, talk, and focus on technology, it's easy to succumb to the very real temptation of forgetting that, at the end of the day, when it's all said and done, it's human beings who use the technology, who in one way or another make it work, and who will ultimately benefit from it.

The hard, cold truth is that technologies live and die on the pedestal of what real-world value those who use them derive from them.

So, the actual success of a given technology will lie not with the technology itself but, rather, with its use and application by real people in real life. It comes down to questions such as the following:

- What are the actual, real-world use cases that people are finding for the technology?
- How easy or hard is it to deploy and use the technology across everyone who has to use it?
- What sort of adoption challenges and hurdles are people encountering in trying to use it?
- How useful and intuitive is its UI – and how enjoyable of a UX is that creating?
- What changes does the technology necessitate – in culture, in attitudes, in processes, and so on?
- What is the actual, real economic benefit of using the technology? Is the business case for it solid or are we operating on a hope and a prayer that it may work as envisioned?

All of these factors will ultimately determine whether a given technology "lives or dies."

This is a reality that's sometimes hard for technologists to understand and swallow. Indeed, it's often harder for technologists to understand and grasp our human nature (irrational as it is) than it is for those who understand human nature to grasp the technology (or at least what they need to understand about it).

Consequently, we have to figure out ways to bridge these two worlds – so that everyone involved in our venture can understand that – as use and leverage new technologies in our solutions – they have to be designed and developed with the end user in mind, and the type of deployment and usage experience that creates for them. This is the bridge domain between human nature and technology, and it's what's required for us to be able to use, integrate, and deploy technology successfully, thus allowing the business we wrap around it to grow and scale successfully.

Back to Intensifi – what are they talking about now?

Back at Intensifi, our friends Ian McAllister, Zoe McPherson, and Watson Afrik continue to talk about – and dream about – their new business and its business model.

They're learning a lot about business model innovation – about how this ultimately means finding novel ways inside the business model to unleash massive new value for their customers – and themselves. They understand that the value they deliver has to go well beyond just a new product or service, or even a new customer experience, so it involves a very purpose-designed business model that lets them unlock maximum value from whatever they do end up delivering.

Consequently, they're asking themselves a lot of questions about what that might look like in the context of the types of problems they want to solve, and the sorts of value they want to deliver. In particular, they're thinking about the following aspects:

- What might be the best ways and venues for establishing and maintaining their customer relationships? Are there new and novel ways of establishing and maintaining those relationships?

- How might they position and brand their business and its offerings to optimally resonate with these customers and their needs? What should its brand promise be, and therefore what message and language should it use to convey that promise?

- What assets and partnerships should they leverage to deliver their solution, and how might they best leverage those? Might there be novel new ways for doing so in their case?

- What might be the best way to monetize their solution – for both them and their customers?

These are clearly questions that they're a long way from answering, but they're at least becoming increasingly aware of the *types of questions* they need to be asking themselves – and, eventually, their would-be customers.

They also continue to be very certain about the central role that certain *technologies* will play in their solution. However, more recently, they've started to learn about how customers' expectations of the UX are changing rapidly – and how many businesses are experimenting with new alternatives for this, ranging from AI bots to XR UIs, to layered UIs, and more. They're quite concerned – probably rightfully so – about whether or not they'll be able to get this part of the business model sorted out right. But they're committed to trying – and to using the right methods for doing so. They're also learning more about the importance of a growth mindset… about things such as having a bias for action, using ongoing experimentation, being aware of their own cognitive biases (including an artificial pro-tech bias), thinking about how they're thinking and rationalizing things, and ultimately being comfortable with being uncomfortable along this journey.

Finally, they realize that they need to be thinking about how to design and build their business from the very beginning so that it will be scalable – able to scale from zero to the maximum without getting stalled by technical scalability issues such as data silos and interoperability problems. Those types of issues would prevent them from being able to scale at the pace they may need to, should they succeed as they hope they will. So, they're committed to doing the necessary homework to ensure this doesn't happen.

Summary

In this chapter, we learned what business model innovation is and what makes a business model innovative. In doing so, we learned a bit about the history of business model innovation, what has changed about it in recent years, and why. This led us to highlight why business model innovation is so important today, in light of the realities surrounding us. Finally, we covered the different ways technology is playing a critical role in business model innovation – as an enabler of novel ways of connecting with customers, delivering value to them, and scaling our businesses.

Understanding these things creates the necessary foundation for being able to move forward to our next chapter, where we'll be exploring exactly when, where, and why a business model is necessary in even greater detail.

To do this, we'll be exploring a functional model of the business model that lets us understand exactly what functions our business model has if we are to succeed at connecting with our customers in ways that unleash massive new value to them and let us scale!

Further reading

- *HBR's 10 Must Reads: On Business Model Innovation*, Harvard Business Review Press, Boston, 2019.

4

A Matter of Reason – When, Where, and Why Business Model Innovation Is Needed

In *Chapter 3*, we learned about what business model innovation is, what makes a business model innovative, some of the history behind business model innovation, including what has changed about it in recent years and why, why business model innovation is so critical today, and some of the important ways that technology is playing a major role inside business model innovation.

Those insights gave us the foundation we needed to be able to move forward to this chapter.

In this chapter, we're going to take a look at the two main scenarios where business model innovation becomes necessary, including the when, where, and why of each case. Then, to expound on this further, we're going to explore a functional model of the business model. Such a functional model allows us to understand exactly what *functions* our business model has to play on behalf of the business if we are to succeed with that business model and thereby unleash massive new value in a way that can scale.

Consequently, we'll cover the following two topics:

- **Anchoring our setting – the two key scenarios**: Countering an imminent threat (a defensive action) and capturing a new opportunity (an offensive action).
- **Unlocking greater value – the Business Model Meta Formula**: A comprehensive functional framework explaining the seven key functions of our business model.

We'll also check in with our friends over at Intensifi to see where they are in their business model thought and exploration process.

Anchoring our setting – the two key scenarios

To begin our discussion, we have to anchor ourselves in the specific scenarios where business model innovation is necessary and warranted, and therefore appropriate.

In particular, business organizations – whether an existing enterprise or a start-up – will generally need, and thus pursue, an innovative new business model for one of two reasons. Let's take a look

Scenario one – countering an imminent threat – the defensive action

The first scenario – relevant only to *existing* business organizations – is where some sort of **existential threat** is impending on a particular business operation being run by the organization.

This is usually on account of one or more changing *external realities* surrounding the organization, where those changing realities are causing that operation's business model to no longer work like it once did. In these situations, because the business model is no longer in synchronization with these realities and the state of its markets, its effectiveness is waning – or has waned – significantly, resulting in highly degraded business performance of the operation.

These changing external realities can include factors such as the following:

- new technologies that enable new uses and applications;
- evolving societal and demographic patterns that give rise to new and/or different market demands;
- new regulatory policies and/or political pressures that change how business has to be conducted;
- shifting economic factors that alter market macro-behaviors;
- countless other factors.

As a result of these changing realities, the operation's existing business model is no longer fit for purpose.

Consequently – and in light of this growing demise of the existing business model – the operation has to **abandon** that business model and start over with a **newer** and far more **innovative** business model… one that fully resonates with where these markets (or newer markets) are presently, and that thus also unlocks far greater value for them.

In some cases, this situation will arise on account of one or more innovative start-ups entering these markets with a radical new business model that undermines the existing, incumbent, business model. In those cases, a new business model becomes fully *necessary* for the ongoing **survival** of this operation; otherwise, it is quite likely to fold – or at the very least, become a mere shadow of its former self.

In other cases, it is simply the natural evolution of organizations as their leaders come to realize that the business they're currently in no longer holds the strategic value it once did, or is no longer of interest to the organization. So, they abandon that path for another, more lucrative one. For example, Nokia began life selling rubber boots, Samsung began life selling fish, and Shell began life selling sea shells – all cases where the organization realized the business they were currently in lacked the potential to scale up to their ambitions, and so they dramatically shifted course.

Scenario two – capturing a new opportunity – the offensive action

The second scenario – relevant to both *existing* organizations and *start-ups* – is where a new **opportunity** arises that the organization or founder team is seeking to capture and capitalize on.

Such new *opportunities* can arise on account of any number of different trends and changes occurring, such as the following:

- new technologies that enable new capabilities;
- shifting demographic and/or psychographic factors and the resultant changes in market expectations and demands arising from those;
- new legal regulations that permit something previously prohibited, or that prohibit something previously unrestricted;
- new economic realities arising in a given market.

And so, as a result of these new opportunities, a **new business venture** is to be launched – either an entirely new *start-up* or a new *division* (or *business unit*) of an existing organization, which can either be kept internal or spun-out on its own.

When this is the case, the new venture will inherently require a **new business model**. This will need to stand out in a *truly differentiated way*, delivering significantly new value to the affected markets and customers. It will also have to be one with a clear competitive advantage that gives it the staying power to be around for a long time.

In these cases, we are starting from **ground zero**, so we have the opportunity to thoroughly research the situation and think long and hard about what might be the best and most optimal business model to use for this new opportunity. This will have to be capable of delivering the maximum possible value to the affected markets (given the capabilities available to us now), and one that likewise allows us to capture as much value as possible for ourselves.

And thus the impetus for an innovative new business model.

Visualizing these scenarios

We can *visualize* these two scenarios via the 2x2 matrix shown in *Figure 4.1*. This figure illustrates three specific cases involving either an *opportunity* or a *threat*, as outlined previously. These cases are as follows:

- **I**: A start-up trying to capitalize on an emerging opportunity.
- **II**: An existing business organization trying to capitalize on an emerging opportunity.
- **III**: An existing business organization trying to address an existential threat and thus ward off its demise.

As this figure also suggests, the lower left quadrant has no relevance since an entirely new start-up doesn't have to deal with an existential threat – given that it doesn't yet exist to be threatened (it will, of course, have to deal with *other threats* after it launches, most notably that of a lack of revenue and thus running out of runway). That notwithstanding, start-ups are sometimes launched to deal with a specific threat to a given region or location, but not to the business itself. Such situations are relatively rare, however:

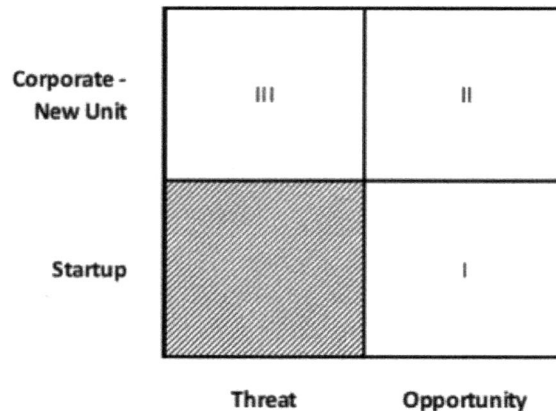

Figure 4.1: A 2x2 matrix reflecting the two scenarios in two different contexts

Now that we understand these scenarios, we can consider two other related and important subjects – namely disruption driven by business model innovation, and the relationship between strategy and business model.

On disruption – a new breed of disruption powered by business model innovation

In thinking about the two preceding scenarios, a question also arises: "Under what conditions are our actions **disrupting** affected markets?" We'll try to briefly address that question here.

In the classic text *The Innovator's Dilemma*, the late Dr. Clayton M. Christensen identified disruption as coming from new entrants into a market in which the functionality of their solution was not as good as that of the incumbent solution, but yet the price of their solution was significantly lower, putting access to it within reach of a much larger customer group. Eventually, over time, that new solution would gradually improve until its capabilities were on par, and ultimately better, than the incumbent solution, thereby displacing that incumbent solution, and in so doing "disrupting" its market.

In this way, disruption was largely a product of new technological capabilities that emerged organically from the *bottom* of a market *upwards* – with lower prices because of inferior attributes at the time – forcing the incumbent players to move progressively further upmarket, until eventually there was only a tiny niche left for them – and eventually nothing.

What we see today, however, is quite different. Today, disruption does not always follow this linear bottom-up origin and trajectory. This is largely on account of the innovative new *business models* being introduced.

In the past, new strategies were just about the **offering** and the **market** – as witnessed in the classic *Ansoff Matrix*, in which it was assumed that everyone would inherently be using *the same industry-standard business model*, given few other options available to them at those times. Now, it is just as much about the **business model** involved – which is *intermediating* between the offering and the market in novel ways that were never before imagined. This is largely because today, we have far more *options* for how to execute a business model than generations before us had.

What we have now is radically innovative new business models entering markets and disrupting the existing players there, nearly overnight – often with little or no forewarning. This was the case, for example, when Uber and Airbnb entered their respective markets, empowered as they were by The Sharing Economy . In those cases, the solutions they offered weren't just "cheaper alternatives" for achieving the same outcome but rather were quite *different* – and in many ways *better* – alternatives right from the start. It was their *innovative new business models*, empowered by newer digital capabilities, that made them so disruptive in these markets. This reality has become an increasingly powerful force in markets today, on account of the ever-increasing rate of technological change and what it enables. And with AI, we can rightfully expect even more business model possibilities than we've ever imagined before.

So, in this sense, business model innovation empowers an **entirely new breed of disruption**, following a **completely different path** than that laid out by Dr Christensen.

Commensurate with this, 2004 to 2011 saw a huge spike in new digitally-empowered business models that ushered in such practices as cloud computing, the sharing economy, subscription-based software models, and so on. Then, following on from that, 2012 to 2023 saw an immense wave of new start-ups leveraging those business models who went on to become "unicorns" (start-ups valued at over 1 billion USD) far faster than any traditional businesses before they ever had. This gave rise to massive new technology companies that ushered in significant new threats to many industries. That, in turn, gave rise to lots of **fear, uncertainty, and doubt (FUD)** and **fear of missing out (FOMO)** in executive suites around the world.

Since that time, however, the dust has settled a bit. The impending doom of many industries that had been forecasted in the 2010s, such as finance, healthcare, and hospitality, for example, has largely given way to the realization that these start-ups and their new business models will continue to **co-exist** with the incumbent players for the foreseeable future. They have *not* entirely disrupted those industries. That being said, however, some industries *have* experienced an implosion – retail in particular – on account of disruptive start-ups with disruptive new business models (with firms such as Amazon and Alibaba being the poster children for this).

So, the takeaway here is due diligence. Wherever we are in this process, and whatever our future aspirations are, we have to look very closely and very carefully at what is occurring in and around the specific markets that we're interested in – including all the different trends and forces at work trying to shape their futures. Then, we have to spend time *thinking about* what those trends and forces *mean* to the future of these industries and their markets – both in the short term and in the long term. This will take some degree of wisdom and discernment. Finally, we have to think about what this means in terms of actual customer *needs*, *expectations*, and *demands* in those futures, and use the methods and practices of this book to work out the right business model to use in each case for each situation.

On strategy – the relationship between strategy and business model

In thinking again about the two scenarios mentioned previously, there is yet another very important and crucial question that arises – namely, "What is the relationship between our strategy and our business model?" Let's address that question.

The most simple answer to this question is that our business model is *a part of our strategy*. Indeed, most management scholars would argue that a key decision factor inside your strategy is the choice of *which business model* you'll use to carry out that strategy – or stated otherwise, which business model will prove most optimal for achieving your strategic objectives? So, in this sense, our business model is simply one of several elements inside our much broader business strategy. Other such elements include the following:

- the choice of which markets and market segments to operate in;
- the choice of what products and services to sell in those markets;
- the choice of how to position our business, its brands, and its offerings in those markets;
- the choice of how to otherwise service our customers in those markets.

This is a rather *meta-level* view of strategy and business model – in which we think of our business strategy as **what** we'll be doing, and our business model as **how** we'll be doing it. Unfortunately, this is a bit of an oversimplification – one that doesn't acknowledge the full relationship between these two constructs.

In practice, the distinction between which factors belong to our strategy and which belong to our business model is not black and white. In reality, most of these factors belong to both – and as a consequence, there'll be a significant amount of *entanglement* between them – meaning that neither exists in *isolation* from the other. Instead, they **co-exist** hand-in-hand with each other since they share many of the same decisions and considerations.

The following choices and decisions appear in **both** our strategy **and** our business model, and therefore belong to neither alone:

- which markets and regions we'll operate in, and therefore what customers we'll serve – *who* and *where;*
- what products, services, experiences, and other offerings we'll sell into those markets – *what;*
- what channel partners we'll use to help us sell our offerings into those markets – *where;*
- how we'll position our business, our brands, and our offerings in those markets – *who* and *what;*
- how we'll service our customers in those markets – *what.*

The **implication** of this is that we have to make these choices and decisions on behalf of *both* our strategy *and* our business model commensurately. The two are entangled at these points of consideration, so it's impossible to separate them from each other. They simply go hand-in-hand and work together as a **symbiotic system** to achieve our business aspirations.

That being said, business leaders often define the "what factors" here in the context of their strategy first, and then the business model inherits those factors from the strategy, with the remainder of the "how factors" being defined more in the context of the business model.

So, while we can think of business model innovation as a *type*, or *subset*, of strategy innovation, the reality is that whenever we dive down into the finer details of either of them, what we find is that most considerations of the two involve many of the same conversations, decisions, and choices. It's just that our business model lays out certain specific details that our strategy alone doesn't define. Otherwise, there's an incredible overlap between the two. Consequently, whenever someone says, "We're pursuing a new strategy," you can be pretty well assured that it involves changes to their business model as well.

A similar and related point is that both strategy innovation and business model innovation require emergent learning and adaptation. Neither can typically be executed and delivered as first intended (especially in a brand-new venture). In most cases, there will simply be far too much that is uncertain and unknowable to be able to do that. This is particularly true whenever we're working with entire value chains of partners and ecosystems. In those cases, the whole milieu becomes that much more complex, fluffy, and necessarily emergent over time.

So, the bottom line here is that whenever we're working on defining a new business model, at the same time and commensurate with that, we have to be working on defining our strategy as well. We can't define one in the absence of the other; they simply have to coexist as a symbiotic set. This may require us to spend some additional time and effort thinking beyond our business model proper – to think also about what other aspects of our strategy we need to sort out – so that its elements will all enmesh properly with those of our business model.

Of course, the best way to establish a strategy in these situations, particularly for a brand new venture, is to have some overall sense of direction and constraints around what we aspire to do and to otherwise allow our strategy to evolve emergently as we grow and learn more about the market situation. In this way, our strategy can adapt agilely to the needs of that situation – including certain aspects of our business model. Both must start with defensible decisions based on sound research, but inevitably we'll learn a lot as we go along, so we'll need to adjust both accordingly (otherwise, we've likely spent too much time over-analyzing our strategy, and too little time in the field learning what we need to know).

Unlocking greater value – the Business Model Meta Formula

Now that we understand the two key scenarios requiring an innovative new business model (and why one is so required in each case), we can start exploring – in far greater detail – the nature of what an innovative business model **does** and how it **does so**.

In particular, what an innovative business model *does* is that it **unleashes massive new value**. Ideally, this will be massive new value on *both sides* of the business model, but at the very least it has to be for the *customer side* (the demand side) if it is to succeed.

We'll start our exploration by diving deeper into this rationale, after which we'll explore a *functional model* of the business model (as opposed to a *structural model*, as we saw in *Chapter 2*) to understand how the business model can achieve this aim – understanding that the business model is, in effect, the logic of how an organization creates, delivers, and captures value.

Why – and for who's sake – do we leverage business model innovation?

As noted in *Chapter 3*, the most fundamental purpose of a business model is to enable the transactional exchange of value between two or more parties.

That being the case, the *reason* that businesses pursue business model innovation is to **unlock far greater value** in that exchange.

As such, an innovative new business model can unlock far greater value for the following aspects:

- just the **business** alone – something businesses may be motivated to do;
- just the **customer** alone – something businesses are typically less motivated to do;
- only **partners** to the business – something, again, businesses are less motivated to do;
- **everyone** – something businesses tend to be *very motivated* to do.

So, the more value the new business model can unlock for *everyone*, the better – a true win-win.

The business organization will want to unlock far greater value for **itself** as this will translate into things such as the following:

- increased market share – and thereby increased sales revenues;

- the ability to enter new-to-the-business markets – and thereby increased sales revenues;

- the ability to create new-to-the-world markets – and thereby increased sales revenues;

- more esteemed positioning – which commands higher prices – and that, in turn, translates into higher profit margins, thereby producing greater profits;

- greater brand equity and awareness – which can translate into any (or all) of these outcomes.

Certainly, any – and ideally *all* – of these outcomes are quite attractive to the business. However, they can be hard to achieve *if* the new business model doesn't also unlock **equally greater (or more) value for the customer** (otherwise nothing is drawing these customers to the business model – to them, it looks and feels just like business as usual).

Let's see what "greater value to the customer" typically looks like (at least in mainstream markets):

- products, services, and/or experiences that are **more relevant** to them – that do things that are of very high value to the customer because they meet a very important (and often missing) need in their lives;

- products, services, and/or experiences that are **more accessible** to them – either on account of broader distribution, lower prices, or other factors (including in combination);

- products, services, and/or experiences that are **more dependable** – that do what is expected of them for the entirety of their lifespans, without interruption or difficulty;

- products, services, and/or experiences that are **more transparent** – that allow the customer to, in a very easy way, know exactly what to expect from them, see exactly is happening with them during their use and consumption, and see what has happened with any instances of them in the past;

- products, services, and/or experiences that fully **live up** to their **brand promise** – whatever that brand promise happens to be (as articulated by the business) – and especially ones that "surprise and delight," which means they *exceed* that brand promise in areas of importance to the customer;

- customer service that **respects** them as human beings, their time as valuable, and their good will as worth keeping.

The more a business organization can deliver *any* – and ideally *all* – of these, the more it will unlock greater value for its customers – and the more those customers will come to demand what the business is selling.

In terms of unlocking greater value for **business partners**, that would typically look as follows:

- increased sales volumes – resulting in greater revenues;

- the ability to extract a higher profit margin (without negatively impacting the business) – resulting in greater profits;

- being able to transact with the business in ways that are far easier, faster, and/or more transparent;

- being able to work with the business to support existing customers and win new customers in mutually beneficial ways.

All of these are ways in which an innovative new business model can unlock greater value for everyone – on both the demand side and the supply side. This should be the ultimate goal and aspiration of any business model innovation effort as doing so will, in the grand scheme of things, ensure the ongoing relevance, resilience, and leadership of the business leveraging it.

The elements of value

When thinking about how our (prospective) customers will *value* what our offerings and solutions do for them, some very useful resources for exploring this are as follows:

- *The Elements of Value*, developed by authors Eric Almquist, John Senior, and Nicolas Bloch of Bain & Company.

- *The B2B Elements of Value*, developed by authors Eric Almquist, Jamie Cleghorn, and Lori Sherer of Bain & Company.

These were both published in the *Harvard Business Review* in 2016 and 2018, respectively.

The first of these laid out 30 distinct "elements of value" relevant to individual consumers, organized into a four-tier pyramid of *functional, emotional, life-changing*, and *social-impact* outcomes – greatly expanding on Abraham Maslow's classic 1943 *hierarchy of needs*. These 30 elements were also studied to determine which were most *important* to achieving business success – something that was found to differ by industry (though *quality* was always the top element regardless of industry).

> **Note**
>
> For an illustration of these 30 elements, reference the HBR article *The Elements of Value* at https://hbr.org/2016/09/the-elements-of-value.

The second of these laid out 40 distinct kinds of value that B2B offerings provide customers, organized into a five-tier pyramid of *Table Stakes, Functional Value, Ease of Doing Business Value, Individual Value*, and *Inspirational Value*. The kinds of value reflected in the base of this pyramid are the more objective forms, whereas those reflected at the top of the pyramid are the more subjective forms. Similar to before, the authors determined, through in-depth research, that the more "high-value elements" included in a B2B solution, the more likely the customer was to repurchase (not surprisingly). And, like before, the authors also determined that the elements valued most by customers varied by industry, though three elements in particular nearly always sat at the top, namely *product quality*, *expertise* (in the customer's business), and *responsiveness*.

> **Note**
>
> For an illustration of these 40 kinds of value, reference the HBR article *The B2B Elements of Value* at `https://hbr.org/2018/03/the-b2b-elements-of-value`.

For those who want to dive *even deeper* into this concept of "value," yet another useful resource on this is the *130+ Value Types Wheel for Sustainability, Business, & Innovation*, developed by Mike Pinder, Founder of Explorer Labs (Belgium) and Co-Founder of Wicked Acceleration Labs (UK). The article on this can be found at `https://www.explorerlabs.co/thinking/130-value-types-wheel-for-sustainabiltity-business-innovation`, while a canvas-type tool for applying the model can be accessed at `https://www.explorerlabs.co/tools-canvases/130-value-proposition-types-wheel`.

Defining our meta formula – the seven functions of a business model

At this point, we're ready to dive deeper – much deeper – into the different *functions* of a business model – not just the structural considerations of *who, what, when, where, how*, and *why* but rather the actual *functional considerations* of exactly what our business model has to do for us. As we do this, we'll still want to think about the when, where, and why of business model innovation, but we'll be able to do so in an entirely new light – the light of the key *functions* that our business model must play.

To do this, we'll introduce a new *model* of our business model – this being a *functional model* known as the **Business Model Meta Formula** – shown in *Figure 4.2*. This functional model will allow us to see and understand the exact *functions* that our business model has to play if it is to be successful at unleashing massive new value in a way that can (and will) scale.

The Business Model Meta Formula

The Business Model Meta Formula is a *functional model* of our business model. As such, it defines the **seven key functions** that our business model has to consistently accomplish for us if it is to be successful. These seven *functions* go well beyond the structural considerations we explored in *Chapters 2* and *3* – to instead define the specific *jobs* that a proper business model has to facilitate, and the specific *outcomes* it has to ultimately produce for us.

The seven key functions of a business model are as follows:

- Market Connection Model
- Unique Value Proposition
- Sustainable Competitive Advantage
- Sales Model
- Profit Model
- Risk mitigation Model
- Business innovation Model.

The following figure depicts the Business Model Meta Formula:

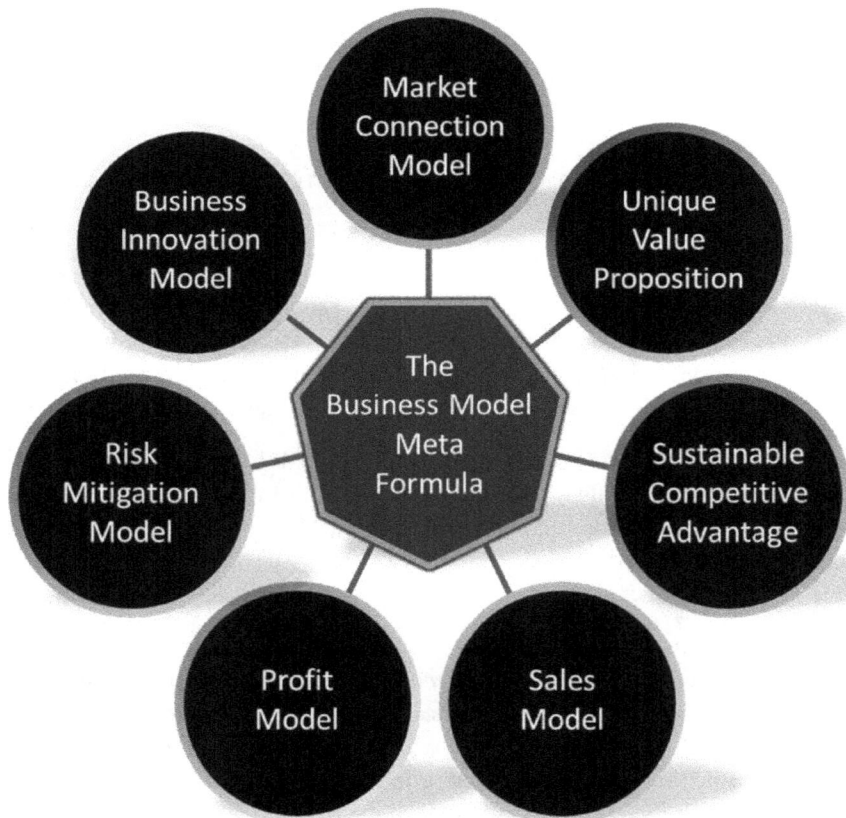

Figure 4.2: The Business Model Meta Formula

Let's explore each of these functions in greater detail, in the order reflected previously.

Market Connection Model

Our **Market Connection Model** involves three fundamentally critical questions and considerations that we have to always start with:

- How attractive is a certain market niche to us?

- How attractive is our offering to that market niche?

- If it is attractive to us, then how do we make our offering as attractive as possible to it – and how can we otherwise connect with the buyers and users in that market niche?

In this sense, our Market Connection Model can be thought of as being like a dating game, or a job interview… the fit has to be right on both sides of the situation and the relationship it involves. If it's not, then no one is going to be happy and it's just going to end up in some sort of turmoil. So, to ensure that it's going to be a happy and harmonious relationship and situation all the way around, we have to get both sides of this equation solved.

Let's explore each of these three considerations in further detail.

How attractive is the market niche to us?

The first thing we have to ask ourselves whenever we're considering a particular market, niche, or industry is, "*Exactly how attractive to us is this particular niche, the market it belongs to, and the industry that serves it?*"

As it just so happens, some industries and markets are inherently more profitable than others (up and down their value chain). That's simply the reality of capitalism and our capitalistic markets as they exist today. So, we have to be thinking very carefully about this before diving into any particular situation. Some industries are just flat-out hard to make a profit in, so those may be industries that we prefer to stay away from unless we have a particular innovation that will, with little doubt, alter that reality somehow.

Furthermore, and beyond the overall industry and particular market, when we look at the specific niche inside that market that we're considering, the same question applies – "*How attractive is it?*" Will it produce the types of revenues and margins that we're hoping for? Does it have the capacity to help us scale – so that we can eventually break out beyond that niche and scale even further? We have to study and analyze this situation before making any real decisions on targeting that particular market and niche. Otherwise, we may end up sinking time, effort, and capital into a situation that won't scale for us as we need and expect it to – not a desirable outcome! So, we have to ensure that whatever niche we're starting with will give us line-of-sight to, and pave the way for, achieving our long-term goals and aspirations. If it doesn't, then we should look for a different niche (and perhaps even an entirely different market) to serve – at least initially (including one that's not overly crowded and too hard to stand in).

Married to this consideration is the deeper question (regarding the problem we're considering solving), *"Is this even a problem worth solving?"* In other words, do enough prospective customers have this problem to justify developing and offering a solution to it? If the number of people who experience this problem is tiny, then it may never allow us to meet our long-term goals and aspirations, and therefore we should probably not pursue it. Likewise, even if the pool of prospective customers is sufficiently large, the other question is, *"How many of them feel this problem acutely enough to invest in our solution for it?"* If the problem, while shared by potentially millions, is only a minor nuisance to them, then potentially not enough people will be interested in investing in a solution to it to make offering that solution worthwhile. We have to study and analyze these questions and considerations very, very carefully – long before ever committing any real resources into developing that solution, let alone a business to monetize it. We need first-hand primary evidence that credibly demonstrates there is a need for this problem to be solved.

A part of this consideration will tie into who the specific customer is. On account of natural price elasticities and market dynamics, high-end luxury customers will give us better margins, but they will be fewer and further between – while low-end value-minded customers will give us much lower margins but show up in masses. So, we have to look at – and think about – which of those segments will best meet our needs, and then figure out if and how we can service that segment sufficiently.

Another additional consideration that we'll have to study, analyze, and consider is – regarding the overall industry involved – *"Where do we sit inside its value chain?"* Are we near the source of original value, but far from the end customer – or vice versa, far from the source of original value yet closer to the end customer? It seems that every industry inherently has a particular pecking order for which end of its value chain makes the greatest margin. Plus, this varies considerably from one industry to the next. In some industries, such as craft coffee, the end seller makes by far the highest margin, while the coffee farmer makes only a tiny fraction of that. In other industries, it's the other way around – such as in the petrol industry, where the oil company makes a much larger margin on every liter of petrol sold than does the gas station selling it. So, we have to consider this situation too and ask ourselves if it is even viable to break into that industry *where* we hope to break into it – or whether the barriers to entry are too great to do so (including being overcrowded). This is, of course, where significant innovation in our business model can help us to overcome such hurdles and barriers. They may also allow us to consolidate more than one role in the value chain as well – a potentially powerful play.

These are the types of questions that we have to ask ourselves on our way to answering the broader question of, *"How attractive is the niche to us?"* The final thing we need to keep in mind when doing this, however, is to not discount the fact that we intend to introduce a major new business model innovation into the situation – one that portends to unlock new consumer behaviors and industry dynamics that didn't exist previously. So, to the extent that we believe this will be the case, we should consider our analysis under two different scenarios… the current "business-as-usual" scenario and the new "business-as-unusual" scenario, impacted as it is by our business model innovation. Then, we can ask ourselves where on this spectrum we believe we'll be able to land, and in what timeframe. At that point, we can make an informed decision about whether or not moving forward in the situation makes sense.

Of course, if we are creating an entirely new industry with an entirely new market in the process – such as is the case whenever an entirely new product category is created, as was the case with the laptop computer and the smartphone – then we have an entirely new greenfield situation to work with and will have to learn as we go along and pioneer that situation. This can be an exciting path to walk, but not one without its share of ups and downs and learning curves to overcome.

Still, we have two other questions we must answer.

How attractive is our offering to this market niche?

Here, our Market Connection Model has to address and answer the **four most fundamental questions** surrounding the market situation at hand:

1. **Who**: Who we are trying to sell to and what is the specific market niche we are targeting? What are the key psychographic factors defining this particular niche – what makes them characteristically unique inside the broader market space? How big of a group are we talking about here (does it affect enough customers to be *a problem worth solving*)?

2. **What**: What is the problem are we trying to solve for these customers? What *outcome* are we trying to deliver to them, and what jobs are we trying to facilitate in that process?

3. **Why**: Why is solving this problem *so important* to them? What makes this outcome, and those particular jobs, so *valuable* to them? How *valuable* are they? How much economic value do they place on solving this problem?

4. **How**: How are we going to solve this problem in a unique, novel, and compelling way for them?

We must fundamentally understand the answers to each of these questions before moving forward. They are foundational to developing a viable solution that will then support a viable business model.

Part 2 of this book is where we'll be diving deep into *how* to study, explore, and ultimately answer these four questions with adequately accurate answers – answers that will allow us to either move forward or else pivot in a way that, in either case, yields high confidence in the paths we choose to take.

How do we make our offering as attractive as possible to this niche – and in that process connect with its customers?

Assuming we've answered the preceding four questions and, having done so, are sufficiently satisfied with the answers we have, the next set of questions – and the next part of our Market Connection Model – deals with how we will *connect with* this niche in a way that gets its customers to purchase and use our solution to solve its problem and meet its need.

Here, again, there are **four key questions** that we have to address and answer:

1. What problem are we *solving* for these customers?

2. Do they *know* they have this problem – or do we first have to *actuate the market* by making them *aware* of their problem (necessary before ever talking to them about a *solution*, let alone *our solution*)?

3. Do they *know about our solution* – and how it solves this problem for them? If not (which is likely in many cases), how do we *make them aware* of it?

4. Why should they – once they are aware of our solution – *buy it* from us and then *use it*?

Given these four questions, connecting with this niche and getting its customers to buy and use our solution will require us to drive **four specific outcomes** in the niche:

1. *Awareness* of their unmet, or under-met, *needs* (problem awareness).

2. *Awareness* of our *solution* to that unmet, or under-met, need (solution awareness).

3. *Demand* for our solution to resolve that need (intent – solution desire).

4. *Adoption* of our solution to meet their need (action – purchase and use).

So, our Market Connection Model ultimately becomes about the combination of choices we'll make, actions we'll take, and other factors we'll use to drive these four outcomes. Together, they ensure that we are offering a real solution to a real problem had by real customers who understand they have this problem – and are willing to invest in resolving that problem, and are aware of our solution for doing so – all in a way that resonates with their innermost needs, desires, and aspirations in this specific situation.

Making the right decisions, taking the right actions, and otherwise using the right factors here will all give us a strong Market Connection Model and thus provide us with the foundation we need for a healthy and profitable business model.

We must do all of this in a way that creates **maximum attraction** of the would-be customers to our solution. We need to make this solution as attractive and compelling as possible to them – so that paying our price for it is more than justified in their minds… they see it as an outstanding value in getting their problem (which matters to them) fully resolved.

Now that we understand the first function of the Meta Formula, let's move on to its second function – unique value proposition.

Unique Value Proposition

Our **Unique Value Proposition** refers to the uniquely novel value that *only* our business can (and will) deliver to its customers. It is comprised of the following three elements:

1. Our offering's **promise** – the distinct *benefits* that our product, service, or experience will deliver to its customers – and that no other organization's offerings can likewise deliver.

2. Our offering's **manifestation** – the actual *form* our offering takes, whether it be a product, a service, an experience, or some other form – and thus the actual *type of value* it is imparting to our customers.

3. Our offering's **fulfillment** of its promise – how our offering *delivers on* its aforementioned promise to achieve its promised benefits and thereby help customers achieve their desired outcome.

Note that our offering's promise will often be tied to a broader *brand promise* associated with the entire brand under which it is being marketed and sold.

The power of a Unique Value Proposition

Defining a compelling Unique Value Proposition is one of the most important functions of our business model. At the end of the day, our Unique Value Proposition has to make it very clear *why* a particular customer will choose us and our offering over the other competing options they have – or in other words, *why* our solution is the one best suited to meet their need.

Consequently, with our Unique Value Proposition, we have to make a *clear promise* to our customers that we will do something on their behalf that **no one else can or will do** – at least not in the way that we will do so, which they may value over other approaches and methods. In this sense, our Unique Value Proposition serves as the bridge connecting us (the value we offer, expressed as key *benefits*) to our customers (the *outcomes* they want to achieve), uniting the two together in a meaningful exchange of value. In short, *our benefits maximize their desired outcomes*.

Implicit in this is the fact that *value* here is defined by the *customer*, not us. Consequently, the attributes of our offering (its form, features, and so on) and the experience of using it only matter to the extent that our customer *values* them (and thus an incentive to *not* over-featurize or over-experiencize them). Ultimately, our Unique Value Proposition has to be valuable and unique in ways that **matter** to our customers, and this typically means it has to be tied to the number-one problem we're solving for that customer.

Furthermore, and all else being equal, the more *valued* (desired by customers) and *unique* (isolated to us) our promise and offering are, the more *compelling* our value proposition will be to these customers.

An important causal chain is involved here:

- the more valued these are by our customers, the more desirable they will be to those customers;
- the more desirable they are, the more we can (potentially) charge for them – within reasonable limits and positioning parameters;
- the more we can charge for them, the more profit we can make from them (keeping in mind the value equation for *all* affected stakeholders);
- the more novel and unique these are to us, the more they will be *differentiated* from anything else in the marketplace – with differentiation being crucial to our long-term competitive advantage.

Being *valued* here is important because our offering must deliver *greater value* to the customer than it *costs them* – if they are to allocate economic resources to secure it. The more *valued* it is to them, the easier it is for them to justify allocating those resources for it – and likewise, the more resources they will be willing to allocate for it.

Similarly, being *unique* here is important because *differentiation* is the key distinguishing factor that lets us stand out in the marketplace as doing something that no one else does – and/or in a way that no one else does – which tends to drive greater value to the customer and thereby allows us to command higher prices and greater profit margins.

This is often where doing what authors W. Chan Kin and Renée Mauborgne – in their 2005 book *Blue Ocean Strategy* – have suggested can play a critical role – namely to find a new "blue ocean" situation to work in that sets us apart from the otherwise bloody "red ocean" of competition around us. This can often be done by being attuned to, and thereafter tapping into, various trends occurring around us and the changing psychographics (consumer motivators) they each portend. By doing this, we can often create a new and uncontested market space that breaks away from the former value-price tradeoff involved, thereby capturing altogether new demand and making our former competition entirely irrelevant to us.

Identifying and meeting the customer's final and ultimate outcome

The preceding attributes – being *valued* and being *unique* – can be easy to achieve if we are first to market with a truly good solution that taps into an unserved or underserved need in the marketplace. This doesn't necessarily mean we are first to market period – but rather first to market with a *truly good solution* (being first to market otherwise is often a detriment as it involves having to undertake new market development, which adds additional risk on top of the already-high risk of having to find new customers for a new offering).

Delivering a truly good solution is why high-quality *needfinding* is so important to business model innovation. One very effective way of doing this is to study and involve our *Early Adopters* as opposed to our mainstream customers. Early adopters tend to be our *Power Users* – the type of *Outliers* that live at the front end of our adoption curve. These individuals will often make the problem situation very clear to us as we explore the different workarounds and other alternatives they're using to augment the situation. That, in turn, tends to give rise to a very clear, specific, and often bold definition of our Unique Value Proposition.

At the end of the day, we have to frame our Unique Value Proposition around what ultimately matters to our customer – meaning that we have to see the Unique Value Proposition through their eyes – and thereafter articulate it in no uncertain terms, stating the specific outcomes and benefits it provides to them.

Of course, if we want to become *good* at developing both Market Connection Models and Unique Value Proposition, then we'll need to dive deep into fields such as *behavioral psychology*, *experience psychology*, and *behavioral economics* to understand the underlying needs, motivations, and aspirations of the customers and markets involved. When we do this, what we'll often find is that most customers' "reason to buy" doesn't stem out of rational logic, but rather out of far deeper emotional needs, resulting in customers' choices seeming irrational to us (but fortunately, predictably irrational).

We'll be looking at these topics in a lot more detail in *Part 2* of this book, where we leverage Design Thinking to get at these underlying latent and emotional needs.

Finally, to truly resonate with our would-be customers, our Unique Value Proposition has to go beyond just enumerating its respective benefits as so many of those benefits will only be *interim benefits* – jobs being done along the way to some final and ultimate outcome. Instead, our Unique Value Proposition has to clearly articulate the **final and ultimate outcome** that our customers will achieve on account of using our solution – or what author Ash Maurya calls "the finished story benefits." We must frame our Unique Value Proposition around this final and ultimate outcome, making it the primary point of focus of our value proposition.

Entrepreneur and podcaster Dane Maxwell (*Dane Maxwell*, www.danemaxwell.com) has defined a good formula for articulating this:

Instant Clarity Headline = End Result Customer Wants + Specific Period of Time + Addressing the Objections

A very classic example of this type of statement comes from the American pizza chain Domino's: *Hot fresh pizza delivered to your door in 30 minutes or it's free.*

So, the more we can articulate our Unique Value Proposition with this type of language, the more our customers will generally understand it, appreciate it, and ultimately engage with it.

Delivering on our Unique Value Proposition

Perhaps it goes without saying – but we'll state it anyhow – that it is of no value to create a particular promise to our customers if we are unable or unwilling to deliver on that promise. That is simply a formula for eventual failure – and is inexcusable, given how much absolute choice customers have today.

It is far better to never make a promise and still deliver on a good value proposition than it is to make a promise and not deliver on it! Whatever we do, we mustn't do that. A bad product, service, or experience will very quickly kill an otherwise great value proposition. So, we have to ensure that we are living up to whatever promises we're making. Otherwise, we shouldn't even enter that market as we'll just be wasting our (and our customers) time and money – not a formula for success.

If we're hoping to build up a brand somehow and then ride on its coattails while we fail to live up to our value proposition, then we're going to be sorely disappointed – very, very little brand loyalty exists anymore these days. With just so much choice available to customers, why would anyone be loyal to a brand that doesn't live up to its promises? Customers today are very quick to abandon any brand that does that. So, we mustn't do that either!

Now that we understand the second function of the Meta Formula, let's move on to its third function – Sustainable Competitive Advantage.

Sustainable Competitive Advantage

Sustainable Competitive Advantage refers to those aspects of our business model that set us apart from other business organizations in a way that cannot easily be replicated. As such, they create an enduring exclusivity and defensibility mechanism for us to leverage.

This can involve things such as the following:

- Sole access to key **resources** no other organization has:

  - a unique business model that no other organization has – and cannot easily duplicate;

  - unique and captive relationships (including captive vendors) that no other organization has – and cannot easily cultivate;

  - a uniquely critical location (physical or digital) that no other organization has – and cannot easily gain access to;

  - unique, proprietary, and captive technologies, and the intellectual property mechanisms to protect them, that no other organization has – and cannot easily develop or work around;

  - other unique intellectual property (including, in particular, trade secrets) that no other organization has – and cannot easily replicate.

- Sole access to key **capabilities** no other organization has:

  - unique knowledge and/or insights that no other organization has – and cannot easily replicate;

  - unique technical or market capabilities that no other organization has – and cannot easily duplicate;

  - a unique level of focus, and therefore focused expertise, in a particular field that no other organization possesses – and cannot easily develop.

- **Control** of key industry or market assets that no other organization has, plus the ability to leverage flexibilities around these that no other organization can:

  - a uniquely high-caliber customer base, of a size and caliber that no other organization has – and cannot easily create;

  - uniquely massive network effects that no other organization has – and cannot easily develop to the same scale;

  - exclusive distribution rights in a particular area or region that no other organization has – and cannot easily secure;

  - full control of a distribution channel (often by absorbing all of its capacity) – thereby preventing others from being able to use it;

  - a unique ability to move up and down the value chain of a given industry (perhaps through flexible vertical integration) in a way that no other organization can – and cannot easily attain.

- Unique organizational **structures** and/or **culture** that no other organization has:

  - a unique organizational culture that no other organization has – and cannot easily replicate;

  - a uniquely low-cost structure that no other organization has – and cannot easily attain;

  - a unique ability to innovate in ways that no other organization can – and cannot easily emulate.

- Unique **brand and product assets** that no other organization has:

  - a unique product portfolio mix that no other organization has – and cannot easily develop;

  - unique product attributes that no other organization offers – and cannot easily duplicate. This leads to consumer benefits such as higher quality, greater durability, greater reliability, lower cost-of-ownership, faster operation, greater convenience, and/or a particularly salient emotional response from using it (any of which can sometimes put an organization in "a market of one");

  - a unique user or customer experience associated with its offerings that no other organization delivers – and cannot easily replicate;

  - a uniquely high level of brand recognition, reputation, and regard that no other organization has – and cannot easily develop to the same level;

  - uniquely high brand loyalty, and thus a captive community of raving fans, that no other organization has – and cannot easily develop to the same scale or caliber;

  - a unique selling proposition that no other organization has – and cannot easily replicate (these are generally associated with the brand and manifest in the form of a slogan – for example, for BMW, "the ultimate driving machine"). As such, they do not take into consideration price or actual customer value;

  - uniquely high-caliber influencer endorsements that no other organization has – and cannot easily secure at the same caliber;

- Numerous others.

Because there are so many different possible differentiators that we can leverage, it's helpful to explore and understand more about what is truly important when leveraging them – so that we can ensure we're using the right *types* of differentiators in the right types of *ways* for our particular situation. We'll do that next.

Building a competitive moat around our business

Because we alone possess these things, it creates a **barrier**, or **moat**, around our business that no other business can cross. As such, it *protects us* from would-be copy-cats copying our business model and solution – including our Market Connection model and our Unique Value Proposition. Consequently, no other business can emulate our Unique Value Proposition – and won't be able to do so for the foreseeable future.

Having a Sustainable Competitive Advantage is a crucial function of our business model – one that's all too often overlooked. What we don't want happening is that we build up a truly great business, only to have our industry's 800-lb gorilla come in the next day, emulate exactly what we're doing, and then take our business out from underneath us! Unfortunately, that happens far too often.

So, the question we have to ask ourselves is, *"What uncrossable moat can we build around our business that makes it completely untouchable by other businesses?"* This, again, can be any of the distinctive *competitive advantages* noted previously – as well as others, and any combination of them.

It's also important that we ensure that our Sustainable Competitive Advantage is, in fact, **sustainable** – that whatever specific advantage(s) we have can be **maintained indefinitely** – without the risk of losing it in the future. We can go on to further strengthen our sustainable competitive advantage by using our growth to accumulate even more of these advantages over time. That should always be a goal of our business – to ensure it will *always* maintain a strong Sustainable Competitive Advantage that it can leverage to win in the marketplace – forever!

Of course, there's also the risk that having such a strong Sustainable Competitive Advantage catches the attention of antitrust / anti-competition regulators who enter the situation and force organizational and/or industry changes on us. We should be aware of that and think about how we will address it, should it occur – and what it ultimately will mean to our current Sustainable Competitive Advantage (such as whether we need a *new* Sustainable Competitive Advantage). Organizations such as IBM, Microsoft, and Intel, for example, have had to redefine their Sustainable Competitive Advantage many times over as either regulators or markets brought an end to a prior one. We may have to do the same should that occur.

Where should we differentiate?

In their 2001 book *The Myth of Excellence: Why Great Companies Never Try to Be the Best at Everything*, authors Fred Crawford and Ryan Mathews revealed a very insightful, and somewhat startling, insight from their extensive research at that firm: of five key dimensions of commercial transaction – those being price, product, access, experience, and service – an organization's ability to lead in a particular market required a very specific formula concerning these dimensions.

Specifically, the organization must dominate in one of them, differentiate in a second, and otherwise operate on par (average) in the other three. Attempting to dominate or differentiate in all five dimensions was a recipe for failure. Consequently, an organization can be entirely average on any three of these – so long as they are world-class on the other two. That will produce market-leading success.

So, the question for us becomes – in our business model – which two of these five dimensions should we try to dominate and differentiate in, using any of the previously listed methods? It may be that, given the particular *types* of differentiations we possess (or intend to eventually possess), it naturally makes sense for us to dominate and differentiate in a particular pair of these five dimensions – certainly, something to study, analyze, and consider accordingly.

What to do on day 1 – before we have a Sustainable Competitive Advantage

Since in the vast majority of cases, a new venture won't possess a Sustainable Competitive Advantage on day 1, what is important when launching a new venture is that we understand the *type* of Sustainable Competitive Advantage our new venture will *eventually and ultimately need to have* if it is to be protected against traditional competitive threats. In other words, we have to understand what our venture's Sustainable Competitive Advantage is going to eventually need to be, and then we have to develop an actionable plan for getting – and staying – there.

This is what author Ash Maurya calls an "unfair advantage story" (referring in his case to what is contemporaneously known as an "unfair competitive advantage," even though, ethically speaking, there's nothing *unfair* about it). Here, the entrepreneur knows the *story* of what needs to happen to achieve success and scale with a truly unfair competitive advantage. And then, from that point on, that understanding serves to prioritize everything they do going forward.

Venture capitalist Ben Yoskovitz describes this similarly – noting that what is needed at this point are the *makings* of an unfair competitive advantage. These will be things that put us on a *different path* from our competition, and therefore give us the "right to play," with a possible "right to win" in our future (*Do You Have an Unfair Advantage?*, by Ben Yoskovitz, Focused Chaos: https://www.focusedchaos.co/p/do-you-have-an-unfair-advantage).

Taking an intentional and focused path to developing our Sustainable Competitive Advantage

So, we mustn't let the fact that we don't *have* a Sustainable Competitive Advantage on day 1 thwart us from launching a new venture. We just need to understand the *formula* for what that advantage ultimately has to be – what our *different path* needs to be – and then develop a game plan for getting there (eventually – before it's too late).

If we embark on a new venture *without* this understanding, then it is quite likely that we'll never develop, and therefore never have, a Sustainable Competitive Advantage. Consequently, we'll remain at risk of being beaten by competitors and thus forced out of business.

Instead, we have to be **very intentional** about *defining* this function upfront (understanding that we don't have it yet) – *and* **extremely thorough** in testing its fundamental assumptions. We do the latter by having a large number of qualified individuals (including, in particular, those with dissenting views from each other) critique it and attempt to poke holes in it. At the very least, we'll then understand the different assumptions it's built on – and how solid those assumptions are or are not. Understanding those weaknesses will allow us to address and rectify them so that we have a strong Sustainable Competitive Advantage that we can work toward developing. Likewise, if we hope to just somehow serendipitously "discover" our competitive advantage along the way, then we may yet again end up very disappointed. This isn't to say that figuring out our sustainable Competitive Advantage doesn't require its share of experimentation – it usually does. But it is to say that we have to be very intentional and focused in that experimentation, and not simply haphazard about it.

This notwithstanding, we should have at least some *basic* type of actual, validated competitive advantage if we hope to launch a new venture. But that *basic* type of competitive advantage can arise out of our Unique Value Proposition, so long as that unique value proposition is genuinely *unique* in its marketplace, backed up by a truly solid Market Connection Model. In any case, *something* has to give us at least a modicum of assurance of success before we take off charging headlong into the new venture. So, it needs at least some *basic* type of competitive advantage.

The next best (initial) thing – obscurity inside a niche

Often – in the very beginning of a new venture – the best **surrogate** for having a Sustainable Competitive Advantage is to pursue a very niche market inside a much larger mainstream market – often a very obscure niche market holed off to itself. In such a "safe sandbox" space, we can work out our problem-solution fit and product-market fit without attracting too much attention from would-be competitors (most of whom will be focused on the mainstream market, not its obscure niches). In this regard, the more incognito the venture can be (hiding off in a corner of the market somewhere), the more opportunity it will have to start building up the assets it needs to create its Sustainable Competitive Advantage. Afterward, it can then slowly and surely start leveraging that competitive advantage to work its way outwards toward the more mainstream market, where it will ultimately use that advantage to take a key leadership position.

Often, the most suitable niches to start in happen to be the most boring, unsexy, and otherwise unattractive ones – as they tend to be the ones with the fewest number of mainstream players operating in them, and therefore afford one that much more obscurity and anonymity whilst trying to establish their initial foothold.

If we think of a normal distribution curve (a bell-shaped curve), the vast majority of mainstream players will all be in the big fat center of that curve. So, new ventures will typically find far better success by targeting either of the tail ends of this curve, where there's *not* a lot of mainstream activity (and where they can thus "hide" while establishing their foothold). These also happen to be the "far corners" of the market that are least well served, and therefore most under-served, or even altogether unserved – making for a potentially lucrative niche where a new venture can establish a real stronghold. This is how many stealthy start-ups have gotten their starts, off the radar screens of large players, only to then slowly and quietly tiptoe their way into the mainstream market until eventually, they catch the attention of these large players, at which point it's typically too late to squash them – at least in any reasonable and legal way.

In any event, the important point here is that, when starting, it is not necessary to *have* a Sustainable Competitive Advantage but rather to develop and validate a clear *understanding* of what that Sustainable Competitive Advantage ultimately needs to be – striving to make it as strong as possible – and then work toward that end state. What we don't want to do is scale up with a weak competitive advantage (especially if we think it's a strong one), only to have it quickly whittled away by very nimble and agile followers. So, getting to a *strong* Sustainable Competitive Advantage is paramount to the venture.

Eventually, and ultimately, after a certain period, the new venture will reach a point of maturity where it will have a Sustainable Competitive Advantage. From that point on, it can leverage that advantage to maximum effect as it will be a crucial function of its ongoing business model.

Be forewarned – it will be tested (eventually)

Finally, every businessperson should be fully aware that once their venture does scale up to a point of significance, its Sustainable Competitive Advantage will be tested thoroughly by copy-cat competitors.

So, the venture will need to defend and, in every way possible, further extend this competitive advantage – such as with new proprietary technology, new intellectual property, and an even stronger brand.

Otherwise, some competitors may resort to unscrupulous means of violating that advantage, such as via intellectual property infringement. This is something that has to always be guarded against.

A key insight – differentiation is the key to Sustainable Competitive Advantage

In reading over the list of competitive advantages, you will notice a specific *theme* that jumps out – namely that they each represent a different form of **differentiation**.

Differentiation has been recognized for decades now as a key source of Sustainable Competitive Advantage. Going back over 40 years, famed academic strategist *Michael Porter*, in his writings, made the following prescient and keen observations:

- Competitive advantage is not about beating rivals but creating *unique value for customers*.

- The true essence of strategic competition is choosing a different path – competing to be *unique*. Competing to be the *best* is a destructive zero-sum game. Competing on *price* is the business equivalent of mutually assured destruction.

- *Uniqueness* is the essence of competitive advantage. Run a different race from your rivals.

- A competitive advantage arises from *differences* in activities performed by companies. Differentiation can come from either performing the same activities better than rivals or choosing a different configuration of activities altogether. In other words, there are two ways to gain a competitive advantage:

  - do things differently;

  - do different things.

- Competitive advantage means you operate at a lower cost, command a premium price, or both. To sustain a premium price, you have to offer something *unique and valuable*.

- Every good strategy has the following (among other things):

  - a distinctive value proposition;

  - trade-offs different from rivals.

- An effective strategy requires the following:

  - a set of choices that nobody else has made;

  - trade-offs throughout the value chain;

  - either/or choices – straddling is usually a mistake.

- Making trade-offs is the linchpin that makes competitive advantage possible and sustainable.

- Strategy doesn't require heroic predictions, but it does require a point of view.

- A strategic value proposition requires a specifically tailored value chain to deliver it.

- Find a unique way to serve your chosen segment profitably.

Each of these points is excellently summarized in the book *Understanding Michael Porter: The Essential Guide to Competition and Strategy*, by Joan Magretta – a recommended read.

Given this understanding, one of the key things we need to be doing whenever we develop a new business model – especially since we're now trying to interject *innovation* into it – is to *use* that innovation to differentiate ourselves and our offerings from those of everyone else we compete against. This includes any *indirect* forms of competition, not just our direct competition, as in reality we have to compete against both. The more we can differentiate ourselves and our offerings (via innovation), the more our Unique Value Proposition will stand out from all the others in the marketplace – and that in and of itself can serve as a key source of competitive advantage! This is something worth keeping in mind.

Another key insight – Sustainable Competitive Advantage is earned, not bought

A second *theme* that jumps out from the preceding list of competitive advantages is that they are all things that must be **earned**. None of them can be easily "bought" or acquired otherwise. This is *why* they often require so much time to develop; few of them can or will arise overnight.

In some cases, however, they can be earned inside of one context (for example, inside one organization) and then transferred to a different context (for example, to a different organization). This is exactly what happens whenever a team of experts develops unique expertise inside a certain organization and then all leave that organization to launch a new start-up together, where they will use their collective expertise to create a competitive advantage right from the get-go (at least a technical competitive advantage, not necessarily a commercial competitive advantage, which will be just as important). Now that we understand the third function of the Meta Formula, let's move on to its fourth function – the Sales Model.

Sales Model

Our **Sales Model** refers to how we will *sell* our offerings. These means will generally depend on the type of industry we're in and the specific markets we're trying to service.

Marketing or sales-oriented?

In some cases – especially those associated with traditional B2C sales – our Sales Model will have to be very marketing-driven. In these situations, we'll rely on active marketing to make customers aware of both their needs and our solution, and then try to drive their demand for our solution. Beyond this, we'll rely on different sales channels to sell the offering – including possibly our own outlets – online and physical – and those of our channel partners.

In other cases – especially those associated with traditional B2B sales – our Sales Model will have to be driven by a much more participatory sales approach. In these situations, we'll generally employ our own sales staff and/or different outside representatives, agents, franchisees, and so on to drive the direct person-to-person sales of our offerings.

Innovating our Sales Model

Both of these approaches are predicated on certain *traditional assumptions* about how sales work in a particular industry and market.

This infers that we may be able to come up with a very *differentiated* and *innovative* way to sell our offerings – something that's quite different and novel from those traditional means of selling. That would be ideal, given our goal of business model innovation.

But whatever means we choose to use, the important matter will be that we work through its details, mechanisms, and inner workings so that we can use them effectively and productively to attain our business' commercial goals and aspirations.

As such, some of the specific questions we'll have to work through for our Sales Model are as follows:

- What channels will we be selling through – physical, digital, mobile, in-house, representatives, franchisees, and so on?

- Will we be able to create a sound, reliable, and repeatable sales process, or will that process be overly dependent on certain individual personalities (something we can't always control or depend on)?

- How straightforward is our sales process, and how many steps will it entail – one, a few, many, or something else?

- Will we be able to sell our offerings at the price we need to sell them at? What will our pricing pressures be, given our branding and positioning?

We'll have to answer each of these questions to work out the details of our Sales Model. Now that we understand the fourth function of the Meta Formula, let's move on to its fifth function – the Profit Model.

Profit Model

Our **Profit Model** refers to how we will make a profit from the activities of our business model – the details of which will determine *how much* profit we can make from that arrangement.

Our Profit Model begins with the revenues we generate from the sales of our offerings (as well as any secondary sources of revenue we have, such as with accessories, extended warranty subscriptions, brand licensing, IP licensing, sponsorships, and advertising), and then takes out our operating and overhead expenses associated with running the business – leaving us with our gross profits. On top of that, we have to (in most cases) pay taxes on those profits, as well as possibly interest on any debt servicing, and possibly other outside fees and expenses that we incur – leaving us with our net profits.

The endogenous and exogenic factors determining our Profit Model

Our Profit Model will ultimately depend on several different endogenous and exogenic factors and considerations, including the following:

- **Our serviceable addressable market and our share of that market**: Is the problem we're solving for a large enough problem inside a large enough market to matter to us? Will it generate the level of revenue we need and desire, and does it have the potential for much larger growth down the road, either through greater market share or ease of entry into adjacent markets?

- **Our Unique Value Proposition**: What benefits are we providing to this market, and toward what final customer outcome? How much does the market value those benefits and outcomes?

- **Our brand positioning and pricing**: Are we luxury, mid-market, or economy? This invokes a price-elasticity consideration – as a luxury brand, we'll command a higher margin, yet sell fewer units; as an economy brand, we'll command a lower margin, yet sell more units. So, the question becomes, aside from any other aspirations and/or goals, "Which combination of positioning and pricing will yield the overall maximum profit for us – and thereby best sustain our business?"

- **Our target customer**: Who is our customer? Closely allied to our positioning and pricing is the question of, "Who are we selling to – is it the luxury buyer, the mid-market buyer, or the economy buyer – and why so?" How do we optimally find and connect with that customer? How do we make that customer a loyal returning customer – and keep them coming back?

- **Our revenue model**: How does our business generate revenue? Will it generate recurring revenues, or will all of its sales be one-offs? Will its revenues be consistent throughout the year – or are they seasonal? Will its revenues be dependent on the actions of a third party whom we have no control over?

- **Our Sales Model and its sales channels**: Where and how are we selling to our target customer? This is affected by how we choose to position ourselves and price our offerings – in that luxury outlets are typically different from economy outlets (though not always), with each being targeted at its particular type of buyer.

- **Our cost model**: What are our **cost-of-goods-sold** (**COGS**), our overall operating expenses, and our overhead expenses? How are these being driven by the choices we've made otherwise in our business model? Do these choices allow us to produce a profit based on the resultant volume and pricing they generate? Does that leave us with the level of profit we need to sustain and grow our business? Does it give us a cost advantage over our competitors?

As we can see, our Profit Model is one of the more complex and entangled functions of our business model – dependent as it is on all these different endogenous and exogenic factors and the choices we'll have to make.

Innovating our Profit Model

There are several key markers of a truly strong Profit Model. In particular, a strong profit model will allow us to do three things:

1. Generate extremely strong gross margins – sufficiently high that we can reinvest a substantial portion of them back into aggressively growing our business, while otherwise operating it efficiently.

2. Generate profits superior to our industry and market norms (what most of our competitors will be achieving), which allows us to innovate and grow faster than anyone else in these markets.

3. Raise our prices as needed without triggering significant market blowback, which allows us to stay ahead of different cost pressures, such as those arising from inflation and supply-chain fluctuations.

So, in innovating our business model, our goal is to maximize our ability to do all three of these – without causing harm or degradation to our business model and those impacted by it.

So, the challenge before us is to look for – and to the best extent possible, find – *innovative ways* to mix up these different factors to produce a very novel, innovative, and differentiated Profit Model. If we can do that, then we can likely unlock additional value for ourselves (in the form of greater profits) that we would otherwise be leaving on the table (and which our competitors are likely leaving on the table).

If we can figure out *innovative ways* to extract that additional profit from our business model – without otherwise taking away from the value we're delivering to our customers and/or sharing with our partners – then it ends up being accretive.. that much more profit we'll have to reinvest back in growing the business that our competitors don't have – thereby allowing us (all else being equal) to outflank and surpass those competitors in performance over time, eventually becoming the undisputed leader in those markets.

That's our ultimate goal for our Profit Model.

Now that we understand the fifth function of the Meta Formula, let's move on to its sixth function – the Risk Mitigation Model.

Risk Mitigation Model

Our **Risk Mitigation Model** refers to how we'll either *avoid*, *mitigate*, or otherwise *manage* all the different *risks* inherent in defining, launching, operationalizing, running, and growing a new business venture.

Every business model has to have a very clear Risk Mitigation Model – beyond all the different functions it otherwise facilitates.

There are *countless* different pitfalls that we'll encounter on our road to success – and we have to have a means of dealing with, and overcoming, every one of them. Otherwise, they'll quite likely jump up and surprise us, yelling "gotcha!" in the process – and that is certainly *not* a situation we'd like to happen.

The common risks and pitfalls we encounter

The most common risks and pitfalls that we encounter in these situations are as follows:

- Solving the wrong problem – or solving a non-existent problem – resulting in no traction at all.

- Not enough customers with this problem / too small of a market – resulting in insufficient traction.

- An inadequate value proposition – our Unique Value Proposition is too weak. Customers' needs aren't strong or compelling enough to motivate them to buy our solution (at least at the price point we have to sell it for) – resulting in insufficient traction.

- An inability to connect with our would-be customers to make them aware of their needs and our solution for those needs – resulting in suboptimal demand for our offerings, and thus insufficient traction.

- Inconsistent demand – demand for our offerings is insufficiently stable and reliable – resulting in unsustainable revenue patterns (based on our current business model).

- Inferior offerings – our offerings fail to live up to their promise (either on account of deficient design or deficient quality), and consequently customers leave and don't return, and eventually our market abandons us – thereby losing our opportunity to grow and scale.

- Encountering legal regulations we were unaware of – we encounter certain regulatory restrictions and/or prohibitions that we were previously unaware of, thereby significantly derailing some key part of our strategy or business model.

- A poor Profit Model – our cost structures are too high, preventing us from being able to extract a usable profit from the business – resulting in the inevitable demise of the business.

- An insufficient sustainable competitive advantage – allowing one or more fast-copier competitors to copy our solution and/or business model and thereby take our market share out from under us – thus losing our opportunity to grow and scale, and potentially spelling the eventual demise of our business.

- Insufficient funding – an inadequate amount of financing to give us the runway needed to work out our product-market fit and thereby turn the corner into profitability (or otherwise secure additional financing to fund a subsequent growth wave).

- The wrong team – putting together a team that either lacks the necessary skills or cannot work together effectively, thus causing the venture to fail from the beginning.

All of these represent potentially existential threats to our new venture and must be taken seriously. This is why our business model has to have this Risk Mitigation Model.

An intentional and explicit set of anticipatory contingency plans

Our Risk Mitigation Model must spell out exactly – very intentionally and explicitly – how we are going to either avoid, mitigate, or manage each of these respective risks and pitfalls. It must spell out how we are going to do the following:

- Ensure we're solving the right problem (a real problem), not the wrong (or nonexistent) one.

- Ensure there's an adequate number of customers for the solution we intend to deliver to justify doing so, and thereby constitute a market for that solution that's sufficient to match our business' goals and aspirations.

- Ensure our value proposition is adequately strong and compelling – because the need it meets and the outcomes it enables are felt strongly enough by its would-be customers to be so.

- Ensure we have the means to connect with our would-be customers and get our message in front of them to drive sufficient awareness of, and demand for, our offerings.

- Ensure that the demand for our offerings will be stable and reliable to match the assumptions and designs of our business model.

- Ensure that our offerings have suitable design and quality to deliver on their value proposition – thereby satisfying (and where it matters most to our customers) and delighting those customers.

- Ensure we're fully aware of and well-versed in each of the respective legal regulations and requirements that we will encounter in the course of launching, operating, and scaling our venture.

- Ensure we have a very strong profit model – one in which we'll be able to extract the desired and intended level of profit from our operations.

- Ensure we have a sustainable competitive advantage that we can use to ward off competition – as well as a plan for leveraging and enforcing that advantage to ensure it's working most effectively and impactfully for the sake of our long-term future.

- Ensure we have sufficient funding to get to the point of profitability and sustainability that we need to get to while giving us the opportunity we need to work out our product-market fit in adequate detail.

A business model without a strong Risk Mitigation Model is an incomplete business model. We should never proceed without first having a very strong Risk Mitigation Model.

Our risk mitigation model is our insurance plan. It gives us (and any possible investors we enlist) the assurance and confidence that we'll be able to overcome any obstacles, pitfalls, and other types of risk that we encounter, and consequently be able to grow and scale our new venture successfully. As such, it will also let us sleep better at night – knowing that we've thought through, and planned accordingly for, all possible contingencies that we might encounter on our path to business success.

Two useful methods for developing our Risk Mitigation Model

Two very useful methods for helping us develop a good Risk Mitigation Model are *scenario planning* and *premortems*.

In **Scenario Planning**, we work to anticipate plausible different *future scenarios* that could occur, and in fact may occur, in a particular timeframe, and then we develop different *strategies and plans* for each one to somehow mash them all together into a single (otherwise healthy and coherent) strategy and action plan that will be robust to any of the scenarios (a meta-strategy). The construction of these believable and plausible future scenarios is generally based on where different trends are heading, and how those trends might all interact with each other, plus whatever other "pressures" are considered plausible in that same timeframe, such as political changes, new and different regulations, changing competitive threats, and so on. Doing this helps us to develop different strategies that are designed to address each of the risk factors outlined previously. It also allows us to consider different *wild card situations* (unlikely but high-impact events), for which we can develop additional *contingency strategies* should such an anomalous situation arise.

In a **Premortem**, we first lay out an intended strategy and plan of attack, and then we imagine that every imaginable thing that could go wrong with that strategy and plan of attack has *gone wrong with it*. With that assumed outcome, we work *backward* to diagnose what might have gone wrong along the way that caused our plans to fail – the causalities involved. Thereafter, we rebuild our strategy and plan of attack with very specific steps and countermeasures integrated into it – each designed to prevent one or more of these causes from ever occurring. This results in a far better and more robust strategy and plan of attack than we would otherwise have. It also offers us the opportunity to entertain each of the risk factors outlined previously and factor those into these new steps and countermeasures – to ensure that we're taking the necessary actions *preemptively* to ensure these risks don't materialize, or if they do, we know how to successfully address and overcome them.

Both of these methods, particularly when used in tandem, can help us to develop very sound and dependable Risk Mitigation Model for our broader business model.

Now that we understand the sixth function of the Meta Formula, let's move on to its seventh and final function – the business innovation model.

Business Innovation Model

Our **Business Innovation Model** refers to the combination of choices we make and actions we take that let us ensure our business is innovating at the pace and scope it needs to – to be able to sustain a true market leadership position.

As such, it asks the question, "How fast are we innovating our business and its value proposition relative to the evolving and emerging needs of the markets we serve? In this regard, are we keeping pace? Are we ahead of the curve? Or are we falling behind the curve? The answers to this question are crucial to our long-term survival and leadership.

We must note that the pace and scope of innovation that's needed in a particular industry and situation is very much a function of that specific industry and situation – particularly in terms of what its customers' needs and expectations are. Integrated circuit manufacturers must innovate at an infinitely faster pace than barber shops do – to use two very distant extremes. Consequently, our efforts to innovate need to match these market and situational expectations. If we innovate too slowly, then we'll fall behind and become irrelevant. But if we innovate too fast, then we may end up spending capital and resources on things those markets don't want and therefore don't value – resulting in a frustrating mismatch between us and the market.

Two outcomes

The answer to the previous question (about pace and scope) will determine two key things for us:

1. how well our business is currently being **perceived** by those on the outside (which will impact its brand image;

2. how well our business can **continue** developing and delivering new and fresher innovations that continue to resonate with our customers of the future, and that therefore continue to meet their evolving and emerging needs in that future.

If our business is *not* innovating at a pace and scope that allows it to remain relevant to those evolving and emerging needs, then it will very likely fall out of favor and become irrelevant to those markets – clearly an undesirable future outcome!

Consequently, the *only way* for us to remain relevant to our markets – and likewise resilient to the long-term changes that will inevitably occur around us – is to be constantly and relentlessly innovating the value we deliver – to ensure we are meeting those evolving and emerging needs and expectations as they arise.

The capability and maturity to do this

Doing this – innovating at this pace and scale – requires that we develop and maintain not only the *capability* for delivering innovation but also a very high level of *maturity* inside those capabilities. This is where the necessary training, experience, and professional certifications can play a significant role in our organization.

Thus, our Business Innovation Model becomes three things:

- the innovation strategy we're pursuing to constantly renew our value proposition and reinvent our business;

- the innovation practices and capabilities we're developing and leveraging to execute that strategy;

- the cadence at which we're delivering on that strategy and thereby succeeding with the innovations we need to ensure our ongoing growth and longevity.

Furthermore, we must constantly refresh this strategy, fortify and extend these capabilities, and drive this cadence if we are to remain the leader we want to be indefinitely.

Transition and recap – from functions to impact

This wraps up all seven functions of the Business Model Meta Formula. As we saw, the Business Model Meta Formula is a functional model defining the seven key functions that every business model has to achieve if it is to succeed. These seven functions go beyond the business model's structural considerations to define the specific jobs that have to be accomplished and the specific outcomes that must be produced.

We now understand each of these seven functions and can see how a particular business model has to address each effectively if it is to be truly innovative and, more importantly, impactful for its situation. This brings us back to the question of how to *innovate* these functions to unlock massive new value for everyone involved – a topic we'll explore next.

But first, just in case you're feeling this framework is a bit theoretical and you'd like to see a practical application of it, don't fear… that's coming. In *Chapters 13* and *14* in particular, we'll see this framework put into real-world use by Intensifi as it goes through the process of step-by-step defining its unique business model using this framework, together with the research insights it will have amassed.

Unlocking value – a better business model

Given our understanding of the *Business Model Meta Formula* and its seven functions, we can circle back to our primary question, "How can we unlock the maximum possible value for everyone involved in our new business model?"

When asking this question, it's very important that we not just try for a simple 3-5% better overall value. Doing that will end up being far too *incremental* to even matter or to register on anyone's radar screen. It simply won't suffice. The business will end up being just another me-too also-ran who somehow managed to eke out yet another 3% of value. That won't cut it – not at all.

Instead, we have to be asking ourselves, "How can we – through our new business model – unlock **10x** or even **100x** greater value to one or more of the impacted parties?" Doing that *will* matter, and *will* register on markets' radar screens as being worthy of paying attention to. Therefore, to matter and to succeed, you have to be thinking in terms of **exponential value gains**. That is the only formula that is going to make a dent in the markets you want to create or penetrate – and that is our goal.

The question of exponential value gain translates into an exploration of how we can innovate **every one** of the seven functions of our meta formula. How can we do the following?

- innovate our Market Connection Model to have an even better, more effective, and more value-liberating market connection model;

- innovate our Unique Value Proposition; to have an even better, more effective, and more value-liberating unique value proposition;

- innovate our Sustainable Competitive Advantage to have an even better, more effective, and more value-liberating Sustainable Competitive Advantage;

- innovate our Sales Model to have an even better, more effective, and more value-liberating Sales Model;

- innovate our Profit Model to have an even better, more effective, and more value-liberating Profit Model;

- innovate our Risk Mitigation Model to have an even better, more effective, and more value-liberating Risk Mitigation Model;

- innovate our Business Innovation Model to have an even better, more effective, and more value-liberating Business Innovation Model.

So, we end up asking this question about a better, more effective, and more value-liberating model for each of the seven distinct functions.

Not only that, we're also taking a step back here and looking at our **entire business model** – not just its functions in isolation – but rather the entire thing **together**, holistically, to ask ourselves, "How can we create new **synergies** between these different functions to liberate even more value yet?" Once again, our goal here will be to achieve **exponential value liberation** (10x or 100x the prior value).

If we can develop a new business model in which not only are one or more (ideally several) of these different functions innovated and thereby individually *value-liberating*, but rather *all of them* are working together in **synchronicity** to unleash **even more**, truly exponential, value, then we will have succeeded in unlocking a truly **innovative new business model** that stands to succeed in ways that others before it never have!

This is precisely what happened in new market situations such as *cloud computing* and *the sharing economy*. In those cases, the business models innovated several different functions all at once.

In the case of *cloud computing*, it was at least four of these functions – namely, the Market Connection Model, Unique Value Proposition, the Sales Model, and the Profit Model.

In the case of *The Sharing Economy*, it was at least six of the seven functions – namely, the Market Connection Model, Unique Value Proposition, Sustainable Competitive Advantage, the Sales Model, the Profit Model, and the Risk Mitigation Model.

As we can see, the more functions that are innovated (together), the more value that's liberated.

Consequently, in general, it tends to be less effective and less impactful when we innovate in just one of these functions, such as in our Unique Value Proposition. In contrast, it tends to be much more effective and far more impactful whenever we innovate in *multiple functions*. In general – the more the better.

So, our challenge here is to try to really examine and dissect whatever business models we're considering for a given situation – and then ask ourselves how we can get creative about each of these different functions – including how they all work together – to unlock exponentially greater value in the marketplace.

If we can find the right meta formula for doing this, then we will have an innovative business model that stands to make a major impact in its targeted markets.

Back to Intensifi – what's happening over there now?

Back over at Intensifi, our friends Ian, Zoe, and Watson have begun putting more focused effort into their business model – including doing a lot of independent research, having conversations and debates about different options, and otherwise ideating possible paths to consider.

They're also starting to understand a lot more about how business models work – including the different functions they have to play on behalf of the business, and how they relate to the business' strategy.

They see this as a great opportunity to think through those different functions and try to nail down something a bit more tangible about each one. Even if those details are more directional than definitive, writing something down about them serves to help their thought process.

They're also starting to invite several different outside experts and experienced entrepreneurs whom they respect to look over and critique this thought process so that they can benefit from those individuals' years of experience and wisdom, and thereby sharpen the pencil on that thought process.

In particular, Ian, Zoe, and Watson are having many different conversations about what they should have for all seven aspects of the Business Model Meta Formula.

At this point, those conversations are yielding more questions than answers – and therefore more options than choices. But that's a great thing – as that is precisely what they should be doing at this point (a divergent activity), given that the team is not yet at the point of trying to *answer* any of those questions. There's still a lot of learning they have to do about their market and their would-be customers before they can do any of that – something that they (and we) are gradually working our way toward in this overall journey.

Summary

We started this chapter with the question (via the title), 'When, where, and why is business model innovation needed (a "matter of reasons")?" We answered that question by exploring two things – the two key scenarios where business model innovation is needed, and the functional jobs that a business model does for us, inside of which we have to seek out opportunities for innovation so that we can, through them, unleash massive new value to both sides of our business model (the demand side and the supply side).

As we learned, our "matter of reasons" starts with, and derives from, these two key scenarios in which business model innovation becomes necessary – namely opportunity capitalization (for both start-ups and corporates) and threat confrontation (for corporates). We also briefly explored how business model innovation is driving a new breed of disruption in these scenarios – a breed that didn't exist 25 years ago. Then, we explored the symbiotic relationship between our strategy and our business model – seeing how the two have to be defined and executed together (never in isolation) so that they can work together effectively.

Finally, we dove deep into the functional aspects of our business model, exploring the seven key functions that every business model has to fulfil if it is to be impactful and sustainable. Specifically, we learned about our Market Connection Model, our Unique Value Proposition, our Sustainable Competitive Advantage, our Sales Model, our Profit Model, our Risk Mitigation Model, and our business innovation model – as well as how all seven of these have to defined and developed together to work properly with each other. Together, these make up our *Business Model Meta Formula*. We ended by learning that a truly innovative business model will seek to innovate in as many of these functions as possible, showing how some of the most impactful forms of business model innovation over the past 20 years have combined powerful innovations inside multiple functions.

All of this – together with what we learned in *Chapters 1, 2,* and *3* – sets the stage for what we'll be exploring next in *Chapter 5*, which specifically deals with how to dissect a business model and from that develop a new and better one. In that context, we'll be looking at a specific process, as well as certain tools, that we can use to dissect an existing business model, study and critique each of its elements and functions, and then build out a new business model that radically improves on the former by introducing innovative changes to both its structure and its functions. Doing this yields the innovative business model we're searching for.

Further reading

- *The Elements of Value*, by Eric Almquist, John Senior, Nicolas Bloch, Harvard Business Review, September 2016, `https://hbr.org/2016/09/the-elements-of-value`.

- *The B2B Elements of Value*, by Eric Almquist, Jamie Cleghorn, Lori Sherer, Harvard Business Review, March-April 2018, `https://hbr.org/2018/03/the-b2b-elements-of-value`.

- *Blue Ocean Strategy: How to Create Uncontested Market Space and Make Competition Irrelevant*, by W. Chan Kim, Renée A. Mauborgne, Harvard Business Review Press, Cambridge, MA, 2005.

- *The Myth of Excellence: Why Great Companies Never Try to Be the Best at Everything*, by Fred Crawford, Ryan Mathews, Three Rivers Press, New York, NY, 2001.

- *Understanding Michael Porter: The Essential Guide to Competition and Strategy*, by Joan Magretta, Harvard Business Review Press, Cambridge, MA, 2011.

The Master Designer – How to Dissect Business Models and Develop New and Better Ones

In *Chapter 4*, we explored the two scenarios where business model innovation is necessary – opportunity capitalization and threat confrontation. We also looked at how business model innovation is driving a new breed of disruption that didn't exist 25 years ago – plus we explored the symbiotic relationship between strategy and business models. We also dove deep into the functional attributes of a business model, exploring the seven key functions that every innovative, impactful, and sustainable business model has to be able to fulfill – known collectively as its *meta formula*.

In this chapter, we're going to explore a process for dissecting and studying existing or prospective business models so that, from those, we can develop far better and more innovative new business models. To accomplish this, we'll delve into a practice that is both deconstructive and reconstructive. In our case, this entails dissecting both the structure and function of a business model, critiquing each element, and then reconstructing a new model that is significantly better and more innovative, ultimately unleashing new value.

We refer to this process as the **Business Model Synthesis Process**, and at its heart is the practice of *reconstructive inquiry*. In reconstructive inquiry, you start with an artifact and then try to learn, through observation, study, and inquiry, what is and is not "good" about that artifact, after which you unpack the artifact further by dissecting it down into its most fundamental parts to examine those parts in isolation. You then work to conceive new variants of those parts that may be able to operate in a better way toward your goal. After, you reassemble those new variants into a new expression of the overall artifact – one that is far better and more effective than the one you began with – one that, in our case, will be capable of unleashing massive new value. Of course, this process only works for modular artifacts. Fortunately for us, business models are indeed quite modular.

That being said, care has to be taken whenever using this approach – to not lose sight of the critical relationships between these modular parts. Otherwise, you can fall prey to Reductionism, Or Reductionist Thinking, in which you see each part as a separate entity in isolation, thus oversimplifying the business model and missing the key points of symbioses between them. Recall that in *Chapter 1*, we stated that business models have to be internally consistent. That still applies here. Nevertheless, we believe this approach to be a good one – so long as those relationships and this constraint are kept in mind throughout.

Therefore, we will explore the following seven topics in this chapter – representing the activities and tools of this process:

- **Understanding the process workflow**: A visual presentation of the overall business model synthesis process.

- **Defining our goal – our starting point**: Articulating the specific outcome we need our winning business model to deliver for us.

- **Exploring our surrogates to create a baseline**: Identifying surrogate business models we can study to create an appropriate context for this work.

- **Dissecting, deconstructing, and critiquing our surrogates**: Taking our surrogates apart and examining them critically to understand what is good and not good about them in our particular context (using evidence-based data as much as possible to minimize the level of subjectivism involved).

- **Starting over – reconstructing a far better business model**: Using what we've just learned to synthesize new business model options that each hold the potential for attaining our goal.

- **Stress testing our options**: Stress testing our different business model options against customer scenarios to find the one option that best attains our goal under the largest number of scenarios (using as much real-world experimental insight as possible).

- **Executing our business model**: Different options for bringing our new business model to life, plus not mistaking a business plan for an actual business model.

We'll also check in with our friends at Intensifi again – to see where they are at this point in their business model innovation journey – including whether or not they're ready to start designing their new business model yet.

Understanding the process workflow

Figure 5.1 illustrates the overall *workflow* of the Business Model Synthesis process, showing its six primary steps and its critical sub-steps along the way:

Step 1	Define our goal for the situation.
	↓
Step 2	Explore our surrogate business models – to create a starting baseline to work from.
	↓
Step 3	Dissect, deconstruct, & critique these surrogates against their & our goals.
	↓
Step 4	Reconstruct elements of these surrogates to create an even better business model for our goal.
↳ **Step 4a**	Start with first principles & trends.
↳ **Step 4b**	Build out our new business model options from these (to test).
	↓
Step 5	Stress test our business model options – to find the 'winning' new business model.
↳ **Step 5a**	Develop our customer scenarios to test against.
↳ **Step 5b**	Run our (simulated) stress tests of options against these scenarios.
↳ **Step 5c**	Choose our 'winning' business model to go forward with.
	↓
Step 6	Execute our new business model.

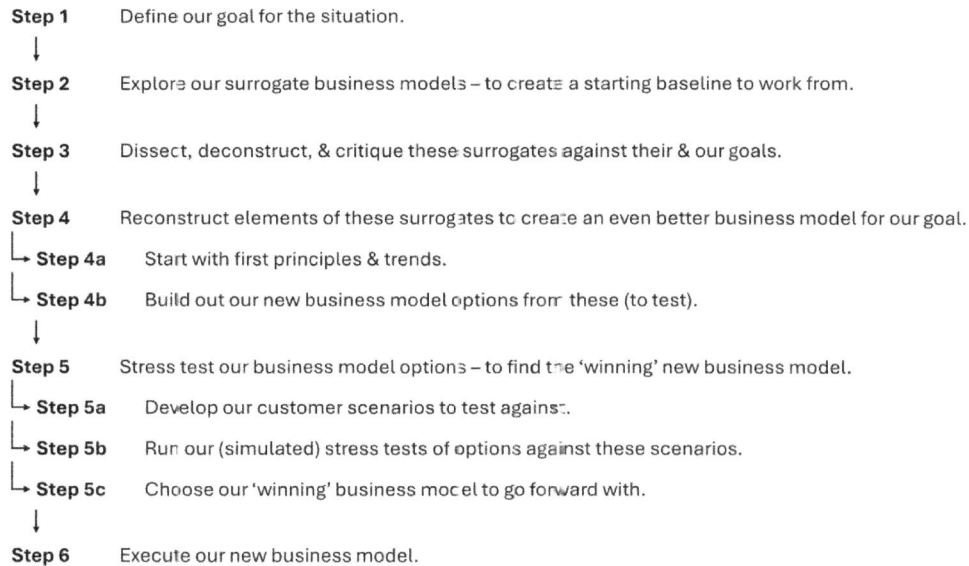

Figure 5.1: The process workflow for the Business Model Synthesis process

The following sections profile each of these steps and their respective sub-steps.

Defining our goal – our starting point

In all cases, our overarching goal here will be to architect an entirely new business model that unleashes massive new value – for both us and our customers/markets.

Beyond that, we must also start by defining and articulating a very specific **goal** for our new business model. After all, how do we determine if the business model we've crafted is truly satisfactory?

This specific goal becomes our "North star" – telling us whether or not we've arrived at a suitable business model that's capable of achieving this goal.

So, for example, our goals for our new business model might be as follows:

- For first-time homeowners, we want to make the process of owning a new home 10x easier than it is today, while at the same time lowering the risk level to lenders by 20x.

- For business leaders, we want to make the process of registering a new business in our territory 1,000x faster and simpler than it currently is and in so doing attract 3x more businesses to our region.

- For those planning their retirement, we want to offer 10x the level of assurance and confidence that exists today concerning their readiness and preparedness for retirement at a specific point in their lives, given their actions today and projections of future events leading up to, and during, that timeframe.

Broad goals like these offer us the litmus test against which we can later *stress-test* prospective new business models to ascertain how well they do or do not achieve our goal.

In each case, we need to be very clear and explicit with ourselves about the specific type of new *value* we're trying to unleash. Is it greater convenience, greater speed, greater satisfaction, greater assurance, greater security, reduced risk, reduced cost, or what? Defining this specific type of *value* is a critical part of setting these goals.

Exploring our surrogates to create a baseline

Once we have defined our goal, our next step is to gather a collection of prospective *surrogate* business models that we believe are relevant to our situation and goal. In other words, they will be different business models that may be able to, in one way or another (perhaps with certain key modifications), attain our goal.

These business models are going to offer us a baseline against which to work throughout the rest of this process.

Is our goal aspirational enough?

If a particular business model already attains our goal, then we could just stop right there and use that business model.

But what that tells us is that, in all likelihood, our goal is simply not aspirational enough… it's already been done. So, if we're trying to do something new and different – something that unleashes massive new value because it hasn't been done before – then no existing business model (at least none that we're aware of) is going to attain our goal. It will be out of reach for each of them.

Indeed, if we don't, to some degree, "aim for the moon" early on here, then in all likelihood, we'll just end up with something incremental and thus incapable of unleashing massive new value. So, we need to be aspirational here – with a very clear vision of something radically better. That is the only way our new business model is going to unleash massive new value into its markets.

Optional – but not really

This and the next major step are our **deconstructive process** – where we'll be breaking down and *analyzing existing business models.*

While these steps and this particular process are optional and can be omitted if desired – jumping straight into *synthesis* instead (the reconstructive process) – they are nonetheless **incredibly valuable** and therefore **strongly recommended**.

This is because they add significant value to the *overall process* by giving us a very strong sense of *context* within which to work, in terms of what else is out there and why it does or not does not work well for achieving our goal. And that sort of *context* will go a long way later on in helping us to stress-test different business model options, given that we'll have a far stronger baseline from which to work when doing so.

Moving on

So, assuming that we'll be taking this and the next step, we'll move forward from here. This involves three specific sub-steps, all of which we'll explore next.

Note

Before doing that, we should mention that this is our opportunity to exercise divergent and analogous thinking in the process – thinking about what's different in each of these business models, and what about them we can reapply to our particular situation (an exercise that can be augmented with generative AI if desired, to help us explore these facets further). It's also our opportunity to be inspired by the different attributes of these respective business models, seeing places and ways we can emulate certain of those facets from different ones and recombine them into a new whole (as opposed to copying a single monolithic business model alone).

Curating our collection

In general, and in most cases, we should aim to select somewhere between four to five different surrogate business models – and certainly, no more than six if possible. This is to keep the process more manageable and time-bound. If this proves challenging, then we should consider lumping different business models together based on their most important similarities.

In most cases, this shouldn't be an issue, but in the end, you'll have to decide how many different overall business models you want to explore. It may be that you explore half a dozen different business models but fail to come up with sufficient insights and inspiration from those to move forward – and so you circle back and repeat these steps with an entirely different set of business models until you eventually arrive at the right business model to use.

Source one – standardized typologies

One source of these surrogate business models can be the standardized typologies that have been compiled and studied in different books and websites – as we explored earlier in *Chapter 2*.

Further reading

Similar resources that highlight the same types of *business model profiles* are **Business Model Pattern Cards**, such as those found at *Business Makeover* (https://businessmakeover.eu/dam/jcr:b8c1e125-2ff4-4dcb-b1a4-3c2920 9dfb90/download_business%20 model%20cards.pdf), *BMI Lab* (https://bmi-lab-shop.myshopify.com/ products/the-business-model-innovation-pattern-cards), and *CIRCit Norden* (https://circitnord.com/tools/circular-economy-business-model-pattern-cards/). Any of these can prove helpful and inspirational to us in this work.

Source two – cross-industry innovation

A second source of surrogate business models is to consider what is known as *cross-industry innovation* – or also as *analogous empathy*.

This refers to solving a challenge, or capitalizing on an opportunity, in one industry by mapping and applying some method or practice used in a different industry to that new situation.

For example, many operating room practices have been improved by studying how race car pit crews operate – and then mapping some of their methods to the operating room environment. The same for fast-food restaurant drive-throughs – they too have modeled aspects of their designs after race car pit crew operations. Certain automobile user interface devices have been modeled after videogame controllers. Similarly, several industries involving queues (of people or things) have innovated their processes by studying how airport luggage handling and carousels operate. This list goes on and on.

So, the same thing can happen with business models. The best way to uncover a powerful new business model in one situation is to identify *other* industries and settings where an analogous type of situation has been successfully addressed, and then study their business models to learn from them and discover what about them can be borrowed and mapped onto, and otherwise adapted for, our new business model. So, this source of alternative surrogate business models should certainly be considered.

Further reading

To learn more about cross-industry innovation, consider reading the books *Not Invented Here* and *Great Leaders Mix and Match* by authors Ramon Vullings and Marc Heleven, respectively – or refer to Ramon Vullings' *Not Invented Here* website, which can be found at www.crossindustryinnovation.com.

Source three – our own concepts

We should also include any new business model designs that we have conceived up to this point in this collection of surrogate business models since we'll want to study and compare those alongside whatever other surrogates we've uncovered.

Doing this will allow us to see and understand how what we're thinking about compares and contrasts with those other business models – what's similar and different about them – and why and how might that make for an important differentiator in our case.

Next steps

Once we've collected and curated these different surrogate business models, our next task is to study and critique each one for its efficacy toward our goal and the casualties behind that presumable *lack of efficacy*.

Our study and critique effort

What we'll specifically be doing here is looking at each business model and asking questions about it, such as the following:

- To what extent could it/might it attain, versus not attain, our goal?

- In what ways might it attain our goal?

- In what ways might it not attain our goal?

- Why might it not attain our goal? What about it fails short in attempting to do so – is it in what is being offered, how that is being created, who is involved in creating and delivering it, how current industries operate in the process, where it is being offered – or some other shortcoming?

- What are its shortcomings in attaining our goal?

- What might be rectified about it to get closer to our goal – and why?

- If those things were rectified about it, how close might it come to attaining our goal?

We'll ask this set of questions for *each* surrogate business model we're exploring.

The final weed-out

When done, and before proceeding to the next step, we may opt to throw out any of these surrogates as being unworkable for our goal, thus reducing the number of business models, or business model facets, that we'll explore and study in our next step.

To do this, we can develop an analysis wall – either real (with Post-It® Notes) or virtual (such as with Miro) – and then ask critical questions about each business model… questions such as, 'How do the attributes of this particular business model fit or not with our situation?" and "Can we pull out certain facets of it to carry forward while eliminating others that aren't relevant or useful to us?" We should ask as many critical questions as possible about each business model and its facets to weed out those that aren't going to be able to attain our goal – leaving us with those with the potential to do so.

Moving forward

With our surrogate business models now selected and defined, we're ready to move on to our next step in the process – namely dissecting, deconstructing, and critiquing these respective surrogates. This is an activity that will reveal all the detailed minutia we need to understand.

Dissecting, deconstructing, and critiquing our surrogates

Once we've finished examining and critiquing our surrogate business models in the way prescribed previously, what we want to do next is **dissect** and **deconstruct** each of those business models (much more so than we might have already done in the process of answering the preceding series of questions) so that we can test them in a much more granular way.

In particular, what we want to do here is break these business models down into their respective constituent elements – so that we can then examine, scrutinize, and critique each of those elements in isolation, in turn.

The *purpose* of doing this will be to uncover those areas in these business models that *can*, and ideally *should*, be altered to unlock massive new value – on both the demand side and the supply side. The more new value that can be unlocked in this process, the more impactful – and generally innovative – the resultant business model will be. The aim will always be massive new value, which will generally involve some type of "breakthrough innovation" on our part.

The trick – two different, yet complimentary, perspectives… structural and functional

The trick in doing this, however, is that we have to – in our situation – dissect and deconstruct *both* the **structural elements** *and* the **functional attributes** of these business models simultaneously. This is not an easy task, but it is the only way we're going to be able to (eventually) architect a new business model that's truly capable of unleashing the type of massive new value we need.

To do this, we'll have to dissect and deconstruct these business models with both frameworks in mind that we explored previously – the structural framework introduced in *Chapter 2* (The Future Lens Business Model Framework) – and the functional framework introduced in *Chapter 4* (The Business Model Meta Formula).

This means we must break down each of these business models into their respective **structural elements**, as follows:

- **Target market**: *who* is being served;
- **Offering space**: *what* they're being served;
- **Customer acquisition**: *where* they're being served;
- **Value creation**: how what they're being served is being *created and delivered* to them;
- **Brand delivery**: what *brand promise* they're being made and what *experience* they're being given to achieve that promise;
- **Value capture**: how *assets* are being used (driving its cost structure) and whether the offering is being *monetized* (driving its revenues);
- **Timing**: *when* (and under what *conditions*) they're being served.

We have to take each respective business model in our collection and dissect it to extract these exact structural elements.

When doing this, we must also consider, discuss, and document exactly how each of these elements is (in each case) being used *together* with one another – as a synchronous and congruent whole – to work together successfully and thereby achieve their collective goal.

At the same time, we must also break down each of these business models into their respective **functional attributes**:

- **Market Connection Model**: how the business and market attract and connect;

- **Unique Value Proposition**: what distinguishingly unique value it promises and delivers on;

- **Sustainable Competitive Advantage**: how it creates a protective moat around the business;

- **Sales Model**: how exactly it sells its offerings to achieve its value capture;

- **Profit Model**: how it goes about extracting the necessary level of profit from its operations;

- **Risk Mitigation Model**: how it prepares for, and ultimately handles, different business risks;

- **Business Innovation Model**: how it ensures it's innovating fast enough to remain a leader.

Here, we have to take each respective business model in our collection and dissect it to extract these exact functional attributes.

Just like in the case of its structural elements, we must consider, discuss, and document exactly how each of these attributes is (in each case) being used *together* with one another – as a synchronous and congruent whole – to work together successfully and thereby achieve their collective goal.

So, as insightful as these two frameworks are as static visual metaphors of our business model, their real power lies in how we leverage them to guide us in analyzing existing business models and synthesizing new ones.

Their respective domains – focused as they are largely on either the *demand side* (Value Proposition) or the *supply side* (Value Delivery) of the business model – create a broad canvas of innovation for us, allowing us to combine their different parts and pieces in completely new ways – not unlike a mosaic – to yield a completely new outcome and result (and thus the "art" of business model design).

In this sense, these two frameworks serve as tools of structured, creative exploration – allowing us to consider these different points of differentiation in countless different arrangements and combinations – so that we can consider and evaluate all of the possible different designs that might work for our situation. Eventually, a winner emerges from this structured and creative process.

As we will see in *Chapter 14*, our friends at Intensifi use this process – in combination with Design Thinking – to explore possible "business model solutions" to the "business model problem" they've uncovered there.

Our goal – to understand and critique what has been done before

Our goal in both of these assessments is two-fold:

1. **Understand** how these different *structural elements* and *functional attributes* each attained their particular goal in their particular situation.

2. **Critique** them to see how well they may or may not be suited for attaining *our goal* in *our particular situation* – and in each case, why or why not.

Together, this understanding and this critique mutually inform us as to *how* these respective elements and attributes may serve us well, and why. It also helps us understand what most likely needs to be altered about them to make them work properly and optimally in our situation and for our goal.

Of course, achieving this understanding and critique will require some very critical and reflexive thinking on our part. In particular, we need to be aware of our human cognitive limitations limiting the breadth and range of analogous applications we're able to see. We inherently tend to be biased and myopic about such things. For that reason, we will benefit immensely from bringing in others who have very different cognitive thought processes from our own – to create a team with significant cognitive diversity – through which we can then study, analyze, and discuss these different business models. This sort of cognitive diversity will often reveal new perspectives and insights that we alone would never have – particularly around new uses and applications of these different facets beyond how they've been used in the past. So, to overcome these limitations, we highly recommend using such a cognitively diverse team for this analogous assessment.

The inter-dynamics – our great effort yields truly powerful new insights

As may be evident by now, trying to work through both the *structural elements* and the *functional attributes* of these business models at the same time isn't necessarily easy; it can prove a bit taxing on the mind.

Nevertheless, it is incredibly **powerful** in its effect. In particular, it *reveals* the inner workings of these different business models like no other method can. It shows us the inter-relationships between their structural elements – their who/what/why/when/where/how – and the functional outcomes they yield. That, in turn, reveals *why* a particular business model works the way it does… what makes it so *successful* in its particular context. These are insights about these business models that we would otherwise never likely obtain.

Indeed, it is these **inter-dynamics** between the structural and functional attributes of a business model that allow it to work effectively… and let it "do its magic." And that is what we are aiming for.

So, for example, in such an analysis, we might see that what made a particular business model so effective was how it did the following:

- understood the inner thought world of its "who" and leveraged that to craft a Market Connection Model and unique value proposition that was insanely irresistible in that market;

- had an incredibly novel approach to the Value Creation Process (perhaps in its use of assets) that created an impenetrable Sustainable Competitive Advantage in its market that no other player could touch;

- truly excelled at its Brand Delivery on account of a highly effective and very powerful Business Innovation Model that kept it at the cutting-edge forefront of its particular industry;

- leveraged a truly unique approach to Customer Acquisition that gave it a Profit Model that was better than any other operator in its field.

This analysis reveals the sorts of insights that we need.

It will also likely show us that in the majority of these cases, it isn't just *one* of these inter-dynamics working *alone*, but rather the presence of *multiple* such inter-dynamics that make a given business model so incredibly powerful and effective (it may also reveal certain elements of *opportunism* and *luck* playing a role in a given case).

And that is the goal that we are working toward here. Ultimately, we have to be thinking and working in terms of these **inter-dynamics** between the structural and functional attributes of our business model – including how we can leverage multiple such *inter-dynamics* synergistically – to really up our game and raise the bar on what can be attained by the right combinations of these inside a particular industry and market!

Of course, we always have to bear in mind that these different structural and functional attributes must – in the end – be fully coherent and internally congruent with each other. In other words, our overall new business model has to be both structurally and functionally coherent if it is to work correctly and be successful.

Abandoning the past – reframing our situation and reimagining a better future!

When we're doing this exercise – especially as we start to turn the corner toward our reconstructive process – it's important that we not let the fact that what we've been examining is **past** business models that limit what we see as being **possible** and **plausible** for the future! Doing so would leave us shackled with unnecessarily restrictive constraints, and we don't want to be constrained by anything that we don't have to be constrained by, which increasingly is less and less.

Indeed, it is often the case that what has been done in the past was done simply on account of taken-for-granted assumptions that no longer hold true – or certain industry orthodoxies that have always been respected (for whatever reason) without really "testing them." When that is the case, we can often turn things upside down and unlock new value simply by breaking through these assumptions and orthodoxies and forging new and even more relevant ones.

This requires us to put on "a new set of glasses" and completely reframe the situation with an entirely different perspective (which is also *why*, by the way, *cognitive diversity* – different ways of seeing and thinking about the world – is incredibly valuable to us at this point… the more we have, the more we'll be able to reframe the situation). If we can successfully reframe the situation with an entirely new perspective, this will often open our eyes to entirely new possibilities that were never even thought about before – and thus the key to unlocking massive new value that markets are willing to pay for.

What this means is that **everything** about the situation and the business model associated with it has to be up for grabs… its *who*, *why*, *what*, *where*, *how*, and *when*. We start over from **ground zero** – looking at who value is being delivered to, why that value is being delivered to them (what problem we are solving for), what value is being delivered to them (solutions, access, services, and so on), where that value is being delivered to them, how that value is being delivered to them (and monetized in the process), and when that value is being delivered to them.

In doing so, **everything** is at stake – there are no "sacred cows". This means that – in terms of *what gets done* and *how it gets done* – we must abandon all of the following:

- Preconceived ideas and notions
- Existing assumptions
- Industry "norms" and (non-regulatory) standards
- Any other taken-for-granted orthodoxies and practices.

Everything must be **reexamined** and possibly **abandoned** – without the cognitive biases that tend to anchor us in either our past or our personal preferences and ideologies. Everything has to be **relearned** from the point of view of the *customer* and the *markets* they constitute. This is not easy to do, nor does it usually come naturally to us. It requires a strong commitment and discipline to do it properly and thoroughly. So, we must be prepared to apply that commitment and discipline to our search if we are to be successful at it. (We also recommend doing some additional research on how to understand your own cognitive biases and how to best overcome them.)

This requires us to go back to **first principles**, which simply means we start over with the *who*, *what*, and *why*: *who* is attempting to achieve a specific outcome, *what* outcome are they pursuing, and *why* is achieving that outcome crucial to them (what value does it deliver)? In particular, the more that we can drill down into their unique "why," the more we can understand their real needs and the *motivations* and *rationales* behind those needs, and therefore the more we can (at least theoretically) deliver a solution and business model that meets those needs.

Once we've done all this reframing and identified any new possibilities in the situation, we can use our imaginations to conceive new options and come up with entirely new variants of these business model's structural and functional attributes – including variants that have never before even been thought about or tried – all because we allowed ourselves to not be bound by the norms, traditions, assumptions, and orthodoxies of an established industry or its marketplace.

In this way, we will often discover the new opportunities we need – by taking an entirely new route – to unlock massive new value in our situation, toward our end goal.

Starting over – reconstructing a far better business model

At this point, we're ready to start the **reconstructive process** – where we'll be *synthesizing new business models*.

We've finished exploring our surrogate business models, as well as dissecting and deconstructing their respective structural and functional attributes to understand what was good and not good about them (for their particular purpose), and we've also reframed our situation through a new perspective, which has potentially allowed us to abandon certain preexisting norms, assumptions, orthodoxies, and other artifacts of the past, as well as our preconceived ideas and notions from both the past and the present. At this point, we're ready to start over and hunt for a new and better business model that will unleash the massive new value we need.

Therefore – given our stated goal and all the new insights we've just amassed – we want to begin envisioning and building out completely new business model architectures that can deliver on that goal – and in the process unleash this massive new value.

Step 1 (our starting point) – first principles and trends

Our starting point for doing this is, once again, and with our ultimate goal in mind, to go back to the *first principles* involved. Here, we must think very deeply about *who* our customers are, what it is they are *really* trying to accomplish (that's in our sphere of control), and *how* we can unlock *maximum value* for them toward that outcome.

If we can discover a new business model that addresses those things in a way that is **very novel** from any before it, then we can very likely unlock massive new value for this customer, and in the process capture a massive step change in value for our organization. This will produce the win-win business model that we're looking for, and that will give us significant success in the marketplace.

There are countless *ways* to hunt for this new value equation – and we will indeed be exploring much more of that (in detail) in the second and third sections of this book – but one approach is to consider the different *trends* happening around us and the signals they're sending us (while likewise understanding the drivers behind these trends). Doing this can often signal a new *opportunity* to rewire the basis of value in the affected market – and therefore the whole basis for competition in that market. If we can restructure the value equation so that it's more in sync with how customer behaviors and desires are *changing and evolving* due to those trends, then we can end up with an entirely *new approach* to that market, and therefore a new business model that better resonates with these customers and their newer needs.

This was, in fact, the whole premise behind the 2005 book *Blue Ocean Strategy*, by W. Chan Kim and Renée Mauborgne – to rewire the fundamental basis of competition in a particular market such that we make our competition *irrelevant* – we're no longer competing with them (because they're still working on the old basis of competition), we leave them behind in the red ocean of weak margins while we embark on a new journey of our own making in a blue ocean of strong margins.

We'll talk more about how to factor in these sorts of trend changes in *Parts 2* and *3* of this book. What is important to understand at this point is that the key to this process is to hunt for important new *clues* and *signals* that reveal to us new ways we can alter our business model to better resonate with where customers and markets are at currently – and where they're heading tomorrow (sometimes quickly).

Step 2 – building out our new business model options

At this point, and given all of the new insights that we will have just amassed, our next step is to simply build out a **variety** of new business models using *new variants* of these respective structural and functional attributes. These will be new business models that we believe *could*, and *may*, have the potential for attaining our goal.

At this point, we aren't worried about trying to *test* these business models for their efficacy in doing so – that will come later on. For now, we just want to build out a wide range of new business model *variations* – using different combinations of differing variants of these respective attributes.

So, for example, with a clear understanding of our *who* and *why* (which should remain *invariant* unless we opt to pivot and target a *different* customer with a *different* need and therefore a *different* motivation), we can try the following:

> Solution **A**, sourced and developed through method **B**, sold and serviced through channel **C**, with brand promise and experience **D**, monetized via method **E** – utilizing Market Connection Model **F**, involving Unique Value Proposition **G**, protected by Sustainable Competitive Advantage **H**, Risk Mitigation Model **I**, and Business Innovation Model **J**, to ultimately achieve Profit Model **K** – all yielding a long-term sustainable, and highly profitable, business model for us.

In this way, we can mix and match *all manner* of different variants of these respective attributes to create *all manner* of different business model options to consider and (eventually) evaluate and choose from. We may create a dozen or more such business model options to ultimately choose from. We should be very open to – and patient in – exploring as many different business models as needed here – until eventually we find the best business model that unlocks the maximum possible value for our situation.

The "secret formula" that we must always keep in mind

As noted earlier in this book, our research – as well as that of others – has borne out that there is a certain **secret formula** involved in business model innovation – at least from a structural standpoint.

That secret formula is that we can only unlock the **maximum possible new value** whenever we alter not *one*, but rather *multiple* aspects of our business model *together* – in synchronicity. Generally speaking, to unlock maximum new value, we have to innovate in at least **three** of the six structural domains noted, as well as in at least **three** of the seven functional attributes noted. It is the **combination** of these multiple differentiators – working together in harmony – that yields a truly innovative new business model capable of unlocking massive new value.

Very similarly, in writing this book, I interviewed Vijay Kumar, the Charles Owen Endowed Chair in Design at the IIT Institute of Design in Chicago, and former Chief Methodologist at Doblin, creators of the broadly recognized *Ten Types of Innovation*. A key insight that Vijay shared with me, and which he and I discussed at length, was that in completing their research for *Ten Types of Innovation*, what Doblin observed (quite consistently) was that for a business to unlock truly breakthrough value, it had to change in *at least 5 of the 10 areas of their framework*. Changing in just one or two of those areas was never enough… there had to be five or more areas of change (types of innovation) to produce a truly breakthrough impact in the situations they were addressing.

We too have made this same observation in our research and experience – as have others working in this field – that innovating in just one part of our business model is **never** sufficient enough to unlock massive new value; it will only incrementally improve that part of our business model; it will not unlock massive new value. Incremental improvements are not our goal here.

Therefore, it is safe to accept this premise – that we will have to alter *multiple* domains of our business model if we hope to unlock massive new value in our situation. It won't be enough for us to innovate in just one or two of these domains:

- A simple product or service innovation by itself won't do it.
- A simple payment method change by itself won't do it.
- A simple change in the distribution method by itself won't do it.

It takes making *multiple* such changes across our business model – in synchronicity with each other – to achieve the truly breakthrough outcome and impact in our marketplace that unleashes massive new value.

So, for example, we may have to make product changes to go hand-in-hand with new payment and distribution methods, while also delivering an entirely brand experience as a result of both of those changes – as well as other changes in our business model – to get to the point of "massive new value" that we're aiming for.

Therefore, whenever trying to innovate our business model, we have to be fully aware of this requirement – and enter the process fully prepared to alter at least **half** (if not more) of our *entire business model* if we expect to unlock the massive new value that we need to.

The tools – using them

In this process of trying to synthesize new business models (our reconstructive process), it will prove very helpful for us to have certain **tools** to use in doing so – beyond the aforementioned frameworks that we've already explored.

Fortunately, as it so turns out, there is a collection of such tools that are widely available to us – ranging from additional frameworks and models to several different canvases we can complete.

These tools help us *visualize* the different elements and attributes of our business model, and by doing so, think through each one and their respective implications to our business' ability to deliver the type of value it's trying to deliver. By doing so, they allow us to quickly and easily *switch out* different attributes in our business model and simulate and test each one for its likely efficacy.

Because there are so many of these and each one warrants a full explanation on its own – and because they also get used for testing (validation) and not just this design effort – they've been collected into a separate chapter of this book – *Chapter 6* (next). There, you will learn about these different tools and how each can be leveraged for a particular activity in the overall design and testing process.

Stress testing our options

Finally, after we've conceived and designed a broad range of different business model *options* – using differing variants of the respective structural and functional *attributes* of our business model – our next and final step will be to **stress test** each of these different options.

The purpose of doing this is to ascertain how well each option will or will not attain the unique goal we've set, and then ultimately choose the *best business model* with which to go forward. That "best business model" may end up being some amalgamation of all the other business models – borrowing bits and pieces of each one and superimposing them together into a final "super business model."

Developing our customer scenarios

The *way* we do this stress testing is by running each new business model option through a set of **simulated customer scenarios**.

First, we need to define the specific *customer scenarios* that we want to use for these simulations. These scenarios might look something like where a prospective customer recognizes a new need they have, and then starts down the classic "customer journey" to do the following:

- **Learn more about their situation**: where our choices around Target Market and Customer Acquisition – plus our Market Connection Model – can, and may, come into play.

- **Research their solution options**: where our choices around Target Market / Customer Acquisition / Brand Delivery / Offering Space – plus our Market Connection Model and Unique Value Proposition – should all come into play.

- **Make a final choice from among these options**: where our choices around Brand Delivery / Offering Space / Value Creation / Value Capture – plus our Unique Value Proposition, Sales Model, Sustainable Competitive Advantage, and Business Innovation Model – will all come into play.

- **Purchases our offering (their choice)**: where our choices around Value Capture / Customer Acquisition / Value Creation – plus our Sales Model / Profit Model / Sustainable Competitive Advantage – will all come into play.

- **Takes delivery of our offering**: Where our choices around Customer Acquisition / Brand Delivery / Value Creation – plus our sales model and unique value proposition – will all come into play.

- **Initially uses our offering**: Where our choices around Brand Delivery/ Offering Space – plus our unique Value Proposition / Sustainable Competitive Advantage / Risk Mitigation Model / Business Innovation Model – will all come into play.

- **Continues using our offering throughout its life cycle**: Where our choices around Brand Delivery / Offering Space / Value Creation / Customer Acquisition – plus our Unique Value Proposition / Sustainable Competitive Advantage / Risk Mitigation Model / Business Innovation model – can, and may, all come into play.

- **Recommends our offering to others in the same situation**: Where our choices around Brand Delivery / Offering Space – plus our Unique Value Proposition / Sustainable Competitive Advantage / Business Innovation will all come into play.

- **Purchases our offering again when needed**: Where our choices around Brand Delivery / Offering Space / Customer Acquisition – plus our Sustainable Competitive Advantage / Business Innovation Model / Risk Mitigation Model will all come into play.

- **Disposes of our offering in an appropriate manner**: Where our choices around offering Space / Customer Acquisition / Value Capture – plus our Unique Value Proposition / Sustainable Competitive Advantage / Profit Model / Risk Mitigation Model / Business Innovation Model – can, and may, come into play.

When considering these different touchpoints along the customer journey, we can define all manner of different simulated scenarios involving the following aspects:

- all manner of different customers who recognize all manner of different needs;

- considering all manner of different solution options (including ours);

- having all manner of different decision criteria (the factors and attributes they care most about);

- purchasing in all manner of different ways (buy, rent, subscribe, and so on);

- buying all manner of different offerings (products services, experiences, and combinations);

- using that offering in all manner of different ways;

- having all manner of different outcomes, results, and experiences from using it;

- needing support and services in all manner of different ways;

- sharing all manner of feedback about it (or lack thereof) to all manner of other prospective customers:

- needing to dispose of this offering at its end-of-life in all manner of different ways.

Here, we have to think through the different scenarios that are most important and relevant to our situation, and then conceive the inputs to these different considerations regarding the customer, their needs, options, brand, solution, use, reconnection, and disposal. From this, we may end up with any number of different unique customer scenarios that we care about that involve any number of unique combinations of these different factors.

There are other methods we can use to develop our customer scenarios – rather than stepping through the customer journey. For example, we can home in on just one particular aspect of the situation that we care about – perhaps the one key aspect that will differentiate us from everything else out there – and then develop a unique customer scenario around that.

Whatever method we use, the point here is to come away with the specific customer scenarios that we care about, and thus want to use in our stress testing.

Running our (simulated) stress tests

Once we have our customer scenarios worked out, our next step is to **stress-test** each unique *business model option* against each respective *customer scenario*. So, we can think of a matrix like the one shown in *Figure 5.2* here, where we pair each prospective business model option against each respective customer scenario that we've defined.

		Customer Scenario							TOTAL SCORE	Notes & Comments
		Scenario 1	Scenario 2	Scenario 3	Scenario 4	Scenario 5	Scenario 6	Scenario 7		
Business Model Option	Option 1	+2	+5	+4	+3	-1	0	-5	+8	Average overall.
	Option 2	+5	+5	+3	+4	0	+1	-3	+15	Strong UVP, SCA, & Sales Model.
	Option 3	+2	+1	+5	+2	-3	-2	0	+5	Note enough market alignment to create customer resonance.
	Option 4	0	+3	+4	+3	0	+1	+1	+12	Sound UVP - less so SCA.
	Option 5	-2	-1	-3	0	0	+4	+3	+1	Deficient overall.
	Option 6	-4	+1	-5	-1	+2	+3	+5	+1	Deficient overall.
	Option 7	-5	-5	0	+2	+4	+4	+1	+1	Deficient overall.
	Option 8	0	-4	+2	-1	+1	+3	+2	+3	Deficient overall.
	Option 9	-1	-4	-5	+1	0	-1	+2	-8	A really poor design - overall.
	Option 10	0	+1	+4	+5	+4	+2	+1	+17	Strong SCA & RMM overall.
	Option 11	+4	+4	+4	+3	+1	+2	0	+18	Very strong MCM & UVP in most cases.
	Option 12	+5	+2	-1	+2	-1	0	+5	+12	Solid UVP & Profit Model.

Figure 5.2: A Business Model Option versus Customer Scenario Stress-Testing Matrix. More specific and detailed notes and comments are suggested.

Then, we run the stress tests. We can do this in one of three ways, each progressing in the actual value it gives us. We can do one of the following:

1. Run them as verbal thought experiments in our group – walking through (verbally as a group) what we believe will happen in each case, given the choice of business model attributes in that case.

2. Use a software simulation tool where we model each business model and each customer (which, in an agent-based modeling tool, are known as "agents"), and then run those simulations to see what happens (this approach requires solid programming skills in such a simulation tool if we hope to have any confidence in its outcomes).

3. Conceive and run real-world "stress test business experiments" in which we use actual real-life subjects to engage with some tangible emulation of that business model (or elements thereof) – to see how well it fares.

As noted previously, each of these approaches progresses in the value it delivers to us. Verbal thought experiments can be an okay place to start for initial (perhaps "weeding out") conversations, but we can't place a ton of value on them. Likewise, simulations can offer us more value, with more reliable insights, but at the end of the day, they're still simulations with certain assumptions baked into them, and those assumptions can, in some cases, turn out to be wrong, leading us down the wrong path.

In truly complex business model situations, it is **only** the actual real-world business experiments that give us the confidence we need to make dependable decisions about our business model. So, the recommendation is – to the extent possible – to find ways to physically emulate and test these different options with actual real-world subjects – to find out how well each one does or does not work under these respective "stressful conditions." Unfortunately in terms of the time, cost, and effort required, this is the only way we're going to be able to have truly solid confidence in the choices and decisions being made here. There simply is no substitute for this type of real-world customer and market feedback in the process.

So, whichever of these approaches we opt to use, the result will be an assessment of each business model option in terms of how well it did or did not attain our goal in each customer scenario – and in each case why it performed so. This is reflected in the scoring (ranging from -5 to +5 in each case) and comments shown in *Figure 5.2*.

What we're looking for

What we're looking for in these assessments is *what* about each of these unique business model options worked well in a *maximum* number of scenarios we explored. In other words, *what* about them and their attributes allowed them to attain our goal (or get closer than the other options) in a maximum number of scenarios?

If we can **isolate** what works so well about one or more of these particular business model options – in terms of their specific structural elements and functional attributes – then we can start toward some sort of convergence where we begin homing in on those details of our business model that work truly well in our particular situation for attaining our particular goal.

Rinse and repeat

We may need to repeat this cycle even further – with even *newer variants* of these business model options (having more *refined* variants of the elements and attributes) and/or *newer customer scenarios* to test against.

As we continue testing, refining, re-testing, refining even more, re-testing even more, and so on, we'll eventually reach a point of convergence where we come upon our final "winning" business model design – the one that we'll use to attain our goal.

Finished – at least for the moment

Once we get to this point of convergence, we're done… finished – at least for the moment.

The "winner" here is the one business model that represents the most stable, optimized value creation / delivery / capture situation for our particular goal, at the point in time it was optimized for.

So, at this point, we have the final business model that we'll start with. We say "start" here because, at this point, all we've done is simulated different options with different customer scenarios – a still very theoretical exercise, even if it's done with actual real-world subjects.

None of this has, as of yet, seen the full light of day – with *real customers* in *real markets* and *real competitive pressures*. It may very well be that meeting such a reality introduces yet other dynamics into the situation – ones that we failed to account for, or weren't able to account for, in our stress tests. And when that is the case, it could change the entire outcome – requiring us to loop back yet again.

In all likelihood, this will happen – at least to some degree.

What really matters

The preceding point is important because, ultimately, it doesn't matter how good our business model looks on paper – or how well it performed in our simulated stress tests.

What really matters is how well it performs in the *real world* – where we have real customers with real needs searching for a real solution, competing against other (real) solutions, and so on. That will always be the litmus test that matters – the one that we have to win against. Otherwise, we will not succeed!

What if this doesn't work and we don't find a winner?

So far, we've assumed the preceding reconstructive process and this convergent stress-testing process will produce a suitable winner… the one best option that "wins out" over all others in our contest for the best business model option. We've also assumed that such a winner will unlock the greatest overall value for every stakeholder affected, and thereby attain the goal we've set for it.

But it's altogether possible that this doesn't happen… that no clear winner emerges – possibly because none of the options we've considered, despite our best efforts, were able to attain our goal.

So, what do we do when that happens? This is an important question.

If and when that happens, we have to start over from the reconstructive process again – circling back with perhaps a new (different) goal, new constraints, and/or new assumptions. Then, we must repeat these respective reconstructive and stress-testing processes (with the same or different customer scenarios) until we eventually find a winner that we're satisfied with.

Alternatively, we conclude that our goal – in whatever form we've chosen to state it – is simply *unattainable*, given current existing capabilities. That leaves us with the question of how to *develop* or otherwise *find* the (newer) capabilities we need to make our goal attainable – and what must we do to develop and/or retain those capabilities.

In most cases, that will become more of a long-term quest than a short-term one – one that may take several years to complete. So, we can choose to invest those years or we can choose to amend our goal based on present existing capabilities (or do both). Whichever we choose, we have to also ensure that we're exhausting *every other feasible means* of unlocking new value in our situation – including by radically reframing the situation and the need it involves

This latter consideration is *why* we have to take a very **human-centered approach** to this whole matter of business model innovation. The only way we're going to be able to adequately reframe our situation and the needs it entails – and thereby define an optional solution and an optimal business model for it – is to work through that situation from a truly *human-centric perspective*.

Fortunately for us, the next two sections of this book address precisely that!

Finally, let's note that, in most cases, if we've defined our goal correctly, and if we've done this process properly, then a "winner" will emerge – a final business model that executes and performs as expected and intended. But that being said, we have to also keep in mind that this is just a "winner for today." The benchmark for "value" will continue to change and evolve, and therefore our new business model will likewise have to evolve dynamically to stay ahead of that reality.

Executing our business model

Once we have the innovative new business model that we intend to use – the one that attains our goal and in so doing unleashes massive new value – we still have the task of executing that business model.

Facing the music

That is where the rubber meets the road, and everything either works as we expected, or – more likely than not – we learn what isn't working about our business model the way we'd thought it would, and thereafter refine it further – including possibly pivoting inside it as we gain new insights through successive rounds of validated learning cycles.

Whatever happens, we'll never know for sure how well our chosen business model works toward our stated goal until we launch our business and put that business model into practice. Then, we'll find out the truth. So, we must prepare ourselves for the harsh lessons of reality, and, at some point, just jump in.

How to – corporates and start-ups

The question is how exactly should we do this?

For start-ups, the answer to that question is typically self-evident… the founders, perhaps with a small cadre of early employees, will simply launch the new business with whatever financing they have and then start hitting the streets to find customers and deliver value to them. They'll do this hoping that their new business model works like they had planned for it to – and expected it to – so that the math ultimately works out for them.

For corporates, however, they have more options to choose from. In particular, there are generally three distinct options they can select from:

1. Launch the new business (with its new business model) inside an *existing* business unit – perhaps as a new division or department in that business unit.

2. Launch the new business (with its new business model) inside a *completely new* business unit – one focused exclusively on, and therefore dedicated to, this line of business (with its new business model).

3. Spin out the new business (with its new business model) as a standalone *business venture* – what is commonly known as a "spin-out venture," or sometimes a "corporate start-up".

Of these three approaches, the first two leverage established skills, resources, and know-how inside the organization to drive and operate the new line of business. This can work well, so long as the new line of business isn't entirely foreign to these types of operations (if so, then the mismatch can spell doom for the new line of business).

The third approach gives the new venture the opportunity and latitude to go out and develop its own (new) skills and know-how to drive and operate its business in a (different) way that's best suited for it. This approach is often best suited in what might otherwise be thought of as a "high-inertia organization" – one heavily mired in traditional and orthodox ways of doing things… ways that may not at all be suited to such a new venture.

With such a spin-out venture, the venture takes on the task – as well as all the risk – of launching this new line of business with its new business model (often a very tech-enabled business model these days) and associated offering(s). The new venture will require appropriate support and resources from the parent organization to do so.

This is often the best approach whenever the parent organization is incapable of making the changes required to be able to execute the new business model – or if doing so represents what it considers to be too great of a risk.

Indeed, if any of the following conditions exist inside the parent organization, then it benefits from using the spin-out venture approach:

- misaligned priorities and motivations around innovation;

- overall cultural barriers to innovation;

- people, time, and resources being torn between the "exploit" and "explore" mentalities;

- **Not-invented-here (NIH)** syndrome;

- a middle management layer of "permafrost," in which middle managers tend to stonewall new initiatives they feel threatened by;

- any other situation that creates an environment that's non-conducive to trialing the new business model.

As with any such undertaking, the new spin-out venture has to be considered an experiment – the key way of learning whether or not, and how well, this new business model works – all else being the same.

So, either way – whether inside the main organization or through a new spin-out venture – the organization has to move forward with such experiments if it hopes to find new business models that can differentiate it in its marketplace and allow it to stand out in ways that resonate with those markets – by unleashing massive new value to them.

Understanding our business model versus having a business plan

Often, whenever a new line of business is being defined, business leaders inherently think that the first thing they need to do is put together a **business plan** for it. And so they immediately jump into that exercise. This thinking is rooted in industrial-era business logic (before today's start-up boom), where businesses operated in very stable and predictable business environments – something that's not so much the case anymore.

So, while having a good business plan is not a bad practice, you have to be *extremely careful* about how that business plan has been developed and ultimately gets used. The reason for this is that all business plans are predicated on certain **assumptions** – and if those assumptions have not been tested and validated, then they may be *wrong*, in which case the business plan isn't worth the paper it's printed on. It's bunk.

A much more important question than "Do you have a business plan in place?" is "What is your business model for this effort – and how have its details been validated to ensure they're the right ones for this situation?" That will **always** be your starting point – long before ever trying to write out a business plan. A large share of new ventures **fail** because the *assumptions* embedded into their business plans were **wrong**, but that fact was never known – because their validity was never tested. Instead, they were simply accepted on blind faith, as though somehow all those assumptions would magically come true.

Consequently, business leaders have to work out exactly what their **business model** is going to be – by testing and validating *each* of its underlying assumptions and hypotheses before using it. They also have to decide, as part of this, the **priority order** of these assumptions – ranking them according to how *critical* they are – and thus what *order* they will test them in (with sound logic) to optimize their use of time in this process (you must always test your most critical assumptions first so that you don't waste time testing less-critical assumptions that ride on these, only to have them invalidated when the more critical assumption prove wrong). This way, once they've done that testing, they can have *high confidence* that their choice of business model details is, in fact, the best and right choice for their situation – long before they ever write out a business plan for it.

Then, when they do finally sit down to write out their business plan, they'll know *exactly* what its underlying assumptions are – including what business model they'll use for it, and why that business model is the best choice for the situation at hand. They can then *defend* that business plan with high confidence, using the hard-earned evidence they've amassed from their in-depth research for its business model. This makes the final business plan far more defensible – and thus far more investible by investors.

Back to Intensifi – where are they now (given all of this)?

Back over at Intensifi – where our friends Ian, Zoe, and Watson are toiling away – the feeling is both optimistic and a bit overwhelmed.

After learning about this process for developing their new business model, they're both thankful for having such a clear process to follow, but also quite cognizant now of just how much hard work lies before them. Nevertheless, they're 100% committed to doing that hard work to ensure they have the most successful new venture possible further down the road.

To this end, as their (preliminary) goal, they have defined the following two-part goal – the first part for individuals (a consumer-focused offering) and the final part for businesses (an enterprise-focused offering) – both of which have to be capable of being executed in a way that yields a sustainably high-profit margin and scale for the venture:

- **For individuals**: To deliver a comprehensive yet affordable service that allows these individuals to achieve their absolute maximum life potential – by giving them access to immense reams of pertinent data and information that has been filtered and curated for them by appropriate AI algorithms. This will help guide them in plotting out their life's trajectory and otherwise advise them in making their key life choices. In the end, they will have lived their lives to their maximum possible potential – personally, professionally, financially, relationally, and otherwise.

- For **business organizations**: To deliver a comprehensive yet affordable service that allows these organizations to achieve their absolute maximum business potential by giving them access to immense reams of pertinent data and information that has been filtered and curated for them by appropriate AI algorithms. This will help guide them in plotting out their organization's strategic trajectory and otherwise advise them in making their key strategic decisions such that at specific points in time, they will have attained their maximum possible growth and impact for that period, given the resources and capabilities they can access and deploy in the intervening time.

They've also identified the following surrogate business models that they wish to study and analyze for this process:

- The business models of successful fitness apps – for example, those of Aaptiv, FitOn, and Jefit.

- The business models of successful financial advisory apps – for example, those of Empower, Simplifi, and Rocket Money.

- The business models of successful career search platforms – for example, those of Indeed, Glassdoor, and Wellfound.

- A cross-industry mashup of different business models featuring the following combinations:

  - The Market Connection Model and Unique Value Proposition of mass-market consumer electronics companies (Apple, Samsung, Sony, LG, HP, and others) in select categories mixed with the Sustainable Competitive Advantage of the world's oldest industrial technology companies (Siemens, Philips, IBM, Toshiba, GE, and others), also in select categories.

  - The Market Connection Model and Unique Value Proposition of Sharing Economy Businesses (Airbnb, Uber, Zipcar, TaskRabbit, and others) mixed with the Sustainable Competitive Advantage and Risk Mitigation Models of enterprise resource planning platforms (SAP S/4HANA, Oracle NetSuite, Acumatica Cloud ERP, Odoo ERP, and others).

  - The Sales And Profit Models of SaaS web service platforms (AWS, Microsoft Azure, and others) mixed with the Business Innovation Models of the world's leading computer chip manufacturers (Taiwan Semiconductor, Nvidia Intel, Broadcom, and others).

- A few concepts of their own:

  - A Market Connection Model focusing exclusively on young upper-middle-class professionals (consumer side) and divisions of large Fortune 500 scale businesses (enterprise side).

  - A Unique Value Proposition involving a comprehensive turnkey platform using sensing and data-collection devices on people, in their homes or businesses, in automobiles, and in any other major assets the party uses (for example, capital equipment) to amass all their data, compare it with a global repository of choice options (strategy options) based on the established goals, and then present the user with a roadmap of optimal decision choices.

  - A Sustainable Competitive Advantage involving intellectual property rights over select methods, plus trade secrets surrounding the actual AI algorithms employed, and finally exclusive partnerships with select key ecosystem partners.

  - A Sales Model involving marketing-driven sales on the consumer side and direct B2B sales on the enterprise side.

  - A Profit Model involving pricing tiers exceeding their cost of operations, with certain specific target margins (potentially different for the consumer and enterprise sides).

- A Risk Mitigation Model that is yet to be determined (they have yet to identify and explore all the different risks that could be encountered – though that is a work in progress).

- A Business Innovation Model designed to keep them at the forefront of this category (whatever that means, per se, as this is yet to be determined).

So, Ian, Zoe, and Watson hope that after studying and analyzing these different business models for their efficacy in satisfying not only their own goals but those of Intensifi as well – including the different causalities associated with their respective structural and functional attributes – they'll be able to start synthesizing new business model options to consider.

However, they don't feel that they are ready to do this quite yet. This is because they aren't entirely sure that they have their goal defined just right yet – and defining your goal *properly* is a prerequisite to being able to study surrogate business models. Indeed, having the *right* goal established is *pivotal* to this entire process. In the case of Ian, Zoe, and Watson, they're rightfully concerned that their two-part goal – especially in the way they've currently articulated each part of it – may not fully align with what each respective target customer wants and needs – not to mention their motivations for wanting and needing these things.

Ian, Zoe, and Watson also want to know more about the different business model innovation tools and models available to them so that they can select and use whichever of those are most appropriate to their particular needs at each stage of this journey.

So, before doing any of this surrogate analysis and subsequent synthesis work, they believe it's important for them to first step back and understand their would-be customers at a far deeper level. This is so that they can truly appreciate and understand the human experience involved – and with it, the very real motivations involved in driving people to use their offering – as well as the motivations that might dissuade them from doing so. Then, they'll be more prepared to address those motivations sufficiently. They believe this step is paramount and that they must take it before going any further, lest they start down the wrong path with inadequate business model options.

So, at the moment, they're going to put a pause on analyzing these surrogate business models, as well as synthesizing any new options, until they've gone through this exercise of understanding their would-be customers' *real* needs and motivations (as well as have the business model innovation tools they need to work with). They believe that, after they've done this, and understand these needs and motivations **thoroughly**, they'll be far more ready and prepared to start analyzing surrogate business models, as well as developing not only new options to consider but also the appropriate customer scenarios against which to test them. This will help them find the best business model for attaining their goal.

The next steps for Ian, Zoe, and Watson are two-fold:

1. To learn about all the different business model innovation tools and models available to them so that they can select specific ones to work with at each stage of the process.

2. To learn about design thinking and human-centered design so that they can do what they need and intend to do here.

It will be fun and insightful to share this learning journey with them.

Summary

In this chapter, we explored a comprehensive process – the *Business Model Synthesis Process*. This was based on the overarching practice of reconstructive inquiry – in which you define your goal, take existing (surrogate) business models, break them down into their respective elements (both structural and functional), and study and critique them for how well they work toward your original goal plus the new one. The next step is to synthesize entirely new business model options around that new goal, after which you stress-test those options against different customer scenarios to find the best business model for your new goal.

This is the process we'll be using to develop your new business model – one that has the best chances of attaining your unique goal, in your specific situation, while also being successful as a real business venture. So, you will need to put effort into learning and mastering this process and becoming fully proficient at it so that you can use it to design the right business model for success in your situation.

In the next chapter, we'll explore a broad historical progression of different business model innovation tools and models that have each been developed and come into use since the start of the 21st century. We'll see how these different tools and models each offer something of value and use to us, and how we can leverage them in different ways to both study and analyze existing (surrogate) business models, and design the new ones we need.

We'll also observe how these tools and models have been developed and come into use since the start of the 21st century. This is a testimony to the fact that business model innovation is itself a child of the 21st century, and as such has come of age during this period (so far).

The Business Model Toolbox
– An Evolution of Tools for
Business Model Innovation

In *Chapter 5*, we explored a process known as the *Business Model Synthesis* process – a deconstructive and reconstructive process we can use to dissect and study existing or prospective business models so that, from that, we can develop far better and more innovative business models capable of achieving *our* particular goal.

At the heart of this process was a practice known as *reconstructive inquiry*, in which we dissect different business models – both structurally and functionally – to understand what is most effective about each of their respective elements. We then use that insight to build out new business model options leveraging the most effective elements of these to create business models that are possibly capable of attaining the stated goal.

Thereafter, we devise specific customer scenarios against which to test those options. And then finally, upon testing them, we select the best business model to use (or some combination of them), resulting in an innovative new business model capable of attaining the stated goal, thus unleashing massive new value to all the parties involved.

In this chapter (designed to support that chapter), we're going to explore the broad historical progression of different business model innovation tools and models – each of which has been developed and come into use since the beginning of the 21st century. These respective tools and models are used to further support our business model innovation *process*. As such, they augment the two main frameworks that we explored earlier – the structural framework presented in *Chapter 2*, and the functional framework presented in *Chapter 4*.

In particular, these tools and models are used in either one of two ways:

- **descriptively** (for analysis) – to study and analyze an existing (possibly surrogate) business model for its unique strengths and weaknesses;

- **prescriptively** (for synthesis) – to design a new business model – one that's purpose-built for a very specific goal and outcome.

Some of the tools and models are better suited for one mode over the other, but most can be used effectively in either mode.

Ultimately, each of these tools and models has something of value to offer us. We'll definitely, therefore, want to use some of them in our own efforts.

In addition to their individual value however, exploring these different tools and models will give us greater context into how the world of business model innovation has evolved over that time – as well as how different parties have gone about thinking about business models, both structurally and functionally, during that time.

In particular, let me point out that the purpose of this chapter is not, per se, to teach you how to use these tools, nor to highlight examples of how they've been used to date. Doing that would be far beyond the scope of this chapter. Each of these tools have their bodies of knowledge and practice (usually collected on some central website) that explain in detail how to use them and that offer case studies illustrating how they've been used to date. Instead, the purpose of this chapter is to highlight these tools for you – so that you're aware of them and where and how they each get applied – as well as to reveal some of the historical progression of thinking around business model innovation over the past 25 years. It is hoped that you take that away from this chapter.

We're going to specifically examine ten distinct tools or models that have emerged since the beginning of the century – used collectively to both *think about* business models, and actually *design and/or redesign* business models to be more effective. Each one of these was – in its own way and at its own time – revolutionary, because, originating out of the startup scene (and that largely on account of the work of Steve Blank), they challenged the dominant dogma of the industrial era macroenvironmental analysis from the 1980s and before. That analysis assumed that there were few *unknowns* in the business model, and so it was simply a matter of *executing* against the knowns. But in the context of startups, this is **never the case**; there are literally hundreds of unknowns that have to be sorted out in the process. And so, the dogma of that day did not fit with this scenario, and thus these tools ushered in a whole new set of approaches for uncovering the unknowns of a startup's business model.

These ten tools are the following:

- **The Business Model Wheel**: Developed in 2005 by Jim Meuhlhausen of the Business Model Institute.

- **The Innovation Radar**: Developed in 2006 by Mohanbir Sawhney, Robert Wolcott, and Inigo Arroniz of The Kellogg School of Management at Northwestern University.

- **The Business Model Canvas**: Developed in 2010 by Alexander Osterwalder and Yves Pigneur of Strategyzer.

- **Lean Canvas**: Developed in 2010 by Ash Maurya of LEANSTACK.

- **Business Model Innovation Factory**: Developed in 2012 by Saul Kaplan of Business Innovation Factory.

- **The Peter Thomson Value Proposition Canvas**: Developed in 2013 by digital strategist Peter J. Thomson.

- **The Ten Types of Innovation**: Developed in 2013 by Larry Keeley, Helen Walters, Ryan Pikkel, and Brian Quinn of Doblin.

- **The Future Lens Business Model Framework**: Developed in 2015 by Anthony Mills of the Global Innovation Institute and Legacy Innovation Group.

- **The Business Model Meta Formula Canvas**: Developed in 2015 by Anthony Mills of The Global Innovation Institute and Legacy Innovation Group.

- **The GInI Business Model Canvas**: Developed in 2016 by Anthony Mills of The Global Innovation Institute and Legacy Innovation Group.

We'll also check in again with our friends at Intensifi – to see how much progress they've made in their business model innovation journey, and where they are as a result of the overall process.

The Business Model Wheel – 2005

The *Business Model Wheel* is a functional model of the business model created by Jim Meuhlhausen, JD of the **Business Model Institute** (**BMI** – www.businessmodelinstitute.com).

Meuhlhausen designed this model with the small- to medium-sized independent business owner in mind – often an individual operating a more traditional service business such as a contract manufacturer, a building contractor, a plumber, and other well-established service businesses, as well as a more contemporary service business too, such as a marketing agency, a website design firm, or an IT firm.

Meuhlhausen based the model on over 4,000 meetings he held with business leaders in these types of firms, after which he studied everything available at the time on business models – in search of the winning elements that would ensure success for any such business. A key realization Meuhlhausen had in this process was that a mediocre businessperson with a great business model would beat a great businessperson with a mediocre business model any day… one simply cannot make up for a bad business model, no matter how smart they happen to be otherwise. (One would be forgiven for assuming that a really smart business person would inherently somehow end up with a really great business model, but Meuhlhausen did not find this to be the case – there was no direct correlation.)

The resulting functional model is comprised of three key zones, broken into eight functional areas. These three zones and eight functional areas are – in order of importance (according to the BMI):

- **Offering**
  - Market Attractiveness
  - Unique Value Proposition

- **Monetization**
  - Profit Model
  - Sales Execution Model

- **Sustainability**
  - Ongoing Competitive Advantage
  - Innovation Factor
  - Avoidance of Pitfalls
  - Graceful Exit.

(The term 'sustainability' here refers to *business continuity* rather than *environmental sustainability*.)

This model – unlike other functional models such as the *Business Model Meta Formula* (which was purpose-designed to be universal) – is focused squarely on **the small- to medium-sized enterprise (SME)**, and as such tends to be less universal in flavor.

The eighth area of this model – 'Graceful Exit' – is designed squarely with the independent businessperson in mind, offering them insights into how to design their business model to make their independent business more saleable when they are ready to exit it. These insights are quite different from those that would be applicable to a high-growth startup that commonly gets bought by a large corporation or else goes on to become publicly traded. In this latter case, the considerations of the business model that will make the business an attractive purchase are those that are already built into its Market Connection Model, Unique Value Proposition, and Sustainable Competitive Advantage – and thus there is no need for a separate aspect of the business model to address this matter.

The Business Model Institute has used this framework as the basis for a relatively in-depth and exhaustive assessment and analysis tool that it created for assessing and studying different business models. In that tool, these, and additional finer areas of the business model, are each scored on a weighted scale based on their relative strength or weakness. The overall business model is then scored to determine how strong it is overall. The outcome of this assessment reflects the strength of the overall business model, plus where its respective individual strengths and weaknesses lie. This allows the business owner to then build on those strengths, while also working to rectify most or all of its weaknesses.

Meuhlhausen featured this Business Model Wheel in the 2013 book *Business Models for Dummies*, which he was contracted to write for publisher John Wiley & Sons. The model is outlined on pages 61-64 of that book.

The 'outsider observation' of this model is that it was designed for, and has been mostly applied to, more traditional SME businesses such as independent wholesalers and retailers (think your local downtown home décor store), independent service providers (think your local favorite restaurant), and so on – and less for high-growth tech startups poised to scale to unicorn status. That being said, most of its precepts are valid for all new business ventures, but some – such as 'Graceful Exit' – may be less so, depending on the founders' intentions (indeed, an IPO for example is far different than BMI's conceptualization of a 'graceful exit').

The Innovation Radar – 2006

The *Innovation Radar* is a business model structural framework that was introduced in the April 2006 issue of MIT Sloan Management Review, via an article entitled *The 12 Different Ways for Companies to Innovate*.

This framework was developed by Mohanbir Sawhney, Robert Wolcott, and Inigo Arroniz, all of whom wrote the relevant article and were at the time associated with The Kellogg School of Management at Northwestern University. The authors' premise was that companies with a *restricted view of innovation* can miss key opportunities to innovate. They therefore created this framework to give companies a 360-degree view of what they at the time termed 'the business system' (the field hadn't quite come around yet to using the phrase 'business model' in the context of innovation) – and thereby help them to avoid this sort of *innovation myopia*.

This was the culmination of a three-year research project the authors undertook involving nine companies – namely Boeing, Chamberlain Group, Conoco Philips, DuPont, eBay, FedEx, Microsoft, Motorola, and Sony.

In their framework – which the authors called *The Innovation Radar* – they break the 'business system' down into the following four core **anchor** areas:

1. Customers – Who.
2. Offerings – What.
3. Presence – Where.
4. Process – How.

They then break the 'business system' down even more granularly into eight additional **dimensions** of business innovation – each spanning in between two of the four anchors:

- In between Customers (Who) and Offerings (What) are *Platforms* and *Solutions*.

- In between Offerings (What) and Presence (Where) are *Brand* and *Networking*.

- In between Presence (Where) and Process (How) are *Organization* and *Supply Chain*.

- In between Process (How) and Customers (Who) are *Customer Experience* and *Value Capture*.

These four *anchors* and eight additional *dimensions* (12 in all) are laid out together on a **360° radar plot**.

The article offers in-depth explanations and examples of each of these anchors and dimensions. Additionally, it provides graded profiles of what were at the time the 4 leading Latin American banks – showing in each case which of these 12 areas that particular bank was strong or weak at, and thus revealing the key differences between them (at least in this regard).

The article can be seen at `https://sloanreview.mit.edu/article/the-different-ways-for-companies-to-innovate/`.

We start to see a pattern emerging here already, with this framework serving as its intermediate point. Starting from the earliest days of the Business Model Wheel conceived right after the beginning of the century, to the Business Model Canvas coming up next (in 2010), we see in this framework the connective thread revealing where the Innovation Community's thought process was evolving from and to at the time. In particular, there was this emerging awakening around the world that innovation wasn't just *product innovation*, but rather far more holistic and multifaceted innovation – embodied perfectly in this framework. That whole thought process is what would eventually emerge, in 2010, as true business model innovation as we know it today.

The Business Model Canvas – 2010

In 2010, Alexander Osterwalder and Yves Pigneur published the book *Business Model Generation*.

This book was the culmination of several years of work the authors invested in the early 2000s into how to think about one's business model *functionally* – so that it could be **purposefully designed** to achieve a certain specific outcome.

Doing this – and having the toolset these authors provided – all of a sudden gave innovators and entrepreneurs a way to break down their business model into its constituent elements – so that, with this, they could then run any number of different 'what-if' thought experiments about their business model. This allowed them to play with the business model and each of its respective functional questions – so that, coming out of the exercise, they could come away with a business model they felt more confident in.

Anecdote

It is interesting to note, as a bit of a side note, that Osterwalder created this framework for his PhD work, but his academic advisors felt that such a framework as this was overly simplistic, and did not reflect good (academic) research. So Osterwalder instead used it to write a very successful book and launch a very successful business based on it. This fact reveals a *further evolution* – from taking the thinking about business model innovation *out of the academic setting* (seen in the prior *Innovation Radar* framework) and *into the real world* of applied business innovation – as well as from the corporate setting into more of an entrepreneurial setting. This brought the Innovation Community's thinking about business model innovation into the light of day, giving it a real face and a voice to work around properly now.

Take 1 – the Business Model Canvas

The key element of their book – and the key reason these authors' work became the phenomenal success that it did (especially when earlier efforts such as *The Innovation Radar* failed to gain similar traction) was the creation and inclusion of the now-famous *Business Model Canvas*, shown in the following *Figure 6.1*.

The Business Model Canvas drew from numerous earlier management insights – most notably Peter Drucker's theories of the firm and Michael Porter's value chain maps – but it put all this into a very well-designed visual format that people found quite easy to use.

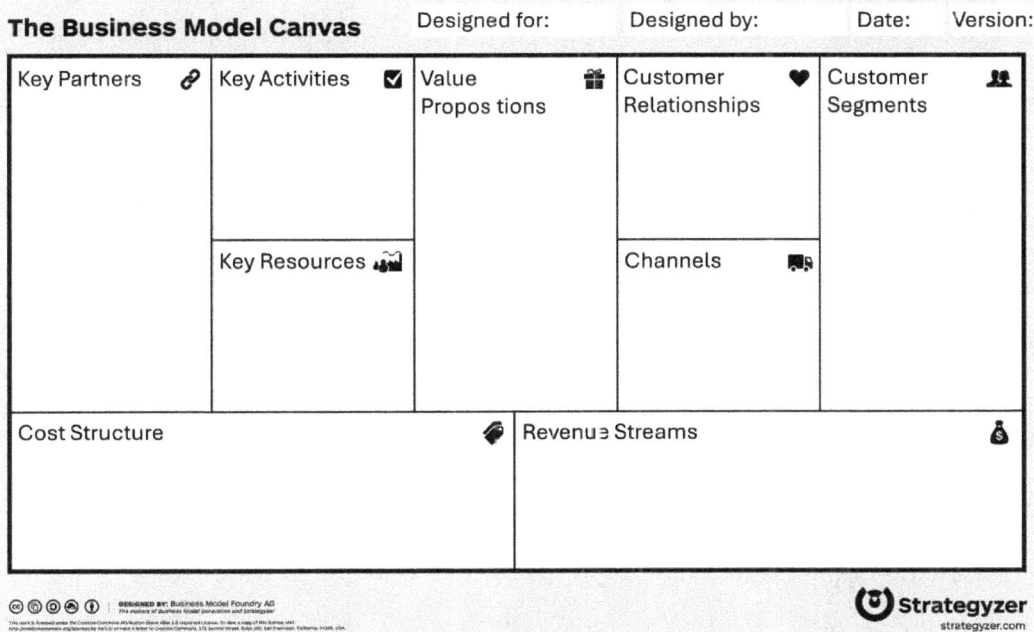

Figure 6.1: The Business Model Canvas. The Business Model Canvas is reproduced here under a Creative Commons license from Strategyzer AG.

Another key departure here from prior business model frameworks was that rather than just being a structural framework for the business model (who, what, where, when, how, etc.), this canvas offered more of a functional view of the business model – looking at certain things the business model had to define, as well as the key questions the innovators would have to answer if they were to be able to activate this particular business model. In other words, it shifted the thinking from being purely analytical (analysis), to being far more practical – what's going to make this business model work, and how are we going to actually execute it?

As such, the Business Model Canvas' **key sections** are as follows:

- **Customer Segments** – who you're serving.
- **Value Propositions** – the match between what you're selling and why people buy it.
- **Customer Relationships** – how you'll find, engage with, and retain, customers.
- **Channels** – where you'll sell, distribute, and service your offerings.
- **Key Activities** – what you must do to operate the business (as modeled).
- **Key Resources** – what resources you must leverage to operate the business (as modeled).
- **Key Partners** – what partners you must enlist to operate the business (as modeled).
- **Cost Structure** – what cost structure you'll incur in operating the business (as modeled).
- **Revenue Streams** – what revenue streams the business (as modeled) will generate for you.

One will notice that the left side of the Canvas generally reflects the supply side of one's business model, while the right side of the Canvas generally reflects its demand side.

That being said, whenever completing the Business Model Canvas, there is no set order in which one is to fill it out. Rather, it's designed to be completed in any order, with each of its respective boxes being considered experimental placeholders where any number of different options can be swapped in and out as required, in no particular order or sequence.

Nevertheless, most experienced Business Model Designers will attest to the fact that nailing down the demand side of the business model is much harder and far more important than nailing down the supply side because if one doesn't have their demand side figured out just right, then it won't matter how well they dial in their supply side, it will all be for naught (which gets to the point of unvalidated assumptions in one's business model). The supply side must of course work with, and make sense in the context of, the demand side, but the demand side is typically by far the most critical to figure out – and the source of most startup failures (indeed, a really sound demand side can make up for many flaws in the supply side).

This activity of experimenting with different combinations of elements in the Business Model Canvas is repeated until one (eventually) arrives at a design they feel good enough about to go out and start doing some real tests and experiments– so that they can prove or disprove the different assumptions and hypothesis underlying it. In this sense, the Business Model Canvas is really just a tool – at least on the front end of the process – for thinking through different options to test and trial – and then on the back end, for documenting one's final business model.

Even though the Business Model Canvas may on the surface seem relatively rudimentary, it was in fact a groundbreaking tool for its time. It was the first such tool that allowed innovators and entrepreneurs to really think through their entire business model in a truly thoughtful way, and in so doing work out different options in a very explicit and intentional manner. No other tool like it existed prior. Prior to this, trying to sort out one's business model was largely a guessing game. It is fair to say, therefore, that many of the startup successes achieved today owe their success to having this tool to help them think through, test, and ultimately work out their business model (or at least their *initial* business model).

The Business Model Canvas is not without its *weaknesses*, however. In particular, what many found in trying to apply it was that it was too far **downstream** in the overall innovation and startup process. So, while it was great for helping those businesses sort out their *product-market fit* (getting the right product to the market, which inherently assumes one has already figured out the right overall *solution* to meet that market's needs), it was *not* so great for helping them to work out their *problem-solution fit* further upstream in the process. It had, in effect, skipped that step, and jumped all the way over to the *product-market fit* situation.

In other words, the Business Model Canvas gives one a good snapshot of their finalized business model to start testing, learning, and refining from, but it doesn't necessarily help them work through the earlier steps required to get there. Indeed, how one (eventually) gets to this point is just as critical as getting to it.

As a result of this shortcoming, people started looking for – and asking for – other similar tools they could use upstream in the process for working out their *problem-solution fit*. This is generally done by undertaking user research to understand those users' needs and pains and thereafter determining how best to resolve those needs and pains – *without* any preconceived notion about *how best* to do so (whether a product, a service, an experience, a regulation, or something else).

This search eventually led to two options – the **Value Proposition Canvas** and the **Lean Canvas** (the latter being covered in the *Lean Canvas* section below).

Take 2 – the Value Proposition Canvas

Thus in 2014, Alexander Osterwalder and Yves Pigneur hit the book trail again – this time in collaboration with their colleagues Greg Bernada and Alan Smith. This time they published the book *Value Proposition Design*, and introduced a new canvas in it – namely *The Value Proposition Canvas* – shown here in *Figure 6.2*.

The Value Proposition Canvas dives far deeper into *just one box* of the Business Model Canvas – namely the *Value Proposition*. Here, the authors define the Value Proposition as being composed of two main parts – essentially the demand side on the right and the supply side on the left.

On the **demand side** – anchored by the customer, or user – it looks at the specific *jobs* they are trying to do in order to achieve some particular *outcome* (concepts drawn from the *Jobs To Be Done*, or *Customer Jobs*, methodologies), the *pains* they encounter in trying to do those jobs toward that outcome, and the *gains* they would value in this process if they existed (language taken directly from the classical *Customer Empathy Map*).

On the **supply side** – anchored by whatever solution the company is offering – it looks at the *products and services* being sold, how those products and services relieve the customer's *pain*, and how they create additional *gains* that these customers will value. Thus, in these authors' economy, the value proposition is made up of the offerings, the pains relieved, and the gains created. However, they do also state, back in the context of the Business Model Canvas, that *Customer Relationships* are a very important element of the overall value proposition – an accurate assessment.

The Value Proposition Canvas can thus be used further upstream in the innovation process to help innovators and entrepreneurs think through their value proposition. In reality, however, there were already *other tools* that did the same thing and addressed the same questions, often in better ways – most notably of which were the *Customer Empathy Map* and *Customer Persona*. So, innovators can choose to use any of these tools at this upstream point in the process to think through their value proposition. None of them, however, will help them test out their value proposition; that they must do on their own, outside of the tools. This is of course true of all the methods and frameworks profiled here... users of them must do their own validation work with boots on the ground – no amount of paper modeling will ever do it for them.

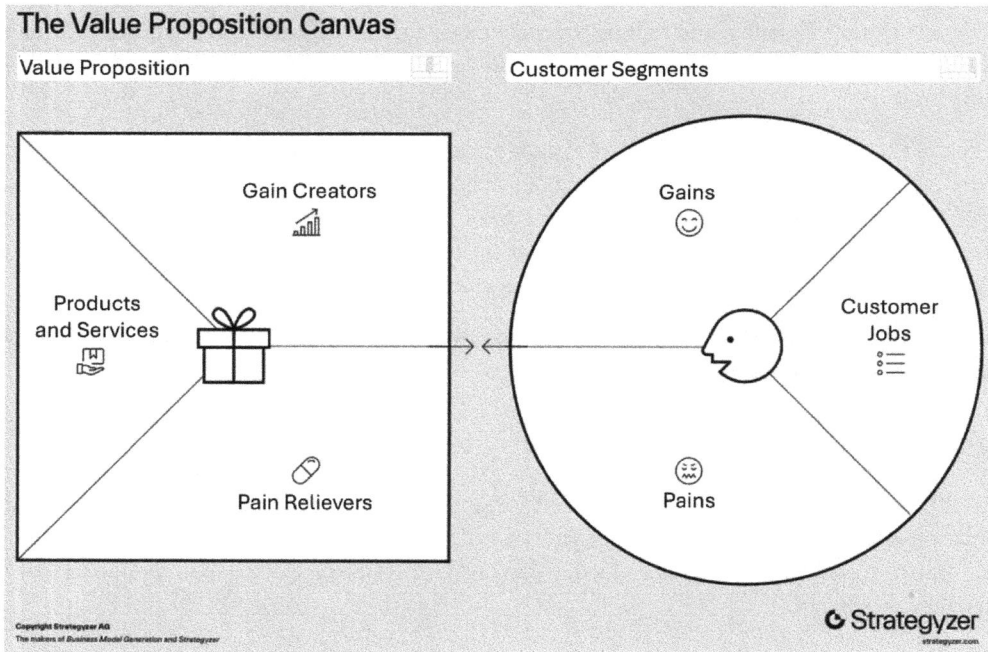

Figure 6.2: The Value Proposition Canvas. The Value Proposition Canvas is copyrighted by Strategyzer.com and Strategyzer AG, and is reproduced here with permission in accordance with these parties' intellectual property rights policies.

Coincidentally, the *popularity* of the Business Model Canvas gave rise to a whole array of different business canvases in use today, for similar thought experiments and design purposes. These include The Mission Model Canvas (Strategyzer), The Staehler Business Model Canvas (Patrick Staehler), The Experiment Canvas™ (Braden Kelley), The Project Canvas (Simon Stubben), The UX Project Canvas (Jim Kalbach), The Resume Canvas, The Content Strategy Canvas, The Customer Journey Canvas, The Data Strategy Canvas, and literally hundreds more.

Essentially *anything* that can be *designed* (such as a business model) can have a *canvas* that lays out its respective design elements. Also, several of these canvases are now integrated into visual team collaboration tools, such as *Miro* (www.miro.com). There are also very generalized Canvas design tools, such as *Canvanizer* (www.canvanizer.com), that allow one to lay out and complete scores of different canvases, including all the well-known ones mentioned here.

Lean Canvas – 2010

In response to the shortcomings of the Business Model Canvas as noted previously, Ash Maurya, founder and CEO of the company *LEANSTACK* (www.leanstack.com), in 2010 developed what he came to call the *Lean Canvas*.

He first published this canvas in an August 2010 article entitled *"How I Document My Business Model Hypotheses"*, and then later expanded on it in his 2010 book *Running Lean: Iterate from Plan A to a Plan That Works* (third edition published in 2022 by O'Reilly).

Tool 1 – the Lean Canvas

The Lean Canvas is a variation on the Business Model Canvas in which Maurya has mashed up different elements of the original Business Model Canvas with elements of the worksheets developed by author Steve Blank in his now-classic 2005 book *The Four Steps To The Epiphany: Successful Strategies for Products That Win*. It was also influenced by the Lean Startup principles espoused by author Eric Ries in his now-classic 2011 book *The Lean Startup: How Today's Entrepreneurs Use Continuous Innovation to Create Radically Successful Businesses* – such as, for example, the fact that startups operate under conditions of extreme uncertainty.

According to Maurya, his main objective in building this new canvas was to make it as *actionable* as possible, while staying very entrepreneur-focused. Consequently, the metaphor he took in his mind was that of a blueprint or tactical plan that could guide an entrepreneur as they navigated their way from ideation to building a successful startup.

Maurya initially experimented with many variations of the canvas, but in the end, he settled on including the following **key sections**:

- **Customer Segments** – the target customers and users.

    Early Adopters – characteristics of the ideal customer.

- **Problem** – this customer's top three problems.

  Existing Alternatives – how these problems are being solved today.

- **Unique Value Proposition** – a single, clear, compelling statement that turns an unaware visitor into an interested prospect.

  High-Level Concept – the Steve Blank analogous formula of "We help (X) do (Y) by doing (Z)".

- **Solution** – a possible solution for each of this customer's top three problems.

- **Channels** – our paths to the customer.

- **Revenue Streams** – the sources of revenue.

- **Cost Structure** – the fixed and variable costs.

- **Key Metrics** – key numbers that will tell you how well your business is doing on any given day.

- **Unfair Advantage** – something unique about your business that cannot be easily duplicated, either by buying it or building it.

Here, there is no delineation, per se, of the demand side versus the supply side; the two are intermixed.

There is, however, a preferred *order* in which the boxes are to be completed – namely the order reflected above, per Ash Maurya. Still, the canvas is a tool containing what should be seen as experimental placeholders, such that once it is initially filled out, any number of different options for its sections can be swapped in and out as needed – until (eventually) a design is found that the Designer feels good enough about to go out and test.

There are a couple of unique elements in this canvas that are worth explaining in further detail – in particular the **Unique Value Proposition** and **Unfair Advantage**. Both of these identify especially important considerations in a business model and make this canvas really stand out.

One's *Unique Value Proposition*, according to Maurya, is the unique marketing promise you make to your customers. It lets them know how you will make their lives better (in ways that matter to them) and likewise sets your solution apart from those of others. It's essentially your brand promise, conveyed using your unique brand message, and crafted in your unique brand language. It derives from the intersection of the Problem and Solution boxes and informs your customer of the benefits your solution will provide them, regardless of whatever features and attributes it uses to do so.

One's *Unfair Advantage*, according to Maurya, is a competitive advantage or barrier to entry you have that cannot be easily replicated by other businesses that follow – whether by copying your business or by buying capabilities from the outside, such as from a partner. While this is an element that's commonly found in many business plans (and sometimes referred to as the 'competitive moat surrounding your business protecting it from outside competitors'), Maurya was very aware that most startups wouldn't have such an unfair advantage defined on day one (meaning that the box would generally start out blank) – but he wanted to encourage them to work towards finding or building this unfair competitive advantage as soon and as quickly as possible. He saw this as being paramount for warding off fast copiers who would try to copy the business should it become successful; otherwise, it remained at risk of being outdone by these copy-cats.

Tool 2 – the Experiment Canvas

Beyond the Lean Canvas, Ash Maurya also created yet another popular canvas known as the *Experiment Canvas*. This nicely designed canvas documents the six key things that any good **business experiment** has to define in order to accomplish its objective of helping work out a certain assumption underlying one's business model. These six things are as follows:

- **Riskiest Assumption** – the riskiest assumption to be tested.
- **Falsifiable Hypotheses** – a statement in the form, "we believe that _____ will drive _____ within _____".
- **Experiment Setup** – the kind of experiment to be used / what is being measured / how many times.
- **Results** – the qualitative or quantitative results of the experiment.
- **Conclusion** – was the result clear and conclusive, and did it validate or invalidate the hypothesis?
- **Next Steps** – the next move to be made.

Other similar **experiment canvases** have also been created by other creators – including the following:

- one by growth strategist Bram Kanstein called the *MVP Experiment Canvas* that's a mashup of Maurya's Lean Canvas and Experiment Canvas;
- one by agile strategist Gust de Backer similar to Ash Maurya's, but in a more of tabular format;
- one by agile strategists Doc Norton and Diane Zajac formatted in a basic 4x2 format;
- one by Braden Kelley (author of *Stoking Your Innovation Bonfire*, 2010, and *Charting Change*, 2016) that lays out the experiment in multiple phases and assigns different learning metrics to the process;
- one by-product strategist Dinker Charak that's very product-centric;
- one by Chris Stone (host of the podcast *Virtually Agile*) designed with a bit more of the scientific method in mind;
- one by biostatistician Sun Kim that's designed around statistical Design-of-Experiments methods;
- and numerous other variations – including those for *agile transformation experiment design* and *culture transformation experiment design* – not to mention countless versions tailored to very specific science and technology domains.

Ash Maurya also created a complimentary canvas – the *Validation Canvas* – that helps to keep track of one's results over successive *rounds* of experiments.

PROBLEM	SOLUTION	UNIQUE VALUE PROPOSITION	UNFAIR ADVANTAGE	CUSTOMER SEGMENTS
List your customers top 3 problems	Outline possible solution for each problem	Single, clear, compelling that turns an unaware visitor into an interested prospect	Something that can't be easily copied or bought	List your target customers and users
EXISTING ALTERNATIVES List how these problems are solved today	**KEY METRICS** List key numbers telling how your business is doing today	**HIGH LEVEL CONCEPT** List your X for Y analogy (e.g. YouTube = Flickr for videos)	**CHANNELS** List your path to customers	**EARLY ADOPTERS** List characteristics of your ideal customer

COST STRUCTURE	REVENUE STREAMS
List your fixed and variable costs	List your sources of revenue

Lean Canvas is adapted from **Business Model Canvas** and is licensed under the Creative Commons Attribution-Share Alike 3.0 Un-ported License.

LEAN CANVAS

Figure 6.3: The Lean Canvas

License

The Lean Canvas is the intellectual property of LEANSTACK and LeanFoundry, and is reproduced here with permission in accordance with these parties' intellectual property rights policies.

The Lean Canvas is adapted from the Business Model Canvas and is licensed under the Creative Commons Attribution-Share Alike 3.0 Unported License.

In passing, it is worth mentioning here, as a relevant side note, that Steve Blank's now-classic and best-selling book *The Four Steps to the Epiphany: Successful Strategies for Products that Win* (republished in 2020) was the first book to ever put forth the idea that startups and new ventures were not simply smaller versions of large companies, but rather something entirely different – an idea that was very novel and eye-opening at the time. Blank pointed out that startups have to search for a viable business model (with many unknowns in the process), whereas existing companies simply execute an already-proven business model (with almost no unknowns). To help find that viable new business model, the book offers a four-step customer-development process that lets startups uncover the flaws in their business and product plans and then correct them before it's too late – as opposed to simply blindly following their original plan. This is where the whole idea of undertaking rapid iterations of customer testing to validate your underlying assumptions originated from. Indeed, Eric Ries – author of *The Lean Startup* – worked closely with, and was mentored by, Steve Blank, such that Blank's thinking and work heavily influenced Ries' thinking and what would eventually become known as *The Lean Startup method*. Blank's book by itself is credited with having launched 10,000+ startups and corporate ventures, with Ries' book giving life to tens of thousands more.

Business Model Innovation Factory – 2012

The Business Model Innovation Factory: How To Stay Relevant When The World Is Changing is a book published in 2012, authored by Saul Kaplan of *Business Innovation Factory* – a community of innovators creating a real-world laboratory to explore and test new business models in healthcare, education, public safety, and consumer experience.

This book presented the *Business Model Innovation Factory* – a collection of 15 principles and other insights about business model innovation, as opposed to being an explicit model or framework of the practice per se.

Structurally, Kaplan identifies the business model as being responsible for how your business *creates value*, *delivers value*, and *captures value* – all other factors are wrapped up inside those.

Kaplan's **15 principles** dealt with such topics as the following:

- catalyzing something that's larger than oneself;
- enabling serendipity – or 'random collisions' between 'unusual suspects';
- pursuing innovation collaboratively, as a team;
- designing the future together, as a team;
- building networks that could be catalyzed for specific purposes;
- using stories to inspire people, and thereby 'change the world';
- making systems thinking appealing and useful to those involved;
- seeing transformation as a creative act in and of itself;
- tapping into people's passions to get them to exceed their own expectations;
- trying to accelerate 'inspiration' inside a group;
- getting beyond incremental 'tweaks' to pursue really impactful outcomes;
- experimenting relentlessly and constantly – to always be learning;
- getting outside the office and into the real world – where the real learning takes place;
- designing for a user-centered world;
- not wasting time in this whole process.

These principles serve as the core of Kaplan's approach to pursuing business model innovation.

Kaplan also named ten reasons why companies typically fail at business model innovation. These range from senior leaders not being sincere about the effort, a myopic focus on just product innovation (not Business Model Innovation), an unwillingness to cannibalize one's existing lines of business, a lack of catalytic individuals inside the organization, an intolerance of catalytic individuals, a fear of career suicide, an inability to forecast a return on the investment, and an unwillingness to do any real-world experimentation. These are of course accurate assessments, but they also apply as well to innovation overall, not just business model innovation.

Finally, Kaplan gives insights into how to set up and operate a formal *business model innovation factory* inside one's organization – as well as how to go about experimenting with new business models in the real world. If for no other takeaway than this, the book is a useful and worthy read.

The Peter Thomson Value Proposition Canvas – 2013

At about the same time, as well as immediately after, Osterwalder and Pigneur launched their Value Proposition Canvas in 2014, a number of *other variants* also emerged on the scene – too many to list here.

One that was quite well received however was the one conceived in late 2013 by Peter J. Thomson, a Digital Strategist based in Auckland, New Zealand. That canvas is shown here in *Figure 6.4*.

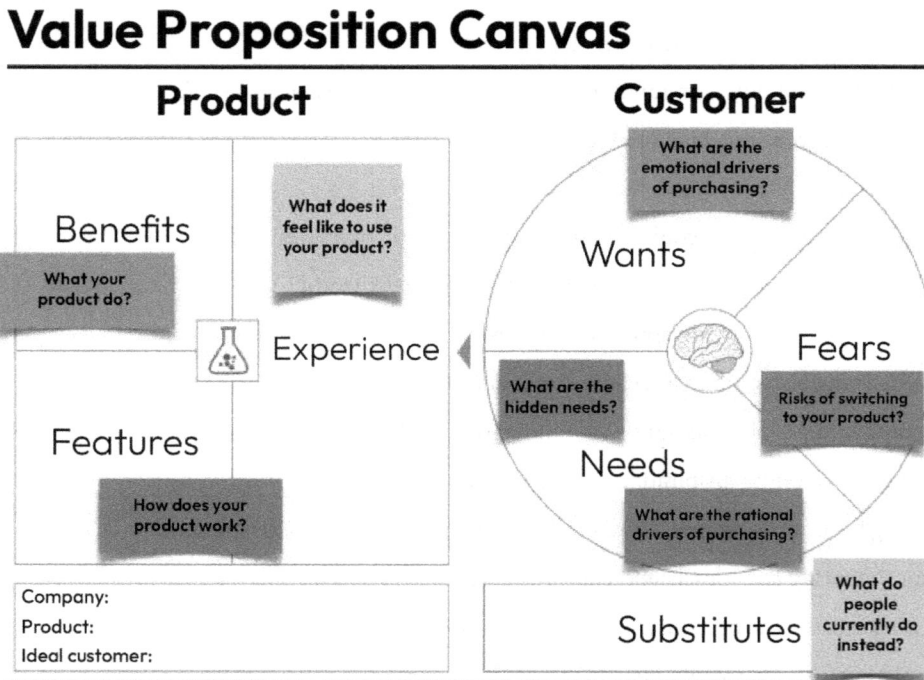

Value Proposition Canvas

Product   ## Customer

Benefits

What your product do?

What does it feel like to use your product?

Experience

Features

How does your product work?

What are the emotional drivers of purchasing?

Wants

Fears

What are the hidden needs?

Risks of switching to your product?

Needs

What are the rational drivers of purchasing?

Company:
Product:
Ideal customer:

Substitutes

What do people currently do instead?

Figure 6.4: The Peter J. Thomson Value Proposition Canvas. Reproduced under Creative Commons.

What we see in Thomson's version is the following:

- The **demand side** (right side) features **Wants**, **Needs**, and **Fears** – behavioral psychology factors. It also features **Substitutes** to highlight the fact that quite often what we are up against are not directly competitive solutions, but rather different types of workarounds and substitutes that are being used.

- The **supply side** (left side) features **Benefits**, **Features**, and **Experience** – direct value proposition factors.

So, in this sense, this variant is a **far more direct attack** at trying to understand both the customer – by looking *directly* at their wants, needs, and fears (the latter of which are often the motivations for the former, as well established in behavioral psychology) – and the solution (product) – by looking *directly* at is features, benefits, and experience for that customer. It also directly identifies the substitutes currently being applied.

Doing this makes this canvas far more **practical** – and thus less theoretical – for the Business Model Designer, compared to Osterwalder's and Pigneur's canvas That, in turn, tends to make it more useful to the Business Model Designer – by reframing everything in far more direct language surrounding the actual human experience involved – looking directly at the customer's psychological state of being, while likewise looking directly at the solution's benefits, features, and experience for them. This is a language that Designers, Innovators, and Product Managers can all relate directly to.

Consequently, Thomson's value proposition canvas has a much more direct and practical application than others, which by comparison seems a lot more abstract and removed from the reality that these professionals must deal with each day.

This is *why* Thomson's value proposition canvas has become so popular – these professionals, in general, find it much more useful and helpful than Osterwalder's and Pigneur's canvas – and consequently, many of them have turned to using it in lieu of that one.

Therefore, whenever we need a more *direct* look at our customer's situation and our solution for addressing that situation, this canvas can be particularly useful and helpful to us. In particular, its **Benefits** and **Experience** entries speak *directly* to aspects of our Unique Value Proposition as defined in the Business Model Meta Formula. It is thus recommended.

You can learn more about Peter Thomson's value proposition canvas in this original blog post about it, found online at `https://www.peterjthomson.com/2013/11/value-proposition-canvas/`. You can also download his free-to-use PDF version at `https://www.peterjthomson.com/wp-content/uploads/2013/11/Value-Proposition-Canvas.pdf`.

The Ten Types of Innovation – 2013

Ten Types of Innovation: The Discipline of Building Breakthroughs was a book published in 2013, written by Larry Keeley, Helen Walters, Ryan Pikkel, and Brian Quinn of Doblin, and based on a research study that Doblin undertook in the years preceding the book.

Its end result was *The Ten Types of Innovation* – essentially a taxonomic classification of the different *types* of innovation that an organization can pursue inside of its business model – those being the following:

1. Profit Model
2. Network
3. Structure
4. Process
5. Product Performance
6. Product System
7. Service
8. Channel
9. Brand
10. Customer Engagement.

Of these 10 types, 9 of them get aggregated into broader groups (Profit Model does not; it stands alone):

- *Network*, *Structure*, and *Process* are aggregated into a group known as *Configuration*.
- *Product Performance* and *Product System* are aggregated into a group known as *Offering*.
- *Service*, *Channel*, *Brand*, and *Customer Engagement* are aggregated into a group known as *Experience*.

Here, *Configuration* makes up most of the supply side of the business model, while *Experience* makes up most of the demand side, and *Profit Model* and *Offering* span both sides.

Inside each of these are a number of what the authors called *Innovation Tactics*. These tactics are, essentially, variations on different elements of the business model, and as such, largely conjure up the standardized business model *typologies* that were discussed in *Chapter 2*, and as seen in places such as *Business Model Ideas* (www.businessmodelideas.com). At the time, Doblin also produced a card deck known as the *Tactics Cards* – with each card reflecting one specific tactic (not unlike how IDEO at one time produced its *Methods Cards* reflecting different *Design Methods*). It should be noted that, since this framework was introduced in 2013, additional 'tactics' have come into play in different scenarios, and so such 'tactics' are certainly not static.

A visual summary of the *Ten Types of Innovation* and its different *Innovation Tactics* – as well as an overview of the *Ten Types of Innovation* containing a case study where five of the ten types have been leveraged – can be found at https://www.deloittedigital.com/us/en/capabilities/creative-experience-design/applied-design-innovation/ten-types.html.

Interestingly, *Ten Types of Innovation* did not set out to be a business model innovation framework, per se – but rather simply an identification and classification of the different *types* of innovation that a business could pursue – plus a recognition of the fact that in order to achieve truly breakthrough results, one has to innovate in *multiple areas at once* – not just in one or two areas in isolation (which can be useful for incremental impacts, but not for breakthrough impacts). In this sense, its nature was more like that of the *Innovation Radar*.

However, this classification of types and this recognition of a key practice ended up being – in effect – a statement about an organization's business model – namely that in order to have a truly breakthrough impact in its markets, it would effectively have to **innovate its business model** in multiple areas and in multiple ways.

Consequently, *Ten Types of Innovation* ends up being a breakdown and critique of one's business model in that its ten types represent the different *areas* of the business model that can be altered to achieve a specific breakthrough outcome. We therefore consider it a framework and tool that can be used for addressing business model innovation. Its real value lies in the fact that it gets teams and organizations to think far more broadly about all the ways they can innovate inside their business model. Doing that expands their thinking horizons well beyond whatever current blind spots they have. It is thus a very good tool for constructive, divergent thinking about one's existing as-is business model.

The Future Lens Business Model Framework – 2015

The *Future Lens Business Model Framework* was developed by Anthony Mills in 2015 for use in his consulting firm Legacy Innovation Group. In 2016 it was repurposed as the *GInI Business Model Innovation Framework* on behalf of the *Global Innovation Institute (GInI)*.

This framework was presented and explored in detail in *Chapter 2*.

What is to be understood about this framework is that it – like several of the other frameworks here – is purely a *structural framework*. It models the *structure* of the business model, and not the more critical *functional attributes* of it. Thus, while it is very useful for answering the key questions of *who*, *why*, *what*, *where*, *when*, and *how*, it does not by itself reveal the magic of how to necessarily 'mix these up' to create the very important *functions* that a business model has to facilitate if it is to truly 'win' in the marketplace. For that, one must use a *functional model* of the business model, such as the *Business Model Meta Formula* highlighted next.

The Business Model Meta Formula Canvas – 2015

The *Business Model Meta Formula* is a *functional model* of the business model developed by Anthony Mills in 2015 for use in his consulting firm Legacy Innovation Group. This model was presented and explored in detail in *Chapter 4*.

Also created with this was a unique canvas tool – specifically the *Business Model Meta Formula Canvas* – shown here in *Figure 6.5*.

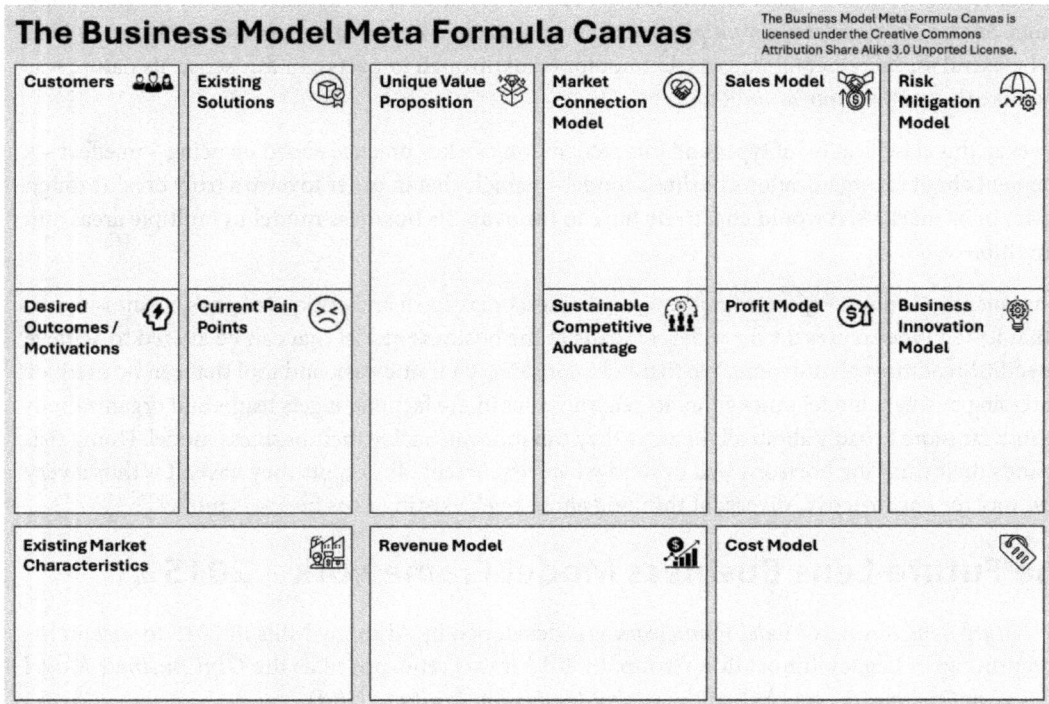

Figure 6.5: The Business Model Meta Formula Canvas

In addition to the seven key functions prescribed by the *Business Model Meta Formula*, this canvas also incorporates seven *additional* attributes of the business model. Four of those deal with the customers involved, one with the overall market, and two with the financials of the business model. In more detail, these are as follows:

1. **Customers** – a profile of the specific customer(s) involved, asking the key question of who, exactly, are we creating value for.

2. **Desired Outcomes / Motivations** – an explanation of these customers' "real reasons for buying," i.e., the specific outcomes and motivators they're trying to satiate, asking the key question of what (specific) outcomes those customers desire – and why so.

3. **Existing Solutions** – a profile of the existing solutions (including indirect ones) that customers currently turn to achieve this desired outcome, plus how long it takes for these solutions to deliver that outcome, and what customers typically pay for such solutions.

4. **Current Pain Points** – a profile of the pain points customers currently encounter – in terms of the specific frictions and pains they experience in their journey of trying to achieve their desired outcome, the ways in which current solutions are difficult and challenging to use, and the ways in those solutions fail to achieve their desired outcome in the manner and/or time period they desire and/or expect.

5. **Existing Market Characteristics** – an in-depth profile of the market involved, specifying what type of market it is, what its present size is in terms of total customers and aggregate revenue, who its major players are and how the market share breaks down between them, and what intermediaries are involved in between those players and their end customers.

6. **Revenue Model** – a profile of the exact revenue engine of the business, addressing such critical questions as how we intend to monetize our solution (the mechanics thereof), how customers currently pay for existing solutions versus how they'd prefer to pay, how much customers are willing to pay for the value they get, and how we can achieve our targeted level of scale in this situation.

7. **Cost Model** – a profile of the exact cost drivers involved in our business, addressing such critical questions as what our upfront cost to develop and launch our new solution will be, what our ongoing costs to operate our business and deliver that solution will be, what the key cost drivers behind those are, including which are most resource and effort-intensive, how we can maximize our ongoing cash flows, and what our expected IROR will be on delivering this solution.

By pairing these seven additional questions with the seven main functions of the Business Model Meta Formula, one can develop a very complete and comprehensive overview of their business model, and then from that develop better insights into just how well they may be able to succeed as a real, viable business in this particular market situation.

We therefore recommend using this canvas whenever applying the Business Model Meta Formula to one's efforts.

Worth keeping in mind is that this – just like the Business Model Canvas and the Lean Canvas – is a proper and detailed *functional model* of the business model. It models the specific functions of the business model that make it unique, set it apart from others, and ensure that it can be sustained over the long run, thereby revealing how the structural elements of the business model get 'mixed up' in a unique way to be able to 'win' in the marketplace. Like every other such model, it is just that… a model. It is not the real world. And therefore while it is useful as a thinking, modeling, and team conversation tool leading up to our validation efforts, it is not a substitute for our real-world validation efforts themselves. Those must always be done.

The GInI Business Model Canvas – 2016

The *GInI Business Model Canvas* is like *The Lean Canvas* – **a derivative** of the original Business Model Canvas of Strategyzer.

The key *difference* here is the **rearrangement** of certain elements on the canvas, plus the **addition** of one other key element that was felt to be missing from the original canvas. This rearrangement was done with the idea of making the tool far more **customer-centric**, and with the cognitive process of reading from left to right in mind.

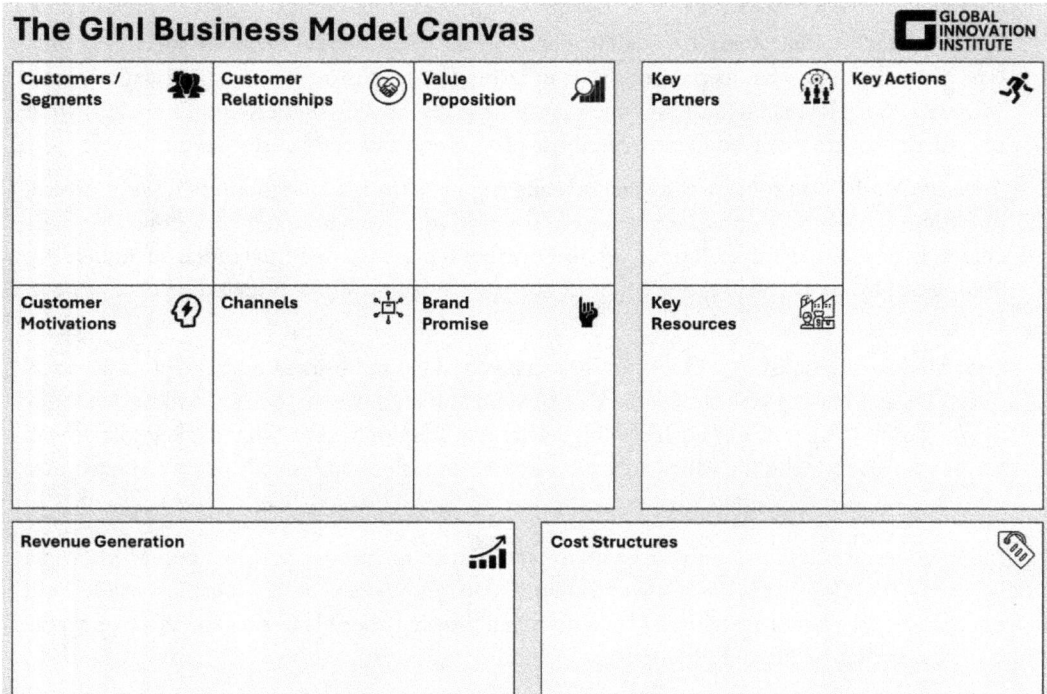

Figure 6.6: The GInI Business Model Canvas. The GInI Business Model Canvas is the intellectual property of Global Innovation Institute, and is reproduced here with permission in accordance with this party's intellectual property rights' policies. The GInI Business Model Canvas is adapted from Business Model Canvas and is licensed under the Creative Commons Attribution-Share Alike 3.0 Unported License.

In particular, all of the *customer-related items* are collected together in the four left-most entries – including **Customers / Segments**, **Customer Relationships**, and **Channels** – plus a new customer-related box was added here focusing on **Customer Motivations**. This latter addition was believed to be crucial because it was felt that Business Model Designers need to always keep their customer's *motivations* (their 'why') front and center before them in this design process, lest they otherwise go off track and forget *why* these customers would be willing to buy from them (their 'reason to buy') – which can lead directly to a business' *right to win* in that situation. Thus, this extremely crucial element was added to the canvas.

Next – in the center of the canvas – are the **Value Proposition** and the **Brand Promise**. Here, brand promise is explicitly included as a statement of branding that can, if so desired, go beyond the value proposition – including any potential slogans that might resonate with these customers' 'reason to buy'.

On the right-hand side of the canvas are aggregated **Key Partners**, **Key Actions**, and **Key Resources**.

Finally, the *sequence* of **Cost Structures** and **Revenue Generation** has been reversed – left and right. The reason for this was, again with the cognitive notion of reading from left to right, one has to tackle the question of *Revenue Generation* **before** they ever worry about their *Cost Structures*. It's not that Cost Structures aren't important – they are – it's just that if one hasn't yet figured out a viable Revenue Model for their business, then their Cost Structures are moot – they don't matter. One could spend all sorts of time trying to sort out their Cost Structures, but if their business doesn't have a viable source of revenue, then all that effort is for naught… it simply won't matter. No business and its cost structures matter if they don't have a sustainable source of revenues. That is not a business. Consequently, we want Business Model Designers to think *first* about what their revenue model is, and then, after they've figured that out, work out a cost structure that affords a good profit margin from that model.

As a result of all these different rearrangements, what we **also** end up with in this particular canvas design is the *demand side* of our business model shown on its left-hand side, and the *supply side* of our business model shown on its right-hand side. As noted previously, figuring out the demand side of our business model tends to be far more **important** – and far more **challenging** – than figuring out our supply side. Consequently, we want Business Model Designers to spend the majority of their time and effort testing and sorting out the different assumptions and intentions of the demand side, before spending an inordinate amount of time working on the supply side. Ultimately, if there is no viable demand side in the business model, then the whole supply side doesn't matter. Furthermore, and especially with purely digital solutions, working out one's supply side tends to be much easier today than it ever has been before. Consequently, we want to spend the majority of our time – at least initially – on this demand side and working out its assumptions and details. Then, once we've done that, we can drill down on the supply side and figure it out to match our demand side. This is *why* the GInI Business Model Canvas is set up in this way.

As a result of these reorganizations and added features, Business Model Designers might prefer using this version over the original Business Model Canvas.

A comparison of tools

The table of *Figure 6.7* below presents a comparison between each of the tools profiled here (12 in all). It arranges the tools according to their *type* – structural or functional – and their *application focus* – upstream, mid-stream, or downstream.

This comparison indicates the following:

- whether the tool is more of a *structural* or a *functional* tool;
- which of the desirability/feasibility/viability domains it helps us to address;

- its main *application(s)* – categorized into four specific activities:
  - Divergent business model thinking
  - Problem-Solution Fit
  - Product-Market Fit
  - Business model execution.

The following can be gleaned from this comparison:

- structural tools tend to be more useful in helping us to pursue *divergent thinking* around our business model;
- functional tools tend to be more useful in helping us to work through the *functional mechanics* of our business model;
- some functional tools – such as the value proposition canvases – are more geared to helping us *upstream* in the area of problem-solution fit;
- other functional tools – such as the Lean Canvas – are geared more to helping us *upstream and mid-stream* in working out both problem-solution fit and product-market fit;
- yet other functional tools – such as the original Business Model Canvas – are geared more to helping us *downstream* in the areas of product-market fit and business model execution.

Based on this comparison, we can see *where* each of these tools fits into the overall milieu of business model innovation work, and thus *where* and *how* we should consider using them each.

No	Tool	Structural	Functional	Desirability	Feasibility	Viability	Divergent BM Thinking	Problem-Solution Fit	Product-Market Fit	Business Model Execution
1	The Innovation Radar	X				X	X			
2	The Ten Types of Innovation	X				X	X			
3	The Future Lens Business Model Framework	X			X	X	X	X	X	
4	The Experiment Canvas		X	X		X	X	X	X	
5	The Value Proposition Canvas		X	X				X		
6	Peter Thomson Value Proposition Canvas		X	X				X		
7	The Lean Canvas		X		X	X		X	X	
8	The Business Model Canvas		X		X	X			X	X
9	The Gini Business Model Canvas		X		X	X			X	X
10	The Business Model Wheel		X	X	X	X		X	X	X
11	The Business Model Meta Formula Framework		X	X	X	X	X	X	X	X
12	Business Model Innovation Factory						X			

Figure 6.7: A comparison of twelve business model innovation tools

Our takeaway

At the end of the day, the preceding set of tools and models are simply that… tools and models that we can (and should) use in our process of business model analysis, discovery, and synthesis. We would do well, therefore, to familiarize ourselves with each of them, and select two or three that best suit our needs and use them for our efforts. As was just seen in the preceding comparison, which tools we use at any one time will depend on which stage of the process we're in at that moment. We therefore need to understand what our specific *goals* are at that point in time and then select the most appropriate tool(s) for our effort at that point.

One will also notice that there is one area in particular of the business model that certain of these tool-designers have really homed in – that of the **value proposition**, or *Unique Value Proposition* to use the language of the Business Model Meta Formula. And therefore, there are tools just for that, such as the many value proposition canvases. This is because our value proposition is really at the heart, or core, of our business model: it entails the core essence of our customers and the core essence of our solution for addressing their unmet needs. Everything else revolves around this value proposition and exists to bring it to life in our markets in a way that makes for a viable business for us.

Consequently, if we don't have our value proposition dialed in just right, then most likely the rest of our business model won't matter… it will just limp along trying its best to make up for a bad value proposition, which is never a formula for long-term success in business. This is why it is so crucially important that we get our value proposition just right – with evidence-based validation – so that we can create the right foundation on which to build the rest of our business.

And finally, one other point to reiterate here yet again is that while these different methods, frameworks, and tools can help us to talk about and think about the respective elements of our business model, none of them will actually test those elements for us. That's something we have to do for ourselves – with real 'boots-on-the-ground' testing, to learn what *really* works and what doesn't. No amount of modeling with the tools will ever do that for us. And so, we shouldn't be lulled into thinking that a business model that looks really great on paper will necessarily work in the real world… it may or may not; only the real world will tell us that.

Back to Intensifi – where are they at this point?

Back over at Intensifi, our friends Ian, Zoe, and Watson are very happy now that they've had the opportunity to learn about, consider, and evaluate the different business model innovation tools and models available to them. This will certainly make their job easier as they start down this path of learning about their would-be customers and the needs and motivations they each have.

They're still in 'pause' mode on the business model synthesis process, preparing as they embark on a learning journey about their would-be customers, but now they're feeling a bit more confident since they have this knowledge in hand.

In fact, they've given some thought and consideration to which of these different business model innovation tools they might like to use – to ensure that, in the process, they're being as thoughtful as possible about their new business model's details. Drawing from that, they've decided that, at least for the time being, they're not ready yet to dive into something like a business model canvas, but they *are ready* to use one or more of the value proposition canvases. This is because they first need to work out a lot more about their Unique Value Proposition and how it may (or may not) actually solve these customers' real problems. Consequently, they've chosen to use a Peter Thomson Value Proposition Canvas until they get further down the road in this process (at which point they think they'll likely use a Lean Canvas to work out more of their business model's details).

And so, as they start down the road toward Design Thinking, they believe they'll be able to (eventually) get inside their would-be customers' heads and hearts – adequately enough to be able to use this value proposition canvas effectively. They also understand that they'll likely find themselves using additional tools and methods as well. In future chapters, we'll see them fill out this value proposition canvas with the new insights they learn and gather.

And so, at this point, Ian, Zoe, and Watson are ready to start learning more about Design Thinking and human-centered design so that they can move forward in this process. They understand at this point why this is so critical: that de-risking their effort by ensuring customer desirability is present (and in what form) – prior to developing a business model, launching a new venture, or taking on an investment – will maximize their odds of success later on when they do end up trying something.

Summary

In this chapter, we've explored a broad historical progression of different business model innovation analysis and synthesis tools that have each been developed and come into use since the start of the 21st Century.

Each unique tool or model in this collection has a very specific goal in mind and therefore serves a very specific purpose. This means that we can leverage them each in different ways – to help support us in our own journey of business model analysis, discovery, and synthesis – specifically by facilitating different *types* of assessment and synthesis in the specific business models we're exploring and considering. Consequently, we will do well to understand them all and the specific value they deliver – so that we can then select those that will serve us the best in our own unique efforts.

We noted that of the different elements these tools let us define, the value proposition is the most central of them all. Thus, the presence of additional tools to work through that one element in further detail. And thus, why we have to really home in on defining this one element, because if we don't get *it* right, then the whole rest of our business model is likely for naught. Getting that value proposition right will inherently require much research and validation on our part as we go through the process. This means a major investment of our time, energy, and effort – but it will pay off in the end once we get back to the rest of our business model innovation efforts.

Given this appreciation for the fact that our Unique Value Proposition is what lies at the heart of our business model, our imperative becomes, first and foremost, to get that part of our business model as perfect as absolutely possible. Nothing beats a business model where what it's selling goes viral and sells itself – in a sustainable way over the long run. And nothing is worse than a business model where no one wants what it's selling, despite its trickery and incentives otherwise. Consequently, we have to get this part of our business model sorted out first if we ever hope to have a truly viable business model for the long run.

This is our point of departure, then, for looking ahead to *Section 2* of this book, where, starting in the next chapter, we'll be exploring what we really need to get our Unique Value Proposition defined properly – namely the practice of Design Thinking, with its underlying design philosophy of human-centered design.

In that chapter, we'll explore what Design Thinking is, together with its essential philosophies and discovery tasks that let us develop empathy for, and ultimately an empathic understanding of, our target customer. Doing that lets us reframe what we originally perceived their challenge to be into one that truly gets at the heart of their needs, desires, and motivations. It is that (eventual) reframing that sets us on the path to understanding our would-be customers in a way that lets us, bit by bit, eventually and convergently, develop a solution for them that meets that need and resonates with that unique motivation.

And that is what we'll need to (eventually) get to a winning value proposition on behalf of our business model – so that we can have a sustainable business venture that grows and scales healthily over time.

Further reading

- *The 12 Different Ways for Companies to Innovate*, Mohanbir Sawhney, Robert Wolcott, Inigo Arroniz, MIT Sloan Management Review, April 2006, https://sloanreview.mit.edu/article/the-different-ways-for-companies-to-innovate/.

- *Business Model Generation*, Alexander Osterwalder, Yves Pigneur, John Wiley & Sons, Hoboken, New Jersy, 2010.

- *The Business Model Innovation Factory: How To Stay Relevant When The World Is Changing*, Saul Kaplan, John Wiley & Sons, Hoboken, New Jersy, 2012.

- *Ten Types of Innovation: The Discipline of Building Breakthroughs*, Larry Keeley, Helen Walters, Ryan Pikkel, Brian Quinn, John Wiley & Sons, Hoboken, New Jersy, 2013.

- *Business Models for Dummies*, Jim Muehlhausen JD, John Wiley & Sons, Hoboken, NJ, 2013.

Part 2 –
The World of
Design Thinking

Part 2 of this book explores Design Thinking – including what it is, its underlying philosophy of human-centered design, and the practices of empathy and empathic understanding that this philosophy calls for. This part also explores how, in order to do Design Thinking properly, we have to be able to think like a Behavioral Scientist… deeply dissecting the actions and behaviors of our subjects so as to understand those subjects' true desires, aspirations, and motivations in the situation of interest.

In addition, this part delves into the details of the Design Thinking process. It uses the vicarious case study of the fictitious venture *Intensifi* to demonstrate this process in full, step-by-step detail – walking you first through the *Problem Space* (the "first mountain" to go up and down) and second the *Solution Space* (the "second mountain" to go up and down). This ultimately leads to a new solution that fully satisfies the wants, needs, and aspirations at hand.

This part contains the following seven chapters:

- *Chapter 7, Thinking Like a Designer*
- *Chapter 8, Thinking Like a Scientist – Centering Our Design around Humans*
- *Chapter 9, Acting Like a Designer – The Design Thinking Process in Application*
- *Chapter 10, Working the Problem Space – Up and Down the Mountain*
- *Chapter 11, Intermission*
- *Chapter 12, Working the Solution Space – Up and Down the Next Mountain*
- *Chapter 13, Design Thinking's Final Act (So Far) – Our New Solution*

7
Thinking Like a Designer

In *Chapter 6*, we explored the progression of different business model innovation tools and models that have been developed and come into use over the preceding 20+ years. We saw how each of those offers something of value so that we can use a selection of them in our process, according to where we are in the process and our specific goals at that point. We also noted that the presence of these points to the fact that business model innovation is indeed a product of the 21st century, and as such has come of age during that time.

In this chapter, we'll begin our exploration of Design Thinking, along with its underlying philosophy of human-centered design – both of which we'll need to eventually get to our Unique Value Proposition.

Specifically, we'll learn what Design Thinking is, including its core philosophy and discovery tasks. We'll see how these empower us to develop empathy for – and ultimately an empathic understanding of – our target customer. We'll also learn how doing this enables us to reframe what we originally perceived their challenge to be – their "surface symptoms" – into one that gets at the real heart of their human needs, desires, motivations, and aspirations. It is this reframing that will ultimately empower us to understand this customer in such a way that we can eventually, bit by bit, converge on a solution that truly meets their needs and aspirations. That is what we will eventually need to get to a winning value proposition on behalf of our business model – so that we can have a sustainable venture that grows and scales healthily over time.

Along the way, we'll take a quick look at some of the history of Design Thinking, some of its well-acknowledged successes, some of its (legitimate) criticisms, and a broader conceptualization of what Design Thinking is becoming more and more as we go forward.

In particular, we'll explore the following seven topics in this chapter – reflecting the key activities of this practice:

- **Design Thinking defined – key insights and why they're important**: Our initial introduction to Design Thinking, explaining what it is fundamentally.

- **Human-centered design – the philosophical foundation**: An explanation of human-centered design and what it means regarding our efforts in hunting for the right Unique Value Proposition.

- **Design Thinking's superpower – reframing problems**: An explanation of the concept of problem reframing and how Design Thinking largely exists to allow us to do precisely that.

- **Understanding and achieving our intermediate goal – empathy and empathic understanding**: An exploration of the process of developing empathy for our subjects, as well as our intermediate goal of cultivating an empathic understanding of them and their situation.

- **Understanding and achieving our ultimate goal – a reframed problem**: An exploration of the process of problem reframing – turning initial issues into properly understood ones that address the most fundamental human needs at work.

- **The takeaway – what Design Thinking means to us**: Our final takeaway, explaining what Design Thinking means to us in our efforts to design and deliver a powerful new business model.

- **Some important sidenotes on Design Thinking**: A collection of additional insights into Design Thinking, including its history, successful uses, proper application, criticisms, and broader understanding.

Once we've learned what Design Thinking is and where it fits into business model innovation, we will be able to "think like a Designer."

We'll also check in with our friends over at Intensifi (Ian, Zoe, and Watson) to see what they're up to. Now that they've gotten a taste of what Design Thinking is and what it can do for them, we'll see what they're thinking about in terms of their plans at this point in their journey and whether these insights have sharpened and honed those plans in any way – and if so, how so.

A final note here is that Design Thinking can be a bit of a dense topic. We'll try to lay it out as best we can, but you'll have to apply yourself to understanding it. We'll see this whole practice put into use in *Chapters 10*, *11*, and *12*, so if you're looking for a real-world application of it to see what it looks like in practice, don't worry – we'll get to that in those subsequent chapters.

Design Thinking defined – key insights and why they're important

In the previous chapter, we pointed out that our Unique Value Proposition is what is at the *heart* and *center* of our business model – and thus we need to nail that down first, dialing it in with a very high level of precision before moving on to the other (still important) considerations of our business model. That is what we're here to do now – to home in on our Unique Value Proposition and dial it in at a super high level of precision and detail.

This begs the question, "How do we do this? How do we dial in our unique value proposition?"

The answer to that is through **Design Thinking**.

This leads us to our next logical question, which is, "What is Design Thinking?"

In this chapter, starting in this section, we're going to answer that question. But before we do, allow me to first point out that, inside the overall "Design Thinking community" (yes, there is such a thing), there has been a lot of debate and disagreement over what, exactly, Design Thinking is – with nearly as many answers are there are askers. So, the answer you will receive here is one that I believe treats each of those different perspectives fairly and respectfully – and as such strikes an objective balance between the theoretical and the practical, as well as between the idealistic and the pragmatic (each representing a distinctive perspective on the subject).

So, with that out of the way, let's then move on to defining Design Thinking.

As we do this, we're going to be talking about designing **artifacts**. The word *artifacts* here is simply a generic descriptor for whatever is being designed. This can be a web page or website, a digital product, a physical product, a service, an experience, or even an entire business and its accompanying organization. So, when we say "artifact," we mean any of these respective (designed) work products.

Defining Design Thinking

Design Thinking is the practice of questioning the assumptions being made behind whatever is being designed – to ensure that those assumptions are, in fact, accurate and correct. Doing this yields optimal design solutions.

This infers that you take first-person **action** to ensure that those assumptions are accurate and correct, and then – wherever they are not – actively pursue the most accurate and correct assumptions to work with instead.

This is all done without presupposing anything whatsoever about either the problem being addressed or the solution being designed – beyond a vague acknowledgment of who the customer is and what their general need appears to be.

In reality, in most cases in Design Thinking, especially when we've been tasked with designing the "right" artifact, we simply start with the assumption that we **do not yet know** what those correct assumptions are, and therefore we have to go out and **discover them for ourselves**. That's how Design Thinking is most commonly practiced today – a properly conservative approach. Design Thinking works for this because it gives us a very methodical and systematic approach that keeps the customer/ user at the very center throughout the process.

The trouble with traditional innovation practices

The trouble with many traditional innovation practices has always been that the "innovators" wanted to simply jump *straight into* brainstorming new ideas for new solutions – without ever asking themselves whether or not the problem they were addressing was even the right problem to start with, understood at the right level. This sort of thinking has its roots in traditional business and engineering school practices, in which students are presented with a canned problem and their task is to find a solution to it (known as the "problem-forward" approach). Real life rarely presents us with such "canned problems."

In these cases, the understanding of the "problem" was based entirely on certain preformed **beliefs** held about it, with those beliefs themselves being predicated on certain **assumptions** about the customer and their need. Such beliefs and assumptions were simply taken for granted, based on whatever experience or other evidence happened to be on hand (or perhaps what they had always been told) – without ever questioning their validity. Often, this was simply prior precedence… "This is the problem we've always tried to solve… so why would we do any different now?" These beliefs and assumptions have their roots in highly traditional organizational cultures and the many cognitive biases that get coddled in such cultures.

Consequently, these individuals have – unbeknownst to them – solved the **wrong problem** – or solved the right problem, but at the **wrong level**. They were solving for what they had always solved for before – and for what everyone else in their industry was solving for. But this wasn't their customer's **fundamental issue or problem**; it was simply a *symptom* of that issue or problem.

Doing this – solving for the wrong problem or the right problem at the wrong level – almost always results in delivering just another "me too" offering – swimming along in the red ocean of disappearing margins, where there is no significantly meaningful differentiation.

What these individuals have failed to realize – beyond the fact that they were not solving the right problem – is that, even more importantly, their organization could be far more successful if they solved the *right problem* – which they could be doing if they would just allow themselves to discover that right (more fundamental) problem in the first place.

This takes discipline and patience – the discipline and patience to say, "No, we're not going to just jump straight into ideating new solutions! Instead, we're going to take the *time*, and put forth the *effort*, to understand the *real problem* at hand (and the user needs behind it) so that we can ensure for ourselves that we're solving the *right problem*, at the *right level*, long before we ever try to ideate any solutions for it!" Discipline and patience are what lie at the heart of Design Thinking as a practice. After all, there's no point in building out a new business model if it involves an offering nobody wants. We can save ourselves a lot of heartache and misery by simply doing it right the first time around.

Our Problem Space always precedes our Solution Space

Another way of stating this is that, historically, many have fallen prey to the temptation of jumping straight into their **Solution Space**, without first exploring their **Problem Space** as they should.

You see, in Design Thinking, *the Problem Space always precedes the Solution Space*, and we don't get to advance to the Solution Space until we've thoroughly explored the Problem Space to understand the situation accurately and correctly! We work our **Problem Space**, and then we work our **Solution Space** – always! This is illustrated in *Figure 7.1*.

① Our Problem Space	② Our Solution Space
Are we solving for the right problem?	Are there currently any solutions on the market that address this problem and need?
Do we understand what the real problem at hand is?	If so, how effective are they? What is deficient about them?
Do we understand our subject and why they have this problem?	Do present solutions address the real need our subjects have – based on their real, fundamentally more human motivations and aspirations?
Do we understand what outcome that subject is trying to achieve?	What work-arounds, if any, are these subjects presently using to address this problem and need?
Do we understand *why* they are trying to achieve that outcome... why it's important to them... what it actually means to them.	What might a better solution look like – one that that delivers the desired outcome while meeting the real need at hand, and while also addressing the underlying motivations and aspirations involved?
How long might this subject have this problem and need... are they ephemeral or permanent?	How can *we* deliver such a solution in this situation???
Do we understand how this need, and its underlying desires, fit with the broader societal structures and narratives happening around us?	

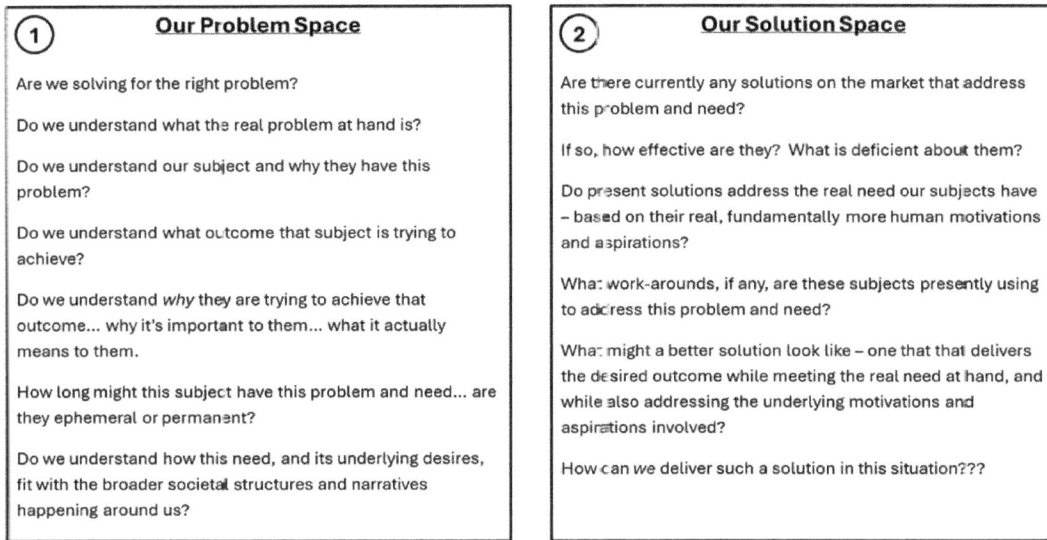

Figure 7.1: Our Problem Space precedes our Solution Space.

Of course, in all fairness, in traditional **new product development** (**NPD**) work, most of the time, the organization is simply working on an incremental advancement to a current product line, in which case that advancement will remain predicated on whatever prior understanding of the problem it was previously predicated on. This is okay for minor generational updates to the product line, but it is not okay for anything beyond that.

Therefore, whenever launching a *new* product line, or significantly *upgrading* an existing product line, you have to start over at the very beginning, with first principles, and rework your Problem Space again – to ensure that you're developing the right solution for a correct understanding of that Problem Space.

We'll explore the actual process for working on each of these spaces in *Chapters 9* and *11*, respectively.

One historical meaning – design "thinking" versus design "doing"

The term "Design Thinking" originates from multiple sources.

One of those is from within the historical Product Design community, in which case it was used to contrast with the idea of "design doing." Design doing – what most Designers were historically expected to do – simply meant to obediently design whatever they were being told to design in the *Design Brief* given to them – without questioning whether or not that "thing" was even the *right thing* to design in the first place.

So, for decades, that is exactly how Design practice was carried out... someone – typically often someone in Marketing or Product Management – would write out a Design Brief for the Designer describing what was to be designed (omitting any explanation of *why* that particular artifact was to be designed, and in the way it was to be designed). They would then hand it over to the Designer, who was expected to design it without questioning it.

Somewhere along the way however (primarily in the 1960s and 70s), there came the realization in the Design community that, more often than not, this approach tended to lead to failed outcomes – products, services, and experiences that simply never managed to grow legs and gain traction with their intended customers.

Consequently, there was a wake-up call saying, *"Hey, as Designers, we have to take responsibility for doing what's right here – for ensuring that what we're being asked to design is the right thing to design, and with the right details for its use."* This shift in mentality is well recorded in the book *Change By Design*, by Tim Brown, Chairman and former CEO of the design firm IDEO.

This shift in mentality shifted *responsibility* for ensuring that the details of the design were correct, from the Marketer or Product Manager, squarely onto the shoulders of the **Designer**. It was here that the Designer was being expected to not just "do as they're told," but rather to put forth time and effort **thinking about** what they were about to design – to ensure that it and its details were *right* and that the assumptions being made behind it were accurate and correct regarding what was needed from this design. And the phrase "Design Thinking" came into use – to distinguish this new responsibility from the more historical one of simply "design doing."

Indeed (and to ratchet that up even further), in writing this book, I interviewed Anne Asensio, World Wide Vice President of Design Experience at Dassault Systemes, and Circular Design Leader at Ellen MacArthur Foundation. A key insight that Anne shared with me, and which we discussed at length, was that when she began her career in Design some decades ago, they all had a very understandable mission: to fulfill the brand signature while addressing their understanding of the customer's expectations based on that brand's stated values. This was a purely functional objective, drawing from the theory of *functionality* in architecture. At that point in history, the sense was that our world was well understood… it was very linear, with a very clear meta-narrative based on the idea of *progress* rooted in capitalism. Consequently, Designers had a very well-established, long-running industry process to follow – one that involved very clear tasks. This meant that everyone doing their job according to that process was sufficient – no one ever questioned the bigger picture. But since that time, this has all changed dramatically! Now, in the postmodern era, Designers are being asked – and expected – to consider a far broader picture, one in which "good design" actually means doing good for *everyone* involved… good for people… good for society… and so on. On top of that, and particularly ever since Design was fully digitized, the pace and intensity of design and innovation have grown dramatically – with every new generation of automobiles, that pace and intensity have increased significantly. Consequently, we now have to question **a lot more** about *what* we're designing. It's no longer just about delivering that brand experience, but rather about figuring out new ways in which to **transform society** into something new and different – meaning that the experience Designers have to try to create is far more *intertwined* with our social structures. As an Automotive Designer, she can no longer just "design cars" – she has to question the societal norms around mobility. This is certainly an entirely different task, one in which the objective of Design is now enormously broader and far more complex. Therefore, it necessitates a radically different approach from before – one in which the Designer has to become an authority on so much more than just functional design – on things that impact society more holistically. And so, as Anne would say in French, those were "*Les* *jours de gloire*" – the glory days. Today, we've closed the door on that chapter and have entered an entirely new one – one involving far more *possibilities* for Design to express itself in new and novel ways, intertwining far more activities and stakeholders than was ever done in that previous chapter.

This reveals one of the more critical limitations of Design Thinking as it has historically been practiced. In particular, in the past, Design Thinking has tended to empathize with only one or two stakeholder groups in isolation (usually the user and/or purchasing customer) and drove its solutions out of that – without ever trying to empathize with the *other* stakeholder groups impacted. This has produced solutions that worked well for the core stakeholder group, but at the same time caused harm to the *other* stakeholder groups. Consequently, modern Design Thinking has to – and more and more is trying to – take a holistic systems-level view of needs, using systems thinking to map out the very complex systems involved and in that process identify specific intervention points where we can create solutions that are good for *all stakeholders*. We'll learn more about this when we cover Humanity-Centered Design.

Yet another meaning – "thinking like a Designer"

Design Thinking also bears its name because it forces us to "think like a Designer" – a practice also known as "Designerly Thinking" and contrasts with scholarly and scientific thinking.

To "think like a designer" means to think in such a way that we take nothing for granted, but instead are constantly in search of new, better, and deeper insights into the situation we've encountered – insights that reveal and characterize that situation at a far deeper level. This is so that we can ultimately devise better ways of arranging the elements of a solution to optimally address that situation and whatever human needs it happens to involve.

This inherently means constantly *challenging* the assumptions we hold (or have been given) regarding that situation, and in that quest, searching for deeper and more absolute truths about it – ones that will lead us to a new solution that ultimately fits best with the situation, as it exists in reality.

Human-centered design – the philosophical foundation

Underlying Design Thinking is a very specific *design philosophy*. That philosophy is known as **human-centered design**.

The **basis** of human-centered design is that the *human* – the recipient or user of the design – must lie at the very **core and center** of our design process. Doing this forces us to study, analyze, and fully understand humans' real needs before ever designing anything for them.

So, it mandates that we place this human at the very **center** of all our efforts – so that whatever we do design is designed uniquely for them, to address the very real and specific need *they* have – typically one that is either unmet or under-met currently.

In the end, this leads to a design process that is 100% fully *human-centric* – or *user-centric* – and that, as a result, yields design solutions that are fully capable of resonating with that user and their unmet human need.

Design Thinking's superpower – reframing problems

When trying to solve a human need, we must solve the **right problem** – one anchored in the human emotions and motivations involved – and not the wrong problem – one based on the superficial surface symptoms, which are, unfortunately, what are most commonly solved for.

It is also important that we solve this problem at the **right level of need**, which is, generally speaking, the lowest and most fundamental need that we can reasonably act on as a solution provider.

In Design Thinking, there are two fundamental realities that we confront:

1. most problems or challenges as we first encounter them are *ill-framed* – meaning they have to be *reframed* from a human-centered point of view if we are to address them correctly;

2. solutions are only as good as the extent to which they solve for the *real problem involved* and in so doing establish the best possible fit between themselves and the needs they're trying to solve for.

These two realities apply regardless of what we happen to be designing – be it a physical product, a digital product, a service, a customer experience, a physical space, or a new business model. In each case, the solution we design has to solve the **right need**, at the **right level**, if it is to produce the best possible fit between the *solution*, *need*, and *those having the need*.

Fortunately, Design Thinking's real **superpower** is that it forces us to "go back to the very beginning and start over" – to go back to the *first principles* and learn from that point onward, abandoning all preconceived beliefs or presumptions about the situation we may have held otherwise.

At this point of reinitiation, we identify the human (user) involved and the need we sense they have, and which we're trying to solve. Then, we use that as our springboard to launch an in-depth investigation into that human and their *real need* to understand both of them at their most fundamental level.

It is that "most fundamental level" that reveals to us this user's "real need," rather than the one we may have initially perceived and thus believed them to have. These two "needs" are often completely different from each other, but the only one that matters is the "real need" that we've just uncovered in that process. Once we understand *that need*, then we can deliver a solution that solves it – and thereby resonates with this user. It's important to understand that these "real needs" are often *subconscious* to our subject... they aren't even consciously aware of them, and therefore can't articulate them to us. So, have to ask, "What's *really* going on here... what is this *really about*?" and undertake research from there to figure out the answer to that question.

This is important. If we **fail** to do this, then in all likelihood, we will do one of two things:

*   solve the *wrong problem*;
*   solve the right problem but at the entirely *wrong level of need*.

In the first case, the solution we offer will most likely be an abject failure in the marketplace.

In the latter case, the solution we offer will most likely be just another "me too" offering… no better than anything else on the market.

Truly impactful solutions – and, by extension, value propositions – require solving both the *right problem* and solving that problem at the *right level of human need*.

This process – of exploring and restating problems from how they were originally perceived to a more accurate statement formulated at the right level of human need – is known as **problem reframing**.

Problem reframing is a fundamental element of Design Thinking. It is the aim and goal of working our Problem Space. After having worked that space, we'll end up with a *newly reframed problem* – one that's stated accurately and at the right level of need, and thus gets to the *real* user need involved, as well as the human motivations and aspirations behind that need – something we'll explore much further in *Chapter 8*

To illustrate this, consider an example where we (initially) observe a young person trying to lose weight and think that their motivation for doing so is simply to be healthy. But in reality, when we start to unpack the situation and peel away the layers surrounding it, we start to get down to their real motivations and aspirations, and therefore their real outcome need, which is instead to be accepted socially by their peers. We can then solve for that aspiration and need – at that level – in a completely different way, perhaps through different clothing, rather than trying to solve the superficial symptom that we'd otherwise be trying to (likely unsuccessfully) solve had we just worked at our original surface level, based on our initial observations.

That is the power of reframing problems into their *real* outcome needs, motivations, and aspirations! Only then can we deliver the *right* type of value proposition that will properly resonate with these subjects.

Understanding and achieving our intermediate goal – empathy and the empathic understanding

Given Design Thinking's underlying philosophy of *human-centered design*, the primary **purpose** and **goal** of putting our design subject (the "human") at the very **center** of our design process is so that we can ultimately develop **empathy** for that subject – in the context of the situation they happen to find themselves at that point in time.

It is this quest for *contextual human empathy* that drives us to use a process like Design Thinking.

Pursuing our intermediate goal – human empathy

If we hope to be able to deliver a solution that truly meets this individual's "real need" – at the level of fundamental human motivation and aspiration – then we have no choice but to develop *empathy* for them (and their situation). This is the **only way** we're ever going to be able to understand their "real need" and its underlying drivers sufficiently enough to develop a solution – and Unique Value Proposition – for them.

What this means is that we have to get "inside the skin" of our subject. We have to put ourselves in a position where we can truly understand **their world from their perspective** – both the problem or challenge they're encountering and whatever solution might be best for resolving that problem or challenge.

Therefore, empathy is a **pivotal concept** in Design Thinking and human-centered design.

Dictionaries define empathy as something along the lines of the act of being aware of, understanding, and being sensitive to – and even vicariously experiencing – the thoughts, feelings, and experiences of another – as well as the capacity for doing so. I would also add that, beyond this, it's also the act of being aware of and understanding the actual *motivations* and *aspirations* behind those thoughts, feelings, and experiences… *why* that particular individual is, under those particular circumstances, actually experiencing those particular thoughts and feelings. That is *true empathy* – the sort that we ultimately have to develop in Design Thinking.

What this means for us as *investigators* is that we'll have to develop – at least for some period throughout our investigation – incredibly deep empathy for the subject at the core of our investigation. This will require us to get up close and personal with that subject – engaging them in all manner of activities to observe them, question them, and otherwise study them – so that we can get to know them and what makes them tick – and then, after that, possibly having them work on solutions together with us. At times, it will require us to make various (temporary) adjustments, to both ourselves and our environment, so that we can fully experience *their world as they do* – allowing us to develop an appropriate empathy for both them and that situation.

It is not until we've done all this that we're able to accurately explore any possible solutions for that particular individual and their unique situational need.

Achieving our intermediate goal – empathic understanding

Developing empathy for our subject and their situation is a process, but not the result. The result occurs when we reach a point in which we possess a complete **empathic understanding** of this subject and its situation.

What this phrase means is that we now **completely understand** this subject and their situation – not from *our* point of view – but rather from *their* point of view. When this is the case, we'll fully 100% understand *why* they are thinking, feeling, and experiencing what they are thinking, feeling, and experiencing in that situation – including their fundamental human motivations and aspirations behind all that.

This all has to occur with 100% complete and total **objectivity** – meaning there can be no judgment whatsoever about what we're learning. It is neither our purpose nor our job in this process to judge whether or not those motivations and aspirations, or the outcome being pursued, are good, bad, or otherwise. It is simply to *understand them from that subject's point of view*. If we find ourselves judging or critiquing their motivations and aspirations, then we've failed to develop the empathic understanding we need.

This requires a certain amount of *compartmentalization* on our part. While our normal selves, thinking in our normal ways, may hold certain attitudes and beliefs about these subjects and their motivations and aspirations, when we put on our "Design Thinking hat," we have to put those aside and commit ourselves to being 100% fully objective in the process, including about whatever we uncover along the way.

This is just as important *during* our investigation as it is at its end. Whenever we're engaging our subjects to learn more about them, there can be no judgment about what we're witnessing or learning – it is purely a learning exercise, nothing more. What we may think or believe about the subject and their motivations and aspirations is entirely immaterial to the process. It is, after all, about them and not us.

Developing this (proper) empathic understanding will serve us well in working both our *Problem Space* (now) and our *Solution Space* (a bit later on):

- In our *Problem Space*, it serves us by letting us properly understand our subject, getting inside their "head" (what they're thinking) and their "heart" (what they're feeling and experiencing) so that we can understand their real outcome need and their motivations and aspirations for having that outcome need.

- In our *Solution Space*, it serves us by letting us test new solution concepts (and thus new value propositions) with our subject, and understand, at a very deep level, *why* one particular solution resonates more with them than does another. The more our solution addresses their *real* outcome need, and their *real* motivation and aspirations, the more it will resonate with them. So, having this empathic understanding allows us to zero in on just that right solution much faster and far more accurately than we ever could without it.

Once we've attained this point of proper empathic understanding, we will have achieved a key intermediate goal for Design Thinking.

Understanding and achieving our ultimate goal – a reframed problem

Our ultimate goal at this point, preceding any thought of a proper and valid value proposition, is to **reframe** the problem we're addressing. That is *why* we developed the empathic understanding that we did – so that we can reframe the problem we're addressing.

Reframing – seeking a more fundamental level of outcome need

In particular, we want to reframe our problem into one that's framed at a more fundamental level of human outcome need – including a complete understanding of the different motivations and aspirations involved in driving it.

To get to that point, we must do the following:

1. start with a large number of *hypotheses* about the situation at hand – hypotheses that try to explain what the actual outcome need is, and why that outcome need is so important to our subject;

2. figure out ways by which we can *test* those hypotheses against reality;

3. and then actually go out and test those hypotheses to sort out *which* of them are accurate and valid (and to what extent), and which are not.

It is this hypothesis development and testing process that is going to allow us – through appropriate investigative work – to uncover *which* of our hypotheses are correct and which are not. This will eventually unlock the key **insights** we need to properly address the situation.

This will require us to spend some time brainstorming all the different hypotheses that could conceivably explain what our subject is trying to achieve and why – a process known as *hypothesis storming*. This is something we have to do with a very open and imaginative mind – not allowing any preconceived notions we might hold about the subject and their situation to artificially limit these hypotheses. Instead, we have to be fully open-minded and broad in considering any number of possible hypotheses, reflecting any number of different outcome needs, motivations, and aspirations. Being as broad as possible at this point can help us to avoid settling on a "local maxima," and instead investigate the full realm of possibilities before us.

As we'll learn in *Chapter 8*, there's a whole somewhat-formalized process for doing this – involving a large number of observation and questioning practices – but we should also be aware of, and appreciate, the fact that this is a *learning exercise*, and as such will often be quite iterative and recursive. We'll develop certain hypotheses, test them, and think we have their answers, but then upon further and deeper investigation, learn that we weren't 100% correct, and so we have to *cycle back and start over* with one or more *refined hypotheses* to learn more – until we eventually achieve this ultimate goal.

Our momentary win – the reframed problem

At the end of our (potentially cyclical) investigation, we'll ultimately arrive at our end point, where we have successfully *reframed* our subject's problem into one that is a more accurate expression of their real outcome need and with it, their real motivation and aspirations driving that need. That is our holy grail.

Getting to this point signifies that we've reached the *end* of our Problem Space – just before entering a liminal space preceding our Solution Space – a critical milestone in our Design Thinking process.

In the vast majority of cases, we will (and should) spend a disproportionate amount of our "Design Thinking time" here in the Problem Space, not in the Solution Space. It is not uncommon to spend 70% of our time here, and only 30% in our Solution Space – figuring out the real problem at hand tends to be a far more challenging task than figuring out how to solve that problem. As Albert Einstein is quoted as so famously saying, "*If I had an hour to solve a problem, I'd spend 55 minutes thinking about the problem and 5 minutes thinking about solutions.*" That's largely what our life will be like during this period of trying to get to this reframed problem.

Once we get to this point, where we're fully confident that we've properly and successfully reframed our problem into one that we can solve through a winning value proposition, we're ready to articulate our new (reframed problem) and then start thinking about our Solution Space for addressing that problem.

It cannot be overemphasized just how **critical** this phase is to our final business model. If we do not successfully reframe our problem or challenge into one that we can solve at a fundamentally more human level, then we'll most likely fail at having an impactful business model. The only way we're going to succeed at this new business model is to have a Unique Value Proposition that truly is unique and that massively impacts our subjects – and the only way we're going to do that is if we get this step done right! So, we must do it right.

The takeaway – what Design Thinking means to us

Our starting point in Design Thinking is to do the following:

1. identify the humans we're trying to solve for, and then center on them;
2. try to understand human needs at a fundamentally more human level;
3. inherently presume we don't know any of the right assumptions yet behind that situation to be able to properly solve it.

Given that our task at hand is to develop a highly compelling Unique Value Proposition to use in our business model, what this ultimately means for us is that we're going to have to go out – presuming we know nothing of any real value yet, other than a vague sense for who our customer is and what issue that "may have" – and discover all those correct assumptions for ourselves.

So, our starting point in developing our *Unique Value Proposition* is to identify the specific customer we want to serve, along with what we "believe" their challenge or problem to be, and then from that point on, to apply the Design Thinking process (with its human-centered design philosophy) to uncovering what that customer's *real need* is. This must inherently include uncovering the most fundamental human motivations and aspirations behind that need. Then, we can define a Unique Value Proposition that delivers a solution that addresses those particular motivations and aspirations – solving for them rather than their surface symptoms – at whatever level of solution we can act on as a business.

Indeed, the more "fundamental" we can get in our solution – by defining a Unique Value Proposition that addresses those most fundamental human motivations and aspirations – then, all else being the same, the more successful we're going to be as a business venture.

By the same token, but on the other side of that token, if we *fail* to do this, if we simply deliver a value proposition that's on par with everything else out there – a "me too" – then it's quite likely that we're going to fail as a business.

Getting a new business venture off the ground takes a bang – and that bang has to come from delivering a truly compelling unique value proposition that solves a real need at a fundamentally more human level of motivation and aspiration. If we can do that – if we can sufficiently address those human motivations and aspirations involved – then we will most likely succeed. And that is our goal here.

Some important sidenotes on Design Thinking

At this point, we understand the essence, purpose, and aims of Design Thinking – what we need to move forward.

However, it's informative and educational to have a bit more insight into the history, success, criticisms, and new evolutions of Design Thinking. Having this will give us a much richer and broader understanding of, and appreciation for, this practice – which, in turn, will offer us greater context for what we'll doing as we go forward.

So, we use the next few pages to look at these points before returning to our main flow of thought.

A bit of history on Design Thinking

What we know today as "Design Thinking" has a long and rich history, dating back almost 150 years.

While the term "Design Thinking" is a newer vernacular dating from the late 20th century, many of its practices were not new. Instead, they derived from user ethnography practices that had been developed and were in use for decades prior, most notably from within the field of architecture. Some of these practices hail from as far back as the 1880s when they were used in Europe by leading Architectural Practitioners of the time. Some of these individuals – most notably Walter Gropius and László Moholy-Nagy – eventually went on, in the 1920s and 1930s, to found and teach at a leading school of Art, Design, and Architecture in Germany known as the Bauhaus (or more formally, *Staatliches Bauhaus*). At the Bauhaus, many of these types of practices were refined and perfected further.

While the Bauhaus itself did not survive the impacts of World War II, it did spawn several other schools in its same philosophical vein – each of which carried on its teachings and practices in various ways. The most notable of these that remain today is the IIT Institute of Design in Chicago.

These philosophies and practices quickly found their way into the world of Product and Industrial Design of the 1940s, 1950s, and 1960s – where a movement emerged that came to be known as "good design." This movement started with the works of such notable Designers of the period as Frank Lloyd Wright, Walter Dorwin Teague, Henry Dreyfuss, Flaminio Bertoni, Battista Pininfarina, and Harley Earl. The movement hit its stride in the 1950s with the works of even more notable designers such as Buckminster Fuller, Arne Jacobsen, Charles and Ray Eames, David Mellor, Raymond Loewy, Luigi Colani, Brooks Stevens, Robin Day, George Walker, Marcello Nizzoli, and Frank Hershey. These Designers hailed from all over the world, and much of their work focused on the emerging consumer products of the day – products such as automobiles, furniture, and consumer appliances – with much of their work being seen as highly innovative and avant-garde for its time. This spirit of good design continued into the 1960s and beyond, with the work of more modern notable designers such as Dieter Rams, Massimo Vignelli, Jacob Jensen, Giorgetto Giugiaro, and, in more recent times, James Dyson and Jony Ive.

Underpinning this movement were certain design theories and practices that were applied to these individuals' work. These theories and practices evolved significantly throughout the period, such that by the 1960s they had given life to a practice known at the time as *Participatory Design*. In Participatory Design, the Designer makes an explicit effort to **integrate** the users of the design directly into the actual *Design Process*. The purpose of doing this was to ensure that the design actually fit its intended use – and users – as ideally as possible.

To give this movement the **tools** it needed to work with, the era also saw the development of what eventually came to be known as *Design Methods* – ways in which to study these users to understand their interactions with the product (including such methods as classical *usability testing*). Many of these methods borrowed from what was already being done in the fields of Architecture and Urban Planning, as noted earlier.

Iterations of this movement in the ensuing decades (the 1980s and beyond) saw such design theories emerge as user-centered design (using cognitive reflection), meta-design (using process methods), and finally what we know today as human-centered design. It eventually came to reflect both a philosophy about design and a design process to accommodate that philosophy. Today, it remains the most dominant design philosophy in use. The early 2000s further saw Industrial Design move beyond just being about the design of *products* – to include the design of *services* and even the much broader design of *businesses* as well.

Today, much of our design practice – which tends to all be labeled under the banner of Design Thinking – was developed in the 1980s and 1990s by professors Robert McKim and Rolf Faste of Stanford University. Their colleague David Kelley subsequently adapted Design Thinking to business and, based on those adaptations, went on to launch, in 1991, the now-famous design firm IDEO. Stanford University's d.school (formally known as the Hasso Plattner Institute of Design) continues to carry the torch for the academic treatment of Design Thinking, which includes its underlying philosophy of human-centered design. Also in 1991, the IIT Institute of Design in Chicago introduced the world's first-ever PhD program in Design.

Several key books and articles were written throughout this period codifying these design theories and practices. These were written by such notable thinkers in the field as John Arnold, L. Bruce Archer, Herbert Simon, Robert McKim, Nigel Cross, and Peter Row.

But Design wasn't the only discipline from which we get the practices of Design Thinking. Indeed, beyond that world, with its focus on user psychology, the world of *Advertising* also made substantial contributions. In the 1940s and 1950s, as this profession was laying down its roots (especially post World War II, where rapidly growing consumer choices meant brands had to woo and sway customers over to their products), key business leaders and academicians in this field made important contributions through the art of *creative thinking*. In particular, in 1939, Alex Osborn, principal of the famed ad agency BBDO, invented the practice we know today as *brainstorming* and contributed even further to the broader world of creative thinking and problem-solving.

Then, in the 1950s and 1960s, academicians such as Sidney Parnes, together with Alex Osborn, gave the world formal **Creative Problem Solving (CPS)**, an overarching practice that brought to life such creative thinking methods as "how might we" questions and countless others – most of which have since been "absorbed" into what we think of today as *Design Methods* (which we'll talk about later in this book). Both Osborn and Parnes wrote several books each covering these topics. CPS still operates today as its standalone practice, run by the **Creative Education Foundation (CEF)** founded by Alex Osborn in 1954 (`www.creativeeducationfoundation.org`). CEF operates the world's longest-running international conference on creativity, known as the *Creative Problem Solving Institute*.

So, what we know today as "Design Thinking" is not new at all – it just has a newer name. And the modern incarnation that we know today largely emerged out of these two camps – the Design Community and the Advertising Community.

Documented successes of Design Thinking

Among those who have applied Design Thinking *properly*, a tremendous amount of business success has been achieved, particularly over the past 40 years.

Of course, and perhaps not surprisingly, there have been thousands who haven't applied it properly, and who, as a result, have not benefited from its capabilities.

However, there are countless case studies documenting and testifying to the power and effectiveness of Design Thinking when used properly. Among those have been the following:

- IDEO's 1999 documentary on ABC's late-night news show *Nightline*, which launched the whole modern awareness of Design Thinking: `https://www.youtube.com/watch?v=M66ZU2PCIcM`.

- Several *Harvard Business Review* articles documenting its success (see the *Further reading* section).

- Several *Fast Company* articles testifying to its power (see the *Further reading* section).

And hundreds more… you only need to do an online search for "Design Thinking success" and you will see many more examples of these.

I have taught Design Thinking to firms ranging from the United States to the United Arab Emirates to Malaysia, and in every case I've been able to help lead the affected organizations into using the practice very effectively for their market situations.

So, Design Thinking can be used very effectively in our hunt here for a compelling new Unique Value Proposition.

Applying Design Thinking properly – with no suppositions about the solution

One of the biggest **mistakes** that would-be *design thinkers* make is to enter into the process having already made up their minds about what type of solution they need (and therefore intend) to deliver – whether it be a product, a service, an experience, a regulation, or some other type of solution.

When they do this, they short-circuit the process because they artificially constrain it to produce some type of solution outcome that may not be the most *ideal* type of solution outcome. This results in a **local maxima** – something that will fail to deliver the maximum possible value to the subjects involved.

Instead, we need to enter this process with our possibilities wide open – completely open to the idea that what we discover in the process is what our subjects need. This could be any of the following:

- a service, not a product;

- a product, not a service;

- an experience, not a service;

- a regulation, not a service;

- and so on – for any type of solution outcome.

When we do this – when we allow ourselves to be fully wide open to deliver **any type of solution**, then – and only then – will we be able to discover and deliver the **absolute maxima**… a solution that truly meets the needs at hand – using whatever form of solution does so, be it a product, a service, an experience, a system, a process, a community, a network, or something else entirely.

So, the challenge before us is to not allow ourselves to be lulled into the belief that we *already know* – a priori – what *type* of solution is going best meet our subject's needs – but instead remain wide open to all the possibilities before us, be those products, services, experiences, systems, processes, communities, networks, regulations, or whatever manifestation of value delivers the greatest possible impact in that situation.

If we can do this, then we will be far more successful (and impactful) in our Design Thinking efforts!

This means that if we currently live inside one of the many bounded domains of innovation – product innovation, service innovation, customer experience innovation, and so on – we'll have to, at least for this period, break out of that domain and rise above it – to let ourselves consider all domains so that we can fully address the "big picture" ahead of us. Doing this may feel very foreign and strange to some of us, but we have to force ourselves to do so if we ever hope to unleash maximum new value to both our customers and our business.

This is also why strong **cross-functional teams** play a key role in this process… having individuals who are skilled in each of these respective domains will allow the overall team to put their minds together to consider all possibilities, and then ultimately deliver the most ideal type of solution for the situation.

The criticisms of Design Thinking

In all fairness and objectivity, Design Thinking hasn't been without its critics.

A big part of this criticism, however, has had to do with how Design Thinking is customarily *practiced* inside Design-oriented firms – and not with the practice itself.

In particular, it's widely acknowledged that there is often an air of *exclusivity* and *superiority* among Designers and Design firms – one that presumes only *they* know how to use the practice, and no one else does. It is this air of exclusivity and superiority that has turned off so many "outsiders" to it. They see the practice as being incredibly exclusionary and non-inclusive, and that rightfully bothers them. Moreover, this attitude has *prevented* some Designers from engaging with their subjects as they should – to learn about them in the way the practice tasks them with doing, thereby causing them to not carry out the practice as it was intended to be done, which is namely in a very participatory and democratic manner.

This reaction has been well documented in several articles in publications by Harvard Business Review, MIT Technology Review, and Fast Company (see the *Further reading* section for more on this).

The *answer* to this very real perception is to go back to what was being promoted in the 1960s – namely *Participatory Design*. In Participatory Design, we work to get *everyone*, and in particular our design subject, involved in the design process – ensuring that it is anything *but* exclusionary.

It should also be noted that this issue has been far less prevalent in the CPS community than it has in the Design Community. The CPS community has, by comparison, tended to be far more open and inclusive in its teaching and use of these methods (the irony in this is that it was the CPS community, not the Design Community, who invented the "how might we" question that was tasked in the *Fast Company* article mentioned previously).

A broader conceptualization – Humanity-Centered Design

In more recent years, there's been an evolution in the overall corporate thought process – from one focusing on a single stakeholder, such as the customer or the shareholder for example, to one focusing on **all** impacted stakeholders – customers, employees, partners, suppliers, shareholders, regulators – and yes, also society at large and the environment it impacts.

This has stemmed largely out of the *Stakeholder Capitalism Movement*, as evidenced in the 2019 *Restatement of Purpose* by Business Roundtable (a coalition of CEOs of some of the United States' largest corporations). This is also well documented in books such as *Conscious Capitalism* (John Mackey and Raj Sisodia, 2013) and *Stakeholder Capitalism* (Klaus Schwab of the World Economic Forum, 2021).

Within the Design Thinking community, this has manifested as a shift – both in our language and our thinking – from *human-centered design* to *humanity-centered design* (sometimes also called *humanity-centered innovation* and *humanity-driven design*).

The inference here is that it is insufficient to apply our human-centered design efforts toward designing for just a single party (the user, or customer). Instead, we have to channel those same energies toward designing for **all of humanity** – for **all** of the affected stakeholders – *including* the earth, which humanity so desperately depends on. After all, what does it profit the world as a whole if we create luxury for a few, but in the process cause pollution, destruction, suffering, and/or corruption for those in the more disadvantaged parts of the world? Doing so does not seem particularly "humanity-centered," does it?

What that means for us and our efforts here – as well as the challenge before us – is manifold:

1. *First and foremost* we have to design for our target subject (the customer, user, and so on). If we cannot succeed as a business because we failed to design for them, then everything else becomes moot.

2. Once we've worked out the most optimal design for *that* target subject – but *before* we execute it – we have to step back and ask ourselves, "How will this design impact all the *other stakeholders* affected… will it be positive or negative – not just in the balance, but for each one individually?"

3. If our design is detrimental to any of those stakeholders, our task is to ask ourselves, "How can we *redesign* our value proposition without losing the magic of what makes it so special for its main subjects, yet at the same time become a better value proposition, and a better business model, for *all* of the affected stakeholders?"

Our goal here is to find a win-win value proposition that does **both** of these. That's our task as true business model innovators and artists. We shouldn't lose sight of this bigger picture involving everyone we're impacting.

Or, as Anne Asensio noted to me, "This is a unique opportunity for Designers to shift from the *pride of their creation* toward *how much benefit they have delivered* and *how much positive impact they're having on the world.*"

Back to Intensifi – where are they now in all this?

When we left off with our friends at Intensifi – Ian, Zoe, and Watson – they had a fairly clear sense of what customers they wanted to serve (a certain group of individual consumers, and a certain group of business customers), plus they had some surrogate business models they were planning to study, but they weren't quite sure about the initial goals they'd set for the platform. This was because they didn't feel like they knew these customers well enough yet to be fully confident that these goals would align with their true wants and needs – not to mention their motivations and aspirations driving those.

So, Ian, Zoe, and Watson now understand that they're going to have to go out and get to know these would-be customers. This is so that, in each case, they can understand and appreciate, what exactly their wants and needs are, as well as the details behind each of those wants and needs… what's driving them to *have* these wants and needs, and *why* is solving those wants and needs of so much value and importance to them.

Moreover, as our trio is starting to learn more about Design Thinking and human-centered design, what they realize now is that what this means for them is that they have to develop *empathy* for these customers and their situation. This is so that, through an empathic research effort, they can develop an *empathic understanding* of these customers and their situation – meaning that they understand these individuals and their needs and desires from *their* point of view, rather than just their own. This is going to require them to "get inside" these customers… to understand what's going on in their heads (their thoughts) and in their hearts (their emotions) – a place from which they can then start to work, in terms of really exploring the Problem Space now and the Solution Space a bit later on.

Indeed, developing this empathic understanding will let our trio start to peel back the layers of each situation so that they can get to the "real problem behind the problem" – or, in other words, to reframe each customer's apparent need into their real underlying human need, motivation, and aspiration. This will then let them deliver a Unique Value Proposition that truly speaks to those needs and aspirations.

To this end, Ian, Zoe, and Watson have identified the following consumer and business parties to serve as their surrogate would-be customers to study:

- **Consumer side**: Five groups – each spanning all ethnographies (gender, race, ethnicity, religion, and so on):

  - High-performing, aspirational sales professionals in their first 5 years of professional practice.

  - High-performing, aspirational finance professionals in their first 5 years of professional practice.

  - High-performing, aspirational engineers in their first 5 years of professional practice.

  - High-performing, aspirational architects in their first 5 years of professional practice.

  - High-performing, aspirational corporate attorneys in their first 5 years of professional practice.

- **Business side**: Six groups – each entailing a different industry and market:

  - Senior leaders in driven, high-performing businesses in the high-tech software sector.

  - Senior leaders in driven, high-performing businesses in the consumer electronics sector.

  - Senior leaders in driven, high-performing businesses in the traditional manufacturing sector.

  - Senior leaders in driven, high-performing businesses in the enterprise services sector.

  - Senior leaders in driven, high-performing businesses in the medical equipment sector.

  - Senior leaders in driven, high-performing businesses in the tier 1 automotive supply sector.

Fortunately for Ian, Zoe, and Watson, they each possess an extensive network of professionals from all over the world. So, they'll be able to tap into those networks to find these individuals and business leaders to spend time with – in each case getting to know them and their situation far better than they do currently.

It's noteworthy to observe here that, on the consumer side, Ian, Zoe, and Watson have put some thought into this and have decided that their best targets will likely be those who are working in large corporate settings. This is because those settings offer these individuals long, multi-tiered career paths to strive toward, thus creating a context in which their platform can offer these individuals maximum value – by helping them to navigate those career paths (and thinking back to the previously stated preliminary goal for this group).

So, what Ian, Zoe, and Watson intend to do at this point is to invest some time and effort in hanging out with these respective would-be customers in their respective environments. Doing this will allow them to shadow and observe these individuals (sometimes up close and sometimes from afar) – as well as talk to them to learn more about what's going on in each situation they're encountering, what thoughts those each entail, and (very importantly) how they each make that individual feel.

What Ian, Zoe, and Watson hope to get out of this is a far deeper understanding of these would-be customers – in terms of what makes them tick, and therefore what's motivating them to pursue certain outcomes under certain circumstances – and/or what is otherwise blocking them from doing so. They believe that understanding these things will allow them to better formulate their goals for the platform, and thus for their Unique Value Proposition, not to mention designing that platform.

As Ian, Zoe, and Watson prepare to embark on this phase of their journey, they'd like to know more about what exactly it is they're looking for. In other words, what sort of "a-ha" will constitute a "success" in each stage of this learning process? To understand that, they believe they need to understand more about the actual consumer psychology involved – as well as how, in each case, that psychology gets shaped and influenced by the different anthropological and environmental structures surrounding them. Fortunately, they've heard that this subject is up next, so they will have the chance to learn more about this before they set out.

Summary

In this chapter, we introduced Design Thinking, including what it is, what its fundamental philosophy is, what its real superpower is, and what all that ultimately means to us as Business Model Designers hunting for a winning Unique Value Proposition.

We also explored the process of developing empathy for our customer in more detail so that we can cultivate an empathic understanding of them and their situation. This is one that's held from *their* point of view, not *ours*. Such an understanding allows us to really "get" these people at a truly human level – because it pulls back the curtain for us on their inner psyche, to show us more about what makes them tick and why so.

We also explored how having this understanding is what ultimately unlocks Design Thinking's superpower of reframing problems into ones framed at a fundamentally more human level – one of real desire, motivation, and aspiration. We also looked at how reframing problems in this way is what ultimately allows us to conceive effective and impactful solutions to these problems – and thus value propositions that deliver what these customers need and desire, regardless of what they might "think" they need and desire otherwise.

In the next chapter, we're going to dive even deeper into the world of **behavioral psychology** – to talk about what ultimately makes up the human psyche and how that gets manifested in our world, starting with each individual's unique *perceptions* of reality, and then culminating in their reflexive *behaviors* in response to those perceptions.

As we'll learn, this is incredibly important to us as Design Thinkers because all we can observe about these people (when we're observing them) is what we see manifested in their *behaviors*. From this, we can sometimes infer what might be their thoughts and attitudes, but we can never really know those for certain without actually engaging them in a more direct and intrusive way. But even then, understanding their thoughts and attitudes is a necessary but insufficient condition for delivering real solutions to them. Instead, we have to get down to their real inner drivers – both at their core level and their "actuated" level. It is these inner drivers that determine both their intrinsic and extrinsic motivations and aspirations and – as we'll see – that, in turn, drive their behaviors.

So, as we'll learn next, our *job* as Design Thinkers is to drill down into our subjects until we eventually understand – to the extent possible – these different inner drivers. It is from *that level* that we'll ultimately be able to define a solution – and thus a Unique Value Proposition – that truly resonates with these individuals – ideally in a way that no other value proposition does.

Further reading

- *Change By Design: How Design Thinking Transforms Organizations and Inspires Innovation*, by Tim Brown, HarperCollins, 2009.

- *The Other Side of Growth*, by Anthony Mills, Editor, Global Innovation Institute, 2020.

- Harvard Business Review, *Design Thinking*, by Tim Brown, June 2008.

- Harvard Business Review, *Design Thinking: What It Is and Why It Works*, by Jeanne Liedtka, January 2013.

- Harvard Business Review, *Design Thinking Comes of Age*, by Jon Koko, September 2015.

- Harvard Business Review, *The Right Way to Lead Design Thinking*, by Christian Bason and Robert D. Austin., March-April 2019.

- Fast Company, *What is Design Thinking*, 2006.

- Fast Company, *'Design Thinking' Isn't a Miracle Cure, but Here's How It Helps*, 2011.

- Fast Company, *Why the Design Thinking process is so important: a primer*, 2022.

- Fast Company, *To advance your career, you may want to think like a designer*, 2023.

- Harvard Business Review (Entrepreneurship), *Design Thinking Is Fundamentally Conservative and Preserves the Status Quo*, by Natasha Iskander, September 2018.

- Fast Company, *Design Thinking's most popular strategy is BS*, by Tricia Wang, June 2021.

- MIT Technology Review (Culture), *Design Thinking was supposed to fix the world. Where did it go wrong?*, by Rebecca Ackermann, February 2023.

Thinking Like a Scientist – Centering Our Design around Humans

In *Chapter 7*, we initiated our exploration of Design Thinking – introducing its essence, its underlying philosophy, its superpower, and what it means to us in our quest for the ultimate and ideal Unique Value Proposition.

In that exploration, we learned about both the need and a process for cultivating *empathy* for our subject, ensuring that, ultimately, we can possess an empathic understanding of them and their situation. We also learned how understanding that situation, and the needs it entails, from *their point of view* (rather than our own) is what is central to tapping into Design Thinking's superpower of reframing problems. Furthermore, we learned that reframing problems is what allows us to go beyond the superficial surface symptoms we encounter to get down to the real "problem behind the problem" – the real need experienced at a human level, involving the different outcomes needed and the motivations and aspirations behind those outcomes.

In exploring those topics, we alluded to, but did not further unpack, the act of "pulling back the curtain" on these individuals to understand their **inner psyche** – thus revealing what makes them tick and why. Therefore, in this chapter, that is precisely what we're going to unpack – the inner psyche of our subjects and what makes them tick, both at their core and in the context of specific situations we find them in.

Key to all of this is understanding **human behavior** in different contexts. To do this, we're going to put on our "Behavioral Scientist hat" and think like a (Behavioral) Scientist. In fact, one big part of "thinking like a designer" is first "thinking like a scientist."

In doing this, we're going to investigate one vein of the world of **Behavioral Science** – namely, the one dealing with, at one end, people's behavioral responses to their *perceived stimuli* and, at the other end, their inherent *motivations* and *aspirations* behind those behaviors, both intrinsic and extrinsic. To facilitate this, we'll introduce a framework we call the **Human-Centered Design Hierarchy of Human Needs**.

We'll wrap up the chapter with a closer look at the specific **outcomes** our subjects are trying to achieve and **why** (in other words, what makes those outcomes so important and, thus, valuable to them). From that, we'll understand that any solution – and, thus, any value proposition – has to satisfy not only *functional jobs* but also, just as importantly (and often more importantly), *emotional* and *social jobs*, and in some cases, *transformational jobs*, empowering our customers to become even better versions of themselves.

All of this is **incredibly important** because if we do not get our "who" just right and their "why" just right, then we'll most likely fail as a business venture. There are so many ways a new venture can go sideways and miss the mark, and certainly starting down the wrong path with the wrong "who" and/ or the wrong "why" will almost always be one of those. So, we cannot emphasize enough this point. It's imperative that we have 100% clarity on who our "who" is and on what their "why" is, long before we proceed to build out a new business model to fit with that "who" and that "why." Being a Behavioral Scientist allows us to crack that "who" and "why."

We're going to break our exploration of these topics down into the following five specific topical areas:

- **Becoming a Design Thinking Behavioral Scientist**: A look at what we have to accomplish if we hope to apply scientific insights to our quest of understanding our subject and then conceiving a winning value proposition for them.

- **The Human-Centered Design Hierarchy – understanding human needs**: A look at all the different sciences that inform our understanding of our subject and their situation, plus a detailed look at how the human psyche works in this context.

- **Understanding the real outcome – the Job to be done**: Exploring a set of methods to codify the specific and unique outcome needs that our customers have, thereby further illuminating their "why".

- **Breaking down jobs – functional/emotional/social/transformational**: An exploration of the different types of "jobs" our value proposition has to deliver on, plus how they relate to one another and the significance they each hold for our ultimate success as a business.

- **What people ultimately buy – better versions of themselves**: A conclusive look at what our subjects ultimately desire, relating to their fundamental human aspirations throughout their lives.

All of this will set us up to, bit by bit, move closer and closer to our ultimate and final Unique Value Proposition.

While this chapter is a bit longer and more on the insights-rich side, rest assured that you'll come away with a clear understanding of the human psychological and sociological considerations within Design Thinking.

We'll also visit again with our friends at Intensifi to see how they're doing at becoming Behavioral Scientists on behalf of their venture, and whether this whole concept of understanding their subject's behavior, aspirations, and motivations is making sense to them – not to mention whether or not they have the patience left to do that.

Becoming a Design Thinking Behavioral Scientist

To do Design Thinking correctly, we must each become, in effect, a "Design Thinking Behavioral Scientist." In that context, we have to study – in-depth – the specific behaviors and attitudes of our subject, and from those, we will try to discern the true aspirations and motivations belying them.

Our task as Design Thinking Behavioral Scientists

Our task as Design Thinking Behavioral Scientists is to use the many design research methods at our disposal (which we'll talk more about in *Chapter 9*) to study our subjects and learn all about their **perceptions**, **attitudes**, and **behaviors** so that, ultimately, we can work our way toward more fully understanding their underlying **motivations**, **aspirations**, and **priorities** – both the *extrinsic* type involved in a specific situation (typically uncovered first) and the *intrinsic* type underlying them (typically uncovered last).

This all *begins* with our *observations* of these behaviors, which is then followed up with deeper *inquiry* into the behaviors in order to hypothesize about what might be the motivations and aspirations behind them (often *filtered* through the subjects' various attitudes). We then ultimately *test* those hypotheses to arrive at what their *true* motivations and aspirations are (which can be manifold).

By doing this, we can come to truly understand our subject and their situation, including what motivations, aspirations, and priorities drive them to pursue the particular *outcome* they seek and why such an outcome is so *important* and *valuable* to them (as well as *how* important and valuable it is to them) – all assessed from *their* unique perspective or point of view, not our own. This is the empathic understanding we strive for.

The ultimate ideal here is to drill down so deep into these individuals' respective psyches as to ultimately understand their true core beliefs and values – those underlying their respective motivations, aspirations, and priorities. The more we can do this – and thus the deeper we can get into this psyche – the better will be the solutions and value propositions we deliver to them, meeting their aspirations in ways that truly (and ideally uniquely) resonate with them. That is our true goal here – albeit one that in most cases we can never fully attain but that, nevertheless, gets as close as we possibly can.

And so, having this empathic understanding, we can start to define a Unique Value Proposition that fully and properly addresses the specific, unique needs, desires, expectations, and preferences our subjects have in this situation. That will allow us to define as perfect of a Unique Value Proposition as possible in the situation – remembering that the reason we're doing all this is to reduce uncertainty in our process, and thereby de-risk it, so that we can ultimately optimize our chances of business success with a positive impact on the world.

Turning Behavioral Science into our secret weapon

One thing that Behavioral Science often does for us as Design Thinking Behavioral Scientists (and as business leaders) is uncover incredibly unexpected, and quite counterintuitive, findings about our subjects and their situation. These findings reveal where their behaviors deviate (sometimes significantly) from what we might otherwise *expect* – unexpected behavioral anomalies that defy conventional wisdom.

As leaders of new business ventures, this is **incredibly valuable** to us, as it gives us extremely valuable and useful insights into our potential customers that our competitors (and any other "competitive options") most likely don't have. We can then **act** on that knowledge – on what we know that they don't know!

Doing this can give us a Unique Value Proposition that in and of itself serves as our Sustainable Competitive Advantage – a value proposition that no one else has and cannot easily duplicate. Indeed, knowledge of these anomalous human behaviors can equal distinctiveness and, therefore, differentiation. This lets us break away from the pack – we're no longer trying to optimize the exact same things they are. We're optimizing things that matter far more than the things they're optimizing. This lets us break out of the "red ocean" of dire competition and into a fresh new "blue ocean" of uncontested opportunity – one that we alone own – simply by rewiring the basis of competition based on this new knowledge. This is powerful indeed!

Dealing with human irrationality

In doing our design research, there are two things that we need to quickly observe and understand:

1. People's *actual* behaviors are often **not rationale** – meaning that the decisions they make (and the actions they take arising out of those decisions) are often not made on a *rational basis*. Instead, they're often made on a much more *emotional* and *intuitive* basis, sometimes leading to choices and actions that are markedly different from what *rational choices* would look like.

2. People's **perceptions** and **understandings** of their *own behavior* are typically immensely **skewed** and **flawed**. What they "think" they do and what they "actually" do are often quite different things. Similarly, in terms of their *reasons* and *rationales* for those behaviors, why they "think" they do the things they do and why they "actually" do them are often quite different from each other.

One of the key implications of this second observation is that when we ask people to explain their behaviors to us, they'll often (unknowingly) lie to us (actually to both us and themselves). This is because what they "think" they know about their behaviors and the reality of those behaviors are two different things. This is something we can sometimes expose to them via *Cognitive Behavioral Therapy*, where we videorecord their behaviors, ask them to explain those behaviors, and then play them back the video recording, revealing to them their own misperceptions about those behaviors (and, to a lesser extent, about themselves). This can be an eye-opening exercise, as it reveals to them certain *cognitive dissonances* occurring in their minds. This (and other methods like it) also lets us, as Behavioral Science Researchers, do a bit more "meta-thinking" about the situation – thinking about how we think about it, including looking at it from both our own and these subjects' perspectives, thus yielding more conscious awareness of the differences between the two perspectives.

As Design Thinking Behavioral Scientists, we have to deal with this unfortunate reality – that our subjects are going to think and act in quite irrational ways that they themselves do not understand and certainly cannot explain.

This means two things – one, that we have to be 100% fully aware of this reality, and two, that we have to go well beyond our own superficial observations to reach down into the deeply emotional and intuitive aspects of our subject and their situation. It is only when we do that – and ultimately get to this place – that we'll be able to cut through the clutter and noise and actually get to the *truth* of the situation. And that is our goal. A classic example of this (discovered by the customer-outcomes community) is the case of people buying a candy bar at the grocery checkout. On the surface, we (and they) may believe the reason for this is that they just want to "have a snack." But the *real reason* for this behavior is to avoid being hangry later on and saying or doing something very irrational on account of low blood sugar, which ends up becoming a career-limiting move. So, in other words, they buy this candy bar at the checkout to save their careers – a much different motivation and aspiration than just "having a snack."

So, be prepared for these different irrationalities. If we go into the process with eyes wide open, then at least we'll have a fighting chance of coming out on the other side with truthful insights we can work with!

Next, to better visualize and understand the human psyche – including both the inherent and contextual manifestations of it – we will introduce a brand-new framework, the *Human-Centered Design Hierarchy of Human Needs*. This will help bring what we just discussed into even greater context.

The Human-Centered Design Hierarchy – Understanding Human Needs

To ultimately and eventually deliver a winning Unique Value Proposition, we're going to have to – as noted in *Chapter 7* – understand our customer and their situation on an incredibly deep level. This includes, in particular, what they're trying to *accomplish* in that situation and *why* doing so is so important to them.

To do this, we're going to have to unpack both the individuals involved and the situational context they're in. This means we're going to have to engage in a certain amount of *design research* on both of these.

For that, we're going to need to tap into several of the different social sciences. In particular, Design Thinking depends on four specific fields of social science (at the very minimum; there are often more). These are as follows:

- **Human Psychology**: In particular, the branch of psychology known as **Behavioral Science**. This focuses on why people behave the way they do, as irrational as that often is, and why people's *actual behaviors* often differ so markedly from their *self-perceived behaviors*.

- **Sociology**: What is occurring socially around our subject that establishes the *social context* in which they encounter certain specific *outcome needs* they need met?

- **Anthropology**: What characteristically defines the "tribe" that our subject belongs to, and what is it about that tribe's *language, culture, customs*, and so on that offers guardrails to define and otherwise shape their particular perceptions of, and behaviors in, the world?

- **Behavioral Economics**: What is happening socioeconomically around our subject that drives certain specific *market behaviors*, within which our subject can, and may, become caught up?

It is this deep understanding of our subject – what is happening inside them psychologically and why – *paired with* an equally deep understanding of their situational context – what is happening around them (and perhaps has been for the entirety of their lives) that defines their (very relative) perceptions and behaviors in that context – that allow us to really understand both them and their situation at a truly *empathic level* (i.e., from *their* point of view and perspective, not our own).

Psychological insights – the science of human motivation

Our first goal here is, thus, to develop a truly deep and empathic understanding of our subject as a human being. To do that, we need a deeper insight into how the human psyche is structured and operates. By having this, we can use science to get inside the head and heart of our subjects.

To do that, we will introduce a new framework – the **Human-Centered Design Hierarchy of Human Needs** – or simply the **Human-Centered Design Hierarchy** for short – as shown here in *Figure 8.1*.

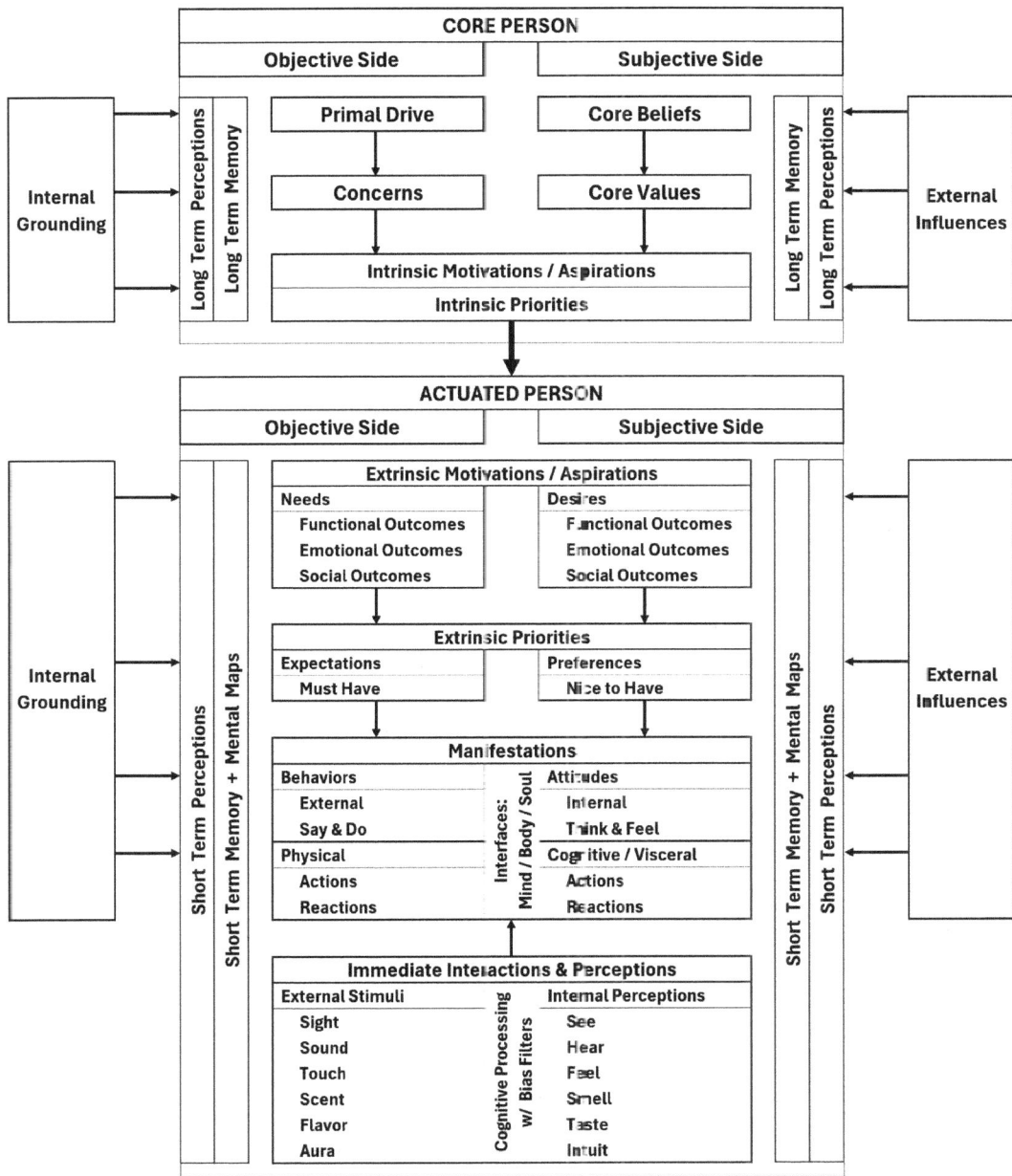

Figure 8.1: The Human-Centered Design Hierarchy of Human Needs

The Human-Centered Design Hierarchy borrows from psychology, sociology, and anthropology to illustrate the structure, nature, and operation of the human psyche.

As such, it is composed of two main elements:

- **The Core Person**: reflecting the individual's core drive, concerns, beliefs, and values and, therefore, their more *intrinsic* motivations, aspirations, and priorities.

- **The Actuated Person**: reflecting the individual's more *extrinsic* motivations, aspirations, priorities, and manifestations, as well as their interactions and perceptions in the contextual situation that occurs.

By understanding our subjects (our potential customers) through this set of lenses, we're able to develop a progressively deeper level of empathy for them and their situation and, thus, a progressively deeper empathic understanding of both.

Let's unpack both of these elements more deeply.

The Core Person

The *Core Person* is made up of an **Objective Side** and a **Subjective Side**.

- Their Objective Side includes their *Primal Drive* (involving such things as survival, food, and shelter), as well as their *Concerns* (involving such things as security, and companionship).

- Their Subjective Side includes their *Core Beliefs* (what they fundamentally believe to be true *about* the world and how it operates), plus their *Core Values* (what they fundamentally hold to be true regarding how the world –and, therefore, the people in it – *should operate*).

Together, these two sides give rise to the individual's **Intrinsic Motivations and Aspirations** (what intrinsically motivates them), as well as their **Intrinsic Priorities** (the relative ordering of importance of everything in their world).

These are all **anchored** by the person's *Internal Grounding* – largely a product of their environment during their upbringing, but also influenced by their own personal disposition. As such, they're largely programmed into the individual's subconscious as a young child and remain with them (to varying degrees) forever. They can, however, also be **influenced** at any given time by *External Influences* in their environment. Both of these (Internal Grounding and External Influences) shape the individual's *long-term perceptions* and, thus, their *long-term memory*. These change much more slowly than their *short-term perceptions and memory* do.

It's worth noting here that all of the major choices and decisions we make in our lives are largely driven out of these intrinsic motivations, aspirations, and priorities. Some of them may be conscious to us, and many of them are subconscious, meaning we're not fully aware of them. We all have, in fact, such conscious and subconscious drivers in our psyche. Consequently, we make many of our choices and decisions without ever being fully aware of our reasons for doing so.

Furthermore, these intrinsic motivations, aspirations, and priorities can each have both positive and negative roots to them – giving rise to both positive and negative choices, decisions, and behaviors in our lives that have, respectively, positive and negative outcomes (for both us and others). So, we can have both positive and negative outcome needs that we proceed to fulfill in either positive or negative ways. Much of this comes down to how aware we are of ourselves and these elements of our psyche, as well as how much we opt to work within them versus actively changing them. Indeed, personal "healing" and the overcoming of past traumas require us to actively change them – so that we can thereafter lead a more positive, fulfilling, and healthy life. Otherwise, if left unchecked, they may not serve us very well.

It's *also* worth noting here that the *extent* to which, and the *rate* at which, you can (and do) alter your intrinsic motivations, aspirations, and priorities will depend on your **deeper motivations and aspirations**. Indeed, research on the *Growth Mindset* versus the *Fixed Mindset* has demonstrated that we are not just static beings (if we choose to not be so) and that we can, in fact, generate new synaptic pathways throughout our lives that serve to (over time) **reshape** our intrinsic motivations, aspirations, and priorities. However, you have to make an active and conscious decision and effort to do this, or have a dramatic life experience that *forces* you to do so; you won't be reshaped on your own without this.

These respective attributes of the Core Person collectively feed into, and thus provide the foundation for, who the *Actuated Person* ultimately becomes and how they consequently see, perceive, and interact with the world around them.

The Actuated Person

The *Actuated Person* is made up of four key attributes:

1. Their Extrinsic **Motivations/Aspirations.**
2. Their Extrinsic **Priorities.**
3. Their **Manifestations.**
4. Their Immediate **Interactions and Perceptions.**

With the Actuated Person – just as with the Core Person – each of these is once again made up of an Objective Side and a Subjective Side.

Within their Extrinsic Motivations/Aspirations, the following applies:

- Their **Needs** make up the Objective Side and include any number of different outcomes they *require.*

- Their **Desires** make up the Subjective Side and include any number of different outcomes they *desire.*

Within their Extrinsic Priorities, the following applies:

- Their **Expectations** make up the Objective Side and include those things deemed to be *must-haves*.

- Their **Preferences** make up the Subjective Side and include those things deemed to be *nice-to-haves*.

Within their Manifestations, the following applies:

- Their Objective Side is made up of two parts:

  - Their **Behaviors**, which are external and manifested in what they *Say* and *Do*.

  - Their corresponding **Physical Activities**, as manifested in both *Initial Actions* and subsequent *Reactions*.

- Their Subjective Side is likewise made up of two parts:

  - Their **Attitudes**, which are internal and manifested in what they *Think* and *Feel*.

  - Their corresponding **Cognitive** and **Visceral Activities**, as manifested in both *Initial Actions* and subsequent *Reactions*.

- There is a layer of **Interfaces** in between the Objective and Subjective Sides, involving the individual's *Mind, Body, and Soul*.

Within their Immediate Interactions and Perceptions, the following applies:

- Their Objective Side involves all of their **External Stimuli** – *sights, sounds, touches, scents, flavors*, and *auras*.

- Their Subjective Side involves all of their **Internal Perceptions** of those stimuli – what they actually *see, hear, feel, smell, taste*, and *intuit*.

- In between the Objective and Subjective Sides, there is a layer of Interface, involving their cognitive processing of these things, including the influence of their own personal *bias filters* on this cognitive processing.

These are all, once again, **anchored** by the person's *Internal Grounding* – largely a product of their upbringing environment but also influenced by their own unique personal disposition. These are also again **influenced** at any given time by *External Influences* in their environment. In this case, this grounding and these influences serve to shape their *short-term perceptions* and, therefore, their *short-term memory and mental maps*. These change much more quickly and more frequently than their *long-term perceptions and memory* do.

Together, these attributes of the Actuated Person derive from, and are the ultimate manifestations of, who the Core Person actually becomes, given the environments, situations, and scenarios they encounter throughout their lifetime.

Unraveling the meaning of the Core Person versus the Actuated Person

What does it actually mean to talk about a *Core Person* versus an *Actuated Person*? Let's try to address and answer that question before going further.

The Core Person represents who the individual fundamentally is, at their very core – what fundamentally defines and drives them – outside of any particular situational context.

These are attributes that are formed largely and mostly during their younger formative years, via their environment, in combination with their own personality and disposition. The individual, of course, evolves and matures to some degree as they age and grow, but these foundations of their psyche are established at that younger age. This is what gives the individual their *Internal Grounding*, which continues to influence their psyche via long-term perceptions and memory – just as some of their *External Influences* do.

Since these attributes are what fundamentally define and drive an individual outside of any particular context, they remain with the individual *throughout* each and every context and situation they encounter. As such, they impact and shape how that individual perceives, and thereafter responds to, every such context and situation.

This is important because, as we place this individual into different contexts, we can *know* – to some degree – the *range* of how they might perceive and respond to that context, based on this fundamental core that defines them. Nothing about it changes from one context or situation to the next (at least not in the short term; in the long-term it can evolve, as noted previously), but it does involve a certain specific **bounded range** of attitudes and behaviors that the individual will exhibit.

In contrast, the *Actuated Person* represents how that person actually shows up and operates in the context of a specific situation. It involves their specific needs and desires in that situation, together with their respective expectations and preferences around those. These – in combination with whatever they happen to be perceiving in that situation – will determine what their attitudes and behaviors end up being in the situation.

As such, the Actuated Person can, and may, look and behave differently in each situation, depending usually on how strong their specific *needs* and *desires* are in that situation and, thus, how much they *value* its outcomes, as well as what experience they encounter and perceive in the situation. If their needs and desires are *low* and the experience is *good*, then this "Actuated Person" will exist at the more **passive** end of the "Core Person spectrum." But if their needs are desires are extremely *strong*, and/or the experience is *bad*, then this "Actuated Person" will quite likely exist on a far more **active** and **vociferous** end of the "Core Person spectrum." Both ends of this spectrum exist inside the bounds of who that "Core Person" is and the particular character they've developed and now possess.

This is *why* some people will characteristically react to a particular situation in one way, while other people will characteristically react to that same situation in a different way. It's the same situation but different "Core Persons" underneath, and thus, markedly different "Actuated Persons" get manifested. This is also why, under the same circumstances, some people go on to become productive members of society while others do not – their "Core Persons" are different from one another.

Sometimes further confounding this is the presence of "front stage" and "backstage" personality manifestations. This is where an individual exhibits, in one context (their "front stage" situation), one manifestation of their personality, and in a different but related context (their "backstage" situation) a very different manifestation of their personality. Both manifestations exist inside the boundaries of the Core Person; it's just that more duplicitous individuals (think politicians, for example) tend to have far broader boundaries than more transparent and objective individuals do. This is something we should be aware of and remain on the lookout for.

So, in the context of our trying to find the right Unique Value Proposition to use, it is extremely important for us to understand this about our subjects – who they fundamentally are as a "Core Person" (or what range is encompassed in our case, which can be quite wide) and who they typically show up as, as "Actuated Persons" in the context and situation that we care about. We have to understand both of these things about our subject if we ever hope to define a Unique Value Proposition that truly resonates with them.

Applying the HCD hierarchy

To *apply* this framework and use it as a tool to understand people and the situation they find themselves in, we have to walk through the overall hierarchy, starting at the very bottom and then working our way upward through it, one step at a time. Let's do so, starting with our subject's Immediate Interactions and Perceptions.

Immediate Interactions and Perceptions – External Stimuli

We will start with our subject's *External Stimuli* (Objective Side). These are the artifacts that express their situation at any given time. They involve the hard artifacts of that reality, including its sights, sounds, touches, scents, flavors, and auras. These are *objective realities*; nothing about them is subjective. They exist the same no matter who experiences them. They are a direct product of the situation at that moment in time.

Immediate Interactions and Perceptions – Internal Perceptions

Then, we consider our subject's *Internal Perceptions* (Subjective Side). This is where things start to get very interesting, as well as diverge from one individual to the next. These are entirely *subjective*. More specifically, they are the subjective perceptions of the previously described *External Stimuli* and, as such, involve (using our six senses) what we as an individual *uniquely* see, hear, feel, smell, taste, and intuit from those External Stimuli.

This point is incredibly, incredibly important and should never be overlooked! It is, in fact, what really matters to our subject – much more so than the *actual reality* before them. You see, each individual perceives reality *differently* from one another – sometimes subtly so, and sometimes markedly so. This is on account of both their *internal cognitive processing* (how their brains are wired and operate), and the specific *cognitive filters and biases* they've come to have as a result of their Internal Grounding and External Influences. Behavioral Science calls this *subjective reality* (that which exists individually inside our respective minds) versus *objective reality* (reality as it actually exists, outside of any human perceptions of it). Both types matter to us, and thus we'll need to discover insights relating to each one. Fortunately, there are both qualitative and quantitative research methods used to explore them both, examples of which we'll encounter in *Chapters 10, 11, and 12*.

Therefore, whenever presented with the exact same sights, sounds, touches, scents, flavors, and auras, two different people will actually see, hear, feel, smell, taste, and intuit two different things! That's the **dilemma** we're dealing with here (good or bad) – each individual sees, hears, feels, smells, tastes, and intuits *differently* from every other individual.

This means that, if we really want to understand our subject and their situation **empathically**, we're going to have to move into talking about their *internal perceptions* of reality, *not* their actual *external realities*, as it is those internal perceptions that actually determine what they *do* with these external realities. In other words, reality itself matters less than do their perceptions of it.

For example, consider the case of Jane and Linda, two attendees at the exact same theatrical performance. Jane, on account of her internal cognition and expectations, deems the performance to be horrible – very poor plot, casting, acting, staging, lighting, costuming, make-up, and so on. Conversely, Linda, on account of her different internal cognition and expectations, deems the performance to be magnificent – outstanding plot, casting, acting, staging, lighting, costuming, make-up, and so on. The objective reality of the performance may be somewhere in the middle of these two extremes, but because two separate individuals, each with their own respective perceptions, experienced it differently, they came away with very different assessments of it. Both sets of cognitive perceptions will have been shaped by the person's Internal Grounding.

Alternatively, consider the case of two students, Mike and Bill, both taking a course together under Professor Entwistle. Both students submit their comparable term papers to the professor, and the professor dutifully grades them using the exact same rubric and standard – in both cases, offering prolific feedback on the respective shortcomings of each paper. Upon getting his paper back, Mike – because of his perception of this outcome – sees it as an insult. He becomes enraged and says, *"How could Professor Entwistle be so nit-picky? Surely my paper is greater than this; he is clearly overlooking my level of intelligence!"* Conversely, Bill – because of his perceptions of this exact same outcome – sees it as a very wonderful growth aid. He is (in contrast) quite thankful that Professor Entwistle has taken the time and effort to help him become that much better of a thinker and a writer. The objective reality was the exact same in both cases, but the two subjective realities were quite different from each other, generally on account of something buried deep down inside their respective Internal Groundings.

We must, therefore, think, talk, and act in the context of these *perceptions*, not of their corresponding realities. That is our first step toward developing a truly empathic understanding of our subject and their situation. In *Chapter 9*, we'll explore more about *how* to do this.

Also note that on both sides of the hierarchy (as shown in *Figure 8.1*), the sixth sense has been included – described as an *aura* and an *intuit* (a perceived aura). This is important because, while a perceived aura and the intuition developed from that perception may or may not be accurate, they nevertheless affect our subject's perception and, thus, influence the attitudes and behaviors they display. They must, therefore, be included.

As we next move upward inside the framework, we encounter our subject's **manifestations**, which are made up of two distinct parts – namely, their *attitudes* (subjective) and their *behaviors* (objective).

Manifestations – Behaviors

We will start with our subject's *Behaviors* (the Objective Side) because they are what we can actually see and observe. Therefore, they hold the key to our being able to work our way up through the rest of the framework.

Behaviors are the **physical manifestations** of what is otherwise going on in our subject's head and heart. As such, they involve two specific *external manifestations* – namely, what they *say* and what they *do*, as well as *how* they say and do what they say and do. All of these are considered their "behaviors."

They also happen in a **physical sequence**. There are our subject's **initial actions** and then (following some response by the "system" involved), their subsequent **reactions** to that system's behaviors, including their *cognitive reactions* (their thoughts) and their *emotional reactions* (their feelings). This way (and this is something we encounter in *Experience Design*), we have this "dance" happening between our subject and whatever "system" they happen to be interacting with in the situation (this "system" can involve people, machines, events, and/or any combination of them). There is this *back and forth* between them – the subject's initial actions / the system's responses to those actions / the subject's perceptions of those responses / the subject's reactions to those perceptions / the subject's subsequent actions / the system's subsequent responses / and so on.

Consequently, as our subject works their way through whatever "steps" and/or "stages" are involved in the situation, there will be this ongoing series of actions and reactions occurring, based on the specific touchpoints and system behaviors that occur. These are the things that we want to observe and make careful notes of, as we're going to use them, later on, to infer far more about our subject and what is happening inside them – in their "inner world."

Behaviors are **super important** to us here because – of everything happening in this framework – they are the *only* attributes that we can actually **observe directly**. Everything else in the framework must be **deduced indirectly** from what we learn about the subject, including, very importantly, from these specific behaviors.

We must be careful, however, because our *observations* of these subjects are themselves colored by *own* particular **cognitive biases and filters** – meaning that the behaviors we observe may or may not be how those behaviors actually occur in reality. We may perceive those behaviors as being of *one nature*, while our fellow Researchers perceive them as being of *a different nature*. This is *why* it's so crucially important to have more than one Researcher involved in our observation and study efforts – so that we can "compare notes" with each other and try to cancel out one another's respective cognitive biases, resulting in an (ideally) more objective assessment of these behaviors. What we *don't want* is our own subjective realities layered atop our subjects' subjective realities, as that will not prove helpful to us at all; it will only lead us astray. So, in the context of our research, our interpretations of our subjects' behaviors and perceptions have to be as objective as possible.

Manifestations – Attitudes

Lurking somewhere beneath our subject's *Behaviors* are their corresponding *Attitudes* (the Subjective Side). It is largely these attitudes that determine their behaviors in response to whatever reality they happen to be perceiving. In other words, there is – to a degree – a one-to-one correlation between their attitudes and their behaviors. Thus, by observing their behaviors, we can at least start to theorize and hypothesize about what their underlying attitudes *might be* – or stated otherwise, their observed behaviors place certain bounds around what their underlying attitudes are likely to be. The more expressive and direct they are, the tighter these bounds can be, but the more reserved and non-expressive they are, the wider these bounds have to be.

Similar to how our subject's behaviors are manifested by what they say and do, their attitudes are manifested by two specific *internal manifestations* – namely, what they *think* and what they *feel*, or in other words, what's going on inside their *head* (their mind) and their *heart*. These thoughts and emotions are incredibly important to us, as they will ultimately determine whether or not we satisfy their needs. If they *think* we're meeting those needs, and if they (more importantly) *feel* that we're meeting those needs, then they will ultimately *believe* that we are, in fact, meeting those needs – at which point we are, for all intents and purposes, actually meeting their needs. This is especially true whenever we're meeting a need that they didn't even know they had before, and in so doing, we are unlocking massive new value for them!

Just as our subject's *behaviors* occur in a *physical sequence*, their attitudes likewise occur in a corresponding (directly correlated) **cognitive and visceral sequence**, involving a sequential series of thoughts and feelings. These occur in response to the exact same stimuli as their behaviors did – the specific stimuli they happen to be encountering in the situation, which in this case serve to drive their resultant attitudes.

Consequently, as that subject again works their way through whatever "steps" and/or "stages" are involved in the situation, there will be an ongoing series of actions and reactions happening, based on the specific touchpoints and system behaviors that occur. In this case, these actions and reactions will involve their specific attitudes, none of which we can observe directly. We can only observe their behaviors directly and then, from those, try to infer what their underlying attitudes might be at each point.

As we'll learn a bit further on, we can test out our theories and hypotheses about these attitudes by (eventually) questioning our subjects (after observing them), trying to dive deep into what *they* believe their attitudes to be (at each step of the process) and seeing whether, in fact, our perceptions are accurate. Irrespective of whether or not they're accurate, they will reveal a lot about what goes on inside our subject's head and heart at each touchpoint. This questioning and other similar research methods can be very effective at exposing, and in some cases explaining, the (sometimes large) gaps that exist between what people say and what they do, or between what they feel and what they think or believe. In turn, that can sometimes further illuminate why some people act on their dreams, while others never do.

Now that we've talked about our subject's manifestations, let's move one more step up the hierarchy to talk about both their Extrinsic Motivations and Aspirations and their Extrinsic Priorities, as these artifacts go tightly hand in hand with each other.

Extrinsic Motivations / Aspirations – Needs

We will begin at the *top* of the Actuated Person with their specific *needs* in a situation (the Objective Side). These "needs" are a form of extrinsic motivation or aspiration and, as such, represent specific *outcomes* that quite literally *have to occur* for that motivation or aspiration to be met. They are mandatory, not optional. If these outcomes do not occur, then the motivation or aspiration has not been attained. They are what are labeled as "pains" in some of the Design Thinking tools we'll use, such as the Empathy Map.

As we will learn later on, these motivations and aspirations can be quite complex in nature, involving any mix of functional, emotional, and social outcomes and, in some cases, even transformational outcomes.

Again, these outcomes are mandatory, not optional. If we do not achieve them, then little else will matter – we will have failed to meet our subject's fundamental motivation or aspiration in this case, a situation that does not make for a viable business operation.

Extrinsic Motivations / Aspirations – Desires

Alongside our subject's *needs* are also their additional **desires** (the Subjective Side). These "desires" are also a form of extrinsic motivation or aspiration and, as such, represent specific *outcomes* that, should they occur, further advance our subject to meet their specific motivation or aspiration. Therefore, they add value to the overall situation.

Unlike needs, desires are optional, not mandatory, but if they are met, they will add additional value to a situation and will quite likely allow our subject to attain their motivation or aspiration more fully, or in a better way. This is something that can prove to be a real **differentiator** for our business – possibly a *Sustainable Competitive Advantage* – so we should always spend time and effort focusing on these as ways to go beyond the "need" at hand and, thus, truly differentiate how our business meets that need. They are what are labeled as "gains" in some of the Design Thinking tools we'll use, such as the Empathy Map.

As we will also learn later on, these motivations and aspirations too can be quite complex in nature, involving any mix of functional, emotional, and social outcomes and, in some cases, even transformational outcomes.

So, together, our subject's needs and desires make up their overall extrinsic motivations and aspirations.

Extrinsic Priorities – Expectations

Within our subject's extrinsic motivations and aspirations (assuming there is more than one), they will *prioritize* their respective needs and desires in a particular order.

First in this order are, of course, their *needs*, as these naturally precede their *desires*. In this sense, we call these needs their **Expectations**. Expectations are outcomes that the subject fundamentally *expects*. They are the "must-haves" in a situation, which are, as noted before, mandatory and not optional. If we do not satisfy these expectations, then we have a no-go situation and won't get any further in trying to service this subject.

In other words, our subject's expectations are the *table stakes* for doing business in this situation – the "cost of doing business." If we don't meet these table stakes, then we're not even in business.

Importantly, since *all businesses* have to somehow meet these exact same table stakes to even be in the game, they, by definition, cannot constitute a differentiator. They are *not* a source of differentiation. All options meet these same expectations more or less equally well; otherwise, they don't last in the market. This is an important awareness to have – one that points to our need to differentiate *elsewhere*.

Extrinsic Priorities – Preferences

Second in our subject's order of priorities are their desires, following their needs. In this sense, we call these desires their **Preferences**. Preferences are outcomes the subject would additionally *prefer to have*. They are the "nice-to-haves" in a situation, which are, as noted before, optional and not mandatory.

Thus, while not satisfying these additional preferences won't necessarily disqualify us from the game, it will limit how successful we can be. If we truly wish to be successful, then we'll strive to meet and satisfy as many of these additional *preferences* as possible – in each case, to a high caliber.

Indeed, it is within these additional *preferences* that we find fertile ground for **differentiation** inside the affected marketplace. The more additional "nice-to-haves" we can satisfy (with everything being equal), the more we can differentiate ourselves, and the greater our odds of success will be. We should, therefore, spend considerable time and effort – once we have satisfied all of the different expectations – working on how we can satisfy as many of these "nice-to-haves" preferences as possible, in order to truly differentiate ourselves in this market.

Summary – the Actuated Person

Now, we've seen how the *Actuated Person* in this framework involves the following elements of our subject:

- **Immediate Interactions and Perceptions**: Their internal perceptions of their external stimuli. In our example, Mike reviewed his returned term paper and mentally processed its implications for him; he perceived it to be an unfair and insulting assessment of his abilities. Bill reviewed his returned term paper and mentally processed its implications to him; he perceived it to be a fair, objective, and professional assessment of his performance in this situation.

- **Manifestations**: Their behaviors and underlying attitudes – what they say and do, and what they think and feel, occurring in a physical and cognitive / visceral sequence, respectively. Mike felt insulted and became enraged; he felt that the professor treated him unfairly; he lashed out verbally about this perception and his feelings surrounding it.

  Bill felt thankful for the constructive input of the professor; he felt that the professor had given him (and presumably everyone else) a fair and objective assessment; he verbally expressed his thankfulness.

- **Extrinsic Motivations and Aspirations**: Their respective needs and desires, in the form of different functional, social, and emotional – and possibly transformational – outcomes. Mike needs acceptable grades in his academic career to continue progressing well. He seemingly needs to feel affirmed that he's more intelligent and capable than his social peers, and he seemingly needs to feel affirmed emotionally as a high-performing student. He does not appear to have any real transformational needs.

  Bill needs a fair and objective assessment of his performance in each case. He does not appear to be overly concerned with his comparative performance among his social peers (this is irrelevant to him as long as everyone is graded equitably). He seemingly needs to feel that he is progressing, learning, and growing academically (as well as a person). He appears to have a transformational need to become an even better thinker and writer and, therefore, a more competent and capable individual.

- **Extrinsic Priorities**: Their expectations and priorities, reflecting their unique prioritization and ordering of these specific motivations and aspirations.

  Mike appears to prioritize his own emotional and social affirmations far above any need to improve as a student or a person overall. Bill appears to prioritize his academic growth as a student far above any particular emotional or social affirmation needs.

What we can also observe about the Actuated Person in this context is that all these artifacts can be, and usually are, informed and influenced by both their Internal Grounding and any External Influences – in this case, via their short-term perceptions and, thus, their short-term memory and mental maps of the world.

Core Person – the Objective Side

Within the *Core Person* – on the Objective Side – we have the individual's **Primal Drive** and **Concerns**. These are the things that fundamentally concern them on a day-to-day basis, thus driving them to pursue whatever motivations and aspirations they happen to be pursuing.

These relate very closely to *Maslow's Hierarchy of Needs*. Thus, where our subject happens to be in that hierarchy at any given time will depend on their particular situation and which of its lower needs are already being met. The more of the lower needs that are already being met, the higher up on the pyramid they can operate – until, at the very top, they can ultimately focus on true self-actualization, which is where, in most cases, we would ideally like them to be (depending on exactly what we're trying to sell to them).

By the same token, if not all of these Primal Drives and Concerns are being satisfied, then they may never get to the specific actuated situation we need them to be in to need and desire the solution we're trying to sell them. In other words, we have to find target customers whose Primal Drives and Concerns are already being sufficiently satisfied so that we can encounter them in the appropriate situation ("actuated"), where we can deliver new value to them, as at that point, they need and desire what we're selling.

Core Person – the Subjective Side

Within the *Core Person* – on the Subjective Side – we have the individual's **Core Beliefs** and **Core Values**. These are extremely important because they ultimately shape what this individual will and will not *desire* and, therefore, what they will and will not *value*. If what we offer does not align with those core values and beliefs, then it will not be seen as a viable option to them, and they will pass on it.

This is *why* we ultimately have to get to know our subjects well enough to thoroughly and clearly **understand** the core values and beliefs they hold, as these ultimately determine whether or not our value proposition is even in the right ballpark to speak to these individuals. If our value proposition is somehow fundamentally misaligned with their unique core values and beliefs, then there will be no way to connect with these individuals as customers. They will find a different option that does align with their core values and beliefs. Many manufacturers and retailers have found this out the hard way when they took positions that countered their core customers' fundamental values and beliefs, causing them to lose significant market share.

This is an incredibly important consideration to muse on for a moment. We have to clearly know *who* the different **customer segments** are, *what* is fundamentally **important** to each one, and what specific core values and beliefs go with those priorities. Only then can we, upon reflection of the specific core values and beliefs we intend to align to, determine *which* of those specific segments we intend to align ourselves with.

Of course, we can always play it safe by attempting to be either *neutral* or *universal* in terms of core values and beliefs, but this does require a tight balancing act to ensure that we *always* remain so, while still being true to our own values and beliefs as a business.

Of equal importance is the fact that who we intend to serve as a customer may in fact have quite different core values and beliefs from those we personally hold. In those cases, if we truly intend to serve those customers, then we will have to put our own core values and beliefs aside and instead work around theirs. Otherwise, if that path is untenable to us, then we'll have to select a *different* customer segment whose core values and beliefs more closely align with our own (which, in some cases, may be a *smaller* customer segment).

Core Person – Intrinsic Motivations and Aspirations

An individual's Primal Drive and Concerns – together with their Core Beliefs and Core Values – ultimately work together to determine what their *Intrinsic Motivations and Aspirations* are and, to sort and prioritize those, what their respective *Intrinsic Priorities* are.

These will be the concerns, drivers, beliefs, and values that ultimately determine *who* and *what* that individual aspires to be and become at each and every point in their life.

This, of course, leaves room for a very broad range of actual manifestations, in terms of things such as the vocation they choose, the spouse they select, the city they opt to live in, the possessions they choose to own, and the experiences they decide to pursue. In each of these cases, the individual's Intrinsic Motivations and Aspirations – and Intrinsic Priorities – will produce the guardrails constraining those range of choices.

For example, if honesty is one of their core values, then they're not going to select thieving as their vocation. If proximity to extended family is one of their core values, then they're not going to relocate far away from their family. If minimalism is a core belief they hold, then they're not likely going to amass opulence, and so on.

Summary – the Core Person

As we have seen, our subject's "Core Person" is comprised of the following elements:

- **Primal Drive**: What fundamentally drives them at any particular point in their life.

- **Concerns**: What core concerns they deal with at any given time in their life.

- **Core Beliefs**: What core beliefs they've come to hold at each point in their life.

- **Core Values**: What core values they've come to have at each point in their life.

- **Intrinsic Motivations and Aspirations**: What intrinsic motivations and aspirations drive them to pursue each respective situation and context they put themselves in.

- **Intrinsic Priorities**: How those respective motivations and aspirations are all prioritized in relation to one another.

Together, these define who our subject is at the most fundamental level.

Our subject's "Core Person" is also informed and shaped by their *Internal Grounding* and *External Influences*, except that, in this case, this happens over far more time, via their *long-term perceptions and memory*. In other words, it takes far longer to shape who a person fundamentally is than it does to influence their attitudes and behaviors in any given isolated situation involving a far more (relatively) minor stake.

This is an important consideration to be aware of, in that we shouldn't count on trying to change an individual's "Core Person" via our business. Our business, although it must *understand* that "Core Person," can, in most cases, only influence and affect the "Actuated Person" – the manifestation of the person we find them in, in the context of the specific outcome-related situation we're dealing with. We can influence that "Actuated Person," via our communication with them, but we cannot, in most cases, impact their "Core Person" in any real way.

Therefore, we must design and structure our business – and its business model – accordingly. Our Unique Value Proposition and our Sustainable Competitive Advantage can speak to *both persons*, but they can only *influence* the latter.

The final caveat

British statistician George Box is credited with having popularized the aphorism – concerning statistical models, and later scientific models in general – that "*all models are wrong, but some are useful.*" This too is true of the Human-Centered Design Hierarchy of Human Needs.

So, in the way of a final caveat about this framework, it – like all such models – will never be 100% correct. There will, at times, be outliers whom it does not characterize fully. Therefore, it is not absolute in its descriptive ability. So, let's not be lulled into a false sense of security when using it, believing that because of how extensive it is, it is absolute in its ability. It is not.

Nevertheless, it can be quite useful in our work, so we should make appropriate use of it, understanding this caveat and the limitations it potentially has.

Now that we understand both our role as a Design Thinking Behavioral Scientist and the Human-Centered Design Hierarchy, we're going to go deeper into the topic of *outcomes*. The whole subject of "outcomes" is indeed one that has attracted tremendous thought energy in the Innovation world over the past 25 years, yielding a range of methods and practices to unpack people's required and desired outcomes, which we'll talk about next.

Understanding the real outcome – the job to be done

At the heart of satisfying our potential customer in a novel way that unlocks massive new value for them is understanding the specific **outcome** – or **outcomes** – they're trying to achieve – and **why** (i.e., why that outcome is so important and valuable to them).

If we can get down to the core essence of *this* – what outcome they want to achieve, and why – in a very *detailed manner* (particularly on the "why" part), then we can eventually and ultimately define a Unique Value Proposition that delivers on that "what" and that "why" in a novel way that no other value proposition does. That is our ultimate goal at this point in the journey. So, to that end, let's explore some core concepts here that unpack this.

Outcome-Driven Innovation® and Jobs-to-Be-Done

In the 1990s, two largely consecutive veins of thought started to emerge, both of which looked at innovation through the lens of (and to a lesser extent, as extensions of) **Total Quality Management (TQM)**. TQM holds that the ultimate arbiter of "value" is the customer, and so while TQM, as it was generally practiced, focused on attaining minimal variation in whatever was being produced, it also recognized that "value" begins by meeting the customer's actual needs, whatever those happen to be.

ODI

The first vein of thought developed into what we know today as **Outcome-Driven Innovation®** (**ODI**) (a registered trademark of Strategyn). ODI was developed by Anthony Ulwick, who, after living through a massive product launch failure at a large tech company, came to the realization that what we should really focus on and discuss (if we want to unlock innovation for our customers) is what *outcome* they're trying to achieve and, along with that, what *process* they're using to attain that outcome (and, to a lesser extent, what products and services they're using to do so).

So, in ODI, we strive to understand the real **outcome** that our subject is trying to achieve and **why**, including what is and is not *important* to them in that process. By knowing this, we can deliver innovations that deliver on that in a far better way. The key to attaining this knowledge is thoroughly studying, dissecting, and understanding the *process* our subjects use to attain that outcome. This is important because, quite often, the outcome we "think" they're trying to achieve – or that it "appears" they're trying to achieve – is not at all the real outcome they're "actually" trying to achieve! This is something their *process* often reveals. So, our job in this case is to discover what outcome they're *actually* trying to achieve (and why) so that we can act on that.

Consequently, we want to forget about what these subjects are presently doing and, instead, focus on the *outcome* they're trying to attain, allowing us to invest our time and energy into searching for a better way of attaining that outcome. In some cases, this will mean abandoning a former approach to the outcome in favor of a new and better approach, thus unlocking greater value for the subjects.

Classical ODI uses a specific methodology. In this methodology, you examine the *process* people try to undertake when they use a particular product or service – their journey toward achieving their outcome (which the product or service plays a role in). By making the *process* the subject of our investigation – rather than the product or service itself – we're able to break that process down into its constituent steps and then study each step in great detail. We do this in search of those places in the process where innovation can unlock new value for the customer. An important part of this is understanding the metrics that customers use to gauge *success* as they go about executing this process, something that formal ODI methodology addresses.

A key activity inside ODI is using User Research to walk experienced users through the process, step by step, to discover which of those steps they deem to be most important versus least important in attaining their outcome, as well as which of them are presently being well-served versus ill-served by current solutions. As it turns out, it's the jobs that exist at the **intersection** of "very important" and "poorly served" that offer the most fertile ground for innovation. It's at these junctions that focused efforts to make a better product or service produce a measurable impact. Focusing on areas that are either unimportant or already well-served (or both) has very little impact and, thus, no payback. The payback comes from addressing this "magic quadrant" of important and underserved. This is illustrated in *Figure 8.2*, which shows that this upper-left quadrant is the zone we need to focus on, as that's where innovation will have the greatest impact on us.

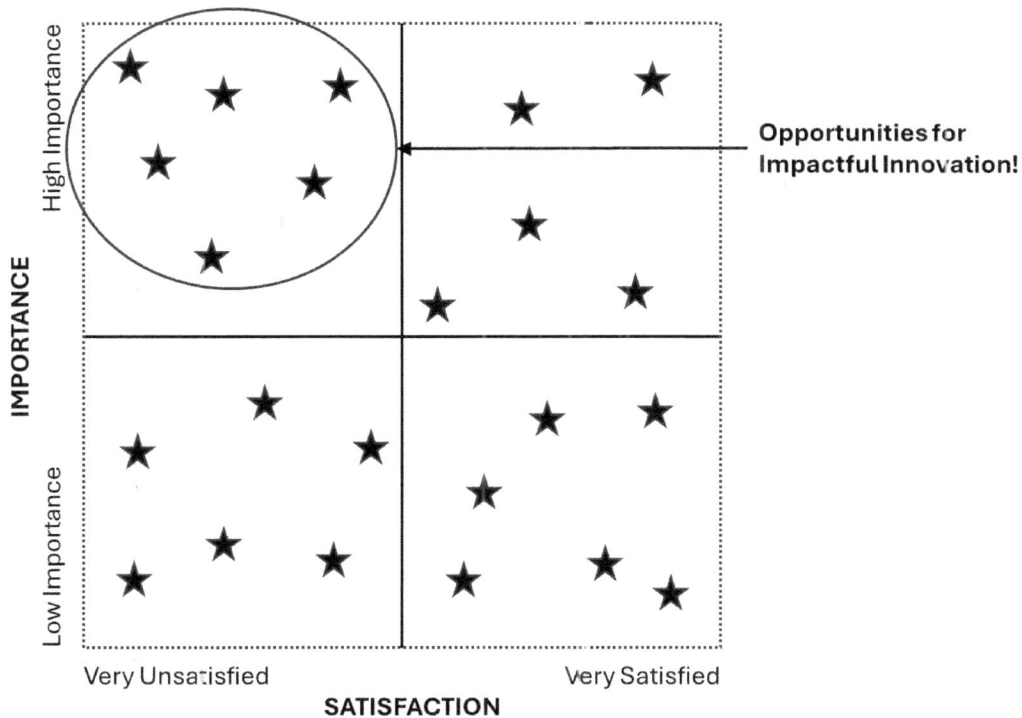

Figure 8.2: The opportunity space for impactful innovation deriving from ODI

The shortcoming of ODI

A major caveat and shortcoming of ODI is that it relies on interviewing users of past and present offerings (products and services) to learn their perceptions of those offerings in the context of using them (and, thus, in the context of the *process* of using them). This, of course, makes it necessary to find individuals who possess that past experience and context. Otherwise, there is no one to interview and study and, therefore, no insight to be gained from the method. And since users can only tell us about whatever prior context and history they have, this means the method is only useful when operating out of that prior history, which tends to lead to better versions of *existing* products and services ("incremental" or "sustaining" innovation), rather than entirely *new* products and services ("breakthrough innovation"). In other words, the method is incapable of telling us anything substantial about new offerings that don't yet exist and which users have no prior context with.

Consequently, if we're contemplating an entirely new product or service category that does not yet exist, the method will have little to no value to us. It can help us understand the *outcome* our customers are trying to achieve, but if we're looking to introduce an entirely new *process* to attain that outcome, then we can't go any further with the method; we'll have to look to other methods for that. Alternatively, we have to really zoom out and talk to our customers in terms of far broader *generalities*, which takes us out of the realm of specifics and into the realm of generalities. That can sometimes be useful, although not always.

Jobs-To-Be-Done

The second vein of thought became what we know today as **Jobs-To-Be-Done** (**JTBD**) or, by its alternative name, *Customer Job Theory*. This practice was pioneered in the 1990s by a community of dedicated practitioners, the most prominent of whom were John Palmer, Rick Pedi, Bob Moesta, Pam Murtaugh, and Julia Wesson.

Like ODI, JTBD focuses on the *outcome* that customers are trying to achieve, except that in this, case it's called the "job". In JTBD parlance, customers "hire" a product or service to achieve a particular "job" for them.

JTBD represented a crucial turning point in the world of product development, as instead of attaching value to what products and services are *in and of themselves*, it instead attached value to what those products and services could *do* for customers – or, more precisely, what they enable customers to *get done* when using them. This is equivalent to saying JTBD places value on how the product or service *benefits* the customer.

JTBD spawned new research practices that focus on *why* and *how* customers use products, as well as how doing so allows them to *attain* their goal(s). That research has repeatedly revealed big gaps between why producers believe customers purchase and use their products and why they *actually* do. That, in turn, has provided tremendous opportunities to dominate the marketplace through innovations that address these "actual jobs." And *that* is JTBD's claim to fame.

The marriage of ODI and JTBD

Over the past 20 years, these two methods, ODI and JTBD, have in many practitioners' minds been largely married together, becoming synonymous – even though they originated from different communities with very different philosophies and practices. This has largely been because much of the literature on ODI, and innovation in general, has incorporated JTBD terminology and concepts inside it, even though both methods contain their own distinctly different practices. Consequently, many people today see the two as one entity.

Our takeaway

The important takeaway for us here is that we have to focus on our customer's "**why**" when they use any product or service, what "outcome" they're trying to achieve, and what "job" they're trying to get done – regardless of what the product or service was actually designed to do in theory.

If we can discover "why" they "hire" a particular product or service, and what "job" or "outcome" they are trying to do by using it, then we can hone in on just the right areas of their situation to innovate on. And *that* is where impactful value propositions arise from! In other words, these methods seek to unveil customers' most fundamental needs and desires – aside from whatever product, service, experience, or other form of value has historically been used – so that we can fully understand those and then innovate around them.

The Job Story

The **Job Story** is a *user-centered storyline* that ties together three pivotally important artifacts of our customer's situation:

1. the situational context involved;

2. the needed or desired job they're trying to achieve in that situation;

3. the outcome that completing that job will produce for them and, thus, their motivation for wanting or needing to complete it.

The *format* of the Job Story is written as follows:

"When __*[contextual situation]*__, I want to __*[desired job]*__, so that I can __*[desired outcome / motivation]*__."

A bit of history

The Job Story was conceived in 2013 by author **Alan Klement** to replace a similar tool people were previously using, known as the *User Story*. The User Story was rooted in a particular *type* of user trying to undertake a specific *action* to attain a specific *outcome*. Klement felt that the *type* of user was, for the most part, irrelevant and that there were too many assumptions being made in this statement, especially around the user and their actions – in particular, how do we even know that those actions are the best ones to attain that outcome? They may not be there may, in fact, be far better actions that no one has yet attempted. So, to address those shortcomings, Klement created the Job Story. Klement also – recognizing the limitations of classical ODI and JTBD methodologies – went on to develop a more expansive philosophy of, and approach to, JTBD, known as *the Self-Betterment concept*.

Our task in using the Job Story

Our task here is to study our subjects until we can confidently fill in the blanks of the Job Story and, by so doing, clearly describe and articulate their specific needs and motivations.

Examples include the following:

*   When looking for a new job, I want to know everything out there that meets my specific, unique criteria so that I can land the best possible career for me and my future.

*   When shopping for a new car, I want to know what other people's experiences have been with each option so that I can make the best possible choice for my needs.

*   When trying to meet a new romantic interest, I want to feel safe in the process so that I can go forward confidently without having to worry about encountering bad actors.

As we can see from these examples, the desired job and the motivation behind it are going to be influenced tremendously by *who* the person is that needs the job and what underlying *concerns, values,* and *aspirations* they happen to have, such as the following:

- An upwardly mobile young professional man is going to have one set of concerns values, and aspirations.

- A single female in a new city is going to have a different set of concerns, values, and aspirations.

- A working couple with busy careers is going to have yet a different set of concerns, values, and aspirations.

- A retired minority senior citizen with health issues is going to have an even more different set of concerns, values, and aspirations.

So, as we can see, there are several very important attributes that we need to establish here that accompany our Job Story, in addition to the Job Story itself. These are as follows:

- *Who* this person is and how to describe them – both *demographically* and (more importantly) *psychographically.*

- At what *stage of life* they find themselves in – school, college, early career, mid-career, young family, retirement, and so on.

- What more specific *situation* they currently find themselves navigating at that stage of life, and what the key *decision and action points* involved in that situation they must work through are.

- What *success* looks like to them in this situation, as well as what is *important* to them in the process of attaining that success.

Thus, while the Job Story is certainly a useful tool to work with, an equally valuable aspect of it is the fact that it forces us to collect and understand other relevant information about our subject, thus helping us to drill down into who they are, and what's going on in their lives, and their particular situation at that point in time. These are precisely the things we need to learn and understand about our subject on our way to discovering their extrinsic motivations, aspirations, and priorities, as well as their deeper intrinsic motivations, aspirations, and priorities.

Demographics versus psychographics – the roles they play (and don't play)

Since we've mentioned here the terms "demographic" and "psychographic," let's take just a moment to define these terms and discuss their value to us so that we're all on the same page:

- **Demographics** consists of those attributes of people relating to their unique *population characteristics,* such as their age, race, ethnicity, gender, religious affiliation, political affiliation, education level, marital status, career, and city of domicile. While these attributes can be useful to make broad sweeping generalizations about any one of these particular groups, there is typically very little correlation between them and the factors that drive each person to pursue a particular type of outcome in their life.

- **Psychographics** consists of those attributes of people relating to their specific *psychological drivers*, such as their values, concerns, interests, motivations, aspirations, and attitudes. *These are the things that ultimately drive people to pursue a particular type of outcome in their lives. They are, in other words, what "makes them tick."*

Thus, of these two, it is the **psychographics** that we care most about – not so much the **demographics**. Our potential customers' psychographics will prove *far more useful and helpful* to us than their demographics, which are more of a secondary concern.

Furthermore, when we think about our markets, and then think about how we can *segment* them into different **customer segments**, the one really unifying construct that matters to us in doing so is not their demographics but, rather, their psychographics – what makes each segment tick and, even more importantly, what specific outcome needs they each have and, therefore, value. A given segment (defined properly) is, generally speaking, not going to have a common set of demographic characteristics, but it is likely going to have a common set of psychographic characteristics.

This is *why* ODI and JTBD are such powerful practices for this type of segmentation. They allow us to profile and segment our market according to their shared *outcome needs* and, thus, underlying *motivations and priorities*. Trying to segment our markets according to their demographics is a futile and pointless task, with very little value. But when we segment our markets according to their specific shared outcome needs, aspirations, and priorities, then we can start to define real solutions that resonate with each and every segment (or at least with those we choose to target). This is something we will do via appropriate research and analysis – in which we survey our overall market to profile its collective psychographic factors, and then divide up the market along specific key psychographic differentiators. Thereafter, we can triangulate our innovations to resonate with the specific key psychographics of the segments we wish to target.

For example, we might find that, of our overall market, when we eventually discern what its most commonly shared outcome needs (and motivations) are – each shared by some portion of the overall market – we end up with four distinct main outcome needs. This means that, for us, we have four distinct market segments, each with its own respective characteristic set of needs, aspirations, and priorities. We can then look at how the overall market breaks down into each of these – perhaps Segment 1 is 60% of the market, Segment 2 is 25%, Segment 3 is 10%, and Segment 4 is only 5% – and thereafter decide whether we want to deliver a solution for all four, or perhaps focus on just the first two. We can also, from those same insights, determine *how* those different solutions need to be unique from each other (which may only be in how they are packaged and presented to the affected segment, or perhaps some other aspect of our business model). The more overlap there is between them, the easier it is to do this.

Thus, ultimately, our potential customers' *psychographic factors* are what we must uncover and understand if we are to so segment our market into these respective segments (each with its own respective set of outcome needs, aspirations, motivations, and priorities).

Supply side versus demand side innovation – an interview with Bob Moesta

In writing this book, I interviewed **Bob Moesta**, President and CEO of the ReWired Group. Bob is a highly respected pioneer of JTBD methodologies and practices. He and I specifically talked about matching the *Supply Side* of our business model to its *Demand Side*, based on a deep understanding of that Supply Side and where our *opportunities* lie in this process. The following is direct input that Bob shared with me:

> The *Demand Side* of our business model reflects what people are willing to **pay** for the **progress** we help them make, while the *Profit Side* (Supply Side) reflects the value our business can extract from doing so. If we aren't delivering real value on the Demand Side (the consumer side), then it naturally proves impossible to have a viable business model on the Supply Side.
>
> Our job, therefore, is to make the Supply Side **fit** the Demand Side. But because the Demand Side is rooted in human behavior – how people behave – it tends to be much more **fixed**. We can't convince customers of anything; they can only convince themselves. So, when we're designing our interactions with these customers, we have to look at what the real *variables* are at work – the things we can operate with to connect with these customers in the way they need to be. Conversely, we have far more **flexibility** on the Supply Side of our business model, meaning that this is where we can more easily innovate.
>
> However, innovation can happen on both sides of the business model, but it looks quite different on the two sides of the equation. Indeed, figuring out innovation on the Demand Side tends to be 10X harder than doing so on the Supply Side, largely because of people's *apparent irrationality*. That being said, we can sometimes find latitude to work with on the Demand Side if we can identify and recognize *non-competition* happening against something in our purview. However, this requires us to understand the entire "competitor set" of indirect "competition" sources. If we can do that, and really understand those sources, then we can have more latitude to position an offering as solving an entirely different *type* of problem (i.e., problem reframing).
>
> As part of this, we have to be *highly attuned* to the **context** in which our business model (or proposed business model) operates, or will be operating. Context creates 50% or more of the value recognized! That is why the *timing* has to be precise for our value proposition; it has to deliver the right offering at the right point in time, according to that particular context and where our customers are in that context (mentally and otherwise). In other words, what concerns and drives them at that point in time, in that particular context?

However, we have to keep in mind that we are still dealing with *context* plus the *apparently irrational behavior* of people – a sometimes complex mix to unravel. What we'll often find is that people's behavior is actually rational; we just don't *understand* that rationale at the time – in the same way that, for example, it turns out people buy Milky Way candy bars at the checkout counter not as a snack or treat but, rather, as a meal replacement/supplement to prevent them from getting hangry and wrecking their careers (a much different rationale, and far bigger driver, than just wanting a snack).

What we should ultimately strive to do then is define a new business model that **changes the context of the day**, the way that Netflix, Uber, and Airbnb so successfully did. This is where looking at the entire business model, plus the business strategy, is so important – thinking well beyond our product and product strategy to, instead, think far more holistically about the overall situation involved and its context, including how our customers; "pain" is wrapped up in a particular context. Then, we can start to deliver innovation via our business model that really matters and impacts!

If we fail to do this, however, and instead spend all of our time focusing on our products and their product strategies, then we'll typically end up with just having *feature creep*, adding new features and functions to our products that offer very little additional value to our customers – something that is *not* a recipe for high-impact success.

A big thanks goes out to Bob Moesta for these insights.

With these insights in hand, we're ready to move on to our next important insight – namely, that not all of our subject's outcome needs are *functional* in nature. Instead, some are *emotional* and *social* in nature, and sometimes even *transformational* in nature. This is something we alluded to earlier, and now we will examine the idea in more detail.

Breaking down jobs – functional / emotional / social / transformational

Back in the "industrial era," the classical mindset was that the basis of competition – what people cared about – was the details of your product or service and, by extension, your *attributes* (features, functions, capabilities, etc.).

Remember when computer manufacturers used to run ads talking about their computers' speeds, feeds, and memory – pure, unadulterated product attributes, and nothing else? They thought that these were what buyers and users cared about, and so they made them the core focus of their advertising efforts.

And then, in 1984, Apple came along and started telling us a *different* story – one about how their products could impact your life and make you into something better than you are today, never once ever mentioning their products' attributes! They got it. They understood that what really mattered to people wasn't what those product attributes were but, rather, what the products could do for them – their **benefits**. Up until that point, everyone had seen product attributes as something that a product "might" do for them (by some sort of correlation). In other words, they left it up to the consumer to make the connection between those attributes and whatever benefit they might derive from them. The manufacturers simply lived in the world of "features, functions, and capabilities" (the stuff they knew intimately), not in the world of consumer benefits (the stuff that mattered to their customers). This was due to not knowing any better, until Apple opened everyone's eyes and showed us a better way (although Apple wasn't the first to do this; they were simply the first to do so in the computer industry – and in a way that had a major impact on society).

What the traditional manufacturers didn't understand at that time was that nobody – save for a tiny cohort of nerds – cared about what their speeds, feeds, and memory were. What they cared about was what those things could do for them, in terms of accomplishing several very important outcomes that they cared about! This is also the difference between taking the internal perspective of what technology we can produce (as a manufacturer or reseller) and the external perspective of what benefits our customers need and, therefore, value. The latter will always resonate with our customers; the former may or may not.

Given this, we're next going to examine three **very important principles** surrounding this reality.

Principle one – outcomes are the only thing that matters to our customer

Whatever type of solution we're offering (be it a product, a service, an experience, or some other type of value), there is one reality that will always be true – namely, that nothing matters to our customers except the **outcomes** they're trying to achieve and the **benefits** associated with those outcomes.

So, in terms of our offerings, nothing else matters except their *ability* to empower our customer to attain those outcomes and their benefits. Everything else is, for all intents and purposes, simply fluff. At the end of the day, what matters to our customers is their *outcomes*, **period**. We can have the fanciest, most elaborate, most expensive, most highly engineered, most precise, highest-quality offering ever produced, but none of it matters if it does not empower our customers to achieve the *outcomes* they want and need to accomplish – in the *way* they want and need to accomplish them.

What this means, then, is that we *always* have to **start with the outcomes** our customers try to achieve (plus an understanding of *why* they want and need those outcomes, and why they're important to them). If we can start with these *outcomes* (and understand the *motivations and aspirations* behind them), then everything else falls into place.

As Steve Jobs so famously said at Apple's 1997 Worldwide Developers Conference, "*You've got to start with the customer experience and work backwards to the technology. You can't start with the technology and try to figure out where you're going to try to sell it.*"

So, whatever we do, we must never start with our offering (the product, service, experience, and so on). We must always start with the customer outcome being sought, working backward from there to wherever that leads us, whether it be a product, a service, an experience, or something else entirely. Wherever it leads us, it has to be on account of those outcomes, and for no other reason!

The implication of this is that we're never ready to start defining our offering until we've first understood who our customer is, what outcome (or experience) they aspire to, and why. We should not talk about our offering's attributes until *after* we have understood all of those things fully, completely, and entirely! Nothing else matters until we understand these things and their relative priorities. This sometimes requires us to "backtrack" with these customers – to work backwards through each respective level of need, peeling back each layer as we go – until eventually, we get to their *real, ultimate need, desire, aspiration, and/or motivation.* Then, and only then, can we start to go forward toward a solution. As we'll see in the next section, some of this relates to what the offering does for them functionally, some of it relates to how it makes them feel, some of it relates to how it makes them look publicly, and some of it relates to how it helps improve their lives. This is indeed the emotional and social appeal of, for example, high-performance automobiles. It's not just about getting from point A to point B; it's about the experience of driving the machine, the thrill of acceleration and cornering, the growl of the engine, and the feeling of prestige whenever people look back at you in their rearview mirror. *These* are the types of real, ultimate *needs*, desires, *aspirations*, and *motivations* we must ascertain if we are to ultimately succeed with our targeted customer.

This also sometimes means that – despite the jobs our potential customers are apparently trying to accomplish today – we have to ask ourselves (and them) if this might not be the opportunity to step back even further and move upstream in the problem definition process… to consider whether or not there might actually be a completely *different* approach (a completely *different* set of "jobs") that they could pursue that would empower them to achieve this outcome in a better way – without ever having to undertake these less-desirable jobs. This is, in fact, where so many new 'white space opportunities' will lie for us and our venture!

So, for example, if we ask an existing customer what they're trying to accomplish, they might say something like, "*I need to drive my car to get to work.*" We can clearly see from this statement that what they really need in this case isn't to drive their car to work but, rather, to get to work in a timely, convenient, and efficient manner – one that affords them the freedom of mobility they value. This may or may not entail them driving a car. They just *assume* it does because it's what they know: it's what they've always done and so inherently presume that this is the way they'll always need to do it. Knowing that their ultimate outcome is to, a) get to work in a timely, convenient, and efficient manner, and b) otherwise have the freedom of mobility they need opens us up to all sorts of different solutions to attain that same outcome, involving potentially products, services, and even explicitly designed enjoyable experiences. We need not be locked into having them own and drive an automobile. And when they no longer need to own and drive the automobile, then all of the "jobs" traditionally associated with vehicle ownership and operation go away – entirely. We're no longer constrained by them, meaning we no longer try to improve on those jobs and make them better; instead, we *replace them* with an even *better* set of jobs that attain our customer's outcome in a far better way.

This is precisely what we must do in our case. We must start with the outcome / benefit they desire and need (and an understanding of why that outcome is so important to them) and then work backward from there toward whatever the best method of achieving it is. This is precisely how Apple ended up with iTunes to empower the iPod – they looked at the overall experience / outcome / benefit holistically and asked themselves what *combination* of products, services, and other forms of value could best attain that ultimate outcome and experience. And *that* is why they succeeded so spectacularly with the platform when all other previous MP3 players flopped entirely. Lesson learned.

Principle two – there are four types of jobs we have to satisfy

Now that we understand it is the *outcomes* and *benefits* of our offerings that matter – not the offerings and their attributes themselves – we can start talking more granularly about the specific **types of jobs** our offerings have to empower our customers to achieve. Doing this will further enlighten us about what is actually happening inside their "inner world" (i.e., their heads and their hearts).

In particular, there are four specific types of jobs that our offerings empower our customers to attain. They are *functional, emotional, social*, and *transformational* jobs. We'll examine each of these in turn.

Functional jobs

As their name suggests, *functional jobs* are the actual **tangible functions** that an offering facilitates and, with it, the associated outcomes those functions produce, such as the following:

- an automobile allows us to transport ourselves, others, and our belongings from one place to another;
- a clothes washer allows us to wash our clothes and get them clean;
- a board game allows us to engage our friends in a friendly, low-stakes competition;
- a winter jacket keeps us warm whenever it's cold outside;
- and so on.

These are all *functional jobs*. They represent the actual tangible functions of the offering – what it fundamentally does for us – including most of the details associated with that, such as how large the automobile is, how many wash cycles the washing machine has, how long the board game takes to complete, and how warm the jacket is.

Ultimately, functional jobs are **table stakes** – the cost of doing business in a particular industry, market, and positioning point, and the things that merely give us a *right to play* in that space. Without them, we can't even participate in the affected market; trying to do so would be a non-starter. Think about it – all automobiles get us from point A to point B, all clothes washers get our clothes clean, all board games entertain us and our friends, all winter jackets keep us warm to the degree we need in their product class, and so on. If they don't, then their producers won't be in business for long.

That being the case, the implication is that, to a certain degree, every participant in this market also produces and sells offerings that attain these *exact same functional jobs*. And when that is the case – when every offering more or less does the exact same thing functionally – then this type of job (and its outcome) ceases to be a competitive differentiator amongst the competing options. This is *why* –

being the table stakes that they are – very few consumers will make their choice to buy based purely and solely on these functional jobs. Instead, they will make them based on other types of jobs the offering provides for them, which we'll talk about next.

Emotional jobs

Emotional jobs involve the specific *emotions* that using (experiencing) the offering elicits within us, before, during, and after using it. In other words, they're about how that offering makes us *feel* – about ourselves and our situation, about those around us, and about the world as a whole.

Does the offering make us feel happy, glad, joyous, peaceful, and assured? Or does it make us feel anxious, frustrated, angry, and depressed? This is the (very important) question at stake here.

To a large degree, how the offering makes us *feel* will be the result of two things:

1. how much we *need*, and therefore *value*, the overall outcome that the offering produces for us, and how much weight we place on it in our lives. The more weight we place on this overall outcome, the more sensitive we will be to how the offering makes us feel in the process of attaining that outcome;

2. how well the offering meets our *expectations* of it (which are often set by the brand messaging used to convey its brand promise, associated with its Unique Value Proposition); the more it meets or exceeds those expectations, the better we'll feel about using it – and vice versa. The more it *fails* to meet those expectations, the worse we'll feel about using it.

Here are some examples:

*   a larger vehicle may make us feel safer than a smaller vehicle does (thereby giving us more peace of mind and confidence when driving);

*   a bigger house may make us feel better about providing for our family than a smaller house does, depending on our overall value system;

*   a more powerful computer may make us feel more assured and confident in our ability to create truly creative work in our job;

*   the opportunity to use business class travel may make us feel more successful in our career than having to use economy class travel does.

Therefore, whether we realize it or not, every offering elicits a particular *emotional outcome* – good, bad, or otherwise – depending on the subject, their situation, their expectations, the results, and their state of mind.

It is within these emotional outcomes that opportunities start to appear for true *competitive differentiation*. The more we can understand the specific and unique emotional jobs that our potential customers need, desire, and value – and the more we can deliver an offering that actually *satisfies* those emotional jobs – the more we can stand out in the field as the true go-to choice among the many different options.

The implication here is that we have to – through appropriate User Research – begin to understand our potential customers' desired and expected emotional jobs, as well as how they want to be made to *feel* whenever owning and/or using our offering. Then, we have to work very hard to deliver on those outcomes much better than anyone else.

This is also why reframing their need into a more fundamental one that we can address (i.e., solving their "problem behind the problem") will often unlock **brand-new emotional outcomes** for them that they never had before – outcomes that absolutely surprise and delight them and convert them into rabid fans of our particular offering and its value proposition.

Social jobs

Social jobs involve how we perceive how others perceive us, usually on account of owning and/or using a particular offering. Thus, they relate to the social value *we place* on what we believe to be the overall social value (in our peer group) of owning or using a particular offering. This is a very subjective thing that depends entirely on the social values that both we as individuals hold and those we believe our social group holds.

These social jobs often arise out of owning and using a luxury or prestige brand (what is known as "conspicuous consumption"), such as the following:

- driving a Mercedes-Benz rather than a Chevrolet;
- wearing an Armani suit rather than a department store suit;
- sporting a Rolex rather than an Swatch;
- living in a large home in an affluent neighborhood rather than a modest home in a middle-class neighborhood.

They can also arise from using a popular or chic brand versus a less-popular brand, or from using a more popular product category versus a less-popular product category – examples of which include the following:

- *working at a large company versus a small company;*
- *driving an SUV versus a sedan (at least in certain countries);*
- *using an Apple MacBook versus a Windows laptop;*
- *affiliating with a winning sports team versus a losing sports team.*

These are all 100% *relative* to who we consider to be our social peer group. Middle-class consumers do not see themselves as "competing socially" with wealthy affluent consumers; they see themselves as competing socially with other middle-class consumers (for example, who has the nicest car in our neighborhood?). Consequently, there are no absolutes in this category, only relatives.

Nevertheless, these jobs are incredibly important to everyone involved, not least because they often tie into the *emotional jobs* being addressed. You certainly feel better about yourself (and by extension about the offerings you use) – both emotionally and socially – whenever you believe those in your peer group perceive you better socially on account of using those offerings. So, these social outcomes will often feed into additional types of emotional outcomes that are important to us.

And so, just as before, whether we realize it or not, every offering elicits a particular *social outcome* – good, bad, or otherwise – depending on the subject, their situation, their peer group, and the results attained.

It is *also* inside these social outcomes that opportunities start to emerge for true *competitive differentiation*. The more we can understand the specific and unique *social jobs* our potential customers need, desire, and value – and the more we can deliver an offering that actually *satisfies* those social jobs – the more we can again stand out in the field as the true go-to choice among the countless options around them.

The implication here is that we have to – again through appropriate user research – come to understand our potential customers' desired social jobs, and how they want to be perceived by and within their social peer group when owning and/or using our offering. Then, we have to work very hard to deliver on those jobs much better than anyone else.

This is also the opportunity to create an offering – and a Unique Value Proposition – that truly resonates with customers and thereby generates "buzz" inside the affected target communities so that whenever someone owns and/or uses our offering, the very act of doing so unleashes for them **major new social outcomes** that they might otherwise be unable to attain. If we can do that, then we can sometimes convert customers *en masse* and scale our business based purely on its social value alone, which is *why* these outcomes are so crucially important to us. We mustn't overlook them!

Transformational jobs

Transformational jobs involve the ways in which owning or using a particular offering **empowers us to transform ourselves into something greater** – by whatever metric happens to matter to us at that point in our lives.

Such *transformations* can come in all sorts of sizes, shapes, and flavors. Characteristic examples include the following:

- attaining a particular level of education, thereby opening up to us new opportunities that otherwise we could not access;
- attaining a higher-ranking job – perhaps one with more prestige and responsibility – empowering us to better ourselves professionally;
- attaining a higher income, empowering us to better ourselves personally and socially;
- losing weight, improving our personal and social appearance.

All of these are transformational jobs that can, and quite often do, allow us to be transformed in some way or another into something "different" – all on account of using a particular offering, such as, in the first case, attending a particular university and a specific degree program.

Unlike emotional and social jobs, not every offering involves a *transformational job*. Some inherently do, while others struggle to do so, depending on a large number of situational factors.

Some offerings are indeed *inherently more transformational* than others. Certainly, university degree programs and similar professional development and certification programs are explicitly transformational in nature, as are dieting programs; they're all designed to help us transform ourselves into something better. Other things, such as owning a particular car for example, don't typically tend to be transformational per se, although there are *indirect ways* they can be – just not immediate, direct ways.

However, the extent to which certain offerings empower us to attain the particular emotional and/or social outcomes we desire can sometimes be transformational in and of itself, especially if and when certain social outcomes afford us a higher social status, and that in turn affords us *new opportunities* to better ourselves. The overall net effect in such situations can indeed be very transformational!

Once again, the implication here is that we have to – through appropriate user research – come to understand our potential customers' desired and expected transformational jobs, and how they aspire to transform themselves into something greater as a result of owning and/or using our offering. Then, we have to work very hard to deliver on those jobs much better than anyone else.

Again, this is why reframing their need into a more fundamental one we can address (solving their "problem behind the problem") will often unlock **brand-new transformational outcomes** for them that they never had before – outcomes that surprise and delight them and convert them into rabid fans of our unique offering and value proposition.

Principle three – each job plays a specific role and has a particular significance

If we study customers long enough and thoroughly enough, and if we truly strive to understand the human behavioral psychology involved at each point, then what we'll eventually come to see and understand is that people do not tend to make their decisions *rationally* – for purely rational and pragmatic reasons. Instead, they tend to make those decisions out of much more *emotional*, and sometimes *social*, bases.

We are indeed **not rational beings**, and we do not, therefore, tend to make purely rational choices and decisions. We are, in fact, very **emotional and social beings**, and so we, more often than not, tend to make very emotional and social choices – ones that make us feel better about ourselves, as well as look better in the eyes of our peers.

Knowing this, on top of the already established fact that the functional jobs involved are merely *table stakes* (and, therefore, not a basis for making a selection from among the competing options), it becomes readily apparent that – of these four jobs – it is, in most cases, the **emotional and social**

jobs that matter the most (and sometimes the transformational ones too). This is because it is these emotional and social jobs – and the emotional and social outcomes they produce – that serve as the true **decision criteria** our customers tend to use in deciding *which* of the competing options they will choose.

Consequently, what this means to us is that, although we absolutely have to nail the functional jobs just right – at the right level of performance and quality – it is in fact these *emotional and social jobs* (and sometimes the *transformation jobs*) that we have to really home in on and ensure that we're doing **far better than anyone or anything else out there**! That is our imperative because these types of jobs are the *true basis of competition*!

If, in fact, we can deliver on those emotional and social jobs far better than anyone or anything else out there, then we're almost *guaranteed* to have a successful business venture. That is the task, therefore, of our Unique Value Proposition.

At the same time, we also have to remain aware of the fact that every choice of product, service, or experience someone makes will typically have some component of **all four jobs** in it, in varying ratios. Sometimes, they're even pursued secretively, such as when people want to make progress in a particular area but don't want anyone else to know about it – at least not until they're finished making that progress. In this way, these jobs and outcomes can be both inputs to, and outputs of, their overall decision process.

We're still left with one very important *big-picture question* that we have to address – namely, why do people *really* buy products, services, and experiences? What do they really want out of all this *overall* – for the sake of their personal and professional lives? That's an important question to answer!

What we have learned is that, ultimately, people don't actually buy "products," "services," or even wonderful "experiences." Instead, what they really buy is "a better version of themselves." As we're going to see, this stems out of their own bigger-picture aspirations, which means that what really matters to them are not the attributes of the products, services, and experiences they purchase but, rather, the benefits these produce for them. This is what they actually buy.

User benefits versus product attributes

In 2014, writer **Belle Beth Cooper** wrote an article in *Fast Company* entitled *Why People Don't Buy Products – They Buy Better Versions of Themselves* (this same article also appeared on *Medium* in 2017).

Cooper began the article by explaining that when Apple first launched the iPod, industry pundits didn't get it; there had already been several MP3 players on the market, none of which were particularly successful, so what made Apple's any different? What those pundits didn't understand, as Cooper points out, was that Steve Jobs, then CEO of Apple, wasn't focused on the product but, rather, on what it did for the end user, namely "1,000 songs in your pocket." This was a statement about *consumer benefits*, not *product attributes*, meaning that Jobs got the point that what would make this category succeed was focusing on the **outcome** it provided for the user – or, in Cooper's taxonomy, how the product could make them a "better person" (even if that only meant a more self-actualized person).

Cooper and her community – like Steve Jobs and his – got the point that the *purpose of the product* isn't the product itself but, rather, how the product can turn an individual into a "more awesome person capable of doing incredible things!" In other words, the point of the product is the *benefits* it produces for us, not anything about the product itself. Consequently, what your business sells is "benefits," not "product attributes."

Cooper attributes the following statement to **Jason Fried**, co-founder and CEO of the firm 37signals (via Twitter from November 2013):

> *"'Here's what our product can do' and 'Here's what you can do with our product' sound similar, but they are completely different approaches."*

Thus, she makes the important observation that a feature is what your product does, while a benefit is what the customer can do with your product. In other words, features are the "what" of our products and services, while benefits are the "why" behind those.

It's useful to note here that these features and benefits aren't an objective reality on their own; they're a part of the customer's subjective reality. In other words, the offerings that people purchase and use do not, in and of themselves, **make them** feel a particular way; rather, they **choose** (consciously or subconsciously) to feel that way on account of owning and using the offering. The external objective artifact leads to an internal subjective feeling. It is the *customer* who decides, or gives themselves permission, to feel a certain way after purchasing and using a particular offering, enabling a particular subjective experience and meeting certain outcome needs they have (good or bad).

Cooper offers several examples of companies that were competently marketing in this vein at the time, including Evernote, Twitter, Nest, LinkedIn, and GitHub. What was common about each of these companies and their respective marketing efforts wasn't just that they were all focused on *benefits* (they were) but, rather, that they framed those benefits in very *transformational language*. For example, LinkedIn's tagline was "*Be great at what you do*"; Nest's was "*Saving energy is a beautiful thing*"; Evernote's was "*Remember Everything.*" In each case, these reflected the mantra that "people don't buy products; they buy better versions of themselves."

Becoming the hero of our own story – an interview with Lisa Rose

In writing this book, I had the opportunity to interview **Lisa M. Rose, MPA**, anthropologist and CX strategy principal at the venture studio City Innovations. Lisa and I discussed what it meant to really "go deep on people" and study their needs and aspirations at a much more fundamental level. Besides talking at length about the process to do this, Lisa and I also spoke quite a bit about what the final outcome of that process would look like. In particular, Lisa made the following wonderful and astute observations about that outcome:

> What we really want to do here is create a solution to an emotionally sensitive problem in someone's life – one where they want to make a meaningful life change. To do that, we have to develop solutions that can, and will (positively) affect their behaviors – to help them make optimal choices that maximize their lives.

And to do that, we have to develop solutions that make people feel **successful**, like a real winner who's taken responsibility for some area of their life (often a very untenable area) and come out on top of that as the victor. This is precisely what Intuit did with TurboTax in the case of helping people file their income tax returns – it made that process such that it didn't suck and even included some key "surprise and delight" outcomes in the process. This made people feel like they could take on their taxes, complete the process successfully, and come out on top as the real winner.

Since this happens in multiple domains of our lives, we have to come to understand each person's respective hopes, dreams, and aspirations in that particular domain – what "being their best" looks like to them in that area. This infers really understanding not only the *functional jobs* they need done there but also, and even more importantly, the *emotional and social jobs too*.

As Designers, we have to understand that the solution lies not with us but with our customers. It's not about us; it's about making the people we're designing for **the heroes of their own journey**! And so, we have to minimize however great we think *we are* and instead focus on *how great our customer can be with the enabling tool we give them*. The story being told here isn't about us as the Designer! It's about the people we're trying to *serve*. It's *they* who need to be in this story, who need to emerge from it as the triumphant antagonist. It's not about us making the tool that made them win; it's about **them using that tool to win**. *They are the hero here, not us* (despite the fact that we made the tool). At the end of the day, as Designers, we have to be able to say, "*You're the winner my friend. You took what I gave you and used it in your own life to become something even greater. You're the hero!*" That's our job as Designers – to make our subject the hero of their own story!

If we can do that – if we can help them become who they aspire to be, and in the process become "the hero of their own story" – then we will, in fact, build **loyalty** with them. The narrative will be, "*If you can enable me to do X and the result is Y – if you can help me do that – then I will be loyal to you, period!*" Moreover, if we can *accelerate* that transformational outcome – to help them become and feel successful even *faster* – then it will be all the more impactful to them, which will in turn develop even greater loyalty from them. And that means both sides win!

A big thanks goes out to Lisa Rose for these outstanding insights.

The Transformation Economy

Taking this concept even further, there's actually a whole new "economy" emerging around this notion of *customer transformation*. It is known as the *Transformation Economy*, and follows on from its predecessor, the *Experience Economy*. There continue to be new books and articles written about it each day.

This is quite different from the genre of *personal transformation* that's been around for decades, in that *personal transformation* was about individual, personal actions we undertake on our own, whereas *customer transformation* is about something that is explicitly enabled and empowered by outside parties via what they provide us. Customer transformation will be a key theme throughout the next two decades.

Our takeaway

The takeaway for us here is that, whenever thinking about our own Unique Value Proposition, we have to ask ourselves, "*How can we offer and deliver something that transforms our customers into more awesome versions of themselves – capable of doing far more than they do today?*" and "*How can we communicate that transformational fact to them in a way that truly resonates with their "reason to buy"?*"

If we can do this one thing – namely, stay focused on the transformational power of our offering and how it will empower our customers to become "better versions of themselves" – then we will at least be on the right path toward defining a powerful and impactful new value proposition.

I believe it is fair to say that, if your business venture can offer its customers something that will transform their lives into something *far better* (moving them closer to self-actualization) – and you can *communicate* that effectively – then it *will* attain business success. But if it fails to do so, then it will have to compete on far less appealing bases (such as price for example) that don't typically yield the same margins, making it much harder of a go as a business.

Seek, therefore, to transform your customer into a better version of themself, making them the hero of their own story, using clear benefits aligned to their unique personal aspirations!

Meanwhile, back at Intensifi...

Back at Intensifi, our friends Ian, Zoe, and Watson – who've been learning the insights of this chapter – have in some ways had their eyes opened to important new perspectives, while in other ways they have had what they already believed to be true reinforced. For example, they already knew and held that, ultimately, their venture had to be about making their customer the "hero of their own journey" (so they really loved having that perspective reinforced), but they didn't quite understand beforehand all the more intricate details of ODI and things such as *the Job Story*, or functional versus emotional versus social versus transformation jobs. Now they do.

So, now they finally feel ready to go out and start studying their potential customers' behaviors and, from those behaviors, try to hypothesize what motivations and aspirations might be behind them, using the Human-Centered Design Hierarchy of Needs they learned about in this chapter, plus the ODI insights they gained here. They believe that, with these fundamental Behavioral Psychology insights now under their belt, they'll finally be able to fully appreciate the human experience occurring in each case they look at, given the situational context surrounding each one. They also feel that they now have the mental framework they need to be able to relate these insights back to their offering and its associated value proposition, allowing them to test the resultant motivations and aspirations against their value proposition to see what sort of alignment there may or may not be.

They're also going to do some more research on these subjects using the resources suggested herein.

As far as actioning what they've just learned, they have now – following up to where we last left off with them in *Chapter 7* – actually starting doing some observational research to study some of the different subjects who represent their prospective potential customers, as defined in the five groups of the consumer side and the six groups of the business side in *Chapter 7*. For example, they've spent some time studying the following surrogate customers (all of whom have volunteered to be so studied), using distant observation, up-close shadowing, and various types of interviews:

- On the **consumer** side, we have the following surrogate customers:

  - **Hunter Bost** – a high-performing, aspirational finance professional in his fourth year of professional practice, working in the banking sector in the United States.

  - **Lee Wong** – a high-performing, aspirational corporate attorney in her fifth year of professional practice, working in the hospitality sector in Hong Kong.

  - **Johannes Pawlowski** – a high-performing, aspirational engineering professional in his third year of professional practice, working in the automotive sector in Germany.

- On the **business** side, we have the following surrogate customers:

  - **Lakshmi Kaur** – a senior business leader in a very high-performing high tech software company in India.

  - **Stephen Wainwright** – a senior business leader in a high-performing manufacturing company in the United States.

  - **George Buchannon** – a senior business leader in a high-performing medical equipment company in the United Kingdom.

For these studies, at least two of our principals were present at any given time (sometimes, all three were), and so Zoe and Ian focused on the two subjects in North America, while Ian and Watson focused on the two subjects in Europe, and Zoe and Watson focused on the two subjects in Asia. This, of course, required them to travel about to these different regions to get themselves to where they needed in each case to study and observe these different individuals.

With the first cohort (consumer side), they've witnessed behaviors such as keeping your résumé up to date, exploring alternative career options (and sometimes even taking calls from corporate recruiters), taking additional graduate degree and professional development programs, pursuing new hobbies, using dating websites and personal networks to meet new romantic interests, exploring a religious faith more deeply, shopping for new homes and new cars, as well as more common products such as clothing, jewelry, and household products.

With the second cohort (the business side), they've witnessed behaviors such as conducting market research, conducting competitive threat assessments, monitoring internal performance indicators, monitoring key industry trends, engaging in traditional strategic planning research and analysis, having strategy off-site sessions, developing new brand and product category strategies, developing new products, and running major marketing campaigns.

What Ian, Zoe, and Watson have begun to learn from these different observations and interviews is that – based on the specific behaviors they're seeing and hearing about when they talk to these individuals – everyone in the first cohort does, by and large, have major life and career aspirations they're striving toward (as they sort of expected), while everyone in the second cohort does, in fact, have key strategic business aspirations they're striving toward on behalf of their organization (as expected).

However, what they're *also* learning in this process – and what they *did not expect or anticipate* – is that in each case, for both cohorts – these aspirations actually stem from of **wildly divergent higher-level aspirations**, involving any number of different **values**, **beliefs**, and **concerns**. This has been incredibly eye-opening for these three – understanding now, as they do, so much more about the Behavioral Psychology going on in each situation.

Given this new revelation, what this means at this point for Ian, Zoe, and Watson is that they feel like they really, really want to walk *through* the proper Design Thinking journey, enabling them to really dig deep down into each of these situations and pull back the covers on these higher-level aspirations. They hope that, by doing so, they can really understand the problem space they're confronting – at that level – and then work toward an appropriate solution space with an optimum value proposition for that problem space, including a more highly refined set of goals for their new platform.

This is something they'll do by learning about the Design Thinking process *proper*, as well as how to properly explore both the problem space and the solution space, thereby coming away with an optimum solution, plus a winning value proposition – one that fully resonates with these customers' "reason to buy". This will, as we're learning, be a solution that helps these customers transform themselves more fully into what they fundamentally aspire to be.

Summary

In this chapter, we explored some very fascinating topics – all stemming from Human Behavioral Science.

We began with our role as (Design Thinking) Behavioral Scientists, including how we can use Behavioral Science to uncover exclusive insights that work as our "secret weapon." We also considered the fact that we'll inherently be dealing with irrationality whenever working with human beings.

We then moved on to an exploration of the Human-Centered Design Hierarchy. We learned that we have to start by observing people and the physical manifestations of their behaviors (what they say and do), which are a conjoined response to both their extrinsic motivations (needs and desires) and priorities (expectations and preferences) and their perceptions of the stimuli before them, which are associated with certain cognitive and visceral attitudes surrounding each touchpoint. They make up the "Actuated Person." We also learned that each person has certain intrinsic motivations and aspirations deriving from their primal drives, inner concerns, core beliefs, and core values, which make up the "Core Person." We saw that the Core Person significantly impacts how the Actuated Person shows up in different situations.

We then dove into the world of ODI and JTBD, where we learned that there are different approaches to studying and understanding our customers' desired outcomes. We also learned that what we really care about here is our subject's psychographics, more so than their demographics. Also, we learned from my interview with Bob Moesta that we need to match supply side innovations in our business model with the demand side needs and expectations that occur.

Then, we explored the concept of "job types," which involves the functional, emotional, social, and transformational jobs that our offering has to deliver for, as well as their relative importance. We learned that the functional jobs – important as they are – are simply table stakes for entry into a given market and, therefore, not a place for differentiation. We learned that it's the emotional and social jobs we can use to connect with our customers, thereby differentiating and competing in that market.

Finally, we took an even deeper look at transformational jobs, where we learned that we have to focus on consumer benefits, not product attributes – a fact that affects both how we design and market our offerings. We learned that our customers ultimately aspire to be a greater version of themselves, the hero of their own story, and thus it's our job to design, develop, and deliver value propositions that empower them to be that.

All of this Behavioral Science insight sets us up to look forward to *Chapter 9*, where we'll explore the actual Design Thinking process in application, including the role and use of its Design Methods. It also sets us up to – eventually – create a winning Unique Value Proposition that succeeds in our marketplace. Moreover, it offers us some very powerful clues toward a Market Connection Model (i.e., how we can connect and resonate with certain markets), plus a Sustainable Competitive Advantage (i.e., how we can develop certain combined capabilities that let us make our customers "the hero of their journey" far better than anyone else). We will take these nuggets of wisdom and store them away for use later, when we have to drill down into those parts of our business model. But for now, it's onward to the Design Thinking process!

Further reading

- *What Customers Want: Using Outcome-Driven Innovation To Create Breakthrough Products and Services*, Anthony Ulwick, McGraw-Hill, 2005.

- *Predictably Irrational: The Hidden Forces That Shape Our Decisions*, Dan Ariely and Simon Jones, Harper, 2009.

- *Thinking Fast and Slow*, Daniel Kahneman, Farrar, Straus, and Giroux, 2011.

- *Replacing the User Story With The Job Story: Too Many Assumptions Are Dangerous*, Alan Klement, November 12, 2013: `https://jtbd.info/replacing-the-user-story-with-the-job-story-af7cdee10c27`.

- *Why People Don't Buy Products – They Buy Better Versions Of Themselves, Belle Beth Cooper, Fast Company*, January 28, 2014: `https://www.fastcompany.com/3025484/why-people-dont-buy-products-they-buy-better-versions-of-themselves`.

- *When Coffee & Kale Compete: Become Great At Making Products People Will Buy*, Alan Klement, CreateSpace Independent Publishing Platform, 2018.

- *The "New You" Business: How to compete on personal transformations*, Lance Bettencourt, Joseph Pine, James Gilmore, David Norton, *Harvard Business Review*, February 2022: `https://hbr.org/2022/01/the-new-you-business`.

Acting Like a Designer – The Design Thinking Process in Application

In *Chapter 8*, we learned about Human Behavioral Science and what it means in the context of Design Thinking.

That included how it requires us to, in effect, become a Behavioral Scientist so that we can properly study and understand our subjects' behaviors, attitudes, aspirations, motivations, values, and so on – those all being things that allow us to develop empathy for our subject, in particular, an empathic understanding of them and their situation. It also included the *Human Centered Hierarchy of Needs*, by which we can observe the behaviors of our subjects – the Actuated Person when in context – to learn about them and their situation and the Core Person behind those behaviors, each replete with their respective extrinsic and intrinsic motivations and aspirations.

We also gained an understanding of our subjects' *outcome needs* and *jobs-to-be-done*, both relating to the worlds of **Outcome-Driven Innovation** (**ODI**) and **Jobs-To-Be-Done** (**JTBD**). That included a consideration of our subjects' *psychographic profile* and their *Job Story*, plus balancing the supply and demand sides of our business model for each situation. We further explored our subjects' different *types* of jobs: their functional, emotional, social, and transformational jobs – plus the fact that consumer benefits (not product attributes) are what allow us to properly address each of these jobs (especially the latter ones). We learned that, in the context of these transformational jobs, our goal is always to make our customer *the hero of their own journey*, or… a better version of themselves.

These are all keen insights into the world of Human Behavioral Science that benefit the journey we're on.

In this chapter, we're going to explore how we actually put Design Thinking *into practice* – how we go from just **thinking** like a Designer to actually **acting** like a Designer. This will include a study of the Design Thinking *process*, an exploration of its associated *Design Methods*, and a look at the crucial role that *prototyping* plays in the process – as well as how *Generative AI* can help us in the process.

By the time we finish this chapter, you should feel ready to dive deeply into both your Problem Space and your Solution Space, which we're going to step through in much greater detail in the subsequent chapters (with an interlude in between). Our goal here is for you to truly grasp this process… what it looks like and feels like, and how it actually gets practiced in the real world.

Topically, our exploration will be the following in this chapter:

- **The Design Thinking process – stages, steps, and micro-learning cycles**: The step-by-step, yet very iterative, process used to undertake Design Thinking.

- **The Design Methods – powerful ways to observe, study, and understand**: The collection of Observe Methods, Question Methods, Experiment Methods, and Study Methods that allow us to carry out Design Thinking effectively.

- **Prototyping in Design Thinking – a critical element in the process**: The powerful and impactful role that prototyping plays in Design Thinking – and how we must make it an inherent part of how we think and work in this process.

- **A little help – how Generative AI can help us**: A look at when, where, and how Generative AI – and AI more broadly – will benefit us in this innovation process.

We'll also check in with our friends at Intensifi to see where they are in their unique Design Thinking journey and how ready they are to start exploring their unique Problem Space and its associated Solution Space via this process, its methods, and the necessary prototyping that they're going have to do.

The Design Thinking process – stages, steps, and micro-learning cycles

We first want to begin with the Design Thinking *process*.

We say "process" because, while there is indeed a certain process that we're going to leverage for pursuing and carrying out Design Thinking, it's one that we don't want to actually think of in a procedural manner. What we mean by this is that Design Thinking is anything but a simple, linear process that we can follow step by step, going from Action A to Action B to Action C and in so doing arrive at our end destination in a very nice, neat, and tidy way. It isn't at all that. Instead, it's a far messier, iterative, nonlinear, circular process that's full of different micro-learning loops. It's also a process that can sometimes be very frustrating as we learn new insights that bring into question prior conclusions we thought we had fully validated. But it's also one that – once we are in fact finished with it – should give us very high confidence that we truly understand the problem or challenge being addressed, and how best to solve that problem or challenge.

It's also important to keep in mind – as we noted earlier in *Chapter 8* – that Design Thinking isn't just a set of procedural methods and practices we can use to explore needs and solutions in a human-centric way, but rather it's a whole way of seeing and engaging with our world... one that forces us to understand and appreciate the human-centricity (and anymore, humanity-centricity) of everything we design – whether for better or for worse. It forces us, therefore, to really pause and think long and hard about everything we're designing – to understand whether or not it is really solving for the true motivations and aspirations involved, and in a way that will positively impact all of the stakeholders involved. Or is it something that is suboptimized in some way, and consequently will miss the mark somehow? That's a very important consideration in this process.

With those points being made, let's dive into our process map for Design Thinking.

Exploring and understanding the five stages of Design Thinking

Let us start by first establishing the fact that over the past 50+ years, there have come to be countless different *process maps* for Design Thinking. Some of these have been overly simplistic – like the classic British Design Council double-diamond model that so many seem to know, or the Stanford University d.school five-step process – while others have been overly complex, with all sorts of nuanced steps and actions interjected along the way.

Without unpacking each of those historical process maps and the reasons behind them, the process map that we're going to use for Design Thinking here is one that I believe fairly represents the *actual process* as it typically gets executed (in proper practice), and accurately reflects each of the important activities and steps that we have to undertake to be successful in Design Thinking.

Figure 9.1 reflects this process. Please take a look at it and study it carefully. As you'll see, it contains the following five distinct stages:

1. Problem Owning
2. Problem Clarity
3. Problem-Solution Interface
4. Value Definition
5. Business Model.

You'll also notice that each of these stages is represented geometrically by a diamond shape. The reason for this is *metaphorical*. In particular, the diamond is a visual metaphor for the fact that, in each case, we tend to begin the process by using **divergent thinking**, including more *inductive* logic, and then, subsequent to that, complete the process by using **convergent thinking**, including more *deductive* logic.

This is true in almost every case, where we first start with lots of *questions* to address the situation and then, through appropriate research efforts, answer those questions to arrive at some definitive set of *answers* with which to move forward onto the next stage of the process.

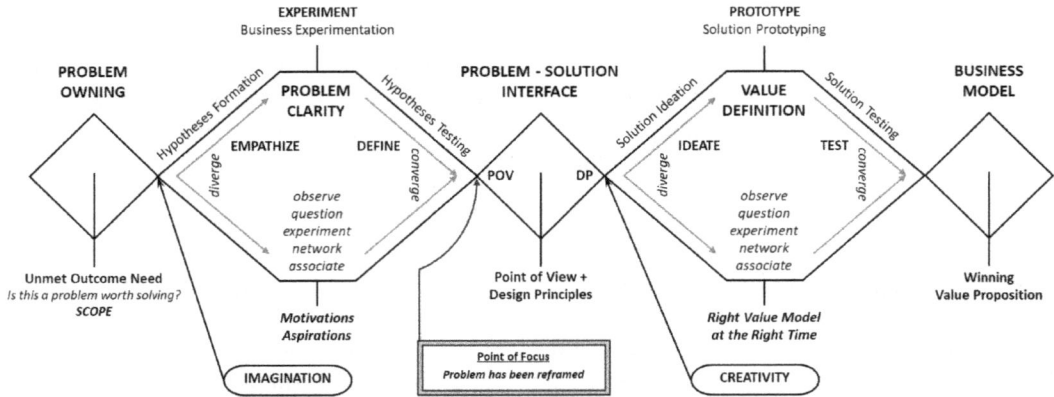

Figure 9.1: The Design Thinking process

Next, we're going to unpack each of these five stages bit by bit to understand what activities are associated with each one and, in each case, why so.

Stage 1 – Problem Owning

Stage 1 is **Problem Owning**. Technically speaking, the classical Design Thinking process doesn't begin until **Stage 2**. *However,* we interject **Stage 1** here – both for full clarity about what has to happen, and to better reflect how Design Thinking *actually* gets executed inside of business organizations.

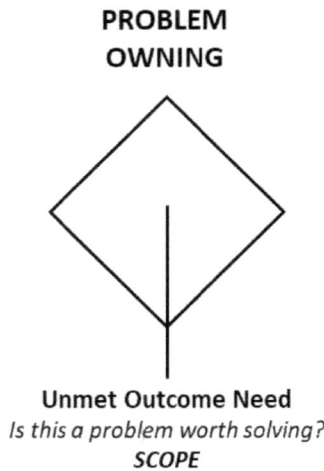

Figure 9.2: Stage 1 – Problem Owning

In particular, no organization or group is going to invest the time, effort, energy, and resources into pursuing this process to unpack a particular challenge or need and come up with a solution for it if – prior to all that – someone doesn't first *own the problem* and in so, doing sponsor the effort (including, in most cases, funding it).

And so, inside any organization or group, someone has to say, *"This is a problem we believe is worth addressing, and therefore we intend to address it, and I'm the one who's going to sponsor such an effort."*

They also have to ask (and eventually answer) the question of whether or not in reality it is a *problem worth solving* for the organization or group. What we mean by this is that the problem or issue affects enough would-be customers – **scope** – such that our defining and delivering a sound solution to it will result in enough of those customers adopting it to justify our cost and effort of doing so – **scale**. Or stated more simply: does the *scope* of this issue offer adequate assurance that a solution to it will *scale* in the marketplace and thereby make for a viable business proposition? If it doesn't, then in most cases there will be little point in addressing it – at least not if our goal is to have a viable business.

Even in the public sector, enough people have to adopt a solution to a problem to make offering that solution worthwhile. Otherwise – if no one is going to use the solution we offer them – then it's a waste of our effort and resources to offer that solution. We're better off trying to understand *why* they won't use the solution, and then addressing that more fundamental issue – which is precisely what Design Thinking is designed to do.

In this stage, there is *divergent thinking* around the problem itself and whether or not it is such a *type* of problem, while there is *convergent thinking* around arriving at a suitable answer to that question. In that process, some of the more *inductive questions* we might ask include: "Is this the right problem to address and solve for at this time?"; "Might there be a different problem that's better to address and solve for, and which we should therefore be trying to solve?"; and "Why is this the most appropriate problem to address and solve for at this point in time... is it a better one to solve for than all the other problems we could try to address and solve for?" The sort of *deductive answers* we're likely to come up with will revolve around, "This is the best and most important problem for us to address and solve for at this point in time because _____."

So, to finish this point, Stage 1 is about someone – or some group – inside the organization or larger group 'owning' the problem or challenge at hand and saying that we care enough about it to invest the necessary time, effort, energy, and resources into studying it and addressing it – and then so sponsoring that effort. In the case of entrepreneurial founders – such as with our case of Intensifi here – this will generally be the founders themselves, working to unpack the specific Problem Space they wish to address and solve for.

Stage 2 – Problem Clarity

Stage 2 is where we begin the classical Design Thinking process, and is all about *working our Problem Space.*

EXPERIMENT
Business Experimentation

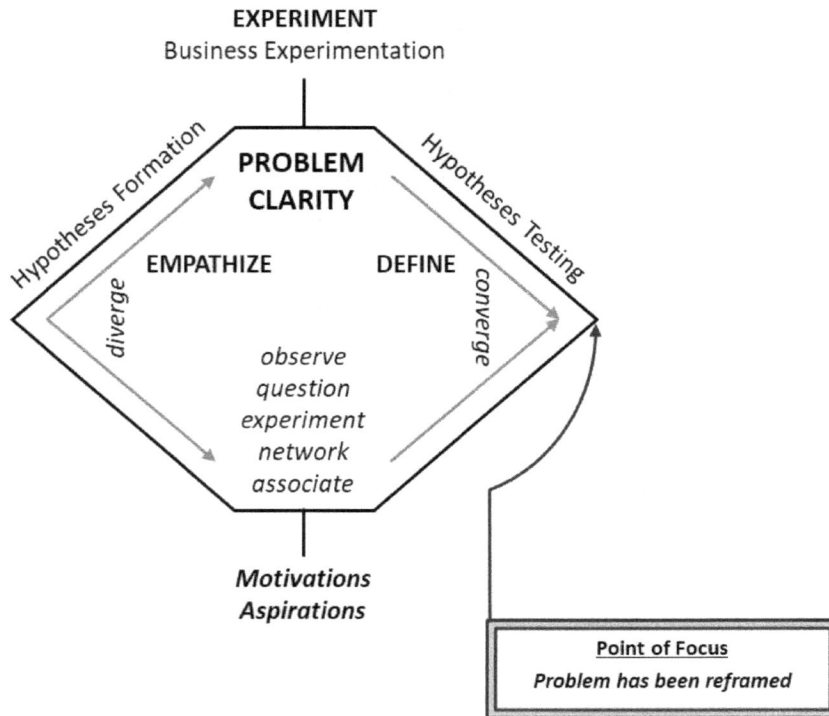

Figure 9.3: Stage 2 – Problem Clarity

The whole point of this stage is to develop *complete clarity* about the **real** 'problem behind the problem' that we're trying to solve. It thus involves, in most cases, *problem reframing* – reframing the original *perceived problem* into a *new problem* that's stated at a much more fundamental human (motivational and aspirational) level – one that gets down the real human motivations and aspirations involved. This is so that we can solve the *right problem* and not the wrong problem – and at the right level of human *need*, such that solving it will matter to both us and our customers.

This stage is divided into three specific sets of activities (steps), each one serving a specific purpose. (Note that in most academic treatments of Design Thinking, only two of these are explicitly called out, however, all three of them actually occur – as they have to for the process to work). These three steps and activities are generically known, respectively, as **Empathize**, **Experiment**, and **Define**. Let's explore each of them further in turn.

Empathize

The first step in Problem Clarity is **Empathize**. The purpose of this step is to develop empathy for our subjects and thus an empathic understanding of them and their situation. Its goal is to (eventually and ultimately) get to the *truth* of that whole situation – to understand what's really occurring behind its scenes – so that we can eventually *act on that truth*.

We do this by developing different *hypotheses* about the subject and their situation – based on whatever preliminary information, insight, and evidence we might have (and, to a lesser degree, our own intuition about the situation). Each such hypothesis sets forth a specific statement about what the real issue, challenge, or problem at hand could, and may, be – none of which have been tested or proven yet – and therefore why they are only just *hypotheses* at this point – a hypothesis being an unproven (and thus lightly held) *assumption*.

This requires us to assume a very **humble posture** toward our subject and their situation – accepting and acknowledging up front the assumption that **we don't know** what their *actual problem* is – but rather we only have certain theories, or hypotheses, about that matter. This may require us to come together as a group to engage in a certain amount of *hypothesis storming* – brainstorming about what these different hypotheses could be.

It will also require us to practice incredible *objectivity* about the whole situation – holding each such hypothesis at arm's length and assuming that, until proven otherwise, we simply don't know whether it is right or wrong. We cannot afford at this point (or at any point for that matter) to let our own biases – cognitive or otherwise – cloud our judgment about them. We must desire and work toward nothing other than the absolute objective truth in the situation.

If we do this step correctly, we should come away with a large number of hypotheses about the situation. The actual number we generate will typically depend on exactly how *complex* the situation is, as there can be any number of different intertangled causalities occurring. The more of those there are, the more we'll need to consider different combinations of possible causalities – and therefore more hypotheses.

As can be seen by the diverging surfaces of the graphical representation in *Figure 9.3*, this step is **divergent** in nature, because it leverages primarily *divergent and inductive thinking* to come up with these respective hypotheses.

Experiment

The second step in Problem Clarity is **Experiment**. The purpose of this step is to define – once we've developed our different hypotheses – how we're actually going to **test** those hypotheses – so as to figure out which are right and which are wrong – and for those that are 'right', exactly 'how right' they are (or aren't).

This is a step that is almost always glossed over in the academic literature on Design Thinking – as though coming up with *how* to test our different hypotheses will just somehow happen as if by magic or simple intuition. But it doesn't usually work that way. Coming up with *how* to test our hypothesis is an equally important and challenging step in the Problem Clarity process – on par with the other steps of this process. That's why we make the point to explicitly address and describe it here.

So, the goal here is to collectively conceive and define a very specific set of **business experiments** that we can carry out to test our different hypotheses for their respective validity. This can be far harder than one might at first think. Indeed, coming up with high-caliber and accessible ways by which to test our hypotheses can be a whole in-depth exercise unto itself. Yet it is one that's crucially important if we're to succeed at the whole Problem Clarity process – and therefore we certainly cannot skip it.

There is in fact an excellent **book** addressing this step. That book is *The Innovator's Hypothesis* by Michael Schrage of the MIT Media Lab (MIT Press, 2014). It lays out, in quite the detail, exactly how to think about, and go about, conceiving and defining affordable and accessible business experiments that teams can use to test and validate their different hypotheses about a particular situation they're considering working on. I highly suggest reading it. It's also where the concept of *5x5 Team Competitions* hails from – in which five teams of five members each compete against each other to each come up with the five best business experiments to run, each for 5,000 USD or less (2014 USD) and in five weeks or less. Schrage's premise in this – and one which I agree with – is that "cheap experiments are worth more than good ideas." This is true because we really don't know whether or not an idea is any good until we've actually run some business experiments to determine that. Otherwise, we're just diving headlong into a situation based on nothing more than untested and unproven assumptions – an incredibly risky approach no matter how good we *think* the idea might be.

Note that these experiments need not be overly complex, time-consuming, or costly. The whole point that Schrage makes in his book is to come up with experiments that we can actually undertake and learn from, without any of them needing an inordinate amount of time, effort, or resources (otherwise they may never get run). In other words, the best experiment is the one that actually gets run.

This step will be both mildly divergent and convergent in nature – in that we'll divergently consider all manner of different experiments that we *could run* – and then convergently decide on certain of those (the ones we deem 'best') to *actually run*.

Once we've decided on our respective business experiments, and defined each one accordingly, we're ready to move on to the next step, which is actually carrying out those experiments to test our different hypotheses. This brings us to the next step.

Define

The third step in Problem Clarity is **Define**, by which is meant to properly and accurately *define the problem*. The purpose of this step is to define the **real problem** involved – moving well beyond whatever superficial surface symptoms we may have originally started with, to the new and properly-reframed *real problem* lying beneath all this – the one that most accurately reflects the real human motivations and aspirations occurring.

We do this by going out and testing our different *hypotheses* using the various *business experiments* we just defined. This will require us to come into contact with **real subjects** (our would-be customers) and undertake these experiments with, and/or via, them. Doing so will allow us to observe and study firsthand their apparent behaviors, reactions, attitudes, and so on in each situation – those all being **indicators** of what is occurring with them in each case. By running these different business experiments, and then observing and properly studying the behaviors resulting from each one, we'll be able to draw conclusions about their associated hypotheses and whether or not those hypotheses are in fact valid – and if so, exactly how valid they are.

Once again, this will require us to be incredibly *objective* in the process – in this case for studying the outcomes and results of each respective business experiment, so as to draw accurate and objective conclusions from each of them. Indeed, we must be 100% objective here, and not let our own biases – cognitive or otherwise – cloud our judgment about these respective outcomes and results. Once again, we have to desire and want nothing other than the absolute objective truth about the situation.

When finished with this process, we should be able to come away with a set of findings that tell us which of our respective hypotheses were in fact valid, and which were not. Having this insight will inform us about what the *actual, real problem* happening here is – and therefore what the actual, real *human need and aspiration* is, as well as what the real *motivations* behind that are. This will then set us up to be able to solve the right problem and not the wrong problem – and to do so at the right level of need and aspiration, not the wrong level.

As can be seen by the convergent surfaces of the graphical representation in *Figure 9.3*, this step is **convergent** in nature, because it leverages primarily *convergent and deductive thinking* to arrive at the most correct set of hypotheses – which at this point will no longer be *hypotheses* (being that they've been proven to be true), but rather *facts*.

Not a once-and-done process!

Now the problem with the preceding explanation of the Problem Clarity process is that right off the bat it probably gives the impression that it is a simple, stepwise, linear process that we can just carry out one step at a time – A, B, C – and that by so doing we'll immediately arrive at our outcome with its commensurate conclusion.

Nothing could be further from the truth! It is in fact *not* a simple, one-time-through, linear process. Instead, it's quite often a very nonlinear, iterative (and usually messy) process – one that typically involves any number of what are called 'micro-learning loops'.

What this looks like in practice is that, at the very beginning, we probably don't even know enough – and thus don't even have enough insight – to know where to start. And so, we just have to start somewhere. So we typically start with certain **guesses** about the situation – and then test those guesses (via select experiments) to learn just how far off (or on) they each were. Then we'll at least start to have enough insight to be able to go through the whole process again – this time with far better hypotheses to test, because this time they'll at least not be *raw guesses* but rather more *well-informed guesses* (but yet still guesses nevertheless).

And so, we'll go through the whole process a second time – to refine our guesses (hypotheses) even further so that then we're set up to go through it a third time and refine our hypotheses further still. In this way, it may take us going through the whole process any number of times – possibly 3, 4, or even 5 times – before we finally feel that we've refined our hypotheses – and our experiments – enough that we can *trust* the final conclusions we reach coming out of it. In other words, in reality it tends to be a very *Bayesian process*. Moreover, each time around, we may be asking slightly different questions and looking at things from a slightly different perspective, so that by the end we've been able to explore every nook and cranny of the space and unearth its most closely held secrets.

In this way, the overall Problem Clarity process is an exercise in **iterative** divergent/convergent hypothesis formation and testing cycles – until eventually, we reach a point of **overall convergence** where we finally trust our conclusions enough to be comfortable with going forward with them. So, although the process is, on one level, alternatingly divergent and convergent, it is, on yet another (higher) level, overall *convergent* towards its final outcome. In this way, what the process will in most cases actually look (and feel) like is something more like what's pictured in *Figure 9.4* – a progressively more convergent sequence of alternating cycles, culminating at the end in an answer that we're finally satisfied with using.

Note also that the process (referring back to *Figure 9.4*) may veer off to the right or to the left – moving in a new direction that we didn't necessarily expect. And so, it won't always follow a straight-line progression as shown here; quite often it will veer one way or the other – into a whole new direction, resulting in a whole new set of insights that we didn't expect. Such is indeed the joy and magic of *problem reframing*.

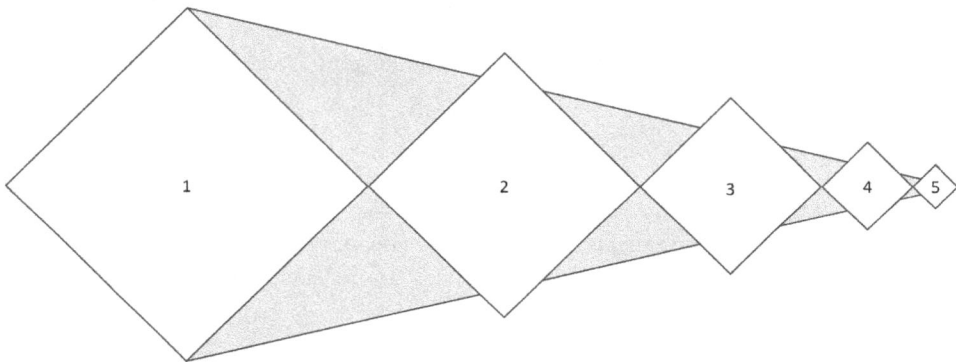

Figure 9.4: What the actual overall convergent Problem Clarity
process generally looks like – with iterative cycles

Of course, we also have to bear in mind that none of us has unlimited time, energy, and/or resources to keep repeating this process *ad nauseum*. And so, we have to always be as intentional as possible about trying to be as focused and as precise as we can be in our respective repeats of the process – so that we can reach our final convergence point as quickly and as painlessly as possible. That being said, it's imperative that we never short-circuit this process and in so doing deprive ourselves of the actual *truth*. Doing that would only produce failure somewhere down the road, which is *not* something we want!

Once we reach the end of the Problem Clarity process for the final time, we will have – as *Figure 9.1* indicates – reached a point of much greater **focus** – one where our problem has now been reframed into a newer and more accurate statement of the problem. That's our official stepping-off point for declaring a specific and unique *point-of-view* that we'll be working with, and then from that point-of-view developing certain specific *design principles* to operate out of – both of which we address next.

In *Chapter 10*, we'll explore the Problem Clarity stage in more detail, largely in the context of our case study with Intensifi.

Stage 3 – Problem-Solution Interface

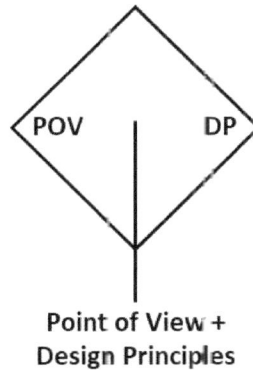

Stage 3 is an intermediate point between **Problem Clarity** and **Value Definition**. It represents a liminal space between working in our Problem Space and moving on to working in our Solution Space.

PROBLEM - SOLUTION
INTERFACE

POV | DP

Point of View +
Design Principles

Figure 9.5: Stage 3 – Problem-Solution Interface

There are two things we do in this intermediate space. Number **one** is we state the specific and unique *Point of View* that we'll be addressing as we move forward. Number **two** is we formulate a specific set of *Design Principles* that we intend to work toward (and adhere to) while developing our solution, so as to come up with a final solution that resolves our newly reframed problem. Let's unpack each of these in turn.

Stating our new and unique Point of View

In the context of Design Thinking, what we mean by the phrase point of view is, specifically, our **subject's** – or **customer's** – point of view about their problem. In other words, it's a statement of their *real problem*, as encountered and understood by them – **from their point of view** – not our own point of view (recall that this was a key element of developing an empathic understanding of them and their situation).

This does not necessarily mean their point of view as they would expressly articulate it if asked to do so. Instead, it means their point of view from a far more **aspirational human level**. *That's* the real point of view we're interested in understanding here – a point of view that reflects the real 'problem behind the problem' involved… or in other words, our newly reframed problem.

So, when we say *Point of View* here, what we mean by this is an articulation of our subject's *real problem* – at the most appropriate level of actionability for us – that we can now try to solve. That's the point of view we're talking about.

And so, what we have to do at this point – prior to being able to go any further – is to actually state, in writing, the specific and unique Point of View that we'll be solving for. Doing this is critically important because it assures a shared understanding, agreement, and alignment between all the different stakeholders involved – one where they're all on the same page about what problem they must solve. Without this alignment, they could, and may, remain fragmented with all sorts of different understandings and interpretations of the problem at hand… not something we can move forward with. And so, we have to stop at this point and explicitly articulate and document this unique point of view so that everyone involved is in fact on the very same page going forward. We cannot move forward until we've successfully done this.

Another thing that having this defined Point of View does for us is it engages and excites our stakeholders to get involved and support our pursuit of a new solution. That's because the best and most appropriate way to convey such a Point of View is to share a narrative about it – one that clearly conveys the emotional pain involved, which we're trying to solve – and one that our stakeholders can get energized to address (versus a purely rational and cognitive expression of the problem, which rarely excites anyone to act on it). So, it's very important that we use our Point of View in this way too – to gain stakeholder support for our efforts.

Once we've articulated and documented our new Point of View, we can then move on to defining our respective *Design Principles*.

Defining our governing Design Principles

In the context of Design Thinking, **Design Principles** refers to a set of *governing principles* by which we intend to design possible solutions to our new Point of View.

As such, they define very specific things these new solutions must do, and very specific outcomes they must facilitate, accommodate, or otherwise help produce. They thus offer guardrails inside of which we have to design – giving us very clear goals for everything our new solutions have to be capable of doing (and often things they must not do).

We'll derive these Design Principles from a very close examination of our new *Point of View*, as well as from all the other new insights we amassed during our Problem Space exploration process. From those inputs, we can distill down a very clear set of principles stating exactly what a new solution for that Point of View **must and must not do**. What this will typically look like is something along the lines of the following:

- A new solution must at all times _____.
- A new solution must be fully capable of _____.
- A new solution must always allow the individual to _____.
- A new solution must offer the individual the choice of _____.
- A new solution must cost no more than _____.
- A new solution must never _____.

By now having these Design Principles in hand, we can proceed to conceiving of possible solutions to our Point of View with **very high confidence** that they will each in fact solve for that Point of View – because any solution that adheres to these Design Principles will *inherently* solve for that Point of View.

Just like before with our Point of View, articulating and documenting, as a group, our new Design Principles is critically important – because it again assures a common understanding, agreement, and alignment (by all the stakeholders involved) around exactly *what* a new solution must and must not do. Without this agreement, the group could, and most likely would, remain fragmented with all sorts of different understandings and assumptions about what our new solution has to do and/or not do. This is, again, not something we can move forward with; we must have this alignment – and so we have to clearly state here at this point in the process our Design Principles, prior to being able to go any further in our overall process.

In *Chapter 11*, we'll explore the Problem-Solution Interface stage in more detail, largely in the context of our case study with Intensifi.

Stage 4 – Value Definition

Stage 4 is the final stage, and therefore ending point, of the classical Design Thinking process. It is all about working our Solution Space.

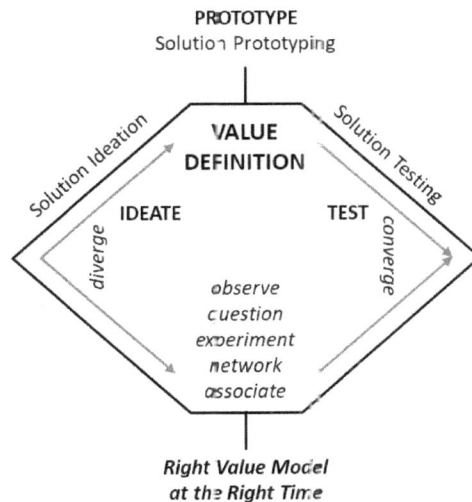

Figure 9.6: Stage 4 – Value Definition

The whole point of this stage is to ultimately define (and eventually design and develop) the most optimal solution possible. This will be one that – more so than any other option considered – fully satisfies all of our respective Design Principles, and thereby optimally solves our subject's problem in a way that's capable of fully resonating with them. In *Chapter 12*, we'll explore the Value Definition stage in more detail, largely in the context of our case study with Intensifi.

This stage is divided into three specific sets of activities (steps), each one serving a specific purpose. (Note that in most academic treatments of Design Thinking, only two of these are explicitly called out, however, all three of them actually occur – as they have to for the process to work). These three steps and activities are generically known, respectively, as **Ideate**, **Prototype**, and **Test**. Let's explore each of them further in turn.

Ideate

The first step in Value Definition is **Ideate**. The purpose of this step is for us to ideate as many possible new solution concepts as we possibly can – the more, the better – so long as they each adhere to our respective Design Principles.

Its goal, therefore, is to create as many new viable, plausible solution concepts as possible, that in each case satisfy all of our Design Principles.

We can do this by holding different ideation sessions and/or workshops with the affected stakeholders – including our outside subjects (the would-be customers). In these workshops, we can present the participants with all of the new insights we unearthed previously in our Problem Clarity efforts – including our new Point of View and the resultant Design Principles. Having this context will give them the insights they need to be able to ideate high-caliber solutions for that Point of View. We would then lead them in various structured ideation activities and exercises to conceive all manner of possible solutions that can (most likely) satisfy each of our Design Principles.

As in the Empathize step, being able to undertake Ideate properly will require us to practice absolute *objectivity* regarding the different solution concepts being proposed. We can't afford to let our own biases – wherever they might originate from – block us from considering all possible viable solutions to our Point of View. This will require us to thus practice humility – acknowledging up front that we really don't know whether or not a particular solution concept is a good one until we've actually prototyped and tested it somehow. Then we can make that judgment – but not before.

Once we're finished with this step, we should come away with a sizeable number of new solution concepts to subsequently prototype and test (for their efficacy in addressing our Point of View). We can choose to either prototype and test *all* of these concepts, or we can instead choose to apply more stringent criteria so as to narrow them down to a more manageable number. The actual number of concepts we intend to prototype and test is up to us, but we certainly want to prototype and test enough of them that we have considered all possible options for our situation. And so, it will be up to us whether or not we want to narrow these concepts down via more stringent criteria, and if so, what those criteria will be (perhaps a more conservative application of our Design Principles).

As can be seen by the diverging surfaces of the graphical representation in *Figure 9.6*, this step is **divergent** in nature, because it leverages primarily *divergent and inductive thinking* to come up with these respective prospective solutions.

Prototype

The second step in Value Definition is **Prototype**. The purpose of this step is two-fold: number one, to build suitable prototypes of our various solution concepts for testing; and number two, to decide how we intend to actually test those prototypes and thereafter design those tests.

This is a step that is almost always glossed over in the academic literature on Design Thinking – as though coming up with representations of our concepts to test and appropriate methods for testing them will all just happen magically somehow. But it doesn't work that way. Coming up with a tangible *artifact* to test and a specific *method* for so testing it is an equally important and challenging step in the Value Definition process – on par with the other steps of this process. That's why we make the point to explicitly address and describe it here.

So, the goal here is to come away with an appropriate collection of prototypes that we can test (representing all the solution concepts we want to test), as well as a suitable set of test methods for doing so (for their efficacy in solving our Point of View). The nature of each of these – our prototypes and our test methods – will depend on exactly what it is we need to validate, and thus what is required to demonstrate success versus failure in that case.

So, in each case, we'll do this by first deciding what exactly we need to test about each prototype – is it their user desirability (perhaps a more aesthetic attribute), their actual usability (a more functional attribute), their ability to adapt to a certain environment (also a functional attribute), or their ability to meet some other requirement? Then, understanding that test need, we'll decide exactly what *type* of prototype we need to build – perhaps a more aesthetic ('looks like') one, a more functional ('works like') one, a quick-and-dirty low-fidelity version, or some other type of prototype. We'll also decide exactly *how* we need to conduct that particular test, and define and document the specific processes and parameters for doing so (our test design). We can, of course, draw from a pool of standardized test methods that we've already predefined for such purposes.

It's important when doing all this that everyone affected agrees on exactly what we're trying to demonstrate in each test, how we intend to go about so testing that, and what success (versus failure) looks like in each case. That way, there'll be no disagreements once our tests are done about how effective each solution concept actually was.

These are all things that we must of course do *prior* to being able to actually test our solution concepts, otherwise we'll have nothing to test and no (defined and agreed-upon) way of testing them. So, if we do this step properly, we'll come away with the prototypes and test methods we need to achieve our specific test requirements.

This step will be both mildly divergent and convergent in nature – in that we'll divergently consider a range of possible prototypes we *could build* to test with, as well as a range of possible tests we *could run* – and then convergently decide on which of those prototypes to *actually build* and which of these tests to *actually run*.

Once we've selected our respective prototypes and built them, and chosen our respective tests and designed them, we're then ready to move on to our next step, which is actually carrying out these tests to validate our different solution concepts via our new prototypes – which brings us to the next step.

Test

The third step in Value Definition is **Test**. The purpose of this step is to actually test our solution concepts – via their representative prototypes – to ascertain their efficacy in achieving the specific outcomes they are each trying to achieve toward our Point of View. Its goal, therefore, is to test out our respective solution concepts (again, via their prototypes), and by so doing eventually converge on the one best solution (which may be a composite, amalgamated solution) that most optimally solves for our subject's (customer's) Point of View. That winning solution will then be the one we move forward into either additional refinements and testing, or toward a final implementation and deployment.

We'll do this, in each case, by running the specific tests we chose in the prior step, in the way we specified in the prior step, and then evaluating each of those test's respective outcomes and results to determine how well the solution concept involved attained its expected and desired outcome toward our Point of View. After running all such tests, we'll then sit down and compare each of the outcomes and results against one another – side by side – to ascertain which of the different concepts performed best toward our Point of View. If we can isolate a single concept that performed most optimally, then we'll most likely be able to move forward with that particular concept. If, however, we cannot isolate such a concept – perhaps because several competing concepts performed equivalently, meaning our tests were comparatively inconclusive – then we'll have to repeat the step with *different* test methods and possibly *different* success criteria – something that will allow us to differentiate between the competing concepts and select a final 'winner' from amongst them.

When finished with this process, we should be able to come away with a single winning solution concept to go forward with. This will sometimes be a composite concept that borrows attributes of other concepts and combines them together into a 'best-of-the-best' type solution.

As can be seen by the convergent surfaces of the graphical representation in *Figure 9.6*, this step is **convergent** in nature, because it leverages primarily *convergent and deductive activities* to arrive at the most ideal and optimal solution possible (from amongst our different competing options).

Also not a once-and-done process!

Once again, the problem with the preceding explanation of the Value Definition process is that it most likely gives the impression that this is a simple, stepwise, linear process that we can just carry out one step at a time – A, B, C – and by so doing we'll immediately arrive at our final solution.

Nothing – again – could be further from the truth! It is in actuality *not* a simple, one-time-through, linear process, but rather a very nonlinear and iterative process that involves its own set of 'micro-learning loops'.

What this looks like in practice is that, in the very beginning (having already iterated our Problem Clarity process several times to arrive at its final Point of View), we'll start out with certain solution concepts that we 'think' may be close – or at least more or less in the right ballpark – for solving our Point of View, and then we'll test those concepts to see how well or how badly they each did. But what we'll **actually learn** in doing this is that **none of them** solved for our Point of View sufficiently! That's an 'ouch'. And so, what we then end up having to do is *repeat* this whole step using the new insights we just gleaned from the first round to further refine our solution concepts (and their respective prototypes) – as well as possibly our tests – and then run those new tests with those new prototypes to see how that round of concepts fare. Quite often we'll end up cycling through this whole set of activities again – a third time – until eventually we've refined our solution concepts down enough that they actually are starting to solve for our Point of View. At that point, we're finally ready to make a comparative evaluation between that competing concepts so as to select from amongst them our final 'winner'.

So, in this way, it may take us going through the whole process multiple times before we finally feel that we've refined our solution concepts – and their respective tests – enough that we can finally *trust* the conclusions we reach coming out of it. In other words, and in reality, it is again a very *Bayesian process* – just like our *Define process* was. Furthermore, each time around, we may be looking for slightly different outcomes and results from our tests, based on the different insights we've been learning up to this point. Ultimately, it will enable us to ensure that we've explored every relevant nook and cranny of our Solution Space, so as to find the single best solution that exists – no matter what corner of that space it happened to be hiding in. This will result in a global maxima and not a local maxima (something we don't want to settle for).

So, in this way, the overall Value Definition process ends up being an exercise in **iterative** divergent/convergent solution ideation and testing cycles – until eventually, we reach a point of **overall convergence** where we finally trust our conclusions enough to be comfortable with going forward with them. So, although the process is, on one level, alternatingly divergent and convergent, it is, on yet another (higher) level, overall *convergent* towards its final outcome. In this way, what the process will in most cases actually look (and feel) like is something more like what's shown in *Figure 9.7* – a progressively more convergent sequence of alternating cycles, culminating at the end in a solution we're finally satisfied with using.

Note also that the process (referring back to *Figure 9.7*), may veer off to the right or to the left – moving in a completely new direction that we didn't necessarily anticipate. And so, it won't always follow a straight-line progression as depicted here; quite often it will veer one way or the other – into a whole new direction that results in a whole new solution we didn't initially expect.

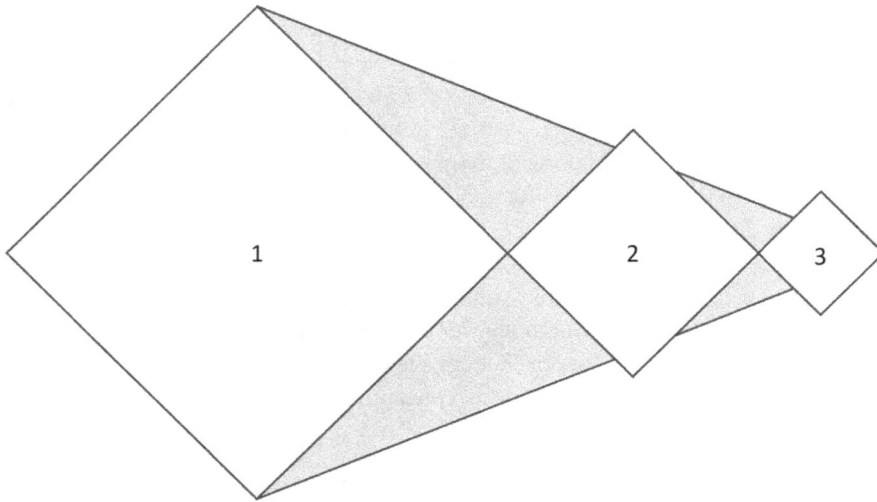

Figure 9.7: What the actual overall convergent Value Definition
process generally looks like – with iterative cycles

Of course – here again – we have to also bear in mind that none of us has unlimited time, energy, and/or resources to keep repeating this process over and over. And so, we have to yet again be as intentional as possible about trying to be as focused and as precise as we can be in our respective repeats of this process – so that we can reach our final convergence point as quickly and as effortlessly as possible. That being said, it's imperative that we never short-circuit the process and in so doing deprive ourselves of the most optimal solution. Doing so could, and may, produce failure somewhere down the road… *not* something we want!

Once we reach the end of the Value Definition process for the final time, we will have – as *Figure 9.1* indicates – reached our final solution which we intend to use to resolve our subject's Point of View. This will be our official stepping-off point for declaring the final solution we intend to deploy, implement, and possibly commercialize.

In *Chapter 12*, we'll explore the Value Definition stage in more detail, largely in the context of our case study with Intensifi.

At this point – the conclusion of Stage 4 – the official *classical* Design Thinking process terminates. We, however, choose to give it a much better 'cherry-on-the-top' ending – as seen in the next section – with an additional, final stage, namely Stage 5.

Stage 5 – Business Model

Stage 5 is an additional stage – following the classical Design Thinking process – that adds to the preceding stages the act of handing off our final solution to a real **business model** so that it can actually be activated and actualized in the market. Otherwise, we just have a new solution with nowhere to go, and no way to become a reality in that market. Our solution needs this business model if it is to in fact become reality.

**BUSINESS
MODEL**

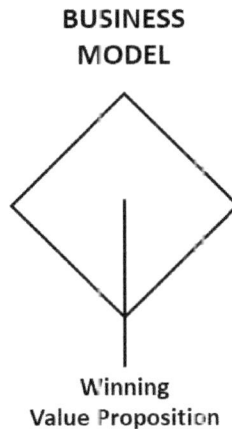

**Winning
Value Proposition**

Figure 9.8: Stage 5 – Business Model

Thus, technically speaking, the classical Design Thinking process doesn't include Stage 5, but we include it here because we believe it's important to not leave the Design Thinking process – a wonderful process otherwise – hanging with nowhere to go. Indeed, the burning question at this point always becomes, *"Okay, now that we have this wonderful new solution, what do we actually do with it... how do we implement it and get it operational?"* Such an important and crucial question cannot be left to happenstance, and thus precisely why we incorporate it here.

So that being said, Stage 5 is about – as indicated – giving our new solution over to a viable business model, so that it can actually be implemented – and in the case of private sector organizations, typically commercialized. At this point, this is predominantly focused on defining the actual **value proposition** we'll wrap around this solution (a *Unique Value Proposition* to be specific, as per the *Business Model Meta Formula*). Here, we call this our "winning value proposition" because it's poised to win in the marketplace on account of its ability to resonate with our would-be customers and their aspirational human need.

This is all the more important because the classical Design Thinking process – as typically practiced – only covers the *Front End of Innovation* – where new ideas get generated and their details fleshed out (which is precisely what Design Thinking does so well). It does **not** cover the *Mid Zone of Innovation* – where the corresponding go-to-market strategy gets defined and developed – nor does it cover the *Back End of Innovation*, where the new solution actually gets launched, operationalized, and scaled in the marketplace – not to mention the business model for any of this. So, we're here to expand Design Thinking into this whole *Mid Zone* and *Back End* space – something we certainly will have done by the end of this book.

Imagination and creativity

You may have noticed in looking over *Figure 9.1* that we call out **two specific practices** in the contexts of Stages 2 and 4, those being, respectively, **Imagination** and **Creativity**. What's going on with these here is the following.

When we enter into Stage 2, we're looking for what might be the issue – and why might that issue be occurring? This is the place where we can really, really benefit from an active and vivid *imagination*.

For our purposes, we define **imagination** as the ability to envision situations and scenarios in our mind that we've never encountered before, and which in reality may not even be possible, but yet we can envision them as though they were possible, and – if we so choose – believe them to be possible in our minds. Indeed, sometimes the more 'impossible' they seem to be, the more breakthrough the ideas they lead to actually are. Per our definition, imagination is an act of the *mind*.

So, we need this ability – the ability to suspend disbelief and believe that anything is possible, as well as the ability to envision these types of things – to help us openly, wildly, and vividly imagine the different types of things that *could*, and *may*, be going on here, and *why* they might be going on. It is precisely that sort of imagination that – whether we realize it or not – allows us to have the genesis of new hypotheses about these situations and their causes. Without our imaginations, we could never, ever begin to formulate new hypotheses about these things. And so consequently we have to exercise *imagination* as we enter into, and work through, Stage 2 for our Problem Space.

Similarly, when we enter Stage 4, we're looking for how we can solve this particular issue, problem, or challenge in a new and novel way. This is the place where we'll truly benefit from strong *creativity*.

For our purposes, we define **creativity** as the ability to combine, or recombine, existing things in a new and novel way to produce something entirely different from what has existed before (at least in the context in which we're using it). So, in this sense, an artist is creative and practices creativity whenever they take paint (an existing item) and paint a scene of something (an existing thing – even if it only exists in their mind, it still has to exist there first) to produce a beautiful new painting of that scene (something that's new and novel). And in this same sense, a novelist is creative and practices creativity whenever they take pen and paper (existing items) and write a story about something (an existing thing – even if it only exists in their mind, it still has to exist there first) to produce an exciting new novel about that something (a new and novel thing in and of itself). So, this is what creativity is for us. Per this definition, creativity is an act of both the *mind* and the *hands*… it never becomes 'creativity' until it leaves the mind and becomes manifest as an artifact via the hands; then it is creativity; otherwise, if it's still only in the mind, then it's imagination and not creativity. Also, per this definition, creativity can be thought of as being akin to 'resourcefulness', though resourcefulness tends to convey more of a utilitarian connotation rather than the more artistic connotation that creativity does; otherwise they're similar.

So, we need this ability – the ability to take existing things and combine (or recombine) them in new and novel ways to produce something entirely different from before – to help us conceive a range of possible solution concepts by which to address our burning Point of View. It is precisely this sort of creativity that lets us ideate and conceive strong new solution concepts that we can then prototype and test out against our respective Design Principles. And it is precisely this sort of creativity that allows us to take the insights we're gleaning from those prototyping and testing efforts to conceive even better, more effective, and more impactful solutions than before. The more creative we can be in these efforts, the more effective and impactful our solution concepts will typically be. And so – whether we realize it or not – it's our creativity that lets us ultimately come up with the winning solution concept we'll take to market and try to succeed with as a business. That is why we need so much creativity here in Stage 4. Consequently, we have to exercise *creativity* as we enter into, and work through, Stage 4 for our Solution Space.

And so, in the Design Thinking process reflected in *Figure 9.1*, we indicate these two practices in those places – imagination preceding Stage 2, and creativity preceding Stage 4 – used as so noted.

The five discovery skills

You may also have noticed in looking over *Figure 9.1* that we call out **five specific activities** in the contexts of Stages 2 and 4, those being the following:

- Observe
- Question
- Experiment
- Network
- Associate.

These five *activities* happen to be associated with five specific **skills** that many prolific innovators often exhibit. These five skills were excellently profiled in the 2011 book *The Innovator's DNA*, by Jeff Dyer, Hal Gregersen, and Clayton Christensen.

In that book, the authors present the findings of an eight-year collaborative study they undertook together in which they sought to gain a richer understanding of disruptive innovators, who they are, and the innovative companies they created. The objective of this study was to discover the *origins* of innovative – and quite often disruptive – business ideas To accomplish that objective, the authors interviewed almost 100 inventors of revolutionary products and services, plus the founders and CEOs of game-changing companies that leveraged such business ideas. This included such leaders as Jeff Bezos, Marc Benioff, Pierre Omidyar, and Mike Lazaridis, amongst others. They also referenced the autobiographies of such individuals as Steve Jobs, Richard Branson, and Howard Schultz. They further studied CEOs who ignited innovation inside existing companies, such as A.G. Lafley, Meg Whitman, and Orit Gadiesh.

As they studied their findings, what they eventually came to realize was that certain consistent patterns of *action* were starting to emerge, reflecting very similar *behaviors* across the entire group. This led to the five primary **discovery skills** that became the basis for their book – skills that allowed these innovators to 'think different', to use Apple's well-known slogan. Without elaborating on all their specific observations about these behaviors (we suggest reading the book) – it all distilled down to these five key behaviors – observing, questioning, experimenting, networking, and associating – with the first four generally resulting in the last one (which involves what is known as 'associative thinking' – or more colloquially, 'connecting the dots'). They also found that, to be effective, these innovators not only had to 'think different', they also had to 'act different' – and thus their explicit *behaviors*, not just *thoughts*.

Now to be completely fair, and to give credit where credit's due, Dyer, Gregersen, and Christensen weren't the first to note and promote these behaviors. That actually happened in the mid-1950s by American Mechanical Engineering Professor **John Arnold**. Arnold was a professor first at **Massachusetts Institute of Technology (MIT)** and later at **Stanford University**, where he was largely the impetus behind what we know today as the Stanford d.school. Arnold was one of the original pioneers (in modern times) in scientifically defining and advancing inventiveness based on the psychology of imagination and creative thinking. He was also an internationally recognized innovator of educational philosophy, leveraging the (at the time quite controversial) case study *Artemis IV* based on science fiction – which gave students a very foreign situation to design for, thus *forcing them* to develop empathy for their very unorthodox subjects.

Arnold believed that creativity could – and should – be improved through a scientific understanding of the *inventive process*. Consequently, he held that improving creativity can in fact be attained through a very deliberate and organized step-by-step process, and to facilitate that process he created a framework involving a combination of *analysis*, *synthesis*, and *evaluation* – clustered into three phases. These are the following three phases (wait for it…):

- **question and observe** – the preparation work;
- **associate** – the production work (it's what creates the end result we're looking for);
- **predict** – the decision-making work of deciding what to do with, and about, what we just invented.

Look familiar? Arnold saw these three phases as a sort of checklist for guiding creative work. He also believed – in keeping with his desire to be very 'systematic' in all this (recall he was using the scientific method) – that an 'associative-thinking machine' could be devised that would assist the engineer in generating new ideas by elucidating all the possible cross-combinations and associations of different attributes of the problem, thereby allowing them to solve that problem in a new and novel way via those new associations (such software does exist today, facilitating what is otherwise known as *morphological analysis*).

So – all this being said – the point being made for our context is that – and this will become increasingly clear as we work through the rest of this chapter and the next three chapters – carrying out our hypothesis formation and testing work in *Problem Clarity*, as well as our solution ideation and testing work in *Value Definition* – will require us to in fact exercise those five activities – observing, questioning, experimenting, networking, and associating. We cannot – and will be unable to – carry out this work unless we commit ourselves to undertaking those five specific activities.

This means we will have to do the following:

- **observe our subjects** to develop hypotheses about what they're trying to accomplish and why they're behaving the ways they are (in each case, and at each point, what their goals and aspirations are, what they're thinking, what they're feeling, why so, and so on);

- **question them and others** about their situation – to test our hypotheses, and to formulate newer and ever better ones to test even further;

- **experiment** with new and different **ideas** – both about the problem and the solution to it;

- **network** with others in our networks to **compare notes** – again, on both the problem and the best solution for it;

- **associate** previously disconnected insights with each other so as to connect the dots and make new **meaning** from it all... the 'aha' moment we want to arrive at in the end where we say, "Ah... I see... I get it now! That's what is actually going on here... !".

That is where we need to get to in each case, and the only way we're ever going to get there is by in fact practicing these five behaviors.

And so, going back to *The Innovator's DNA*, it's helpful if, in the context of undertaking this work – and acknowledging, as those authors did, that each of us has stronger skills in certain of these behaviors and weaker skills in others of them – we can put together a team where their respective strengths and weaknesses all complement and otherwise compensate for each other. For example, not always but commonly, introverts are better at observing than extroverts whilst extroverts are sometimes more adept at questioning than introverts (though introverts often formulate some of the most impactful questions). Extroverts also often have larger networks to tap into, whereas introverts often have deeper and higher-quality networks to use. So, each of these respective traits and skills can balance out and complement one another. In the end, we'll want a team that – as a whole – is capable of doing all five of these activities incredibly well – so that as a whole we can fully benefit from the entire Design Thinking process.

From process to methods

Now that we understand the five stages of the Design Thinking process, as well as the role that imagination, creativity, and the five discovery skills play in the process, we can turn our attention over to the actual toolbox for this process – namely the Design Methods.

As we'll see, there's an immense wealth of methods we can leverage to help us carry out this process.

The Design Methods – powerful ways to observe, study, and understand

While it's incredibly helpful that we now have a defined process for undertaking Design Thinking, the reality is that carrying out that process involves tasks that are quite different from the ordinary everyday tasks we're generally accustomed to. Indeed, doing so successfully involves tasks that will be quite foreign to most of us. Consequently, we need a set of *methods* by which to carry out these tasks. That's where Design Methods come into play.

Design Methods are the *toolbox*, if you will, of Design Thinking. They incorporate a broad array of research, analysis, and synthesis practices used to carry out the tasks associated with Problem Clarity, Problem-Solution Interface, and Value Definition. As such, they empower teams to be able to properly and adequately explore their Problem Space so as to arrive at the right Point of View, and then subsequently work their Solution Space so as to arrive at the most optimal solution per their Design Principles. Without Design Methods to support this work, teams would be unable to carry out Design Thinking effectively.

Collectively, Design Methods have been intentionally developed and formulated over many years by many different people, largely starting in the 1950s. Several of the research-oriented methods borrow directly from the world of classical market research, as well as more modern user research.

Categorizing the Design Methods

Design Methods is an incredibly rich area of knowledge, encompassing nearly 200 different methods. Given this fact – and the reality that certain methods are used for certain specific purposes – different parties have, over the years, devised different approaches to categorizing them. Schools such as the IIT School of Design and Stanford d.school have had their approaches, while different consultancies have likewise had their approaches, and so on – each according to a specific logic pertaining to how they get used.

In my work in applying and teaching Design Thinking over the years, I've found that Design Methods generally get used for one of four types of tasks. Consequently, I've chosen to cluster them according to those task types. These four categories and their respective explanations are as follows:

- **The Observe Methods**: We use these methods to watch and observe our subjects, making very keen observations of their specific behaviors (and sometimes their apparent attitudes). These observations can be done from afar, or up close, but we never want them to interfere with or otherwise influence the behaviors we're trying to observe (lest we get false signals). From those observations, we can then start to build out certain hypotheses about our subject's problem and their effectiveness in trying to apply certain solutions to that problem.

  Observation is limited, in that it can allow us to observe people's actual behaviors, but it likely won't reveal to us the underlying causalities of those behaviors. For that, we require other methods.

- **The Question Methods:** We use these methods to engage directly with our subjects (by questioning them) in an effort to gain more immediate access to their specific thoughts, attitudes, and opinions, each of which is informed by their past experiences and present needs – meaning they have a contextual basis here. Questioning our subjects can begin to reveal their inner motivations and aspirations, which will often explain, to a degree, the causalities of their behaviors.

- **The Experiment Methods**: We use these methods to undertake any number of experiments surrounding our situation of interest – including experiments with our subjects, to see how they react to a particular scenario, or how they react to a new concept we're considering, and experiments with ourselves, to find out for ourselves how a particular situation feels, or to see how well a particular solution works, and so on. Running these types of experiments can reveal much deeper insight into our subjects' needs, desires, aspirations, motivations, and even their values and beliefs.

- **The Study Methods**: We use these methods to undertake any number of evaluative tasks aimed at learning a particular situation better and thereby creating a shared understanding of the different aspects of the situation within our broader team. These often require that our whole team engages together in creating design artifacts that describe or explain either a present situation or a desirable future situation.

Of course, you'll probably notice right off the bat that three of these categories – *observe*, *question*, and *experiment* – relate *directly* to three of the five discovery skills covered in *The Innovator's DNA*. The fourth category – *study* – also relates as well, in that it's the place where we'll typically use *associative thinking* to associate all the different insights we've culled from the first three sets of activities to ultimately come up with the innovative new ideas needed to address and resolve our problem.

Sequencing the Design Methods

Understanding these four types of Design Methods – and applying each one in its right place – will certainly allow us to carry out the Design Thinking process most effectively and impactfully.

We must be careful however to not mistake this categorization for a chronological sequence per se. While it's true that, in general, we will want to do *observational work* first (to seed our hypotheses) and then *questioning work* thereafter (to test and refine those hypotheses), followed by certain *experimentation* and *study efforts* to further refine our insights (and eventually converge on the right hypothesis), the reality is that this order as presented does not necessarily reflect the exact chronological sequence in which we'll use the methods. Especially because this whole process tends to be so *iterative*, it may very well be that we use certain Study or Experiment Methods to help us understand where we need to undertake additional observation and questioning work – using those types of methods. And so, in this sense, we'll often end up moving back and forth between the different methods, in any sort of sequence, until we eventually arrive at our end goal.

Ultimately, we'll end up interweaving the different Design Methods we need to use – in whatever sequence makes the most sense for our situation – to learn what we need to learn from them, and thereafter be ready to deliver a winning value proposition from our efforts.

Applying the Design Methods

We furthermore need to be aware that, while some Design Methods can be useful across the entire spectrum of activities we do in this process, other Design Methods will be more relevant to certain specific stages and steps in the process, given their goals and the types of tasks they characteristically involve.

We can say the following in particular:

- certain methods are better suited for the Problem Clarity stage;
- other methods are better suited for the Value Definition stage.

And similarly:

- certain methods are best suited for divergent activities (forming hypotheses and ideating solutions);
- other methods are best suited for convergent activities (testing hypotheses and testing solutions).

We can consider this *visually* via a matrix – as shown in *Figure 9.9* – where we can associate any given method of any particular type, according to our four clusters on the vertical axis, to any particular activity – divergent or convergent; Problem Space or Solution Space – according to our four key steps shown on the horizontal axis.

This will become more apparent as we explore each method type in further detail.

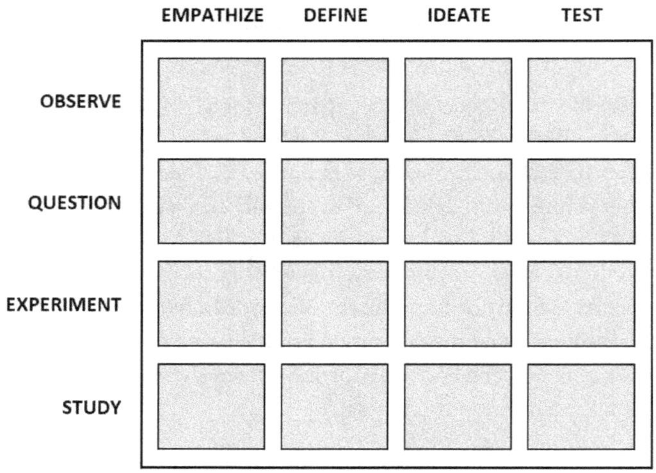

Figure 9.9: A Design Methods matrix

Finally, it is to be noted that, while most of these methods represent specific actions we'll undertake, a minority of them – such as Beginner's Mindset and Absence Thinking, for example – involve instead a certain specific **mindset** we are to adopt: a specific way of thinking and seeing mentally so that we can get our minds into the right frame to be able to do observational, questioning, experimentation, or study work in a particular way, with a particular mental frame of mind. Using those methods will filter our work through a completely different set of mental filters than we normally use, resulting in a completely different set of outcomes than we would otherwise achieve. And that is typically a good thing!

A deeper look at the Observe Methods

In Design Thinking, we use the Observe Methods to keenly and intensely watch and observe our subjects – typically inside a particular context, situation, and/or environment. We'll do this so as to collect useful insights about them and their situation.

Each Observe Method has a specific name and process to it. *Table 9.1* lists 15 Observe Methods in common use, and in each case indicates which steps they are best suited for.

1	Still Photo Survey	Empathize
2	Fly On the Wall	Empathize
3	Absence Thinking	Empathize / Define
4	Behavioral Archeology	Empathize / Define
5	Spatial Behavior Mapping	Empathize / Define
6	Business Ethnography	Empathize / Defne / Point of View
7	Digital Ethnography	Empathize / Define / Point of View
8	Contextual Inquiry / Shadowing	Empathize / Define / Point of View
9	Cultural Probes	Empathize / Define / Point of View
10	A Day In the Life	Empathize / Define / Point of View
11	Guided Tours	Empathize / Define / Point of View
12	Time-Lapse Video Survey	Empathize / Define / Point of View
13	Social Network Mapping	Empathize / Define / Point of View
14	Workarounds	Empathize / Define / Point of View
15	Customer Hacks	Empathize / Define / Point of View

Table 9.1: The Observe Methods

From afar versus up close

In some cases, we'll observe our subjects from afar, without intruding on their situation. It can at times be important (especially initially) to be able to observe our subjects without intruding on or intervening in their situation – because in those cases we need to be able to make very objective observations of them in an accurate context of their environment and their specific product/service/experience use case. Intervening in any way on that situation could disturb this contextual objectivity and thereby void any observations.

In other cases, we'll engage directly and up close with our subjects, such as by shadowing them. This is so that we can examine them and their situation and activities more closely, and thereby develop a deeper insight into their apparent needs, motivations, priorities, and values, amongst other factors.

In both cases, the Observe Methods allow us to observe true behaviors as accurately as possible.

What observations reveal – and do not reveal

Observations – using the different Observe Methods – will reveal our subjects' *behaviors*. What they will not necessarily reveal however are the *causes* of those behaviors (depending on what can and cannot be inferred from our observations).

That's typically where the *Question Methods* come in. They allow us to probe and question, and thereby develop deeper insights into the *causes* behind what we have observed. Consequently, observation work typically precedes questioning work – at least initially.

Taking care to ensure objectivity in our observations

In using the Observe Methods to do observational work, we must be very careful about our observation process. This is because the human mind automatically filters out a significant portion of the information our senses take in, generally doing so in a subconscious manner that we're not even aware of, thus resulting in various cognitive biases and misperceptions.

We have to be cognizant of this fact, and thus careful and diligent to avoid such misperceptions. This often means we'll need to step back and observe situations with 'fresh eyes'. And in fact, sometimes, if we find that we're too close to a particular situation to be able to observe it in a fully objective manner, we'll need to find others who are more removed from that situation to help us observe it. Such assistants will often spot certain behaviors and other details that our own minds gloss over – thereby ensuring we don't miss important behavioral clues in this process.

A deeper look at the Question Methods

In Design Thinking, we use the Question Methods to engage directly with our subjects – questioning them about certain things so as to gain direct access to their thoughts, beliefs, and attitudes. These will all be informed by their past experiences and present needs – meaning the answers they give us will have a contextual basis.

Question Methods include a number of different ways of engaging and querying our subjects. These range from direct verbal interviews, to associative and classification methods, to co-creation methods. Each of these will yield a slightly different snapshot of our subjects' cognitive processes and emotional states, as well as their contextual experiences that over their lifetimes have formed these.

Each Question Method has a specific name and process to it. *Table 9.2* lists 28 Questions Methods in common use, and in each case indicates which steps they are best suited for.

1	Focus Groups	Empathize / Define / Point of View
2	Draw The Experience	Empathize / Define / Point of View
3	Conceptual Landscapes	Empathize / Define / Point of View
4	Collaborative Mind Mapping	Empathize / Define / Point of View
5	Collage	Empathize / Define / Point of View
6	Personal Inventory	Empathize / Define / Point of View / Design Principles
7	Unfocus Groups	Empathize / Define / Point of View / Design Principles / Ideate / Test
8	Participatory Design / Co-Creation	Empathize / Define / Point of View / Design Principles / Ideate / Test
9	Journal / Diary Study	Empathize / Define / Point of View / Design Principles / Test
10	Camera Journal Study	Empathize / Define / Point of View / Design Principles / Test
11	Contextual Interviews	Empathize / Define / Point of View / Design Principles / Test
12	Empathy Interviews	Empathize / Define / Point of View / Design Principles / Test
13	Behavioral Interviews	Empathize / Define / Point of View / Design Principles / Test
14	Extreme User Interviews	Empathize / Define / Point of View / Design Principles / Test
15	Foreign Correspondents	Empathize / Define / Point of View / Design Principles / Test
16	Kano Analysis	Empathize / Define / Point of View / Design Principles / Test
17	Collaborative Sketching	Empathize / Define / Point of View / Ideate / Test
18	Five Whys	Empathize / Define / Point of View / Test
19	Question Laddering	Empathize / Define / Point of View / Test
20	Why-How Laddering	Empathize / Define / Point of View / Test
21	Behavior Sampling	Empathize / Define / Point of View / Test
22	Narration	Empathize / Define / Point of View / Test
23	Card Sort	Empathize / Define / Ideate / Test
24	Free Listing	Empathize / Define / Ideate / Test
25	Word Concept Association	Empathize / Define / Ideate / Test
26	Random Name Generation	Empathize / Define / Ideate
27	Primary Quant Research	Empathize / Define / Test
28	Stoke	Ideate

Table 9.2: The Question Methods

Using the Questions Methods to add insights to our previous observations

We'll commonly use the Question Methods following the Observe Methods. This is so that we can add additional insights to our prior observations.

Doing this typically allows us to test and refine our various hypotheses about our subject and their situation. This is because the answers they provide to our questions will often reveal deeper insights into their true needs and motivations – and sometimes even their higher-level aspirations. Those sorts of insights will typically help to explain at least *some* of the causalities behind the specific behaviors we observed.

Using the Question Methods to develop a psychographic profile and deeper insights

After completing our questioning activities, we'll often be able to construct a relatively complete picture of our subjects' composite psychographic profiles, including their specific values, priorities, attitudes, and outcome requirements.

Those insights may help to explain further the motivations behind certain specific behaviors we observed, as well as the motivations behind particular needs surrounding a particular offering's usage.

A deeper look at the Experiment Methods

In Design Thinking, we use the Experiment Methods to conduct any number of business experiments for our Problem Space, as well as any number of solution experiments for our Solution Space.

Thus respectively, we undertake these experiments to evaluate certain hypotheses and likewise to test the efficacy of certain solution concepts.

Each Experiment Method has a specific name and process to it. *Table 9.3* lists 9 Experiment Methods in common use, and in each case indicates which steps they are best suited for.

1	Bodystorming	Empathize / Define / Point of View / Design Principles / Ideate / Test
2	Role-Playing / Informance	Empathize / Define / Point of View / Design Principles / Ideate / Test
3	Try It Yourself	Empathize / Define / Point of View / Design Principles / Ideate / Test
4	Empathy Tools	Empathize / Define / Point of View / Design Principles / Test
5	User Scenarios	Define / Point of View / Design Principles / Ideate / Test
6	Scenario Testing	Define / Point of View / Design Principles / Ideate / Test
7	User Testing	Define / Point of View / Design Principles / Test
8	Usability Testing	Define / Point of View / Design Principles / Test
9	Café Testing	Define / Point of View / Design Principles / Test

Table 9.3: The Experiment Methods

Why we experiment – three key purposes

We'll generally undertake our experimentation for one of three purposes:

- The first purpose is to determine how our subjects respond to a particular situation or scenario, including their behavioral reactions to certain hypotheses and/or solution concepts. This sort of experimentation is done directly with subjects.

- The second purpose is to be able to experience our subjects' situation for ourselves firsthand, so as to develop empathy for them and that situation. This sort of experimentation we'll do on ourselves.

- The third purpose is – in the case of solution testing – for purely functional purposes, to see how well different solution concepts perform against each other along different criteria, and thus their functional efficacy in satisfying certain of our Design Principles.

Field experiment or lab experiment?

Some experimentation we'll need to conduct inside a lab – such as an innovation lab inside our business – so as to have a controlled environment in which to work. Other experimentation we'll need to conduct in the field, where we can assess our subjects in their actual context.

The latter approach often provides the most reliable insights, though real-world environments can at times make it challenging and difficult to control for confounding factors.

And that is where internal labs come in. With their ability to control for and possibly exclude certain factors – such labs can prove incredibly helpful, especially when we're trying to deeply understand the behavioral causalities associated with a certain scenario.

Consequently, we suggest using both approaches – as required and as deemed most appropriate. This infers of course that we'll need some sort of lab in which to undertake those lab experiments. Thus, we must ensure that we have access to such a laboratory or equivalent resource.

Ultimately, we'll need to look very closely at what it is, specifically, that we're trying to learn from each experiment, and then ascertain whether that experiment will be best conducted in the lab or in the field, and in each case why so. We'll then need to design and conduct each such experiment accordingly.

A deeper look at the Study Methods

In Design Thinking, we use the Study Methods to undertake any number of evaluative tasks aimed at further studying the problem we're addressing and/or the solutions we're promoting for resolving that problem.

In each case, our objective is to learn more about that problem or solution, as well as to create a shared understanding in our business of the different aspects of the problem or solution – including what an ideal solution outcome would look like (one that optimally satisfies all our Design Principles).

Study Methods often require us to work together in our teams to create specific *design artifacts* that we can use to describe and explain either a current situation or our ideal alternative situation (the ideal future state).

Each Study Method has a specific name and process to it. *Table 9.4* lists 55 Study Methods in common use, and in each case indicates which steps they are best suited for.

1	Beginner's Mindset	Empathize / Define
2	Secondary Research	Empathize / Define
3	Persona	Empathize / Define / Point of View
4	Empathy Map	Empathize / Define / Point of View
5	Story Share and Capture	Empathize / Define / Point of View / Design Principles
6	What? How? Why?	Empathize / Define / Point of View / Design Principles / Ideate
7	Storyboarding	Empathize / Define / Point of View / Design Principles / Ideate
8	Concept Models	Empathize / Define / Point of View / Design Principles / Ideate
9	Metaphor Mapping	Empathize / Define / Point of View / Design Principles / Ideate
10	Cross-Cultural Comparisons	Empathize / Define / Point of View / Design Principles / Ideate
11	Stakeholder Analysis	Empathize / Define / Point of View / Design Principles / Ideate
12	Process Flow Analysis	Empathize / Define / Point of View / Design Principles / Ideate / Test
13	Swim Lanes	Empathize / Define / Point of View / Design Principles / Ideate / Test
14	Cognitive Task Analysis	Empathize / Define / Point of View / Design Principles / Ideate / Test
15	Anthropometric Analysis	Empathize / Define / Point of View / Design Principles / Ideate / Test
16	Error Analysis	Empathize / Define / Point of View / Design Principles / Ideate / Test
17	Value Webs	Empathize / Define / Point of View / Design Principles / Ideate / Test
18	Analogous Empathy	Empathize / Define / Point of View / Design Principles / Ideate / Test

19	Alignment Model	Empathize / Define / Point of View / Design Principles / Ideate / Test
20	Affinity Analysis	Empathize / Define / Point of View / Design Principles / Ideate / Test
21	Saturate and Group	Empathize / Define / Point of View / Design Principles / Ideate / Test
22	Ecosystem Visualization	Empathize / Define / Point of View / Design Principles / Test
23	2x2 Matrix	Empathize / Define / Ideate / Test
24	Position Map	Empathize / Define / Ideate / Test
25	Activity Analysis	Empathize / Define / Test
26	Rapid Facilitation	Empathize / Ideate
27	Storytelling	Empathize / Ideate
28	Barrier & Trend Mapping	Empathize / Ideate
29	Desired Experience Model	Empathize / Ideate
30	Piggybacking	Empathize / Ideate
31	Brainstorming	Empathize / Ideate
32	Point of View Madlibs	Define / Point of View
33	Point of View Analogy	Define / Point of View
34	Point of View Want Ads	Define / Point of View
35	Critical Reading Checklist	Define / Point of View
36	Brand Swap / Brandcasting	Define / Point of View / Design Principles / Ideate
37	Design The Box	Define / Point of View / Design Principles / Ideate
38	Six Thinking Hats	Define / Point of View / Design Principles / Ideate
39	Historical Analysis	Define / Point of View / Design Principles / Ideate
40	Era Maps	Define / Point of View / Design Principles / Ideate
41	Long Range Forecasts	Define / Point of View / Design Principles / Ideate
42	Predict Next Year's Headlines	Define / Point of View / Design Principles / Ideate
43	Tangible Futures	Define / Point of View / Design Principles / Ideate
44	Scenario Planning	Define / Point of View / Design Principles / Ideate / Test
45	Collaborative Inspection	Define / Point of View / Design Principles / Ideate / Test
46	Collaborative Sketchboards	Define / Point of View / Ideate
47	Constraint Imposition	Define / Point of View / Ideate
48	HMW? Questions	Define / Point of View / Ideate
49	Powers of Ten	Define / Point of View / Ideate

50	Backcasting	Define / Point of View / Ideate
51	Concept Videos	Define / Point of View / Ideate / Test
52	I Like, I Wish, What If	Define / Point of View / Ideate / Test
53	Feedback Capture Grid	Define / Point of View / Ideate / Test
54	Competitive Product Survey	Define / Design Principles / Ideate / Test
55	Indirect Benchmark	Ideate / Test

Table 9.4: The Study Methods

Regarding the preceding four sets of methods – the Observe Methods, the Question Methods, the Experiment Methods, and the Study Methods – attempting to explain these, method by method, is unfortunately beyond the scope of this book. We will however – in *Chapters 10, 11,* and *12* – be exploring certain of them in the context of our case study with Intensifi and its team using them. Otherwise, there are other helpful resources you can access that offer detailed explanations of these. The most comprehensive of such resources would be the *Applied Innovation Master Book* from **Global Innovation Institute (GInI)**, and perhaps the second most-useful one would be the book *101 Design Methods* by Vijay Kumar (interviewed in *Chapter 3* of this book). You can also do an online search for any of these methods and find detailed explanations of them and their respective application.

It's important also to *not be overwhelmed* by the sheer number of these Design Methods. Instead, select a few to use, master them, and then, over time, move on to learning and using other methods. Mastery comes through practice, not through memorization. In due season, you will master a number of different methods and be able to use each of them effectively.

Embracing the value Design Methods offer

All Design Methods work – whether it be observation work, questioning work, experimentation work, or study work – is not necessarily challenging or overly difficult to undertake, but it will generally require considerable time, effort, energy, and focus to complete properly.

That being the case, using Design Methods can at times seem daunting – especially when we're down in the weeds trying to complete our work. To counter this, and so as to not feel completely overwhelmed by these efforts, we must also stay focused on our bigger picture – namely the goal of a winning value proposition.

This is one of the reasons why so many organizations don't pursue this work. They don't understand Design Methods or their value – nor how to leverage them effectively in the stages of their project work. Consequently, they pressure teams to move on to ideating solutions without ever taking the time to first properly work their Problem Space, because doing so will require them to spend additional time making the necessary observations, asking the necessary questions, conducting the necessary experiments, and studying the situation sufficiently to be able to develop the required clarity around the problem and then the proper focus for the solution.

For this reason, you and your teams should be prepared to push back on this pressure should it be encountered, so that your work can properly benefit from the methods.

Knowing how to select the right Design Methods to use

One of the biggest challenges we'll face in this process is knowing exactly *which* Design Methods to select and use – especially given the sheer number of them.

To address this, there are two key pieces of knowledge and understanding we'll need to develop and possess:

1. what stage and step of the Design Thinking process we're in, and therefore what type of work we need to do at that point to achieve its specific *goal* – observation, questioning, experimentation, study, or some specific combination of these;

2. the type of insight or outcome each Design Method (or at least a majority of them) delivers – allowing us to then match up our specific insight or outcome *need* to what a specific Design Method delivers, and thereby select the method (or methods) that best delivers on what we need to achieve by that point.

Of course, in practice, we don't always know everything upfront that we'll need to learn throughout our journey, but we should at least know enough to tell us where to get started. We can then evolve our learning path as we gain new insights, which will usually point us toward additional new learning areas we need to explore further.

The important point here is to know what we need to learn or achieve at any given point and what each Design Method allows us to learn or achieve so that we can then select those that allow us to reach our objective.

This choice does of course have strategic implications for us – because the insights we develop, which will ultimately guide the innovations we deliver and the business model we use to do so, themselves have key strategic implications. Consequently, we must always strive to understand the key strategic implications of the decisions we'll be making from these insights, and then select our methods carefully to ensure that we are in fact developing as high of a caliber of insights as we possibly can from the process.

Creating our Insights Plan

When embarking on our design research efforts, it's generally a good idea – as well as proper practice – to first put together an **Insights Plan**. This plan outlines what we wish to learn, and how we intend to do so.

An Insights Plan is simply a plan that lays out our specific learning objectives, the research methods we intend to use (at least initially), the order in which we intend to use them, the required insights each method is expected to deliver, and how those insights will be woven together to form a complete and proper understanding of the situation we're evaluating.

In the case of Design Methods, our Insights Plan will specify which Design Methods we intend to use, in what order we intend to use them, the insights or outcomes each method is expected to produce, and how as a team we'll piece those insights together to produce a coherent, shared, and empathic understanding of our subject and their situation.

Having such a plan upfront will allow us to plan out our work and then follow through with a sound course of action, understanding that such a plan is a living artifact. This means that as we go along and learn new insights, we'll likely find it necessary to modify our plan to learn additional insights – quite often in an iterative manner.

Our Insights Plan thus serves as the charter that keeps our team working together and moving in the same direction as we tackle our specific challenge. For this reason, we should always develop such a plan prior to diving into our design research.

Prototyping in Design Thinking – a critical element in the process

Besides using the *Design Thinking process* and the countless different *Design Methods* to support that process, there is one other incredibly important activity necessary to complete a proper Design Thinking effort. That activity is **prototyping**.

Prototyping literally means – as its name suggests – building different types of *prototypes* of various artifacts involved in our undertaking. Those artifacts can be things required to help us properly explore our Problem Space, such as props for our hypothesis testing – or things required to help us properly explore our Solution Space, such as mockups of proposed new solution concepts we've conceived. In both cases, Design Thinking requires us to build appropriate prototypes to be able to execute its work properly and sufficiently. It's an integral part of the process.

Making prototyping inherent to how we operate in Design Thinking

In Design Thinking, prototyping is paramount. It lets us move ideas and concepts out of our own heads and into the open – tangible artifacts in the physical world that others can see, hear, feel, smell, and possibly even taste for themselves, thus creating a shared insight and understanding amongst all our stakeholders!

Consequently, there is no substitute for good prototyping in Design Thinking… no shortcuts or easy ways around their necessity. We have to build and use prototypes if we ever hope to do Design Thinking well!

However, what we're actually after here is something even more. What we really want to do is go beyond the physical act of just building prototypes per se (using whatever steps are necessary to do so) – to instead making 'prototyping' our inherent way of thinking and operating in this process – one that fully permeates everything we do toward our goal of a superior end solution.

If we can do this – if we can make prototyping our inherent way of thinking and acting – then it will become second nature to us; we won't even have to think about it. Anytime something we're trying to accomplish will benefit from a prototype, we'll just inherently build a suitable prototype for it – no hesitation whatsoever. That's where we need to get to – to inherently building prototypes whenever and wherever they're needed. Thus, I encourage you to strive for that sort of *prototyping flow state*.

Understanding the different purposes of prototyping

If we were to ask someone with a more traditional R&D mindset what the purpose of prototyping was, they would most likely say something along the lines of, "to validate the technical performance of a new product."

However, in Design Thinking, we realize that testing isn't just about functional performance testing, but rather, and more often than not, about human acceptance and usability testing. This is quite a different type of testing – one that involves as much psychology as it does physics. Consequently, in Design Thinking, the purposes of a prototype are likewise different – and generally far broader.

In particular, in Design Thinking, we say that prototyping has twelve specific purposes (with some overlap between them). Those twelve purposes are as follows:

- **Build to Learn**: Prototypes used to inquire, observe, and learn… especially to learn new things via a *Beginner's Mind*.

- **Build to Empathize**: Prototypes used to develop an empathic understanding of our subject and their situation/world. These can be replicas of things we've observed in the field – so that we can 'live in them' ourselves to develop that empathy.

- **Build to Clarify**: Prototypes used to test our hypotheses about our subject and their situation. They can also be used to engage subjects in a simulated environment via a prototyped artifact.

- **Build to Think**: Prototypes used purely to engage our mind's *analysis and synthesis engine*. Indeed, having something tangible to turn over in our hands helps our minds to better understand a concept. And then, as our mind suggests new thoughts about it, we can go prototype these to see what comes out of it. Even if nothing does per se, doing this will still keep our minds exploring for more ideas.

- **Build to Engage**: Here, prototypes are used to engage our subjects in all manner of conversations and collaborations; drawing them into both the problem exploration work and the solution ideation work via these prototypes.

- **Build to Collaborate**: Prototypes used by groups to create together, to learn together, to resolve ambiguity together, to ideate together, and to test together. We should always make in-situ prototyping a core aspect of how we collaborate in our teams and with our subjects.

- **Build to Communicate**: Prototypes used to help us communicate our insights, findings, and ideas with each other – so that as a team we can deepen our shared understanding of the meaning of these things.

- **Build to Compare**: Prototypes used to undertake comparative evaluations between proposed new solutions and existing or surrogate solutions – any of which we can use to figure out how to solve our subjects' problems more effectively.

- **Build to Iterate**: Frugal (AKA 'quick and dirty') prototypes – used to test out new ideas quickly and cost-effectively so that we can learn what doesn't work about them and why. We can 'rinse and repeat' this activity as often as we need to achieve eventual convergence.

- **Build to Decide**: Prototypes used to enable us to come together as a team and synthesize our insights and findings so that, collectively, we can make the necessary decisions we need to make to move our effort forward toward convergence.

- **Build to Prove**: High-fidelity prototypes used to validate the customer efficacy and functional performance of new solution concepts.

- **Build to Inspire**: Prototypes used to cast a new vision that speaks to our shared humanity and thereby compels us to go forward.

As we set about building and using prototypes – perhaps each with a specific purpose in mind – we'll eventually come to understand two things. First, we'll learn just how powerful prototypes can be – as they rally people together around some key new insight or takeaway. Second, we'll come to see how that any given prototype can more often than not be used for multiple of these purposes; they certainly are not mutually exclusive of each other – a fact that makes them that much more powerful and impactful to our efforts.

Two important considerations about prototyping

There are two important considerations we need to be aware of in Design Thinking. They are the following.

Prototype fidelity and resolution

In Design Thinking, prototypes will range in their fidelity, or resolution – from the very low to the very high – in keeping with their respective purposes and applications:

- Low-fidelity (low-resolution) prototypes will be very conceptual in nature – often just a 'rough and dirty' representation of some concept made out of simple materials like paper, or a drawing.

- High-fidelity (high-resolution) prototypes will be very realistic in nature – often featuring much of the same functionality and other attributes the real-world artifact they represent does.

The fidelity used in any particular scenario will need to be commensurate with the objective we're trying to achieve there. This usually relates to where we are in the progression of our overall process:

- Early on, when we're trying to test out different hypotheses via customer interactions with various mock-ups, those mock-ups can be quite simple and coarse in nature. This allows us to build new ones on the fly and thereby rapidly explore new hypotheses as we proceed along.

- Toward the end of our effort, where we're trying to validate competing solution concepts, our prototypes will need to be far higher in fidelity – with much more complete and accurate functionality, so that we can obtain more accurate results from them.

- In between these two stages, our prototypes will need to have an intermediate level of fidelity.

In this way, we should match the resolution to the need, but otherwise keep that resolution as low as possible – so that we can explore our Problem and Solution Spaces as quickly, easily, and broadly as possible.

Prototyping with a purpose

Often we'll want to isolate just one factor of our situation – so as to ascertain how changing that particular factor affects the outcome of a certain test. When that is the case, we'll use what is known as **OFAT testing** – or **one-factor-at-a-time testing** – a practice also known as 'prototyping with a purpose'. Using this practice allows us to understand that factor in greater detail – including how sensitive our situation is or is not to it.

OFAT testing can be very helpful whenever we need to break down a particular problem into a set of smaller (and more easily tested) sub-problems. Doing this can allow us to study each part of the overall problem in isolation, and by so doing understand the role that each part plays or doesn't play in that overall situation. That in turn can help us to achieve convergence much faster (whether in the Problem Space or the Solution Space), as well as with higher confidence in our final outcome.

Understanding the different types of prototypes

Given the twelve purposes of prototyping noted previously, and the fact that we require a range of prototype *types* and *resolutions* to be able to meet our needs at each stage of our process, there are in fact a specific set of prototype *types* that we should be aware of. Each of these offers a particular resolution and carries with it a characteristic purpose or application. Let's explore each of them in turn.

Conceptual prototypes

These are prototypes – quite often a diagrammatic or schematic drawing – that illustrate the conceptualization of some relatively complex artifact – often a large 'system' or similar construct.

They're used to either describe and analyze a current situation, or else conceive and design a new and better situation around that particular artifact.

Paper prototypes

These are prototypes built using paper, markers, Post-it™ Notes, and other similar simple 2D materials. They let people easily organize their thoughts, articulate new ideas and concepts, visualize abstract concepts together, and brainstorm new insights together – all so that the group can collaboratively explore a question or concept together.

Their simplicity lets teams use them to quickly explore and evaluate different concepts together, with very little cost and no risk. They're often the natural starting place from which teams will kick-start their Design Thinking effort, where they're used to engage with subjects and each other to better flesh out the Problem and Solution Spaces.

Frugal prototypes / quick and dirty prototypes

These are prototypes that one is able to build quickly and easily using materials readily available to them.

They allow teams to quickly assemble variations on an idea or concept to share in their work. Though low in fidelity, they're still very capable of communicating that idea or concept effectively. This lets teams interact with subjects and each other to quickly evaluate and refine new ideas and concepts together.

Scale-model prototypes

These are prototypes that make use of a scaled version of an artifact. Their scaling can be either up (of a very small artifact such as a molecule) or down (of a very large artifact such as a power plant) – in both cases bringing the artifact into a scale that teams can easily handle and manipulate.

They're used to bring the artifact under study into a size proportion that teams can more effectively comprehend, and thereby study. By studying the artifact at a scale they can wrap their minds (and often arms) around, teams are able to identify and confirm key issues, as well as to collectively explore new options for solutions that may better meet the needs at hand.

Appearance / 'looks-like' prototypes

These are prototypes that physically resemble the appearance of a particular real artifact. They generally do not possess full functionality, but rather only convey a representative appearance.

Their objective is to allow teams to understand the extent to which their appearance conveys their intended meaning, purpose, or expectations to those who will purchase and/or use the artifact. Teams can use them wherever they want to gather feedback on the appearance of a particular artifact.

Wizard-of-Oz prototypes

These are prototypes in which some aspect of the functionality of the artifact is emulated by a hidden resource. To the observer, they appear to be functioning as one would expect of the real artifact. However underneath, they're actually being operated by a hidden resource – most commonly a human faking what would otherwise be an automated operation.

These are used to test out certain concepts with subjects (involving the functionality of concern) without having to actually build a fully-functional prototype, thereby saving teams tremendous time, money, and effort in the process (especially when the underlying hypothesis is found to be incorrect).

They can thus be very useful whenever a team needs to learn more about a particular area or type of functionality prior to being ready to invest the time, effort, and capital required to produce that functionality in its true form.

Functional / 'works-like' prototypes

These are prototypes that deliver the full functionality of a real artifact – either through the same mechanism as that artifact, or through some other (interim) mechanism.

They often look nothing at all like the actual artifact is to look, but they nevertheless prove very useful for evaluating the functional performance of different concepts.

Teams will often use them, therefore, in the final test step of their Value Definition work, where they're trying to understand the functional performance of different competing solutions. In fact, they're generally necessary if a team is to make an accurate comparative evaluation between competing concepts and thereby find the single best solution to their problem.

Behavioral prototypes

These are prototypes used to ascertain the behaviors of subjects (would-be customers) – often in the context of how they interact with a particular product, service, or experience.

Teams commonly use these for the following types of work:

- empathy work – to study, learn, and understand customer behaviors and the reasons behind them;
- define work – to test customer behaviors against certain hypotheses and thus test their validity;
- ideate work – to help stimulate their brainstorming of new solution concepts;
- test work – to test out different solution concepts with customers and see what behaviors they elicit.

Experience prototypes

These are prototypes used to simulate a particular customer experience and/or the immersive environment in which that experience takes place.

This is important, because being able to appreciate and evaluate a particular experience – set in its proper context and environment – demands that it be prototyped and staged for subjects to explore and experience firsthand – just as they would the real experience. The prototype must thus be capable of projecting a high degree of perceived realism to those encountering it – meaning that the artifacts used in it must be capable of seeming real, and the people delivering it must be capable of portraying the real delivers.

User-driven prototypes

These are prototypes (typically of new solution concepts) in which actual end users have been engaged to help design and develop them. This tends to produce prototypes that are highly effective at revealing these users' mental models of their situation and their need in that situation.

By doing this, teams gain insights not only from observing users use these prototypes, but more importantly, from observing them actually design and develop the prototypes – watching very carefully what they create and how they go about doing so, and then finding out why they created what they did… what their specific rationales and motivations were. This reveals immense insights into how they see their problem, how they think it should be resolved, and why they think it should be so resolved.

By specifically looking at how users think about solving their problem, and by understanding the reasons behind that, a team can gather deep insights into these users' collective psyche – thereby allowing them to better understand the fundamental needs, desires, aspirations, motivations, priorities, values, and beliefs involved – all very powerful for delivering a winning solution concept.

Prototype application and fidelity

As a consequence of both the Design Thinking process itself (with its respective stages and steps) and the preceding series of purposes, what we'll actually find in the course of carrying out this process is that we end up using prototypes to do each of the following (and more):

- Test out our hypotheses through different business experiments.
- Refine our Point of View and Design Principles through various comparative evaluations.
- Visualize and communicate different solution concepts to the affected stakeholders.
- Validate some of these concepts through various solution tests.

And in that process, our prototypes will range in 'fidelity' – including the following:

- low-fidelity prototypes – used to create a shared understanding;
- medium-fidelity prototypes – used to let us and our subjects 'try things out';
- high-fidelity prototypes – used to validate the technical performance and efficacy of various solutions.

We'll find that – whatever the need at hand – there will always be an appropriate type of prototype to satisfy it. That reality lets us use prototyping *throughout* the Design Thinking process.

When in doubt, prototype and test – the undeniable power of prototyping

Prototyping is one of the easiest – and yet most effective – things we'll do in Design Thinking, producing paybacks *many times* the time, effort, and cost we invest into it. By removing ambiguity, and by creating tangible shared understandings amongst the different stakeholders involved, it makes our innovation process far better and less risky, and thus far more intelligent.

We must resist the temptation, therefore, to ever rush through this process and skip our prototyping work, believing (erroneously) that we'll somehow be able to achieve the same outcome through simple mental and verbal exercises. We cannot afford to do that! Instead, we have to resolve to do our prototyping work… to put in our time at our Prototype Shop making whatever is required to advance our cause.

There is a philosophy amongst some startup investors – namely that they won't invest in a new venture unless the founders have some *"dirt under their fingernails."* What this means for us is that we have to be knee-deep in the prototyping trenches doing this work on behalf of our own venture.

Understanding this, we can see why making prototyping a foundational way of life in Design Thinking is so incredibly powerful for us. If we succeed at prototyping and testing, then we'll succeed at Design Thinking, and if we succeed at Design Thinking, then we'll succeed at business. It all begins with the mentality and mantra of, "When in doubt, prototype and test!" Adhering to that mantra will serve us well.

In all cases, action is required. Just talking about prototypes won't put something tangible in front of us, or our customers. We have to get some "dirt under our fingernails" – by prototyping early and prototyping often. That will be our recipe for success here!

A little help – how Generative AI can help us

Over the past two decades, **Artificial Intelligence (AI)** has – as a comprehensive category of technology – been a boon to innovation and innovative business models. On the back end, we've had AI pattern recognition and predictive analytics tools letting us deliver breakthrough solutions that were never before possible. Its impact on the world of research and development has been nothing short of incredible – especially in areas such as disease diagnosis and drug discovery! And now on the front end, we have Generative AI tools empowering us to be ever more insightful and creative. Let's take a look at exactly how Generative AI in particular fits (and does not fit) into our Design Thinking effort.

As a resource for more comprehensive insights

Because Generative AI tools are built atop **Large Language Models (LLMs)**, they're able to incorporate massive amounts of preexisting knowledge and data – making for an exhaustive body of knowledge overall.

Consequently, when we're trying to cultivate a deeper contextual understanding of our subject's situation, we can query these tools about specific details of those situations and they can – assuming they've been trained on language models containing that contextual information – provide us with the answers to our queries using natural language narratives we can understand.

Doing this can reveal to us new insights and information that we didn't previously have – simply because our own base of experience hasn't been nearly as exhaustive as the potentially centuries' worth of experience encapsulated in these models – especially for the particular context we care about here.

Therefore, tapping into their knowledge bases – conveyed to us in these easy-to-understand natural language narratives – can fill in some of the important and missing bits of information we need to understand our subjects and their situation better. In this sense, Generative AI tools can help us to reach a point of empathic understanding that much quicker.

As a stimulus for enhanced imagination

A Generative AI tool, whether textual or visual, can – within certain bounds that we can generally tailor – spit out for us anything we ask it to, whether real or imagined. So, for example, if we ask a textual tool like OpenAI's GPT-4 to describe a scene that can't actually exist in our own world – like, say, humans on Mars naturally breathing the Martian atmosphere – then it can certainly do so. Or if we ask a visual tool like Stability AI's Stable Diffusion to render a scene that can't actually exist in our own world – like, say, someone being teleported via quantum teletransportation – then it can certainly do so. There's no limit to what these tools can describe or render to us, other than that of our own imaginations. This of course requires us to use *our own imaginations* to come up with the prompts describing these scenes, but so long as we have a vivid enough imagination to do so, there's no limit to what we can have the tools portray for us.

This benefits us because, by using the tools in this way, we can spur our imaginations even further. So, for example, we might tell the Generative AI to portray a particular non-realistic scene that we've imagined, and it does so, and then the resultant imagery triggers an even more imaginative thought in our minds. In this way, we can use these tools to, in effect, amplify our own natural imaginations and thereby make them that much more vivid and expansive.

So, in terms of the work that we're doing here, trying to really understand situations and what's going on behind their scenes, as well as possibly ideating far-fetched ideas for addressing them somewhere down the road, having a tool that can, in effect, amplify our imaginations can prove to be a crucial asset to us. We should therefore use them in this way whenever and wherever doing so proves helpful in our journey. In particular, if we ever find ourselves feeling 'stuck' in a particular place in the process, then we may be able to use one of these tools to further spur our imaginations and help us get 'unstuck'. They should thus be used in that manner as well.

The caveat we have to keep in mind here is that all of this depends on *our imaginations*. The AI tools (at least at this point in their development) don't have imaginations of their own per se – nor any real impetus to use an imagination were they to have one. It starts and ends with *our imaginations* – the AI tools simply sit in the middle and help us to amplify those imaginations.

Not as a direct resource for novel ideation

Finally, where Generative AI tools do **not** shine is as a direct source of *novel ideas*.

While we can always query these tools to ask, "How might I solve this problem?", or "How would Ronald Reagan have solved this problem?", or something along those lines, the answers we're going to get are all rooted in the **past**… in prior things that people have already done at this point. What we need *instead* are usually new and novel ideas for new and novel actions that no one has ever done before – something these tools cannot give us, because they lack the ability to foresee the future as well as the ability to imagine, per se, new ways of solving a problem that haven't been tried before.

Moreover, because the statistical algorithms they use to query their LLMs (under the covers) look for instances of answers that have a high probability of occurrence (meaning many sources agree on them), they will always tend toward the middle of the pack... the most mainstream of answers. They will almost never return the outliers in their data, because that's not how they're programmed to work; they're programmed to look for the most commonly held answers and report those. This is unfortunate in our case because so much of innovation relies on understanding and trying to solve for the *outliers* on both ends of the distribution pool; it's those *outliers* who often hold the "aha!" nuggets of insight we need – nuggets that we can't get from the mainstream population. So, unfortunately, Generative AI tools will, by and large, fail us in this regard. This reality was reflected in a study conducted by **Boston Consulting Group** (**BCG**) and reported in September 2023. That study found that Generative AI's relatively uniform output can reduce a group's diversity of thought by 41% (reference: https://www.bcg.com/publications/2023/how-people-create-and-destroy-value-with-gen-ai).

So – as a combined result of having only the past to draw from and using statistical probability algorithms to look for the most common of answers – we'll almost never get something that's new and novel and that hasn't been tried before. We're on our own for that. This naturally limits these tools' usefulness in this context.

There is one "yeah, but..." here that we haven't mentioned. That is namely that we can use Generative AI tools to help us develop a **cross-industry** perspective. So, say, for example, we query a tool and ask it to tell us "how the electrical power industry would solve the problem we're experiencing in the cosmetics sector" – or "how the airline industry would solve the particular problem we're experiencing in the agricultural sector" – and so on. We can use Generative AI tools in this way to help us mix and match different solution approaches used in the past in one context in a *completely different context*. Doing that can, in some cases, reveal to us novel ways to solve a particular problem (at least in our 'other' industry or sector) – and that can prove to be the impetus for a new approach we actually end up using. So, we'll give Generative AI bonus points in this context.

At the end of the day, how much value we get out of Generative AI in this context will depend on where the tools are in their evolution, and how we end up using them. We just have to bear in mind these specific limitations at this point in their evolution.

AI hypothesis testing – a new era for lean startups

Besides Generative AI, we can also use back-end AI tools to help us test certain hypotheses we've formulated. In particular, we can set them up to explore existing data sets for applicable evidence that a particular hypothesis is or is not true (we say 'applicable' because whatever they conclude has to be generalizable to our population of interest). Doing this stands to measurably accelerate the world of lean startups.

This is something that's enhanced even further when we use these tools to create what are known as 'agent-based models' – where they're programmed to synthetically imitate what certain humans think, believe, and do, and as such can be used to test out new ideas and concepts with those synthetic populations. So long as they're programmed accurately (meaning they accurately reflect these humans' real irrational behaviors), they can be used in this way very effectively.

This point was well made in an August 2023 interview with Steve Blank, the father of lean startups, published on *TechCrunch*, and found at `https://techcrunch.com/2023/08/30/artificial-intelligence-lean-startups/`.

The long-term risks of using AI in our innovation work

There's also the inherent risk in the world of Design Thinking that coming to rely *too heavily* on AI to do our thinking for us will lead us all down a path of least regression – toward common 'me-too' solutions.

If this were to happen, it would cause us to lose our own innate human imagination and creativity. That's a risk we should very much be aware of – and always strive to guard against. No matter how much we might enjoy using AI, and Generative AI in particular, at the end of the day what makes our solutions and business models genuine, unique, diverse, and human are their innate human characteristics – the ones born out of only the human mind, with its inherent imagination, creativity, and the will to use both. We must never let ourselves become so complacent as to replace these with AI (in any form), as doing so will only lead to a world of overt homogeneity – not something we should aspire to as humans.

The near-term and long-term ethical risks of using AI

Finally, there's also a very clear and present ethical danger in relying too heavily on AI (of any form) to do our thinking and innovation work for us. In particular, AI models do not, generally speaking, encompass the full breadth of human ethical considerations, not to mention our moral considerations. Consequently, they have a tendency to make decisions (and even take actions if allowed to do so) devoid of such considerations.

This can lead to all sorts of negative consequences for our secondary and tertiary stakeholders – including our communities, the communities on the other side of the world, and the planet as a whole, just to name a few.

We must guard against this therefore – ensuring that all insights and decisions reached via AI, as well as all actions taken based on those insights and decisions – take into full consideration this complete breadth of ethical and moral considerations – so that in innovating we never lose our humanity or our soul. This will – at least for the foreseeable future – always require real human oversight and intervention to ensure.

Back to Intensifi

Okay… back now to our friends at Intensifi. What do *they* think about all this Design Thinking process, methods, prototyping, and Generative AI stuff?

Well, as it so turns out, they're quite happy to learn that there's a specific process they can use for doing all this, plus they're likewise very happy to learn that there's this massive arsenal of Design Methods they can leverage for this work. Concerning the role of prototyping in this effort – they're rather enlightened. This was something they didn't quote realize before. They're also very thankful to understand how they can leverage Generative AI in this process, as well as the inherent limitations of these tools to be aware of.

They realize now that they're going to have to spend some time really thinking through how they intend to take on this whole process. This will start with their Problem Space, from which they'll then be able to develop the right Point of View – as well as the right Design Principles to use. And then, following all that, they're going to have to figure out how they'll tackle their Solution Space in order to come up with their final value proposition.

As we noted in *Chapter 8*, they've already identified certain subjects they've been traveling around spending time with, so as to develop a greater and deeper empathy for them and their situations. This has included, to date, the three individuals on the consumer side (Hunter, Lee, and Johannes), as well as the three individuals on the business side (Lakshmi, Stephen, and George). This has been, and continues to be, an incredibly helpful exercise to them, as they're learning all sorts of insightful and helpful things about these specific subjects. Of course, they realize that they'll eventually have to open up this group to an ever-large set of subjects if they're to have a representative sampling of their market.

But what they more importantly realize now is that it's not enough just to get to know these different subjects and what makes each of them tick (though that's incredibly important). Instead, they have to now really start formulating their specific hypotheses about these individuals and their rationales, motivations, and aspirations – so that, in each case, they can fully characterize their Problem Space the way it needs to be characterized. This will include segmenting their market into different segments (submarkets), each of which may have its own unique and differentiated set of needs, aspirations and motivations – and therefore its own unique *Point of View* to address. That of course would mean a unique set of *Design Principles* for each one, though the question at that point becomes one of how those different *Points of View* might all be **combined** such that *one set of Design Principles* was able to address them all. But, alas, that's getting ahead of themselves.

In the next three chapters, we're going to explicitly walk this journey together with Ian, Zoe, and Watson, as they seek to undertake the Design Thinking process, stepping, in turn, through Problem Clarity, Problem-Solution Interface, and Value Definition to thereby, in turn, unpack their Problem Space, discover the right Point(s) of View, define their Design Principles, and ultimately explore their Solution Space to arrive at a final endpoint. In that process, they'll choose certain specific Design Methods to use, which we'll have a front-row seat watching them employ – different ones for each of the respective stages. They'll also start building some prototypes to work with as well – again different types for different stages, purposes, and activities.

Having this opportunity to watch Ian, Zoe, and Watson walk through this process, using these methods (and possibly some Generative AI exercises as well) will allow us to really understand the process in detail, as well as certain of the Design Methods and how those *types* of methods get used in each case. This will make the whole process very *tangible* to us. And that's where we leave off in anticipation of *Chapter 10*.

Summary

In this chapter, we've explored the Design Thinking *process*, Design *Methods*, the role of *prototyping* in Design Thinking, and the role of *AI* (especially Generative AI) in Design Thinking. This gave us a very high-level overview of how these things work together to empower Design Thinking and make it function as expected and intended.

In particular, we learned that there is in fact a clear process for undertaking Design Thinking, though that process is often incredibly iterative and messy in nature, and certainly not a simple linear one. It involves 'owning our problem', exploring our Problem Space to reframe that problem into a proper Point of View, formulating specific Design Principles for how to solve that Point of View, and then exploring our Solution Space to discover an optimal solution that resonates with our subjects and their most fundamental needs in this case.

We similarly learned that there are scores and scores of different Design Methods we can leverage in this process – each being best suited to a particular activity in the process. We saw how these methods can be clustered into four main types – according to the type of activity they each involve – those being *observe*, *question*, *experiment*, and *study*.

Along with this, we learned the power and role of prototyping in Design Thinking – how we have to make prototyping a fundamental element of how we think and operate in this process, as it's paramount to doing the process properly and well. *"If in doubt, prototype and test!"*

Finally, we learned about the assistive role of AI in this process, and how we can use it to augment our work.

As we've seen, Design Thinking is an incredibly powerful approach to addressing problems from a truly human-centered perspective. By giving us its underlying philosophy of human-centered design, its process, and its plethora of Design Methods, it lets us develop and test hypotheses about our subjects' problem, so that in the end we can solve that problem in the most ideal manner possible – producing a solution that truly resonates with these individuals and their unique need.

In *Chapter 10* (up next), we're going to go even deeper into the whole **Problem Clarity** stage – walking 'up' the divergent mountain of 'empathize', 'across' the peak of 'experiment', and 'down' the convergent mountain of 'define' – all hand-in-hand with Ian, Zoe, and Watson of Intensifi – and most likely in an iterative manner. This will allow us to more fully understand and appreciate that stage, including certain of the pertinent Design Methods and how they each get used, plus different types of prototypes and their uses – to ultimately arrive at a point where we've reframed our problem to give better focus on the situation.

Further reading

- *GInI Applied Innovation Master Book*, Anthony Mills, editor, Global Innovation Institute, Grand Rapids MI, 2017, www.gini.org/aimb.

- *The Innovator's Hypothesis: How Cheap Experiments Are Worth More Than Ideas*, Michael Schrage, MIT Press, Cambridge MA, 2014.

- *101 Design Methods: A Structured Approach for Driving Innovation in Your Organization*, Vijay Kumar, Wiley, Hoboken NJ, 2012.

- *The Innovator's DNA: Mastering the Five Skills of Disruptive Innovators*, Jeff Dyer, Hal Gregersen, Clayton Christensen, Harvard Business Review Press, Boston MA, 2011.

Working the Problem Space – Up and Down the Mountain

In *Chapter 9*, we explored how to put Design Thinking into practice – how to go from "thinking" liking a Designer to "acting" like a Designer. That included the Design Thinking process, the Design Methods, and the role of prototyping in Design Thinking – as well as the role of Generative AI in Design Thinking. This allowed us to see how these different pieces work together to empower Design Thinking and make it work as expected – even when it is highly iterative and messy at times. That gave us the insight we needed into how to work our Problem Space and our Solution Space – as well as further confidence to explore both.

In this and the next two chapters, we're going to dive deep into these spaces. We'll do this by walking through the overall process together with Intensifi – in each case looking at what they're trying to achieve, which Design Methods they opt to use (each of which will be explained as they're encountered), any prototypes they choose to use along the way, and the specific outcomes they achieve from each activity. Doing this will offer us very clear insights into what the actual process looks like, and how it works in the real world to produce an empathic understanding of our subject and their situation. It will also give us far greater insight into how the Design Methods are used – including those used for observation, questioning, experimentation, and study. Plus, it will show us how the different types and fidelities of prototypes get used in the process.

In this chapter, we'll specifically look at Intensifi's Problem Space via the "Problem Clarity" stage (Stage 2) of the Design Thinking process. In particular, we'll explore the following three topics:

- **Divergence – hypotheses formation – or what could the need be**: In this section, we'll explore the divergent activity of formulating hypotheses about our subject, their situation, and their real-world need – including the use of inductive logic to do this.

- **Business experimentation – deciding and planning how to test our hypotheses**: Here, we'll explore how we think about testing our hypotheses, and thus develop a plan for doing so.

- **Convergence – hypothesis testing – determining the real need**: Finally, we'll explore the convergent activity of testing our hypotheses to arrive at the most accurate and correct one(s) – and thus a correct understanding of our Problem Space – including the use of deductive logic to do this.

Upon completing this chapter, we will have thoroughly explored Intensifi's Problem Space with them. (Or will we have? You'll need to read the subsequent chapters to find out for certain!)

Note that, in the way of setup, Ian, Zoe, and Watson of Intensifi have now recruited a broader team of "early employees" (actually just volunteers at this point, though ones committed to their cause). Altogether, they've assembled a team of 16 individuals to help them undertake the research and analysis of this stage (the Problem Clarity stage) since otherwise it would be overwhelming (and too unreliable) for just three people. They require this broader group to get a much better read on, and comprehension of, the situation they're trying to address, and thus its correct hypotheses.

Divergence – hypotheses formation – or what could the need be?

The Problem Clarity stage is about trying to sort through the murkiness of problems as we first encounter them, and the many "symptoms" that we first see on their surface so that we can (eventually) get down to the real *problem behind the problem* – the one that properly articulates our subject's **aspirations** and **motivations**, and therefore their truly desired **outcome**.

Our point of entry into this stage is working to "empathize" with our subject – an activity we'll do by formulating different hypotheses about them, their situation, and what their real need (aspiration, motivation, and outcome) might be. Doing this will require us to observe them, and then use inductive logic and reasoning to try to hypothesize what might be going on (hypotheses that we'll test later on; we have to formulate them first):

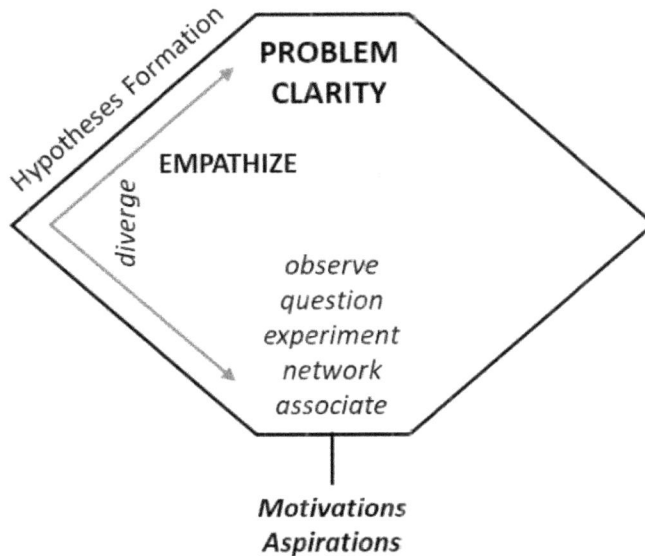

Figure 10.1: The divergent Empathize step of the Problem Clarity stage

Doing this will take the team through the divergent Empathize step of the Problem Clarity stage.

Appreciating Intensifi's goal at this point

In Intensifi's case, the team has a general sense of the type of solution they want to offer, but this is largely driven by what they know they can theoretically do with newer AI technology (the "push" of the situation). It is *not yet* – at this point – rooted in a proper understanding of the **market need** that will create the necessary "pull" for that capability and their specific solution.

That is what they're here to do now: develop a deep, rich, and complete understanding of this market need, in all its various nuances, among all its different players. This involves formulating hypotheses about the people involved and their underlying needs – something Intensifi will leverage its imagination to kickstart.

Revisiting who Intensifi's subject is

In pursuing any innovation – and especially a business model innovation – we have to always start with our "who" – who it is we're trying to solve a problem for. Doing so is critical. If we fail to properly match our "what" and "why" with the right "who," then we'll end up solving for the wrong "who" – and the problem we end up solving for (their problem) may not be the one with the greatest market potential. That's not something we want to do. So, it's always crucial that we clearly define our "who" before doing anything else – or at least consider the fact that we still have to discover which "who" has the biggest problem in the market, for which a solution will thus have the maximum chances of success in terms of scaling up into a real business.

As noted previously, Intensifi has hypothesized – based on all their prior collective experiences – that their "who" will be a range of upwardly-mobile professionals – covering a wide range of different ages and career stages – each of whom aspires to optimize their life choices to extract as much success and happiness from their lives as possible. This will include all genders, races, and religious and ethnic groups.

So, while Intensifi remains open to "discovering" any other type of "who" here, they'll be focusing primarily on studying these types of individuals as their subjects and would-be customers.

Intensifi's learning plan – 8 Design Methods

To undertake the work of formulating their hypothesis, the team has decided to employ the following eight Design Methods (drawn from the three method types indicated). They've chosen these in particular because they believe these specific methods will allow them to maximize their overall learning in this situation:

- **Observe Methods**:
  - Business Ethnography
  - Behavioral Archeology
  - Workarounds
  - Customer Hacks

- **Question Methods**:
  - Draw The Experience
  - Free Listing

- **Study Methods**:
  - Beginner's Mindset
  - Saturate and Group.

Next, we'll explain each of these methods, how the team is using them, and what outcomes they attain from them – including the final hypotheses they extract from them.

Observing – Business Ethnography

What it is: Business Ethnography is an anthropological approach (a derivative of cultural anthropology) that involves closely observing both individual and group behaviors in the full context of a particular situation of concern.

It's used because it gives us rich insights into our subjects' behaviors when interacting with a particular "system" (which could be our business, our brands, our products and services, or an experience staged we've around any of them). Since people's stated and actual behaviors are often quite different from each other, it's important to watch and see what people *do and say* within real contexts and real timeframes, rather than simply accepting what they say they do (or don't do) – an approach that may lead us astray. It can also reveal unmet or unsatisfied needs our subjects have, and therefore opportunities to deliver innovative solutions for those needs.

Since the constraints of real-world business innovation make it impractical to spend years living "in the field" with our subjects watching and observing them, the way that true ethnography dictates, Business Ethnography is our next most appropriate substitute. With its brief stints of field observation, it is both within our reach and capable of yielding a surprising amount of insight about our subjects. How long we spend observing them will depend on how strategically important our effort is, and how much is at stake. For many efforts, it may only be a matter of weeks, but for some efforts with high strategic value, it can be several months.

There are also varying shades of Business Ethnography, depending on how far we want to keep our distance for objectivity, versus how up close we want to get for detailed accuracy. Consequently, the method uses different approaches, including observations, interviews, having people record in diaries, and exploration of artifacts. Regardless of which approaches we use, they're all aimed at understanding our subjects' routine behaviors and their particular customs and rituals more deeply, including their beliefs, values, and myths underlying them. To make these observations, we may spend time posing as subjects ourselves so that we can watch others inconspicuously.

How Intensifi uses it: Intensifi's team spreads out and observes different professionals using (or trying to use) different "life optimization" methods, platforms, and tools, which at this point each focus on just a specific aspect of their overall life situation, such as (and most commonly) financial optimization tools (such as those offering robo-advisors on wealth-management investment decisions to make at different stages of someone's life). Other platforms and tools in this category include those for health and fitness, career-building, mate-finding, family planning, business strategy, hobbies, and so on. None, however, attempt to help users evaluate their lives holistically over their entire lifespan.

So, in particular, certain members of the team here focus on finance, others on career, others on health and fitness, others on marriage and families, others on business, and so on. In each case, they attend user groups, read online forums, and generally – to the best extent possible – observe individuals using these tools in different contexts to see what they're doing (and sometimes saying) with them, and why so – including their apparent frustrations with those tools' respective limitations. The team would ideally love to "snoop" on users behind the scenes, but since they don't have access to these companies, and doing so would violate privacy rights in many cases, they obviously can't do that, so they're a bit limited in that regard.

Intensifi's insights: Intensifi learns that different individuals are interested in optimizing these respective areas of their lives, so they invest in these platforms and tools and use them to varying degrees, according to their proficiency with them (which tends to be proportional to the time they spend learning how to use them), with varying degrees of satisfaction with the actual outcomes (many of which can take years to evaluate).

The team also observes that users don't typically trust these platforms and tools in their entirety, and consequently tend to supplement them with actual human advisors, such as financial advisors, career advisors, business advisors, fitness trainers, and so on – an important insight about the platforms and tools and their effectiveness (or lack thereof) in achieving these users' ultimate goals.

Observing – Behavioral Archeology

What it is: Behavioral Archeology is used to infer insights about people's lifestyles, habits, rituals, values, and priorities. It involves a close examination of the specific artifacts and environments involved in their situation, as opposed to an observation of the individuals themselves.

This being the case, we study these artifacts and environments closely in search of evidence of how they figure into our subjects' lives – studying things such as their wear patterns, overall organization, and specific placements. This can reveal pertinent aspects of their lifestyles, habits, rituals, values, and priorities, which can, in turn, help us to further understand what motivates them (a hint of their overall psychographics). This is useful for understanding how we might innovate around these particular artifacts and environments.

How Intensifi uses it: Intensifi studies the specific environments, activities, and artifacts their subjects are using – which primarily involve using digital tools at home or work, and human advisors in direct one-on-one interactions. They look very closely at different subject's respective lifestyle activities and the "rituals" they employ in those situations – as well as the specific artifacts they use and how they use them. From this, they try to infer certain specific values and priorities these subjects have – and thus their psychographic motivations.

Intensifi's insights: Intensifi learns (not surprisingly) that certain people tend to spend time at home and work using different digital platforms and tools to help them try to optimize certain parts of their lives.

What they also learn however – perhaps more insightfully – is that these same people tend to "socialize" the outcomes they obtain from these platforms and tools in some way – by sharing them with either their trusted friends and family in confidence or with paid professional advisors. What the Intensifi team has learned here is that these individuals are generally looking for *validation* of those outcomes, and even more so, of the specific *decisions* they're planning to make based on them – hoping for signals that either *affirm or refute* those decisions and the reasoning behind them. This is a critical insight as it reveals that while these individuals all wish to use automated tools to help them make critical life decisions, at the end of the day, they don't trust these tools carte blanche – and so seek means by which to "second guess" them with their own "gut" and the wisdom and "gut" of other humans whom they do trust and generally respect. This points to a key trust and confidence issue going on. Indeed, even with these "second opinions" affirming their decisions, the team has observed that some subjects don't always follow through with actually making those decisions – they still don't have the full confidence they need to do so and trust that the outcome will be as it's projected to be (a type of *uncertainty paralysis*).

Observing – Workarounds

What it is: Whenever the artifacts that people engage with, whether those be people (our staff) or a certain product or service, have shortcomings associated with them, users often find their *own* workarounds for dealing with those shortcomings – often manifesting as unintended or modified *uses* of the artifact. These reveal where such shortcomings exist, and thus the presence of an unmet or unsatisfied need associated with them. These needs are often around a specific "job" that has to be done to achieve the intended outcome. So, they represent possible opportunities for us. If we can deliver an innovation that eliminates the shortcomings, and thus the need for such workarounds, then we may be able to capitalize on the situation and deliver a differentiated offering with a unique brand experience that both builds our brand and commands a higher profit margin.

A related concept is that of desire paths. Desire paths reflect wherever a group of people actively demonstrate a shared interest in creating a *different* pathway (a way of doing something) that *deviates* from whatever affordances we originally provided them in our official designs. The presence of desire paths usually points to a ready opportunity to improve a design and potentially deliver an innovation.

Thus, as we set out to observe our subjects, we should keep a keen eye open for any hint of a workaround being used. If we sense that a workaround is being used, we should zoom in on that situation and explore it further to fully understand the workaround, why it is being used, and what it is about the artifacts that are not delivering on our subjects' needs. We can then take this back into our need-finding conversation.

How Intensifi uses it: Intensifi, while otherwise observing their subjects, also looks for specific workarounds they happen to be using to get around certain limitations and/or restrictions of the methods, tools, and practices they're presently using – both automated and human.

Intensifi's insights: Intensifi learns that certain subjects are indeed using specific workarounds in their life-optimization efforts. Here are some particular workarounds to consider:

- Trying the tools, but then just giving up on them and resigning themselves to not optimizing that particular area of their life (the "oh well" crowd).

- Augmenting the tools with additional add-on tools that are used to undertake more detailed and in-depth analysis of a situation, thereby bringing greater granularity to the decision process they're facing.

- Using multiple competing tools (for the same application) and comparing their outcomes to see how they compare and contrast to each other – as a way of affirming or refuting their respective suggestions.

- Hiring professional advisors to operate the tools for them (or even more capable versions) since they lack confidence in their ability to use them correctly and achieve the right outcomes from them.

- Skipping the tools altogether (even though they own them) and instead relying on professional advisors to guide them in their decision processes using more traditional human heuristics based on their expert experience and guidance.

What these workarounds tell the Intensifi team is that none of the tools by themselves work 100% satisfactorily for users who want to make real-life decisions from them (non-serious users who are just "playing around" don't care as much, but then again, they aren't the majority in this case). So, the tools often require various workarounds to permit serious users to achieve the specific goals they have.

Observing – Customer Hacks

What it is: Whenever *lead users* are involved in a particular situation, they'll often go about developing their *own* innovations around current offerings. This is especially true in environments such as software and online platforms, where lead users are equipped to do their own programming and plug into the platform via APIs.

So, we should study these "hacks" and look for any opportunities to possibly integrate them into our offerings wherever doing so makes sense. This often opens us up to proven new value extensions that can further perpetuate our offerings in the marketplace with very little effort or risk on our part.

How Intensifi uses it: Intensifi, while otherwise observing their subjects, looks for any specific "hacks" their "power users" have developed to get around the specific limitations and/or restrictions of the methods, tools, and practices they're currently using – both automated and human. One way they do this is by "snooping" on certain social media sites such as Reddit and other user forums to find these "power users" and see exactly what they're doing, why, and how.

Intensifi's insights: Intensifi learns that their very advanced subjects are using certain "hacks" in their life-optimization efforts. This mainly involves them building out analysis models (often in spreadsheets) that combine the different inputs from the respective life-optimization tools (investment management tools, career-building tools, shopping tools, and so on) to come up with some sort of a more holistic optimization algorithm that lets these different domains impact each other, thus avoiding (hopefully) any local maxima.

They also find that these subjects are constantly updating their analysis models with current information and data – including things such as stock trends, political events, new products and services, and more. What the team learns is that these subjects are very concerned with their tools and models always having access to the latest and most pertinent information in their analysis – so that their analyses are always accurate at any given time.

They also find that many of these subjects are in network with each other (like a private club, often on social media sites such as Reddit) where they share their hacks. They further find that these subjects are keeping detailed records of their prior analysis and decisions – so that they can always look back on them and have them be explainable, meaning the logic and rationale behind them are fully understandable and defensible.

What these hacks tell Intensifi is that these serious "power users" are dissatisfied with any one tool's ability to make recommendations that take into account *all* of the choices and decisions they have to make and that thus balance those out in a fully optimized and holistic manner. While these particular subjects are a minority in the overall population of subjects, their needs do represent points of value that all subjects would most likely appreciate and value. So, these insights represent a major gap in the marketplace begging to be addressed.

Insights summary – Empathize Observe Methods

The following table summarizes Intensifi's Empathize insights so far, as derived from these **Observe Methods**:

Insights Summary – Empathize – Observe Methods			
Observe Method 1 Business Ethnography	Observe Method 2 Behavioral Archeology	Observe Method 3 Workarounds	Observe Method 4 Customer Hacks

Key Insights

- People use tools at home and at work.
- People socialize their results with others.
- Currently no tool works all around for their entire life (or business).
- People use many work-arounds...
  - giving up
  - augmenting tools with other tools
  - using multiple tools together
  - advisors run the tools for them
  - professional advisors in lieu of tools.
- Advanced users are using 'hacks'... spreadsheets, models, etc.
- Advanced users are constantly updating their models (manually).

Areas of Concern (Pain)

- Trust of Platform – accuracy.
- Satisfaction – ease of use.
- Satisfaction – performance.
- Need for validation...
  - of prescriptions
  - of their final decisions.
- Automatic access to the latest & most pertinent information.
- Current state of the market does not allow balanced trade-off assessments between all factors.

Areas of Desire (Gain)

- Optimizing the different areas of their life (or business).
- Socializing their results with others they trust.
- One tool they can always trust.
- Ability to do balanced trade-off assessments with all factors.

Figure 10.2: Empathize Insights – Observe Methods

Next up are their **Questioning Methods** for additional Empathize insights.

Questioning – Draw the Experience

What it is: This method is used to reveal how people conceive of and order certain activities and/or experiences they encounter. Since different people will often conceptualize these differently from each other, this method can be useful in debunking any one particular set of assumptions around how a particular group of people conceptualize a particular activity or experience.

To carry out this exercise, we'll ask subjects to visualize the activity or experience for us by drawing it out as a diagram. After different subjects have each diagramed their particular conceptualization of the activity or experience, we can start to put together a compilation of the different conceptualizations and thus better understand the *range of ways* in which different subjects conceive and order the activity or experience. This lets us become aware of these conceptualizations and how far apart they *range* – such that when conceiving of a new solution, particularly of the product or service experience involved, we can be sure to take all of these conceptualizations into account, thereby delivering a solution that potentially resonates with the broadest possible range of customers.

How Intensifi uses it: Intensifi hosts a series of five workshops with different cohorts of subjects. In these workshops, the subjects come up with their conceptualization of the overall "life-optimization process." As part of this time, these subjects are asked to draw in isolation, and thereafter, for the rest of this time, they're asked to do so in the presence of others, after which they share their respective drawings with the overall group and explain the details behind them. This, in effect, results in a set of low-fidelity paper prototypes.

Intensifi's insights: Intensifi learns the full range of conceptualization of the overall "life optimization process" from a range of subjects. This tells them that some people, on one end of the spectrum, see it very simply as just taking advice from experts (paid or otherwise) and trusting that advice, while others, on the opposite end of the spectrum, see it as being an incredibly intricate and complex undertaking involving modeling countless scenarios and situations to determine the best options and combining those with an extremely broad range of expert inputs and suggestions based on an extensive amount of research they've done on their own. These are often the more analytical and critical thinkers in the group, which in some cases, though not always, correlates to the level of education they have, with more educated individuals tending toward this end of the spectrum and less educated individuals tending toward the prior end of the spectrum. In between these two ends of the spectrum are the majority of subjects, who hold varying perspectives reflecting differing levels of complexity in the process. This at least informs Intensifi as to the range of different perspectives about the process, and "who's who" in the "pecking order" of users here. From this, they believe they could develop a profiling tool that would let them test would-be customers and learn which type they are, in terms of where they fall on this spectrum of different perspectives (something they may eventually do later on).

Questioning – Free Listing

What it is: Free Listing is used to reveal subjects' associations between a categorical topic and specific terms.

Here, the subjects are provided with a particular category or topic and then asked to write down as many terms as they can relating to that category or topic within some predefined timeframe. Afterward, the subjects' lists are examined in comparison to each other to reveal where certain terms occur *repeatedly* across subjects and what their relative *ordering patterns* are. This reveals which terms, overall, have the strongest association with a particular category or topic. We'll typically debrief afterward with each cohort of subjects to expose the patterns that emerged and discuss what that might say about their relative preferences and expectations for, say, the attributes of a solution to their situation.

As with other Classification Methods like this, the subjects involved must have prior experience with the category or topic of interest so that they can have the necessary context for creating these lists. Otherwise, they'd have no context for being able to do so.

How Intensifi uses it: Intensifi hosts a series of four workshops with different cohorts of subjects. In these workshops, they give the subjects (verbally) a topical word (one at a time) and have them write down – for that word – as many other terms as they can think of relating to the topic, within a set amount of time. In particular, the team has selected eight specific topical words to use – to see what thoughts they each trigger in their subjects' minds. The eight topical words they've chosen are as follows:

1. Success
2. Health
3. Wealth
4. Prestige
5. Happiness
6. Career
7. Marriage
8. Family.

Following each workshop – and after all the workshops have been completed – the team compares the outcomes of each to see what associated terms tended to show up repeatedly, and what their respective ordering patterns were.

Intensifi's insights: Intensifi learns that the following word associations tended to show up – in these orders:

- Success: Power, rank, prestige, wealth, happiness
- Health: Fitness, strength, stamina, success, happiness
- Wealth: Money, real estate, bank accounts, homes, cars, clothing, security
- Prestige: Fame, fortune, wealth, fashion, influence, power
- Happiness: Family, wealth, success, power, influence, security
- Career: Power, rank, success, prestige, recognition, influence, wealth, progress
- Marriage: Love, family, fulfillment, happiness, companionship, security
- Family: Love, happiness, joy, fulfillment, security.

Based on these respective lists, Intensifi can see that their subjects assign different attributes to each area, but that there are also certain *overlaps* across the areas – including those of power, influence, wealth, rank, prestige, success, love, happiness, fulfillment, and security. This starts to clue Intensifi in on the specific attributes of our lives that people may want to ultimately optimize on; at least that's a hypothesis.

Insights summary – Empathize Question Methods

The following table summarizes Intensifi's further Empathize insights derived from these **Question Methods**:

Insights Summary – Empathize – Question Methods		
Question Method 1 Draw The Experience		Question Method 2 Free Listing
Key Insights • A full range of understandings about what overall 'life optimization' or 'business optimization' means to people. • A range of interest / skill / desire on how deep to go & how serious to be about it. • More educated users tend to be more serious / go deeper – and vice versa. • Majority fall into the middle of this spectrum. • Subjects equate different attributes to success; overlaps lie in power, influence, wealth, rank, prestige, love, happiness, fulfillment, and security.	**Areas of Concern (Pain)** • Tools are too simple for some; too complex for others; and varying degrees of these for the majority. • Not 'succeeding' on the metrics that matter most to each user (as established by their goals) means 'not succeeding' at all.	**Areas of Desire (Gain)** • Ability to assess the user type (sophistication) and match them to a comparable solution configuration to use (extensibility). • Ability to attain multiple measures of 'success' – including outcomes like power, influence, wealth, rank, prestige, love, happiness, fulfillment, and security – amongst others.

Figure 10.3: Empathize insights – Question Methods

Next up are their **Study Methods** for additional Empathize insights.

Studying – Beginner's Mindset

What it is: Beginner's Mindset – also known as *Think Like a Four-Year-Old* – is a mental framework in which we put aside everything we know about a given subject or situation, together with all of our preconceived notions about it, so that we can once again see the world through the eyes of a four-year-old and ask some fundamental questions about it, such as "Why is it this way?" and "Why can't it be that way?", forgetting that we are supposed to "know" the answers to these questions. It invites us to abandon all conventional wisdom and start over and challenge every underlying assumption we have about the situation.

Doing this lets us break away from the stronghold of conventional thinking, of the entrenched thought patterns that have led to today's problems and their inadequate solutions, and instead set out on an unlimited number of new thought patterns that presume the things we normally believe are "necessary" are *not necessary*. This opens us up to the sort of 10x breakthrough thinking that leads to disruptive business models that stand current business models on their heads and completely rewrite the rulebook for a certain industry. It's the type of thinking that led to the Sharing Economy business models like those of Uber and Airbnb disrupting the conventional business models of crass consumerism and high-volume consumption.

This is important because it's often the *only way* we can break out of our own "baggage" of past experiences, established mental models, and deep expertise – perspectives buried deep down inside us. While those can be assets under any other circumstance, at the moment, they're our liabilities. Because the world continues to change and societies' prevailing socioeconomic propensities continue to evolve, our assumptions about how the world works end up quickly becoming outmoded – misconceptions and misplaced stereotypes. As such, they artificially limit how well we're able to reconceive the world, as well as constrain how much empathy we're able to develop for those not like us.

To resolve this, we hit the reset button and assume a beginner's mind – a posture of wonder and curiosity in which we're once again truly curious about the world and how it operates. This means we put aside whatever biases and judgments we've otherwise developed over our lifetimes so that we can approach the challenge with radically fresh, open thinking. As we proceed to observe and question our would-be customers, we must do so without bias and without the influence of whatever value judgments our experience has told us to have toward their attitudes, behaviors, circumstances, decisions, values, issues, needs, and motivations. This means there are no right or wrong answers, only answers… the realities of the situation are what they are. This requires us to *question everything*, especially the things we believe we already know and understand about the situation… the things normally familiar to us. We must forget such things and instead ask our would-be customers how *they* perceive the world – get inside their heads and understand how they construct *their worldview*. So, we come at this like a four-year-old would, asking "Why?" about everything, and then behind every answer asking "Why?" yet again. In doing this, we're looking for new patterns, new themes, and new lines of thought – anything that will reveal to us a radically different way of seeing the situation.

When finished, we'll likely have learned a thing or two about how our would-be customers see and process the world (very likely different from how we see and process the world). This lets us completely reframe our thinking into radical new thought patterns that potentially lead to breakthrough business models.

How Intensifi uses it: Intensifi adopts this particular mindset while doing *each* of its respective Observe and Question Method exercises. This helps them set aside all preconceived notions they have about the situation and instead see it with completely new fresh eyes like their subjects do… the way a four-year-old would. That, in turn, opens them up to more fundamental lines of questioning than they would otherwise pursue in this work.

Intensifi's insights: In this case, Intensifi's insights are the same as those mentioned previously, only this method has greatly enhanced those insights, leading to new insights they may not have attained had it not been for layering this mindset (method) on top of them.

Studying – Saturate and Group

What it is: Saturate and Group is an exercise in which the team first works to "space saturate," meaning they saturate their collective workspace with tangible and visual pieces of information by using things such as Post-it™ Notes headlining key findings and photos they've collected of characteristic customers. They then work to cluster those pieces of information together into related *themes*. The first step allows them to space-saturate. The second step allows them to synthesize their collective information together.

Doing this lets the team collectively share the products of their work (observing and questioning fieldwork, market research, and other tasks) and collectively unpack their thoughts and insights arising out of those. They do both of these by saturating their workspace with these pieces of information and then grouping them to see what *patterns* and *themes* emerge from them. There can be *many* such patterns and themes, and thus numerous ways of grouping them. As the team does this – as they synthesize their respective work products together – their collective insights will start to yield a deeper and more meaningful understanding of their subject and that subject's needs. This is important because understanding begets empathy. This ultimately lets the team conceive an all the more well-informed Solution Space whenever that time comes.

Furthermore, space saturation plays an important role in influencing the team's collective psyche. By simply surrounding themselves with this saturation, there's a tendency for them to both embrace a deeper understanding of the subject and be inspired to solve that subject's problem. This is precisely why, inside many organizations, major NPD projects will set up "war rooms" where all of the team's guiding documents are pasted all over the walls – it drives the team members' psyches forward in delivering meaningful results. In this case, the team's collective workspace may be one or more walls in such a room, or possibly mobile workboards that they can move from place to place as their project evolves.

Saturate and Group can be leveraged at various points throughout the Design Thinking process. Using it will help the team always move forward in the same direction and at the same pace so that they can most effectively achieve their objective.

How Intensifi uses it: At the end of their Observation work, the team saturates their workspace with photos, Post-it™ Notes (containing key observations), and other tidbits from their work. They then try to group these into preliminary related thematic groups. Similarly, at the end of their Questioning work, the team further saturates their workspace with additional artifacts, including interview summaries, subject profiles, photos, and more. Then, the team once again works to group all these into related groups reflecting certain key themes that are emerging. This visual arrangement makes the emerging themes all the more visible and real to the team.

Intensifi's insights: In this case, Intensifi's insights are the same as those mentioned previously, only this method has greatly enhanced their ability to formulate these insights and the key themes they represent. This leads to very specific insights that they otherwise wouldn't have attained had it not been for augmenting the rest of their work with this particular method.

Insights summary – Empathize Study Methods

The following table summarizes Intensifi's Empathize insights derived from these **Study Methods**:

Insights Summary – Empathize – Study Methods	
Study Method 1 Beginner's Mindset	Study Method 2 Saturate and Group

Key Insights	Areas of Concern (Pain)	Areas of Desire (Gain)
• The same as before – but greatly enhanced by using these specific methods on top of the others.	• The same as noted previously.	• The same as noted previously.

Figure 10.4: Empathize insights – Study Methods

That wraps it up for Intensifi's Empathize efforts (at least at this point).

Their results – the official hypotheses

The Intensifi team has undertaken these 10 methods, and from them developed the following 10 hypotheses about their subjects and those subjects' needs and desires in this situation:

1. **Holistic optimization**: People want a single platform that lets them optimize all aspects of their lives – their career, marriage, family, wealth, lifestyle, and so on – all in one place and all at once. Also, there are certain key attributes that people ultimately want to optimize throughout this process – crossing over these different domains of their lives. These include power, influence, wealth, rank, prestige, success, love, happiness, fulfillment, and security.

2. **Easy, but extensible, usage**: Most people expect the platform to be easy and intuitive to use – walking them through the process step by step. However, others (more power users) expect the platform to be highly extensible, with "expert mode" options for them to use in gaining more advanced functionality from the platform. So, the platform must feature beginner, intermediate, and advanced user modes to accommodate all users' expectations.

3. **Current data**: People expect such a platform to automatically pull in all the latest and most current data and information from around the world – in areas such as stocks, tax law, political trends, business news, wealth management practices, the newest products and services, and so on – anything and everything relevant to the types of life-optimization decisions they need to make at any given time. This dynamic daily data upload must be entirely automated and transparent to the end user.

4. **Platform augmenters**: People are willing to augment the platform with additional data-collection devices (hardware) that supply the platform with data and allow it to operate optimally and seamlessly for the user – including personal health data collectors, home data collectors, vehicle data collectors (using the OBD ports), and so on.

5. **Platform trust**: People worry about whether or not they can and should trust the platform with their critical life decisions (a major issue). They need some sort of assurance that the prescriptions the platform gives them will be the best ones for them and their lives – without having to wait for 20 years to find out. This also raises the question of liability – if a user can prove that a prescribed course was not the most optimal one for them, can they then sue the platform provider?

6. **Platform socialization**: People want to be able to socialize the recommendations and prescriptions they're being given by the platform so that they can "compare notes" with one another, and seek affirmation or correction on certain specific decisions from individuals they trust.

7. **Platform security**: While socialization is important, people also expect the platform to be incredibly secure – using every known form of advanced user authentication possible – given the vast amount of personal information that will be embedded in it. Otherwise, it can, and likely would, become a haven for Identity Thieves, which would completely and utterly undermine society's trust in the platform.

8. **Platform customization**: People want to be able to customize the platform in ways unique to their particular tastes and needs. While the platform must allow users to define their own unique goals and tastes (in each affected area – such as wealth, career, spouse, city to live in, and others), it also needs to include the ability to define additional, more nuanced, details, such as their risk comfort level, their preferred brands and vendors, and any other constraints they wish to impose on the platform.

9. **Platform ecosystem**: People will value having the platform also be a clearinghouse for a far broader ecosystem of product and service providers so that they can access them directly within the platform. At the same time, this raises the ongoing question of whether or not the ecosystem partners chosen and featured are the best ones for their particular life situations.

10. **Platform financing**: People are willing to pay commissions on the wealth and other gains they acquire on account of using the platform – versus just paying a flat subscription fee.

Business experimentation – deciding and planning how to test our hypotheses

Next, based on the preceding hypotheses, the team wants to select business experiments they can run to test out each of those hypotheses. This is a crucial stage as being able to test out our hypotheses to either prove or disprove them (or else discover their degree of *validity*) is **pivotal** to ultimately arrive at a proper understanding of the problem at hand. So, these experiments must be selected, designed, and executed very carefully so that they can reveal accurate insights to the team.

It's also important that each experiment be designed to be as simple, cost-effective, and quick as possible so that the team can learn *at speed*, with sufficient velocity to move toward convergence quickly and effectively:

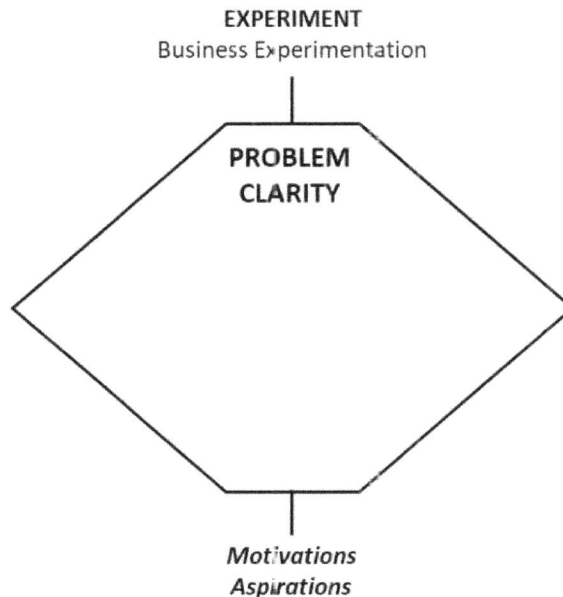

EXPERIMENT
Business Experimentation

PROBLEM CLARITY

Motivations
Aspirations

Figure 10.5: The convergent Define step of the Problem Clarity stage

This point in the process lets the team think through how best to test their respective hypotheses, and thereafter define specific Design Method based experiments to do so.

Understanding Intensifi's goal at this point

At this point, Intensifi's goal is to consider different Design Methods they can leverage to conduct their business experiments – or else design other types of business experiments to use – so that they can execute these Design Methods (and/or other experiments) in the next step to test out their different hypotheses.

Intensifi's test plan – 16 Design Methods

For these respective business experiments, the team is once again calling upon, and building on, certain Design Methods. In particular, and after careful consideration, they've chosen to use the following 16 Design Methods for these experiments (taken from the three method types indicated). They've selected these in particular because they believe these specific methods will allow them to maximize their learning toward the convergence they seek

Observe Methods:

- Contextual Inquiry / Shadowing
- Digital Ethnography
- Cultural Probes

Question Methods:

- Unfocus Groups
- Question Laddering
- Five Whys
- Contextual Interviews
- Empathy Interviews
- Extreme User Interviews

Study Methods:

- Activity Analysis
- Storyboarding
- Cognitive Task Analysis
- Cross-Cultural Comparisons
- Story Share and Capture
- Six Thinking Hats
- Empathy Map.

Convergence – hypothesis testing – determining the real need

Having selected the 16 Design Methods listed previously to use for their business experimentation efforts (and having defined the exact details of each experiment), the team must now actually undertake and execute each of those respective Design Methods / experiments:

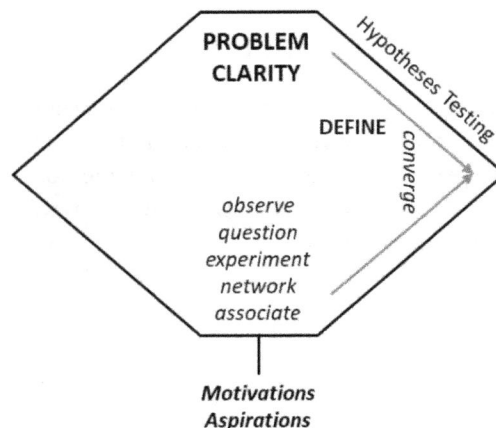

Figure 10.6: The convergent Define step of the Problem Clarity stage

Doing this will take the team through the convergent Define step of the Problem Clarity stage.

Understanding Intensifi's goal at this point

At this point, Intensifi's goal is to **test** their respective hypotheses to ultimately discover *which* of them are accurate and correct, and which of them are less so – and therefore which hypothesis, overall, best describes their subject and the situation they're encountering.

This "one best hypothesis" will usually end up being an amalgamation of different hypotheses mashed together into one. In any event, the final hypothesis that's selected must be capable of describing the situation at hand and all the causalities associated with it. This means it must be capable of fully articulating the exact *aspirations* and *motivations* our subject has, and perhaps what intrinsic *needs* and *values* those stem out of – as well as what *functional*, *emotional*, *social*, and *transformational* jobs they are trying to accomplish in the process.

This is an insight that can only be arrived at via appropriate testing through business experimentation.

Intensifi's testing work – the 16 Design Methods

To carry out the work of testing their hypotheses, the team has chosen to employ the 16 Design Methods noted earlier. In each case, they will undertake these methods with an appropriate number of subjects (which can sometimes be large).

Let's go over each of these methods, how the team is using them, and what outcomes they achieve from them – including their conclusions about their respective hypotheses.

Observing – Contextual Inquiry / Shadowing

What it is: Contextual Inquiry, also known as Rapid Ethnography or Shadowing, is similar to Business Ethnography except that now we move much *closer* to our subjects, to observe them more closely firsthand. This allows us to obtain an up-close exploration of their routines, rituals, habits, interactions, and natural language, including an understanding of the meanings they ascribe to certain activities and their associated artifacts. This is a useful way of revealing otherwise unknown issues inside people's rituals and the circumstances they encounter in particular contexts. It may also reveal opportunities to deliver innovations that help them in these situations by positively affecting or complementing their behaviors and actions.

Since we'll be engaging up close with our subjects, tagging along with them (possibly shadowing them), this is no longer an inconspicuous at-a-distance observation, but rather a direct, up-close observation. As such, we must secure their permission and cooperation since they'll be aware that they're being observed. Once we've secured that, the next thing we must do is engage with them in a way that puts them at ease so that they can undertake their normal routines without modification – something that's important to us so that we can make *accurate observations* of them and these situations.

First, we'll walk them through a standard set of activities designed to put them at ease, such as introducing ourselves and our effort and engaging them in routine conversation to build trust and rapport with them (which gains us access to their natural habitats and activities without having them be altered in any way). After that, we'll work to evoke stories from them about specific experiences they've had, to explore their emotions, values, and motivations. We'll often question specific statements they make – to draw out even more detailed nuance and insights about their values and motivations – and ask questions such as, "Why was that important to you?"

In undertaking this method, we will want to spend as much time as we can interacting with as many different subjects as possible who have relevant experiences. Doing so will allow us to collect the breadth and depth of insights we need to ensure that our overall observations can be properly *generalized* to a whole population.

How Intensifi uses it: Intensifi's team shadows several different subjects to see how they use the different life-optimization tools and platforms, and why they do the things they do. They also organize certain group meetups for power users to use the tools in proximity to each other so that they can compare notes with one another and learn even more insights from shadowing them in that particular context.

Intensifi's insights: Based on directly shadowing these individuals, both in isolation and in the group setting, Intensifi learns that the hypotheses they've set forth do seem to be holding water thus far. None of these hypotheses were refuted, and no additional hypotheses were created from this effort.

Observing – Digital Ethnography

What it is: Digital Ethnography is a type of Contextual Inquiry that's undertaken *online* or via a *mobile app* and intends to innovate around an online or mobile environment, such as those used in social media sites, news sites, and gaming platforms. The objective is to understand both users' *stated* needs, desires, aspirations, and priorities, as well as their *actual* online behaviors, so that we can then correlate the two for actionable insights.

To undertake Digital Ethnography, we usually do two things. First, we make direct online or in-app *observations* of actual user behaviors (actions and/or conversations) and document these accordingly, including the contexts, environments, activities, and any unique vocabulary involved. Second, we may interview select users to better *understand* their behaviors and the needs, desires, aspirations, and priorities behind these behaviors. Putting these together, we can form a relatively complete composite of these users' psychographic profiles. As in physical ethnography, these may be different for each respective market segment. Using these insights, we can then design better online and mobile user experiences for users.

How Intensifi uses it: Before engaging in this method, Intensifi implemented an online observation tool that allows them to remotely observe users' activities inside certain platforms, as well as direct permission from them to do so. Given these, Intensifi spends time "watching" how users use these platforms and tools and makes copious amounts of notes from that. Immediately afterward, they engage in conversations with each user to discuss what they did on the platform, how they did it, why they did it, and how satisfied they were with both the process and the outcome they achieved.

Intensifi's insights: Vased on doing this type of digital observation and follow-up discussion, Intensifi learns what these subjects liked and didn't like about each platform – both the activity of using it and the outcome it produced for them. This gave the team some further insight into specific UI considerations to use later on. Otherwise, they found that the hypotheses they set forth seemed to be holding water. None were refuted per se, and no additional hypotheses were generated from the effort.

Observing – Cultural Probes

What it is: Cultural Probes is a field-study method where we go out and observe and study different *cultures* firsthand. This lets us make direct observations of each cultural group of interest and thereby develop a deeper understanding of their respective rituals, environments, and artifacts, and how they compare and contrast to one another. That, in turn, will help us to better understand each respective group's unique values, beliefs, and attitudes.

Depending on how many cultural groups we want to study, how much time we have, and how many team members we have, we can disperse our team in several ways. Generally speaking, we'll undertake a Cultural Probe by assigning each person on the team a particular cultural group to study, and then have them go out to make direct observations of that group – collecting evidence of behaviors and artifacts occurring in the group. Afterward, we study these to evaluate the different behaviors and artifacts, and thereby develop certain perceptions of the values, beliefs, and attitudes involved. As needed, we may follow these up with direct interviews to fill in more details around specific observations and develop a richer understanding of them.

Having a Cultural Probe of the different cultural groups we must solve for is important when the time comes for us to formulate our Point of View. That Point of View must always, in all situations, be informed by all of the cultural factors and considerations the solution has to address.

How Intensifi uses it: Intensifi sends out members of its team – in pairs – to get closer to certain specific "cultural groups" in their subject pool. In this case, these "cultural groups" are segmented according to life stage – high schoolers, college students, early young professionals, early-mid-career professionals, late-mid-career professionals, late-career professionals, early retirees, and late retirees – eight groups in all. Each pair of observers spends time getting closer to their specific group and observing them do the things that align with the aspiration of "life optimization," including conventional activities such as traditional research and courtship. As they do so, they take pictures and lots of notes on the rituals, activities, environments, and artifacts they're seeing. When done, they reconnect to compare notes with each other about the respective groups.

Intensifi's insights: Intensifi analyzes these observations via the Cross-Cultural Comparisons method. See that method (later in this chapter) for their resultant insights.

Insights summary – Define Observe Methods

The following table summarizes Intensifi's Define insights so far, as derived from these **Observe Methods**:

Insights Summary – Define – Observe Methods		
Observe Method 1 **Contextual Inquiry**	**Observe Method 2** **Digital Ethnography**	**Observe Method 3** **Cultural Probes**
Key Insights • There are certain things that users like & dislike about each existing platform – both their use & the results they produce. • The 10 hypotheses appear valid. • None are invalidated. • No new hypotheses generated.	**Areas of Concern (Pain)** • Bad UI designs. • Unreliable and thus unusable platform results.	**Areas of Desire (Gain)** • Certain specific UI design and configuration details. • Reliable, and therefore usable, outcomes from the solution.

Figure 10.7: Define insights – Observe Methods

Next up are their **Questioning Methods** for additional Define insights.

Questioning – Unfocus Groups

What it is: An Unfocus Group is similar to a Focus Group in that it consists of a workshop setting with different individuals (typically 1, 2, or 3 days long). The similarities end there, however.

First of all, in an Unfocus Group, an attempt is made to constitute the group with as *diverse* a set of individuals as possible, including young, old, wealthy, poor, educated, uneducated, and diverse races – leading to a diverse set of perceptions. This highly diverse group is then tasked with working together in the workshop.

Secondly, a stimulating range of materials is used in which the participants are asked to create various artifacts together (from those materials) representing different conceptualizations of the topic involved. Some of these may be warm-up / ice-breaker exercises, but they will become increasingly more challenging.

The idea is to initially help everyone release their inhibitions, but eventually open up to much more creative thinking. Ultimately, the workshop seeks to encourage creative, rich – and in particular, *divergent* – contributions from the participants. Throughout the workshop, and particularly toward its conclusion, the workshop leaders will lead the group in a very engaging, diverse, and thought-provoking conversation about the topic of concern, trying to draw out as many diverse perceptions and opinions about it as possible, and have these each build on one another to ultimately produce a rich mosaic of shared understanding.

The main takeaway here is a deeper insight into the range of different perspectives around the topic of concern. This can potentially help us formulate new solution concepts that resonate with the widest possible audience.

How Intensifi uses it: Intensifi assembles as broad and as diverse of a group as they can find, to come in and engage with them in a two-day Unfocus Group. On the morning of Day One, they talk about the overall goals, aspirations, and motivations involved in trying to optimize a person's life – or at least the various aspects of it. On the afternoon of Day One, they ask the group to create artifacts individually (from the materials they're provided). On the morning of Day Two, they ask the group to create artifacts once more, but this time doing so together (again, using the materials they're provided). On the afternoon of Day Two, they lead the group in a conversation talking about these topics and having them explain their different artifacts to the group. All of this – both the artifacts and the conversations – reveals the breadth of mental models and conceptualizations of these topics that are represented by such a broad and diverse group.

Intensifi's insights: Intensifi learns that, while these individuals are very diverse from one another, coming from all sorts of different backgrounds and groups, there is a bit of a shared value among them – namely that everyone involved, no matter who they are, where they've been, and where they think they're going wants to, in some way or another, better optimize their life. Each of them has different goals for doing so… some want to optimize their marriage the most, others want to optimize their health the most, others yet want to optimize their career the most, and so on. But regardless of their actual goal, it seems to be a universal truth that they all want to optimize their life in some way. Moreover, Intensifi learns that even though different people have different primary goals for doing this, they are not averse to having other areas of their lives also optimized at the same time. That just becomes the "icing on the cake" for them… a surprise and delight element. These are all incredibly helpful and useful insights for Intensifi.

Questioning – Question Laddering

What it is: Question Laddering is a planning method that's used to plan out the series of interview questions someone will be using in their interviews. It suggests certain specific question *constructs* to start with, thus allowing us to ensure we're capturing the right *types* of questions we need to get the insights we're looking for. Having these questions planned out in a structured manner ahead of time allows us to then focus on actually *asking* them during the interviews so that we can get the answers we need. This allows us to hone in on the specific aspects of the situation we're most interested in learning about.

In this method, the subject list (across the top) is *Who, What, Where, When, Why,* and *How*. Similarly, the state / action list (along the left-hand side) is *Was, Did, Is, Can, Will, Would,* and *Might*. These are matrixed together so that each box yields an individual question construct. These constructs are then used as the *seeds* for the actual questions we intend to ask.

Some of these questions deal with *past* states and past actions (was, did), some with *present* states and present actions (is, can), and some with *future* states and future actions (will, would, might). This past/present/future nature flows from left to right, making the questions on the left (those about the past) simpler and thus easier to answer, and those on the right more complex and thus more challenging to answer. Those in the middle (about the present) have a more moderate level of complexity.

This offers us a quick and simple way to structure our interview questions, as well as to combine questions in a variety of ways so that we can uncover more complex answers about the situation we seek to learn about. Used properly, it lets us chain together a set of questions that go progressively deeper and deeper into the situation until we're finally able to get to the real heart of the matter – the "a-ha point" we seek.

How Intensifi uses it: The Intensifi team uses this method to plan out the different interview questions they'll use later on when undertaking Contextual, Empathy, and Extreme User Interviews. This seeds those methods with question sets such as, "When do you find these platforms and tools helpful?", "Why do you tend to use these platforms and tools?", "Who else do you know that would benefit from using these platforms and tools, and why so?", "In what ways are these platforms and tools meeting, or not meeting, your present needs?", "Can you think of ways these platforms and tools might be even more valuable to those who use them?", and so on – for a large array of different questions to explore under different contexts.

Intensifi's insights: Being that this is a planning exercise rather than a learning exercise, Intensifi doesn't learn anything directly from it, other than how best to think about their hypotheses and the questions they have surrounding those, so that they can frame their questions accordingly.

Questioning – Five Whys

What it is: Five Whys originated in the **Toyota Production System** (TPS) as a problem-solving methodology. In that context, it was used to drill down into a problem to get to its root causes. Here, instead of being used to solve problems, it's used to probe people for their truest values, priorities, and motivations. As such, it isn't used in isolation, but rather in a broader interview context, such as in the ones Intensifi will carry out.

In Five Whys, we probe down into the problem and people's perceptions of it by repeatedly asking them questions such as "Why?," "Why is that?", "What caused this?", or "Why is that important to you?" This forces them to reexamine their motivations and reveal the underlying reasons for their attitudes and behaviors.

Drilling down into people's motivations allows us to continually peel back the layers covering up their deeper underlying motivations until we eventually expose their deepest motivations. Such motivations tend to reveal people's truest needs and desires. This is important because we'll otherwise end up focusing on the *symptoms* of the problem, rather than the real problem itself. In this context, we must expose the real underlying needs, motivations, and values involved so that we can address them at an appropriate level.

By asking these questions repeatedly – Why? Why? Why? Why? Why? – whether three times, five times, seven times, or however many times at each step, we'll move down *one level of need* until we eventually get to the level of need we're looking for and can act on. In this way, we gain the insights needed to be able to address the real problem in a way that can make a real impact in these individuals' lives.

How Intensifi uses it: Intensifi – in the context of the interviews it eventually undertakes – incorporates this act of drilling down into their subject's underlying motivations – one layer at a time – until they eventually get down to these people's actual, real motivations, aspirations, needs, and desires. This shows them what they *actually* need to act on, rather than trying to act on any specific symptom they've otherwise observed.

Intensifi's insights: Being that this is an embedded activity to be used inside the interview methods, and not a direct learning activity itself, Intensifi does not learn anything directly from it. Thinking about it does, however, prepare the team for being able to use the practice and ask these types of questions when they are inside those interviews later.

Questioning – Contextual Interviews

What it is: Contextual Interviews are direct user interviews that are conducted *within* the context of the situation of interest. They involve going out into the field and engaging directly with our subjects *in their context*. This contrasts with us bringing them from the outside (their context) into our organization (our context) to discuss their situation. Even if we attempt to reconstruct their context via a simulated environment in our lab, the result isn't generally the same as they will not be in the same mental frame of mind there as they are when in their context. Therefore, direct fieldwork is mandatory to get an accurate read on this.

Contextual Interviews are similar to Contextual Inquiry, except that instead of shadowing our subjects across a certain period and space to observe them, we're now focused on understanding a more limited set of activities but in a deeper manner. Therefore, we'll station ourselves in a confined setting where we can observe any number of subjects coming and going throughout a particular situation or experience. From that vantage point, we will first observe subjects engaging in the situation and note the specific behaviors they exhibit (what they say, what they do, how they interact, their body language, and so on). After this, we'll then select some of the subjects and engage them in an interview discussion about the situation or experience – what they perceived happened, why those things happened, what they did, and why they did what they did. So, any shadowing will be limited in scope – breadth is traded off for depth around the situation or experience.

The sort of dialog these interviews generate, while seemingly straightforward, can reveal important gaps between subjects' expectations (their desired or intended outcomes) and the actual outcomes they get. It can also reveal their thought processes, including those behind any workarounds they had to use. These often end up being nuanced observations and insights that can only be had when pursued *inside* the context of the situation. Otherwise, they'd be lost if we tried to recreate them after the fact in another setting – meaning that for all practical purposes, it's impossible to gain these insights in any other way.

How Intensifi uses it: Intensifi observes certain subjects engaging in more traditional "life optimization" tasks (sometimes without their knowledge), as well as other subjects engaging in the use of various "life optimization" platforms (in that case with their knowledge). In both cases, after observing each group, they approach and engage certain subjects to discuss what just took place... what they did, why they did it, what they said, why they said it, what outcome they were trying to achieve, what results they ended up with, how that made them feel, how satisfied they were with the process they used, whether or not they believe there might be a better process to use, and so on. Intensifi also takes the opportunity here to discuss the tenets of their respective hypotheses with these subjects – asking them how they believe others will perceive each of them (as opposed to asking how they perceive them since the former tends to elicit a different cognitive response than does the latter, and thus tends to produce much more accurate and reliable answers).

Intensifi's insights: Intensifi learns that the outcome people are (ultimately) trying to achieve in each case is the optimization of some situation associated with the particular domain of life they were just trying to operate on. They also learn that, in the majority of cases, these individuals were not satisfied with the process they felt they had to use to pursue such aims and were only moderately satisfied with the outcomes they attained from them. In all cases, they believed that these outcomes were only moderately optimal for the short term, and in no cases were necessarily optimal for the long term, as neither they nor these practices had any way of foreseeing the long-term future to even begin to estimate such an outcome. Finally, from testing their hypotheses on these subjects, they learn that while all subjects value most of the tenets they've put forth, certain subjects value some of those tenets more so than they do the others.

Questioning – Empathy Interviews

What it is: Empathy Interviews are direct interviews, though not necessarily conducted inside the context of the situation or experience of interest. They're often conducted *after the fact* in an alternative setting. This is useful for those situations where it isn't practical to engage subjects in situ in a certain context, such as when they're running late for a plane, in an emergency scenario, or when dealing with situations that play out over a long period, such as loyalty programs do.

Aside from being conducted *outside* the context, we're trying to uncover and understand our subjects' thoughts, emotions, and motivations, as well as their perceptions of their own and others' behaviors. By understanding these motivations and perceptions, and the choices they make, we can better understand their needs and thus know how to deliver an innovation that speaks to those needs.

There are certain key practices we must adhere to whenever we engage in empathy interviews:

- Always ask open-ended questions that elicit further discussion. Never ask closed "yes or no" questions.

- Keep questions concise; otherwise, subjects can get lost inside long, complex questions.

- Ask only one question at a time, on only one topic at a time. Never layer multiple questions together, as doing so can cause confusion.

- Always ask neutral questions. Never use wording that would suggest a right or wrong answer as subjects will almost always go for "the right answer" to satisfy their perceived expectations and avoid embarrassment.

- Never, ever, suggest answers to a question. There is often the compulsion, whenever a subject pauses or hesitates, to offer a "for instance…" Do not do this as subjects will often – wittingly or unwittingly – go along with whatever suggestions we make to seem agreeable with their perceived expectations. If the answers are not *their answers*, then don't use them.

- Always speak in terms of *specific* instances and occurrences… never in generalities. Draw this out with queries such as "Tell me about a time when you…"

- Encourage subjects to tell stories and draw those out. Listen – inside those stories – for their tensions, pains, and frustrations. Try to understand what obstacle or unmet/unsatisfied need triggered those emotions and how intense they were. Seek to understand precisely what expectations were unmet, and why those expectations were important to them. Even if their stories aren't true, they reveal how these individuals understand and think about the world (their worldview), as well as their cognitive processes in processing their perceptions of reality. That is what we're after, rather than any absolute truth per se.

- Strive to understand the "why" in each conversation. Even if we believe we know the answer, ask subjects why they do the things they do and why they say the things they say. Also, ask them why a certain outcome is important to them (which reveals their values and motivations). Sometimes, their answers will surprise us.

- Allow room for silence – the "pregnant pause" or "7-minute lull." While we'll often feel the compulsion to fill such gaps with more questions, we have to check ourselves and not do this. Silence is often the golden opportunity for subjects to recompose their thoughts and undertake the necessary introspections they require to recall prior feelings about a situation, which may reveal something deeper yet from within their subconscious. This silence also imposes a certain pressure on them to "come clean" about the situation and thus be more forthcoming than they might otherwise be.

- Pay close attention to subjects' body language, facial expressions, and nonverbal cues. These reveal their true emotions about the situation, regardless of what they say otherwise. If so trained, we can use **Neuro-Linguistic Processing (NLP)** to further read their body language and infer insights from it.

- Watch for the inevitable *inconsistencies*. What people say they do and what they actually do are often very different from each other. Such inconsistencies reveal insights into the *dissonance* between their cognitive and visceral behaviors. This sometimes translates into having to deliver *one innovation* but yet market it as a *different innovation* so that people don't get hung up on their subconscious biases.

- Allow a line of questioning to go on for as long as it needs to get down to the nugget we're seeking, or until the subject has exhausted their ability to answer it further.

- Be prepared to capture subjects' responses. Since it's impossible to simultaneously engage a subject and take detailed notes of our conversation, it's generally best to have two researchers – one to act as an interviewer, asking the questions and steering the conversation, and the other to act as a scribe, recording the replies. Alternatively, we can use a recorder to record the conversation and transcribe it later on.

Moreover, given that the time we have with each subject is limited and thus valuable, we must extract the greatest possible value out of that time. This requires us to be prepared by planning out the specific flow and sequence of questions we'll ask. While we may not get each one of those questions asked, and while we should allow room for spontaneous subject-led conversations (which sometimes produce serendipitous insights), we should nevertheless have an engagement plan in place and be prepared to carry it out. That plan should aggregate related questions together and order these questions in a way that they build on each other to create a deepening level of insight, especially around our subjects' emotions. They should allow for a natural flow in the conversation – including allowing adequate open space for the inevitable "why" and "tell me more" set of questions. This allows us to most effectively walk our subject through a coherent, flowing conversation that builds out a useful story to interpret.

How Intensifi uses it: Intensifi invites a large number of subjects whom they've gotten to know through this journey, to engage them in Empathy Interviews. In each case, they use the questions they prepared earlier (via Question Laddering) to guide the interview conversation, trying in all cases to elicit stories from these individuals' experiences. They have these subjects draw out those stories to reveal their emotions involved, what ultimately drove such emotions, and how they each related to that individual's motivations and aspirations for doing these things, as well as how well those motivations and aspirations (and thus their needs) were and were not satisfied in each case. Intensifi also uses this opportunity to weave in certain questions about their hypotheses – to test those hypotheses against these individuals' experiences.

Intensifi's insights: Intensifi learns that people's real motivation and aspiration (and thus need) in each case has been to optimize some particular aspect of their life (even if they didn't necessarily call it that). They also learn that in almost all cases, there were emotions of hopefulness, partial satisfaction, and (quite often) disappointment. In the latter case, this was because either the methods or tools they used didn't deliver on what they had hoped for, or if they did, the individuals had no way of correlating such outcomes back to those methods and tools, versus being just sheer coincidence, which led to disappointment either way.

Intensifi also found that the hypotheses they've set forth seem to be holding water – except for possibly one – dealing with paying commissions to finance the solution (some subjects seemed to have strong reservations about people's willingness to pay that way). Otherwise, none of the other hypotheses were refuted, and no additional hypotheses were generated from the interviews.

Questioning – Extreme User Interviews

What it is: Extreme User Interviews involves – as its name suggests – interviewing "extreme users." Extreme users generally consist of two groups:

- **First-Time Users**: Those least familiar with the product or service.
- **Lead Users**: Those most familiar with the product or service.

These two types of users sit at opposite ends of the user spectrum.

First-Time Users have little or no exposure to the product or service of concern and thus know very little or nothing about it. They tend to bring *fresh eyes* to using the product or receiving the service.

Lead Users, on the other hand, are the "innovators" on the Diffusion-of-Innovation adoption curve – those who are the first to buy the latest version of an offering and who thereafter become its most engaged and prolific users. Therefore, they are extremely familiar with the offering. These users are highly valuable to us – because they push those products and services to their extreme limits, serving as a real-world source of functional validation for them. If the offering has any hidden shortcomings, these users will find them (and let us know about them). In this sense, Lead Users can be some of a business's greatest allies in ensuring the efficacy of the offerings they offer, which is precisely why some organizations explicitly sign up Lead Users and have them field test new products and services for them before rolling them out to the broader market – such as when athletic equipment companies sign up athletes to test out new equipment before making them widely available, or when airlines first try out a new service on extreme frequent flyers to get their feedback.

Both of these extreme users – First-Time Users and Lead Users – are capable of uncovering and highlighting design deficiencies and providing suggestions for improvements and refinements in an offering. First-Time Users do so out of a pure framework of what their *needs* are. Lead Users do so out of an innate understanding of what they believe the offering *should do*. Likewise, given time, both of these users will likely come up with certain workarounds for the offering – First-Time Users because it does not fully satisfy every job they need to get done and thus they engage in extreme behaviors; Lead Users because they want to "hack" the offering and make it even better. Because extreme users' needs are often amplified relative to ordinary users, their workarounds and "hacks" are often much more notable and extreme as well.

So, we should identify and engage extreme users and have them use our product (perhaps a prototype) or receive our service (perhaps a simulation) and then evaluate their experiences, both by observing them in context and by interviewing them afterward. By studying their workarounds and "hacks," we can often draw out more clearly what their real needs are – needs that may not surface when dealing with ordinary users in the middle of the Adoption Curve (the Early and Late Adopters), but needs that nevertheless apply to the entire population. This additional clarity around needs can then serve as the inspiration for new opportunities to deliver better value and better meet all users' needs. Extreme users can also sometimes spur more radical new ideas that we can capitalize on. In those cases, we need only ensure these will resonate with the ordinary users we are otherwise designing for (and who represent the bulk of our buying population).

Given that products and services often have numerous aspects to them, at times, it may be difficult to find truly extreme users for all of these aspects. To make the process simpler, we can hone in on certain specific aspects of the offering and then work to identify a panel of extreme users for just those aspects. These aspects would relate to a specific user need being addressed.

How Intensifi uses it: Intensifi invites a large number of extreme "lead users" they've gotten to know through their journey to engage in these particular interviews. In each case, they use the questions they prepared earlier (via Question Laddering) to guide the conversation so that, in each case, they can elicit stories from the individuals' experiences. Since these individuals are extreme Lead Users (of different platforms and tools), it is very easy to draw out their (very specific) expectations of these platforms and tools (as well as their underlying motivations, aspirations, and needs) – as well as their intense frustrations and disappointments with using their platforms and tools – not to mention their countless hacks and workarounds for dealing with their respective limitations and restrictions (some being quite arcane). Intensifi in particular uses this opportunity to test their hypotheses with these Lead Users – to learn their unique viewpoints on them, given their in-depth expertise and experience surrounding the hypotheses.

Intensifi's insights: Intensifi learns that these Lead Users' true motivation and aspiration is to optimize their lives as much as possible and that they are incredibly frustrated with several aspects of them, including that they have to use several different unrelated platforms and tools to optimize each area of their lives (one for health and fitness, one for wealth management, one for career planning, one for relationships, and so on), that none of them share data, and thus at best allow them to *suboptimize* their lives, and that, in general, they all have specific limitations and restrictions that prevent these individuals from extracting as much value as they'd like to from them. So, overall, they're disappointed and frustrated that there isn't one platform or tool that lets them do this in the way they want – to optimize their overall life, holistically and thoroughly! When asked "Why continue to use these different platforms and tools?", the answer seems to be for lack of anything better to use in their decision processes. They feel it's high time someone used the power of AI available to us today to do just this! Many of them have offered to share their models and hacks with any organization willing to do so (or try to do so).

Intensifi also learned from these Lead Users that all of their hypotheses appear to be accurate – except for the one noted earlier. In particular, these Lead Users affirmed the fact that even they, the Lead Users, wouldn't be willing to pay commissions on their gains from using such a platform, but would only be willing to pay a set subscription price on it – as agreeing to do otherwise (pay commissions) could open them up to a lot of uncertainty around what they were obligated to pay, and they weren't willing to sign up to that level of uncertainty. Thus, the need for certainty (a known subscription price) was more important to them than the possible upside of amassing great wealth from the platform. None of their other hypotheses were refuted, and no additional hypotheses were generated from these interviews.

Insights summary – Define Question Methods

The following table summarizes Intensifi's further Define insights derived from these **Question Methods**:

Insights Summary – Define – Question Methods					
Question Method 1	Question Method 2	Question Method 3	Question Method 4	Question Method 5	Question Method 6
Unfocus Groups	Question Laddering	Five Whys	Contextual Interviews	Empathy Interviews	Extreme User Interviews

Key Insights	Areas of Concern (Pain)	Areas of Desire (Gain)
• Despite all of the diversity involved – all users share a common goal... to optimize in some way. • Their specific (relative) goals differ, but inside those goals they all want the right balanced formula for optimization & success. • People appreciate having their secondary, tertiary, and so on goals also optimized alongside their primary goal(s). • Currently no way of correlating *actual outcomes* to prescriptions. • 9 of the hypotheses appear valid. • 1 hypothesis appears to be invalid. • No new hypotheses generated.	• Not being able to optimize their life (or business) holistically according to their goal prioritization in a balanced, harmonious way. • Frustrated with having to use several noninteracting tools to optimize each area independently (non-correlated), resulting in unbalanced trade-offs that don't achieve their goal priorities. • Emotions of disappointment and hopelessness from the current tools.	• Having each area of their life (or business) optimized according to their goal rankings – first priority, second priority, etc. • One solution that optimizes *all areas simultaneously* in an integrated, balanced way – so as to achieve their goal priorities. • A way to correlate *actual outcomes* to the solution's prescriptions (causality).

Figure 10.8: Define insights – Question Methods

Next up are their **Study Methods** for additional Define insights.

Studying – Activity Analysis

What it is: Activity Analysis is a planning method that's used to plan out insights development work. In particular, we select a specific scenario or experience we want to explore and then, based on its flow, develop a comprehensive list of the stakeholders, participants, actions, tasks, artifacts, and interactions involved. Once we've identified all of the stakeholders and participants and the particular actions/tasks/interactions they're each involved in, we can map out a plan of action for the order in which we need to interview them, as well as the issues we need to explore with them, and in what order.

This is an effective planning method that we can use at any point in our Design Thinking work, but it has particular usefulness up front in planning out our empathy research for Problem Clarification. It also becomes a part of our broader Insights Plan, which lays out all of the Research and Design Methods that we intend to use, including any Market and/or Secondary Research efforts we intend to pursue.

How Intensifi uses it: Intensifi studies how they have observed subjects attempting to undertake "life optimization" activities – including both traditional tasks and the use of digital tools. From this, they've mapped out the specific stakeholders, participants, actions, tasks, artifacts, and interactions involved. This helps them to ensure they're not missing anything relevant in their respective interviews, observations, and analyses there of.

Intensifi's insights: Intensifi identifies the following attributes:

- **Primary stakeholders**: Platform vendors, service providers (advisors, and so on).

- **Secondary stakeholders**: Banks, retailers, manufacturers, fitness clubs, social clubs, employers, and more.

- **Participants**: Direct users, indirect users (spouses, families, coworkers), and those in relationships with users.

- **Actions**: Subscribing to digital platforms, securing professional services, and making and acting on decisions.

- **Tasks**: Using and maintaining digital platforms, using professional services, and socializing results.

- **Artifacts**: Digital platforms, outcome results, and reports (with recommendations/prescriptions).

- **Interactions**: Users with each other, users with their social connections, and users with service providers.

Intensifi ensures that they cover all of these attributes in their respective observations, interviews, and analyses thereof – especially as they try to test their respective hypotheses.

Studying – Storyboarding

What it is: Storyboarding is a visual method that's used to illustrate a particular *storyline* (generally for a group engaged in a workshop or other similar event) – just as has been done in the movie-production field for decades.

Storyboards are used to illustrate a particular customer experience or scenario so that the group can develop a shared understanding of that experience or scenario. Often, after we've storyboarded an *existing or baseline scenario*, we explore *revisions* of that scenario that aim to resolve a particular challenge or obstacle and thus better meet our subjects' needs.

Storyboards typically involve a set of discrete illustrations depicting a sequence of *events*, or competing or complimentary *scenarios*. They serve to illustrate the *interactions* that are happening in a particular experience or scenario – where the subject exhibits particular behaviors, what the result of that is, what behaviors the organization / product / service exhibits in response, the results of that, and so on. As such, storyboards are an incredibly useful tool for bringing the customer experience to life so that we can wrap our minds around it and the needs it points to, and then begin to think about ways in which to address the shortcomings it presents.

If desired, we can employ a skilled illustrator to facilitate the storyboarding exercise for us (though in reality, anyone can create a storyboard, so long as their illustrations are comprehensible to the group). So, the need for artistic skills is not a limitation preventing us from using the method. However, if those skills are available to us, using them can often make for a more fun and engaging storyboarding exercise.

How Intensifi uses it: Intensifi holds a workshop with its core team and certain trusted external advisors to explore – and ultimately storyboard – what they've seen to be subjects' attempts at undertaking "life optimization" type activities. They retain a professional Illustrator to help them with this.

Intensifi's insights: Intensifi identifies two distinct storyboards – one that focuses on people using more traditional (human analog) methods for this activity, and one that focuses on people using more modern digital platforms and tools for the activity.

In each case, the team storyboards the user's journey showing exactly what they do, what happens along the way as they do these things, what their respective reactions and emotions to those events are, and what occurs by the end of their journey. Doing this helps everyone on the team appreciate the user journey these individuals are encountering – including, very importantly, their emotions along the way. That, in turn, helps the team to have greater empathy for these subjects, which serves them well in working through their hypothesis testing. It also lets them see *where* and *why* most of these hypotheses should be true.

Studying – Cognitive Task Analysis

What it is: Cognitive Task Analysis is a User Research method that's used to understand subjects' mental models and cognitive processing tasks for engaging in a particular scenario or experience. Here, after carefully studying how subjects engage in that particular scenario or experience, we list and summarize – for each touchpoint – their respective sensory inputs (visual, auditory, tactile, olfactory, and gustatory), decision points, and resultant actions. The idea is to better understand their actions and cognitive processes in completing a particular task.

In any particular scenario or experience, these actions and cognitive processes happen through an intertwined set of events occurring between the subject and whatever "system" they are interacting with (including both human and non-human systems). Here, the subject begins with a particular cognitive process, then initiates a set of actions, after which the system responds, including possibly giving feedback indications to the subject, followed by the subject perceiving and interpreting those indications through additional cognitive processing, after which they act again, with this whole process repeating until the scenario/experience has completed.

By studying the cognitive task processing of subjects engaging in a particular scenario or experience, we can develop insights into their needs. We can also discover where in that scenario or experience certain obstacles or bottlenecks occur, which can lead to error states in which the situation does not resolve correctly, and thus the subjects' needs are not adequately met.

This method allows us to build out a much more complete understanding of our subjects' mental model of their situation – their understanding of themselves, others, their environment, and the "system" they are interacting with – thus allowing us to better understand them and their situation.

How Intensifi uses it: Here, Intensifi focuses on subjects who use digital platforms and tools. In these cases, they walk through the "dance" that these users do as they go back and forth in using a particular platform or tool. As they do this, at each touchpoint, they map out what these individuals are thinking cognitively and feeling emotionally, as well as what they see, hear, physically feel, smell, and taste, what their perceptions of those inputs are, what they do and/or say, how the system they're interacting with responds to them, and how this cycle repeats until the situation is completed.

Intensifi's insights: Intensifi sees that there is a *lot* of cognitive processing that has to occur in this process, as well as a *lot* of interactions with the particular platform or tool being used. They also note that this creates many possibilities for highly negative emotions in the process, with only a few opportunities for positive emotions (meaning the scales are, in general, weighted toward a more negative than positive experience).

In terms of their hypotheses, understanding these things lets the team see why and their first eight hypotheses are most likely to be accurate.

Studying – Cross-Cultural Comparisons

What it is: Cross-Cultural Comparisons is a study method in which we try to draw out the differences between different cultural groups in terms of their values, attitudes, and behaviors, as well as the unique artifacts they use to demonstrate them. We do this by documenting our experiences in a given culture, plus published accounts of these cultures. The more contributors on our team who have exposure to these different cultures, the richer and more complete our observations will be and the differences they reveal.

We'll commonly use this method in our Problem Clarity work whenever we have to address a problem facing an unfamiliar market – or if we're trying to solve for the entire global market. These comparisons serve as our means of understanding the different cultural factors at work in each market, plus how these impact whatever solution we ultimately deliver. This is especially important when we have to formulate our Point of View later on, as that Point of View must always be informed by the totality of the cultural factors and considerations we have to solve for.

How Intensifi uses it: Intensifi simply uses this as a method of analysis for their prior Cultural Probe work.

Intensifi's insights: Intensifi finds that the overall aspiration and motivation of "life optimization" appears to be universal across all "cultural groups," but the specific activities they're focused on in any particular group are (not surprisingly) correlated to whatever is occurring at that particular stage of their life – school choices, career choices, employer choices, spousal choices, investment choices, location choices, hobby choices, purchase choices, and so on. This would seem to affirm Intensifi's first seven hypotheses. It is neutral toward the others, refuting none of them, and generating no further hypotheses per se.

Studying – Story Share and Capture

What it is: Story Share and Capture is a group study method in which the members of the team, having each gone out and conducted observational and questioning fieldwork, come back together into their shared workspace to share their stories. As they do this, they start to saturate their workspace with different pieces of information and other artifacts from this work.

Doing this serves three specific purposes. First, it lets each team member get up to speed on what the other team members have been seeing and hearing in their respective fieldwork. In this case, each team member recounts what they've seen and heard and tells various user stories illustrating certain points that stuck out to them. This is valuable even if the whole team has participated in the same fieldwork as how each person experiences and perceives what they saw and heard can be different because they're each being filtered through a different series of cognitive biases. Second, by listening to their fellow team members and thinking about what's being said, and by probing them for more information on various points, team members can draw out even more meaning and nuance from these respective experiences than they had originally derived, making the overall exercise that much richer in insight. Third, by collectively capturing the respective details of the different subjects and the situation, the team begins to saturate their workspace together.

As the various team members are sharing, the rest of the team will be writing down headlines on Post-it™ Notes, which they'll eventually paste up in the team's shared workspace. This begins (or adds to) their space saturation effect. Each headline will include things such as interesting tidbits they observed, things they had encountered that surprised them, and perhaps characteristic quotes that certain subjects gave them. As they paste these up on the wall, they can also be physically grouped to illuminate certain specific patterns and themes that emerge from them. This helps to initiate the team's eventual synthesis process.

Teams will want to leverage this method at various points throughout their Design Thinking work as doing so will help them ensure they're on the same page with what each person is doing and learning so that they can all maintain a shared understanding of their collective subject and that subject's needs.

How Intensifi uses it: Intensifi uses this practice every time their team goes out and does fieldwork – including Contextual Inquiry, Digital Ethnography, Cultural Probes, and the three interview types (Contextual, Empathy, and Extreme User).

As a result of using this method, the team has saturated their workspace with quite a lot of "snippets" representing all manner of important insights resulting from both their fieldwork and their lab work. These include critical observations, characteristic quotes, and poignant and/or surprising insights.

Intensifi's insights: In looking over their shared workspace, Intensifi believes that the evidence seems to be mounting to affirm all but their last hypothesis (the one contested earlier). Thus, they're feeling quite strongly about their first nine hypotheses at this point.

Studying – Six Thinking Hats

What it is: Six Thinking Hats is a conceptual framework method that's used to help teams structure their convergent thinking efforts so that they can examine a situation from new and different perspectives. It allows teams to see their challenge through new perspectives and in so doing develop deeper insights into it.

With this method, situations are explored through six distinct perspectives. The White Hat focuses on data; the Red Hat focuses on emotions; the Black Hat focuses on caution; the Yellow Hat focuses on optimism; the Green Hat focuses on creativity, and the Blue Hat focuses on process. By forcing our team to explore its challenge and the various situational elements through these six different defined perspectives, we are drawn away from our old ways of seeing and thinking about the situation and toward new, possibly unfamiliar, ways of seeing and thinking about it. This sometimes results in new perspectives and a deeper understanding of the situation. If our team finds these particular perspective definitions to overly constrain their effort, then we can (if we like) create perspective definitions ("lenses") through which we can see and think about the situation. It may be that some other type of "lens" is what our team needs to unlock the hidden perspective they need. Therefore, we can define and use any given set of lenses we wish to use when undertaking this exercise.

How Intensifi uses it: Intensifi uses this method to study their respective observations and takeaways from the different observational and questioning work they've done up to this point. In particular, they explore these through the lenses ("hats") of *data* (what data is needed and is being used, and why?), *emotions* (what emotions are being elicited, and why?), *caution* (what precautions do users believe they need to take, and why?), *optimism* (what hopes are users experiencing, and why?), *creativity* (in what ways are users being empowered – or not empowered – to be creative in these situations, and what effect is that having?), and *process* (what processes are users having to use, and how do they feel about those processes – are they happy or unhappy with them?).

Intensifi's insights: By doing this, Intensifi gains deeper insights into the actual tasks and activities their subjects have to step through to achieve their goal, how they feel about those tasks and activities (what emotions they each elicit), what "systems" they're trying to use – successfully or unsuccessfully – to complete these tasks and activities, how effective they believe they're being at those tasks and activities, and what fears and concerns they're encountering in the process. This, in turn, helps to further solidify the majority of Intensifi's first nine hypotheses.

Studying – Empathy Map

What it is: An Empathy Map is a tool that's used to synthesize certain observations of our subject, reflecting what they are encountering in the situation of interest. These observations relate to several areas of internal cognitive and emotional processing, as well as to certain external influences. Documenting these helps to create a deeper understanding of the subject's needs and motivations in the situation.

The primary Empathy Map has an upper section and a lower section. The upper section is divided into four quadrants – top, bottom, left, and right, with an X pattern segregating them. In the very center is typically a small window that captures any relevant demographic and similar information about the subject.

Based on our observations and engagements with these characteristic subjects, we would populate these four quadrants of the upper section as follows:

- **Think and feel**: A snapshot of what is going on in their head and heart. It asks questions in the context of the situation, including, "What cognitive, and perhaps even subconscious, thoughts do they appear to be experiencing?", "What emotions do they seem to be experiencing?", and "What might these say about their values, beliefs, and motivations?"

- **Say and do**: A snapshot of their demonstrated behaviors. It asks questions in the context of the situation, including, "What are they saying to those around them (representative quotes, defining phrases, and so on)?", "What actions are they demonstrating?", and "What might these say about their needs and the outcomes they seek?"

- **Hear**: The environmental influences their minds are taking in via the aural pathways. It asks questions in the context of the situation, including "What things are they hearing that may be influencing their thoughts, emotions, and behaviors?", "What music and news programs are they listening to (and why)?", "What marketing messages might this be exposing them to?", "What are their friends, family, neighbors, and coworkers saying to them?" and "How might those all influence them?"

- **See**: The environmental influences their minds are taking in via the visual pathways. It asks questions in the context of the situation, including "What things are they seeing that may be influencing their thoughts, emotions, and behaviors?", "What books, magazines, movies, television programs, news shows, and live events are they encountering?", "What marketing messages might this be exposing them to?", "What are they seeing friends, family, neighbors, and coworkers doing?", and "How might that influence them?"

Since our subject's thoughts and emotions, and thus their values, beliefs, and motivations, can't be observed *directly*, we have to try to infer those by paying careful attention to the many clues they offer, such as their choice of words, their tone of voice, their facial expressions, and their overall body language. However, when doing this, we have to be cognizant of the fact that we are filtering this through our biases, so we have to try to bypass those biases and instead be as objective and nonjudgmental as possible. This allows us to get as accurate of a read as possible on their situation.

The lower section of the Empathy Map reflects additional insights that we've developed around our subject and their needs. These insights may arise out of direct observations of a subject attribute (those aspects reflected in the four quadrants mentioned previously), tensions/pains/frictions they appear to be having, unusual behaviors they're demonstrating (such as workarounds), observed contradictions and disconnects between two or more of their attributes, such as incongruity between what they say and what they do, and so on. Since these insights intend to relate to our subject's needs, this section is often broken down into two parts – pains and gains. Pains represent the tensions and frictions they need to have alleviated – taken away so that they no longer encounter them. Gains represent additional opportunities to deliver even more value in ways that resonate with their ultimate goals and values (often the "surprise and delight" features). Both need types should be expressed as "need statements" and not as "solution statements." In other words, they should be action (verb) based statements in the subject's voice, expressing the outcome they seek to accomplish (and why). They should never speak of how that outcome is to be achieved as that will be for us to define later.

Some versions of the Empathy Map finish by reflecting (at the bottom) a characteristic *Job Story quote* from the subject. This quote summarizes the entire Empathy Map by laying out the situational context ("when") and explaining both the activities they wish to engage in ("I want to") and their reason for doing so, which is the actual outcome they seek to achieve ("so that I can"). So, this Job Story quote captures the ultimate goal and motivations of our subject, together with their beliefs of what has to be done to attain that goal. This will prove useful later on when we want to contemplate solutions to the statement. The only consideration we'll have to be careful of is to ensure that we don't let their statement of the activities they believe they have to do ("I want to") limit the solutions we conceive for attaining that goal. There might be completely different sets of actions that lead to that same outcome – perhaps a far better set of actions – our subject has absolutely no awareness of, but which we may be able to conceive and deliver. This means we must focus on the primary outcome our subject seeks – keeping that rigid – while otherwise considering the actions part very malleable. In either case, our solution, whatever it ultimately ends up being, must solve their pains and should also look for available opportunities to deliver against their gains.

How Intensifi uses it: Intensifi completes an Empathy Map to document the *characteristic aspects* of all the subjects they've been observing and interviewing. This Empathy Map reflects the overall sense of what these people are hearing, seeing, thinking, feeling, saying, and doing – as well as their characteristic pains and associated gains. It also reflects a characteristic *Job Story quote* from these composite subjects, which is as follows: "When I am selecting and planning my life details, I want to ensure all areas of my life are optimized in harmony so that I can achieve my maximum overall life potential." This last statement in particular seems to articulate these subjects' underlying human motivation and aspiration – to achieve their maximum overall life potential – or, in other words, to be all they possibly can be in life, and achieve everything they possibly can achieve. As we can see, they are very achievement-oriented individuals:

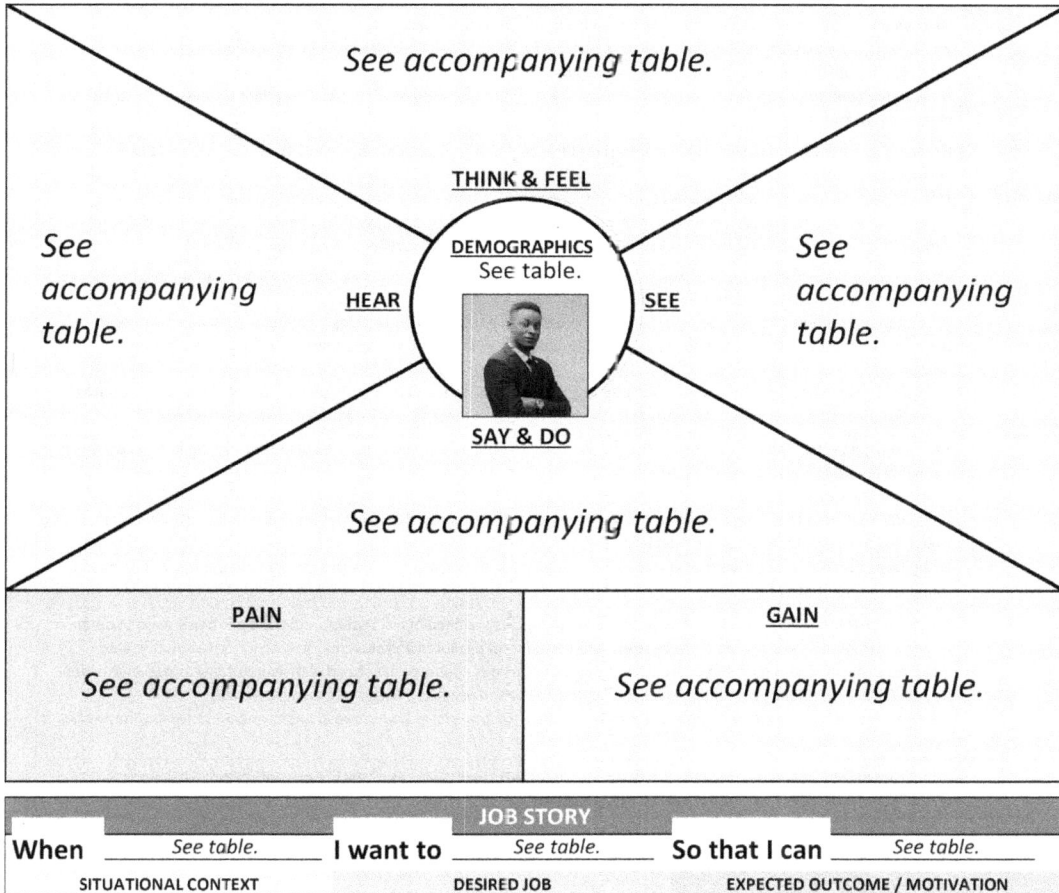

Figure 10.9: Intensifi's Empathy Map of their characteristic subject

This accompanying table elaborates on the preceding figure.

DEMOGRAPHICS	Aspiring Upwardly-Mobile Professional
HEAR	He hears others talk about their successes and accomplishments in life. While he has his as well, he'd really like to have more. He also hears others talk about how they use advisors and certain tools to optimize some area of their life, like their health or their financial investments. But these are all fragmented. What he doesn't hear anyone talk about is one tool, platform, or service that will let him do all of this in one place – even though he keeps asking people he knows and trusts about this. No one seems to have an answer. He also hears about retirement planning a lot – about ensuring he and his spouse will be safe and secure in retirement. He'd really like to hear about something that does this in concert with all other aspects of his life.
SEE	He sees others being very successful – and balancing their overall lives well. While he's not necessarily dissatisfied with his situation, he'd like to see himself being more successful overall – and balancing his life better, to succeed in each area of life. He also sees online and on TV the 'rich and famous' and it makes him wonder what 'hack' he might be able to use to move closer to that status.
THINK & FEEL	He wants to optimize and maximize each area of his life – so that he can lead a happy and fulfilled life, and feel like he's being successful in everything he does. This includes his health, wealth, marriage, family, friends, career, home, city, hobbies, friends, possessions, and more. When he feels that he's doing this well, it makes him feel safe, secure, and happy. When he feels that he's not doing this well, it makes him feel anxious, frustrated, and unhappy. So he wants to make sure he's always doing this well!
SAY & DO	He has spoken with his financial advisor, his fitness trainer, his career coach, and his trusted friends about ways to manage his life more holistically and comprehensively. He's been telling them that he's been watching the progress of AI systems and – being a technical professional himself – believes that there has to be a way to leverage that to integrate all those areas somehow and optimize his life more holistically. He's also been doing all manner of research online, looking for platforms and/or tools that will allow him to do this, but he hasn't found anything yet, which makes him frustrated. He knows there 'has to be a way' to do this somehow!
PAIN	He is a real go-getter, and consequently strongly wants to maximize each and every area of his life – his health, his wealth, his career, his marriage, his possessions, etc. – all in harmony with each other. He is very frustrated that there is currently no way / no system / no service that will support him in trying to optimize / maximize everything about his life in a holistic manner. He believes that doing this should be technically feasible, given the right input data and the right algorithms, but he hasn't found such a solution yet!
GAIN	He also recognizes that if he did have such a solution to this aching need of his, that he could use it in many ways to optimize his life – including finding the best purchase options for different products and services. And so if such a solution also included some kind of ecosystem of providers he could shop with – perhaps in concert with an automated concierge – then this could further expedite his finding and securing the goods and assets he needs to maximize his life. He also sees the value in networking with other like-minded 'optimizers' to learn special hacks and tricks for maximizing his performance in this context.
JOB STORY	When I am **selecting and planning my life details** / I want to **ensure all areas of my life are optimized in harmony** / so that I can **achieve my maximum overall life potential**.

Table 10.1: Empathy map details

Intensifi's insights: By building out this Empathy Map, the Intensifi team can put a real face and voice to what they've been learning in their empathy work here. It also reinforces the validity of their first nine hypotheses.

Not Studying – Persona

Coincidentally, one Design Method the team has chosen *not* to use (at least at this point) that often is used is the **Persona**.

A Persona, or Composite Character Profile, is a synthesized profile of a particular subject group of interest. Each such profile is expressed as a composite semi-fictional character representing that subject group and thereby embodying their common attributes. Those attributes are typically psychographic and need-based, but they can also be demographic. Personas are based on observations of real individuals and serve as the archetype for understanding different customer groups and what makes each particular group tick.

The reason the team has chosen *not* to use a Persona here is because their perception is that the overall psychographics involved – and thus the aspirations and motivations – are all very broad, and consequently do not differ significantly from one group to the next. In other words, this is a very homogenous market in terms of its overarching outcome needs and the psychographic motivational factors involved.

What *is different* between the respective segments of this group lies in the area of optimization relative to their age and level of career and life progression – with younger subjects being more focused on early-life and early-career considerations, such as a first job, marriage, a first home, and so on; and older subjects being more focused on later-life and later-career concerns, such as sending their children to university, maximizing their retirement savings, and otherwise enjoying a pleasant lifestyle in the moment. So, what is true in this case is that each segment has a **very consistent goal** – namely to optimize their life mostly for the particular phase of life and career they happen to currently be in, but also, to a lesser degree, for their overall life. This does not change between the respective segments, other than *which* specific life stage is being emphasized most at a particular time; otherwise, their goal always remains the same.

Consequently, building out the Personas of each respective segment offers no particular value to the team as doing so doesn't reveal anything new that they don't already know, nor is there any significant difference between the segments from a human motivational standpoint. Thus, building them here is deemed unwarranted.

Insights summary – Define Study Methods

The following table summarizes Intensifi's Define insights derived from these **Study Methods**:

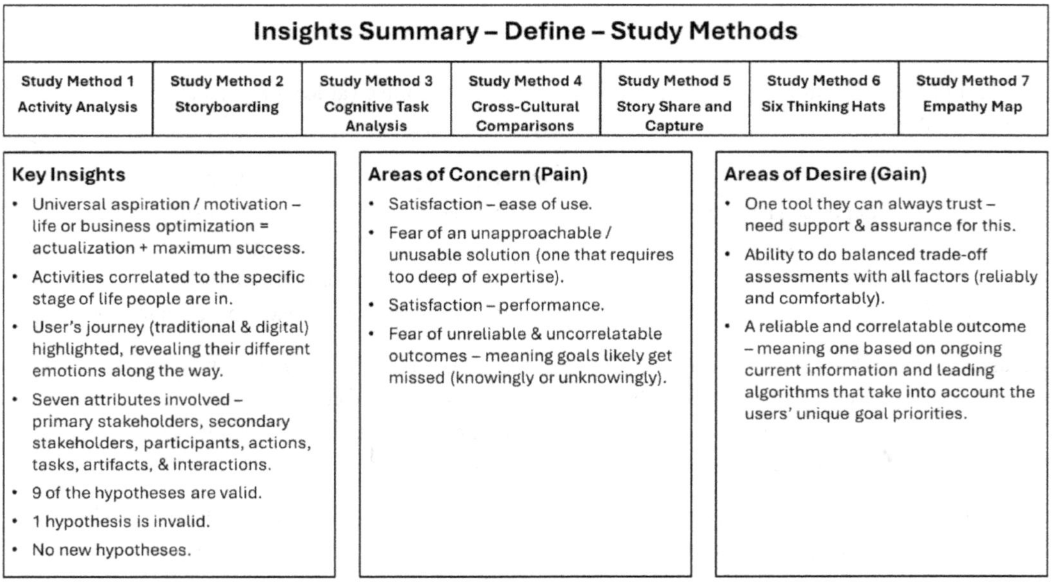

Insights Summary – Define – Study Methods						
Study Method 1	Study Method 2	Study Method 3	Study Method 4	Study Method 5	Study Method 6	Study Method 7
Activity Analysis	Storyboarding	Cognitive Task Analysis	Cross-Cultural Comparisons	Story Share and Capture	Six Thinking Hats	Empathy Map

Key Insights

- Universal aspiration / motivation – life or business optimization = actualization + maximum success.
- Activities correlated to the specific stage of life people are in.
- User's journey (traditional & digital) highlighted, revealing their different emotions along the way.
- Seven attributes involved – primary stakeholders, secondary stakeholders, participants, actions, tasks, artifacts, & interactions.
- 9 of the hypotheses are valid.
- 1 hypothesis is invalid.
- No new hypotheses.

Areas of Concern (Pain)

- Satisfaction – ease of use.
- Fear of an unapproachable / unusable solution (one that requires too deep of expertise).
- Satisfaction – performance.
- Fear of unreliable & uncorrelatable outcomes – meaning goals likely get missed (knowingly or unknowingly).

Areas of Desire (Gain)

- One tool they can always trust – need support & assurance for this.
- Ability to do balanced trade-off assessments with all factors (reliably and comfortably).
- A reliable and correlatable outcome – meaning one based on ongoing current information and leading algorithms that take into account the users' unique goal priorities.

Figure 10.10: Define insights – Study Methods

That wraps it up for Intensifi's Define efforts (at least at this point).

The result – Intensifi's new insights

Based on all of their preceding empathy work, and upon reaching convergence at this point, the team concludes the following:

- Their first nine hypotheses were *correct*:

  - Holistic Optimization

  - Easy, But Extensible Usage

  - Current Data

  - Platform Augmenters

  - Platform Trust

  - Platform Socialization

  - Platform Security

  - Platform Customization

  - Platform Ecosystem

- Their last (tenth) hypothesis was *incorrect* – that of "Platform Financing." Here, the consensus from the research was that users would *not* be willing to pay for a solution via a commission basis as agreeing to do so would open them up to too much uncertainty – a risk most would not be willing to take on.

- No additional hypotheses were generated from their work.

This brings them to the point where they can start thinking about articulating the "real problem" they're addressing – in other words, their subjects' collective *Point of View*. This acts as our segue into the next chapter.

Summary

In this chapter, we dove deep into the Problem Clarity stage of Design Thinking. We did this by walking the journey with our friends at Intensifi – exploring their Problem Space with them.

By doing this, we worked through the divergent Empathy step with them, where they (and we) used various Design Methods to cultivate empathy for their subjects (their "would-be customers"). This was done so that they could formulate relevant hypotheses – a process in which they leveraged inductive logic by integrating all of their observations and learnings into a coherent set of presumptions. At the end of that, we saw Intensifi define what they believed would be their hypotheses to move forward with.

Then, we saw Intensifi decide how they would go about testing those hypotheses through other Design Methods and saw them execute those Design Methods in the convergent Define step, where they (and we) used those methods to ultimately define their final hypotheses. This was a process in which the team leveraged deductive logic by testing each of the hypotheses against specific observational, questioning, and study exercises they undertook to validate or invalidate each one. What they eventually deduced from those exercises was that nine of their original 10 hypotheses were accurate, while one of them was not.

At each step of this journey, we looked at what Intensifi was trying to achieve, how they went about doing so, and the specific outcomes they attained in the process. This gave us a clearer insight into what the Problem Clarity stage looks like and how it works in real life to arrive at that empathic understanding we so desperately seek of our subject and their situation.

We came away with a far better understanding of Intensifi's subject – including a much deeper understanding of their underlying motivations and aspirations – and therefore their "real need" – regardless of whatever type of solution (and thus value proposition) Intensifi ultimately offers them.

It's worth noting that *formulating* hypotheses can be relatively straightforward… it only took Intensifi eight Design Methods to do so. However, *testing* those hypotheses (for validity) is much **harder** to do. To that point, it took Intensifi twice as many Design Methods – 16 to be exact – to test its hypotheses, and it wasn't until some of the later Question Methods that they started to discover an invalid hypothesis (where they focused on that hypothesis). This is, in most cases, characteristic of the Design Thinking process.

We should also note that this process – as we've just encountered it, being focused squarely on *human beings* – can be fully scaled to any size and/or complexity of endeavor, regardless of the sector, industry, or market. We simply have to break down the respective elements of our overall challenge into discrete parts that we can test, and thereafter integrate the resultant insights. Wherever elements are intertwined or otherwise entangled, multiple tests may be required under differing scenarios to disentangle their impacts on each other. But by following the process methodically and carefully, teams can unpack their Problem Space and come away with a usable hypothesis to work with, regardless of the situation – so long as that situation revolves around human needs and aspirations.

We should further note that this process – just like the overall Design Thinking process – is just as valid for *non-business* human-oriented endeavors as it is for *business* ones. The context – business or non-business – is irrelevant. So long as the situation involved revolves around human beings and their specific *needs* and *aspirations*, the process is fully relevant and works as described.

With this information, we can move on to the next chapter. There, we'll walk alongside Intensifi in the process – via additional Design Methods – of defining their prospective customers' *Point of View*, and then subsequently the *Design Principles* they'll use in conceiving possible solutions for that Point of View. This is an intermediate stage (the "intermission," if you will), before moving into their Solution Space via Design Thinking's Value Definition stage.

We're clearly "deep in the weeds" of figuring out Intensifi's Unique Value Proposition, but rest assured we'll eventually come up for air and get back to their overall business model, ensuring that it ends up being as innovative and impactful as possible.

Further reading

- *The Innovator's Hypothesis: How Cheap Experiments Are Worth More than Good Ideas*, by Michael Schrage, MIT Press, Boston, 2016.

Intermission

In *Chapter 10*, we went deep into the Problem Clarity stage of Design Thinking, where we walked side-by-side with our friends at Intensifi to explore their Problem Space with them. There, we worked through the divergent Empathy step by using different Design Methods (and inductive logic) to cultivate empathy for their subjects and ultimately reach the point of hypothesis formation. At that point, we saw Intensifi define what they believed to be their respective hypotheses to test. We then saw them select certain Design Methods to use in testing those hypotheses. Finally, we worked through the convergent Define step using even more Design Methods (and deductive logic) to affirm their nine final hypotheses.

At each step of that journey, we looked at what Intensifi was trying to achieve, how they went about doing so, and the specific outcomes they attained. Doing that gave us clearer insights into what the Problem Clarity stage looks like and how it works in reality. That resulted in a much deeper understanding of Intensifi's subject – including a far better understanding of their real motivations and aspirations – and thus their **real need**.

In this chapter, we're going to explore and work through the third stage of the Design Thinking Process – namely the **Problem-Solution Interface**.

In this stage – which is a bit of an "intermission," if you will, between working our Problem Space and working our Solution Space, we'll be doing two things. First, we'll be defining our **Point of View** (technically our *subject's* Point of View) about the problem; second, we'll be establishing our **Design Principles** for solving it. Consequently, we've divided the chapter into these two key sections, according to those actions:

- **Our Point of View on the problem**: A compelling and useful restatement of our subject's *reframed problem* – one that inspires action on our part to address and resolve.

- **Our Design Principles for the solution** Actionable principles we'll adhere to in conceiving and defining possible solutions to our Point of View, thus informing and guiding the different solution options we consider.

As we explore these two actions, we'll come to understand what they each entail, the critical role they play in the overall Design Thinking process, and how to go about doing them. As before, we'll be doing this collaboratively with our friends at Intensifi, using certain Design Methods to carry out the activity.

Our Point of View on the problem

Stepping into the Problem-Solution Interface stage, as we are now, our first order of business is to take everything we just learned in the Problem Clarity stage and turn that into a compelling and useful Point of View that articulates our problem in just the right way.

PROBLEM - SOLUTION
INTERFACE

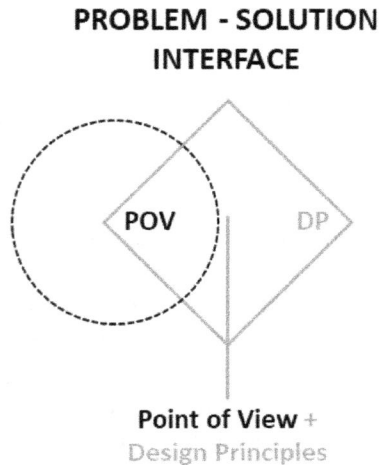

Figure 11.1: The Point of View step in the Problem-Solution Interface stage

Doing this will set us up to define our Design Principles thereafter. This is what we will explore now.

Taking stock of where we are now

In *Chapter 10*, we walked alongside Ian, Zoe, and Watson, plus the rest of their team (16 people in all), as they defined and tested their respective hypotheses about their particular subjects and the situation they were encountering.

Having tested and refined their hypotheses to arrive at their final hypotheses, the team has now finished working through its Problem Space (or so they believe). As a result, they've arrived at a point of clarity and focus around the problem they're trying to solve for.

This brings them to the third stage of the Design Thinking process – an intermediate place in between the Problem Space and the Solution Space where they will have to formally codify their Point of View and establish their supporting Design Principles.

Understanding the Point of View – what it is

Our **Point of View (PoV)** is a new articulation of the problem we're solving for – one that reframes the original problem we encountered into a newer problem that more accurately reflects our subjects' *actual* needs, desires, and motivations.

The name literally means to present that problem from the Point of View of our subjects' innermost needs, desires, and aspirations, as well as all the motivations behind them. As such, the PoV is our thesis – a statement of guiding beliefs if you will – about what we understand that subject's **real problem** to be.

When defining our PoV, it's important that we state it in such a way as to be *actionable* for both us and our organization. This is because it will ultimately shape the guiding Design Principles we will end up using to generate new ideas for solution concepts to consider later on.

Consequently, a sound PoV will be one that does the following:

- drives focus by correctly framing our subject's *real problem*;
- captures the imagination of all the stakeholders involved;
- inspires both our team and our broader organization to act on the opportunity it represents;
- allows our team to revisit and reformulate it as we learn through additional (repeated) action steps.

It's important to note here that our PoV ends up being the **rallying cry** for our organization and its ecosystem (including any potential investors we have) – **its call to action** to act on the specific opportunity we're presenting it with. Consequently, it's important that our PoV is stated in a way that is very *compelling* to each of the stakeholders we have to convince (or "sell") on the opportunity. Otherwise, if it's not, then we may lose their support for it. Another way to look at this is that our PoV has to tell a compelling story that moves these stakeholders to take action (including spending money) on this opportunity.

The Point of View must remain fluid (for now)

While our team will use its PoV to move forward from this point (into Design Principles and ultimately into Value Definition), there can at times arise situations where, in the course of our work, we uncover new insights that we didn't encounter before, and those new insights lead us back to restating our PoV.

Though this doesn't occur every time, it does occur often enough that we have to be aware of its possibility. It is certainly not out of the ordinary. Consequently, we need to be aware that it can occur to us, even if our original PoV was good.

We're next going to work through the process of developing a PoV with Intensifi, which will give us an example of what the PoV looks like and how we can go about developing it.

Using Design Methods to define our Point of View

Defining and articulating a good PoV isn't as easy as it may seem on the surface. Fortunately (for everyone involved), there are a number of Design Methods that have evolved for use in this situation.

In this case, we're going to journey with Ian, Zoe, and Watson – and their entire team – as they call upon certain specific Design Methods to help them define their unique PoV.

In particular, they've chosen to use the following six **Study** Design Methods:

- Powers of Ten
- Point of View Madlibs
- Point of View Want Ads
- Point of View Analogy
- Critical Reading Checklist
- Design The Box.

Next, we're going to explain each of these methods, how the team is using them, and what outcomes they attain from them. Eventually, we'll arrive at their final and formal PoV.

It's important to understand that developing a high-caliber PoV is paramount to having **confidence** in the Design Principles we will eventually develop and use later on (and thus, the solutions we will eventually consider). For this reason, it is important for us to leverage these types of Design Methods to help us, in fact, craft such a high-caliber PoV.

Study – Powers of Ten

First, we'll cover what it is. Powers of Ten is a reframing method that allows teams to zoom in and out on a particular situation they're addressing. It lets them take one or more pieces of that situation and contemplate it at increasing and/or decreasing levels of magnitude, thus giving them a very different perspective on the situation.

This spurs contemplative questions to address. Such questions can be either absolute or relative. For example, they might ask, "What if we had to make our widget 10X smaller than it presently is?", or "What if completing Task B had to take only one-fourth as much time as it currently does?", or "What if Service X had to cost less than $99?", or "What if customers didn't have to be physically present?", or "What if this experience had to engage 40X more people than all our other experiences?". All of these are examples of Powers of Ten.

Teams can use this method for both insights development work and ideation. For insights development, they can use it to extrapolate their subjects' observed behaviors from one situation onto a different one, contemplating what it might look like for that same behavior to be cast into, for example, a scenario where the subject had to finish in one-tenth the time, or where the subject had to spend 20X more money. In this way, they can contemplate how the behaviors they've observed in one scenario might potentially map onto a completely different scenario of a substantially larger or smaller scale. For ideation, they can use it to help stimulate their creative thinking, in which case it serves as a source for artificial constraints. So, in that case, consider a scenario where participants are asked how they might solve the problem such that the solution was 10X more effective than any solution currently on the market. This new (extreme) constraint would start to percolate all manner of new ideas in their minds, some of which might be realistic while others not. But these nevertheless stimulate a large number of new ideas (being that the aim is generally quantity over quality at this point). This can be especially useful whenever an ideation session begins to lose steam.

Powers of Ten also captures the essence of 10X breakthrough thinking. Here, if a team is asked how to make something 10% better, then in most cases, their efforts will only tend toward incremental thinking. However, if that same team is asked to come up with a way to make the solution 10X better, not just 10% better, then it is typically forced to abandon all current approaches to solving the problem and instead focus on entirely new and different approaches for solving the problem. That is breakthrough thinking, and it often leads to breakthrough solutions that win big in the marketplace.

Next, let's discuss how Intensifi uses it. Intensifi wants to use this method to help them think about their subject's situation at different scales of magnitude. In particular, they want to ask the question, "How can we make our customer's outcome 10X (or even 100X) more effective and impactful than anything currently available to them does?". They believe that addressing this question, framed in this way (at 10X and 100X scales in particular), will help them to work through their PoV more impactfully, which will in turn produce a better and more impactful statement of that PoV.

Next, we'll look at Intensifi's outcome. Intensifi uses this method in conjunction with the other methods noted below. As a result, the team comes away with what it believes is in fact a far better, and more impactfully stated, PoV. Several specific points the team draws out from this method include the following:

- A comprehensive integration of all life areas in their solution – which represents a 10-20X multiple of value over the isolated solutions presently available.

- An integration of leading-edge AI capabilities to make their solution's prescriptions 10-100X more effective and impactful than anything currently accessible in the market.

- Reach up to 100X more customers than current isolated solutions reach together.

The resultant PoV is reflected in their final PoV statement noted later in this section.

Study – Point of View Madlibs

First, let's explore what it is. A *Point of View Madlib* is a generative scaffolding method teams use to help them in developing their PoV. In using it, the team draws on its earlier empathy and problem definition work, where they will have identified and clarified their subject's need through a number of different Design Methods.

In this method, a facilitator writes the Madlib on a large flipchart or whiteboard for the team to collectively see and work on while they're working together to develop their PoV. This Madlib – similar to the Job Story – captures three key elements of the PoV, namely the subject, their need, and, in this case, a surprising insight the team has uncovered about these.

The format of the PoV Madlib is thus as follows:

{Subject} needs to {subject's need} because {surprising insight}

In this case, the need is a verb statement and the insight is something the team has intentionally synthesized (as opposed to an obvious observation) – so that they use it as a real springboard for new PoV options. Since the surprising insight is the real linchpin of the whole Madlib, it should create a Madlib that is intriguing, engaging, and able to capture the *tension* in the PoV.

Some examples might be as follows:

- Adult male athletes need a new class of performance sports shoe that makes them feel invincible – one with a brand promise that inspires and a brand experience that delivers.

- Junior High School students need to eat a healthy diet so that they look good and feel socially accepted, as social acceptance is of paramount importance to their emotional health. Physical health begets emotional health.

- Middle-aged adults need a health insurance plan that gives them assurance of maintaining a certain lifestyle into their nineties, which gives them the peace of mind they need to have less stress in their lives.

Using this format, the team experiments with a number of different combinations by varying each of the three elements. They'll repeat this until they feel they've exhausted all the possible options that make sense to them. They'll then test these for congruity with what their own collective intuition is telling them and ultimately settle on one PoV statement that most *accurately* conveys the PoV they want to use.

As seen in the preceding examples, the final PoV must be actionable – something they and their organization can use to define a well-focused innovation – as well as inspirational – something that will compel all the stakeholders involved to deliver on the opportunity.

Next, let's discuss how Intensifi uses it. Intensifi's team uses this method to work through different Madlib combinations to consider.

In this case, their key *surprising insights* were as follows:

- While subjects want to optimize their lives across their entire lifespan, they naturally seek to optimize it *most* for whatever phase of life they're currently in.

- People are more than willing to augment themselves and their possessions with data-tracking devices if they believe that doing so will help the solution help them attain their maximum potential.

- People ultimately do not trust automated solutions to produce truly optimized results – ones that let them reach their maximum potential – for them. Consequently, they find themselves second-guessing these solutions' recommendations, usually via different types of social comparison with others ("What are others doing that's working for them, and how does that compare to what I'm being told to do?").

- People like the act of socially comparing themselves to others (whether or not they admit it) – to see whether they are rising above or falling below their particular "litmus test" for success in that phase of their life.

- People quite often do not have the level of risk appetite and tolerance that they claim to have; behind the scenes, they play it much safer than they otherwise portray themselves as doing.

- While there is a small cohort of lead users who do all their own research and make all their own choices, the majority of users aren't quite so motivated. They look to a solution to do that research and make certain choices for them – including the selection of different products and services. This is why they appreciate a "pre-curated ecosystem" of vendors to shop with and purchase from.

Consequently, some of the team's **Madlib options** end up being as follows:

- Aspiring young professional needs to maximize their career prospects because they want to ensure that they attain a high career status with lots of power, prestige, and income, and by so doing have the freedom to spend money and experience life to its fullest.

- Upwardly mobile businessperson needs to maximize their overall career journey across different organizations because they aspire to be a highly successful and well-recognized CEO someday.

- Rising high-potential leader needs to maximize their social and political clout because they aspire to be a powerful politician and exert maximum influence over policies and organizations in their purview.

- All-star senior executive needs to maximize their stock vesting options in their organization because they wish to retire as a billionaire.

- Aggressive business leaders need to optimize their organization's business strategy so it can crush its competition and become the undisputed leader in its markets.

Intensifi's outcome is the next point of focus. Intensifi uses these different Madlib variants of their PoV to help them define and articulate their final, formal PoV – reflected in the final version noted later in this section.

Study – Point of View Want Ads

First, let's discuss what this is. A *Point of View Want Ad* is a generative method teams use to help in developing their PoV. It involves writing a **want ad** about their customer and that customer's need. This approach, by accentuating a particular customer and the important character traits of that customer, tends to be quite intriguing and makes for a more playful and engaging way of experimenting with possible PoV statements than a direct Madlib does.

In this case, the PoV Want Ad interjects the team's customer and that customer's need directly into the want ad, together with key insights about that customer the team has distilled through its empathy and synthesis work.

A typical format used for PoV Want Ads would thus look like the following:

{Descriptive customer characterization} seeks {ambiguous method for meeting implied need, with added flavor reflecting customer insights}

Thus, an example might be as follows:

Serious career-minded working mother seeks a network of progressive, upwardly mobile professional women. Must be serious about both career and family, and not afraid to take on a man's world on its own terms. Will exchange support and mentorship. All ages welcome. No namby-pambies.

This approach to framing a PoV can be very playful, and can often offer a team the opportunity to play with a lot of nuance in expressing the statement. The final PoV the team ultimately chooses, however, will still need to demonstrate clarity into both their customer's problem (reflecting how it has been reframed) and how their organization intends to deliver on that problem – including the unique Brand Experience that sets the stage for the particular Design Principles they'll use.

This method makes for a useful complement to PoV Madlib and PoV Analogy, and will sometimes yield a more intriguing and inspiring PoV.

Next, let's talk about how Intensifi uses it. Intensifi's team uses this method in a workshop setting to come up with different want ad variants of their PoV.

Let's also mention Intensifi's outcome. Intensifi generates several different want ad variants of their PoV. A characteristic example of these want ad PoVs is the following:

Aspiring young professional seeks a readily accessible solution they can use to optimize every area of their life simultaneously. The solution must be capable of assessing everything about them, as well as everything occurring in the world around them. It must use those to make suggestions that let them optimize every area of their life in a balanced and holistic way. Life potential maximization is the goal; solutions that cannot deliver on that promise need not apply!

The gist of these want ad PoVs is integrated into the team's final PoV, as noted later in this section.

Study – Point of View Analogy

First, let's talk about what it is. A *Point of View Analogy* is a generative analogy method teams use to help them in developing their PoV. It makes extensive use of analogies, metaphors, and similes – analogies for conciseness in comparing different ideas, metaphors and similes for creating rich mosaics of meaning around those ideas.

Here the team – while conducting its synthesis work earlier on – will strive in particular to notice and capture useful and relevant metaphors for the situation they're encountering, as well as relevant analogies that can be drawn between their subject's situation and other similar situations.

Having collected these different metaphors and analogies, the team will then lay them out in their workspace and (via a facilitator) look for ways in which they can mash them up to create the particular mosaic of meaning and insight they're searching for on behalf of their PoV. They can then use this as either a source of inspiration for stating PoV options, or else embed the metaphor *directly* into their PoV. Whichever approach they use, their final PoV has to be concise and compelling. It must also articulate a strong directive for how they intend to go about solving their subject's problem.

PoVs that embed analogies are often seen in the digital technology world, where the analogies are to other well-known digital platforms. For example, for a new platform that intends to deliver on a business' need for a better visual marketing platform, the PoV might be as follows.

Serious consumer-driven businesses need a fresh modern visual marketing platform that's the Instagram of the business world.

Since the human mind responds so well to analogies and metaphors, this method often leads to very inspiring and compelling PoVs. Teams can thus use it as one more means of helping them synthesize an impactful PoV.

Next, let's explore how Intensifi uses it. Intensifi's team actually started with this method earlier on – when it was out doing its Empathy and Define work in **Stage 2**. There, the team made a special effort to observe specific details about their subjects. Those subjects' situations, in their minds, could give rise to relevant analogies, metaphors, and similes to possibly use at this point.

As a result, the team did, in fact, curate a list of specific analogies, metaphors, and similes to impart into their PoV. Those include the following:

- Customers not having the integrated life solution they really want and need is like trying to cook a meal without knowing the right ingredients to use nor being able to measure any of those ingredients. The final outcome will be unpredictable and is likely to be suboptimal and not live up to its full potential.

- Having a comprehensive all-life integrated solution would be like having an all-seeing genie who watches out for them and their interests at all times.

- Having a solution that is capable of assessing past, present, and emerging information and making customized recommendations just for them and their life traits based on that is like having a personal coach or advisor who knows them better than they know themselves while at the same time knowing everything happening in the world around them. This is also kind of like having their own personal omniscient being that happens to be working for them.

- What customers would really like is a **Generative AI for Life Optimization**.

Intensifi's outcome is as follows. As a result of doing this, the Intensifi team was able to generate the following analogous or metaphorical statement to possibly use in their final PoV:

Customers want a comprehensive all-life integrated solution that works like an omniscient "generative AI genie" who is also their friend, mentor, coach, and advisor. This solution should always give them the best possible advice in each area of their life, given the circumstances surrounding them, which then lets them live their best possible life – one where they attain their maximum potential at every point in life.

Thus, the analogous takeaway from this is that the solution has to operate like both of the following:

- an omniscient generative AI genie;

- a trusted friend, mentor, coach, and advisor who is capable of doing this.

These analogous insights prove extremely helpful, valuable, and useful to the team. They show up in various ways in the team's final, formal PoV, which is reflected in the final version noted later in this section.

Study – Critical Reading Checklist

Let's explore what it is. A *Critical Reading Checklist* is an evaluative method teams use to determine whether or not they've arrived at a **usable, high-quality PoV** that they can move forward with. The method walks them through a set of *four fundamental questions* about their PoV to answer. These are aimed at ensuring their PoV is in fact insightful, focused, actionable, unique, meaningful, and inspiring!

The four fundamental questions of the Critical Reading Checklist are as follows:

1. What's the real issue here? What's our team's unique take on it?

    - What mental model are we using to frame this issue?

    - Is it truly user-centric, outcome-based, and insight-driven?

2. Says who exactly? How valid is our particular PoV?

    - Is our take supported by research findings from an appropriately representative set of subjects?

    - Is it an accurate distillation that we can generalize to the entire population of subjects?

    - Does it apply to our mainstream, outside of the outliers and extreme users we interviewed?

3. What's truly new or novel about our PoV? What new value does it bring to the situation?

    - Has our team articulated its findings in a fresh new way? Or do we need to be more precise?

    - Are our findings truly rooted in the context of our customer and their unique outcome needs?

4. Who cares here? In what ways is our PoV even significant at all?

    - Is our team truly excited about it?

    - Does it represent a problem that's truly worth solving to us? If not, why not – and what are we going to do about that?

As the team works through this list of questions, they'll likely find that they have to repeatedly reframe and rephrase their subject's situation until they're finally confident that they've nailed it correctly (as evidenced by the checklist). If they do not feel that their PoV is unique enough, then they'll have to work toward trying to be more specific in how they articulate it.

While the Critical Reading Checklist is useful for helping teams think through the quality and potential impact of their PoV, it's not a tool that in and of itself can help those teams resolve deficiencies in the PoV. For that, they'll have to secure additional outside assistance.

When they are finished with the method, the team should ideally be very excited about their PoV. If they aren't, then there's likely still something wrong with it, and they'll want to secure additional input on it. Or it may be that, despite all efforts at reframing the problem, in the end, it simply isn't a problem that's worth solving for them. This could be because it is not an opportunity that will engage their organization and make for a compelling business case. When that's the case, the team should report this and give their reasons for reaching such a conclusion (at which point the effort will typically be abandoned).

Next, we'll discuss how Intensifi uses it. Intensifi's team uses this method to evaluate different versions of their PoV and, by so doing, ensure that each one passes muster with respect to these four fundamental questions.

Anything about those PoVs that does not pass muster gets eliminated – and any deficiencies the method points out are subsequently addressed (sometimes via additional work).

Intensifi's outcome is as follows. In the end, Intensifi's team used this method to ensure that their final PoV was in fact as follows:

- extremely customer-centered, need-based, and insight-driven;
- reflective of extensive research across a broad sampling of subjects, and thus fully generalizable to all;
- extremely specific to the unique contextual needs and desires of their subjects;
- reflective of a problem that is in fact worth solving to them, stated in an interesting and compelling way.

This, in turn, has given Intensifi strong confidence in their final PoV, as noted later in this section.

Study – Design The Box

Let's discuss what it is. *Design The Box* is a creative synthesis method used to help teams clarify their thinking around a common, shared vision for the solution they'll deliver – including its associated Brand Experience.

Here, the team, working together, will create a "box" (package) for their solution that's intended to be representative of how they would package it for retail sale. As an alternative to creating the physical package, the team can also just create a digital rendering of it.

Product packaging is intended not only to secure a product but also to convey a certain *brand image* or *brand message*. Team members would thus decorate and annotate the package with colors, designs, a product name, a brand tagline, perhaps key features and benefits, and so forth. These package design elements would thus be an expression of both the brand's *Visual Brand Language* and, more importantly, its *Brand Promise*.

By creating this tangible touchstone artifact, what Design the Box therefore does for a team is that it forces a conversation within the team about the things that matter most about their solution and about the Brand Promise it is intended to deliver. This helps the team envision and articulate a shared vision for their solution – what their solution will ultimately do for their customer (which is, after all, the essence of a Brand Promise).

Teams generally use this method whenever working on their PoV and Design Principles. By helping the team flesh out the specific Brand Promise they want to deliver, the method clarifies for them what the associated Brand Experience needs to be like, and thus the Brand Experience Lens they'll want to use when setting down their Design Principles, which will guide the new solutions they pursue. Design the Box is thus a powerful – and efficient – method for helping teams reach clarity on both their PoV and their Design Principles.

Next, let's discuss how Intensifi uses it. The Intensifi team spends some time together in a workshop thinking through all their prior research and what it has taught them about their subjects, as well as those subjects' situations in light of the type of solution they hope to deliver – and the sort of Brand Experience they'd like to create via that solution.

From those insights, the team has defined a number of key brand attributes they can leverage in both their PoV and their subsequent Design Principles. They use those insights to design a faux "package" for the solution that reflects each of these brand attributes. The team likes the end result it produces!

Intensifi's outcome is as follows. As a result of doing this, the team has crafted the following respective brand attributes for their solution and its packaging/marketing:

- **Brand Experience**: The one source for ultimate, all-encompassing maximized life.
- **Brand Experience Lens**: We are the ones who deliver ultimate, all-encompassing maximized life.
- **Brand Name**: Intensifi.
- **Product Name**: Life Max 1.
- **Brand Promise**: Our solution – more than any other option available to you – will empower you to optimize each area of your life – in harmony and balance with one another – so that at every stage of your life, you can achieve your maximum possible potential.
- **Brand Imagery**: Bold, aspirational achievements – at each stage of life.
- **Brand Language**: Bold graphics, sharp graphics, "power colors".

- **Brand Colors**: "Power colors" such as black, red, and purple, with dashes of bright green, yellow, and orange.

- **Brand Tagline**: Your life maximized – today!

- **Key features and benefits**: A solution that learns and knows everything thing about you, plus your goals and aspirations, and that every day ingests new data and information about current and emerging trends around you so that you can use it at any given time with full confidence to optimize each area of your life in harmony – in the ways you want – without ever having to worry about privacy and security.

- **Other**: A solution that's considered affordable by the vast majority of aspiring professionals – priced according to their present life stage and the scope of their ambitions at that stage.

The team then seeks to weave these respective brand attributes into their new PoV and Design Principles as they articulate each one.

The outcome – Intensifi's final, formal Point of View

Having undertaken the six preceding Design Methods, the Intensifi team finally sits down to develop and write out the final, formal PoV that they'll use (at least at this point).

That final, formal PoV is stated as follows:

- This we know… that aspiring business-minded individuals – from the earliest to the latest career stage – seek a solution that empowers them to achieve their *maximum potential* in both life and business. – by giving them the extensible toolset and the ongoing knowledge they require to simultaneously optimize every area of their life and business – with full confidence that the decisions and choices it leads them to will in fact result in their achieving *maximum overall success* – as clearly demonstrated by the many others before them who have achieved similar maximum life success by using the solution.

- We further know that the *reason* these individuals seek this solution is because they want the confidence – at each stage of their career and life, but especially at the *end* of their career and life – that they have in fact made every possible choice and decision in life they could to attain *the maximum possible success available to them* so that, ultimately, they can look back on their life with complete satisfaction and joy, and with absolutely zero regrets.

- We also know that these individuals want to *conceptualize* such a solution as being a sort of "omniscient *Generative AI for Life* genie" who's also their very trusted friend, mentor, and coach.

- Finally, we know that these individuals value certain specific *attributes* in such a solution – those being the following:

  - **comprehensiveness** (covering all areas of life and business);

  - **extensibility** (customizable according to each person's preferred approach to using it);

- **connectivity** (using myriad devices to incorporate relevant data from our personal world);

- **currency** (able to incorporate all the latest news and data from around the world every day);

- **dependability** (our ability to have full confidence in its prescriptions);

- **sociability** (our ability to socialize our prescriptions with others whom we trust and value);

- **networked** (including a curated ecosystem of providers we can choose from and engage with);

- **private and secure** (all information is protected and inaccessible to unauthorized parties);

- **accessibility** (our ability to afford the solution depending on our current life stage).

Consequently, we as a business intend to deliver a solution to this PoV, as we believe that doing so will lead to maximum success as a new business venture.

Confident... but still aware

Before going any further in the Design Thinking process, it's worthwhile to pause here and note that we've undertaken fairly exhaustive research by this point, including several validation experiments. This means that we can have relatively high confidence that our PoV is accurate, though not necessarily complete, as there's still the risk that it's incomplete in some way. This is because it's straightforward to be exhaustive in what we already know to test for, without being aware of what *else* we should be testing for when we didn't know to do so. Thus, we can move forward with, on one hand, high confidence in our current PoV, but on the other hand, our eyes wide open to the fact that there could still be something else we've missed so far.

Our Design Principles for the solution

Our second order of business here in the Problem-Solution Interface stage is to define the specific Design Principles we'll use in ideating new solutions. This is something we'll do based on the new PoV we just created.

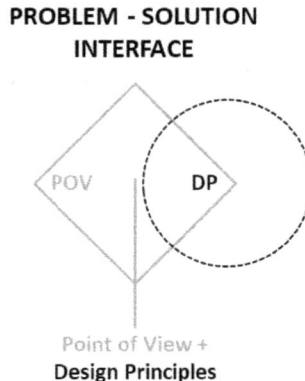

Figure 11.2: The Design Principles step in the Problem-Solution Interface stage

Doing this will, in turn, set us up to be able to conceive any number of possible viable solution concepts to that new PoV. Thus, this is what we will explore now.

Taking stock of where we are now

We've just walked alongside Intensifi as its team defined its final, formal PoV (at least at this point).

Having done this, they are halfway through the Problem-Solution Interface stage (this intermediate stage we find ourselves in right now).

Their next step in this stage will be to take that PoV and use it to define the Design Principles they'll use in going forward. That's what they (and we) will do next.

Understanding Design Principles – what they are

Design Principles reflect the *strategies* we intend to use in solving our subject's problem, according to the PoV we've just established to articulate that problem.

As such, they reflect the set of beliefs we hold regarding what an ideal solution must ultimately *be* and *do* to solve that problem. They are otherwise independent of any specific solution.

Our Design Principles are therefore a guiding statement of *beliefs* – a *thesis* – regarding the following matters:

- The *type of solution* we intend to deliver against our understanding of the problem.
- *Why* we believe that the type of solution is, in fact, the *best way* to address the problem.

Thus, while our PoV established the nature of our problem, our Design Principles establish the nature of our solution – including its Brand Experience and design attributes that ensure it delivers on that experience.

In defining our Design Principles, we will, in effect, translate our findings and PoV into a specific set of **design directives**. Though still abstract, these directives establish certain *imperatives*, and thus actionable *guidelines*, prescribing specific attributes of our solution – things that it must have and/or do in order to optimally solve the problem we're addressing. They thus capture our effort's *design intent*.

So, for example, our Design Principles might state, "Our solution must enable our customers to do X", "our customers must have access to capability Y", and/or "Our solution must not incur Z".

As a litmus test then, a sound set of Design Principles is one that will do the following":

- Fuel the ideation of potential solutions by suggesting numerous "how might we" questions.
- Provide a reference point for evaluating the various competing solution concepts.
- Prevent us from pursuing solutions that want to be "all things to all people" – a mistaken aim.

- Empower us to make decisions both independently and in parallel with one another.
- Guide all of our remaining Design Thinking efforts from this point forward.

Being a statement of beliefs about the type of solution we believe we need to deliver, Design Principles also define a vision for the Brand Experience we hope to deliver, and thus also for the Customer Experiences we intend to stage. They do this by providing the directives we'll use in shaping the solution we ultimately conceive, design, develop, and deliver for this opportunity. They thus define the *Brand Experience Lens* through which we'll cast that solution – and in so doing, define how we will deliver our brand.

Another way of thinking about our Design Principles is that they establish constraints around our solution – what it must *be* and *do*. Those constraints are necessary when working to come up with the best solution for the problem or need we're addressing, since violating them will produce a suboptimal solution that doesn't fully satisfy that problem or need. By adhering to our Design Principles, the solution we produce will be able to deliver the desired and intended Brand Experience for our customers who use the solution. Also, since our Brand Experience applies broadly to the entire brand under which the solution is to be delivered, it adds another layer of constraints on how the solution is delivered.

A team can develop its Design Principles in a couple of ways. They can, for example, simply restate their customer's needs as *solutions* rather than as *needs*, without losing sight of the customer. Alternatively, they can extract their Design Principles from various solutions the subjects they surveyed found compelling, using the specific attributes of those solutions that *resonated* with these subjects and then abstracting those into unique Design Principles.

By following and applying our Design Principles, we'll be able to head into the next stage of the Design Thinking process – Value Definition – armed with the guidelines we require to be able to explore possible solutions and settle on the one solution that best solves our problem with its signature PoV.

Defining the Design Principles

Now that we understand what Design Principles are, we can walk alongside the Intensifi team as they strive to define their particular Design Principles to address their unique PoV. These will be the principles the team applies in working to conceive possible solutions to that PoV.

Here, the team needn't use any particular Design Method per se – aside from those they've already used up to this point. This means they can jump straight into defining their Design Principles based on the discussions they've already had regarding their PoV and what any solution must do to solve that PoV.

Using that approach then, the team has defined the following 15 Design Principles to solve for their PoV. In particular, a solution must do the following:

1. work for business-minded individuals at *each stage* of their career – from the earliest stages (going back to high school) to the latest stages (up to, through, and beyond retirement);

2. empower its users to achieve their maximum possible potential in both *life* (personal matters and outcomes) and *business* (their business' performance and outcomes) – meaning it has to work for both *life-planning* and *business strategy development* using the same interface;

3. operate across *every area of life* – including health, wealth, relationships, marriage, family, employer, career, location, possessions, hobbies, and so on – leaving no area of life untouched;

4. operate across *every area of business* – including strategy, culture, sales, marketing, innovation, R&D, operations, hiring, development, salaries and benefits, and so on – leaving no area of business untouched;

5. provide the user with an *extensible* and *customizable* set of tools and options to work with at any given time – including whatever *knowledge* they require to use in the process at that time;

6. present itself as – in effect – a type of omniscient *Generative AI for Life and Business* genie who is also the user's most highly trusted friend, mentor, and personal life / business coach;

7. provide *connectivity* to various devices used to collect and incorporate relevant data from the user's personal world;

8. ensure *currency* with all the latest news and data from around the world each day;

9. offer an *ecosystem* of select partners to procure certain products and services from – vendors who match the user's present life stage, status, aspirations, and needs;

10. lead users to the most optimal *choices* and *decisions* for that point in their life or business that will ultimately lead to *maximum success* from that point onward;

11. instill *full confidence* in the choices and decisions it leads the user to, based on a demonstrated record of past success and performance;

12. give the user the ability to *socialize* their prescriptions with others they trust, and whose opinions and insights they value;

13. be *private* and *secure* – preventing any unauthorized access at all times, with no exceptions;

14. be *accessible* and *affordable*, in accordance with the particular life stage the user is presently in – meaning it will, in effect, scale with them, their career, and their aspirations over time;

15. instill, at any given point in the process and journey, absolute *satisfaction* and *joy* within its users, with *no regrets ever*.

As a business, then, we intend to deliver a solution that fully adheres to these 15 Design Principles. We believe that doing so will lead to maximum success as a new business venture.

Moreover, when we do actually deliver this solution, we will of course use it in the ongoing operation and growth of our own venture – so that we do in fact attain the maximum possible success as a business over the long run.

Confident but still open-minded

At this point, we can have fairly high confidence in our Design Principles. This is because they emerge directly out of the exhaustive research and validation work we've undertaken so far. They therefore relate directly and concretely to the insights we gathered in that work.

So – just as in their corresponding PoV – we can have relatively high confidence that our Design Principles are in fact accurate, but less so that they are necessarily complete. You see, just like with the PoV, there's always the outside chance that we missed something (something we didn't know to look for), and so there's always the risk that, though accurate in and of themselves, they remain incomplete. This is something we'll have to remain aware of as we go forward. We want to do so with, on one hand, high confidence in these Design Principles, but on the other hand, our eyes wide open to the fact that there could still be other relevant principles we've missed so far.

All of this validated learning effort – as encapsulated in our PoV and Design Principles – provides the insights we need to inform our next-step decision-making – including whether or not to go forward.

Is this still a problem worth solving?

At this point, having fully codified our PoV and its accompanying Design Principles, we and our organization must do one last thing, namely revisit the question of whether or not this new problem – as it has now been reframed and is properly understood (and thus needs to be solved for) – still represents a sound opportunity for us that we wish to pursue; a *problem worth solving* in other words. This is a question about how this specific opportunity links back to our broader organizational strategic intent. Is it a fit for that intent or not? Does it satisfy all of our qualifying criteria?

In most cases, the answer to this question will still be "yes". However, in some cases, it may become clear that the new problem (the properly reframed version of it), or how it needs to be solved, is no longer the type of problem that our organization wishes to address (or is prepared to address). Otherwise, it may represent a different sort or scale of problem that won't make for a sound business investment. In those cases, the endeavor would come to an end at this point and we'd move on to a different, hopefully more lucrative, opportunity.

This demonstrates that the Problem-Solution Interface stage involves the sort of **smart innovation work** that prevents organizations and entrepreneurs from going down unprofitable paths that lead to market failures. This is a very important takeaway in and of itself for us to understand.

Going forward

Now that Intensifi has its PoV and Design Principles, it's ready to move on to exploring possible new solutions to its PoV – its *Solution Space*. That's what it will do next in *Chapter 12*, so stay tuned.

Summary

In this chapter, we learned about the Point of View and the Design Principles – what they are, respectively, and what function they each serve.

In particular, we learned that the PoV is a specific, actionable, and inspiring restatement of our would-be customer's reframed problem. As such, it reflects what their need and/or desire is, why they have that need and/or desire, and why solving for it is a worthwhile endeavor for us.

Likewise, we learned that the Design Principles are a specific set of beliefs about what an ideal solution has to be and do in order to solve the problem. As such, they provide specific constraints on the solution that point to clear strategies to use in solving the problem.

To illustrate both of these, we walked alongside Intensifi as it used certain specific Design Methods to help it flesh out its ultimate PoV, and thereafter craft a set of actionable Design Principles it can use in conceiving possible solutions in the next stage of the Design Thinking process.

This tees us up for our next point in the journey. In *Chapter 12* (up next), we'll dive into the Value Definition stage of Design Thinking to learn – alongside Intensifi – all about how that stage works – both divergently and convergently – to conceive, prototype, and test possible new solutions to the problem and thereby bring the Design Thinking process toward its eventual conclusion.

Working the Solution Space – Up and Down the Next Mountain

In *Chapter 11*, we explored the third stage of the Design Thinking Process – namely, the **Problem-Solution Interface**. In that context, we took an "intermission" between our Problem Space and our Solution Space to refine our *Point of View* (an articulation of our subject's reframed problem) and our *Design Principles* (actionable principles we'll use to guide the solution options we entertain). This allowed us to understand the role each of these play in the Design Thinking process, as well as how to go about developing them (which we did together with Intensifi using certain of the Design Methods).

In this chapter, we're going to explore the fourth stage of the Design Thinking process – namely, **Value Definition**. This is where we work through our Solution Space. This stage is about using creativity and divergent thinking to resourcefully ideate possible new solutions (according to our Design Principles), practical insights to prototype those solutions, and then convergent thinking to test them so as to reveal the best one. We'll come out of this process with a ultimate solution concept that best addresses our subject's real (reframed) problem – according to the Point of View that we articulated for them. This solution – when properly presented and marketed to them – should resonate with them because it resolves their real need, together with their underlying motivations and aspirations. In this process, just like before, we'll call upon certain Design Methods, as well as the five discovery skills (observe, question, experiment, network, and associate), to help us work through the process correctly and arrive at its intended outcome.

As we work through this stage and its respective tasks, we'll come to understand what each task involves and how to go about doing it. As before, we'll be doing this collaboratively with our friends at Intensifi, using select Design Methods to carry out their activities. As we (eventually) approach the end of this stage, the conclusion of the Design Thinking process will start to come into sight for us – which is, namely, turning that solution into a real (winning) value proposition (which we explore in *Chapter 13*) and wrapping a full (innovative) business model around it (the subject of *Chapters 14* and *15*).

In this chapter, we'll specifically explore the following three topics:

- **Divergence – solution ideation – what could be the best solution**: An exploration of the divergent activity of conceiving (ideating) possible solutions to our (real) problem – including the use of inductive logic for doing so.

- **Validation – deciding and planning how to test our options**: An exploration of how to think about prototyping and testing our possible new solutions, and thus develop a plan for doing so.

- **Convergence – solution testing – finding which solution is best**: An exploration of the convergent activity of testing out our possible different solutions to arrive at the one solution (or combination of solutions) that best resolves our subject's real problem – including the use of deductive logic to do so.

When we finish this chapter, we will have thoroughly explored Intensifi's Solution Space with them (albeit not without a detour along the way… as we'll soon find out)! We'll also come away with a complete understanding of the critical role the tasks of this stage play in the overall Design Thinking process.

Divergence – solution ideation – what could be the best solution

The Value Definition stage is about trying to creatively and resourcefully contemplate and consider all of the possible different **solutions** we can come up with to our PoV so that, ultimately, we can test most or all of them against our subject's *real needs* (using those subjects) so as to arrive at the **one best solution** (or combination of solutions) that will fully meet those needs and therefore resonate with them.

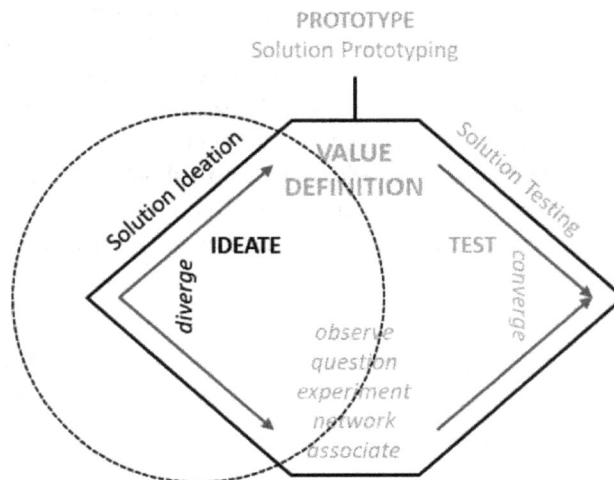

Figure 12.1: Starting at the Ideate step of the Value Definition
stage to ideate possible new solutions (divergent)

Our point of entry into this stage is working to conceive and consider as many possible solutions to our problem as possible – an activity we'll do by collectively brainstorming possible solutions using different methods and techniques that ignite fresh new thinking about the problem (something our PoV has also hopefully done at this point). Doing this will require us to do lots of thinking about this problem and what motivations and aspirations are behind it, and then use inductive logic to conceive new solutions that address those factors.

Appreciating Intensifi's goal at this point

At this point, Intensifi's goal is to ensure they are ideating solution concepts that are all rooted in a proper and correct understanding of the **market need** they're addressing – solutions that create the necessary "pull" from inside that market, so that adoption of the final solution comes easily and naturally and doesn't require an excessive "push" effort from them. This will ensure – all else being right about their business model – maximum adoption of the solution and, therefore, maximum growth and scaling of their new business venture.

This is what they're trying to do now… develop solution concepts that are most capable of resonating with as many subjects as possible in this market space – a task they'll leverage their creativity to do.

Recalling the need to begin unbounded – with no presuppositions

Before embarking on this stage, Intensifi's leadership is reminded of what they learned back in *Chapter 7*, namely, that they must – if they hope to maximize their chances of success here – begin unbounded, with no real presuppositions about the specific *type* of solution they'll have to offer. It could be a product, a service, an experience, a community, or some combination of all these. At this point, they're allowing themselves to remain wide open to all possibilities, so that they can (hopefully) arrive at the best possible solution (and thus value proposition), whatever that ultimately ends up being. Doing so will maximize their overall chances of business success.

This is also one more reason why these leaders are extremely thankful for the highly cross-functional team they've assembled around them. They feel very confident that this cross-functional team will allow them to be as objective and as open-minded as possible – considering all solution concepts from a broad range of perspectives and experiences – so as to arrive at very high caliber solution concepts whatever form and manifestation they each take.

Intensifi's ideation plan – 12 Design Methods

To undertake the work of ideating possible new solutions, the team has decided to employ the following 12 Design Methods – each bucketed into one of three method types. They've chosen these in particular because they believe these specific methods will allow them to maximize their creativity and resourcefulness here, and thereby ideate as many possible new solution concepts as possible. In particular, Intensifi will be using three Question Methods, one Experiment Method, and eight Study Methods, as listed here:

- **Question Methods**

  - Kano Analysis

  - Collaborative Sketching

  - Participatory Design / Co-creation

- **Experiment Methods**

  - User Scenarios

- **Study Methods**

  - Competitive Product Survey

  - Analogous Empathy

  - Brainstorming

  - Constraint Imposition

  - Piggybacking

  - Alignment Model

  - Predict Next Year's Headlines

  - Brand Swap / Brandcasting.

Next, we'll explain each of these methods, how the team is using them, and what outcomes they attain from them – including the final set of solution concepts they develop from them.

The Question Methods

Intensifi starts with the three *Question Methods*. They'll use these methods to query their subjects further so as to gain better clarity around what might be viable solution concepts to consider.

Kano Analysis

What it is: Kano Analysis is a quantitative survey method used to understand would-be users' preferences surrounding certain specific product or service attributes and their relative priority. Researchers will often use this method to help guide them in solution refinement, as they seek to prioritize the relative attributes of their solution and otherwise develop their specifications for it.

Here, survey respondents are asked to consider a number of different product or service attributes, and then bracket them into either "must-haves" or "nice-to-haves," and then within each of those groups, to order them further according to their respective level of *value*. In this way, researchers are able to understand would-be users' *preferences* and *priorities* – including which attributes are necessary to ensure their complete satisfaction, and which can be used to create additional delight beyond that.

Kano Analysis – like all other Question Methods – requires the respondents to have an appropriate base of context from which to be able to answer its questions. This means they need to have full familiarity with the products or services involved. The method cannot be used when dealing with *new* product categories for which respondents have no prior context unless possibly there is a comparable product category that they do know and which can be used as a surrogate, in which case the researchers will be projecting feedback from one domain onto a new one. In those cases, the onus is on them to ensure that doing so produces reliable results.

How Intensifi uses it: Intensifi uses this method to ask its subjects to think back to prior solutions they've used or consumed to help them optimize certain areas of their lives or businesses, and then, based on that, to prioritize the specific set of attributes Intensifi has defined for them – as well as add any of their own they felt were important and which Intensifi did not offer. Their goal in doing this is to see what attributes subjects deem to be most- and least-important in the grand scheme of things, with the hope this will help illuminate the nature of a solution to offer them.

Intensifi's outcomes: Intensifi gains the following results from this exercise – each list being listed in order of most to least important:

- Must-haves: dependable (reliable) maximization, current insights, extensible (customizable), private, comprehensive, sociable, and downtime value.

- Nice-to-haves: fully connected, secure, affordable, access early on, and reliable future predictions.

From these lists, the team sees the sorts of priority that subjects are placing on these respective attributes, which kind of tells them that there may likely be elements in the final solution that are software, services, and possibly even hardware (of their own or of others).

What was surprising to them, however, was the mention of several other (new) attributes they had not previously identified – including *downtime value*, *access early on (in life)*, and *reliable future predictions*. These each showed up multiple times among participants but had not before, and, therefore, hadn't made it into the team's current PoV or Design Principles. So, for the moment, the team "sticks a pin" in this new insight and holds onto it as fodder for further discussions later on.

Collaborative Sketching

What it is: Collaborative Sketching is a participatory co-creation activity that's used to either better understand subjects' perceptions of a particular design and how it relates to their particular needs, desires, values, and motivations, or else to engage a team in trying to create a shared vision of some ideal design concept. As a practice, sketching helps participants express their ideas in a very *tangible* way. That, in turn, tends to bring clarity around design objectives and solution requirements.

Collaborative Sketching is conducted inside an open workshop. Here, the group is first presented with the specific design challenge or problem statement. Then, each subject proceeds to sketch their own thoughts about the design space, including its deficiencies and potential design solutions. Next, the whole group discusses their respective reasons for drawing particular design solutions. Subsequently, they all sketch new, revised versions of their concepts, possibly incorporating certain of the shared dialogue that they just had. Subjects can iterate on their design solutions as much as they want, to explore countless different concepts, approaches, combinations, and refinement of their ideas.

With a cohort of subjects, these sketches will provide researchers with insights into the individuals' unique needs, desires, values, and motivations – as well as an understanding of how they *perceive* certain design solutions resonating or not resonating with those needs, desires, values, and motivations. With a team that's seeking a shared vision, as they go through the exercise, the workshop leader will work to steer them toward a common shared vision of the ideal design solution. This may require any number of *iterative* sketching sessions to move them in that direction and, ultimately, arrive at the shared vision they seek.

Organizations sometimes run these workshops twice – first with outside subjects to better understand their needs and motivations, and secondly, with the affected internal team to work toward a shared vision that resonates with those particular needs and motivations.

How Intensifi uses it: Intensifi uses this method to engage recruited subjects in collaborative sketching workshops. They actually conduct two different workshops, the first being focused on life optimization, where participants are presented with the design challenge of conceiving a solution that uses the latest technologies and capabilities to empower people to fully optimize their entire lives, and the second being focused on business optimization, where participants are presented with the design challenge of conceiving a solution that uses the latest technologies and capabilities to empower business leaders to optimize their organization's holistic business performance, according to their key strategic goals.

Intensifi's outcomes: Intensifi gained some useful insight from these workshops. In both cases, participants seemed to be leaning toward online platform tools as a possible primary source of value and interaction, with augmenting services as a possible secondary (support) source of value and interaction, while also acknowledging the critical role that hardware devices will have to play to integrate relevant data about users and their bodies, possessions, assets, and environments. There didn't seem to be a clear consensus, however, even after discussing each participant's specific reasons for sketching what they did – around which form of value would be best, and therefore, which should actually be the primary, secondary, and tertiary, nor how exactly users should interact with them all, other than that everyone acknowledged that some type of technological devices, tools, and platforms will somehow have to be a part of the equation to achieve the aims of their design challenge.

Participatory Design / Co-creation

What it is: Participatory Design, or Co-creation, is a workshop method where both the researchers and their external subjects are paired together to work on designing and co-creating a new solution together. By incorporating actual subjects into this conception process, the goal is to yield solutions that accurately reflect their real needs, expectations, and priorities.

The workshop commonly proceeds in three stages. In *Stage 1*, the group collectively explores the challenge or problem of concern together, and the Design Space surrounding that, including what the current customer experience happens to be like. In *Stage 2*, the group engages in an exploration of what the ideal solution or ideal customer experience might look like, and why it would be such (which often reveals the underlying needs, motivations, values, and priorities involved). In *Stage 3*, the group collectively explores different ways of achieving that ideal solution/experience, testing each concept against the subjects' needs to see how well they do or do not address those needs and thereby resonate with these subjects. In the latter case, additional latent needs can surface that weren't surfaced previously, adding further to the constraints around a final solution.

Once the workshop is complete, the researchers will typically walk away with a much clearer understanding of that particular cohort's needs, desires, values, priorities, and motivations – based on the range of inputs they provided. These will then serve as guiding constraints in ideating and validating a final solution for them.

The researchers can repeat this workshop with any number of different cohorts if each one represents a different market segment, since each segment may have its own unique set of needs, desires, values, priorities, and motivations. The researchers can then look toward a solution that satisfies the largest superset of these different needs, so as to deliver a solution that's capable of resonating with the broadest possible market.

How Intensifi uses it: Intensifi uses this method to explore, more directly, specific *types* of solutions with participants – anchored, respectively, in standalone digital tools, online platforms, concierge-style services, hardware devices, and more. The team specifically wants to understand how people might respond to different types of solutions, and how much certain technologies, such as AI, can be a part of those solutions before they start to feel overly obtrusive.

Intensifi runs two different workshops with the method – one on personal life optimization and one on business optimization. In each of them, they ask participants to think not so much about *themselves* and how they *personally* might respond to each of the solutions, but rather how they believe *others* in those situations (different "personas") will respond to them. It was done this way for two reasons. First, psychologically, people tend to answer more accurately (and more objectively) when talking about other people versus themselves. Second, it overcomes the hesitation that people otherwise have when needing to talk about themselves (which requires a high level of vulnerability on their part – something not every subject is always ready to give).

Intensifi's outcomes: In both workshops, Intensifi spent considerable time with participants discussing the nature of the different types of solutions – again, standalone digital tools, online platforms, concierge-style services, hardware devices, and more – plus the role that certain technologies (especially AI) would or would not play in them. Intensifi then had participants – one option at a time – walk through the simulated mental exercise of using that type of solution, to get their perceived reactions to how they believed certain specific personas would respond to them.

From this, the team learned that most participants believed the different personas would be a bit reticent and cautious about the intrusiveness of the technology (AI in particular) on their lives and business. But otherwise, they seemed to believe that these users should be comfortable with the technology, so long as they believed they remained in control of it, and what it did or did not do with their lives (or businesses) and data. Similarly, they felt these users would be comfortable relying on different concierge services so long as these remained affordable and within reach to them, without starting to override the purpose of the solution in the first place.

Consequently, the exercise gave the team fairly good confidence that at least the technological elements of the solution would be acceptable so long as they were framed and presented in a way that made the users feel in control of them (at least on the surface) and that solutions involving mixed modalities would likely be acceptable so long as users saw the value of them from an overall holistic standpoint.

Insights Summary – Ideate – Question Methods		
Question Method 1 **Kano Analysis**	**Question Method 2** **Collaborative Sketching**	**Question Method 3** **Participatory Design / Co-Creation**

Key Insights • Online tool primary interaction point. • Services secondary interaction point. • Generally comfortable with the tech (so long as it's not too intrusive).	**New Ideas (Solution Concepts)** • A solution that addresses the user's concern over the technology becoming more intrusive than they're comfortable with. • Solution Must-Haves: • Dependable, reliable maximization • Current insights • Extensible platform • Private • Sociable • With downtime value. • Solution Nice-To-Haves: • Fully connected • Secure • Affordable • Access early on • Reliable future projections.

Figure 12.2: Insights Summary for ideation using the Question Methods

The Experiment Method

Intensifi next moves on to the one *Experiment Method* they chose. They'll use it to try out different concept ideas with their subjects and get their reactions to them.

User Scenarios

What it is: User Scenarios is a method used to test proposed new solutions and their usage experiences. Here, the researchers storyboard a very character-rich storyline illustrating the *context* for using a particular solution, this being that solution's *User Scenario*. They repeat this for each proposed scenario. Thereafter, they *compare* and *critique* each such storyline against one another. This lets them consider and evaluate the essence of each possible scenario in the broader context of their expected solution usage, as well as in the context of one another. To be most effective, researchers can also bring in subjects and have *them* evaluate and critique these scenarios – to offer *their* feedback and reactions to them. This can often be more useful than internal reviews and critiques.

Researchers often find this method useful when contemplating different hypotheses about the situation – what's right and wrong about each imagined scenario, and which scenario best represents peoples' reality as they perceive it. They also find it valuable when evaluating different solution concepts against each other – which concept produces a User Scenario that best meets users' needs and removes their frictions and pains.

How Intensifi uses it: Intensifi uses this method to reinforce their Participatory Design workshop efforts. In this case, they're also running two different workshops – one on personal life optimization and one on business optimization. Here, however, they storyboard specific user scenarios with participants and ask them to think not about *other users*, but rather, about *themselves personally and specifically* – how they believe *they* will respond and react to these different scenarios. The character-rich storylines the team creates really help to bring the different scenarios participants will encounter to life so that they can project themselves and their own lives into them.

Intensifi's outcomes: Intensifi's outcomes from this activity were similar to those they obtained from their Participatory Design workshops, except that participants seemed to be a lot less reticent and cautious about how they believed they would react to the intrusiveness of the technology (AI in particular) on their lives and business. It seemed that when thinking about themselves rather than others, participants tended to be a lot more "adventurous" and not as risk-averse as they imagined others would be (which points to a clear difference between how people perceive their own attitudes and behaviors, and how they perceive those of others).

Here, participants felt quite comfortable with lots of technology, so long as they (again) felt that they remained in control of it and what it did or did not do with their lives (or businesses) and data. Likewise, they again felt comfortable relying on different concierge-style services so long as those remained affordable and within reach, and didn't start to override the whole purpose of the solution in the first place.

These participants also wondered, with each of the solution concepts, what value they would be getting from them during periods of relative stability in their lives or businesses – where they weren't needing to make any major life or business decisions with them. Would they just be dead costs during those times? Here, again, was this question the team encountered earlier during their Kano Analysis, where people were concerned about the value of the solution during "lulls" in their situation… something the team made a note of to come back to.

Insights Summary – Ideate – Experiment Method

Experiment Method 1
User Scenarios

Key Insights

- Users are comfortable with the tech so long as *they* are in control of it.
- Users are comfortable with the services so long as they are affordable & within reach.

New Ideas (Solution Concepts)

- A solution that addresses users' concerns / cautiousness about the intrusiveness of the technology.
- A solution that addresses users' concerns over whether or not the solution has any value during periods of stability (no major new decisions being needed).

Figure 12.3: Insights Summary for Ideation using the Experiment Method

The Study Methods

Intensifi finally moves on to the eight *Study Methods* they've selected. They'll use these methods – some on their own and some with their subjects – to study the overall Solution Space further and develop clearer insights into it.

Competitive Product Survey

What it is: A Competitive Product Survey is a study method where the researchers go out and collect information on their organization's competitors' products and services, as well as possibly secure instances of those for themselves, so that they can evaluate them firsthand (both qualitatively and quantitatively). This allows them to build a database of competitive offerings so that they can compare all the various competing options in a particular category against each other – often feature by feature, function by function, attribute by attribute, and positioning by positioning.

This sort of information – once the researchers have fully absorbed it – can do three things for them. First, it can help them fully understand all the options their customers have available to them in the marketplace at that point in time. Second, it can help them paint a useful backdrop for new solutions (at least for incremental solutions) by understanding the full superset of capabilities, features, aesthetics, prices, sizes, weights, and so on in the marketplace. This lets them understand the breadth of the current Solution Space in use, including whatever the "state-of-the-art" happens to be at that time for this category. Third, from a benchmarking standpoint, it lets them clearly understand where their organization's current solutions (if they exist) fall within that superset – are they at or near the top, the bottom, or somewhere in the middle? This lets them know where the organization is starting from presently, though it is not necessarily where the organization should end up once they're done – depending on this starting point.

Having this information in hand, researchers can establish new functional performance standards and other benchmark targets they wish to pursue in a new solution. The only consideration they must be careful about is not allowing these to constrain them to *incrementalism*, as say, pursuing a 20% performance improvement on a particular attribute – an incremental improvement – may actually lead them to consider only incremental innovations. If what their organization in fact seeks is a *breakthrough* innovation, then these functional performance standards and other benchmark targets may be entirely irrelevant, because such a solution would solve the problem in such a radically different way that an entirely different set of performance attributes would be required. When that's the mandate, the researchers must focus their collective mind instead on how to define that breakthrough solution and not on how to incrementally improve on existing performance standards.

How Intensifi uses it: Intensifi uses this method to go out and benchmark all the existing *partial* life optimization solutions on the market – including those for health and wellness, investing and wealth management, career development, hobbies, business improvement, and so on. This has them studying vendors such as Quicken, Wealthfront, eMoney, MindBody, ActiveHealth, CoachHub, Zavvy, DevSkiler, and literally hundreds of others – all to understand their respective tools, platforms, offerings, user interfaces, and business models.

Intensifi's outcomes: From doing this benchmarking research, Intensifi builds out a database of different solutions where they profile the specific capabilities of each, together with their user interface models and their respective business models. Based on this, Intensifi has a foundational knowledge of everything out there and where each piece fits into the broader puzzle. They can build on this to understand how different solution ideas they have match or exceed the capabilities of these solutions, meaning they know where the "bar" is set in each case, and what functional outcomes they must meet or exceed (ideally exceed).

The team also notes that more and more of these solutions are incorporating various types of AI, including Generative AI, but also many backend machine-learning algorithms that let the solutions become increasingly personalized to the end user with passing time and increased usage. They take special note of this.

Analogous Empathy

What it is: Analogous Empathy is a method used to draw out analogous solution spaces (products, services, experiences, and so on) that serve as either strong or weak examples of particularly critical areas of a team's Problem Space. They're used to help teams develop a deeper shared understanding of those areas by seeing firsthand cases where the area is particularly *well-served* and possibly cases where it is particularly *poorly-served*. The team can then project those insights into *their* Problem Space as a starter for what is *possible* in a particular area (though they're also free to go *beyond* these examples).

To get the most out of this method, the team should – once they've identified an analogous space and have gone out and studied it – bring all that information back into their workspace and build out an *Analogous Empathy Inspiration Board* from it, saturating the board with pictures, key observations, new insights, representative quotes, and so on. This will help them to develop a deep *shared understanding* of that analogous space.

How Intensifi uses it: Intensifi uses this method to search for other domains with analogous solution spaces that they can compare to and then researches those domains to learn the specific details of each one, which they then bring back into their situation to spur the conceptualization of new solutions in their domain. They are, in particular, looking for other domains where the subject's comprehensive needs are met holistically.

Intensifi's outcomes: Intensifi identifies several domains where the subjects' needs are being met more or less holistically – including certain medical systems that deliver holistic medical care, comprehensive travel planners who deliver comprehensive turnkey travel arrangements, and several high-end concierge services that offer life-enhancement services to the wealthy and affluent.

Based on undertaking analogous benchmarking of these different providers and their solutions, two things become immediately apparent to the team: number one, that completely transparent many-to-many communication channels are paramount to the solutions even working (ideally without the need for a centralized hub to coordinate the communications); and number two, that all of the data embedded (or to be embedded) in the associated systems must be thoroughly architected to be fully usable in each part of the overall system, thereby avoiding any interoperability issues between datasets and the associated digital tools. Ancillary to this, and recognizing the fact that many legacy sources of data (which will still be needed) will in fact *not* adhere to that architecture, is the need for data scrubbers that take this legacy data (including its unstructured data) and restructure it into forms that fit into the new architecture.

On top of this, the team also recognizes that central to any holistic approach working properly is a clearly defined hierarchy of heuristics with very clear rules for how they all interact with one another. For example, if two or more optimization goals conflict with each other, then which one commands the highest priority, and which one is assigned the lowest priority, and how are they ordered and ranked otherwise? Plus, what is the overall relative prioritization of the optimization agenda and how are different conflicts to be handled (and under what conditions is user involvement required versus not required)? This is important because it highlights the centrality of the need for some type of governing AI to govern and administer this set of hierarchical heuristics with its potentially complex interplays – despite whatever type of solution might be offered otherwise.

Backcasting

What it is: Backcasting is an ideation method that teams use to brainstorm innovations that get them from a present state (today's situation) to a desired future state (tomorrow's situation) by working backward from that future state to the present state. Here, teams begin by visualizing an ideal future state where all of their subjects' pains, frictions, and tensions have been entirely eliminated, and potentially in which additional gains have been created for these subjects. They'll typically write a storyline reflecting a day in the life of their subject under this ideal future state. They may even storyboard or physically mock-up that ideal future state so as to truly bring it to life. Of all the exercises, this one can truly engage the team's imagination.

The team then explores and captures all the details of the innovation that gets their subject from the present state of affairs to the new state of affairs, and precisely how it does that. That results in the definition of their new solution, which, in turn, allows them to articulate all the necessary assumptions, actions, and outcomes that have to happen to bring that solution to life.

Teams can use this method to great effect because most people find it easier to first imagine an ideal future state and then work backward from that state than to take a present state of affairs and try to work forward. The reason for this is because of how the human mind works. Imagining an ideal future state engages a part of the brain associated with the imagination, which is quite capable of imagining anything we want it to. By having this ideal future state fixed in one's mind, the mind has a destination that it wants to work toward. This destination tends to "pull" the rest of the mind toward it. A different part of the brain – that is associated with creativity – then goes to work and can be incredibly resourceful in coming up with all sorts of ways to get to that new destination. Backcasting engages both of these brain centers and allows the different areas of the mind to work together to get us to our destination. In contrast, without the mind pulling us toward a destination, it becomes much more challenging for the brain's creativity center to know what to work on Thus, our creativity is never fully engaged without first having this destination, which is precisely why the use of the imagination (to imagine our destination) must always precede the use of creativity (to figure out how to get us to our destination).

How Intensifi uses it: Intensifi uses this method to cast a vision for what it wants to see in the future and then uses that method to help its team think through the things it must do to achieve that vision.

Intensifi's outcomes: Intensifi defines as its vision a world in which millions of people all over the world are living life, and running businesses, to the maximum of their respective potentials (though this does raise a question about the knock-on effect to those individuals and businesses who don't use its solution… will they somehow have their lives and businesses minimized as a result of not using this solution when others are? Will they care?).

Based on this vision, Intensifi recognizes the need for whatever solution they offer to be completely *scalable* all over the world – to everyone who wants it – without prejudice or discrimination around who can access it. They realize this puts a particularly heavy burden on them – given the projected power of their solution – to ensure its democratization – so that it can't be "captured" by various powers, political or otherwise, and allowed only to some while denied to others (therefore, they realize this isn't going to be without its barriers in certain countries). This then poses the question to them as to which type of solution – platform, standalone tool, service, product, and so on – will best permit that to become true, something they will continue to ponder going forward.

Brainstorming

What it is: Brainstorming is a generative group method that uses collective thinking to generate new ideas. It lets a group come up with numerous new ideas and concepts that they most likely would never have come up with were each individual to work on their own to think up new ideas. In this sense, brainstorming's real power lies in the fact that it is a *group method* – it leverages the *collective* thinking power of an entire group. Because the different group members all listen to one another and give consideration to each person's ideas, their thinking is able to build on the group's overall collective thinking, and thus their ideas all build on each other. As a group, therefore, they're able to produce substantially more and better ideas than they ever could if each person were to work alone in isolation.

Teams will commonly – over a period of time – conduct countless brainstorming sessions, often of different types and flavors for different goals and objectives, and often in short sprints, so as to not overly exhaust their minds (the work can be very mentally taxing). Consequently, brainstorming sessions tend to define for the team those specific periods in time where they collectively engage only the generative parts of their minds, placing the evaluative parts on "pause." This allows them to generate a large number of high-caliber ideas, without regard for their efficacy at this point (that consideration comes later). In this sense, brainstorming can become a real ritual for teams.

Great practices for facilitating brainstorming sessions are broadly published and, therefore, not reproduced here, other than to say that teams should take advantage of those practices to ensure their brainstorming sessions are as effective as they can be. They should also use them to guard against the many possible pitfalls this method is prone to, such as groupthink, bandwagon effect, and countless other collective cognitive biases the method tends to attract to itself (each of which *can be* guarded against). After each such brainstorming session, the team will need to "harvest" out certain winning concepts that they then explore and evaluate further.

How Intensifi uses it: Intensifi uses this method by inviting in a few additional parties and, based on everything it has learned thus far, brainstorming potential solution concepts to test.

Intensifi's outcomes: From this method, and after numerous ideation sessions and subsequent harvesting, Intensifi identifies five main solution concepts it wishes to test. In each case, the concept allows the user to establish all of their life or business goals and, thereafter, access detailed guidance on how to achieve those, given their inherent capabilities, capacities, and resources. These five main concepts are as follows:

1. A native digital app/tool that can be operated independently (in other words, it is not dependent on being constantly connected to cloud servers to operate and deliver its outcomes). This would operate on existing computers and smart devices. This tool would interface with external hardware devices (as needed) to periodically collect relevant data from them.

2. An online digital platform that uses constant connection to cloud servers to operate and deliver its outcomes. It too would operate on existing computers and smart devices and tie into their respective privacy and security systems to enhance its own online privacy and security. This platform would constantly interface with external hardware devices to collect pertinent data from them.

3. A concierge service in which humans (augmented by various technological tools behind the scenes) operate at the primary interface level and serve users to ensure they are each achieving their desired and expected outcomes and results. This service would interface with select external hardware devices (as needed) to collect relevant data from them.

4. A separate, dedicated physical device that users carry around and use to engage with the system, with all processing being done locally on the device, and the device otherwise connecting online mainly to pull in refreshed data on an as-needed basis. This device would interface with other external devices – either constantly or as required (per user preferences) – to collect pertinent data from them. Inspiration for this comes from devices such as the Rabbit r1 and Humane Ai Pin.

5. A combination of all of the aforementioned, with each part operating in sync with the others to do whatever it does best to deliver the most optimal overall user experience possible, thereby ensuring that users at all times have access to the most current and relevant guidance possible, including the knowledge and ability to apply it most effectively with extremely high confidence and assurance of the outcomes.

Each of these must, of course, deliver on Intensifi's stated Design Principles. That being said, Intensifi understands that some of these concepts will inherently deliver on certain Design Principles better than will others. That's one reason why the team is also considering a composite solution because they suspect that being able to achieve all of their Design Principles may very well require some type of hybrid solution.

Intensifi intends to test each of these solution concepts against subjects for their respective efficacy.

Constraint Imposition

What it is: Constraint Imposition is any place where a team places intentional *constraints* on their solution ideation efforts – something they do to help better focus that effort and, ultimately, produce better, more high-caliber ideas than they would otherwise. This may at first seem counterintuitive, but it has been born out in many research studies and elsewhere that using constraints in this way does in fact work. Imposing constraints (chosen intentionally by the team to focus their efforts toward ideas that are truly of value to their task) will, in the end, help produce the largest number of high-value ideas pertinent to their challenge. The specific constraints they choose, and when and where they apply them, are also important. Thus, the team must be very intentional in choosing and using them.

Teams can, of course, choose to apply and remove constraints *at will*, any time they desire. Thus, in the interest of trying to spark a new line of thinking, they may choose to append a new constraint on their efforts to see how that might steer the line of thought and what new ideas it might stir up. When finished with that line of thought, they might likewise move on to applying *yet other constraints*, each in succession and one at a time, so that, when finished, they'll have conceived a large number of new ideas. Brainstorming leaders should thus come to brainstorm sessions prepared with a list of constraints they can opt to try – constraints that they have thought through for their value in moving the team toward the types of solutions needed.

The same also applies in early prototyping, where researchers "build to think." Here, by constraining the time they have for each prototype and possibly the materials they can use, they will often come up with many low-resolution prototypes that help to spark their thinking.

How Intensifi uses it: Intensifi uses this method while brainstorming to consider efforts to make individuals' lives and businesses 10–100X more successful than they are today. Doing this has ruled out many incremental evolutions of current offerings, ensuring that Intensifi takes a truly fresh new approach to achieving its goal.

Intensifi's outcomes: Intensifi's use of this method results in solution concepts that conceptually leapfrog everything current partial life optimization solutions do and, instead, work together holistically to in fact deliver 10–100X more success than anything presently can. This is reflected in each of their five main concepts.

Piggybacking

What it is: Piggybacking is a specific method used inside of brainstorming that lets individuals build their new ideas directly on top of other people's new ideas.

To use this method, the team hosts several timed silent ideation sprints. Within each of these, every person – working alone and in silence – creates a set of new ideas and records them on a piece of paper (this, by itself, is also known as *brainwriting*). At the end of each round, they pass that set of new ideas to another person in the group (often the person to their right if arranged in a circle), and that individual then proceeds – in the next round – to list additional new ideas that specifically *build upon* the prior person's ideas (again working alone and in silence). This process is repeated again and again, each time with a new person building on all the prior person's respective ideas. This will commonly go on for five or six rounds, depending on the time available.

Once the group is done with this part of the exercise, they'll then share openly across the group all of the different ideas that were generated and why certain ideas were built upon certain other ideas.

Teams can make good use of this method, as the ideas it generates tend to be of a very high caliber, and often lead to entirely new concepts that the team had not previously considered, and thus offer fodder for additional concepts they can try out. It's particularly helpful whenever the team is engaged in the *Ideate* step of Value Definition, especially if they happen to get stuck at this point.

The method benefits greatly from using the broadest possible cross-section of participants, including any number of "outsiders" – as cognitive and experiential diversity produces the highest possible caliber outcomes.

How Intensifi uses it: Intensifi uses this method to help everyone in its brainstorming sessions ensure they are first starting out with a great collection of new ideas by brainwriting as many as they can, and then using those to piggyback off of each other and consider as many possible new ideas as possible.

Intensifi's outcomes: Via this very powerful method, Intensifi is able to maximize both the quantity and quality of new ideas they generate as a group. This results in the set of new ideas that they came away with from the previous Brainstorming.

Alignment Model

What it is: An Alignment Model is a method teams use to highlight the *relationships* between subjects' tasks and the attributes of a particular product, service, or experience. It lets teams understand the key activity / attribute relationships, and thus spot where weaknesses and gaps exist that reflect a possible innovation opportunity.

To build an Alignment Model for a particular customer experience or scenario, the researcher first breaks down the subject's activities into discrete tasks, which they'll arrange into columns across the top of a work-board. Depending on the activity, there can be any number of different tasks, and thus task columns. Next, using these different task columns, they enter all the different product, service, or experience attributes into every column they impact. Such attributes might include features, functions, aesthetics, dimensions, weight, content, duration, and so on. Each such impact must be assessed in the context of this subject's needs and desired outcomes and can be both positive in nature, such as supporting features, or negative in nature, such as detracting characteristics. They will thus indicate this nature with either a + or -, respectively, or *0* if neutral.

When finished, the researcher has a completed Alignment Model showing where and how each specific attribute impacts each respective task, reflecting in one place where all the different attribute-task touchpoints exist and what their nature is. This can quickly highlight two things. First, wherever a gap exists, there is the possible opportunity to deliver a new innovation that positively closes that gap. Second, wherever a negative impact occurs (a weakness in the solution), there is the possible opportunity to deliver a new innovation that turns that into a positive impact. Depending on which tasks subjects consider to be most important to them (often where their expectations are highest), and which tasks they deem to be most underserved, the second situation often provides an even more powerful opportunity than the first.

Teams can use Alignment Models both in Problem Clarification work, where they help to understand the weaknesses of present solutions (and thus a potential source for subjects' pains), and in Value Definition work, where they help to map out new solution attributes that resolve confirmed pains and better meet customer needs. In both cases, the tool helps to frame the team's discussion around specific *solution attributes*, which allows them to eventually arrive at the most ideal set of attributes to deliver on their Point of View.

How Intensifi uses it: Intensifi uses this method to walk through the conceptualized customer experience of using each type of solution it is considering, identify the specific solution attributes involved, and then think through how to optimize each of those for the most ideal customer experience possible.

Intensifi's outcomes: Using this method, Intensifi comes away with a specific set of attributes for each of the five types of solutions it is considering, as noted previously under *Brainstorming*. These include such attributes as specific User Interface parameters (such as intuitiveness of use), specific UX parameters (such as speed of processing and returning results, and extensibility), specific cost parameters (upfront and ongoing costs), specific privacy and security parameters, specific device interoperability parameters, and specific overall customer experience parameters – as well as others.

Predict Next Year's Headlines

What it is: Predict Next Year's Headlines is a very informative and engaging exercise teams can use to help their organization develop a useful *Brand Experience Lens* through which to formulate its PoV and new solutions to that PoV. Since, at this point, the team has completed its Problem Clarification work with its supporting Market and User Research, the exercise can be well-informed and capable of marrying those insights with how the organization wants to go forward in the ensuing future.

Here, the team first recruits a panel of key internal stakeholders to join them in this exercise. Next, that broader team spends time together projecting their organization into the foreseeable future by coming up with *idealized news headlines* for the ensuing years. These headlines reflect different *scenarios* the organization wants to play out. Having these helps the broader team, and the organization overall, to better understand how they need to go about delivering their particular brand (or cause), as well as how they need to develop and enrich certain relationships further.

Teams can use this method whenever trying to ideate new solutions. It serves to inform the particular Brand Experience the organization wants to deliver in those solutions, and thus the Brand Experience Lens through which they will need to conceive and articulate those solutions.

How Intensifi uses it: Intensifi uses this method to have a fun workshop break for just themselves to think through the type of brand promise, brand message, and brand language they want to convey for the sort of value proposition they aspire to. This is a welcome respite from having to recruit so many other outside subjects to interview and work with.

Intensifi's outcomes: In this workshop, the Intensifi team generates the following key future headlines:

- Intensifi stuns the world with the first ever truly comprehensive life- and business-optimization solution.

- Entire product categories collapse as Intensifi gives the world "one solution to rule them all".

- One company finally figures out what to (really) use AI for – meet Intensifi!

- Never again fall short of your potential – Intensifi unlocks maximum possibilities!

Out of these types of headlines, it becomes increasingly clear to Intensifi that what they want to do is deliver a brand whose promise, message, language, positioning, and actual solution are all about optimizing people's lives and businesses in a way that was never possible before – even for the average professional, not just the wealthy and affluent. It wants to be that business that can truly say, "We make your dreams come true!" – and sincerely mean it for all who dare to pursue those dreams of optimization. It wants to be the business that can say, "Where every day is the most important day of your life!", and then deliver on that with astounding outcomes and results. This means that whatever solution Intensifi offers, it has to be 100% capable of delivering on its promise of always-on maximum optimization across a person's entire lifespan.

Brand Swap / Brandcasting

What it is: Brand Swap and Brandcasting offer teams a way to collaboratively explore different variations on their PoV as they address a particular challenge or opportunity aimed at resolving a specific problem.

Here, team members engage in a discussion in which they imagine their solution being designed, developed, marketed, and delivered by some other well-known organization with a highly-recognized brand.

Representative questions put forth might thus be as follows:

- How would Disney solve this problem?
- How would Amazon solve this problem?
- How would Starbucks solve this problem?
- How would Nike solve this problem?
- How would Apple solve this problem?

And on the examples would go.

The idea here is that because each one of these organizations has its own respective Brand Experience Lens through which it will cast a solution (so done to deliver a consistent brand experience to its customers), it would solve the problem in a particularly characteristic way for that brand.

Thus by exploring their subjects' problem through these different Brand Experience Lenses, teams are often able to develop a better sense of how *they* want to solve the problem, and in a way that delivers a particular brand experience on behalf of their brand or cause in the market. This often allows them to deliver the type of innovation that optimally resonates with their particular customers and/or with the types of customers they aspire to gain. It also plays a role in how they ultimately go about *positioning* the solution they conceive and, thus, influences the commercialization strategy they ultimately use in taking that solution to market.

How Intensifi uses it: Intensifi uses this method to further refine and reinforce its own brand identity.

Intensifi's outcomes: By thinking through how other parties they respect – such as Apple, Starbucks, and Virgin, for example – might deliver this solution, the team is able to reinforce its own brand identity, seeing it as a mashup of those parties, and in each case, recognizing the *absolute primacy* of the customer experience.

Insights Summary – Ideate – Study Methods								
Study Method 1 Competitive Product Survey	**Study Method 2** Analogous Empathy	**Study Method 3** Backcasting	**Study Method 4** Brainstorming	**Study Method 5** Constraint Imposition	**Study Method 6** Piggybacking	**Study Method 7** Alignment Model	**Study Method 8** Predict NY's Headlines	**Study Method 9** Brand Swap / Brandcasting

Key Insights

- Team understands the complete 'competitive landscape' of options.
- An increasing number of solutions are using AI (of different types).
- Different domains are being served well, but in isolation of each other – e.g. medical, travel, wealth, etc.
- Clear vision... a world where millions of people all over the world are living life / running businesses to the maximum of their potential.
- Team wants to do things never before possible! Always on maximization!
- Certain key attributes are crucial... overall CX / UX / cost / privacy & security / interoperability / more.

New Ideas (Solution Concepts)

- Solution must be globally scalable to everywhere in the world – without prejudice.
- Solution must feature transparent many-to-many communication channels.
- Solution must have a clearly-defined hierarchy of heuristics w/ clear rules for how they each interact w/ one another.
- All data must be architected to be fully usable in all parts of the solution (no interoperability issues).
- Solution needs data scrubbers to clean up & use legacy data.
- Solution must leapfrog everything else out there by working all domains simultaneously & holistically – to deliver 10X - 100X more success for users.
- **5 Main Concepts:**
  1. Native digital app / tool
  2. Online digital platform
  3. Concierge service
  4. Dedicated physical device
  5. Combination of all of the above.

Figure 12.4: Insights Summary for Ideation using the Study Methods

The final outcome at this point – the new solution concepts

Having undertaken the preceding Design Methods, Intensifi's team has now conceived the following proposed *solution concepts* to address their subjects' PoV:

- A native digital app/tool operating independently on existing computers and smart devices, and interfacing with external hardware devices as needed to periodically collect relevant data from them.

- An online digital platform operating on existing computers and smart devices, tying into their respective privacy and security systems to enhance its own privacy and security, with constant connections to cloud servers and external hardware devices to collect and process data in real time, all the time.

- A concierge service where humans operate at the primary interface level and service users to help them achieve their desired results. These services will use various technological tools, plus interface with select external hardware devices as needed, to fulfill the requirements of each user.

- A separate, dedicated physical device users carry around and use to engage with the system, with the end user being given control over where and how this device interfaces with external servers and other devices to achieve its objectives.

- A combination of each of the aforementioned, with each part operating in sync to do whatever it does best so as to deliver the most optimal outcome possible for the end user.

In each case, the concept is to allow the end user to establish each of their life and/or business goals and, thereafter, access detailed guidance on how to achieve those goals, given their own inherent capabilities, capacities, and resources. In so doing, each concept will satisfy all of Intensifi's Design Principles.

Validation – deciding and planning how to test our options

Given the set of new solution concepts the team has now conceived, the next question becomes one of how to prototype and test those solution concepts for their respective efficacy, impact, and likely adoption by the target subjects. This is the **climax point** of this stage – in between *Ideate* (divergence) and *Test* (convergence).

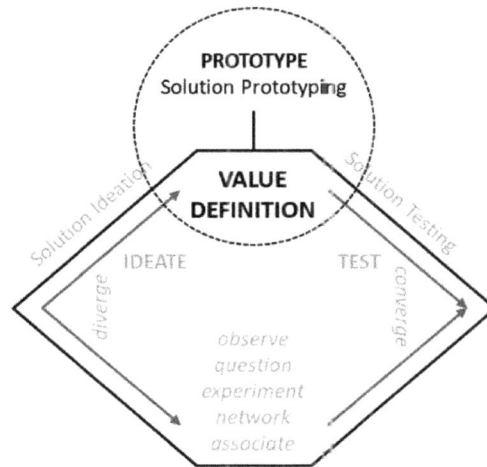

Figure 12.5: Moving on to the Prototype step of the Value Definition stage – where we decide how to prototype and test our new solution concepts

After putting some thought into this, the team has decided that it will call upon the following seven Design Methods – each bucketed into one of three method types – and use the specific type of prototypes indicated with each one. They've chosen these in particular because they believe these specific methods will let them best test each solution concept for its efficacy in addressing their subject's need (as espoused in their PoV), and thereafter come out with the best possible solution or combination of solutions. In particular here, Intensifi will be using three Question Methods, two Experiment Methods, and two Study Methods, as listed next.

- **Question Methods**

    - Why-How Laddering – no prototypes required.

    - Behavioral Interviews – no solution prototypes needed; subjects will use existing offerings as surrogates.

    - Narration – no solution prototypes needed; subjects will use existing offerings as surrogates.

- **Experiment Methods**

    - Role-Playing – low-fidelity physical mock-ups.

    - User Testing – early digital mock-ups simulating the functionality of the (digital) solutions.

- **Study Methods**

    - Concept Videos – conceptual videos using animations generated by Generative AI.

    - I Like, I Wish, What If – prior physical and digital mock-ups reused.

Convergence – solution testing – finding the best solution

The Value Definition stage is about trying to creatively and resourcefully contemplate and consider all of the possible different **solutions** we can come up with to our PoV so that, ultimately, we can test most or all of them against our subject's *real needs* (using those subjects) so as to arrive at the **one best solution** (or combination of solutions) that will fully meet those needs and, therefore, resonate with them.

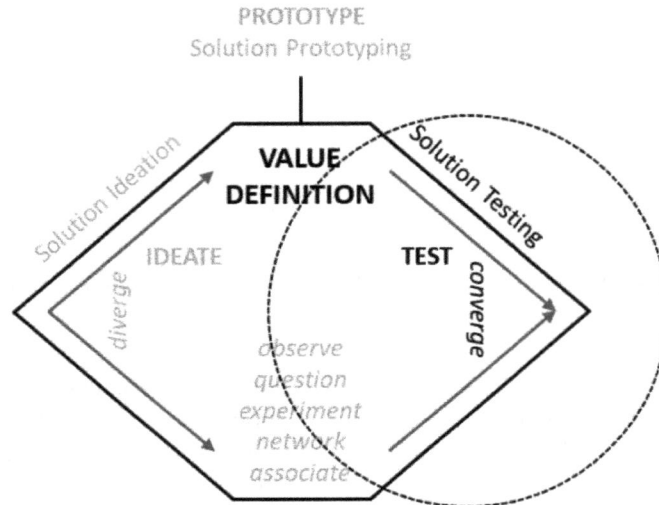

Figure 12.6: Moving into the Test step of the Value Definition stage
to test out our new solution concepts (convergent)

Our point of entry into this stage is working to conceive and consider as many possible solutions to our problem as possible – an activity we'll do by collectively brainstorming possible solutions using different methods and techniques that ignite fresh new thinking about the problem (something our PoV has also hopefully done at this point). Doing this will require us to do lots of thinking about this problem and what motivations and aspirations are behind it, and then use inductive logic to conceive new solutions that address those factors.

Appreciating Intensifi's goal at this point

At this point, Intensifi's goal is to ensure they are ideating solution concepts that are all rooted in a proper and correct understanding of the **market need** they're addressing – solutions that create the necessary *pull* from inside that market, so that adoption of the final solution comes easily and naturally, and doesn't require an excessive *push* effort from them. This will ensure – all else being right about their business model – maximum adoption of the solution and, therefore, maximum growth and scaling of their new business venture.

This is what they're trying to do now – develop solution concepts that are most capable of resonating with as many subjects as possible in this market space – a task they'll leverage their creativity to do.

Intensifi's validation plan – seven Design Methods

As noted previously, Intensifi's team has decided to call upon seven Design Methods (listed earlier) to test out its different solution concepts and try to find the best new concept to proceed with.

The Question Methods

Intensifi starts with the three *Question Methods*. They'll use these methods to query their subjects so as to gain better clarity around which of the different solution concepts they've conceived resonate best with them.

Why-How Laddering

What it is: Why-How Laddering is a common variant of *Question Laddering* and is similarly used to structure interview questions and other exploratory dialogues so that they unfold in a way that lets the researcher develop the details and abstract aspects of the situation they're exploring. This lets them ensure they're capturing a complete understanding of the subject's story as they engage with them in dialogue.

In this case, the researcher starts with a meaningful need that the subject has and writes that down. They then *ladder up* by asking the "Why?" behind this need, phrasing that answer as yet another need. For example, Statement: "The customer needs A." Question: "*Why* do they need A?" Answer: "Because they really need B." Statement: "The customer needs B." They then repeat this process again and again, in each case, writing the new need above the prior one. At some point they reach a particularly abstract need that is common to almost everyone, which is their stopping point... the top of their subjects' need hierarchy. This is not unlike the *Five Whys Method*, except that there remains a second part to this process.

In the second part, the researcher fills in "How?" questions so that they're sure to capture pertinent details of the subject's story. Where they went *up* with the "Why?" questions, they now go *down* with "How?" questions. For each "Why?" question, they build out branches around the "Why?" that let them flesh out useful and relevant details via the "How?" questions. As the subject relates to them the "Hows" of each "Why?", the researcher develops a more complete and comprehensive view of the subject's situation, needs, motives, values, attitudes, behaviors, and beliefs. The researcher can, as they desire, zoom in or out in this process to any particular level of detail. Thus, if they happen to hit upon a particularly salient need that they wish to explore in greater detail, they can easily do so (given sufficient time).

This two-stage laddering process is important because, as a general rule, asking "Why?" questions tends to yield more vague and abstract answers, whereas asking "How?" questions tends to yield much more specific answers. The researcher will need both if they are to build out a complete and comprehensive understanding of the subject and their situation. The abstract answers are the more *meaningful* ones... the real "meat" the researcher is looking for, but unfortunately, they're not always the most *actionable* ones for the organization. It is usually the more concrete and specific "How?" answers that tend to yield the actionable insights an organization can work with. They tell the researcher exactly *what* it is the subject likes and dislikes and usually *why so*. This then gives them some idea of how they might consider developing a solution for that, or at least provides them with useful constraints they can leverage in their Value Definition efforts. Researchers can thus benefit from integrating this laddering into all of their questioning work, as doing so will ensure they capture a complete and actionable story they can use.

The only caveat here is that the researchers have to be careful in how they apply the "How?" answers they obtain. While it's invaluable to have these detailed insights into subjects' likes and dislikes and other preferences, the researcher must not let those insights blind them to the possibility of a completely *different* set of "hows" these subjects aren't aware of – in the sense that their "hows" speak of the specific *tasks* subjects believe need to be done. It is the *researcher's* responsibility to determine the best "hows" for achieving a particular outcome. Consequently, the researcher mustn't let these "How?" answers constrain their thinking to be only *incremental* in nature. If what they really want to deliver is a *breakthrough solution*, then they'll likely have to translate those likes and dislikes into a completely *different* set of "hows" for achieving that outcome. In any situation, the researchers have to consider this matter and remain cognizant of how they use their new insights.

How Intensifi uses it: Intensifi uses this method to structure the question set they intend to use when testing out different solution concepts with subjects.

Intensifi's outcomes: Using this method, Intensifi comes away with questions such as the following:

- Why did you decide to use Solution X?
- Why was achieving that outcome (that Solution X enabled) important to you?
- Why was achieving that particular life goal (that the preceding outcome enabled) important to you?
- How, specifically, did you achieve (or are you achieving) that life goal?
- How, specifically, is the outcome of Solution X empowering you to achieve that life goal?
- How, specifically, are you actually using Solution X to attain its outcome?

Based on leveraging these and other similar questions, the team encounters the answers they were somewhat expecting. But they also encounter some other important answers – and insights – that they didn't expect. In particular, there was a recurring theme where subjects expressed that they wished they had used these solutions to pursue these goals earlier on in their lives or business careers – going back as far as even when they were in high school. This is an insight that did not surface in Intensifi's earlier research, so they've made a special note of it.

Behavioral Interviews

What it is: Behavioral Interviews are used to study people's *perceptions* of their behaviors, including their interactions with various products, services, and environments, as well as the people and systems that make up those things. Here, researchers ask the subjects to recount their specific behaviors, as opposed to their opinions or preferences about something. Subjects may also be asked to *demonstrate* how they recently completed a particular task, the artifacts they used in doing so, and the obstacles, or friction points, they encountered in trying to do so. This can yield very useful insights – especially around the friction points – that hint at new innovation opportunities.

In conducting these interviews, the researchers are as interested in people's *perceptions* of their behaviors as they are in their *actual behaviors*. This is because subjects often idealize their experiences and, in so doing, recount behaviors that are *different* from their actual behaviors (which can be documented by video recording them). In other words, what subjects *say they do* and what they *actually do* are often two very different things. Researchers must be deeply aware of this and, consequently, take the answers they receive with an appropriate "grain of salt," understanding that these *perceptions* are primarily what they're after.

After each interview, the researcher may then, in fact, play back for a subject the video recording of their actual behaviors, and then explore with them *why* there may have been differences between their perceptions of their behaviors and the realities of those behaviors. Those differences can at times reveal certain cognitive biases and dissonances that point to opportunities to modify some product or service to better resonate with what subjects actually want and need.

How Intensifi uses it: Intensifi uses this method to interview people about how they use existing (partial) life optimization solutions, what specific behaviors they do and do not exhibit when using them, and why so.

Intensifi's outcomes: Intensifi learns that people honestly believe they are taking control of their lives and businesses by using these (partial) solutions – largely because they have no context for knowing any different (that something more comprehensive might be available). This belief makes them feel empowered – at least to a level. Intensifi also learns that most users of these (partial) solutions don't feel like they're getting as much value out of them as they could be, because doing so would require spending more time and effort using the solutions than they are willing to carve out of otherwise trying to live their lives or operate their businesses.

Interestingly, they also learn that people are unsatisfied with existing solutions because they feel like they only benefit at certain specific times in their lives when they need to make certain specific decisions, otherwise, they're not delivering any value to them when that is not the case, which means they're usually paying some subscription cost for them even when they aren't being used. Respondents indicate that in order for a new solution to deliver an optimal experience for them, it either has to have a way to not have such "lulls" or else not charge them for when there are such lulls. This was a new insight for Intensifi and one that's in line with the signals they detected earlier on in their Kano Analysis and User Scenarios. So, at this point, Intensifi is starting to get a bit concerned that maybe they missed something important early on since nothing about their PoV, Design Principles, or current solution concepts addresses this concern.

Narration

What it is: Narration is a method used to study users' motivations, perceptions, concerns, and cognitive reasoning while engaged in a certain process or task. Here, the researchers interview the subject in situ, inside the context of carrying out the particular process or executing the task. As the subject goes about performing that process or executing that task, they describe aloud to the researcher precisely what they are thinking.

Narration can be useful for studying *mental reasoning processes*, but only to the extent that subjects are cognizant of what they are *thinking* during a particular process or task. If that process or task is relatively new to them, it will require focused and explicit cognitive processing on their part. In this case, they will likely be very *aware* of what they are thinking. If, however, that process or task is very familiar and routine to them, such that it no longer requires conscious thought on their part but has been assumed by their subconscious mind, then they would likely be unable to describe very well what they were thinking, as they would, in fact, not be thinking in any front-of-mind cognitive sort of way. For this reason, it's usually best to undertake Narration with users who, while not entirely new to a particular process or task, are still relatively new to it… new enough that they still have to think about it. This allows the researchers to collect the sort of insights they're looking for.

By capturing subjects' task-inspired thoughts, researchers can usually infer certain motivations, perceptions, concerns, and reasoning patterns behind them. These insights can then be used in validating certain hypotheses and solutions.

How Intensifi uses it: Intensifi uses the method to have cohorts of recruited subjects reflect to them their use of existing (partial) optimization solutions while using them. There are two cohorts – one for life optimization, and one for business optimization. The team hopes to learn how well these insights affirm or refute what subjects told them during their Behavioral Interviews.

Intensifi's outcomes: Intensifi learns that users do in fact feel a sense of control from using these solutions, even though in each case these are only partial solutions addressing one part of their life or business. They also learn that many users feel a bit short-changed because they feel like there is so much more they could be doing with these solutions if only doing so did not require so much time and effort on their part. So, in other words, the subjects feel frustrated with how limited many of these solutions are on account of how much actual manual effort they require from them as the user.

Intensifi also learns something from these studies that they didn't expect – namely, that users wish these solutions could, and would, actually *forecast* future evolutions of different situations in their lives or businesses to foresee different scenarios that could and may play out in the future, and then let them compare different strategies against each other, inside of each scenario, to figure out which ones will work best under multiple different scenarios (in other words, basic Strategic Futuring work). This is something that subjects never brought up in the other interviews Intensifi conducted, largely because (the team believes) they weren't in context in those cases. But now that the subjects are in the context of trying to use these solutions, they do in fact (multiple times) bring up this shortcoming. This is also something that concerns Intensifi, because it's something the team didn't catch before, and thus is not reflected in their PoV or Design Principles (or present solution concepts, per se). They've thus made a very special note of this, recalling that the same issue was also flagged in their Collaborative Sketching effort (which must have triggered the same thought at that time).

Insights Summary – Test – Question Methods		
Question Method 1 Why-How Laddering	Question Method 2 Behavioral Interviews	Question Method 3 Narration

Key Insights	Areas of Special Need / Attention
• Very similar user expectations as uncovered during ideation. • But users also desire having the solution earlier on in their life or business. • Users do derive a sense of 'control' in their lives or business from using various piecemeal solutions to address different areas of concern in each case. • But most users are oblivious to how disjointed their current piecemeal solutions are & thus how suboptimized & unbalanced their lives are compared to what they could be. • The limited value of current solutions doesn't lead users to master them and extract the full value from them. • Users especially call out lulls in their lives when they feel they don't get any real value from these solutions. • Users want the solution to forecast plausible future scenarios to work on.	• Having access to this holistic solution much earlier on in their lives or businesses. • Ensuring the solution delivers value all the time – even during periods of lulls in people's lives and/or businesses. • The capabilities of a solution need to be extensive and compelling enough to motivate users to invest a lot more time & effort mastering them for their full benefit. • Forecasting plausible future scenarios to consider & plan toward.

Figure 12.7: Insights Summary for Testing using the Question Methods

The Experiment Methods

Intensifi next moves on to the two *Experiment Methods* they've selected. They'll use these to try out the different solution concepts they've conceived with their subjects and get their reactions to them.

Role-Playing

What it is: Role-Playing, also known as *Informance* (for *informative performance*) and *Be Your Customer*, is an informative, engaging, and often entertaining method that teams use to help their organizations better understand their own perceptions of their customers and/or would-be customers, as well as to try out potential new customer experiences.

In this method, the team first recruits a panel of internal stakeholders to join them in the exercise. They next have these stakeholders describe, outline, and/or (preferably) act out what they believe their customer's typical experience is like in interacting with the organization, its brands, and its offering (if desired, they can video record these enactments for later review). Props are used wherever needed to aid the exercise. Once all of the stakeholders have gone through the exercise, the team then attempts to draw out specific *contrasts* between what has been presented and the reality of how customers *actually* perceive this experience. They can do this in any number of ways, such as, for example, having customers observe the enactments and provide their feedback on them (a dose of reality), acting out customers' real experiences themselves for the stakeholders to watch (based on what they've witnessed firsthand), or having the stakeholders watch video recordings of actual customer experiences so that the differences can be clearly noted. Any of these can be effective.

Teams often use this method to help their organization see, understand, and appreciate the nature and scope of the problem or situation they're confronting. It also helps the broader group of stakeholders to themselves develop a deeper sense of empathy for these customers, and potentially raise other issues pertinent to the situation. In both cases, this method allows the team to get certain insights communicated broadly across the organization – so that they can build a shared understanding within the organization of the situation and of certain problem / solution concepts and their respective implications to both the organization and these customers (or would-be customers).

Once these steps have been done, teams can further use the method to test out any number of newly proposed experiences. Here, they'll have the panel of stakeholders act out the specific actions of a particular proposed experience to see how the situation and its experience actually play out. Here again, they can, if they so desire, have actual customers watch and critique these role plays to get their immediate feedback on them.

Teams can leverage this latter application as a means of business experimentation for testing early hypotheses for accuracy, as well as solution testing for comparing competing solution concepts against each other.

How Intensifi uses it: Here, Intensifi wants to take cohorts of subjects who've never been exposed before to the idea of a holistic life or business optimization solution using AI to help them achieve complete and total optimization (via extensive automation), and actually expose them to just such a concept to see what their reactions and responses to it will be. This includes walking them through a simulation of each solution using different prototypes. The team hopes to explore many different nuances and details with these subjects.

Intensifi's outcomes: Intensifi again identifies two cohorts – one for life optimization and one for business optimization. In each case, and for each main solution concept, the team develops a low-fidelity mockup of the solution. For digital tools, these are wire-frame UI mockups. For services, these are actors acting out the service they'll deliver to the subjects. And for hardware devices, these are cardboard mockups decorated to look like an actual device. In each case, the subjects are asked to use their imaginations to fill in any missing details as best as they can.

By walking these "fresh eye" subjects through each solution concept, using each type of low-fidelity mockup, the team learns that, overall, the subjects conceptually love this new idea of overall, holistic life or business optimization. They are, however, at the same time very anxious and reticent about how challenging and difficult using such a solution might be, given the sheer number of goals one must define in it, the sheer number of interfaces one has to create to it so that it can collect all available data on them and their property or assets, and the sheer number of options they will need to entertain in making all of the associated trade-off decisions that an optimized life or business will inevitably present them with. When the team (eventually) lets them in on the secret that much of that work will be helped along by extensive AI automation, the cohorts seem to be a bit more at ease about this. Nevertheless, it is a valuable insight to take away from this.

The cohorts' feedback otherwise seems to affirm everything that's already reflected in Intensifi's PoV and Design Principles, and which each of their solutions thus strives to provide. For completeness, the team also runs these cohorts through a role-play involving the final composite solution having a mixture of digital tools, hardware devices, and services. From this, the team observed what they had suspected – namely, that a solution using a mixture of touchpoints like this should be most capable of delivering maximum value to users, and thereby achieving all of Intensifi's Design Principles at once.

Finally, in exploring the many details and nuances of each respective solution, two other issues again arose – namely, that subjects want access to such a solution very *early on* in their lives and careers, and that they're concerned that paying for such a solution over their entire lives may in fact turn out to be a less-than-optimal investment, given that there will inevitably be periods of stasis in their lives – times when they won't need to make any major life decisions, and thus don't need the solution. The Intensifi team is now really starting to get concerned about this input, given that they missed it before. They've made a very careful note of it.

User Testing

What it is: User Testing is a foundational User Research method teams use whenever either testing out various hypotheses in the Problem Clarification phase, where they're working toward convergence on a correct hypothesis, or when testing out various solution concepts in the Value Definition phase, where they're working toward convergence on an ideal solution concept.

Here, the team brings in a cohort of subjects and has them each engage with different prototypes, mock-ups, and simulations of the various products, services, and experiences. This can involve recreating a particular use case in the laboratory where subjects trial prototypes of product concepts, acting out the delivery of various service concepts, or perhaps simulating the staging of various customer experiences. In each case, the team seeks to deeply engage the subjects in the simulated experience so as to watch and observe their behaviors and reactions, as well as to solicit their direct feedback on what they do and do not like about each concept, and why so. In the Problem Clarification phase, this helps the team develop deeper empathy for these subjects by better understanding their needs, desires, values, and motivations. In the Value Definition stage, this helps the team gauge how well each concept meets the subjects' needs and delivers the experience they're striving to deliver. From there, it allows the team to further refine each concept, and perhaps meld certain concepts together to move closer to their ultimate solution.

The more accurately a team can emulate the affected products, services, and experiences, including their environments and use cases, the higher the quality of the learnings they take away. For this, they must be very intentional in how they stage and execute the exercise. They will know they're succeeding at this when it's clear that they have transported their subjects out of their normal realities and into these new scenarios and environments. If subjects aren't entirely familiar with these scenarios and environments, the team can help to explain the context as needed, but they should – as much as possible – leave it to the subjects to figure these out for themselves so as to not bias the activity. Under no circumstances should the team reveal their reasoning for a particular prototype or simulation, as that would assuredly "poison" the experience. The team should also not "correct" subjects' engagement with the prototypes and simulations. If they are misusing them, let them do so (so long as it's safe), and make note of the fact that how to use the product or receive the service is not sufficiently intuitive. If, after some time, they still have not comprehended how to engage with it, and allowing them to carry on in this way will rob the team of valuable feedback they need, then the team can step in and help them understand the proper usage intended.

While subjects are engaging with a particular prototype or simulation, the team may have a Questioner query them to find out what they're thinking and perceiving while experiencing that prototype or simulation – just as in the Narration Method. After each subject has had an opportunity to fully experience a particular prototype or simulation, the Questioner would then interview them and have them walk the team through what they had just experienced. They would solicit feedback on how the experience made them feel and why, together with the ways in which they felt the experience did or did not meet their needs and why so. They may also solicit detailed feedback around specific features and attributes of the product, service, or experience – to see how well users understand their purpose and function, and how well users were able to take advantage of them.

In soliciting this feedback, the team should identify one person per group of subjects to act as the Questioner. This prevents subjects from getting overwhelmed by too many people asking them questions all at once. Another individual on the team serves as a scribe to record their reactions, behaviors, and feedback. Some members of the team will need to act out certain roles in staging particular scenarios, environments, services, and experiences. Other team members will need to serve as pure observers (sometimes from behind a two-way mirror to be less conspicuous). Observers can also video record these sessions for future reference.

How Intensifi uses it: Intensifi uses this method to do more extensive testing of the digital solutions they've proposed (a standalone app and a cloud-connected platform). In each case, they've had digital mockups made, and will use a User Research Lab to observe their subjects trying to use each solution to see how well doing so goes for them, and whether, in fact, any additional insights can be gathered from such observations.

Intensifi's outcomes: Intensifi learns – partly surprisingly and partly not so surprisingly – that users do in fact start to feel overwhelmed rather quickly when trying to bite off the whole tool set at once, meaning focusing on all areas of their lives or business up front in the beginning. They come to realize this "everywhere all the time" approach up front is a bit much for most users – even with the AI system helping them.

They consequently realize that they'll have to build into whatever solution they offer a *roadmap* that walks the user through the solution one part at a time – in a specific order according to the user's personal objectives and priorities. This way, the user can focus on one part at a time, and in so doing, enter everything they need to enter, and connect everything they need to connect, over time – until, eventually, they finish it all and can start optimizing everything all at once from that point on.

They also learn – after letting certain "power users" (those who took a strong liking to the concepts) use these mockups for an extended period of time – that once they got their entire lives or businesses modeled in them, they too started asking about future projections so that they could make certain decisions *preemptively* before they needed to. Subjects especially asked about this in the domain of wealth management, where they wanted to know what stocks and other assets to invest in well ahead of time. Since this now seems to have become a recurring theme the team didn't hit on earlier, they've made a special note about it.

Insights Summary – Test – Experiment Methods	
Experiment Method 1 Role-Playing	**Experiment Method 2** User Testing
Key Insights • Users really like the key concept behind this proposed solution. • Users are a bit anxious & concerned however about how challenging & difficult it might be to use such a solution, given all the factors involved... multiple goals, data interfaces, and trade-off options they have to define. • Users like that extensive AI automation can help them with this. • Users want access to this solution early on in their lives and/or businesses. • Users concerned about the value of the solution during periods of stasis in their lives or businesses.	**Areas of Special Need / Attention** • Super high caliber AI automation to help users define and manage all the different factors involved. • Having access to this holistic solution much earlier on in their lives or businesses. • Ensuring the solution delivers value all the time – even during periods of stasis in people's lives and/or businesses.

Figure 12.8: Insights Summary for Testing using the Experiment Methods

The Study Methods

Finally, Intensifi finishes with the two *Study Methods* they've chosen. They'll use these methods to collectively study their different solution concepts with their subjects and get their further responses to each concept.

Concept Videos

What it is: Concept Videos are videos produced to tell a story about a new solution. They're intended to convey a particular vision for how people might use that solution in the future. As such, they tend to not focus on the specific details of the solution's *attributes* (its functions, features, aesthetics, and so on), but rather on the *context* for the solution and the *benefits* people would accrue from using it.

Teams can use this method to explore different solution possibilities. To do this, they'll make a short film about each solution and then play those films for different subjects to get their responses to them – searching for those concepts that strike the strongest chord with these subjects. While viewing each video, subjects rank each one according to select predefined criteria. After watching all of the videos, the team then hosts an open group discussion on what the subjects liked and disliked about each concept, and why so. This can provide highly valuable feedback on the different concepts, especially for those that aren't so easily prototyped and tested at this point. It also helps the team ensure the subjects understand the big picture for each concept and don't get lost in the minutia of its exact manifestation. As such, the method is often used in the early stages of concept evaluation, whereas detailed prototype evaluations are used in the latter stages of concept evaluation.

How Intensifi uses it: Intensifi uses this method by having a video-production firm create simulated concept videos for them demonstrating each solution and how it will work in the life of the user to empower them to optimize their life and/or business. Each such video is relatively brief – only about 3 or 4 minutes long per video.

Intensifi then recruits two new cohorts of subjects who once again have never before been exposed to the idea of a holistic life or business optimization solution using AI to help them achieve complete and total optimization (via extensive automation), and then exposes them to just such a concept, using these videos, to see what their respective reactions and responses to them will be.

In this case, Intensifi is particularly looking to see how these respondents' reactions will differ between the different solution concepts they're presented with

Intensifi's outcomes: Intensifi finds that respondents respond positively to all five solution concepts, as presented to them in the five different short videos. They also find that – after seeing all five videos, representing all five concepts – the subjects responded most positively (by far) to the final composite concept that used a mixture of digital tools, hardware devices, and concierge-type services to help them achieve their goals. Respondents noted the perception that they believed this approach would allow them to achieve their goals most effectively and most impactfully, with the least amount of effort overall – assuming it is actually delivered in the seamless manner portrayed in the video.

Respondents also noted in each case that they believed these solutions would benefit them and others the most if they could have access to them as early on in their lives as possible (or at least as is reasonable). Some even suggested starting users with it as early as 12 years old; others felt that 16 might be a more reasonable starting point. This, again, is one of the recurring (missed) themes borne out in several of Intensifi's solution tests so far. Intensifi is definitely sitting up and paying attention to this point by now.

I Like, I Wish, What If

What it is: I Like, I Wish, What If is a simple method teams use to solicit, collect, and curate feedback from any number of sources on specific solution concepts they're considering. The method involves having its subjects review these concepts and then formulate **I Like, I Wish, What If (IL/IW/WI)** statements about each one.

The format of this statement tends to encourage open and clear feedback, especially since feedback is generally best when given in the form of situational and emotional statements such as "*It sometimes seems as though these concepts may be missing the financial consideration*" rather than in the form of absolute and factual statements such as "*None of these concepts will ever be cost-effective.*"

This feedback is typically solicited in a group setting, in which participants are invited to critique a particular set of solution concepts and provide their feedback on them. The feedback is thus offered in this form, stating what they like about each concept, what else they wish were true about each concept, and then suggesting the "What if" part, such as *"What if we added this other service to the mix and made the overall customer experience that much better by shifting these touchpoints off the customer's plate and onto our business?"*

This method lets reviewers give their feedback in a very open, honest, and constructive way that tends to build on each concept more than it takes away from them. This feedback can be gathered from any number of reviewers – typically a handful to potentially dozens. As each bit of feedback is being offered, the team should listen carefully and consider what is being said (they should have one person acting as a scribe so that the majority of them can focus their energies on listening and not on writing). The team need not necessarily respond to each bit of feedback, but they may do so if they feel that having a deeper conversation about a particular point will bring greater value or clarity to the effort – something they'll need to exercise judgment on.

Overall, the method can provide teams with very useful insights into further refining their solution concepts to become even better and smarter innovations. As in the context of Co-creation, the team may also want to invite various external stakeholders and would-be customers into the conversation – to ensure they have the right outside voices weighing in, and so that the feedback doesn't suffer from internal myopia or groupthink.

How Intensifi uses it: Intensifi uses this method by recalling a number of their prior subjects from the other tests that involved exposing subjects to the whole idea of a comprehensive life or business optimization solution (Role Playing, User Testing, and Concept Videos), and then, while presenting each respective solution concept to them, asking them to give their feedback on each one using the "I Like, I Wish, What If" format.

Intensifi's outcomes: From doing this, Intensifi gets the following sort of *characteristic feedback* on each respective solution:

- **Solution 1**

    - I Like… that by it being more isolated, I can feel better about its privacy and security.

    - I Wish… that I could know it was always up to date with the latest information and data.

    - What If… it has a set schedule for connecting, collecting data, and then disconnecting?

- **Solution 2**

    - I Like… that by it being always connected, I can feel good about its accuracy and relevance.

    - I Wish… that I could ensure it was secure so that no other parties could hack into it and steal my data.

    - What If… we use the closest thing available to quantum cryptography to ensure its privacy?

- **Solution 3**

    - I Like… that I have a real person to speak to and work with whenever I want that.

    - I Wish… this wasn't the only means of access, as sometimes I just want to work alone in privacy.

    - What If… the service part was always there, but the user had the option of a digital or human interface?

- **Solution 4**

    - I Like… that there is something tangible to handle to make the whole thing seem more real and alive.

    - I Wish… I didn't have to carry around yet another device when I already have one that can be used.

    - What If… we have both the physical device and a mapping of it onto other, more conventional devices?

- **Solution 5**

    - I Like… that I get the best of all interface options here – online, physical, and human.

    - I Wish… there was a clear roadmap explaining to me how they all work together most effectively.

    - What If… we publish a set of use cases highlighting the best way to use this for different goals?

Insights Summary – Test – Study Methods	
Study Method 1 **Concept Videos**	**Study Method 2** **I Like, I Wish, What If**
Key Insights • Users respond positively to all 5 concepts, but they respond most positively to the last concept – a composite solution featuring a mix of online platform, hardware, & services. • Users will benefit the most if they can have access to this solution earlier on in their lives and/or businesses – starting anywhere from 12 - 16 YO. • Users value very high-level privacy & security in this type of solution. • Users want assurance that its data & info are all current, as they value its outcomes being accurate & relevant. • Users appreciate automatic update schedules. • Users value access to real human support when needed – and they like the idea of having the choice of either a human or online (digital) interface. • As far as hardware goes, users prefer to use their existing devices, not a new separate device.	**Areas of Special Need / Attention** • Ideal solution will involve a composite of an online digital tool, some kind of hardware interface, and augmenting services – with the hardware leveraging present devices (no new separate devices). • Having access to this holistic solution much earlier on in their lives or businesses. • Being able to extract value from the solution via either a digital or a human interface (when & where desired). • Providing the highest levels of privacy and security possible.

Figure 12.9: Insights Summary for Testing using the Study Methods

Taking stock of the situation

At this point, the original plan was to be done with the Design Thinking process… to walk away with their one best solution concept. However, Intensifi realizes that if they were to do that – if they were to just take what they have right now and press ahead with it – they'd probably be missing a potentially critical element of that solution, and more importantly, of their broader value proposition. They understand that missing that could throw off their entire value proposition – and thus their entire business model – leading to failure, not success, something they obviously don't want. And so they realize it's time to "take their licks" and cycle back into the Design Thinking process again.

Hitting a roadblock – their unexpected result and a major U-turn

As we can surmise by now, Intensifi hit a bit of a roadblock in the preceding test process. Quite to their surprise, they learned from those seven tests that *none* of the solution concepts they'd conceived so far **fully achieves** their goal of solving their subjects' *entire needs*. It would seem they get most of the way there, but not all of the way, as highlighted by the new issues that surfaced during the last step.

This was rather a shock to the team, and it raised a major red flag for them. It told them that they somehow missed something important earlier on in their process! And that realization stops them dead in their tracks, leaving them feeling somewhat deflated! In fact, of the 16 team members they began with, two of them have chosen to depart the team at this point, as they don't feel that things are going the way they had desired and expected, and so they opt to not spend any more time on this effort with the team. Sometimes, such is the nature of figuring out one's new venture… the hard work is not for everyone.

So, what to do now?

Accepting iteration – a normal part of Design Thinking

This is one of the points that we discussed back in *Chapter 9*, where we pointed out just how iterative the Design Thinking process can be. What this particular result is telling the team is that, somehow, they missed one or more important hypotheses back in the Problem Clarity stage. Consequently, their PoV is either wrong or incomplete, and thus their Design Principles are likewise either wrong or incomplete.

So, that being the case, what they have to do now is start all over back at square one – except that now they still have all the key insights they've already learned, so they won't be throwing those away; they'll just be working to add to and further clarify those insights with additional new insights. So, let's consider what factors the team apparently missed before – so that we (and they) can get on with the situation.

Seeing the new factors they missed before

Based on what the team has now learned from their initial (failed) Solution Testing step, they believe the following three factors are also at play in their situation:

- Access to the solution earlier on in one's life or business (at a younger age, or at an earlier career point).

- The question of whether or not the solution has any value during times of stasis with no major decisions.

- The desire for a solution that can exercise foresight into plausible future scenarios to plan for.

These are each a new insight that drives a new *assumption* (*hypothesis*), and those new assumptions will each have to be tested for their own respective validity or invalidity.

The team has consequently now formulated – based on these additional observations – the following new, **hypotheses** that they will have to test (hypotheses they apparently missed the first time around):

- **Early access:** Subjects want access to the solution early on in their lives – starting in high school or university (before they can even afford it in the way that a working professional can). This lets them get a head start on optimizing their lives from way back then, and in particular, helps them to understand – given their unique interests and capabilities – what college major they should pursue and what type of career they'll be best suited for and satisfied with. This means there'll need to be versions of the platform that are initially free (to high schoolers) and otherwise within reach of university students.

- **Usage lulls:** Subjects are concerned about the fact there will sometimes be long lulls in their lives or businesses – periods of stasis when things are stable and no major decisions need to be made (things are going well with their career, their marriage, their family, their health, their wealth management, and so on – so they don't really *need* the solution during those times). So, they're a bit concerned about having to pay for the solution during those times – and whether or not they're getting adequate value from it during those periods. This seems to require an invitation and ability to engage in constant "micro-tuning" of their lives or businesses – so that they can in fact derive value from the solution during those times. It may also be the place where different paid tiers are warranted – ones for times of major decision analysis, and others for periods of minor micro adjustments.

- **Future foresight:** Given the solution's daily updates of data and information from all over the world, subjects expect it to be able to foresee key trends and possibly even events in the near future, and alert them to how those are (or may be) changing the circumstances surrounding their lives or businesses and thereby impacting the prescriptions they were previously given, to now be different prescriptions that they should change to. They also want the solution to give them the ability to explore different plausible future scenarios and then, based on those, explore and think through different strategies to use now to set them on a course for an optimum future under any of those different scenarios.

Formulating these additional hypotheses is equivalent to the team going back into the *Empathize* step of the Problem Clarity stage.

The detour – going back to the Define step – their new testing plan

Given what has transpired up to this point, the Intensifi team must now cycle back to (and through) the *Define* step of the Problem Clarity stage to prototype and **test** these additional new hypotheses, and from those tests, learn the right insights about them (are they or are they not correct?).

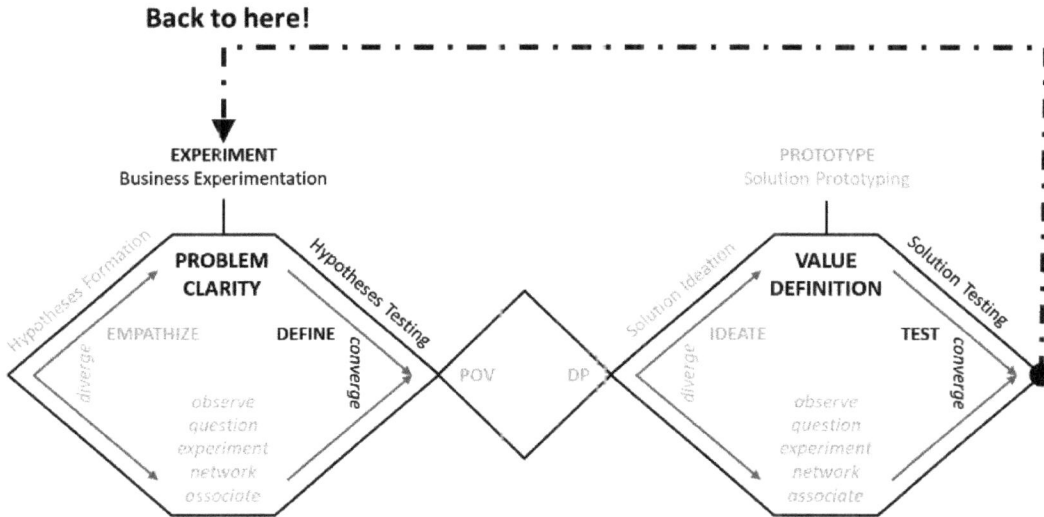

Figure 12.10: Going all the way back to the Define step of the Problem
Clarity stage with their new hypotheses to test

To do this, the team must once again engage in **hypothesis testing** work, using some of the *same* Design Methods they used before, plus four additional ones – namely, *Absence Thinking, A Day In The Life, Scenario Testing*, and *Storytelling*. The team chose these additional Design Methods in particular because they believe that they – plus the ones they used before – will let them best test out their newer hypotheses for validity, thus ensuring they've overcome the blind spots they missed before. These methods force the team to stop, step back, and think much more critically about the situation than they did before – asking what in particular is missing in their subject's *use* of a solution. These additional methods are bucketed into one of three method types – two Observe Methods, one Experiment Method, and one Study Method, as listed here.

- **Observe Methods**
    - Absence Thinking
    - A Day In The Life

- **Experiment Methods**

  - Scenario Testing

- **Study Methods**

  - Storytelling.

Let us profile these four new methods they'll be using and see how they'll be using them.

The Observe Methods

Here, Intensifi starts with the two additional *Observe Methods* they've chosen. They'll use these to (re)observe their subjects in an effort to preliminarily test the additional hypotheses they developed about the situation to see whether these observations indicate these hypotheses' validity or invalidity.

Absence Thinking

What it is: Absence Thinking is a conceptual practice used in both Observing and Questioning Methods. The idea is for the researcher to think about and take note of those things that are *not* present in the situation they're observing… things that are absent or missing from the situation that they might otherwise expect to be there. Thus, they consider questions such as the following:

- Who is not here that could or should be here, or that one might expect to be here?

- What is not here that could or should be here, or that one might expect to be here?

- What statement is not being said that could or should be said, or that one might expect to be said?

- What action or behavior is not being done that could or should be done, or that one might expect to be done?

- What timeframe is not being used that could or should be used, or that one might expect to be used?

- What place or environment is not being used that could or should be used, or that one might expect to be used?

- What situational context is not being invoked that could or should be involved, or that one might expect to be invoked?

In each case, the researcher will follow up with the question of "Why?" and repeat that line of questioning as far as they can – until they reach the real "aha" insight they're looking for.

This can be a powerful method for revealing the unarticulated needs in a situation – the underlying outcomes that people have but don't realize they have, or don't realize could even be possible to satisfy. Organizations often capitalize on these insights with new innovations – potentially even new product or service categories that give rise to entirely new markets (which often disrupt older business models).

How Intensifi uses it: Intensifi uses this method while revisiting some of their prior observations and questioning of subjects (with refreshed observations and questioning). In this case, they specifically think about the following:

- Might the potential solution be missing from people's early lives and careers; if so, why?
- Might the potential solution be missing an ability to deliver value during periods of stasis; if so, why?
- Might the potential solution be missing the ability to deliver foresight, when it should; if so why?

This lets them really hone in on the three new hypotheses they're trying to test, while always remaining alert for any new insights pertaining to their other hypotheses, or even to newer hypotheses they may have missed.

Intensifi's outcomes: Intensifi finds that – yes, indeed – all three of these things do in fact appear to be missing from the equation when they should be there based on people's articulated and unarticulated needs. In particular, they learn the following.

- Younger subjects do in fact express a desire to have access to such a solution early on in their lives, well before they've even decided what to do with their lives (as they believe that having it will help them to evaluate their strengths, interests, and propensities and point them in the right direction for that).
- Mid-life and mid-career professionals do in fact have a legitimate concern about paying for a solution during periods where they may not need it… when there is relative stability.
- Older subjects do in fact express a desire for certain foresight capabilities – especially as they're trying to think about retirement – when to do so, how to plan and save for it, and so on. They express that they believe having such a capability would help them immensely in this area, and not only that, but by doing so, it would give them far greater peace of mind knowing what to expect under different scenarios.

A common theme the team sees between the first and third points is that subjects seem to really want the ability to look long into the future and use such an AI-empowered tool to help them plot the course for their lives or businesses deep into the future. This is especially pronounced at the early beginning and later end of one's professional life and career. It is much less pronounced in the middle, where a different concern arises – namely, the ability to derive sufficient value from the solution during that period.

A Day In The Life

What it is: A Day In the Life is a variant of Contextual Inquiry that's focused specifically on observing the normal daily routines of particular subjects. This can be a useful means for revealing unexpected issues and obstacles in people's normal routines and in the circumstances they encounter every time they do those.

In this method, the observer goes about carefully cataloging the subjects' activities throughout their day, and the contexts in which they encounter and experience those activities. They'll do this across the entire course of a typical day. They'll also generally do this with as many different subjects as possible who have relevant circumstances so that they can collect an adequate breadth and depth of insights to ensure their overall observations are generalizable to the full cohort of interest (the market segment).

How Intensifi uses it: Intensifi uses this method to study the three distinct cohorts they seem to be zooming in on – high schoolers, mid-career professionals, and mature professionals. In each case, they ask to mirror them, not on just any ordinary day per se, but rather specifically on a day when they're trying to gather insights on how to plan their futures (for their lives and/or businesses). The team wants to see what this particular "day in the life" of these individuals looks like presently – and what solutions they currently use – and in particular the following:

- How the younger cohort is or is not using solutions to figure out their early lives and careers.

- How the middle-aged cohort is or is not using solutions during this phase of their life/career.

- How the mature cohort is or is not using solutions during that phase of their life/career.

Intensifi's outcomes: Intensifi observes the following:

- The younger cohort is relying largely on other peoples' advice to guide them… teachers, parents, coaches, counselors, clergy, and so on.

- The middle-aged cohort is using different piecemeal solutions to manage each area of their life (health, career, money, marriage, and so on) – but on the whole, they're really doing this sporadically… a few years on this, a couple of years on that, and so on. Nothing seems to be sticking with them consistently over the long run, and in the end, they end up questioning whether or not each one ever really helped them all that much, and thus whether or not they got their money's worth out of them.

  In terms of prioritizing these, the team learns the following:

  - for men (a larger market in this case), the main focus tends to be on solutions that help them optimize their careers, health, and hobbies;

  - for women (a smaller market in this case), the main focus tends to be on solutions that help them optimize their marriage, families, friendships, and health.

- The mature cohort is now focusing much more on financial planning solutions than anything else, given that they now have retirement in sight and have become far more fixated on optimizing that stage of their life.

These observations appear to strongly affirm new hypotheses 1 and 2 and weakly affirm new hypothesis 3.

Insights Summary – Define – Observe Methods

Observe Method 1 Absence Thinking	Observe Method 2 A Day In The Life

Key Insights	**Areas of Concern (Pain)**	**Areas of Desire (Gain)**

• Confirmed missing insights:
  • Subjects want access early on in their lives – especially young users trying to figure out what to do with their lives.
  • Professionals don't want to pay for a solution they aren't using (during lulls… period of stasis).
  • There is a desire for Foresight capabilities – especially amongst older users looking toward retirement.
• Younger users rely on other's advice.
• Current solution usage is sporadic.
• Older users focus largely on wealth.
	• Current solutions are overly short-term oriented (the 'here & now')… they don't help look out into the future to forecast long-term scenarios.
	• Any potential new solution also runs the risk of being likewise if it does not explicitly address this shortcoming.
		• A very strong desire – especially among younger and older users – to have long-term scenario forecasting capabilities to plan against.

Figure 12.11: Insights Summary for Defining (Take 2) using the Observe Methods

The Experiment Method

Next, Intensifi moves on to the one additional *Experiment Method* they've selected. They'll use it to try out different solution concepts with their subjects to see whether the additional attributes of these concepts validate or invalidate their new hypotheses about the situation.

Scenario Testing

What it is: Scenario Testing is a method used to collect *feedback* and *reactions* from subjects (would-be customers) to different possible scenarios and the solution concepts they represent.

Here, one first creates – for each scenario they want their subjects to evaluate – a deck of cards explaining the scenario and how it flows. Once they have those in place, they then bring in cohorts of subjects and show them the different sets of cards explaining the different scenarios and the solution concepts they each represent. Sequencing each scenario on discrete cards allows them to walk their test subjects through each scenario in a very *methodical and procedural manner* – so that they can ensure they understand the scenario and how it works, and so that they don't get confused by trying to take it all in at once. After they present each scenario, they'll solicit and record the subjects' reactions and feedback to it. If desired, they may sequence the order in which they present the different scenarios according to some important criteria, such as, for example, increasing complexity. After they've presented all of the scenarios, they'll then invite their subjects to reflect on all of them and to compare and contrast them to each other to find out – comparatively – what they liked and disliked about each one. This can sometimes lead to hybrid scenarios / solutions that best fit their broader needs.

This is a useful method for presenting different User Scenarios to would-be customers/users and gaining valuable feedback from them. Since one can conduct the exercise in a very methodical and procedural manner, they can have high confidence in their ability to connect cognitively, and to some extent, emotionally, with these subjects. This generally produces high-caliber insights. This can also prove useful later on whenever they're trying to work on the Design Principles for our final solution design.

How Intensifi uses it: Intensifi defines four distinct scenarios they wish to test with subjects. These are as follows:

- **Scenario 1**: A tool or platform that lets users optimize their entire life holistically across all its facets, at any given time, with extensive customizability, optional augmenting hardware, and an ecosystem of service partners, that is expensive to use.

- **Scenario 2**: A service that lets customers optimize their entire life holistically across its many facets, at different points in time, including optional augmenting hardware and an ecosystem of additional service providers, that is expensive to use.

- **Scenario 3**: A tool or platform that lets users optimize their life holistically across its many facets, at any given time, but without much customizability, without augmenting hardware, and without an ecosystem of service providers, that is very inexpensive to use.

- **Scenario 4**: A service that lets customers optimize their life holistically across its different facets, at different times, but not including optional augmenting hardware and an ecosystem of additional service providers, that is very inexpensive to use.

In each case, they include use cases for early, mid, and late-career situations.

Intensifi then uses the method to do two distinct things:

1. **Number one**: To test subjects' reactions to different attribute arrangements, so that they can gauge their value trade-off priorities among the different attributes of a solution.

2. **Number two**: To test subjects' reactions to different early-, mid-, and late-life / career situations, so that they can see the extent to which these subjects do and do not resonate with certain particular use cases and applications in each stage of life/career.

Intensifi's insights: Intensifi learns the following from this method:

- In all cases, the majority of subjects are in fact price-sensitive, and thus not too keen on options that are expensive to use, and therefore gravitate far more strongly toward solutions that are less expensive (more cost-effective) to access and use.

- In most cases, subjects value customizability and extensibility, and in fact, it seemed that the older and more sophisticated they became, the more they tended to value these attributes.

- Subjects also tended to value additional augmentative services more as they became older and more mature as, at those stages, they were more able to afford such services, as well as less inclined to do as many of these activities for themselves as they did when they were younger.

- Young users seemed to resonate with the idea of having a solution early on in life (such as in high school) so they could hopefully use it to figure out their life/career path.

- Mid-life / mid-career professionals seemed to resonate with the idea of having a way to customize the solution to get just what they needed from it, when they needed it, without losing sight of the fact that it lets them optimize all areas of their lives all at once.

- Later-life / later-career (mature) professionals seemed to resonate with the idea of using a solution to look well out into the future and plan for different future scenarios in their lives.

All of these observations seem to affirm both Intensifi's original hypotheses plus their three new ones.

Insights Summary – Define – Experiment Method		
Experiment Method 1 Scenario Testing		
Key Insights	**Areas of Concern (Pain)**	**Areas of Desire (Gain)**
• Most users are price-sensitive… steer away from expensive options. • Younger users like the idea of having access to the solution early on so they can use it to help figure out where to go in life. • Users value customizability / extensibility in the solution – especially mid-life professionals willing to invest time in mastering it. • Older users like the idea of long-term forecasting to explore options. • Users value augmenting services – increasingly so as they grow older and can afford more of them (and are less willing to do them themselves).	• An overly expensive solution that ends up being out of reach and only for the most wealthy and affluent. • Not having access to the solution early on enough in their lives to have a significant impact on their lives. • Not having the extensible capabilities needed to model and evaluate complex scenarios and decisions.	• An affordable, extensible solution that lets them plot their life course from beginning to end – looking at different plausible future scenarios at each stage – and optimizing for each season of their life.

Figure 12.12: Insights Summary for Defining (Take 2) using the Experiment Method

The Study Method

Finally, Intensifi moves on to the one additional *Study Method* they've chosen. They'll use it to share different solution concepts with their subjects (in a compelling and relatable format) and get their responses to each one, again in an attempt to either validate or invalidate the additional hypotheses they've developed here.

Storytelling

What it is: Storytelling is a very useful method because stories engage the listener's mind, as well as often their heart. They especially engage the areas of the mind associated with our imaginations, such that when stories are told, our minds wake up and listen… engaging with that story. Stories are very much hard-wired into the human psyche, and as such they – especially when told well – have the power to connect people to ideas in a very human way. Indeed, a well-told story that reveals surprising information with a deeper meaning and some human emotions thrown in will impact the listener not only intellectually but also emotionally, and sometimes even spiritually.

In crafting a compelling story, teams must understand what it is they want to tell about their particular challenge, and then skillfully weave together a narrative around that challenge that both stimulates the listener intellectually and moves them emotionally. Their story needs to convey a sense of purpose in resolving this challenge and must relate that purpose to something that matters to the listener at a human level. Given that the details of how to develop and convey great stories are very well documented elsewhere, we won't go into that here, other than to say that a great story will always involve action, conflict, and transformation, with transformation being the most important element. In our case, these stories are used to help us and others develop empathy for our subjects so that we can better understand them and their situation. In doing this, the stories reveal important details about these subjects and their situation that pull back the curtain on their emotions, motivations, and aspirations that lie beneath their behaviors.

When developing our stories, we can draw directly from the Empathy Map we created. What our subject thinks, feels, says, and does defines who that character is. Their needs (pains and gains) define the conflict in their story. And the insights we've amassed, plus the solution concepts we've conceived, together define the transformation in the story. That story is, in other words, built right into the whole Design Thinking process. A team should be able, therefore, to develop and tell a very compelling story around their subject and that subject's situation, and should be able to relate, in a human way, how they'll be able to deliver transformation through those insights and solutions. When they're done, and if they've told a great story, then they should have been able to sell their solution to whomever it resonates with.

How Intensifi uses it: Intensifi uses this method to tell different stories to different subject cohorts – stories specifically about individuals using their solution at different points in their lives, under differing circumstances. After each story, they query the group, initially via written assessments and subsequently via verbal discourses, to gauge their reactions to that story. The team is trying to see which cohorts connect with which stories – and why so in each case. They want to use this to further infer specific insight into each cohort's respective aspirations and motivations around the solution.

Intensifi's outcomes: Intensifi finds – not surprisingly really – the following results:

- Younger subjects connected with stories of younger individuals using the solution early on in their lives to figure out and navigate their path into adulthood, and thereafter, to navigate university and then their early careers.

- Middle-aged subjects connected with stories of adults using the solution to optimize the specific areas of their lives they cared most about – whether that was health, career, wealth, marriage, family, hobbies, or whatever. In general, however, their measure of affinity to these stories was slightly weaker than that of the younger and older subjects.

- Older subjects connected with stories of accomplished senior professionals who were near or at the pinnacle of their careers and were looking forward to subsequent stages of their lives.

- In all cases, the subjects seemed to admire the protagonists of these stories and how they used the solution to achieve some important life goal as well as the transformation that led them through. They seemed to resonate with the fact that such a solution allowed the protagonist to become "the hero of their own story" (to borrow a phrase from *Chapter 7*).

All of these insights seemed to affirm all of the team's hypotheses thus far. So… so far so good.

Insights Summary – Define – Study Method		
Study Method 1 Storytelling		

Key Insights	Areas of Concern (Pain)	Areas of Desire (Gain)
• Younger users connect with stories of having access to the solution early on in their lives – so they can figure what to do with their life. • Middle-aged professionals connect with stories of optimizing each area of their life according to the priority balance of that stage of their life. • Older users connect with stories of using it plan out their retirement for maximum wealth and freedom. • All users connect with the idea of 'being the hero of their own story'!	• Not having access soon enough to help guide the life direction. • Not having the ability to balance out prescriptions according to a prioritization order and algorithm. • Not having the ability to plan for the longer-term future.	• Access early on. • Holistic optimization – at each stage of life. • Future foresight & long-term planning.

Figure 12.13: Insights Summary for Defining (Take 2) using the Study Method

The result – Intensifi's new insights

At this point, the team has run both these repeated and new *Define* business experiments and thereby tested their new hypotheses. What they learn from doing this is that they were in fact correct… that there are these additional factors at work. Consequently, their three new hypotheses – *Early Access*, *Usage Lulls*, and *Future Foresight* – did in fact prove to be accurate.

Therefore, the team will now proceed with a total of **12 accepted hypotheses**, rather than just their original 9. This makes their total set of accepted hypotheses the following:

- Early Access

- Holistic Optimization

- Easy but Extensible Usage

- Current Data

- Platform Augmenters

- Platform Trust

- Platform Socialization

- Platform Security

- Platform Customization

- Platform Ecosystem

- Platform Foresight

- Usage Lulls.

These are, therefore, the specific issues they'll need to confront as they go forward.

Back to the Problem-Solution Interface stage... again

Given their new additional *accepted hypotheses*, the team changes their reframing of the issue slightly, leading to an *alteration* of their original PoV.

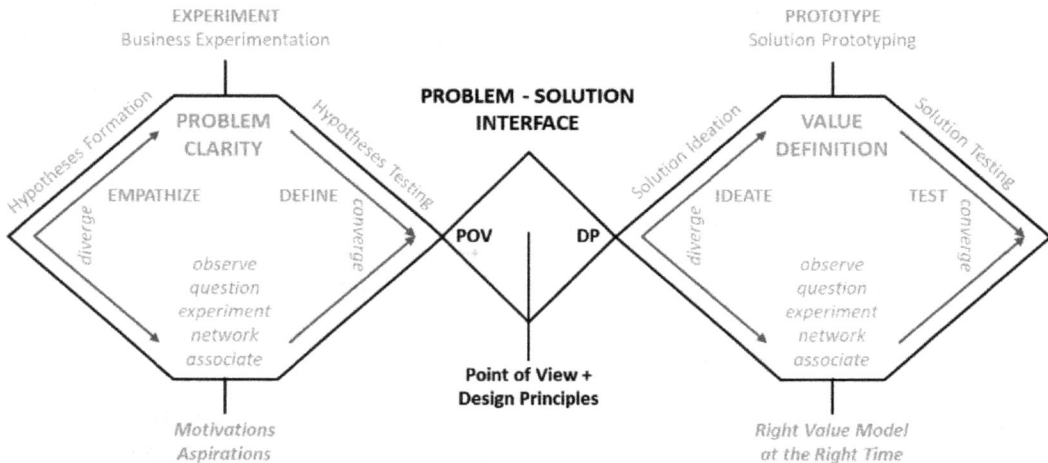

Figure 12.14: Revising their Point of View and its associated Design Principles

In particular, they've reworked that PoV to now state the following:

- This we know... aspiring business-minded individuals – from the earliest to the latest career stage – seek a solution that empowers them to achieve their *maximum potential* in both life and business – one that gives them the extensible tools and ongoing knowledge they require to simultaneously optimize each and every area of their life and business – with full confidence that the decisions and choices it leads them to will result in achieving *maximum overall success* – as clearly demonstrated by the many others before them who have achieved similar maximum life results by using the solution.

- We further know that the *reason* these individuals seek this solution is that they want the confidence – at each stage of their career and life – but especially at the *end* of their career and life – that they have made every possible choice and decision in life they could to attain *the maximum possible success available to them* – so that, ultimately, they can look back on their life with complete satisfaction and joy, and with absolutely zero regrets.

- We further know that these individuals want to *conceptualize* such a solution as being a sort of "omniscient *Generative AI for Life* genie" who is also their very trusted friend, mentor, and coach.

- We finally know that these individuals value certain specific *attributes* in such a solution – those being the following:

  - *comprehensiveness* (covering all areas of their life and business);

  - *early access* (the opportunity and ability to use the solution very early on in their lives);

  - *extensibility* (customizable according to each person's preferred usage approach);

  - *connectivity* (using myriad devices to incorporate relevant data from their personal world);

  - *currency* (able to incorporate all the latest news and data from around the world each day);

  - *dependability* (their ability to have full confidence in the solution's prescriptions);

  - *foresight* (the solution's ability to construct plausible future scenarios for them to plan against);

  - *perpetual value* (the solution's ability to deliver clear gains and wins even during periods of stasis);

  - *sociability* (their ability to socialize their prescriptions with others whom they trust and value);

  - *networked* (incorporating a curated ecosystem of providers they can choose from and work with);

  - *private and secure* (all information protected and inaccessible to unauthorized parties);

  - *accessibility* (their ability to afford some version of the solution at each stage of their life).

Consequently, as a business, we intend to deliver a complete solution to this PoV, as we believe that doing so will empower our venture to attain maximum success.

Now, based on this newly revised PoV, the team has defined the following four additional Design Principles to use:

1. provide access *early on* in users' lives – starting ideally in early high school, and in some cases even sooner;

2. provide the ability to perpetually *micro-tune* one's life by delivering valuable insights on even the smallest of decisions – showing users how even small decisions can often have *big impacts* on their future;

3. constantly monitor for *new opportunities* that definitely will be of interest to the user and alert them to these as soon as they become known;

4. project trends and drivers into the future to create *plausible future scenarios* at different points in time for the user to plan and strategize against, so that they can feel *prepared* for almost anything that lies ahead, and so that they can make more reliable forecasts about their *own future* – with this including their own personal trends such as their health and finances, as well as exogenic trends such as stock markets, interest rates, political changes, and so on.

This results in a total of 19 specific Design Principles the team will use – these plus the 15 others from before (refer to that section to review those). Intensifi thus intends to deliver a solution that fully adheres to all 19 of these Design Principles, as they believe that doing so will allow their venture to achieve maximum success.

And now back to the Ideate step – their new ideation plan

Having run through the preceding steps, Intensifi's team now arrives *full circle* back to where they started this stage… namely at the *Ideate* step of the Value Definition stage. Here, they'll once again ideate possible solution concepts, but this time around, they'll be certain to work off of their newly *revised* PoV, plus, of course, work according to their newly *expanded* set of Design Principles. Based on these new Design Principles, the team will ideate new and/or revised solution concepts that incorporate each of the principles.

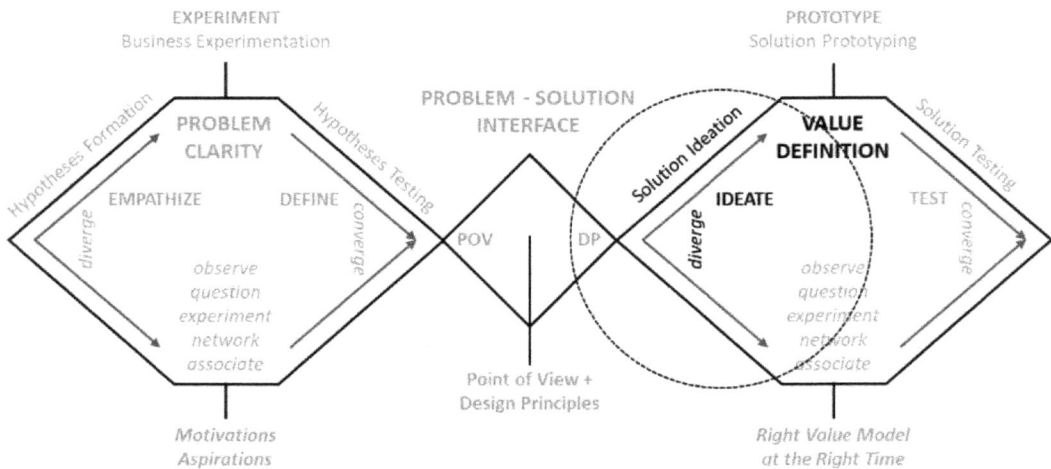

Figure 12.15: Back again to the Ideate step of the Value Definition stage

To do this, the team will once again engage in *ideation and brainstorming activities* using some of the same Design Methods they used before, plus two additional ones –namely, *Empathy Tools* and *Collaborative Sketchboard*. They've chosen these additional methods in particular because they believe these methods will force them to have even greater empathy for – and engagement with – their subjects, as they try to empathically co-create solution concepts with them. These additional methods are bucketed into two method types – one Experiment Method and one Study Method – as shown here.

- **Experiment Method**

  - Empathy Tools

- **Study Method**

  - Collaborative Sketchboard

Let us profile these two new methods they'll be using and see how they'll be using them.

The Experiment Method

Intensifi now starts out with the one additional *Experiment Method* they've chosen. They'll use it to help them, as the innovators here, to conceive new solution ideas reflecting even greater empathy for their subjects.

Empathy Tools

What it is: Empathy Tools involve physical and/or digital augmenters that researchers use in their empathy work whenever the problem they're addressing exists due to certain limitations a market segment has which they themselves don't have. These tools help them better understand certain aspects of these subjects' lives, and thereby develop a deeper sense of empathy for their unique challenges and obstacles – challenges and obstacles they and the general population don't generally face.

Many of the Empathy Tools available are aimed at helping researchers understand the plight of people with various disabilities and special conditions. Examples include "fat suits" to appreciate the challenges of severely obese people, weighted gloves to appreciate the challenges of those with musculoskeletal disorders, and clouded glasses to appreciate the limitations of those with eyesight issues. Such aids are often used in the development of new medical devices intended to help patients deal with the limitations of these conditions.

Beyond this, researchers can also conceive of any number of different Empathy Tools to help them appreciate a particular challenge associated with a certain problem that they themselves don't generally encounter. Any time they need to cast themselves into the role of a particular subject – and that subject, in the context of consuming a particular solution, is fundamentally different than themselves – these researchers will benefit from tools that augment their ability to enter into the situation. This can occur, for example, when the researcher is designing for a profession they don't have, for a hobby they don't engage in, or for a religious celebration they don't observe, and so on. Thus, any tools such as these that can help them to enter into these subjects' experiences can help them to develop better empathy for those subjects.

How Intensifi uses it: Given the nature of its likely solutions, Intensifi is taking a slightly different tact to this method. What it's doing, in particular, is – for each of its team members – creating fake life situations for them that they must "enter into" (at least mentally) and then, while in that particular persona, try using the different mock-up solutions they used before – looking for specific weaknesses or gaps in them.

Here are some examples:

- some team members take on the persona of a high school student with a part-time job and limited bank account and other resources – to see what different solution concepts feel like in that frame of mind;

- other team members take on the persona of a university student looking for career direction – to discern the same thing;

- other team members take on the persona of a mid-career professional trying to balance health, marriage, family, relationships, finances, hobbies, and so on – to see what different solution concepts feel like under those conditions;

- other team members take on the persona of a business leader trying to optimize their business performance in both the short-term and long-term futures;

- other team members take on the persona of a senior professional trying to look forward to other stages of their life, beyond their professional career – to again discern the same thing.

By each team member taking on the mental persona of these different subjects (this being their "empathy tool") and then trying out different solutions in each situation, they're able to gain a lot of insights into what does and does not work well in each respective situation – and why so. All this without having to use outside subjects.

Intensifi's outcomes: Intensifi learns that what the users in most of these situations value most is the ability to access an online (yet secure and private) cloud-connected platform that allows them to input all of the current information (about themselves, their health, their finances, their relationships, etc. – basically, a digital twin profile), as well as their respective goals and aspirations that that stage of their life, and then have the platform analyze all that for them, show them some of the different ideal options before them, and then make expert recommendations tailored just to them.

The team also learns that while high school and university students likely cannot afford augmented services (and thus have little value for an ecosystem of providers), mid-career professionals can, and senior professionals can even more so, such that as each user gets older and more experienced, they increasingly come to value these augmented services and the curated ecosystem of providers they involve.

The team further learns that as users become increasingly sophisticated over time, they increasingly value the ability to customize the platform to their preferences and liking, and thus they value its extensibility more.

Finally, the team learns that all users see the value in connecting their smart connected assets and possessions into the platform so that the platform can help them manage and optimize those – including replacing them with even better ones when they each reach their respective end of life.

These are indeed a wealth of insight just from putting themselves into these users' respective shoes, using all of the knowledge they've attained elsewhere in the process so far.

Insights Summary – Ideate – Experiment Method

Experiment Method 1
Empathy Tools

Key Insights	New Ideas (Solution Concepts)

• Users value most the ability to:
  • access the solution online;
  • create a *digital twin* of themselves and their possessions & assets;
  • define their *goals & aspirations* for that period of their life / business;
  • be shown *options* to consider;
  • have the solution offer a balanced, optimized *prescription*.
• As users get older, the more they value (and will use) *augmenting services* from the ecosystem.
• Users value *customizability* increasingly as they become more *proficient* with the solution.
	• A solution that – in addition to everything else already defined – is also:
	  • accessible online;
	  • highly extensible / customizable;
	  • includes a strong ecosystem of providers of augmenting services;
	  • provides for the creation of a detailed *digital twin* of the individual or business and all their corresponding *assets / possessions*;
	  • lets the user define a prioritized set of *goals and aspirations* for that particular phase of their life or business – to analyze against;
	  • offers the user different *options* to consider;
	  • provides a balanced and optimized prescription based on the user's digital twin, goals, and relevant events occurring around them.

Figure 12.16: Insights Summary for Ideation (Take 2) using the Experiment Method

The Study Method

Intensifi next moves on to the one additional *Study Method* they chose. They'll use it to help them co-create with their subjects new solution concepts that maximally resonate with those subjects, given all the different Design Principles they're working with now.

Collaborative Sketchboard

What it is: Collaborative Sketchboard is a participatory co-creation method. It lets a team work collaboratively to lay out their collective insights and work toward a common vision of a solution together. It's commonly used in UI/UX work.

In this method, the team uses a large piece of paper – often a long strip of butcher paper hung up on a wall – and by working together, sketches various pieces of their work in turn. All sketching is thus done collaboratively and not individually. Using a large piece of paper like this gives the team the opportunity to roll up their work afterward and take it elsewhere to share with others who need to understand it. To begin the actual working session, the team first starts by posting all of their defining criteria, such as their collective discovery findings and insights. They will agree on these as their guiding criteria prior to moving on so that, as they proceed, they're consistently working from a common framework of criteria.

The team next selects a nearby space on the paper and begins sketching (often using Post-It™ Notes that they can later rearrange) the various elements of potential design solutions. They may begin with these in the form of thumbnail sketches and evolve them into more detailed sketches as they proceed. As they work through the exercise, they will layer many different design options on top of one another... until they eventually reach some convergence on a single concept. That final concept represents a common understanding within the team of the high-level definition of their design solution. When finished, the team will be able to walk away with a common vision of their solution and a common ground for why it is the best solution.

How Intensifi uses it: Based on all the insights the team has amassed so far (particularly those they just learned in their Empathy Tools exercise), Intensifi invites in a fresh cohort of subjects and lays out for them all of their defining criteria – specifically, their PoV and their 19 distinct Design Principles – and asks them to engage together in a Collaborative Sketchboard. Here, they all start ideating solutions and writing their details on different Post-It® Notes and placing those on the sketch board. The overall group takes several pauses to aggregate the ideas and cluster them together and then proceeds again in successive waves until they feel they've reached adequate convergence on different ideas and concepts.

Intensifi's outcomes: Having given this group their PoV and Design Principles up front, Intensifi comes out of this exercise with several important insights and takeaways – including the following:

- With the emerging capabilities of AI, the distinction between human-delivered services and AI-delivered services starts to blur, and consequently, many of the services that have historically been delivered by outside human advisors can now potentially be delivered by similar outside AI advisors – depending on the specific service involved.

- Subjects seem to want some type of digital interface to be the primary interface to a solution, but beyond that, don't necessarily care whether the solution is more isolated (standalone) or integrated (cloud-connected), so long as it delivers the same outcome and achieves the same goal. That being the case, different flavors are still viable but may or may not create a significant enough differentiation to even matter per se.

- Subjects seemed to recognize where concierge-style services could become increasingly important and valuable as users became older, more mature, and more financially well-off. The consensus seemed to be this could be baked into specific tiers of a solution – versions with and without them – or else versions with a limited range of them and other versions with an expansive range of them, depending on the details.

- Subjects also noted in their concepts that users need to feel there is a very high ROI from the solution – not just financially but also with the assurance that it empowers them to maximize their overall happiness by optimally balancing their health, career, family, hobbies, finances, and so on, based on their individual priorities. The group similarly highlighted the fact that in order for the brand to be sustainable, it cannot afford to have cases of abject failure amongst users. Thus, there seemed to be a call for some type of *Quality Assurance* built into the solution so that if certain users were not using it properly or well, they could either be guided back into its proper usage, or else marked as bad users (via some type of rating system) so that the world could see that any bad outcomes were the result of them misusing the solution, rather than an issue with the solution itself. The team felt this was an important consideration to take away and work on as well. In fact, from this, they added a twentieth Design Principle.

Arising out of this exercise, the team's twentieth Design Principle became the following:

1. Ensure proper usage of the solution at all times (for example, through appropriate guidance, localized monitoring, and/or user recognition and incentives).

Insights Summary – Ideate – Study Method

Study Method 1
Collaborative Sketchboard

Key Insights

- AI may have a role to play in terms of automated advisory replacing traditional human advisory.
- Stand-alone vs. cloud-connected doesn't seem to be a point of differentiation.
- Different tiers can be designed – lower tiers with fewer optional services; higher tiers with more optional services.

New Ideas (Solution Concepts)

- A solution whose primary user interface is digital.
- A solution that provides some sort of guardrails to ensure users are using it correctly. When it sees that they're not, it guides them back into using it properly (the 20th Design Principle.
  This allows people to overcome the fear of not getting their expected value from the solution on account of not being able to use it properly.

Figure 12.17: Insights Summary for Ideation (Take 2) using the Study Method

Defining their new concepts

From the preceding *Ideate* steps, Intensifi has defined the following solution concepts to its new PoV that it wishes to test:

1. A dual-interface platform – both online and a smart device app – operating at a user-selectable degree of online (cloud) connectivity, using both the native platform's privacy and security systems and its own, and connecting to external hardware devices so as to collect their data – and that otherwise bears all the key digital features prescribed in the Design Principles.

2. A concierge service in which humans interact as the primary interface and thereby serve users in helping them to achieve their desired results, with the servicers using various technological tools behind the scenes, as well as interfacing to select external hardware devices as needed, to fulfill their requirements to the user – and otherwise delivering all the service features prescribed in the Design Principles.

3. A dedicated physical hardware device that users keep with them at all times and use to engage with the system, with the user having control over when, where, and how the device interfaces with external servers and other devices to achieve its objectives – and that otherwise delivers all the key digital features prescribed in the Design Principles.

4. A combination of the preceding solutions, with each element functioning in sync with the others to do what it does best in order to deliver the most optimal outcome possible for the user – and that otherwise delivers all the digital and service features prescribed in the Design Principles.

In each case, the idea is to allow the end user to establish each of their life and/or business goals and, thereafter, access detailed guidance on how to attain those goals, given their own inherent capabilities, capacities, resources, and desires. In doing so, each concept will satisfy all 20 of the stated Design Principles.

Note that each of these solution concepts must at this point be treated as separate and independent concepts – even if later on they end up being combined into a broader and more comprehensive solution package. This is because they each need to be tested independently for their respective efficacy, with minimal confounding and entanglement between them to skew the findings (but also understanding that sometimes their efficacy arises out of their symbioses with certain other concepts). In the end, once all the concepts have been tested, those showing positive efficacy can be combined into an overall more comprehensive solution package, in which case they each then become simply a feature or function of that broader solution. This is just not something to be decided quite yet in the process.

Finally, back to the Test step again – their new validation plan

The team finally comes back to the *Solution Testing* step of the Value Definition stage, where they'll be prototyping and testing their new solution concepts to determine their respective efficacy and impact in addressing their new PoV and revised Design Principles. These results will serve as an indicator of each concept's likely adoption and use by the targeted subjects.

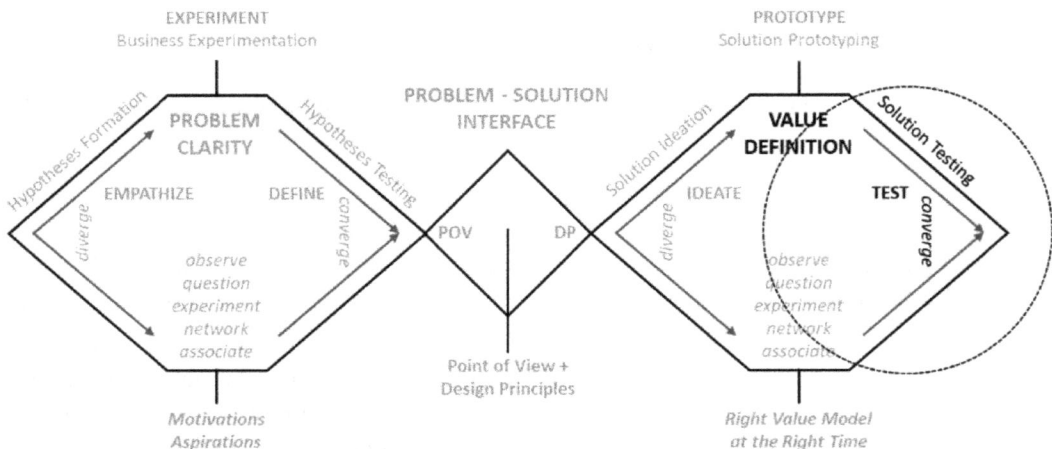

Figure 12.18: Back again to the Test step of the Value Definition stage

To do this, the team will once again engage in **Solution Prototyping and Testing** activities using some of the same Design Methods they used before – plus four additional ones – namely, *Usability Testing, Café Testing, Collaborative Inspection*, and *Feedback Capture Grid*. They've chosen these additional methods in particular because they believe these methods will let them better engage their would-be customers/users in helping them to evaluate the efficacy and resonance of each concept. These additional methods are bucketed into two method types – namely, two Experiment Methods and two Study Methods – as noted here, together with the types of prototypes they'll each use:

- **Experiment Methods**

  - Usability Testing – digital mockup with simulated capabilities and augmented services.

  - Café Testing – digital mockup with simulated capabilities and augmented services.

- **Study Methods**

  - Collaborative Inspection – digital mockups plus bits of the prior wireframe mockups.

  - Feedback Capture Grid – digital mockups plus bits of the prior wireframe mockups.

Let us profile these four new methods they'll be using and see how they'll be using them.

The Experiment Methods

Here, Intensifi uses the two additional *Experiment Methods* they've chosen. They'll use these to assess and evaluate the *usability* of the respective solution concepts they've conceived.

Usability Testing

What it is: Usability Testing is a variant of User Testing – often used in the context of UI/UX work – where subjects are asked to *use* specific elements of the user interface of a device, such as those of a physical product, a website, or a mobile app (anything with an embedded or remote UI), and their actions are subsequently observed and recorded so that the researchers can understand the efficacy of these interfaces.

In these tests, subjects are asked to complete certain real-world tasks on the product (either a production model or a prototype if it involves a concept not yet in production). While they're doing this, team members watch and observe what they're doing. They may ask for certain feedback from subjects while they're in the process of each task (such as in the Narration Method, where they're asked to think and work out loud), and will almost always solicit detailed feedback from them after they're finished with each task (as in the Behavioral Interview, where they're asked to relate their perceptions of the task and their actions). This exercise does not typically require overly large groups to collect useful feedback, as there will often be high uniformity within any particular market segment. It should be repeated, however, for each segment of interest, as there will often be differences in perceptions and preferences between those segments.

This method is also used for competitive benchmarking, in which researchers have subjects use the UI of different competing models from competing businesses and collect their feedback on each one so as to make a comparative assessment of the best and worst, and to establish where in that spectrum their design falls. From there, engineering teams can attempt to dissect each model's design and establish correlations and causalities between specific design features and certain user perceptions (which may or may not prove fruitful). Businesses at times do this to establish best-in-class design baselines against which they judge all new designs. If their engineering teams are successful at establishing correlations, they can also be able to develop new design guidelines that help to move their designs toward those best-in-class characteristics.

How Intensifi uses it: Intensifi quickly develops a digital mock-up of a digital solution concept that features reconfigurable attributes that simulate different variations of the many Design Principles, plus simulated human services as an augmented form of value. The team then recruits subjects (representing the different age cohorts they've since discovered) to come into their lab and test out this mockup and its variants with them – playing out the different attribute variations to get subjects' feedback on each one.

Intensifi's outcomes: Intensifi learns that subjects, in general, really like the digital solution concept, and that different age cohorts have differing preferences on the details of each Design Principle. For example, young users seemed less discerning, and therefore less demanding, about privacy, security, and extensibility, while older users seemed to much more expect, and therefore demand, these things. This means the team could either a) solve for the most demanding user group and then have that apply to all users; b) offer increasing/decreasing levels of these attributes at different price/feature tiers; or c) make those attributes entirely user-configurable. This decision will depend on certain cost/value / branding trade-offs the team will need to study.

Intensifi also finds – consistent with their other research findings – that the older, more mature, more sophisticated users recognize more value in the augmented human services and ecosystem of service providers, as well as the foresight capabilities mentioned earlier (which were emulated in this mockup).

Finally, all users seemed to universally grasp and value the conceptual notion of an "omniscient *Generative AI for Life* genie" who was likewise your trusted friend, mentor, and coach. They all seemed to place a high value on the following attributes:

- *comprehensiveness* (covering all areas of their life and business);
- *currency* (able to incorporate all the latest news and data from around the world each day);
- *connectivity* (using myriad devices to incorporate relevant data from their personal world);
- *dependability* (their ability to have full confidence in the solution's prescriptions);
- *sociability* (their ability to socialize their prescriptions with others whom they trust and value);
- *privacy and security* (all information protected and inaccessible to unauthorized parties);
- *accessibility* (their ability to afford the solution).

This all made the team feel like they were starting to move toward some convergence with better confidence.

Café Testing

What it is: Café Testing – also known as Guerrilla Usability Testing – is a variant of User Testing in which the researchers literally sit in a café and ask random passers-by (perhaps those who appear to likely have the necessary experience) to evaluate a particular design, usually in exchange for paying for their beverage. This highly-effective approach tends to produce useful feedback in a fraction of the time, and at a fraction of the cost, of traditional in-lab User Testing. It obviously can't be used for every type of product, but it is generally useful for digital products such as websites and mobile apps, and possibly for other small, handheld products such as photo equipment, gaming consoles, and drone controls. The same test is also sometimes conducted in bars where subjects tend to be more relaxed and move at a slower pace.

Teams – whenever dealing with small handheld products or digital devices – can make good use of this rapid, cost-effective approach to User Testing, while also collecting high-quality feedback from a broad cross-section of subjects.

How Intensifi uses it: Intensifi repeats their prior research using the exact same digital mockups, except this time around, they recruit perfect strangers at different cafés and brewpubs to try out the solution with them (after, of course, explaining the concept to them).

Intensifi's outcomes: Intensifi finds that, first of all, these random subjects really love the whole concept of such a holistic life optimization solution – framed as it is as an "omniscient *Generative AI for Life* genie" that they can use to optimize every area of the life simultaneously, with high assurance that doing so leads them to attain their highest possible potential.

Aside from that, their takeaways seem to be a bit more sporadic in this case, depending on who exactly they spoke to, as there was less "filtering" happening here than there was in their curated cohorts for their workshops. What this tells them is that really homing in on their specific target subject (the aspiring professional) is their first order of business, as this solution and all its details don't seem to resonate quite as strongly with less aspirational people (many of whom they find in the brewpub) as they do with more aspirational people. So, now they know for sure that they really have to target the "more aspirational" people in the market.

In terms of the actual simulated digital tool, most subjects seemed to like it and what it was able to do for them. They did – more so than the in-lab subjects – seem to emphasize more the value of the sociability of the solution… being able to share its prescripts with their friends and colleagues and "compare notes" with each other. This affirmed for the team the need to emphasize this attribute even more, so as to potentially capture customers with a solution that they might not otherwise capture were this attribute missing.

The remainder of the feedback here seemed to echo what the team had learned previously in their other exercises, regarding their PoV and Design Principles.

Insights Summary – Test – Experiment Methods	
Experiment Method 1 **Usability Testing**	**Experiment Method 2** **Café Testing**
Key Insights • Everyone seems to understand & grasp the idea of an 'omniscient Generative AI for Life or Business' concept. • Users really like the digital solution concept. • Different age cohorts have different preferences around each Design Principle. • Older users place more value on the augmented service provider ecosystem and their respective services. • Older users place the most value on foresight exploration capabilities. • Everyone values privacy, security, comprehensiveness, currency, connectivity, dependability, sociability, and accessibility.	**Areas of Special Need / Attention** • Their target customer is clearly the *high-aspiration professional* (at any age). Non-aspirational people won't value their solution. • Different tiers / packages are required for different life stages. • The solution must at all times ensure comprehensiveness, currency, connectivity, dependability, sociability, privacy, security, and accessibility. • Sociability is an especially strong attribute amongst many user groups.

Figure 12.19: Insights Summary for Testing (Take 2) using the Experiment Methods

The Study Methods

Intensifi now uses the two additional *Study Methods* they've chosen. They'll use these to solicit and collect additional feedback on the respective solution concepts from different subjects – to see which one receives the most positive responses from them.

Collaborative Inspection

What it is: Collaborative Inspection is a group examination process in which a broad group is brought together to collaboratively review and inspect a particular innovative work product, such as a prototype solution concept.

The Collaborative Inspection session is typically led and moderated by a Lead Reviewer and includes a designated Recorder and Time Keeper. The Lead Reviewer has a preset agenda for the session, and based on that, leads the broad group through the collaborative review process, typically exploring and discussing one attribute of the solution at a time (a feature, a function, a piece of content, an appearance, and so forth). The session thus follows a methodical and systematic review sequence to ensure that all necessary attributes have been adequately inspected and critiqued.

The secret sauce behind Collaborative Inspection lies in the breadth of the group brought together. This group will include researchers, designers, business stakeholders, subject matter experts, technologists, and perhaps most importantly, end users (customers). Because so many different perspectives are represented, the inspections tend to be very thorough and very effective in catching oversights, misses, and misplaced assumptions – things the team by itself may never catch. It also affords the opportunity for the effort's stakeholders to come together and have a meaningful conversation about possible solutions, which can sometimes uncover deeper insights into the broader Solution Space. The method thus helps teams properly vet each solution concept and either refine it further or weed it out from further consideration.

How Intensifi uses it: Here, Intensifi knowingly recruits an incredibly diverse group of professionals from an incredibly broad array of industries, fields, and vocations – artists, teachers, engineers, academic philosophers, research scientists, designers, business leaders, salespeople, yoga instructors, and so on – and, as a group, walks the entire group through their digital solution mockup, plus parts of their other (prior) wire-frame mockups, and solicits their feedback on each attribute.

More specifically, the group explores one attribute at a time and asks for group feedback/discussion on that attribute to flesh out each one's respective pros, cons, likes, dislikes, benefits, drawbacks, and other "*But did you think about this?*" considerations that the team might've missed earlier. Having such a diverse group, marked by such *cognitive diversity*, is precisely the right place to ask for this type of "last-minute sanity check" feedback, as this is where one will most likely succeed in getting that sort of feedback.

Intensifi's outcomes: Intensifi learns that there were, in fact, certain insights they had missed earlier – most notably the fact that certain professions (sales, engineering, and design, for example) tend to value this type of solution and its capabilities more so than do other professions (teachers and fitness instructors, for example). This tells them they should (mostly) focus on, and market to, these (typically higher-paying) private sector corporate roles versus those operating more in the public sector or public service fields… something they had sort of considered previously, but never really gave it that much serious thought.

Intensifi also learns that the more analytical professions such as scientists and engineers, for example, are (not surprisingly) more picky and selective about things such as the data the solution is using (is it of sufficiently high quality? Is it biased or skewed?) and the choice of ecosystem partners being used. Similarly, the more "artistic" professions seemed to be more concerned with things such as early access, opportunity discovery, and ongoing day-to-day value. These new observations give the team more insights into how to potentially package and market versions of the solution to different professions (in other words, which attributes to emphasize and/or deemphasize in each case).

Feedback Capture Grid

What it is: Feedback Capture Grid is a visual categorization method that teams use to capture and categorize the evaluation feedback given to them on various ideas and concepts by different reviewers at an evaluation event. It's useful when evaluating potential solution concepts (as well as in other applications).

In this method, prior to soliciting and collecting feedback from reviewers, the facilitator first constructs, on a blank piece of paper, a 2x2 grid defining four quadrants. They then label each quadrant and, subsequently, use those quadrants to collect four different *types* of feedback, according to the following pattern:

- Quadrant 1 – Upper LH – plus symbol (+): Used to capture the things reviewers liked or found notable.

- Quadrant 2 – Upper RH – delta symbol (Δ): Used to capture reviewers' constructive criticisms.

- Quadrant 3 – Lower LH – question mark (?): Used to capture questions the review raised.

- Quadrant 4 – Lower RH – light bulb (¤): Used to capture other new ideas the review spurred.

+	**Δ**
Things the reviewers liked / found notable.	Reviewers' constructive criticisms.
?	**¤**
Questions the reviewers raised.	New ideas the process spurred (from reviewers or the team).

Figure 12.20: The Feedback Capture Grid

Teams can use the method to capture real-time feedback on different solution concepts. Its use lets them be very systematic and intentional about how they capture this feedback. Especially when reviewing the feedback later on, this visual diagramming really helps to quickly digest, understand, and apply the feedback that was given. To be most useful, teams should attempt to solicit and collect good feedback in *all four quadrants*, but especially in the *top two quadrants*.

How Intensifi uses it: Intensifi integrated this method into their prior Collaborative Inspection workshop as a means of capturing the participants' feedback on each attribute.

Intensifi's outcomes: Intensifi got all four types of input on each attribute, but in particular, the following:

- certain attributes got more likes (for example, those of comprehensiveness, connectivity, and foresight);

- certain attributes got more constructive criticisms (for example, the value of the solution at all – some perspectives saw it as just a tool to fuel people's vanity – the value of the solution during "down times," the value of certain augmentative services, and the value of certain customizations);

- certain attributes got more questions (for example, why the need to feed all of our personal, private data into the solution, and why the need to have ourselves and all of our digitally-enabled possessions constantly connected to it);

- certain attributes got more new ideas (for example. why not package and market unique versions of the solution for each profession… an engineer's version, a teacher's version, an architect's version, and so on). These were all ideas that the team committed to going back and discussing and debating on their own afterward – to work out for themselves their value and viability.

Insights Summary – Test – Study Methods	
Study Method 1 Collaborative Inspection	Study Method 2 Feedback Capture Grid
Key Insights • As a whole, certain professions value this type of (holistic) solution more so than do other professions. • As a whole, the more analytical professions are more concerned about the data being used in the solution. • As a whole, the more artistic professions are more concerned with early access, opportunity discovery, and the day-to-day value of the solution. • There may be the opportunity to package & sell unique profession-specific versions of the solution... an engineer's version, a teacher's version, an accountant's version, etc. This can have pros & cons.	**Areas of Special Need / Attention** • Primarily focus on / market to private sector corporate roles. • Different customer groups need different solution attributes emphasized to them – according to each one's specific interests, preferences, and points of concern. • Comprehensiveness, connectivity, and foresight are attributes that generate a lot of positive responses from all would-be customers. • May have to work harder to sell attributes like value during stasis, customization, and augmenting services. • May have to work harder to explain the need for constant, comprehensive data feeds in the solution.

Figure 12.21: Insights Summary for Testing (Take 2) using the Study Methods

The outcome – Intensifi's winning solution

Okay… so the team has now finished going through the *entire Design Thinking process* and they believe they are finally at a point of convergence with their final solution concept. This is a good thing because, quite honestly, at this point, the team is exhausted and very much "workshopped out." They probably couldn't do too much more of this if they had to, which is a valid point. At some point, all teams have to call it "done" and move on so that they can move ahead to the next step in their venture.

Given this, and based on everything the team has learned so far throughout the journey, they've decided that their final solution (the winner) will be a **hybrid digital/service solution**.

The **digital platform part** of this solution will *do* the following for the user:

- serve as the user's very own personal, "omniscient Generative AI for Life/Business" mentor and coach;

- let users – at each stage of their life, career, and business – optimize each and every aspect of that life or business simultaneously, according to certain specific heuristics established by their own personal goals and priorities, so that they can attain their maximum possible potential at that stage of their life or business, as well as in their future ahead, and thus attain their greatest possible success;

- cover each and every aspect of their life comprehensively – health, family, career, marriage, finances, relationships, hobbies, life planning, and so on;

- cover each and every aspect of their business comprehensively – strategy, finance, operations, HR, R&D, and so on;

- deliver 100% fully personalized prescriptions for each user, allowing them to attain the maximum possible return on the specific knowledge, skills, and resources they possess, according to their stated goals and priorities, and in accordance with all of the opportunities and options surrounding them (which the solution will always know about);

- let users socialize their personalized prescriptions with others so that they can gain those individuals' feedback and advice, which can sometimes add additional flavor and nuance to them;

- guide the user in how to use the solution most effectively during both major and minor decision periods, and therefore, how to use it during both major decision and transformation periods and all of the lulls occurring in between. This will empower them to micro-tune their lives and businesses at all times, which can prove incredibly important since some seemingly minor decisions do in fact snowball into far broader consequences later on in life or business – ones having a major impact on them (the details of which the solution will foresee and inform them about);

- offer a range of extensible features that let users customize the solution to work the way they prefer, with varying levels of user control versus solution control (according to the user's preferences), as well as varying levels of depth and nuance that let users be more or less detailed in their unique goals, aspirations, and decision rules for each area, per their preferences and desires;

- offer specific modules for undertaking foresight analysis on the data it has about the user and their world so that the user can then explore different plausible future scenarios inside the solution and, by doing so, develop plans and strategies that are robust to each such scenario.

The **digital platform part** of this solution will further *work* in the following ways:

- have users input, and as needed update, their personal attributes (physical characteristics, test scores, degrees, certifications, etc.), as well as connect to each of their respective digitally-enabled devices to likewise input and constantly update those datasets;

- constantly amass, assess, and incorporate the latest pertinent information and data from around the world to integrate into the user's personal prescriptions for their life or business;

- use proven AI heuristics to deliver absolute confidence that the personalized prescriptions given are in fact the most optimal ones for that particular user, given the choices and decisions they've made so far, and the other driving factors affecting their environment and world;

- apply the most current, contemporary, and proven privacy and security measures to ensure 100% absolute user privacy and complete security over the user's data inputs and prescription outputs;

- use an online digital (cloud-connected) platform plus a mobile app that together function as the main interfaces to the solution (the team envisions that most input and decision work will occur on the online platform, while most monitoring work will likely take occur on the mobile app);

- require no dedicated hardware other than the devices the user already owns and uses – except where required to digitalize certain of their assets, in which case, existing third-party IOT devices are outfitted to these assets to collect and transmit the desired information and data on them.

The augmenting **services part** of this solution will offer the following:

- different tiers of optionally-available human concierge services that undertake certain actions on behalf of the user, to expedite and ease their attainment of certain specific goals and objectives in their life or business;

- an ecosystem of curated providers that allow the user to access and procure certain specific products, services, and/or experiences they require for attaining certain specific goals and objectives at that point in time.

And in terms of *how* the overall solution will be *offered* to customers, it will be offered as follows:

- different versions will be offered with varying feature sets for differing stages of life, career, and business – rudimentary versions for early adults, intermediate versions for mid-life adults, and highly advanced, customizable versions with additional features for later-life adults – in each case, reflecting the unique goals and aspirations of that particular life stage, while being fully accessible to every life stage:

  - a *free starter* version for high-school students that helps them navigate their educational and career paths at that point in their lives (while also getting them started on the solution);

  - a *paid, but still very affordable* version for university students that helps them further navigate their more specific career path looking forward;

  - a *slightly more expensive* version for young professionals that helps them to navigate the early days of their career and start to figure out their respective relationships (possible mates, etc.);

  - an *even more expensive* version for mid-life / mid-career professionals that helps them maximize their success in career, marriage, finances, health wellbeing, and so on throughout that stage;

  - a *premium, premier version* for more mature, later-stage professionals that helps them maximize their success in late career and on into retirement and beyond;

- similarly differentiated versions will be offered with differing feature sets for different types of professionals – those tailored to the more analytical fields and those tailored to the less analytical fields;

- within each of these, different pricing tiers will be offered with different feature and capability sets, so as to offer something to everyone who desires it, and thus make the overall solution accessible to each person who wants it at a specific stage in their life or business, while also being extensible in a way that grows and scales with them as they progress throughout their life and career, or as their business progresses throughout its respective stages of launch, growth, and maturation;

- special incentives will be offered to encourage users to use the solution routinely – such as promotions with select ecosystem partners, and possibly even "gamified recognition" in the platform for those who opt into that.

Taken as a whole, this describes exactly the solution that Intensifi intends to offer from this point forward.

However, this is just the solution in its "raw form" so to speak. We still have yet to translate and package that into a proper "value proposition" that reflects each of the elements and pieces of a correct value proposition – not to mention defining Intensifi's *Unique Value Proposition* that's going to help them win in the marketplace. That is what we need to do next.

Thus, in *Chapter 13*, we will explore and unpack this solution in more detail – including by extrapolating it into a proper and formal *Unique Value Proposition* for Intensifi to use inside its business model. But for now, this brings us to the end of the formal Design Thinking process for the solution, and therefore, to the end of this chapter.

Summary

In this chapter, we explored Intensifi's Solution Space with them. We did this by first working through the *Ideate* step of the Value Definition stage to ideate new solution concepts, after which we developed a validation plan to use in testing those solution concepts – along with the types of prototypes we'd use in each case – and then we worked through the *Test* step of the Value Definition stage to test out those concepts and thereby find the winner.

Only we didn't find a winner. Instead, we found a problem – namely, missing hypotheses. This forced us, as is quite common in the Design Thinking process, to have to cycle back to thinking through what we missed earlier on (thus giving us new hypotheses to test) and then testing those new hypotheses to see whether they were in fact correct – which, luckily for us (and Intensifi), they were. We then had to alter our PoV and amend our Design Principles accordingly to reflect these additional realities. After this, we started the whole Value Definition stage all over again... ideating new solution concepts, deciding how best to test and validate each one (including what prototypes to use), and then doing so – all using our array of Design Methods.

Coming out of this, we (and Intensifi) eventually arrived at the winning solution concept. This whole forward-backward "oops we missed something" journey is indeed very indicative of the actual Design Thinking process (although sometimes it's not even this neat; sometimes it takes three or four iterations to get it right).

jmNext, we need to translate this solution concept into a proper *value proposition* – and more specifically, into a *Unique Value Proposition* that Intensifi can leverage in its new (innovative) business model – recalling that their goal in doing so will be to "unleash massive new value" for their would-be customers. So, we'll see in *Chapter 13* whether they can start to do that with this solution concept, as doing so will require them to think through how to take that value proposition to market and actually activate it with real customers. That will also bring them back to the point where they need to get back to defining the balance of their business model – using both the structural and functional considerations we explored earlier – our segue into the remainder of this book.

Design Thinking's Final Act (So Far) – Our New Solution

In *Chapter 12*, we literally experienced the Value Definition stage of Design Thinking – walking vicariously alongside Intensifi as they worked through their Solution Space in the hunt for the most optimal solution. We also encountered with them the not atypical recursion in this process, where somewhere down the road we realize we missed an important insight earlier on, and so have to cycle back to a prior step to address that. In their case, there was the realization – after having already done solution ideation (Ideate) and solution testing (Test) – that they'd missed several possibly important customer considerations that they shouldn't overlook. And so, they turned those observations into new hypotheses and proceeded to re-execute the prior three steps until they came back again to where they had begun, at which point they finished the process successfully.

This brought them to the point where they had defined their "winning solution" for the current point in time (something that has to be regularly revisited) … the end of the *traditional* or *classical* Design Thinking process.

And so, this raises the questions… "What's next?" "Where do we go from here?" Those are the questions this intermediate bridge chapter aims to answer, recalling that our goal here is to find not just the right solution, but ultimately the right business model by which to take that solution to market and operationalize it as a business. It's one thing to have a winning solution to sell, but it's an entirely different thing to have a winning business model by which to sell it. Missing either one can lead to failure.

Here are, specifically, the topics we explore in this chapter:

- **All Done (For Now) – Here's Our Solution**: An exploration of the implications to our business model of having defined a winning solution.

- **Where Do We Go From Here?**: A brief exploration of where we need to be looking and what we need to be thinking as we marry the world of classical Design Thinking with Business Model Innovation.

We'll also check in again with the team over at Intensifi – to see if they've recovered yet from their Design Thinking activities, and if they're ready to buckle their seatbelts and hit the throttle again.

All Done (For Now) – Here's Our Solution

At this point, Intensifi has defined its "winning solution" (for now) – and has done so in quite extensive detail, making it very clear what they're aiming for, given everything they've just learned about their subjects in this process. So let us review that new solution again.

Recalling Intensifi's solution

Recall from *Chapter 12* that Intensifi's new solution – the full details of which are outlined at the end of that chapter – is a **hybrid digital / service solution**. Recall further that the digital platform part of the solution works in certain ways and does certain things for the user, while the services part of the solution also does certain things for the user. Finally, recall from Intensifi's specifications that the entire solution is to be offered in a certain, specific set of ways so as to reach the maximum number of market segments in ways that resonate with each one.

Collectively, these points define the solution that Intensifi intends to offer, against the detailed Point of View it defined following its Problem Clarity stage. They (and we) realize of course that there is still more to be learned – especially once they turn this into a real offering and start trying to sell it (reality has a way of bringing stark clarity to whatever we still have wrong). But for now, this is the solution definition they're working toward.

A solution versus a business – appreciating the difference

If we (and Intensifi) were just using the *classical* Design Thinking process, then we'd be all done now, as we have our winning solution.

But as the astute reader of this book, you'll quickly realize that this is the difference between an inventor (someone who creates a solution) and an entrepreneur (someone who turns that solution into a successful commercial enterprise). And *our goal* here is not only a successful commercial enterprise but a *very successful* commercial enterprise. And so, we have to have more than just a "solution" to do that.

We therefore have to go beyond just the solution – to thinking about how that solution is to be a part of, and relate to, our far broader business model. This is the mental transition we need to start making at this point.

Envisioning Intensifi's value proposition – the Value Proposition Canvas

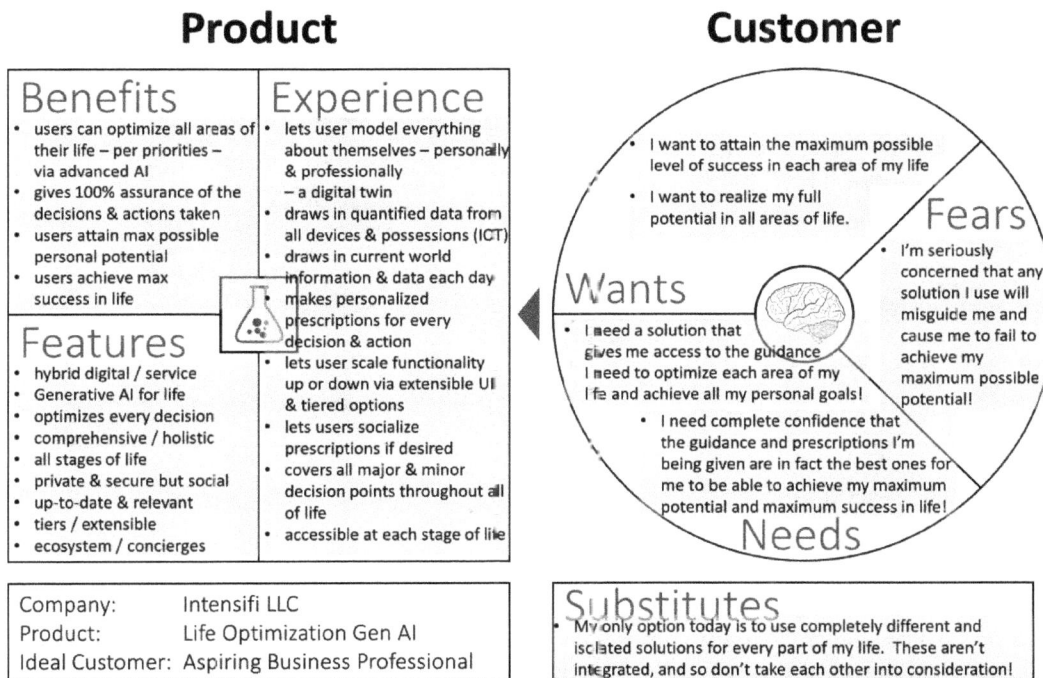

Recalling from *Chapter 6* that Intensifi's intention at this point was to pause and map out their value proposition on a **Peter Thomson Value Proposition Canvas** – to see what new insights mapping it out would reveal to them – let us now have Intensifi do that.

Figure 13.1 shows a Value Proposition Canvas for Intensifi's *individual value proposition*.

Value Proposition Canvas

Product

Benefits
- users can optimize all areas of their life – per priorities – via advanced AI
- gives 100% assurance of the decisions & actions taken
- users attain max possible personal potential
- users achieve max success in life

Experience
- lets user model everything about themselves – personally & professionally – a digital twin
- draws in quantified data from all devices & possessions (ICT)
- draws in current world information & data each day
- makes personalized prescriptions for every decision & action
- lets user scale functionality up or down via extensible UI & tiered options
- lets users socialize prescriptions if desired
- covers all major & minor decision points throughout all of life
- accessible at each stage of life

Features
- hybrid digital / service
- Generative AI for life
- optimizes every decision
- comprehensive / holistic
- all stages of life
- private & secure but social
- up-to-date & relevant
- tiers / extensible
- ecosystem / concierges

Company:	Intensifi LLC
Product:	Life Optimization Gen AI
Ideal Customer:	Aspiring Business Professional

Customer

Wants
- I want to attain the maximum possible level of success in each area of my life
- I want to realize my full potential in all areas of life.

Fears
- I'm seriously concerned that any solution I use will misguide me and cause me to fail to achieve my maximum possible potential!

Needs
- I need a solution that gives me access to the guidance I need to optimize each area of my life and achieve all my personal goals!
- I need complete confidence that the guidance and prescriptions I'm being given are in fact the best ones for me to be able to achieve my maximum potential and maximum success in life!

Substitutes
- My only option today is to use completely different and isolated solutions for every part of my life. These aren't integrated, and so don't take each other into consideration!

Based on the work of Steve Blank, Clayton Christensen, Seth Godin, Yves Pigneur, and Alex Osterwalder. Released under creative commons license to encourage adoption and ideation. No rights asserted.

Figure 13.1: The Value Proposition Canvas for Intensifi's individual value proposition

As we can see from this canvas, the "product" here (Intensifi's individual solution) involves certain specific features that allow its usage to create a particular user experience, while also delivering certain specific benefits. All of these connect directly to the "customer" profiled here. In particular, that experience speaks directly to allaying their fears, while those benefits directly address their respective wants and needs.

Figure 13.2 shows a Value Proposition Canvas for Intensifi's *business value proposition*.

Value Proposition Canvas

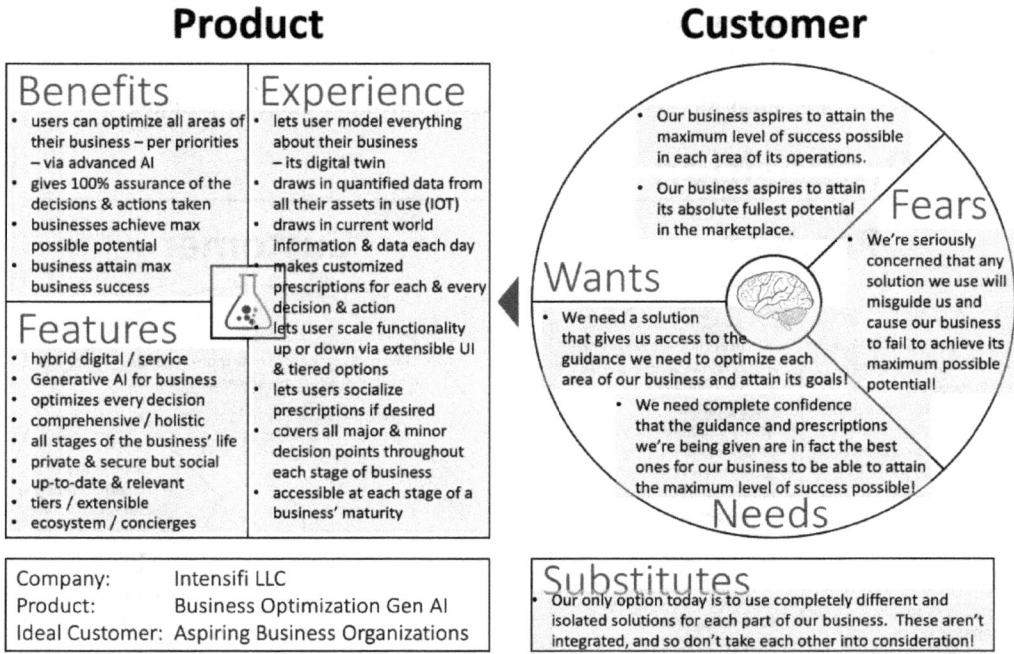

Product   ## Customer

Benefits
- users can optimize all areas of their business – per priorities – via advanced AI
- gives 100% assurance of the decisions & actions taken
- businesses achieve max possible potential
- business attain max business success

Experience
- lets user model everything about their business – its digital twin
- draws in quantified data from all their assets in use (IOT)
- draws in current world information & data each day
- makes customized prescriptions for each & every decision & action
- lets user scale functionality up or down via extensible UI & tiered options
- lets users socialize prescriptions if desired
- covers all major & minor decision points throughout each stage of business
- accessible at each stage of a business' maturity

Features
- hybrid digital / service
- Generative AI for business
- optimizes every decision
- comprehensive / holistic
- all stages of the business' life
- private & secure but social
- up-to-date & relevant
- tiers / extensible
- ecosystem / concierges

Fears
- Our business aspires to attain the maximum level of success possible in each area of its operations.
- Our business aspires to attain its absolute fullest potential in the marketplace.
- We're seriously concerned that any solution we use will misguide us and cause our business to fail to achieve its maximum possible potential!

Wants
- We need a solution that gives us access to the guidance we need to optimize each area of our business and attain its goals!
- We need complete confidence that the guidance and prescriptions we're being given are in fact the best ones for our business to be able to attain the maximum level of success possible!

Needs

Substitutes
- Our only option today is to use completely different and isolated solutions for each part of our business. These aren't integrated, and so don't take each other into consideration!

Company: Intensifi LLC
Product: Business Optimization Gen AI
Ideal Customer: Aspiring Business Organizations

Based on the work of Steve Blank, Clayton Christensen, Seth Godin, Yves Pigneur, and Alex Osterwalder. Released under creative commons license to encourage adoption and ideation. No rights asserted.

Figure 13.2: The Value Proposition Canvas for Intensifi's business value proposition

As we can likewise see from this canvas, the "product" here (Intensifi's business solution) involves certain specific features that allow its usage to create a particular user experience, while also delivering certain specific benefits. All of these connect directly to the "customer" profiled here. In particular, that experience speaks directly to allaying their fears, while those benefits directly address their respective wants and needs.

So, what we can observe from these two Value Proposition Canvases is the following:

- Their customers' *wants*, *needs*, and *fears* are all laid bare for us to see in plain light (no doubts).

- These *needs* directly reflect these customers' *outcome needs* (aspirations).

- These *wants* directly reflect their *motivations* driving those outcome needs.

- These *fears* directly reflect these customers' concerns and inhibitions around *not being able* to attain those needs – a form of "pain" associated with the situation.

- These *features* represent all the specific (intended) attributes of our solution (which in some cases we may care more about than customers do – remember this is down at Level 3).

- These *benefits* are what tie our solution back to these customers' *wants* and *needs*.

  This *experience* is what determines whether or not our solution and its benefits actually achieve these customers' *needs*, and thereby deliver on their specific *wants*.

  If this *experience* proves this out, then we have succeeded; if it doesn't, then we have failed!

Understanding the first four of these insights certainly reinforces our empathy for these customers. Plus, it helps us to develop the empathic understanding we need of them and their situation.

Understanding the last three of these insights clearly reveals how well our value proposition does or does not unlock massive new value for these customers – and thus allows them to attain their needs and wants in a powerfully unique and novel way that no other party can or does today.

These are all powerful – and mostly reinforcing – insights that serve to bring tremendous clarity to the whole situation, on both the customer wants/needs/fears side and the features/benefits/experience side. It serves therefore as a great litmus test of whether or not our value proposition should resonate with these customers.

While this canvas does indeed speak to what makes our value proposition a *great one*, it doesn't necessarily speak to what makes it a *unique one* – or in other words, a truly *Unique Value Proposition*. For that, we have to go beyond the canvas and look at what is in fact truly unique and differentiated about our particular value proposition… what makes it unlike anyone else's value proposition.

On to the Unique Value Proposition

While we'll focus on the majority of the actual business model in *Chapter 14*, for now, we want to at least start by extrapolating Intensifi's new solution into a formal and proper **Unique Value Proposition**, since we and Intensifi have what is needed to do this now – namely, their *Point of View*, their *Design Principles*, and their *solution* that emerged out of those No further work is required to define this Unique Value Proposition.

Let us therefore recall from *Chapter 4* that the Unique Value Proposition is defined in the following manner, drawing from the **Business Model Meta Formula** introduced there.

Recalling the Unique Value Proposition's definition

One's Unique Value Proposition is defined as the **uniquely novel value** that *only their business can (and will) deliver to its customers*. As such, it is comprised of the following three elements:

1. Their offering's **promise** – the distinct *benefits* their solution delivers to their customers that no other organizations' solutions can deliver.

2. Their offering's **manifestation** – the actual *form* their solution takes, whether it be a product, a service, an experience, or some other form – and thus the actual *type of value* it imparts to these customers.

3. Their offering's **fulfillment** of its promise – how it actually *delivers* on this aforementioned promise to achieve its promised benefits and thereby help these customers attain their desired outcome.

There are also a few other important points we need to recall here regarding the Unique Value Proposition:

- It must connect us and the value we unlock to the specific outcomes our customers want to achieve – functional, emotional, social, and transformational.

- As such, it has to make a very clear promise to those customers that we will be doing something for them (in relation to those outcomes) that no one else can or will – certain specific and unique benefits.

- The more valued (desired by our customers) and unique (isolated to us) our promise and offering are, the more compelling our value proposition will be.

- The more novel and unique our promise and offering are, the more they will differentiate us from everything else out there – with differentiation being crucial to our long-term sustainability.

- It should be informed by all the *workarounds* that current Power Users and Early Adopters use and the hacks they craft to overcome the shortcomings of present solutions for their outcome needs – shortcomings that they're acutely aware of.

- It must emphasize the "finished story benefits"… the final and ultimate outcome it helps customers achieve in their situation.

With these insights in mind, we can start to see an important **nuance** emerging here – namely, that it isn't just about the *solution* we offer, but rather, and more importantly, about how we *frame* that solution – something we'll do by thinking very critically about thes things:

- what specific outcome(s) our customers are trying to achieve – we must always start with those;

- what "pain" our customers are currently encountering in trying to achieve those outcomes;

- what promise do we make about alleviating that pain and making the attainment of these outcomes far easier;

- how, exactly, we espouse that promise – as it must be in language they understand and resonate with.

This is very important because, quite often, Innovation Teams get the whole idea and point of a value proposition wrong! They want to talk about their solution's *features*. But it's not about those features or what they do per se… it's about us doing the above and nothing else! This is – as we so clearly noted in *Chapter 8* – an entirely different level of abstraction in our thinking process!

So **if** we can formulate our Unique Value Proposition with these four points in mind, **if** we can explain the benefits of our solution and how those benefits allow our customers to attain their desired outcome – especially their main, final outcome, and **if** we can do so in emotional, lifestyle-oriented language (how does it make me a "better version of myself" and thus "the hero of my own story"?), then very likely we can transform our "winning solution" into a truly powerful Unique Value Proposition that wins over customers' hearts, minds, and wallets – and by so doing, makes for a very successful business venture.

That is indeed something that will be worth plugging into our business model!

And so, given this insight, we can take what we know of Intensifi's Point of View, Design Principles, and defined solution and, based on those, start to define its Unique Value Proposition.

Prepping for Intensifi's Unique Value Proposition

Given Intensifi's articulated Point of View, Design Principles, and final solution, we can make the following preliminary observations about their particular situation:

1. Intensifi's would-be customers' **primary outcome need** is to achieve their individual maximum potential in life, given what they have to work with, and in so doing attain the maximum level of success possible for them. This is Level 1.

2. Stemming out of this is a key **secondary outcome need** – namely, to have *100% complete confidence* that the decisions they're making, and the actions they're taking commensurate with those decisions, are in fact those that will *optimize* their lives in a comprehensive, holistic, and balanced manner so that they can in fact attain that primary outcome need. This is Level 2.

3. And stemming out of this is a very important **tertiary outcome need** that speaks directly to Intensifi's *solution* – namely, that they need some type of "solution" they can procure that will empower them to achieve that *secondary outcome need* so that, in so doing, they achieve their *primary outcome need*. This is Level 3.

So here we see that Intensifi's solution is actually way down at the tertiary level of these people's needs, not even at their secondary level, and nowhere near their primary level. This is *why* if Intensifi were to go off and start talking about their solution in isolation and all its wonderful attributes and capabilities, they wouldn't even begin to resonate with these prospective customers.

Instead, they have to get past that temptation and move up to talking about these customers' *primary outcome need*, with subtle hints toward their secondary outcome need, and even subtler hints toward their tertiary outcome need (the solution). Thus, the **benefits** they articulate for their solution must clearly link to this *primary outcome need*, less so to the secondary one, and even less so yet to the tertiary one. Consequently, the **promise** they and their solution make must speak *directly* to this primary outcome need, less so to the secondary outcome need, and even less so to the tertiary outcome need.

Interestingly, when we and Intensifi were working through the Design Thinking process, we were actually way down in the weeds of figuring out their new solution at that tertiary level. And why was attaining that solution so important? It was important because having that solution (Level 3) gave would-be customers the confidence and assurance that they could in fact attain Level 2, and being able to attain Level 2 (well) further gave them the confidence and assurance they could likely attain Level 1. So we see this direct connection between all of them.

But as a business enterprise, we cannot operate purely at Levels 1 and 2 if we hope to actually sell something. Instead, we have to get down to Level 3 to define a solution that we can actually sell.

But when it comes time for us to *market* that solution – as well as to define our Unique Value Proposition – we have to tie that Level 3 solution up to our customers' Level 1 needs, as doing so is the only way we'll ever connect with them emotionally and motivate them to buy our solution.

With that all understood now, let us move on to defining Intensifi's Unique Value Proposition.

Defining Intensifi's Unique Value Proposition

Given the points just made, the purpose and definition of a Unique Value Proposition, and everything we know so far about Intensifi's Point of View, Design Principles, and final solution concept, a suitable articulation of their Unique Value Proposition for individual customers would be the following (and/or other variants thereof).

Unique Value Proposition - Individuals

At Intensifi, we empower aspiring, achievement-oriented professionals to attain their maximum possible potential in life, and by so doing achieve maximum success for themselves and their loved ones.

We give you 100% confidence that the decisions you're making, and the actions you're taking, are in fact the ones that will optimize your life in a comprehensive, holistic, and balanced manner, thereby allowing you to attain this goal in both your personal and professional lives.

Our advanced solution uses leading-edge AI capabilities to deliver unrivaled life-decision clarity that nothing else even begins to match. With its private and secure online platform, easy-to-use and extensible user interface, broad curated ecosystem of partners, and optional concierge services to augment your own actions, you can easily attain your maximum life success with us. Learn more today!

Similarly, a suitable articulation of their Unique Value Proposition for business customers would be the following (and/or other variants thereof).

Unique Value Proposition – Businesses

At Intensifi, we empower aspiring, growth-oriented businesses to attain their maximum possible potential in all their operations, and by so doing achieve maximum success for all their stakeholders.

We give you, the business leader, 100% confidence that the decisions you are making, and the actions you are taking, are in fact the ones that will optimize your business in a comprehensive, holistic, and balanced manner, thus allowing you to attain this goal throughout your organization.

Our advanced solution uses leading-edge AI capabilities to deliver unrivaled business-decision clarity that nothing else matches. With its private and secure online platform, easy-to-use and extensible user interface, broad curated ecosystem of partners, and optional support services to complement your business' own actions, you can easily attain maximum business success with us. Learn more today!

And so, we see that these articulations of Intensifi's Unique Value Proposition only *vaguely* hint at the details of their solution. They certainly do not go into any detail on those (but those details are discoverable for whoever wants them). Instead, they focus mainly on the key **value** they are unlocking for these customers – value that truly matters to them, and value that no one else can or does unlock for them (at least at this point in time… assuredly, imitators will eventually come along; Intensifi just has to stay ahead of the game in that regard).

Consequently, Intensifi's *solution* – defined as it is in great detail at this point – actually lives in the *shadow* of its Unique Value Proposition. It is in fact their Unique Value Proposition that really matters. Their solution is simply the *means* by which they will deliver on that Unique Value Proposition.

This is *why*, of course, businesses must always remain focused on their Unique Value Proposition and how that relates to their customers' and would-be customers' actual outcome needs. Organizations that get overly fixated on their solution (and all its many nuanced details, features, and attributes) often lose sight of their customers' outcome needs. This becomes problematic when those needs change. If the organization is not (at all times) attuned to those outcome needs, then they'll miss those changes and just keep on pumping out the same old solution as they always have. They'll go straight when their customers turn left. Consequently, they'll become out of sync with those customers and eventually irrelevant to them, unless they too change course in sync with these customers – something they can only do if they are attuned to their outcome needs, and something they will inherently do if they are indeed value-proposition-oriented and not solution-oriented.

The final outcome – a Unique Value Proposition plus a winning solution to back it up

So now we have **both** Intensifi's clearly articulated *Unique Value Proposition* (both individual and business versions) and their very specific *solution* by which they will deliver on that Unique Value Proposition and thereby back up the unique and novel *promise* they've made within it.

Quite interestingly, when we compare these (collectively) to the 30 *Elements of Value* alluded to in *Chapter 4*, what we see is that, together, they actually deliver, in one way or another, on **all 30** of those types of value. The same with the 40 *B2B Elements of Value* in the case of the business solution. This truly is, then, a very comprehensive and complete value proposition / solution set from Intensifi.

This is the outcome that we (and they) need at this point so that we (and they) can start to think far more broadly – beyond either of these – to the much broader overall business model we ultimately need to define!

One minor side note here is that while our Unique Value Proposition is clearly something we'll use for marketing our solution to its would-be customers, it's not something we'll use when pitching our business to prospective investors. Investors don't care so much about what our Unique Value Proposition is; they care whether or not there is a sizeable enough market that cares about that Unique Value Proposition to buy into it. That's an entirely different question. We mention this because it's often a point that Entrepreneurs and Innovation Teams don't understand, and therefore get wrong. Don't make this mistake in your case.

Where do we go from here?

At this point, we've made an *entry* into the broader business model – because we had what we needed to do so.

In fact, this is something that your team can do too – simply by emulating everything Intensifi has done up to this point. I invite you and your team to spend some time "mad-libbing" your own Unique Value Proposition using this same three-part structure (and its connecting rules) as was prescribed herein.

But we still don't yet have what we need to embark on defining the *remainder* of the business model.

Consequently, in Intensifi's case, they've now defined their Unique Value Proposition, but they have yet to define (referring back to the *Business Model Meta Formula*) the following:

- Market Connection Model
- Sustainable Competitive Advantage
- Sales Model
- Profit Model
- Risk Mitigation Model
- Business Innovation Model.

Some of these – like the *Risk Mitigation Model* and the *Business Innovation Model* – are largely internal to the business, and can be defined according to however the business' principals wish to operate the business, though they do have to be informed by the nature, character, and rhythm of the different markets the business operates in.

Others of these – in particular, the *Market Connection Model*, the *Sales Model*, the *Profit Model*, and the *Sustainable Competitive Advantage* – must stem directly from customers' *needs*, *desires*, and *aspirations* – just like the *Unique Value Proposition* did. **However**, in their cases, those *needs*, *desires*, and *aspirations* can (and often will) show up in *different ways* than they did in the Unique Value Proposition – with different *priorities* and different *emphases* placed on different factors, compared to how they were treated inside the solution and Unique Value Proposition.

So, obviously, where we go from here is out into our broader business model – considering both the structural and functional elements that we explored earlier. But – unlike what far too many business operators in the past have done – we cannot simply do so by making **blind assumptions** about what these different elements of our business model should be, based as those assumptions may be on some past history and experience we happen to have – or based on the possibly erroneous assumption that what we learned about our solution informs these too. It may or may not, but blindly assuming that it does is an incredibly risky and very likely erroneous path to go down.

Instead, we have to stop, sit down, and think really hard about how we're going to take our new Unique Value Proposition into the marketplace and activate it as a real business. Doing this will require some additional new learning on our part. And for that, we'll once again need a very disciplined approach to our learning.

This is where – as we're about to see in *Chapter 14* – we must call upon Design Thinking again, using its processes and methods to help us undertake a methodical and disciplined approach to learning the additional insights we need for these other parts of our business model. Using Design Thinking here again will allow us to successfully define our business model *in its entirety* so that we can leverage that overall business model for the maximum success of the venture we're chasing.

This is our segue into the last section, and final three chapters, of this book… where we will "Design Think" again.

A quick peak in on Intensifi

Following their intensive months-long effort at using the (iterative) Design Thinking process to formulate and test their hypotheses, come up with a correct Point of View, translate those into specific Design Principles, and ultimately ideate and validate solutions to arrive at their final solution, the Intensifi team was quite exhausted.

Consequently, the entire team took two weeks of leave and went on vacation (separately) to "come up for air" and recharge their batteries – which at this point, they've successfully done.

Upon reconvening back in their office, the team used what it had learned in the solution research, plus the Value Proposition Canvas shown above, to visually map out their new value proposition. Then, going beyond that, they used the definition of a *Unique Value Proposition* from the Business Model Meta Formula to define their own Unique Value Proposition – the result of which was also shown above.

So, at this point, the Intensifi team – still 14 dedicated individuals (though some do have growing time pressures) – is fully committed to working through the *rest* of their business model with the exact same fervor, dedication, and discipline as they did in the case of their solution and its resultant Unique Value Proposition. They are preparing themselves therefore (mentally) for this final big push of their journey – prior to actually launching the new venture and finding out what happens thereafter.

The team is thus very eager and ready to move forward. They are indeed genuinely excited about all they've learned so far, and where they are in this journey and process, as well as what the rest of it has in store for them. So, let's go forward with them!

Summary

In this chapter, we recalled Intensifi's new solution from *Chapter 12*, noted that we must transition here from being an inventor (solutions) to being an entrepreneur (businesses), and used a Value Proposition Canvas to map out Intensifi's new value proposition visually.

We then used the definition of a *Unique* Value Proposition from the Business Model Meta Formula of *Chapter 4* to prepare for, and ultimately define, Intensifi's own Unique Value Proposition – which the team can now drop into the rest of its overall business model.

In looking ahead to *Chapter 14*, we're going to encounter the reality that the rest of our business model requires its *own* dedicated research and learning – apart from whatever we've already undertaken for our solution – if that overall business model is to be defined in a way that truly resonates with our prospective would-be customers. And for that, we're going to look at Design Thinking again – but this time in the service of defining the rest of our business model, which can look and feel a bit different from when we used it to define our solution. Get ready for another exciting journey.

Part 3 –
The Worlds Merged

Part 3 of this book merges the world of business model innovation and Design Thinking together into one complementary practice that gets used to define the totality of our business model – beyond just its "winning solution." It shows us, therefore, how to leverage all of the insights we learned about Design Thinking and its processes and methods to define our Unique Value Proposition, our Market Connection Model, our Sustainable Competitive Advantage, our Sales Model, our Profit Model, our Business Innovation Model, and our Risk Mitigation Model. This results in a complete and coherent business model – both functionally and structurally – that is in all ways human-centered, and which therefore has the maximum possible chances of success in the market.

Part 3 also shows us how to go about *executing* our new business model and thus bringing it to life. This includes the fact that introducing it to the real world will inevitably teach us some additional insights about it that we didn't catch in our original discovery process – a reality we must be prepared for so that we can agilely adapt as needed.

Finally, *Part 3* describes how we can take this merged process and institutionalize it across an entire business – making it a consistent process that gets used over and over to generate multiple ongoing successes for the organization. This part finishes with a short look at what the future of human-centered business model innovation holds for us.

This part contains the following three chapters:

- *Chapter 14, Back to Business Model Innovation – à la Design Thinking*
- *Chapter 15, Execution – Bringing Our Business Model to Life*
- *Chapter 16, The Final Outcome – Consistent Ongoing Success*

Back to Business Model Innovation – à la Design Thinking

In *Chapter 13*, we used several ingredients – namely, Intensifi's new solution, their Point of View, their Design Principles, a value proposition canvas, and elements of the Business Model Meta Formula that we explored in *Chapter 4* – to frame out at least one piece of their overall new business model – their *Unique Value Proposition*. These ingredients supplied us with the inputs we required to do this.

But this left us with only one part of the overall business model. While, alone, it is good, it is very unlikely that it will unleash the massive new value that a truly innovative and comprehensive holistic business model can. Our next task therefore – and what we'll be focusing on in this chapter – is building out the *rest* of our business model.

To do this, we'll need a process. Fortunately, we have such a process – the *Business Model Synthesis* process that we introduced and explored in *Chapter 5*.

However, there's a caveat to using this process (one we didn't really mention back in *Chapter 5*). The process begins with our unique *goals* for the business model – and so using the process requires that we first have such goals. Our problem – at least at this point – is that we don't have those goals yet (not in any real solid and reliable form anyhow). In fact, we don't even know yet what these goals should be, so how can we discover and define such goals?

That's where Design Thinking comes in (again) – as we're about to thoroughly find out in this chapter. So, just in case you thought we were done with Design Thinking… think again. We're not.

This chapter is the culmination of the marriage of Business Model Innovation and Design Thinking… where the two ultimately come together to support each other and, in doing so, enable an incredibly powerful and impactful approach to Business Model Innovation.

In particular, in this chapter, we explore the following five points relating to this stage of our journey:

- **We have a solution… now what? Using Design Thinking yet again!**: Realizing that the *rest* of our business model (not just our solution) has to be human-centered too if it is to resonate.

- **Design Thinking our business model – applying Design Thinking to business model design**: Setting ourselves up to use the Design Thinking process on the Business Model Meta Formula to answer all of the functional and structural questions of our new business model.

- **Our new Problem Space – what business model does our market need?**: Using the Design Thinking process, together with select Design Methods, to work through the Problem Clarity stage for each function of the business model and come out at the end with a set of Design Principles by which to define those respective functions as part of a holistic and congruent business model.

- **Our new Solution Space – the best business model**: Combining Design Thinking with the Business Model Synthesis process to step through the Value Definition stage and come out with a new business model that meets the entirety of our collective Design Principles set.

- **The outcome – a new business model that delivers results**: The articulation of a final business model that spells out the detailed actions of each function, and that answers all of the structural questions of our business model – resulting in a business model that's special and that unleashes massive new value.

In this process, we will once again walk vicariously alongside our friends at Intensifi, as they demonstrate, via their new business model, exactly what this process looks like and how it gets executed. When finished, you will understand clearly how to leverage Design Thinking for holistic business model design – resulting in a new business model that will resonate with your markets and customers over the long term.

We have a solution… now what?

Let us start by first looking at where we are now.

In *Chapter 2*, we learned that there are six key structural questions our business model has to answer, as follows:

- **Who?** – Who we will serve and, therefore, deliver value to (our main customer).

- **What?** – What we will serve them (our offering).

- **Where?** – Where and how we will find and connect with them (our channels).

- **How?** – How we will conceive, create, produce, and deliver this value for them (our value factory).

- **Why?** – Why we will do all of this (the unique problem we are trying to solve for them).

- **When?** – When we will do all this (which may be now or later/at certain specific times or always).

We also learned, in *Chapter 4*, that there are seven key *functions* our business model needs to fulfill, as follows:

- Market Connection Model
- Unique Value Proposition
- Sustainable Competitive Advantage
- Sales Model
- Profit Model
- Risk Mitigation Model
- Business Innovation Model.

Of these, we (and Intensifi) have so far answered three of the structural questions:

- **Who?** – The aspirant professional seeking to optimize their life and maximize their success.
- **What?** – A solution they can easily use that gives them complete confidence in the decisions and actions being pursued such that, through those decisions and actions, they can attain this lifelong aspiration.
- **Why?** – Because they want to optimize their life in an overall holistic and balanced way that lets them achieve 100% of their full potential in life and thereby attain the greatest level of success possible for them – with the belief that doing this will give them maximum personal fulfillment and enrichment in life.

We've likewise defined one of the functional elements so far – namely, the **Unique Value Proposition**.

These all derive from Intensifi's solution, which, in turn, derived from their original *Point of View* and *Design Principles* (which live alongside the solution and equally inform these other points).

Next, let's look at where we need to go.

We thus still need to answer the remaining three structural questions:

- **When?** – When we will deliver our new solution to these customers (both overall and in their lifetimes).
- **Where?** – How and through what channels we will find and connect with these prospective customers.
- **How?** – How we will conceive, create, produce, and deliver our new solution to these customers.

And we still need to define the remaining six business model functions:

- Market Connection Model

- Sustainable Competitive Advantage

- Sales Model

- Profit Model

- Risk Mitigation Model

- Business Innovation Model.

In thinking about the structural framework that we looked at in *Chapter 2* – the *Future Lens Business Model Framework* – this means we've defined approximately 2/3 of the *Value Proposition* side of the framework (the Target Market and the Offering Space, but less so the Brand Delivery), and none of the *Value Delivery* side of the framework (Customer Acquisition, Value Creation, and Value Capture).

To address and answer those remaining points, we could (as noted previously) easily leverage the *Business Model Synthesis* process that we introduced in *Chapter 5* – looking at these different elements in other (surrogate) business models – except that we don't yet have clear goals for each of these points to test the surrogates against, nor have we defined any explicit customer scenarios to test out our new business model options against.

So, in terms of putting first things first, we first need to discover and define these specific goals prior to being able to do anything else.

But how to do so? The answer to that lies in our prospective customers.

Back to Design Thinking – once again

Hopefully, it should occur to us at this point that it's just as important for the remainder of our business model to be human-centered – that is, anchored in the specific aspirations and motivations of our subjects – as it was for our solution and *Unique Value Proposition* to be if we hope for that overall business model to resonate with these customers. And so, hopefully, it occurs to us to again turn to Design Thinking's problem/solution exploration process to solve the remainder of our business model – so that it too can resonate with our customers and unleash the maximum possible value for both them and us.

Fortunately for us, we now understand and can execute the Design Thinking process – and we realize that the *Design Principles* from that process are, in effect, goals. Indeed, our Design Principles tell us precisely what a solution must *be* and *do* to solve for our Point of View. Therefore, they constitute the mandatory goals for this solution. What a fortunate coincidence indeed!

Design Thinking the rest of our business model

Given our need for specific goals for the remainder of our business model – attributes we can find in the form of *Design Principles* – our task at this point will be to apply the rich problem exploration process of Design Thinking to this final act of designing the remaining structural and functional attributes of our business model.

To that end, we turn again to Design Thinking – except that now, in this case, we'll be treating these remaining structural and functional questions as our *Problem Space* (actually, as their own separate and independent sets of *Problem Spaces*) – meaning that we need to uncover and articulate a proper Point of View about each one, using our test subjects as we did before.

This difference means that rather than probing our subject's behaviors, attitudes, and perceptions about their need for a solution, we'll instead be probing them about *when*, *where*, *how*, and under what *circumstances* they'll actually procure, access, and use our solution… all of the other business model attributes surrounding that solution.

More formally, this means that we'll be probing those behaviors, attitudes, and perceptions to determine what will be our ideal for each of the following:

- Market Connection Model
- Sustainable Competitive Advantage
- Sales Model
- Profit Model
- Business Innovation Model
- Risk Mitigation Model.

This is precisely what we'll be doing next. We will – vicariously through Intensifi again – walk through the Problem Clarity stage for these respective business model attributes.

In particular, since the functional model of the business model (the *Business Model Meta Formula*) offers us a more formalized and structured framework to operate within – with its well-defined functional chunks that also encompass the remaining structural questions we have – we'll be using that model to work through the Problem Clarity stage rather than the structural model of the *Future Lens Business Model Framework*. Doing this will, in the end, address and answer both our functional and structural questions at once (and prevent us from having to undertake repetitive, non-value-adding iterations of the process).

Again, we will treat each of these functions as its own respective *Problem Space* – meaning that each one will get its own Point of View and its own corresponding set of Design Principles – though there can always be overlap between and among any of them.

Our new Problem Space – what business model does our market need?

At this point, we're going to dive into the Problem Space of the overall business model. We'll do this step-by-step – one function at a time.

For each function, Intensifi's goal will be to uncover the **most optimal design possible** for that function – the one that, in harmony with all the other functions, unleashes the maximum possible value to the prospective customer, in a way that these customers will readily see, understand, and appreciate (or in other words, that maximally resonates with them). This will yield the most innovative and impactful business model possible.

In each case, we'll lay out the following activities by the Intensifi team:

- the *Empathize* methods they use to help them formulate their hypotheses about this function;
- he specific hypotheses they end up formulating and are therefore putting forth for testing;
- the *Define* methods and business experiments they use to help them test out these hypotheses;
- a summarization of their findings from these respective tests;
- their resulting Point of View about this particular function;
- their corresponding Design Principles for this function.

Note that since we explained and demonstrated certain Design Methods in detail in *Chapters 10, 11,* and *12* – to give us a sense of what Design Methods look like and how they're used – we won't be explaining the Design Methods used here in similar detail, as doing so is beyond the purpose of this chapter.

We must also note that Intensifi is not starting this process from scratch, and therefore is not entering into it blindly. The team already possesses significant insight based on having previously worked through the process for their solution and Unique Value Proposition. However, it would be very presumptuous of them to assume that they already know *everything* they need about the situation to define the rest of their business model. They do *not* know everything they need to know to do that. And so, they must – as a matter of proper **discipline** – walk through this process again for each business model function, to answer the remaining functional and structural questions correctly. They will do this in a particular order, starting with their Market Connection Model and ending with their Risk Mitigation Model, as this order seems most logical to the team.

Exploring Intensifi's Market Connection Model

Intensifi starts with its *Market Connection Model*. You can refer to *Chapter 4* for the complete definition and explanation of this function.

Empathize Methods used

Intensifi uses the following Empathize Methods to help it synthesize new hypotheses about its Market Connection Model:

- **Persona**: Contrary to their initial inclination, Intensifi now knows enough about each of the respective ethnographic/psychographic groups they've identified that they finally complete a Persona for each one. This helps them to better visualize, understand, and empathize with each of these groups.

- **Business Ethnography**: In which they study further the behavioral patterns of the different customer groups they've identified to understand more about their motivations and aspirations.

- **Digital Ethnography**: In which they study further the online digital behaviors of the different customer groups they've identified to understand more about their motivations and aspirations in this context.

- **Stakeholder Analysis**: An exploration of who all the stakeholders are in each situation, what's in it for them, and how Intensifi may be able (or not able) to satisfy their particular motivations.

Hypotheses formulated

Intensifi formulates the following hypotheses about its Market Connection Model:

- Middle and junior high school students want a comprehensive solution like theirs to help them figure out what courses to focus on in high school.

- High school students want a comprehensive solution like theirs to help them figure out what to do with their lives and how to plan for college and beyond.

- University students want a comprehensive solution like theirs to help them figure out which major to pursue and what careers to pursue following college – in line with their natural interests and abilities.

- Young working professionals want a comprehensive solution like theirs to help them figure out how to start and navigate their careers for maximum professional success, their familial relationships for maximum personal success, their financial choices and decisions for maximum financial success, their lifestyle choices and decisions for maximum health and fitness success, and more.

- Mature working professionals want a comprehensive solution like theirs to help them figure out how to maximize their financial performance in preparation for eventual retirement and the freer lifestyle it will give them.

- Retired professionals want a comprehensive solution like theirs to help them figure out how to manage their retirement years, how to plan their estates for their heirs, and other end-of-life-type decisions.

- There is some "mystery group" out there that would value Intensifi's solution, which Intensifi just hasn't discovered yet.

- Small business enterprises want a comprehensive solution like theirs that lets them optimize the operation and future growth of their business.

- Medium-sized business enterprises want a comprehensive solution like theirs that lets them optimize the operation and future growth of their business.

- Large business organizations want a comprehensive solution like theirs that lets them optimize the operation and future growth of their business – or of certain specific business units within it.

- Consulting firms want a comprehensive solution like theirs that they can use to sell consulting and other value-added services to their different clients.

In each of these hypotheses, Intensifi is interested in learning not only *absolute answers* but also more nuanced *quantitative insights*. In other words, they want to know not only whether the hypothesis is true or false but also to what extent it is true or false for each group, and thus how many members of that group feel strongly about it, feel not strongly about it, or are ambivalent about it. This helps them gauge the overall interest level inside each group, which translates into the effective market size of that niche, and thus whether or not that niche represents one that's worth pursuing for Intensifi.

Define Methods and business experiments planned and used

Intensifi uses the following Define Methods and business experiments to help it test its new hypotheses about its Market Connection Model:

- **Primary Quantitative Research**: In which they retain a Market Research firm to undertake select quantitative research for them to quantify the relative size and strength of each respective customer group they've identified.

- **Focus Groups**: In which they host different groups representing the different customer groups they've identified to talk qualitatively about why certain behaviors exist and what drivers underlie them.

- **Unfocus Groups**: In which they mix up each group to make them as diverse as possible and then explore different life scenarios with the group to get their respective perceptions and reflections on each scenario, what is occurring in it, and what the affected persons in it should or should not do with respect to the type of comprehensive solution Intensifi has proposed.

Findings summarized

Intensifi has summarized the findings of these respective experiments as follows:

- practically no interest at all from the middle and junior high school students – too few are even thinking this far ahead at this point to worry so much about what they'll be focusing on in high school. They figure that they and everyone else in their group will just figure it out once they get there;

- strong interest from the high school students – they understand and see the value of this solution in helping them to figure out their life goals and paths, but only about 25–30% believe that people in their group would justify investing in it, even if it is priced for high school students (slightly more if it were to be free somehow);

- moderately strong interest and alignment from the university students – they see the value in the solution and understand how they could use it, but just less than half feel that those in their group would actually invest in it (others would continue to rely on intuition, guessing, and traditional guidance);

- very strong interest and alignment from the young working professionals – the solution seems to really resonate with the key aspirations and motivations of their life at this point in their life (noted previously). A majority (about 70%) feel that people in their group would invest in it;

- very strong interest and alignment from the mature working professionals – the solution seems to really resonate with the key aspirations and motivations of their life at this stage of their life (noted previously). A large majority (about 80%) feel that people in their group would invest in it;

- surprisingly, very little interest from the retired professionals – most felt that people in their group would have gotten their future affairs more or less figured out and in order by now, and so are really just interested in living out the rest of their lives in peace, without worrying so much anymore about maximizing or optimizing their life. In other words, they've kind of gotten past the point of worrying about that anymore;

- while there may very well be some other mystery group waiting to be discovered for Intensifi's solution, so far, none of their efforts have turned up such a group – yet the team doesn't let go of the possibility that such a group could appear at some point in time, and so they believe it's best to keep an open mind and remain opportunistically ready to pursue such a group should they be discovered;

- lukewarm interest from small business enterprises, strong interest from medium-sized business enterprises, and extremely strong interest from large business organizations;

- similarly, extremely strong interest from professional consulting firms.

Point of View formulated

Intensifi thus formulates the following Point of View about its Market Connection Model.

In terms of the **primary market niches** that Intensifi and its solution can attract and solve well for, they are as follows:

- Mature working professionals
- Young working professionals
- Large business organizations
- Professional consulting firms.

In terms of the **secondary market niche** that Intensifi and its solution can attract and solve moderately well for, they are as follows:

- University students

- High school students

- Medium-sized business enterprises.

In terms of **non-starter market niches** that Intensifi and its solution will *not* attract, and therefore should *not* invest its time, energy, and resources on, they are as follows:

- Middle and junior high school students

- Retired professionals

- Small business enterprises.

In each case, Intensifi can **maximize** the attractiveness of its solution by understanding the unique and specific **psychographic aspirations and motivations** of each respective group, and thereafter configuring, packaging, and marketing its solution according to those.

Intensifi must also be aware of, and attuned to, **secondary customers** in each case – other *stakeholders* who may impact and influence the purchase and use decision of the solution. For example, there may be a way to offer incentives (commissions) to high schools to purchase the solution and have their guidance counselors use it with their students as a more powerful tool for helping them work through their life goals and paths. Likewise and similarly for universities, who have similar guidance counselors for their students.

Design Principles defined

Intensifi defines the following Design Principles (goals) for its Market Connection Model:

- Focus *first and foremost* on the mature and young working professionals (individual solution) and the large business organizations and consulting firms (business enterprise solution).

- Focus *secondarily* on university and then high school students – together with their schools, parents, counselors, coaches, and other mentor stakeholders (individual solution), and the medium-sized business enterprises (business enterprise solution).

- *Ignore* as target markets the middle and junior high school students and retired professionals (individual solution), as well as the small business enterprises (business enterprise solution).

- In each case, *configure, package, and market* the solution in a way that is uniquely tailored to that particular group and its unique motivations and aspirations for that stage of its life.

- In all marketing communications, highlight the *benefits* the solution delivers toward achieving that group's unique *outcome goals* – with special emphasis on the *emotional jobs* in play.

- Wherever doing so makes sense, use *targeted marketing channels* that cater directly to a particular target group, along with marketing and brand language that speaks directly to their unique motivations and aspirations (and outcome goals).

These Design Principles represent the specific goals Intensifi will use when defining its final Market Connection Model for its new business model

Exploring Intensifi's Sustainable Competitive Advantage

Intensifi next works on its *Sustainable Competitive Advantage*. You can refer to *Chapter 4* for the complete definition and explanation of this function.

Empathize Methods used

Intensifi uses the following Empathize Methods to help it synthesize new hypotheses about its Sustainable Competitive Advantage:

- **Absence Thinking**: Thinking about which types of professionals may need this type of solution the most, and yet don't have it. It's missing from their personal and professional lives but should be there.

- **Customer Hacks**: Another look at which of these groups, and which specific professions, have attempted hacks with other solutions to get them to interoperate for a broader and more holistic set of prescriptions than the user can otherwise get from them.

- **Storyboarding**: Developing different storyboards of different prospective customers to walk through their use story with them – in each case, testing different points of differentiation in that journey to try to see which points might be most salient and important to them as they proceed.

- **Empathy Interviews with Five Whys**: More in-depth discussion with subjects about their specific behaviors and priorities – this time, in search of specific areas of the business model where domination and/or differentiation might make a measurable difference to these prospective users/customers.

Hypotheses formulated

Intensifi formulates the following hypotheses about its Sustainable Competitive Advantage:

- What matters most to our target markets (and therefore, where we should focus on dominating and differentiating) is **product** – its technologies, attributes, and user experience.

- What matters most to our target markets (and therefore, where we should focus on dominating and differentiating) is **experience** – the overall customer experience, the brand experience, and the product experience we create.

- What matters most to our target markets (and therefore, where we should focus on dominating and differentiating) is **access** – people's ability to find, afford, secure, and use our solution.

- What matters most to our target markets (and therefore, where we should focus on dominating and differentiating) is the **price** – its price being much lower than what people might expect, and much lower than any other competing option in the marketplace.

- What matters most to our target markets (and therefore, where we should focus on dominating and differentiating) is **service** – how well we service and support our customers over the long run.

- Intensifi will be able to develop proprietary *knowledge* and *capabilities* inside our organization that no other organization will be able to emulate.

- Intensifi will be able to develop a unique *culture* in our organization (for example, one that's always hungry, agile, and nimble) that manifests in additional value to our customers that no other organization can replicate.

- Intensifi will be able to develop a compelling *brand* that no other organization can replicate.

- A suitable "obscure niche market" to begin in would be _____ (many occupational options are considered here, such as doctors, nurses, physician's assistants, attorneys, designers, engineers, scientists, stock brokers, teachers, architects, building contractors, and more).

Define Methods and business experiments planned and used

Intensifi uses the following Define Methods and business experiments to help it test its new hypotheses about its Sustainable Competitive Advantage:

- **Kano Analysis**: Exploring the different facets of the business model with test subjects – in particular, the offering, its usage experience, ways to access it, its price, and the customer service around it – to see which of these facets prospective customers seem to value the most and which the least.

- **Scenario Testing**: Testing different scenarios with subjects involving different mixes of domination and differentiation to gauge their respective reactions to each scenario and see which scenario their particular group appears to respond best to.

- **Ecosystem Visualization**: A mapping of Intensifi's anticipated *internal and external ecosystem* and the *push* and *pull* forces that cause elements of that ecosystem (including their own staff) to come and go under different situations – impacting their culture, know-how, and capabilities.

Findings summarized

Intensifi has summarized the findings of these respective experiments as follows:

- In their primary target groups of young and mature professionals, the two most critical differentiators by far are product and experience – much more so than price, access, or service.

- This is the same for the two primary target groups in the business enterprise market segment – product and experience.

- In their secondary target groups of university and high-school students, the two most critical differentiators appear to be price and access – more so than product, experience, or service.

- Likewise, for their secondary target group in the business enterprise market segment (fortunately), price and access are the most critical differentiators.

- There is nothing concrete that Intensifi can find in their research that guarantees their ability – within the overall industry and market ecosystem – to develop proprietary knowledge, capability, or culture that other organizations cannot replicate. That hypothesis appears to be squarely wrong (and perhaps a bit pompous), even though Intensifi believes they'll give it their best effort to do so (they just can't bank on it at the moment, given how many future unknowns remain at this point).

- While there are indicators that indicate Intensifi can build a compelling brand that others cannot replicate, the evidence indicates that doing this will take a certain (longer) period of time, and so this isn't something that will create an impenetrable moat around their business on Day 1.

- Though not entirely definitive, the testing with different subjects seems to indicate that (for the individual solution) specific occupational niches that may be worthwhile starting in are the ones where the prospective customers are both *aspirational* (driven) and *analytical*. For this reason, they believe that an initial early emphasis on engineering and finance professionals represents two strong obscure niches to start in.

- By certain similar parallels, initial emphasis in the business enterprise market segment should likely be on manufacturing and consulting firms.

Point of View formulated

Intensifi thus formulates the following Point of View about its Sustainable Competitive Advantage:

- In Intensifi's primary target groups of young and mature working professionals, plus large business enterprises and consulting firms, Intensifi must focus squarely on the offering and the experience – with the intention to dominate on experience and differentiate on offering.

- In Intensifi's secondary target groups of university and high-school students, plus medium-sized business enterprises, Intensifi must focus on price and access – with the intention to dominate on access and differentiate on price (the offering in these cases can just be de-featured versions of their core offering).

- Given that Intensifi's primary target groups are believed to be far *larger* and much more *profitable* than their secondary target groups, their main focus *overall* must always be on experience and offering, less so on access and price, and least of all on service (not that their service will necessarily be bad; it just won't be an area of differentiation for them).

- Intensifi should choose certain obscure niches to begin where the prospective customers are both aspirational and analytical. Key examples of this in the individual market segment would be engineering and finance professionals. A key example of this in the business enterprise market segment might be manufacturing firms. Focusing on these obscure niches gives them the opportunity to further refine their business model and offering so that they can develop, over time, a much stronger Sustainable Competitive Advantage with their offering, its technologies, and their own know-how around those.

Design Principles defined

Intensifi defines the following Design Principles (goals) for its Sustainable Competitive Advantage:

- Above all else – and especially when targeting the primary markets – focus on dominating the market in experience and differentiating on offering.

- When targeting the secondary market, define alternative packages that emphasize access and price – including possible incentives to the additional ecosystem stakeholders involved – such as school administration and consulting firms, for example.

- In the individual market segment, focus initially on occupational groups that are both personally and professionally aspirational and inherently analytical

- In the business enterprise market segment, focus initially on organizations that have strong growth aspirations and entail a significant amount of analytical planning, operations, and growth work.

These Design Principles represent the specific goals Intensifi will use when defining its final Sustainable Competitive Advantage for its new business model.

Exploring Intensifi's Sales Model

Intensifi next works on its *Sales Model*. You can again refer to *Chapter 4* for the complete definition and explanation of this function.

Empathize Methods used

Intensifi uses the following Empathize Methods to help it synthesize new hypotheses about its Sales Model:

- **Digital Ethnography**: A look specifically at how their targeted subjects procure and pay for current digital solutions and their related services today – the specific mechanisms used.

- **Extreme User Interviews**: Interviews with *extreme users* of present solutions to find out what they in particular like and don't like about when, where, and how they purchase these present solutions – and whether they have any particular hacks or workarounds they use to make this process and experience much better for them.

Hypotheses formulated

Intensifi formulates the following hypotheses about its Sales Model:

- The individual customers who see the value in Intensifi's solution are only in _____ (to be tested for North America, Latin America, Europe, Asia, Africa, the Middle East, and Australasia).

- The business customers who see the value in Intensifi's solution are only in _____ (to be tested for North America, Latin America, Europe, Asia, Africa, the Middle East, and Australasia).

- Individual customers prefer to purchase directly from Intensifi.

- Rather than purchasing directly from Intensifi, individual customers prefer to purchase indirectly through a third-party vendor, such as a value-added reseller who bundles additional products and services with Intensifi's offering.

- Rather than purchasing directly from Intensifi, individual customers prefer to purchase through a third-party service provider who provides expert services directly associated with the Intensifi solution – thereby empowering these customers to most effectively and easily use the Intensifi solution.

- Individual customers prefer to pay a one-time upfront purchase fee that's good for a defined period of time, and thereafter purchase additional future updates and/or upgrades whenever they want them.

- Individual customers prefer to purchase an annual subscription that automatically renews and keeps them up to date all the time with any updates to the offering.

- Individual customers prefer to purchase a monthly subscription that automatically renews and keeps them up to date all the time with any updates to the offering.

- Individual customers prefer to have a certain amount of additional services prepackaged with the core offering they purchase.

- Individual customers do not prefer to have a certain amount of additional services prepackaged with the core offering but, rather, prefer to purchase those separately whenever they want them.

- Individual customers wish to purchase the solution early on in their lives and be given some type of loyalty benefit that makes it more affordable or useful to them as time goes on – with more benefits accruing the longer they use the solution.

- Individual customers value and respect targeted marketing and advertising that's targeted directly at them, based on their prior online behaviors and habits.

- Business customers prefer to purchase directly from Intensifi.

- Rather than purchasing directly from Intensifi, business customers prefer to purchase indirectly through a third-party vendor, such as a value-added reseller who bundles additional products and services with Intensifi's offering.

- Rather than purchasing directly from Intensifi, business customers prefer to purchase through a third-party service provider who provides expert services directly associated with the Intensifi solution – thereby empowering these customers to most effectively and easily deploy the Intensifi solution.

- Business customers prefer to pay a one-time upfront purchase fee that's good for a defined period of time, and thereafter purchase additional future updates and/or upgrades whenever they want them.

- Business customers prefer to purchase an annual subscription that automatically renews and keeps them up to date all the time with any updates to the offering.

- Business customers prefer to purchase a monthly subscription that automatically renews and keeps them up to date all the time with any updates to the offering.

- Business customers prefer to have a certain amount of additional services prepackaged with the core offering purchase.

- Business customers do not prefer to have a certain amount of additional services prepackaged with the core offering purchase but, rather, prefer to procure those separately when they need them.

- Business customers wish to deploy the solution broadly across their enterprise, rather than using it in only isolated pockets of the organization.

- Business customers value and respect targeted marketing and advertising that's targeted directly at them, based on what is publicly (and potentially otherwise) known about them.

- This is the sort of solution business customers will attend trade conferences in search of.

Define Methods and business experiments planned and used

Intensifi uses the following Define Methods and business experiments to help it test its new hypotheses about its Sales Model:

- **Focus Groups**: Hosting groups representative of each individual and business customer group to explore their perceptions around these different sales and marketing approaches – in particular, which of them they believe individuals or organizations in their group will be most receptive to and responsive to.

- **Scenario Testing**: Testing out a range of different sales and marketing scenarios with a broad range of subjects to gather their respective reactions and responses to each one – in particular, to see which of them each group seems to most prefer and not prefer (sorted by target group).

- **Customer Journey Mapping with Cognitive Task Analysis**: An explicit step-by-step study and exploration of everything that each respective target customer will be seeing/hearing/ thinking/feeling/doing/saying as they navigate the purchase and use of Intensifi's solution – thus understanding all of their cognitive and emotional experiences as they work through this process.

Findings summarized

Intensifi has summarized the findings of these respective experiments as follows:

- Individual customers who recognize the value of Intensifi's solution appear to be located primarily in North America, Europe, and Australia, with the Middle East being a close follower.

- Business customers who recognize the value of Intensifi's solution appear to be located primarily in North America and Europe, with Latin America being a close follower.

- Individual customers prefer to purchase directly from Intensifi rather than through any other (third-party) source – even when they otherwise value access to those other resources.

- Business customers prefer to purchase directly from Intensifi, though they are (nearly equally) open to purchasing through other third-party value-added resellers or service providers, so long as the experience remains a positive one for them.

- Individual customers prefer to purchase a monthly subscription plan with automative cloud-delivered updates provided on a regular ongoing basis.

- Business customers prefer to purchase an annual subscription plan with automatic cloud-delivered updates provided on a regularly scheduled basis.

- Individual customers prefer to not have additional services prepackaged with the core offering but, rather, be able to purchase those separately whenever they need or want them.

- Business customers prefer to have a certain group of additional services prepackaged with the core offering they purchase – specifically around helping them implement and deploy the solution as needed in their enterprise.

- Individual customers do in fact wish to purchase the solution early on in their lives and then be given some type of loyalty benefit that makes the solution more affordable and/or more useful to them as time goes on – with more benefits accruing the longer they use it.

- Business customers wish primarily to deploy the solution in only isolated pockets of the organization rather than broadly across the enterprise. In particular, they wish to concentrate its use in those places where strategic decisions get made in the organization.

- Individual customers do in fact value and respect targeted marketing and advertising that's targeted directly at them, within certain reasonable limits (not seeming like stalking).

- Business customers also value and respect targeted marketing and advertising that's targeted directly at them – again, within certain reasonable limits.

- This is in fact the type of solution business customers will attend trade conferences in search of, with the hopes of finding something like this.

Point of View formulated

Intensifi thus formulates the following Point of View about its Sales Model:

- Intensifi's primary individual customers will be found in North America, Europe, Australia, and the Middle East.

- Intensifi's primary business customers will be found in North America, Europe, and Latin America.

- Intensifi's individual customers want to buy directly from Intensifi – the solution only, with no prepackaged services – and on a monthly subscription plan with automatic updates.

- Intensifi's business customers want to buy directly from Intensifi, but are also willing to purchase through third-party sources – the solution plus certain prepackaged services for implementation and deployment – and on an annual subscription plan with automatic scheduled updates.

- Intensifi's individual customers want the opportunity to buy the solution early on in their lives – and when they do so, they expect to be given a loyalty benefit that makes the solution more affordable and/or more useful to them over time – with more benefits accruing the longer they use it.

- Intensifi's individual customers value and respect targeted marketing and advertising that's targeted at them, so long as it doesn't feel like they're being stalked.

- Intensifi's business customers value and respect targeted marketing and advertising that's targeted at them, so long as it is within reasonable and acceptable (and legal) limits.

- Intensifi's business customers will attend trade conferences and shows in search of a solution like this – in the optimistic hopes of eventually finding one.

Design Principles defined

Intensifi defines the following Design Principles (goals) for its Sales Model:

- For both market segments, focus all sales and marketing efforts on North America and Europe only at this time – nowhere else (laser-like focus is critical early on).

- For the individual market segment, offer a direct-purchase solution that's purchased on a monthly subscription basis with no prepackaged services.

- For the business enterprise market segment, offer the choice of either a direct-purchase solution or a third-party purchase solution – both purchased on an annual subscription basis with prepackaged services for implementation and deployment.

- For the business enterprise market segment, create a commission/discount structure for third-party partners as a strong incentive for them to maximize their sales efforts on this offering.

- For the individual market segment, offer a customer loyalty program that involves rewarding early purchasers and long-time users – with benefits increasing the longer a customer stays with Intensifi.

- For both market segments, use targeted marketing and advertising within reasonable constraints – using information on each target secured from publicly available sources, and placed in specific channels aligned to that respective target.

- For the high-school market, work to have the schools pay for the solution so that a base version of it (with limited functionality) can be offered to the students at no charge, and then an upgraded version offered at a price, with certain commissions returning to the school (this being a Freemium variant that has the potential to lock in certain students for life).

- For the business enterprise market segment, participate in appropriate business conferences and trade shows (as a sponsor/advertiser) where Intensifi can connect with prospective business customers.

These Design Principles represent the specific goals Intensifi will use when defining its final Sales Model for its new business model.

Exploring Intensifi's Profit Model

Intensifi next works on its *Profit Model*. You can refer to *Chapter 4* for the complete definition and explanation of this function.

Empathize Methods used

Intensifi uses the following Empathize Methods to help it synthesize new hypotheses about its Profit Model:

- **Value Web**: In which Intensifi maps out all of the exchanges of value in its solution's ecosystem to see where the balance of power and influence lie with respect to what the ultimate customer values and is willing to pay for, and all the activities required to deliver that value to them.

- **Competitive Product Survey**: In which Intensifi does some research into not only other (partial) solutions on the market but also what sort of profit margins their sellers are apparently making (all derived from published public information).

Hypotheses formulated

Intensifi formulates the following hypotheses about its Profit Model:

- Its overhead to operate and expand its platform (once initially built) will be minimal and not capital-intensive – giving it a more favorable profit margin.

- Its need to source different sources of daily financial and other news insights and data will represent a sizeable overhead that cuts into its overall margins but should be manageable.

- The sales and marketing overhead it incurs to drive outreach and relationships with its prospective markets will be heavily offset by the significant revenues it generates.

- It can charge a price that yields a very attractive profit margin to it (>60%) – having chosen to *not* differentiate on price (partly because the evidence it has seems to indicate that price is not a primary determiner of purchase intent).

- The price structure will need to be tiered to be within reach of each target market – meaning that different versions of the solution will need to be configured accordingly for each one.

Define Methods and business experiments planned and used

Intensifi uses the following Define Methods and business experiments to help it test its new hypotheses about its Profit Model:

- **Secondary Research**: Intensifi spends time gathering as much insight as it possibly can, culling data and information from all sorts of sources on the financial performance of similar business operations, and uses these for comparative purposes against their respective hypotheses.

- **Foreign Correspondents / Focus Groups**: Intensifi hosts a set of *Focus Groups* with "foreign correspondents" from different consulting firms – large and small – across North America and Europe, with each focusing specifically on one of its target markets. Intensifi in particular tests its respective hypotheses with these diverse and well-experienced individuals to gather their particular perspectives and insights on them relative to the specific target market they serve.

Findings summarized

Intensifi has summarized the findings of these respective experiments as follows:

- The primary actors identified in Intensifi's *value web* are itself, its data/news source providers, its service partners, and any outside sales agencies it engages. Being that Intensifi maintains a strong direct relationship with all customers (even when they purchase through a third-party source), it is felt that Intensifi will always own the relationship; consequently, the balance of power will remain with it.

- Its assumption that its overhead to operate and expand its platform (once built) will be minimal and not capital-intensive – giving it a more favorable profit margin – would appear to be accurate and correct.

- Its assumption that its need to source different sources of daily financial and other news insights will represent a sizeable overhead that cuts into its margins would likewise appear to be accurate and correct – but something that seems to be manageable, such that Intensifi can keep it within reasonable constraints while still delivering the necessary performance the platform needs.

- Its assumption that its overhead for sales and marketing will be heavily offset by the significant revenues these efforts generate would also appear to be accurate and correct.

- Finally, its assumption that it can charge a price that yields a very attractive profit margin to it would appear to be accurate and correct as well.

Point of View formulated

Intensifi thus formulates the following Point of View about its Profit Model:

- For its primary markets of young and mature business professionals and large business organizations and consultancies, Intensifi can charge a premium price for a premium solution – yielding a very large profit margin, sometimes upward of 200%. These customers have a high **lifetime value (LTV)** and a relatively low **customer acquisition cost (CAC)**.

- For its secondary markets of university and high school students and medium-sized businesses, Intensifi must charge a more discounted price for a more value-oriented configuration of the solution – yielding it a less desirable but still healthy profit margin of around 50% or so. These customers have a more moderate LTV and a slightly higher CAC.

- Intensifi will incur overhead for its engineering and design (ongoing solution development), daily data and information sourcing, sales and marketing, and general administration – but it understands these costs sufficiently to know what its financials should look like and it believes they will, overall, produce the profits desired.

Design Principles defined

Intensifi defines the following Design Principles (goals) for its Profit Model:

- Offer a premium solution at a premium price for its primary target markets.

  Expect a very high LTV/CAC ratio from these customers.

- Offer a value-oriented solution at a discounted price for its secondary target markets.

  Expect a more moderate LTV/CAC ratio from these customers.

- Structure operations to maintain the desired and targeted (overall) profit margin required to sustain ongoing growth. In the beginning, Intensifi will likely pour these profits back into even greater sales and marketing (and market-learning) efforts so that it can scale up more quickly and attain a larger scope, eventually shifting gears to a more profit-retaining mode once it attains a particular scale in the market.

These Design Principles represent the specific goals Intensifi will use when defining its final Profit Model for its new business model.

Exploring Intensifi's Business Innovation Model

Intensifi next works on its *Business Innovation Model*. You can once again refer to *Chapter 4* for the complete definition and explanation of this function.

Empathize Methods used

Intensifi uses the following Empathize Methods to help it synthesize new hypotheses about its Business Innovation Model:

- **Absence Thinking**: Intensifi uses this simply to think about, "What level and areas of innovation are missing from this space that should be there, or that we might expect to be there?" This is so that they can think about where missing voids potentially exist (beyond the novel things they're already doing), and thus where additional new opportunities might lie for them in the future.

- **Role Play**: The Intensifi team acts out using the new solution as they've envisioned it and then assumes they've been using it for some time now such that it has become normalized to them. They then ask themselves, "Okay… what's next… what additional new value needs to be unlocked for me at this point, now that I've attained this new threshold in my life?" This lets the team think about what sorts of additional innovations they might have to pursue in the future, and thus what sorts of research and development efforts will be required.

- **Predict Next Year's Headlines**: Intensifi uses this as yet another exercise (undertaken in their case at the 1-year, 2-year, 5-year, 10-year, and 20-year marks) to engage their collective imaginations and help them dream up what might be next after what they're currently pursuing, to try to get some feel for the specific innovation cadence they'll need to be pursuing in the near and distant future.

Hypotheses formulated

Intensifi formulates the following hypotheses about its Business Innovation Model:

- Intensifi's solution will be quickly emulated by others (especially with the assistance of AI tools to help them reverse-engineer it), meaning comparable competition will rise quickly.

- To remain at the leading edge of this market and its ability to absorb/adopt new iterations of the solution, Intensifi will need to release a major new version of it (with additional new capabilities and functions) *annually*, with not insignificant incremental updates provided *quarterly*.

- Intensifi will need to quickly ramp up its engineering and design groups to operate at this particular pace and scope.

- Intensifi will have to constantly engage users – especially its *extreme users* – to constantly learn of areas for improvement and opportunities for innovation. It can never afford to lose touch with actual user outcome needs and the specific human motivations and aspirations behind those – understanding that these may in fact *change* from what they are today because having this solution versus not having it can significantly alter what customers see as being *possible* and thus *attainable*, thereby changing what they desire and expect from such a solution.

- Intensifi will need to leverage its innovations in its marketing to reinforce its user experience reputation (recall this is its intended point of domination) as well as its brand image – over time, building out a strong and widely-recognized brand that becomes known and in-demand globally, thus strengthening its Sustainable Competitive Advantage.

Define Methods and business experiments planned and used

Intensifi uses the following Define Methods and business experiments to help it test its new hypotheses about its Business Innovation Model:

- **Foreign Correspondents / Focus Groups** – In hosting the prior *Focus Groups* with foreign correspondents, Intensifi used these foreign correspondents to also help it think through the possible *future evolution* of this specific solution space – where it might go in the future and what the implications of that might be to its environment (including Intensifi) and what sort of additional innovation will thus be required to extend the solutions into that direction and remain ahead of the market's needs, desires, and expectations.

- **Scenario Planning** – Based on all the *trends* Intensifi foresees around this particular solution space and their respective *drivers* (the *critical uncertainties* in particular), Intensifi defines certain *plausible future scenarios* at different points in the future (again, at 1-year, 2-year, 5-year, 10-year, and 20-year marks), with progressive causal chains between each set. They then explore the implications of those different scenarios to this market, as well as think about where this particular solution space might ultimately go, and what sorts of innovations they'll have to develop in light of that.

Findings summarized

Intensifi has summarized the findings of these respective experiments as follows:

- The Foreign Correspondent Focus Groups seemed to all agree that Intensifi's solution will in fact be emulated very quickly by others – meaning that comparable competition will rise quickly and Intensifi has to be prepared to act accordingly.

- The Foreign Correspondent Focus Groups likewise seemed to agree that for Intensifi to remain at the forefront of this market and its ability to absorb/adopt new iterations of the solution, Intensifi will have to release a major new version at least *annually* and not insignificant updates *quarterly*.

- Both the Foreign Correspondent Focus Groups and Intensifi's Scenario Planning exercise seemed to affirm the belief that Intensifi will have to quickly ramp up its engineering and design groups to operate at this specific pace and scope.

- Both methods likewise affirmed that Intensifi will have to constantly engage its users – especially its *extreme users* – to constantly learn of new areas for improvement and innovation and that it is indeed quite possible that these users' motivations and aspirations change over time on account of having this solution, so their expectations of the solution will likewise change – meaning that Intensifi has to stay very much on top of this evolving situation as it unfolds.

- Intensifi's Scenario Planning effort seemed to affirm the belief that Intensifi has to leverage its innovations in its marketing so as to reinforce its user experience reputation and brand image – to over time build out a strong and very widely-recognized brand that becomes known and in-demand globally (thus strengthening its Sustainable Competitive Advantage).

Point of View formulated

Intensifi thus formulates the following Point of View about its Business Innovation Model:

- Intensifi's solution will be emulated quickly by others – meaning that comparable competition will rise quickly and Intensifi has to be prepared to act accordingly.

- To remain at the forefront of this market, Intensifi will have to release a major new version of its solution at least *annually* and not insignificant updates to it *quarterly*.

- Intensifi needs to quickly ramp up its engineering and design groups to operate at this pace and scope.

- Intensifi will need to constantly engage its users – especially its *extreme users* – to constantly learn of new areas for improvement and innovation opportunities.

- It is definitely possible that its users' motivations and aspirations will change over time – on account of having this solution – meaning that their expectations of the solution will likewise change and so Intensifi needs to stay on top of this situation as it evolves and unfolds.

- Intensifi needs to leverage its innovations to reinforce its user experience reputation and brand image and thereby build out a strong, widely-recognized brand that becomes known and in demand globally.

Design Principles defined

Intensifi defines the following Design Principles (goals) for its Business Innovation Model:

- Prepare for comparable competition to rise quickly with similar offerings by readying the Innovation and R&D functions to turn out ongoing updates and improvements at the requisite pace and scope.

- Ramp up these Innovation and R&D functions accordingly to be able to operate at this pace and scope.

- Prepare to release a major new version of the solution at least *annually* – as well as notable updates to it at least *quarterly*.

- Constantly engage users – especially *extreme users* – to constantly learn of new areas for improvement and innovation opportunities that allow Intensifi to maintain a market leadership position.

- Always be prepared for the fact that customers' motivations and aspirations may change over time, and with that, their expectations of this solution – and thus stay atop these evolving drivers so as to address them proactively and preemptively.

- Leverage its innovations at all times to reinforce its user experience reputation and brand image and, in doing so, build out a strong, widely-recognized brand that becomes known and in demand globally.

These Design Principles represent the specific goals Intensifi will use when defining its final Business Innovation Model for its new business model.

Exploring Intensifi's Risk Mitigation Model

Finally, Intensifi works on its *Risk Mitigation Model*. You can again refer to *Chapter 4* for the complete definition and explanation of this function.

Empathize Methods used

Intensifi uses the following Empathize Methods to help it synthesize new hypotheses about its Risk Mitigation Model:

- **Value Web**: Used as before in defining the Profit Model.

- **Stakeholder Analysis**: Used as before in defining the Market Connection Model.

- **Competitive Product Survey**: Used as before in defining the Profit Model.

Hypotheses formulated

Intensifi formulates the following hypotheses about its Risk Mitigation Model:

- Its Market Connection Model is weak/faulty/errant. The **Total Addressable Market** (**TAM**), **Serviceable Addressable Market** (**SAM**), and **Share of Market** (**SOM**) assumptions it's made so far are errant and wrong – meaning the business will be enable to gain adequate traction to scale.

- Its Unique Value Proposition is insufficiently compelling to get prospective customers to buy it – or at least a significant enough number of customers to matter.

- Its Sustainable Competitive Advantage (now and in the future) is neither sustainable nor competitive, and therefore will not produce the moat around its business that Intensifi needs to protect it from encroachment by others (especially larger competitors).

- Its Sales Model is somehow flawed and won't work as expected and planned.

- Its Profit Model is flawed and won't produce the profits Intensifi expects – perhaps because some element of its cost structure was underestimated.

- Its Business Innovation Model is flawed and will not produce the results and outcomes required of it over the long term.

- Its Risk Mitigation Model is flawed and therefore insufficient to ward off all the risks it will encounter on its journey from launch to traction to scale.

Define Methods and business experiments planned and used

Intensifi uses the following Define Methods and business experiments to help it test its new hypotheses about its Risk Mitigation Model:

- **Primary Research** – All of the *prior research* that Intensifi has undertaken up to this point, on both its solution / Unique Value Proposition and the rest of its business model – is used now to validate all of the assumptions it has made so far about this business model.

- **Secondary Research** – Intensifi has undertaken significant *secondary competitive benchmarking* to validate all of the business and operational assumptions it has made so far.

- **Foreign Correspondents / Focus Groups** – In hosting the previous *Focus Groups* with foreign correspondents on behalf of the Profit Model, Intensifi also used these foreign correspondents to help it validate the *other elements* of its business models and all the assumptions underlying them – looking for very candid "gut reaction" feedback on each of them – to ensure they each pass the "smell test" with these respective, well-experienced professionals for what makes for good business fundamentals.

Findings summarized

Intensifi has summarized the findings of these respective experiments as follows:

- Based on all of the primary and secondary research it has conducted, Intensifi believes the insights it has generated thus far are all acceptably accurate and complete, and therefore, that all of the assumptions it has made so far are reasonably accurate.

- Based on all of the feedback it received during its foreign correspondent Focus Groups, Intensifi feels sufficiently confident that its overall business model – including each of its respective functions – is sufficiently sound and acceptable at this point in time. They each passed the gut reaction/smell test from the majority of the foreign correspondents for having sound business fundamentals.

- The feedback received from the few dissenters in the Focus Group has been given very serious consideration for what possible *additional risks* they might represent, and what Intensifi should do about them should they actually materialize (in other words, Intensifi has used these dissenting insights to define certain contingency strategies to potentially use should the need arise to do so).

Point of View formulated

Intensifi thus formulates the following Point of View about its Risk Mitigation Model:

- Intensifi has studied, evaluated, and considered all of the pertinent business risks before it and has developed appropriate primary and secondary (contingency) strategies to address each one (within the means currently available to it) – and will continue to do so.

- Intensifi's intended business model – including each of its respective functions – would appear to be based on sound business fundamentals and thus carries acceptably low risk (all to be finally validated upon actual launch).

- Intensifi's intended business model – anchored as it is in its novel new Unique Value Proposition and solution – is in fact expected to unleash massive new value for its marketplace – as well as potentially disrupt other existing solutions and their companies.

Design Principles defined

Intensifi defines the following Design Principles (goals) for its Risk Mitigation Model:

- Proceed with the business model assumptions it has vetted so far, while constantly monitoring outcomes and results and thereafter adjusting/pivoting as needed.

- Continue to seek out even more means by which to strengthen every function of its business model – in particular, its Market Connection Model, its Unique Value Proposition, and its Sustainable Competitive Advantage.

These Design Principles represent the specific goals Intensifi will use when defining its final Risk Mitigation Model for its new business model.

The combined Design Principles and answers to our remaining structural questions

As can be easily seen, the preceding set of Design Principles – especially when taken together as a whole – directly addresses and answers our remaining structural questions.

In particular, we find the following answers to those structural questions:

- **When?** – When will we deliver our new solution to these customers (both overall and in their lifetimes)?

  - For the individual market segment, Intensifi will attempt to capture these individuals while they are still young – ideally in high school, but if not then, while in university – so that Intensifi can demonstrate to them the value and benefit of its solution and hopefully lock them in as ongoing lifetime subscribers for the remainder of their professional careers.

  - Intensifi will otherwise (for this market segment) offer its solution to any professional at any point in their life/career – so that anyone can benefit from it starting from wherever they happen to be at that point in their life.

  - For the business enterprise market segment, Intensifi will work to capture these prospective customers at any point in their growth trajectory – from pure start-up to long-established enterprise. Since its solution is equally valuable and beneficial at any stage of development, Intensifi is not at all picky about which stage of development these business customers happen to be in; it will service all of them equally.

- Intensifi will work to have its marketing outreach connect with these prospective customers at certain opportune moments in time – for example, when individuals are doing (or have recently done) an online search for optimization solutions (whether financial, health, relationship, or another category), when individuals are trying to contact advisors, consultants, and/or mentors in these areas, when business leaders are attending certain trade shows and business conferences, and so on.

- **Where?** – How and through what channels will we find and connect with our prospective customers?

  - For individual customers, purchase directly from Intensifi, with no intermediaries.

  - For business enterprise customers, either purchase directly from Intensifi or through a third-party reseller offering additional complementary services bundled with the solution (and therefore, cultivating key partnerships with certain select resellers, such as consulting firms, for example).

  - Direct targeted marketing and advertising to both market segments.

  - Select conferences and trade shows for business enterprise customers.

- **How?** – How will we conceive, create, produce, and deliver our new solution to these customers?

  - Intensifi will develop and produce the solution itself via its own internal Innovation and R&D groups – with the exception of the platform's ecosystem of vetted service providers who, in each case, will sell and deliver their own respective services.

  - Intensifi will deliver its solution directly to customers, even if they initially purchased it through a third-party reseller. Intensifi will own the relationship between itself and each of its customers so that it can always control the narrative surrounding its story.

  - Intensifi will partner with certain service providers – such as professional consultancies – to make its solution as widely available in the marketplace as possible, but always ensuring the use of reputable market channels for the sake of its brand integrity.

  - For the secondary university and high school markets, Intensifi will partner with the schools to make its solution widely available to students at little or no direct cost to them, by having the schools underwrite the blanket subscription cost, while also offering them incentives to help sell the upscaled version of the solution to their students.

Consequently, we now have all of the structural questions of Intensifi's business model answered… *who*, *what*, *why*, *when*, *where*, and *how*. We're ready to move forward with these (and this is likewise an invitation for us to answer these remaining questions for our own new business venture).

This brings us to the end of our Problem Space for the overall business model. At this point, we've worked through the Problem Clarity stage of Design Thinking for the balance of our business model – mainly using the functional framework that we have. As a result, we now have a very clear set of Design Principles we can use in moving forward toward ideating possible *options* for our business model and then testing those to find the best option.

Achieving an internally congruent business model

Recall in ideating and testing new options something that we emphasized very heavily back in *Chapter 2* – namely, that it's crucial for our business model to be **internally coherent and congruent**. In other words, all parts of our business model have to work in harmony with each other to produce the desired and intended outcome.

This is why it is not advisable at this point to try to just hodge-podge our Design Principles together without further thought, reflection, and consideration. Doing that *could* result in a business model that's not internally congruent between its respective elements, and which therefore fails to achieve its intended outcomes and results.

It is far better – and very advisable here – to continue in the Design Thinking process and work through the Value Definition stage *properly* –to arrive at an internally congruent business model.

As we're about to see, this is something we'll do next by juxtaposing the *Business Model Synthesis* process with this particular stage of Design Thinking. We do this using **surrogate business models** (which are known to already be internally coherent) and considering those against our respective Design Principles (goals) to see which ones (or which parts of them) might work best for our particular situation. We further do this by being very careful to ensure that if and when we do select different elements of more than one business model, the final result remains internally congruent.

Our new solution space – the one best business model

We're now entering into the Solution Space of our business model, where we'll take our collective Point of View and Design Principles from the prior stage and apply them to the Value Definition stage of Design Thinking.

Unlike what we did in our prior case of the *Problem Space* (in the Problem Clarity stage), here, we do *not* want to address the individual functions individually (in a disintegrated manner) – as doing so could result in an internally incongruent business model. Instead, at this point, we need to look at the business model more holistically to ensure that we're working toward an internally congruent business model.

To do this, we'll leverage the Business Model Synthesis process to help us work through the Value Definition stage, as it calls for using surrogate business models that are already known to be (more or less) internally congruent. So, we'll next walk through doing this one step at a time – doing so again vicariously with Intensifi as they execute the process.

Step 1 – Using this process to ideate

In *Step 1*, we'll apply the Business Model Synthesis process to conceive a range of different business model options to choose from. This is a specific approach to the *Ideate* step of the Value Definition stage of Design Thinking. In this case, we're using other surrogate business models as our inspiration and fodder for new business model ideas to consider here. This will result in new business model options to further test.

The surrogates

In Intensifi's case, what the team chooses to do to seed this process is to use certain of the **standardized typologies** found in some of the *Business Model Pattern Cards* (refer to *Chapter 2* for a more thorough discussion of these, plus *Chapter 5* for examples of them). Using those cards, the team selects, considers, and evaluates the following 24 standardized business model typologies as their starting surrogates:

- **Behavioral Segmentation**: Identifying groups of customers (market segments) based on their unique behaviors (and the motivations and aspirations underlying those), and then focusing the offering (or different variations thereof) on certain of those market segments.

- **Customer Analytics**: Mining, analyzing, and applying data about customer behaviors to refine the solutions being offered to those customers, as well as the marketing messages being used to communicate their value and benefits to these customers.

- **Solution Provider**: Offering a complete package that fulfills a customer's unique needs, in which the solution consists of multiple distinct products and services working together.

- **Bundling**: Selling multiple products together for a single price, thus allowing customers to obtain a package of solutions at a price that's lower than purchasing the individual offerings separately, thereby producing economies of scope for the business.

- **Versioning**: Selling different versions of the same offering to different customer segments at different prices, recognizing that each type of customer has unique needs.

- **Orchestration**: Combining and coordinating the activities of different independent parties with the aim of offering a joint solution for the need at hand.

- **Revenue Sharing**: Working with other businesses to deliver an offering together, and sharing the risks and rewards (revenues and profits).

- **Business Alliance:** Collaborating with other organizations to achieve a common goal – typically because there's a certain synergy between them involving a common customer base with complementary needs that can be satisfied by their respective complementary offerings.

- **Affiliation**: Creating sales for other parties by linking from one's own offering to those parties' offerings, such that when customers purchase from those other parties due to this referral, the referrer collects a share of the resultant revenue.

- **Platform:** Operating an infrastructure that connects two or more interdependent groups so that they can interact with each other commercially.

- **Long Tail**: Selling a large number of unique products for which there is relatively low individual demand, yet collectively taking a noticeable share of the broader market with them.

- **Experience Selling**: Selling not just a product or service but, rather, a complete experience – often created through a set of events surrounding the offering.

- **Content Curation**: Collecting, organizing, and curating useful information about a particular topic for customers to help them find and select the information they find most interesting, relevant, and/or valuable.

- **Subscription Licensing**: Licensing the offering's use as an ongoing recurring subscription (with ongoing upgrades and support) rather than selling it directly as a one-time monolithic purchase (with no upgrades and limited support).

- **Freemium**: Giving customers a free (basic) version of the offering, while a smaller group purchases the premium version with the more advanced features and functions if and when they need it, producing sufficient profit to cover the cost of serving all customers.

- **Add On**: Providing a basic offering at an attractive price and subsequently charging customers for each additional feature or function, such that customers can configure their own personalized solution.

- **Cross-Selling**: Selling new products or services to the existing customer base, thereby reducing the cost of customer acquisition and yielding more revenue per individual customer.

- **Lock-In**: Customers depend on a specific vendor for the offering, such that switching to a different vendor will be very costly and/or significantly inconvenient.

- **Pay Per Use**: Charging customers for the actual usage of the offering whenever its usage can be metered in discrete measures such as time, distance, clicks, calls, and so on.

- **Dynamic Pricing**: Pricing the solution on a flexible basis depending on different (usually external) factors, which necessitates being able to assess and track those different factors.

- **Advertising**: Generating additional revenue by selling advertising time/space on the platform associated with the solution, and then forcing customers to watch those paid advertisements on the platform, typically in exchange for getting to use the free or low-cost version of the solution.

- **Self-Service**: Letting customers undertake some portion of the offering generation process themselves, resulting in lower costs, higher margins, and greater customer engagement.

- **Data as a Service**: Collecting, amalgamating, analyzing, interpreting, and transforming (non-customer) data into useful information that can be sold to third parties for a profit.

- **Leveraging Customer Data**: Collecting, packaging, and reselling customer data to third parties for additional profit.

The team believes that each of these likely contains one or more elements that could possibly address their particular situation well. Of course, the team also understands that no single one of these archetypes alone represents the entirety of a given business' business model but, rather, only a main or core element of it.

The additional Design Methods

Intensifi also leverages the following Design Methods to further *augment* their ideation and conception effort:

- **Constraint Imposition**: Used to *focus* their ideation onto the specific *types* of customer benefits and value they wish to deliver – so as to not go off on tangents that miss that critical point.

- **Backcasting**: Used to envision their *ideal future state*, and then try to work backward from there on how to *attain* that ideal future state.

- **Powers of 10**: Used to force the team into "10X thinking," in which they ask themselves how they can make each facet of the business model – and the solution it delivers – 10X (or even 100X) *better* than anything else currently available to customers.

- **Piggybacking**: Used to build on each other's *personal thoughts and ideas* about this new business model and its unique elements.

- **Brainstorming**: Used to collectively ideate new business model ideas together.

- **How Might We? Questions**: Used to spur "How might we?" types of thoughts and ideas about the new business model.

The resulting design elements

From these, the following are the specific *design elements* (each culled from a different surrogate business model) that seem to resonate strongly with Intensifi's unique goals in this case (understanding that any business model chosen has to conform to their respective Design Principles). They are divided into those that are outwardly customer-facing and those that are inwardly organizational or ecosystem-facing.

The outward, customer-facing design elements are as follows:

- **Solution Provider**: The team recognizes the value of offering a comprehensive turnkey package to their customers, made up of their platform plus other complimentary services as a complete solution.

- **Behavioral Segmentation**: The team sees the value and usefulness of segregating their customers into different market segments based on their unique behaviors and the motivations and aspirations behind them so that they can tailor variations of the solution to each one.

- **Versioning**: The team sees the value of selling different versions of their offering to different customer segments at different prices in accordance with each one's unique needs.

- **Subscription Licensing**: This is the model the team believes will likely work best in their situation – for both them and their customers.

- **Freemium**: This is something the team is entertaining in the context of servicing the high-school market, albeit with a likely twist where the schools underwrite the cost so that it is free to the students.

- **Add On**: This is something the team is entertaining, albeit more so in the context of tiered packages rather than as *a la carte* add-ons per se.

- **Experience Selling**: Given that one of Intensifi's Design Principles (goals) mandates they "dominate on experience," this is an area they must definitely focus on. They don't just want to deliver a great customer experience; they want to actually stage a purposefully crafted experience that their customers will return to over and over again (they have a lot of work to do to figure out how to do that, however).

- **Content Curation**: This is something the team sees as being vital, but more so in the context of integrating this content and its information into their solution's *analytics*, rather than for direct consumption by customers, though they figure that if they're pulling it in anyways, they may as well as make it directly consumable by users as well – something they'll continue to look at and think about.

- **Customer Analytics**: The team sees the value of mining, analyzing, and applying data on their customers' behaviors to refine their solution and marketing messages to each segment.

- **Long Tail**: This is a *maybe* for the team… something they're entertaining for now but are unsure of.

The inward, organizational- or ecosystem-facing design elements are as follows:

- **Business Alliance**: The team sees the value in collaborating with other organizations that have well-regarded brands and who wish to achieve a common goal together – wherever there is a synergy that benefits their mutual customers. In Intensifi's case, examples might include certain stock brokerages, certain health-optimization organizations, and certain relationship-oriented platforms.

- **Affiliation**: The team certainly sees the value in creating sales for the highly-vetted and curated partners they choose for their exclusive *ecosystem* of service providers, and thereafter collecting referral commissions from these partners.

- **Platform**: The team likewise sees the value in operating an *infrastructure* that lets their customers connect directly with this ecosystem of service providers – thereby making the affiliation process very smooth and frictionless.

- **Bundling**: This is a *maybe* for the team… something they're entertaining for now, but are unsure of.

- **Advertising**: This is something the team is contemplating as a means of offsetting the lower prices of bottom-tier offerings.

- **Data as a Service**: This is something the team sees value in, in which they can take the *aggregate* data about each customer *segment* and find suitable customers willing to purchase it.

The resulting business model options

Based on these different elements, the team is now considering seven distinct *business model options* that contain these elements in different configurations – each representing a slightly different mix of value and benefit to the end customer, as well as a slightly different profit model for Intensifi. These are reflected in the matrix of *Figure 14.1*, organized into the previous two groups. Some of these are considered *variable* elements (meaning they have varying degrees of applicability), while others are considered to be *non-variable* (meaning they're more or less universally applicable in this case).

Element	BM Option	1	2	3	4	5	6	7
	Solution Provider	X	X	X				X
	Behavioral Segmentation	X	X	X	X	X	X	X
	Versioning	X	X	X	X	X	X	X
	Subscription Licensing	X	X	X	X	X	X	X
	Freemium	X	X	X		X		X
	Add On	X	X	X	X	X	X	X
	Experience Selling	X			X			X
	Content Curation	X		X	X		X	X
	Customer Analytics	X	X	X	X	X	X	X
	Long Tail			X			X	X
	Business Alliance		X			X		X
	Affiliation	X	X	X	X	X	X	X
	Platform	X	X	X	X	X	X	X
	Bundling				X	X	X	
	Advertising			X			X	X
	Data As a Service	X			X			X

Figure 14.1: The seven business model options Intensifi is considering

The team believes that each of these business model options can be internally congruent – so long as the appropriate measures are taken in each situation.

Step 2 – Using this process to test

In *Step 2*, we'll leverage the Business Model Synthesis process to test out these seven business model options against real-life *customer scenarios* (artificially enacted as they may be).

This is a specific approach to the *Test* step of the Value Definition stage of Design Thinking – in this case, using customer scenarios as the framework for the testing process, and generally combining those with additional Design Methods.

The additional Design Methods

Intensifi uses the following additional Design Methods to help them facilitate their option testing efforts:

- **Role Play**: Used to have recruited test subjects (representative of each market segment) work through trying to attain their specific (assigned) goal within each business model.

- **Empathy Interview**: Used to unpack the test subject's thoughts, emotions, and perceptions in each situation as they tried to apply the defined business model to their specific goals of that scenario.

- **Try It Yourself**: Used to let the members of the Intensifi team try out each business model option themselves – to see how they each felt as they tried to attain their specific goal in that scenario.

The customer scenarios

For this testing, the team has conceived 34 specific customer scenarios they want to test each business model option against. These 34 scenarios are shown together in *Figure 14.2*, broken out by market and customer segment. Some involve the customer being new to the platform/product category (no matter the point of life or business they're at), and some involve the customer being familiar with it already.

The testing workshops

To undertake its option testing work, Intensifi recruits several groups of test subjects from both their own network and a market research agency and engages them in a series of test workshops.

In each workshop, the test subjects are asked to role-play the specific scenario so that the team can test it out under as realistic of a simulation as possible (given where they are in the process). To simulate the platform, the team uses sets of UI markup cards. To simulate the associated services, the team hires individuals from the actual respective roles (for example, financial advisors, personal trainers, etc.) to participate with them and play out their customary roles in the context of this particular platform.

Given how many different customer scenarios there are to test, the team does a "divide and conquer" in which they divide up into six separate groups (two or three members each) and each group takes on one of the six customer segments. That group then works on its customer segment's respective scenarios (ranging anywhere from three to seven scenarios).

Inside their respective workshops (all taking place at the same time in the same general location), the group leads their respective test subjects through the activity of using the platform for their particular goal and interjects the attributes of that particular business model option into the role play. To minimize any bias with the test subjects, they are rotated around to the different groups such that it isn't always the same group testing out each option (it was believed that doing this would maximize the overall objectivity of the activity).

The following image shows the individual market Customer Scenarios Intensifi tests.

Market	Customer Segment	No	Scenario Context	Scenario Goals	Prospective (Potential) Helper
Individual	Mature Business Professionals	1	New to solution / category	Plan out new details for future career / family / health / financial / other areas as a baseline starting point given their current situation.	Various / None
		2	Familiar with solution / category	Update / refine career / relationship / health / financial / other areas in the portfolio based on updated information and/or goals.	Various / None
		3		Optimize their marriage and family situation as they look to transition into empty-nesting	Marriage Counselor
		4		Optimize their overall health and fitness for the long term.	Health & Fitness Platforms for Senior Adults / Personal Trainer
		5		Optimize their financial and wealth-building performance.	Finance & Wealth Platforms / Wealth Advisor
		6		Balance their overall life with their very long-term goals in mind.	Various
		7		Plan for their eventual retirement with very specific goals in mind.	Finance & Wealth Platforms / Wealth Advisor
	Young Business Professionals	8	New to solution / category	Plan out details for new career / new relationships / new health goals / new financial goals / etc.	Various / None
		9	Familiar with solution / category	Update / refine career / relationship / health / financial / other areas in the portfolio based on updated information and/or goals.	Various / None
		10		Find the most ideal spouse and enter into a lifetime relationship with them.	Matchmaking Platforms
		11		Optimize their marriage and family situations - including their performance as a spouse and parent.	Marriage and Parenting Platforms / Marriage Counselor / Parenting Advisor
		12		Optimize their overall health and fitness for the present time.	Health & Fitness Platforms for Young Adults / Personal Trainer
		13		Optimize their financial investments for maximum long-term wealth	Finance & Wealth Platforms / Wealth Advisor
		14		Balance their overall life with their long-term goals in mind.	Various
	University Students	15	New to solution / category	Assess personal strengths / explore possible career and university paths.	University Career Counselor
		16	Familiar with solution / category	Affirm current major and career path - or else explore different ones.	University Career Counselor
		17		Balance school with health and dating relationships	Various / None
		18		Minimize school loan debt over the course of their university career	Financial Advisor
	High School Students	19	New to solution / category	Assess personal strengths / explore possible career and university paths.	Guidance Counselor.
		20	Familiar with solution / category	Update / refine future career or university paths with new or revised information and insight.	Parents / Teachers / Guidance Counselor
		21		Explore universities to consider, and specific majors to pursue at those universities.	Parents / Teachers / Guidance Counselor / University Admissions Counselor

Figure 14.2: The 21 individual market Customer Scenarios Intensifi tests

The following image shows the business market Customer Scenarios Intensifi tests.

Market	Customer Segment	No	Scenario Context	Scenario Goals	Prospective (Potential) Helper
Business	Large Corporate Business	22	New to solution / category	Plan out the details of a new business strategy to optimize overall performance and achieve maximum growth potential.	Strategy Advisor / Consultant
		23	Familiar with solution / category	Update / refine overall business strategy based on updated information and/or goals.	Strategy Advisor / Consultant
		24		Optimize the business' innovation strategy and efforts to drive maximum future growth.	Innovation / Innovation Strategy Consultant
		25		Optimize the business' operations to drive maximum profit takeaway.	Business Operations Consultant
		26		Foresee the business' future and optimize its innovation and operations activities for the most optimum future outcome.	Various / None
		27		Plan for the public listing of the business.	Specialty Financial Advisor
	Medium-Sized Business	28	New to solution / category	Plan out the details of a new business strategy to optimize overall performance and achieve maximum growth potential.	Strategy Advisor / Consultant
		29	Familiar with solution / category	Update / refine overall business strategy based on updated information and/or goals.	Strategy Advisor / Consultant
		30		Optimize the business' innovation strategy and efforts to drive maximum possible future growth.	Innovation / Innovation Strategy Consultant
		31		Optimize the business' operations to drive maximum profit takeaway.	Business Operations Consultant
		32		Foresee the business' future and optimize its innovation and operations activities for the most optimum future outcome.	Various / None
		33		Plan for the public listing of the business.	Specialty Financial Advisor
		34		Plan for the eventual sale of the business.	Specialty Financial Advisor

Figure 14.3: The 13 business market Customer Scenarios Intensifi tests

Once each group is finished, they reconvene to compare notes with each other and debrief one another about their respective findings surrounding the different business model options.

Leveraging the Lean Canvas

In addition to conducting their test workshops for each respective business model option, the team also completed a **Lean Canvas** for each option – just as they had tentatively planned to do (see *Chapter 6*).

Doing this helps to further aid their thought process, by illustrating where and how each option is similar or different from the others and the impacts and implications of those respective similarities and differences (which can be minor given how much has already been defined by the solution and Unique Value Proposition).

An example of the Lean Canvas for their final business model is shown in *Figure 14.4*.

PROBLEM	SOLUTION	UNIQUE VALUE PROPOSITION	UNFAIR ADVANTAGE	CUSTOMER SEGMENTS
Aspiring pros want to: • optimize each area of life commensurately; • achieve max success; • have complete confidence in actions. Aspiring business want: • optimize each area of the business / strategy commensurately; • maximize growth & positive impact; • have complete confidence in actions. Existing Alternatives Piecemeal solutions that only optimize one part of this in isolation.	Composite offering: 1. online digital platform with advanced AI / ML capabilities + many user-desired features for holistic optimizing. 2. Curated ecosystem of service partners. **KEY METRICS** New subscribers per day / week / month / year. Overall ARR. LTV / CAC ratio. Ecosystem engagement & consumption. Customer success rate.	We empower aspiring, achievement-oriented professionals to attain their maximum possible potential in life & thus maximum success – with 100% confidence in the decisions made. We empower aspiring, growth-oriented businesses to attain their maximum possible potential & thus maximum success for all stakeholders – with 100% confidence in the decisions made.	Defining/compelling CX. Unrivaled AI capabilities. Segmentation via customer analytics – w/ versioned solutions. High caliber ecosystem. **CHANNELS** Individuals Direct sales & marketing Indirect partner sales Businesses Direct sales & marketing Indirect partner sales Conferences / shows.	Individuals • Mature aspirant professionals • Young aspirant professionals • University students • High school students Business Organizations • Large corporate enterprises • Mid-sized businesses Early Adopters Aspiring, success-oriented parties.

COST STRUCTURE	REVENUE STREAMS
Operating / maintaining / improving the core platform. Innovation and R&D to grow the platform / solution over time. Overhead for sales, marketing, & admin. Sales commissions to partners for bundled offerings. Sales commissions to schools for student upsells.	Primary Direct recurring subscription fees – monthly & annual. Indirect Partner purchases on behalf of clients – ongoing / recurring. Secondary Referral commissions from ecosystem partners. School systems purchase solution for students – ongoing / recurring annually.

Lean Canvas is adapted from **Business Model Canvas** and is licensed under the Creative Commons Attribution Share Alike 3.0 Unported License.   **LEAN CANVAS**

Figure 14.4: The Lean Canvas for Intensifi's final business model

The outcome – a new business model that delivers

Once we've done all of the previous testing of business model options against our different customer scenarios – as well as used whatever other evaluative tools we wish to use in the process, such as a Business Model or Lean Canvas – we're finally ready to evaluate those options (perhaps by a forced ranking) and thereby select the winning business model that we'll use going forward.

We can break this business model out by each of its respective functions, and from those, articulate its specific structural attributes – ensuring in the process that the resultant business model remains internally congruent between its respective constituent elements.

In Intensifi's case, having done their testing on each respective business model option against their collective set of Design Principles (goals), as well as considered each option on a Lean Canvas, they've finally settled on a single specific, albeit multifaceted, business model to use. They call this business model their "Experiential Curated Allied Solution Provider" business model. It is represented by the following functional attributes.

Defining the Unique Value Proposition

Intensifi's *Unique Value Proposition* is as we outlined in *Chapter 13* – with one variant for each of the two market segments of individual and business customers. Both variants were aspirational in nature, empowering customers to attain their maximum possible level of success in the situation of interest. Both also assured absolute confidence in the decisions and actions being prescribed, resulting in a balanced, holistic, and comprehensive approach to life or business optimization. It also spoke of a solution that leveraged advanced AI to deliver unrivaled decision clarity that nothing else available could match.

All of this was predicated on the solution that we similarly profiled in *Chapter 12* – a hybrid, digital, cloud-based platform plus aligned service options that allows users to simultaneously optimize every aspect of their life or business according to their unique goals and priorities at that time. This was done via personalized AI prescriptions based on knowledge of both the individual or business and what is occurring in the world around them. It was furthermore a solution that gave users lots of latitude and flexibility around when, where, and how they leveraged it – including how extensive of a feature set they wanted to use in it, and whether they wanted to use it in a formal foresight mode to explore different future scenarios. In keeping with users' expressed desires, it was available to them early on, as well as throughout their lives, with solution options suited to each stage.

Defining the Market Connection Model

Intensifi's *Market Connection Model* borrows elements from the following surrogate business models: Customer Analytics, Behavioral Segmentation, Content Curation, Experience Selling, Affiliation, Platform, Business Alliance, Versioning, Subscription Licensing, Freemium, and Add On.

Using these elements, it achieves Intensifi's six Design Principles that specify which customer segments are to be its primary and secondary targets (and non-targets), and how to package and market a solution specific to each of those segments.

Accordingly, this model builds the following specific activities into the business model:

- Using customer *analytics* to constantly study and profile its customers and then *segmenting* them into distinct segments according to their unique psychographic outcome needs (jobs to be done), and thereafter, packaging and marketing a solution that speaks *directly* to those needs.

- Curating specific content for the customer for *two distinct purposes* – the primary purpose being for use in the AI optimization algorithm for the constant holistic environmental adaptation required of such a platform, and the secondary purpose is for direct customer consumption.

- Creating an explicit *experience* around the platform by using it to help each segment achieve their respective goals – including importantly their emotional *jobs to be done*, and in the context of social sharing with their peer and advisor network, as desired.

- Facilitating access to highly-valued optional services from a curated ecosystem of service provider partners, thus creating a platform business with affiliations to each of these respective partners.

- Curating direct alliances with specific businesses whose brands and offerings likewise resonate with the targeted market segment.

- Offering different tiers of solution options to the different market and customer segments (all involving a subscription licensing model) – starting at Freemium and going all the way up to a highly advanced version – depending on which segment they're in and their unique goals at that particular stage of their life or business (as well as their available budget to invest in the platform and time to invest in using it).

Defining the Sustainable Competitive Advantage

Intensifi's *Sustainable Competitive Advantage* borrows elements from the following surrogate business models: Experience Selling, Solution Provider, Platform, Affiliation, Customer Analytics, Behavioral Segmentation, Versioning, Long Tail, and Business Alliance.

Using these elements, it achieves Intensifi's four Design Principles that mandated that Intensifi dominate on experience while differentiating on offering, leverage ecosystem stakeholders to get its solution embedded deeply and early into its secondary markets, and seek out individual and business groups that are both highly aspirational and growth-oriented to cater to.

Accordingly, this model builds the following specific activities into the business model:

- Delivering a compelling and defining customer experience that brings customers back to the solution over and over again – to constantly and perpetually optimize their lives in ways that let them achieve their maximum possible level of success and fulfillment.

- Delivering an offering that is truly differentiated from anything else available on the market by way of its unique AI-based capabilities and its uncanny accuracy in specifying just the right life or business prescriptions at just the right moments in time (including major alerts whenever needed) that let its customers attain a level of success and fulfillment unmatched anywhere else.

- Using customer analytics and behavioral segmentation to target very specific customer groups who possess a strong growth orientation and are highly aspirational in their life or business.

- Offering segmented solutions that speak to each customer group, at each stage of their life or business, from beginning to end, with suitable features and functionality tailored to their specific needs at that particular stage of their life or business.

- Leveraging suitable partners in a *platform/affiliation* manner to deliver additional value-added services tailored to each respective customer group (meaning that each customer group *only* sees the partners and services curated for their particular group, and not those curated for the other customer groups).

Defining the Sales Model

Intensifi's *Sales Model* borrows elements from the following surrogate business models: Solution Provider, Platform, Affiliation, Customer Analytics, Versioning, Subscription Licensing, Freemium, and Business Alliance.

Using these elements, it achieves Intensifi's eight Design Principles that specify focusing on North America and Europe only initially, offering individuals a monthly subscription direct-purchase offering with no prepackaged services, offering businesses an annual subscription direct- or third-party purchase offering with prepackaged services, creating a commission structure for third-partners partners to incentivize them, using targeted advertising based on customer analytics, and engaging in distinct business arrangements or marketing activities tailored to each market segment.

Accordingly, this model builds the following specific activities into the business model:

- Offering a monthly subscription, direct-purchase solution for North American and European individuals, with no prepackaged services, but plenty of optional services from the partner ecosystem.

- Offering an annual subscription, direct- or third-party purchase solution for North American and European businesses, with prepackaged deployment and implementation services, plus the additional optional services of the partner ecosystem.

- Defining an explicit commission and discount structure for the company's third-party partners to incentivize them to sell Intensifi's solution.

- Defining a customer loyalty program for the company's individual customers to incentivize them to subscribe early on and remain with Intensifi over the long run (with increasing benefits accruing to them the longer they're with Intensifi).

- Levering customer analytics to craft marketing messages tailored to each segment's unique needs and aspirations for the solution and for that point in their life or business.

- Defining a special high school and university program in which the schools underwrite the cost of the solution, so as to be able to provide it to their students free of charge, while also receiving commissions on any students they upsell to the paid version – a true win-win ecosystem affiliation approach.

- Participating in suitable business conferences and trade shows in North America and Europe to reach new business customers.

Defining the Profit Model

Intensifi's *Profit Model* borrows elements from the following surrogate business models: Solution Provider, Versioning, Subscription Licensing, Platform, Affiliation, Customer Analytics, Freemium, Long Tail, and Business Alliance.

Using these elements, it achieves Intensifi's three Design Principles that specify that the company offers a premium solution at a premium price to its primary markets (with the resulting high LTV/CAC ratio), offers a value-oriented solution to its secondary markets, and structures its operations in a way that maintains an overall targeted profit margin capable of sustaining its ongoing and indefinite growth.

Accordingly, this model builds the following specific activities into the business model:

- Offering a premium solution at a premium set of price points to its primary targeted markets.

- Offering a value-oriented solution at a more discounted set of prices to its secondary targeted markets.

- Structuring its operations overall – between these two markets – to maintain an average overall profit margin that's sufficiently healthy to empower the company to continue its ongoing future growth trajectory (something that's helped in the short run by winning more primary market customers, and in the long run by locking in more secondary market customers).

Defining the Business Innovation Model

Intensifi's *Business Innovation Model* borrows elements from the following surrogate business models: Solution Provider, Experience Selling, Customer Analytics, Behavioral Segmentation, Long Tail, Content, Curation, Add On, and Business Alliance.

Using these elements, it achieves Intensifi's six Design Principles that specify that Intensifi is to do the following:

1. quickly ramp up its Innovation and R&D functions;

2. keep those functions operating at a strong and healthy pace each year;

3. release a major new release annually and significant upgrades quarterly;

4. use its extreme users to help it stay ahead of the market;

5. remain prepared for the reality that its customers' motivations and aspirations may evolve and change over time (and thus the need to remain constantly attuned to them);

6. leverage its innovations to maintain its strong brand image and reputation so as to sustain ongoing demand for its solution globally.

Accordingly, this model builds the following specific activities into the business model:

- Building and operating a strong and capable Innovation and R&D capability inside the business to drive the innovations needed to maintain a market leadership position in the category.

- Maintaining a rapid pace of innovation development and launch – releasing major new versions of its solution each year, with significant updates each quarter.

- Engaging its lead and extreme user communities to stay at the very forefront of customer needs, and thus ahead of the mainstream market curve.

- Remaining constantly in tune with the evolving needs, motivations, and aspirations of its customer base as they (potentially) change over time – to constantly retune its solutions accordingly.

- Using its innovations to constantly reinforce its positive, progressive brand image, and thereby drive and maintain a globally-recognized brand with very strong demand.

Defining the Risk Mitigation Model

Intensifi's *Risk Mitigation Model* borrows elements from the following surrogate business models: Solution Provider, Experience Selling, Content Curation, Customer Analytics, Behavioral Segmentation, Versioning, Add On, Long Tail, Business Alliance, Platform, and Affiliation.

Using these elements, it achieves Intensifi's two Design Principles that specify that Intensifi proceeds with the assumptions it has so far but constantly monitors the actual outcomes and results and adjusts them or else pivots the business accordingly, while at the same time, constantly seeking out other ways to mature and further strengthen its overall business model.

Accordingly, this model builds the following specific activities into the business model:

- Proceeding with the assumptions Intensifi has vetted so far, but constantly monitoring actual outcomes and results, so as to adjust or pivot the business accordingly – if/as needed.

- Constantly seeking out additional means by which to mature and strengthen its overall business model, especially those that matter the most at any given time – its Market Connection Model, its Unique Value Proposition, and its Sustainable Competitive Advantage.

Completing the structural business model

As was noted in the prior main section, we've now answered the main structural questions of Intensifi's business model – *who, what, why, where, when,* and *how.* Consequently, we can now profile Intensifi's business model using the structural framework of the *Future Lens Business Model Framework.* That profile would be as follows:

- **Target Market**: Aspiring, growth-minded individuals and businesses – the former spanning high school students to senior business professionals, and the latter spanning medium-sized to large enterprises, who, in each case, aspire to attain their maximum possible potential and thereby experience the maximum level of success attainable for them.

- **Offering Space**: A composite digital (online, cloud-enabled) AI + service platform that leverages advanced AI capabilities fed by a constant, steady stream of information and data to create personalized prescriptions for people's lives and business strategies in accordance with their unique goals and aspirations. This will be in a manner that fully balances each goal and aspiration according to their specified priorities – while also delivering a curated ecosystem of service providers who further augment the value customers derive from the solution – all structured in different capability tiers tailored to the unique needs of each respective market and customer segment.

- **Brand Delivery**: The promise (and the fulfillment of the promise) that customers will be absolutely confident in the prescriptions they're being provided – that these prescriptions will, under all of the circumstances at hand, absolutely ensure the maximum possible success of that individual or business in accordance with their own personal goals, aspirations, and priorities.

- **Customer Acquisition**: Via targeted advertising and marketing, and via both direct and partner sales channels, as well as certain unique "early lock-in" models, the company will find and engage every possible customer in its targeted regions early on in their lives, and retain them as lifelong raving fans throughout their lives – at least up until they reach retirement age, and sometimes beyond.

- **Value Creation**: The in-house development and constant renewal of the intended digital solution, combined with the services provided by the business' curated ecosystem of service providers, access to whom is facilitated by the overall platform.

- **Value Capture**: Very unique "early lock-in" models used to engage ecosystem stakeholders such as schools to help the company lock in future customers at an early age (thereby assuring high overall lifetime value) – combined with premium, high-profit margin solutions for its primary market customers (thereby assuring current high margins) – all working in harmony to assure the ongoing, lifetime profit maximizations of the overall business operation.

This is Intensifi's structural business model. We will, of course, want to define the same structural model for our own new business venture as well.

Understanding the role of metrics

Thus far, we have not discussed *metrics* for our business model – though they did show up in the Lean Canvas example we looked at previously. This isn't because metrics aren't important to our business model; they certainly are. They are how we'll eventually gauge how well our business model is or is not working, and so they matter very much to us.

But we haven't discussed them yet because we can define metrics that measure just about any business model we come up with. And so, the choice of metrics themselves is not a key part, per se, of defining our business model. The metrics are, however, very important to our business model – as some business models will be easier to measure than others, and more importantly, some business models will produce better results on the key metrics that matter than others.

It's just that for two or more competing business models, the metrics may be *the same*, as is the ability to measure them. And so the choice of metrics does *not* become a deciding factor in which of those business models we choose; they're the same in all cases.

Of course, one or more of those business models may perform better on these metrics than the others, and so that's a consideration that may allow us to select one over the others – though, in reality, making that judgment at this point is often conjecture. We really won't know for certain how well they each perform until we test them in the real world.

Consequently, we need to look at our goals for the business, decide which metrics matter most to those goals, and then measure those particular metrics. Obviously, we want the business to prosper, grow, and be successful, so we'll need normal operating metrics to gauge those performance factors. But beyond those normal operating metrics, there'll often be *other metrics* we want to measure that gauge something unique to our particular business model. For example, I suspect that Intensifi will be very interested in tracking the actual success rate of their customers over time, and consequently, their satisfaction level with the solution. This is what will drive viral word-of-mouth marketing for them. If the word gets out that their solution really works and people are attaining great success because of it, then they will certainly let the world know about it. Likewise, if their solution isn't working and people are encountering failure with it, then they will certainly let the world know about that too. Either scenario will impact Intensifi's brand and reputation, which will impact its ultimate scale and success in the long run, so you'd better believe that Intensifi probably cares about this metric.

Likewise for our own business model. We'll want to figure out what special and unique metrics matter most to our business, and thereafter try to measure those. We can, if we want, try to use the expected performance against these metrics as a decision factor in our choice of competing options – so long as we understand that doing so involves untested conjecture at this point (short of other experimentation beyond what we've already done).

Is this the right business model?

Finally, there are a couple of additional questions we'll want to address and answer prior to moving forward. These questions are designed to help us ensure we have developed the best and most optimal business model for our particular situation using the preceding process.

Let us tackle each of these two questions in turn.

What's special about this business model?

The first question is, "What is so *special* about this particular business model?"

This question is designed to ensure we do have a very *sound and innovative* business model – one with the following:

- a truly unique and compelling Unique Value Proposition – one that uniquely meets our customers' outcome needs and makes them the heroes of their journey;

- a truly attractive and compelling Market Connection Model – one that works both ways, market-to-business and business-to-market;

- a truly sustainable and competitive Sustainable Competitive Advantage – one that is truly forward and innovative in its thinking – or at least the seeds of this, with a clear line of sight to what has to be done to solidify it over time;

- a truly sound Sales Model that leverages both new avenues (innovation) and proven business channels;

- a truly effective Profit Model that ensures a high likelihood of yielding an above-par profit margin;

- a truly impactful Business Innovation Model capable of keeping our business moving at pace indefinitely;

- a truly useful Risk Mitigation Model that ensures the business adapts and learns rapidly and nimbly.

If we can answer in the affirmative to each of these points, and we feel really good about our business model – both in how innovative it is and in how sound it is in terms of its business fundamentals – then we can feel confident in proceeding forward with it. If we cannot answer in the affirmative to each of these points, then there is likely something deficient in our business model… it is not "special" enough (yet), and we would do well to circle back and uncover what is still deficient about it and work to remedy that prior to moving forward.

Will it unleash massive new value?

The second question is, "Will it unleash *massive new value* for both us and our customers? If so, why and how?"

Recalling that the whole point of business model innovation, in the beginning, was to unleash massive new value for both us and our customers, this question is designed to ensure that the business model we've just finished defining does in fact do that. Thus, we need to pause at this point and ask ourselves this one simple question… does it or does it not unleash massive new value for both us and our would-be customers?

If it does – and we understand clearly why and how it does – then congratulations… we have (so far, at least on paper) attained business model innovation.

But if it does not – or if we aren't clear on *why* or *how* it does so – then there remains a big risk inside our business model. It may *fail* to unleash this massive new value – in which case, we don't have business model innovation and our business model is not likely to attain what we want or need it to. Moving forward with such a business model would be a huge mistake on our part! We have to – before going any further – get this matter right, meaning we have to go back and figure out what we missed – what's still a deficit about our business model – and then figure out how to rectify that so that it will unleash this massive new value. So, here again, we need to circle back and figure out what exactly is wrong with the business model. Is it in the *who*, the *why*, the *what*, the *when*, the *where*, or the *how* – or in some combination of them?

That is why we ask this question at this point in the process. It's a final gating litmus test that helps us ensure we've done everything we possibly can up to this point to ensure we have defined a truly innovative and impactful business model – one that's rooted in human-centered design and that delivers unique, desirable, and sustainable value to all stakeholders in a viable business format. If we can pass this litmus test, then we are ready to move forward.

In Intensifi's case, given that everything in our world – from our homes to our offices, to our belongings, even to our bodies – will eventually be mirrored by a digital twin in the virtual world that AI can operate on, the team feels the time is right for their Unique Value Proposition and that they have, after all of their exhaustive Design Thinking work here, defined a truly unique, compelling, and innovative business model that will unleash massive new value for both them and the customers they end up serving.

Are we done now?

At this point, we are finished *defining* our innovative new business model. Excellent! The process we've just demonstrated with Intensifi is precisely the same process your own venture will use to discover its unique and innovative business model. It simply needs to replicate this process with the same focus, vigor, and discipline that Intensifi has.

Yet we've not even *begun* to build, launch, and operate our new business venture! Those are two completely separate things! One is (comparatively speaking) a theoretical exercise, while the other is the reality of the real world – which is sometimes kind and sometimes cruel.

So, everything we've done so far has been essentially theoretical – despite our best attempts at using real subjects in real (simulated) scenarios to test out our business model options – and despite our best attempts at using the Design Thinking process and its methods to define our Unique Value Proposition and its corresponding solution. As the saying goes, "The proof is in the pudding."

And so, the real world of executing our business model awaits us. It's time for us to get out of the lab and out into the real world – where we'll take our innovative new business model and see whether it works the way our experimentation has so far indicated it would… to see whether it does in fact unleash massive new value for everyone involved.

We may find that everything in the real world works exactly as our experimentation indicated, and so we move forward precisely as planned. Or – just as likely – we may find that many things in the real world don't work quite like our experimentation indicated, and so our shiny new business model gets a few "black eyes" in the process. We'll never know until we actually get out into the real world and launch it to find out.

This brings us to the topic of our next chapter – executing our innovative new business model.

Summary

In this chapter, we learned how to use Design Thinking for overall, holistic business model design – so that we could design a new business model that resonates with our markets and customers over the long term.

We did this by combining the Business Model Synthesis process with the Design Thinking process. There, we started by conceiving various hypotheses about each function of our business model (using certain Design Methods), which we then tested using other Design Methods, to, in each case, arrive at a specific Point of View about that function so that we could ultimately craft corresponding Design Principles for the function.

Using those Design Principles as our goals for each function, we then stepped through the Business Model Synthesis process via select surrogate business models to see how well each of their designs satisfied our specific goals. From that, we were able to distill our own new business model – an amalgamated version of our own creation that borrowed different elements from many of these surrogates – to yield a final business model design that does the following:

- attains all of our goals (*Design Principles*);
- is internally coherent and congruent;
- is truly special and unique;
- is poised to unleash massive new value to both us and our markets.

This showed us how to leverage Design Thinking for overall, holistic business model design work – insight we can now go out and apply broadly anywhere we need to.

This brought us to the point where we're now ready to transition onto the topic of *Chapter 15* – which is actually executing our business model. There, we'll walk through everything we need to do to prepare for executing our business model, actually execute our business model (going to market), and thereafter, follow through by tracking our business model's performance and adjusting it accordingly. All of this will ultimately lead us to a sustainable business venture that grows and scales healthily over time.

15

Execution – Bringing Our Business Model to Life

In *Chapter 14*, we learned how to take Design Thinking far beyond just the immediate solution we want to offer and apply it holistically to our entire business model. Doing this allows us to have not only a solution that resonates with our target customers but also a comprehensive business model that does so as well. This is crucial if we hope to unleash massive new value and, in so doing, achieve maximum success for our venture.

We accomplished this by merging the Business Model Synthesis process with the Design Thinking process to yield a new business model design that does the following:

- achieves each of our respective goals (defined via our Design Principles);
- is internally coherent and congruent across the entire business model;
- is truly special and unique;
- is poised to unleash massive new value to both us and our markets!

In this chapter, we're going to explore what comes after that, namely actually *executing* this business model and the preparation that goes into doing so. Topically, we'll walk through the following three key points:

- **Preparation – preparing to execute our new business model**: Everything we need to do to plan and prepare for deploying and executing our new business model.
- **Going to market – executing our new business model**: Actually executing our new business model and taking it to market.
- **Following through – tracking and tweaking our business model**: Following through by tracking our business model's actual performance and adjusting it accordingly.

Doing this will ultimately lead us to a sustainable business venture that grows and scales healthily over time.

We'll also take a look at what this process looks like for Intensifi, including their own preparations, their initial lean execution, and their ongoing follow-through. In doing that, we'll see a new dilemma the team encountered in the process that they hadn't initially considered, and how they chose to address that dilemma (and what it meant to their business model). We'll also have a very brief glimpse at how this has all worked out for Intensifi.

Preparation – preparing to execute our new business model

At this point, we now have a new business model design. This will be one that we believe, based on our extensive Design Thinking research and validation work (via its many Design Methods and appropriate mockups and prototypes), will actually work in the marketplace to unleash massive new value on account of one or more innovative elements within it.

Now it's time to prepare for executing that business model.

Starting out (together)

If the new venture is to be an independent start-up, then the first task will be for its Founders to establish a proper Founder Operating Agreement amongst themselves (if they haven't already done so). This agreement spells out such points as the following:

- exactly how the business is to be structured amongst the Founders;
- who is to have what role in the venture;
- who is to have voting rights in the venture, and what those rights are;
- how equity is to be divided amongst the initial Founders.

If the new venture is to be a corporate venture, then the first task will be for its leaders to create a proper Venture Operating Charter documenting how it is to operate in the context of its parent organization. This addresses such questions as the following:

- Is it to be a standalone business, a captive part of an existing business unit, or the captive subject of an entirely new business unit?
- How is its decision-making to be handled… autonomously, semi-autonomously, or by corporate overseers?
- How are its financials to be accounted… independently, or as part of a sponsoring business unit?

These decisions must all be settled and their answers properly documented prior to proceeding any further. Doing this will ensure there is full clarity between all the affected parties on how the venture is to be operated going forward. That, in turn, will prevent otherwise inevitable misunderstandings and disagreements later on that could derail the effort.

Defining the basics

The next – and much simpler – task in this process will be undertaking the routine work of setting up the new legal business entity if we haven't already done so (if it is to be a start-up or separate corporate entity). This includes such steps as the following:

- creating its Articles of Formation / Organization;
- filing for its official business license;
- establishing the necessary bank accounts;
- and so on.

All of these tasks are routine and nothing out of the ordinary.

Defining our initial go-to-market strategy

Prior to launching our new venture with its new business model and new solution, one of the things we'll need to do at this point is to sit down and fine-tune our exact *go-to-market strategy*. By this, what we mean is deciding things such as the following:

- Are we going to tackle *all* of our market and customer segments at the very beginning, or start with certain ones and then expand outward from there (sometimes the added focus on a smaller number of segments can prove very helpful and beneficial)?
- Are we going to develop *all* of the planned capabilities of our solution at the very beginning, or start out with certain ones (to get to market faster) and then quickly expand them post-launch as we learn more?
- Are we going to develop our *entire ecosystem* at the very beginning, or just certain parts of it, and then expand it further as we go forward and learn more?

As we can see, these decisions are all intertwined with one another, and each will play a potentially critical role in how much initial traction we're able to attain – particularly in our most important segments. We therefore must study and analyze our situation very carefully, and make these critical decisions very carefully – including in light of the brand promises and brand positioning we wish to create.

In general, the less solution development work we can do pre-launch and at-launch – and the more we can do post-launch – to allow ourselves to learn in the *real world* as we go along, the more *efficiently* we'll utilize the capital available to us, and the more *quickly and effectively* we'll home in on all the right details. This is in fact the essence of modern innovation practice – to move as much of our overall learning process *upstream* in our innovation efforts as possible, learning early on our incorrect assumptions and then correcting them before they become costly to us. We do this by limiting how much pre-market solution-development work we do based on as-yet fully unproven premises, and move as much of that work as we can into the post-launch phase, where we can quickly learn from the real world (for which there is no substitute). We should keep this in mind whenever fine-tuning our initial go-to-market strategy.

Furthermore, in our initial go-to-market strategy development work, we will often encounter *new issues* that we hadn't given consideration to previously. This isn't to say that our earlier Design Thinking work was deficient in any way; it wasn't. It's just that it was more focused on certain specific elements and functions of our business model. Now that we're about to hit the road running, new issues tend to materialize that we hadn't considered before. This is okay, so long as we pause at this point to address them intelligently and sufficiently, which we can generally do based on the many insights we developed during our earlier Design Thinking work (so that the work did set us up for addressing these issues at this point). We'll see an example of this later on when we look at Intensifi's path to market.

Developing our venture's primary solution

The next, and more involved, task will be taking the different structural framework elements that we've created so far and, from them, building out our new core solution.

In the case of digital solutions, developing them has become an increasingly simple task with the advent of low-code, no-code, and AI-assisted coding tools, together with the many available and extensive cloud service capabilities. We should of course use these tools everywhere it makes sense to do so.

It's also important when building out our new solution that we constantly seek the feedback of would-be users along the way so that their inputs can be incorporated into its many details. The feedback of power users and other outliers in particular will prove very helpful to us, by allowing us to see where certain details do and don't work (and why). We may, in fact, learn certain nuances that appear counter to our initial findings, in which case we'll have to dig deeper to understand what exactly is going on and potentially adjust course accordingly.

Once the initial version of our solution is finished, it's ready to be launched and used to operate our venture's Unique Value Proposition.

Not long after launching it, we will of course initiate the ongoing and indefinite journey of expanding and improving on it in countless ways. We'll do this in accordance with the additional new opportunities that stem from the market's ongoing evolution and the deeper insights we uncover along the way.

Seeding our venture's new ecosystem

The next step – though it need not sequentially follow the others; it can and should be done in parallel with them – will be to begin seeding our venture's *ecosystem of partners*, whomever that involves, and whatever it is to look like.

Increasingly today, markets are continuing to fragment into more and more small *micro-markets* in which customers are demanding uniquely customized services that meet their specific needs. Consequently, almost no venture today can operate in isolation, apart from an enabling ecosystem. More often than not, this enabling ecosystem will prove critical to the execution of its business model, and therefore to the life of the venture. This is something we must be fully aware of.

In writing this book, I interviewed Shawn Crowley, Co-CEO of the digital solutions firm *Atomic Object*. A key insight that Shawn shared with me, and that we discussed at length, was that creating this ecosystem of partners to operate with has become (and continues to become) increasingly critical. Here's what Shawn said:

> While historically we didn't see as much of this – because businesses wanted to own the entire ecosystem so that they could minimize their risks and capture more of the overall margin – today that's changing. There's this dance occurring in which businesses are asking themselves, "Do we want to take twice as long to get to market to develop this entire (potentially risky) endeavor ourselves – or do we want to get to market faster to capture less margin, but do so faster, while spreading out our risk? Do we want that (potential) first-mover advantage now?" Even in pure digital domains, there seems to be much more appetite today to work with partners – even with different SAAS companies working together because that way they can meet a market need more holistically than they could alone. Plus it gets them both to market faster than they would otherwise. This was seen at the 2023 Consumer Electronics Show, where there was a lot more talk about companies looking to integrate consumer electronics into their products – and thus talk about partnering to do so.

This offers clear evidence that partnership ecosystems have become an increasingly critical element of almost all venture's business model.

In many cases, seeding our new *ecosystem of partners* will prove to be the most challenging task before us at this point, but one that is obviously critical to the ongoing survival and thriving of our venture. Its seriousness and importance must therefore be understood, and it must be pursued vigorously.

Securing the necessary funding

The initial funding required to support our venture's pre-launch phase – while its solution is being developed and its ecosystem is being built – must come from somewhere. This can be funded directly from the Founders, investments from friends and family, or possibly investments from an Angel Investor or Angel Syndicate, should there be good connections to one of them.

Whatever the source, an equally important step in this phase will be to secure the necessary funding. This will give the venture the runway it requires to develop its solution and ecosystem and thereafter market and sell them so that it can ultimately start generating revenue.

Once our venture has started generating some revenue, it can then decide what growth trajectory it wishes to move onto – a slower revenue-funded trajectory, or a faster and more aggressive venture-funded trajectory. But that is a decision for a bit later. Today, the immediate need is to get to where the venture can start generating revenue so that it can cover most or all of its operating expenses.

Going to market – executing our new business model

Once we've done all of the preparatory steps, the day finally comes when it's time to start our clock.

This is Day 1.

Where our real learning begins

At this point, we will – according to the initial go-to-market strategy that we chose – actually start marketing and selling our new solution, thereby activating its Unique Value Proposition for our targeted customers.

This is where – despite all of the efforts we've put forth so far – our real learning begins.

We have to understand that what Design Thinking has done for us so far – including using it to develop our overall business model so that it *too* is human-centered – is that it has, based on all of the insights it provided us, significantly improved our chances of success (and, by the same token, reduced our chances of failure).

But it *has not* – because it *cannot* – guaranteed our absolute success. This is because so much is still left up to the thousands and thousands of exogenous circumstances that we could never begin to account for in a simulated environment, as well as the hundreds of endogenous factors amongst the Founders and early employees that we could never begin to account for (such as, for example, just how good our staff is at marketing and selling).

So, whatever we enter into Day 1 with is an optimal (and innovative) business model and solution that has the highest possible chances of success that we could ever hope for at this point, but still no absolute guarantee of success. Much, much learning remains before us.

This is why Steve Blank so famously stated, *"No plan survives first contact with customers."* And, indeed, there simply is no substitute for real-world learning, which is what we'll be doing now.

The Lean Start-up transition

Day 1 is where, in effect, we transition from our earlier simulated *Design Thinking world* to the real-world efforts of a *Lean Start-up*. In a Lean Start-up, the understanding is that, despite our best efforts so far, there remain thousands of untested and therefore unproven factors that we simply cannot account for anywhere else other than in the real world. This is just as true for a corporate venture as it is for an independent start-up – there's no difference in this reality for either one.

We therefore begin with some initial offering – call it a *Minimum Viable Product* if you like (or call it whatever you wish), but it's something that is far less than our full-blown intended offering – and we begin with certain market and customer segments that we want to test and learn from. We then work through rapid, iterative learning cycles with those segments – trying (intelligently, not randomly) different details with them so as to learn what works and what doesn't, and why so. Wherever something doesn't work, we pivot to different actions based on our newly acquired insights from that experience.

At this point, we are no longer working on *unproven assumptions* – or even *assumptions* at all – we are working on *reality*: what the real world tells us. We may go through any number of different rapid learning cycles like this until eventually we converge on a final business model and solution that achieves everything we aspired to (or else some other aspiration if we learn that our original one was misplaced or unattainable – something we should've already learned if we're using the process taught in this book).

Hopefully, this won't be too far off from the version we created using Design Thinking, but we must work through this process with a completely open mind – accepting that at any moment something could change or we could learn a new insight that negated a previously-held belief we had formed. When that occurs, we must not let our *cognitive bias* get in our way. We have to accept the evidence that reality gives us and conform to it accordingly if we hope to succeed at unleashing the massive new value we're trying to unleash.

As part of this whole early (Lean Start-up) transitionary process – and well beyond – we'll have to start assessing the performance of our business model. Doing this will allow us to continue innovating and improving it further still, which brings us to the next phase of our journey.

Following through – tracking and adjusting our business model

The final critical action that we need to undertake throughout the first several years of our new venture is – using appropriate metrics – tracking the performance of its business model and adjusting it as necessary to further improve on those metrics. This is the process known as *scale-up*, as opposed to *start-up*.

Doing this will allow us to constantly refine our business model until, eventually, we've optimized each function of it, and in the process achieved maximum performance from it (for a given period of time). It will also let us ensure that we're constantly unleashing massive new value for each *new customer* who comes to us, which means we'll have to constantly be *innovating* and otherwise *improving* on that business model.

Common measures of business model performance

Some very common examples of appropriate business model performance metrics are as follows:

- Number of new customer subscriptions (of each type) each month
- Percentage growth in new customer subscriptions (of each type) for each month

- Number and percentage of customers terminating their subscription each month (attrition)
- Number of total customer subscriptions (of each type) cumulatively
- Percentage growth in total customer subscriptions (of each type)
- Revenue growth each month – value and percentage
- Total annual revenue (historical)
- Total annual recurring revenue (forecasted)
- Profit growth each month – value and percentage
- Total annual profit (historical and forecasted)
- Running profit margin by customer type
- Running **Customer Acquisition Cost (CAC)** for each customer type
- Running **Lifetime Value (LTV)** for each customer type
- Running LTV/CAC ratio for each customer type
- Customer satisfaction/delight ratings
- Viral marketing growth each month
- Running brand recognition each quarter
- Attainment of CSR objectives each quarter.

As we measure these different metrics each month, we'll want to be constantly looking for new strategies and actions that allow us to maximize each one. Our goal in all cases will be to unleash the maximum amount of value possible for all impacted stakeholders. In the case of our business, we'll be reinvesting that value back into further future growth and positive impacts in the world.

Converging on a final business model

Eventually, after some period of time in the early years of our venture, and as we work toward expanding into our other market and customer segments with our completely capable solution, things will begin to converge toward a more stable and final business model to employ. This is what the scale-up period is all about.

This period gives us the opportunity to do several things within and on behalf of our business model, including the following:

- refine and perfect our Market Connection Model to each of our market and customer segments;
- refine and perfect our Unique Value Proposition for each of our market and customer segments;
- refine and perfect our Sales Model with each of our market and customer segments;

- refine and perfect our Profit Model in the case of each of our market and customer segments;

- solidify our Sustainable Competitive Advantage in each of our market and customer segments;

- activate our Business Innovation Model on behalf of each of our market and customer segments;

- activate our Risk Mitigation Model in the context of each of our market and customer segments.

At the end of this initial phase (which will often be the first several years of the venture's life), we should eventually arrive at a more stable business model that works as we had hoped it would, and that therefore achieves all we've aspired for it to achieve in terms of unleashing massive new value for us, our customers, our partners, and all other stakeholders involved.

Intensifi's path to market

Let's now take a look at Intensifi's journey through a series of steps. As we'll quickly see, new issues often arise while preparing to face this reality – ones that we didn't necessarily anticipate or prepare for. And so we have to remain agile throughout this process, as Intensifi does in this case.

The solution

For Intensifi's primary solution, the team will be building out an online, cloud-based digital platform.

This solution involves all of the attributes specified in *Chapter 12* (and reiterated in *Chapter 13*).

The go-to-market strategy

For Intensifi's initial go-to-market strategy, the team has decided to limit the scope of their focus at this point, focusing only on corporate customers and senior professionals (the premium customer segments in each respective market segment: business and individual).

Starting at the very top in each market segment – though more demanding – will give them the opportunity to learn inside a more profit-rich environment and thereby maximize their ongoing runway as they continue to learn and evolve, prior to moving into the more profit-lean segments, where learning has to be even more efficient. It will also give them a bit more of an *obscure niche* to hide in while they work on otherwise strengthening their Sustainable Competitive Advantage.

The ecosystem

For Intensifi's ecosystem, the team had determined earlier that this will entail a broad ecosystem of service partners, each delivering a particular service that complements the Intensifi platform and offers additional value to the end user.

Their plan is to have a different cohort of service providers for each customer type – premium ones for large corporates, value-oriented ones for medium-sized businesses, premium ones for senior professionals, mid-range ones for young professionals, and value-oriented ones for university students. In each case, the scope and pricing of the services will be matched to the needs and budgets of that particular customer.

The Intensifi team must therefore invest the time and effort necessary at this point to establish their initial ecosystem, in anticipation of their eventual launch, since they'll need to launch on Day 1 with at least some portion of this ecosystem in place.

In particular, since the team has decided in its initial go-to-market strategy to focus on only its two most premium customer segments, they initially only need to establish the specific ecosystems designed to service those two segments. Over time, as they begin to expand into their other targeted segments, they will have to develop the necessary and appropriate ecosystems to service those segments as well.

Their big dilemma

In preparing to activate these early elements of its planned business model, Intensifi encounters a particular *dilemma*.

Specifically, recalling that Intensifi's *intention* is to dominate on experience, it has always had the aim of making its solution – including its underlying platform and the associated service partner ecosystem – as easy and as straightforward to use as possible (a very positive overall experience). However, the team encounters a dilemma in this regard, stemming from the trade-off between the platform's powerful *capabilities* and its *ease of use* – the former sometimes tending to confound the latter.

While Intensifi's platform will itself simplify many aspects of using it to achieve the user's stated goal, there remains far more that can be done with it – especially when augmented with the accompanying services – than the typical user is willing (and in some cases able) to learn. This is especially true the deeper the user goes into the technicalities of each facet of their lives – the technical financial details, the technical health and nutrition details, the technical relationship and family dynamics details, and so on. Most users simply can't do this (at this level) alone. At some point, they need *help* if they hope to truly attain maximum success with the platform.

Consequently, Intensifi has considered three options for addressing this situation:

- leave it entirely to the end user – focus their efforts on just providing the platform and then let the end users figure out how to use it themselves, on their own;
- offer a complete turnkey "done-for-you" service in which in-house experts at Intensifi create the life-optimization models for each user according t their specific goals;
- create an expert marketplace in which a portion of their overall service ecosystem involves a set of *expert advisors and agencies* who help users build, optimize, and operate their optimization models to achieve maximum outcomes and results.

Intensifi selects option three. They believe that the first option will not engender customer delight (it's not the product experience they want to create) and thus not long-term success for them, and that the second option simply isn't scalable for them (at least, not easily). Consequently, they see the third option as being the best overall path forward; plus, it creates a symbiotic business model in which multiple stakeholders win something out of it, including (most importantly) their customers attaining the brand promise of an optimized, full-potential life with maximum success. It is therefore the only option that makes any real sense to Intensifi.

Of course, adopting this option represents an additional facet to Intensifi's business model that they hadn't fully fleshed out during their earlier efforts, though they were incidentally aware that something like this could be required as part of the overall partner ecosystem they were planning. We see, therefore, that in the early stages of planning out one's go-to-market strategy, additional needs arise that have to be addressed, and that leads to yet further evolutions in the final business model used.

Intensifi's Expert Advisor Marketplace

Intensifi thus defines its *Expert Advisor Marketplace* as a curated selection of Intensifi-approved life-optimization *experts*, each of whom offers a specialization in one or more of the affected areas – finance and investing, health and nutrition, family and parenting, business strategy, and so on. Intensifi models this marketplace after similar programs at companies such as Shopifi, Squarespace, and Webflow. As in those programs, each Advisor in the marketplace is carefully vetted and formally approved by Intensifi.

These Advisors are set up to help users along a *spectrum* of different services – from simple advice and guidance to complex model-building for them in their overall life (digital twin) model. This works well because Intensifi has designed these models to be *modular* in nature, such that different modules can be swapped in and out of them at will, such as those for finance, health, and parenting, for example, while the overall heuristic engine balances the resulting prescriptions according to the user's defined goals.

These Advisors – just like in any other freelance marketplace – get rated by customers, and consequently can be sorted by their customer ratings and reviews, their level of experience, their prices, and other criteria. Once selected, the user contacts and engages the Advisor directly without the need for Intensifi's direct involvement – though Intensifi does monitor these engagements just like in any other freelance marketplace, and retains the right to extract commissions from them should they choose to do so in the future (a potential future business model enhancement for them).

Intensifi of course oversees the development and curation of this marketplace, but all engagement details get handled directly between the parties involved. This approach greatly simplifies matters for Intensifi, allowing it to focus just on facilitating these connections, while otherwise staying focused on advancing its core platform.

The resultant symbiotic business model

The Intensifi *Expert Advisor Marketplace* creates what is known as a **symbiotic business model** – a true win-win-win business model between Intensifi, its customers, and these service providers. Such a business model creates the conditions required for the overall ecosystem to thrive and become a healthy, self-reinforcing one. Let's look at the details:

- Intensifi signs on more customers (and therefore generates more revenue) because these customers have the assurance they need that they can get the assistance they require to succeed with the platform; in essence, having this marketplace reduces customers' barriers o entry with the platform;

- service partners gain new clients that they would otherwise never have, producing a steady new stream of revenue for them;

- customers get the assistance they require to achieve maximum success with the platform – and thereby attain their maximum life potential and maximum life success – as desired, and as promised by Intensifi;

- Intensifi makes more profit because it costs them very little to facilitate this marketplace, and most of its patrons come from the wealthier and more premium tiers of its customer base (meaning the higher-priced, higher-margin subscriptions);

- the support Advisors give to customers leads to overall greater customer success with the platform, thus encouraging its lifelong use, and with that, a resultant greater LTV for each customer of Intensifi.

The expected *total economic impact* of this facet of Intensifi's business model is expected to be incredibly large over time, especially as the marketplace grows in size.

Intensifi Academy – one last twist

To ensure complete success with its *Expert Advisor Marketplace*, Intensifi further determines that it must ensure all Advisors have the requisite skills to perform as expected and thereby help Intensifi's customers attain their stated goals.

To ensure this, Intensifi intends to establish *Intensifi Academy*. This (additional) online platform will deliver a wide range of training courses covering everything relating to Intensifi – from operating its platform to extending its platform via the inherent options, to building the necessary functional modules that plug into the overall heuristic (digital twin) model, and more. Also, after completing a demonstration examination for each course (demonstrating their mastery of the subject), Advisors will receive a corresponding certification indicating this, which they can then display on their respective profiles in the marketplace.

By equipping these Advisors with the in-depth knowledge they need, Intensifi will ensure the overall caliber of its marketplace, so that customers will be able to trust it and those they find there. This will further boost customers' satisfaction and delight, and consequently Intensifi's brand recognition and regard.

Of course, Intensifi Academy represents yet another facet of Intensifi's business model that they hadn't foreseen or envisioned earlier on during their initial efforts, though they certainly understand now its necessity for ensuring the caliber of this part of their overall business model. Thus, once again we find in the early stages of planning out our go-to-market strategy additional needs that require addressing, thus leading to yet further evolutions in our overall business model.

Intensifi's Day 1 – the launch

Intensifi succeeds at completing all of the previously mentioned planning and preparation tasks – including defining its operating agreement, completing its basics, finalizing its initial go-to-market strategy, developing its new platform (an early lean version), establishing its initial partner ecosystem (including Version 1 of the Expert Advisor Marketplace and Academy), and securing the necessary funding to underwrite its earliest pre-revenue days.

Based on having done all this, Intensifi launches. It has its Day 1.

At this point, Intensifi has its initial platform and its initial ecosystem and so it starts marketing and advertising its solution and, even more importantly, the benefits that solution delivers, in language that matters to, and thus resonates with, its initially-targeted customer segments. Shortly thereafter, the sales begin, resulting in its first wave of actual revenue.

Shortly thereafter, Intensifi starts applying the specific early metrics it has chosen to gauge the performance and success of its business model to date. In particular, it is looking at things like this:

- Number and percentage growth in new customer subscriptions monthly
- Total number and percentage growth in customer subscriptions cumulatively
- Monthly revenue growth
- Total annual revenue (running)
- Monthly profit growth
- Profit margin by customer type
- LTV/CAC ratio by customer type
- Customer satisfaction / delight ratings
- Monthly viral marketing growth
- Quarterly brand recognition ratings.

Intensifi's Day 2 – the evolution

Based on what the team has been learning from its aforementioned assessments, the venture continues to evolve and adapt its solution, its business model, and how it markets and sells those to its targeted customers.

Eventually, it unfolds the rest of its business model, covering both overall market segments (businesses and individuals) and all six customer segments completely – more or less as originally planned in each case.

Its metrics appear very healthy, and so it would seem that everything the team learned earlier on about its would-be customers, their pains, needs, aspirations, and motivations, as well as Intensifi's own solution and business model – all via Design Thinking, Human-Centered Design, and the methods described herein – was indeed accurate and on the mark. It is producing the success it promised.

Intensifi's Day 3 – the future

Intensifi goes on to have a very rich future. To learn more about this, and to see what this new venture eventually achieves, stay tuned for its final chapter, detailed at the end of *Chapter 16*.

Summary

In this chapter, we explored the several steps required – after defining our initial human-centered business model – to activate and execute that business model in the real world. This included working out our Founder Operating Agreement, registering our business as a formal and legal entity, defining our initial go-to-market strategy, creating our primary solution, seeding our ecosystem, and securing any funding needed to help us underwrite these efforts.

We noted that in the process of defining our initial go-to-market strategy, new issues will sometimes arise that we hadn't considered before, and so we have to address them at this point. We also noted that, in most cases, we can address these issues by successfully using the insights we've already developed through Design Thinking.

We noted too that seeding our initial ecosystem will be one of the most important, though potentially hardest, steps we'll have to undertake at this point. It is considered crucial considering how *dependent* innovations today tend to be on the proper functioning of an ecosystem to deliver them well.

We further noted that our real learning starts in the *real world*, where we'll learn immeasurably more about our business model than we ever could in the prior simulated scenarios we explored. We saw that this leads our new venture – even if a corporate venture – through some version of a *Lean Start-up transition* based on a set of validated learning cycles and subsequent adjustments (pivots) to its business model.

Finally, we noted that we have to assess the *performance* of our business model over time using appropriate *metrics* so that we can eventually converge on a final business model that we'll stay with for the foreseeable future.

We concluded by observing Intensifi's path to market through this process. This ended up involving certain new additions to their business model on account of additional considerations that arose during their initial go-to-market strategy development work. Such is often the case in reality.

In *Chapter 16* (our final chapter), we'll look back across our entire journey and see how we can use this process over and over again for constant, repeated success for the serial entrepreneurs and corporate intrapreneurs amongst us. This includes institutionalizing it inside of corporate organizations, marrying it to strategic foresight and futuring efforts, and applying it to digital transformations. We'll wrap up with a look at where human-centered business model innovation is likely to go in the future.

We'll also learn a very interesting plot twist about our now-good friends at Intensifi and see where their venture ends up somewhere down the road. This will be their testimony to the true power of human-centered business model innovation. Stay tuned for the end!

Further reading

- *No Plan Survives First Contact With Customers – Business Plans versus Business Models*, Steve Blank, 08 April 2010, www.steveblank.com, `https://steveblank.com/2010/04/08/no-plan-survives-first-contact-with-customers-%e2%80%93-business-plans-versus-business-models/`.

- *Scaling Up Corporate Startups: Turn Innovation Concepts Into Business Impact*, `Frank Mattes, Dr. Ralph Christian Ohr, Lean Scaleup UG, 2018.`

The Final Outcome – Consistent Ongoing Success

In *Chapter 15*, we explored the steps required to activate and execute your human-centered business model. That included tasks such as working out the initial Operating Agreement, registering the business, defining its initial go-to-market strategy, creating its primary solution, seeding its ecosystem, and securing the funding needed to underwrite its early-stage activities. We noted that new issues often arise when defining our initial go-to-market strategy, which we have to address using the insights we developed in this work before going forward. We also noted that seeding our initial ecosystem is one of the most important, albeit potentially hardest, steps we'll have to undertake at that point. We also noted that the *real learning* begins once we get into the real world, where we'll learn immeasurably more about our new business model than we ever could in the simulated scenarios we explored so far. We saw how this leads a new venture – even a corporate venture – through some version of a Lean Start-Up transition, based on a set of validated learning cycles and subsequent adjustments (pivots) to its business model.

In this final chapter, on designing the human business, we're going to look back on our journey and see how we can leverage this whole process – the one that we just learned – for ongoing and repeated successes. This is important, as being able to do so is a necessity for both serial entrepreneurs and long-term corporate intrapreneurs.

In particular, we're going to explore the following five topics together:

- **Appreciating the final and repeatable outcome of this process**: Understanding that the final outcome of this process has, in most cases, a far higher probability of success and, since it's a repeatable process, that using it as such can lead to ongoing and indefinite successes (a higher "hit rate").

- **Making this happen consistently inside our organization**: A look at how we can institutionalize human-centered business model innovation inside larger corporate organizations.

- **Applying human-centered business model innovation to digital transformation**: A look at how we can leverage human-centered business model innovation to get back to first principles, in order to deliver winning digital solutions and business models in the context of a broader digital transformation.

- **Winning today, tomorrow, and the day after tomorrow**: A look at how we can marry human-centered business model innovation to our strategic foresight and future efforts.

- **Reflections – where do we take this in the future?**: A look at where human-centered business model innovation may be going in the future and how we can journey forward with it.

We're also going to learn a very interesting plot twist about our now-good friends at Intensifi, as well as see where their new venture has ended up somewhere down the road. This will be their testimony to the true power of human-centered business model innovation, so stay tuned to the very end!

Appreciating the final and repeatable outcome of this process

When we look back over this whole process that we've just explored together – from dissecting our business model structurally and functionally, to understanding the human psyche, to mastering the Design Thinking process, to then extending that process to our entire business model – what we can see is that the human-centered business model innovation process – as presented in this book – is one that stands as incredibly effective and hugely impactful.

Indeed, it is a process that, through many direct and indirect uses of its principles and practices, has proven itself to be **highly effective** when executed with proper discipline and focus. I (the author) have personally used it to establish several successful new business ventures, as well as to understand why other ventures that I've launched in the past weren't quite as successful.

Consequently, what you must do as a business leader is to emulate this process, using whichever of the Design Methods best suits your needs and purposes and the types of insights you need to develop at the time, for each stage of the process. If you emulate this process as we've just witnessed Intensifi execute it, then you and your organization too will be able to greatly increase the odds of success from it.

A broader extension of the Design Thinking process

This process is, in effect, an *extension* of the now well-honed and well-proven Design Thinking process to the broader and more comprehensive structural and functional elements of your business model. This works because there's no reason why the practices and methods of Design Thinking (used to define winning solutions) cannot also be extended and applied to the remainder of your business model, as long as there is a way to define and address that business model's discrete elements – something we've provided here.

Indeed, by so defining our business model in terms of its structural and functional attributes, as we've done here, we have the discrete elements we need to be able to leverage the Design Thinking *process*. The end result – as we'll see later with Intensifi – is in most cases business success, albeit not without additional learning and adaptation once we get into the real world. Experience has shown that using this process – while not a 100% guarantee of success – does significantly **increase** our chances of success once we actually hit the marketplace. This is because we hit the marketplace with a business model and a corresponding value proposition that have both been well-tested and well-validated for their market and business viability. For example, common mistakes that entrepreneurs and corporate intrapreneurs often make include the following:

- not understanding the real aspirations, motivations, and needs of their subjects (their "reason to buy"), so they launch solutions that go after the *wrong outcomes*, which of course do not resonate with these subjects, and so the subjects never adopt their solution;

- failing to understand how would-be customers prefer to *purchase and use* a solution, so they package it in a completely wrong way that's never able to drive marketplace adoption of it;

- failing to understand all the different *hurdles and barriers* that potential customers will face in trying to change to their solution (especially from an *ecosystem* standpoint), so they never address those hurdles and barriers to help the customers overcome them and adopt their solution.

Each of these are mistakes you can avoid **if and when you use the process taught herein**. Doing so gives you a value proposition and a business model that lets you actuate your solution in the marketplace (because it resonates with customers' true needs, wants, desires, and aspirations) and, at the same time, makes it easy for them to procure, use, and otherwise adopt your solution. In other words, it gives you the "right to play" in this particular market space, and also a "reason to win" in it.

A very repeatable – and institutionalize-able – process

The even greater takeaway here is that this is a process that's **incredibly repeatable**. It's a structured and repeatable process that lets us learn the necessary insights quickly, cost-effectively, and on demand. Consequently, once we've learned and mastered the process – including the many Design Methods that help support it – we're able to leverage it *repeatedly* to produce **ongoing, sequential successes** – one after the other. This includes, just as importantly, using it to learn where we need to *kill* certain endeavors and *not* take them to market. Both represent wins for an organization because they both yield capital efficiency for it.

This repeatability is *why* the process can be so effectively **institutionalized** inside of business organizations. It's a process that any business leader (with sufficient patience and care) can learn, and a process that those with the dispositions for discovery-oriented work can execute consistently well. This leads to ongoing, indefinite success for an organization applying it.

Making this process happen consistently in your organization

Given that the process for human-centered business model innovation (as taught herein) is a learnable and repeatable process – one that can be used over and over again for repeated successes – it's one that can be institutionalized inside any organization.

To do so, there are a number of important *principles* that must be adhered to, as well as a number of important *activities* that have to be undertaken. These are both explained next.

Applying the guiding principles

To institutionalize this process, you need to adhere to the following eight principles:

1. This process is incredibly well suited to any situation where an organization wants to take the time to define, develop, and deliver a truly *breakthrough business model* to address a particular unmet, unsatisfied, or emerging market situation.

2. This process requires a certain amount of *time, energy*, and *effort* to execute. Generally speaking, it cannot be rushed if it is to succeed. The months it may require to execute are almost always compensated by the years of languishing market failures that it *avoids*.

3. This is *not* a linear process. Each step of this process – as well as the process as a whole – must be allowed to be *iterative*, especially in its convergent stages (where new insights often arise that were missed previously). Since new insights are constantly being learned throughout the process, teams often have to step back and revisit a prior decision before being able to move on to their next step. We sometimes call this giving teams the *headroom* they need to think and the *elbow room* they need to experiment.

4. Throughout this process, the five *discovery skills* (observing, questioning, experimenting, networking, and associating) will be constantly called upon. They each play a crucial role in being able to execute the process well.

5. *Imagination* and *creativity* should each be applied in their respective best places – where they best serve the process. Imagination is the domain of imagining different ideal states, which is very useful for forming different hypotheses and assumptions about a situation. Creativity is the domain of resourcefully contemplating new solutions to a problem, which is very useful in brainstorming new solution concepts. When used in their respective places, both of these serve the process well.

6. Learning somewhere in this process that a particular line of business being pursued is *not* going to be viable – and thus *not* pan out – is **not a failure**; it's a **learning step**. That sort of learning is *normal* in this process. Not all proposed lines of business that are subjected to this process are going to work out. It's the job of this process to learn that and prevent the organization from going any further down that path. If and when it does so, it represents a **success** for an organization – in that it just prevented the organization from suffering untold losses down the road. That, in turn, allows the organization to move on to other efforts that may in fact prove far more viable and worthwhile.

7. Organizations should *never* try to "cram" this process inside their normal, routine Product Development efforts. It is not well suited for that, as such routine efforts demand a relatively fast pace with quick convergence, typically involving an extrapolation of some existing business model and offering. In other words, those endeavors are built on an *existing problem-solution construct*. This means they assume that the problem, and therefore its ideal solution, are already well understood from the very beginning. This process, in contrast, requires far more time and effort, as it involves *reframing the problem* into a completely new one, leading to a completely *different* type of business model and solution.

8. Organizations *should*, however, try to institutionalize the *thinking* behind this process into their culture. This will be one where they're always working out of a desire for *empathy* for their customer so that, whenever appropriate, they can in fact reframe *perceived problems* into *real problems*, delivering fundamentally better value for their customers (and new ones too).

Adhering to these principles will allow an organization to deploy this process effectively. Moreover, using these principles will empower the organization to embed the human-centered design philosophy and way of thinking into their corporate psyche and culture. That, in and of itself, can pay back huge dividends in the long run.

This is important because all organizations tend toward corporate inertia. Once they have success, they sit back and exploit that success endlessly – known as the "exploit" (versus "explore") mode. This is great for them, so long as it doesn't distract them from always asking, "*What's next?... How can we stay attuned to our markets' evolving needs, desires, and expectations, as well as to any new situational opportunities arising around us?*" Otherwise, they'll be at risk of being disrupted by others who do ask these questions (such as, in a sense, the now-famous *Innovator's Dilemma*). This is precisely why Steve Jobs said in his 2005 Stanford commencement speech (quoting from the final issue of *The Whole Earth Catalog*), "*Stay hungry, stay foolish.*" Staying "hungry" – via the Design Thinking mindset – lets us remain fresh and up to date, and therefore, we are able to leverage both incremental and disruptive innovations as needed to ensure our ongoing, long-term survival in the world.

Undertaking the necessary activities

To institutionalize this process), the following seven activities have to be pursued:

1. Establish a formal **function** in the organization (a group of people) that "owns" this process and serves as its hub. This function serves as the process' *Center of Excellence*, operating as the experts in the process who train others on it, including coaching them on how to use it as they work to do so.

2. Establish the necessary **roles** to support this function. This should be individuals who enjoy processes such as these and teaching and mentoring others in the process.

3. Onboard key **stakeholders** to the effort, starting with its main *Sponsor*. Identify the main Sponsor of the process and get them working to promote its adoption wherever it's appropriate in an organization. Also, identify other important stakeholders and recruit them to serve as *Champions* who support its use in their areas of the organization (wherever it's needed).

4. **Document** the process, including how it is to be executed in the specific context of a particular organization. This may, on account of various structural, cultural, and other organizational factors, involve slight variations on what has been presented herein (although it is likely not too far from it).

5. **Disseminate** the process, via its documentation, its training, its coaching, and its overall promotion. Ensure that everyone in an organization who needs to understand and use the process has the opportunity and ability to do so.

6. **Use** the process everywhere in an organization that it has a role to play. Furthermore, track its usage, how it's being used, and the outcomes it produces.

7. **Publicize** the results of using it, both internally inside the organization and, in certain cases, outside the organization. Its success stories will help maintain its widespread adoption and use over time.

By undertaking these activities – together with the aforementioned principles – an organization can fully *institutionalize* this process and have it become a repeatable one inside the organization.

Over time, it is to be expected that an organization will become increasingly more mature and capable with the process, as more and more individuals and teams master it and its methods. Eventually, it can – if the appropriate discipline is maintained – become an ingrained element of how the organization operates in the context of launching new lines of business. It also helps the organization steer away from innovation and business model design "theater" (with their endless pitfalls), ensuring instead that it is always profitably delivering and recapturing new value in and out of the marketplace – a crucial outcome for ongoing success.

Applying human-centered business model innovation to digital transformation

Much has been written and taught about *Digital Transformation*, including how dismally unsuccessful so many of its efforts have been. Certainly, Digital Transformation holds the promise and hope of a far better future – for both a business and its customers (a win-win). But getting there is a path that's often fraught with stumbles and downfalls. Fortunately, there's a way forward based on the things taught in this book.

Avoiding the big mistake of "digitalizing today"

One of the clear themes that commonly underlie the aforementioned failures is the very tempting tendency to simply digitalize one's *existing business model*, with its current practices and processes. This is regardless of how good or bad these happen to be, as well as how digitalizing them may make them better or worse.

Doing this – especially digitalizing bad processes – is *never, ever* a recipe for success. Instead, it's often a recipe for just *amplifying* the current shortcomings of those processes, turning them into even bigger and more glaring failures. Consequently, you should never, ever just mindlessly digitalize your existing business model and its practices without first giving them both a lot of thought and consideration, looking at where they can be altered and streamlined for a far better customer experience.

Starting over – going back to first principles

The way we do this is by going back to the very beginning and starting over with **first principles**.

This means starting over with the very basic questions, "*What is our customer trying to achieve here?*" and "*What are we doing on their behalf to help facilitate that outcome?*"

We do this by forgetting everything we currently know about a situation and about how we *currently* address that customer outcome, **starting over** from *ground zero* with a brand-new and far more effective **digital-native process** (not a digitalized version of our current process). Crafting new, better, and much more effective *digital-native processes* produces a **far better customer experience** than our customers currently have, and certainly far better than they'd have if we just digitalized our existing processes.

This is very important because organizations often only get one chance to get this right before it's too late, especially if they're a new venture of some sort. Simply digitalizing some existing business model or process can turn into a very expensive (and fatal) failure. Therefore, it's imperative that we do *not* do this and, instead, start over with an entirely new digital-native business model and process that are well-suited to the situation.

It's inherent in Design Thinking

Now, the thing is, starting over at ground zero with first principles is inherently *built into* the Design Thinking process, on account of the human-centered design philosophy that undergirds it.

In that process, we forget **everything** we *believe we know* about the current process and situation and assume a *Beginner's Mindset*. In so doing, we start over from ground zero and learn all about what *outcome* our customer is trying to achieve, as well as why that outcome is so important and valuable to them. Those *are*, indeed, the first principles of our particular situation.

And so, to the extent that we require changes to our broader *business model* for the sake of Digital Transformation, this human-centered business model innovation process is in fact the process we're going to want to use. We will simply apply it to whichever of the functional attributes of our business model warrants reworking.

Therefore, what we must do in this context is to use this process while keeping in mind that an important element of our goal is to replace certain existing (non-digital) practices and processes with far better *digital* practices and processes that achieve the desired outcome. This will, more often than not, result in a far better and much more streamlined customer experience – usually one with fewer steps and actions, on account of the digital information being shared across the business model.

The human-centered business model innovation process is, thus, one that will prove very beneficial and pivotal to a successful Digital Transformation effort.

Winning today, tomorrow, and the day after tomorrow

If this process is to be one that will continue to serve an organization for decades to come, then it should not be used in isolation. Instead, it should be married with appropriate *strategic foresight and futuring* efforts so that it can address **emerging situations** well before they become mainstream. Failing to do this can mean an important new window of opportunity is missed, or perhaps a major new challenge is not addressed in adequate time to be effective – neither outcome is desirable.

Understanding the respective purposes of foresight and futuring

The purpose of **strategic foresight** is to scan your environment and horizon for signals of trends and events happening in and around them that stand to *impact* an organization, its environment, and its work at some point in the future. Based on those signals, the organization then analyzes those trends and events (and their drivers) so that they can construct multiple *plausible future scenarios* at different points in the future. This helps them to avoid the fallacy of assuming and expecting *one future* (the linear extrapolation of their present) and, instead, entertain the much more valid notion that our future can involve any number of different scenarios – each of which needs to be understood, contemplated, and possibly prepared for.

If the purpose of strategic foresight is to *understand* the range of plausible future scenarios before us, the purpose of **strategic futuring** is to *prepare* for those future scenarios. As such, this involves an organization casting a compelling vision for its future, engaging in collective prospection about its options for that future (with the goal of always increasing its optionality), and finally, engaging in strategy development efforts to define actual strategies to use today, shaping and impacting the future to become more like what the organization wants it to be (known as its *normative future*).

Merging these with human-centered business model innovation

Understanding this, it starts to become increasingly apparent that it can prove difficult to apply the human-centered business model innovation process if we don't understand the possible futures that we apply it to. In other words, studying only today's situations limits us to addressing only today's situations. It doesn't do a very good job of helping us to address *tomorrow's situations*. It is only by *studying* tomorrow's (potential) situations that we're able to address those prospective future situations. That is indeed the difference between *insight* and *foresight*.

Consequently, if we are to extend the use of human-centered business model innovation *beyond* the insights that we're able to gather today – to instead start thinking about the emerging situations and needs of tomorrow and what their most ideal business models might be – then we have to *combine* these respective practices. This can be done by role-playing the situation where a particular future scenario is assumed to be our current reality, and then trying to unpack that situation in as much detail as possible via this process. Of course, role-playing that situation as though it were our current reality means we'll have to make certain *assumptions* about the scenario in terms of what it looks like and how it operates. But at least making such informed and intelligent assumptions about the future will get us further ahead (often much further ahead) than not exploring them at all.

Thus, if we can develop the skill of fleshing out different future scenarios and then studying them with the same fervor and focus that we use for our current situations, we'll be able to extend and apply this process to help us plan and prepare for our future. That, in turn, will let the process serve us for decades yet to come.

Reflections – what about the future?

A final set of questions I'd like to leave us all with are, "*Where do we take human-centered business model innovation in the future?*" and "*What might it look like 10, 20, 30, or even 50 years from now?*" I'd like to address that with a set of tenets if I may.

Tenet one – our future is human

To start with, our future will always be human. It will, therefore, be human-centric as well. This is something we must keep in mind as we march forward into an ever more technologically advanced society, anchored in AI and other key technologies. Our future will always be human.

This is because we are ourselves human and, as such, desire and crave human relationships and interaction. Thus, the more immersed we become in our different technologies, the more we'll have to cultivate deep human relationships, resulting in all manner of human-centered scenarios ahead of us.

In fact, human attributes such as caring, empathy, love, and trust simply *can't* be replicated inside of technology. They're innately human attributes – meaning they will never *truly* exist inside of a machine, only inside humans.

Likewise, machines cannot experience what humans experience in the ways that humans experience them. They can't be accepted to their preferred university, hired into their dream job, get fired from that job, fall in love, get married, have children, and so on – not in the way that a human being can. Therefore, the future will always be human – meaning we'll always need human-centered business models to address real human needs.

Tenet two – humans operate in tribes

For reasons both psychological and anthropological, human beings tend to think and operate in terms of "their tribe." We are, in essence, **tribal beings**; we have the need to "belong" (even if only in our minds) to certain groups possessing certain distinguishable identities. We then derive some element of our own personal identity from that tribe.

Therefore, when thinking about solutions and the businesses that deliver those solutions, we should think in terms of these "tribes," as that is where people will draw their associations to the solutions. For example, take Red Bull (the energy drink). It's tribe – as so well established in its marketing efforts – is the extreme athlete. Now, in reality, most people who actually consume this beverage are *not* extreme athletes, but that is nevertheless the tribe they associate with. The same with Harley Davidson. Most people who ride its motorcycles don't necessarily bear the appearance of a hardened biker, but nevertheless, that's the tribe the brand is associated with, and therefore those who use its offerings have at least some aspect of their identity associated with that tribe. In other words, whenever I use the offerings of Brand X (name your favorite iconic brand), I'm a part of its tribe. This sort of identity association is, in reality, how many consumers tend to operate. It's clearly a process that's driven out of social and emotional associations, not out of purely functional needs.

In writing this book, I interviewed Erica Eden, founder of Citizen Collab in New York City and former Director of Global Design Innovation at Pepsi. When discussing what organizations and entrepreneurs tend to get *wrong* in the process of developing their business model (and thus what should they be doing *differently*), Erica shared the following incredible insight with me:

> Innovators need to start with the tribe – not the brand. The consumer groups are already out there, and their need is already out there – so you can work on solving a real problem that group already has! But you first need to *identify* that group. And you do this via their "tribe." Finding a "tribe" of people is far better than trying to talk to, or research, the masses. The tribe will inform you on behalf of the masses! And where do we find the "tribal spokespersons" for these "tribes"? They're the outliers on the very front end of these groups – those at its extreme front (its extreme users). Find the problem they're having, and then turn solving that problem into something that's premium and desirable for the masses. But also use these extreme users as the "tribal spokespersons" – the identifying persona – for the tribe, as doing so will help to draw in the masses to the tribe.

So, in thinking about (in terms of the future) who to solve problems for, which of their problems to solve, and how to solve those problems, look for where you can identify a "tribe" with a commonly-held need that a tribal identity can be built around. Doing this will, in most cases, unlock even more value in the market.

Tenet three – technology will increasingly aid us

While the future will always be human, we'll increasingly use technology in our human-centered business model innovation process. AI in particular will help us to better understand our fellow (emotional and irrational) human beings as we work with the process.

It's fair, therefore, to accept that different machine learning models and Generative AI tools will become increasingly embedded inside the different tools we use to study, analyze, and understand human behaviors. This is especially true of those behaviors rooted in contexts such as behavioral economics, which have a statistical base. AI tools are becoming increasingly better at teasing out the hidden patterns in such behavioral data, as well as at detecting the different influencing factors involved (possible causalities).

Even at the individual level – such as what we encounter when doing User Research – AI tools such as emotion detection can help us (with increasing accuracy) detect the actual emotions that our subjects experience at any given time. By using such tools, we can get a better read of their emotional and visceral responses to things, which adds further depth and richness to our learning. That, in turn, makes our learning that much more specific, precise, and accurate, resulting in an even better business model to use.

These are just a couple of examples. Ultimately, there'll be countless more (and new) ways that we'll leverage technologies to aid us in this pursuit of the human-centered business model.

This all being said, we should never expect this process to become 100% fully automated. Since it's actually about humans, it will always require humans to set and pursue its distinctive goals. And indeed, as we continue to offload so much of our cognitive work to machines, we'll be left to focus (that much more intensely) on the specific *human* and *social* elements of that work.

Tenet four – human-centered business models will become increasingly important

While it may seem counterintuitive at first, given how much AI and other technologies are being integrated into our lives and work, the reality is that – precisely because our future will be human – the presence and use of human-centered business models will, in the future, become increasingly important to us.

Indeed, in time, all technology will become commoditized. This means the *only way* businesses can truly stand out in such a landscape is by becoming increasingly more human themselves. That, in turn, will require their business models to, over time, become increasingly more human-centric.

Wasn't it, after all, a big part of the original hope and dream of Digital Transformation that we (i.e., businesses) would deliver far better business models that leveraged digital technologies to streamline both our business and customer experience, resulting in a better outcome for both parties (plus a more loyal and growing customer base)? It was indeed! The problem there, however, was that we focused too much on the technology and not enough on the humans. Now, by leveraging that technology, while focusing on the humans involved, we can in fact deliver a human-centric digital business model that actually achieves this hope and dream.

And so, our future will see the rise of the truly human-centered business model. This will be an innovative business model that truly stands out from the crowd and unleashes massively more value than ever before thought possible – all because it marries the technology to the human, with the human at the center.

We must also not forget that in order for there to be human-centered business models, there also have to be flourishing humans in our world. This means that we have to also leverage these business models to continue addressing all of the things that threaten us as flourishing humans – things such as climate change, poverty, disease, political conflict, and the other burdens upon humanity. Thus, these business models will be, in many ways, also humanity-centered business models.

The takeaway – how can, and should, we evolve alongside this?

Given these tenets and the imminent rise of the fully human-centered business model (as the primary means of standing out in an otherwise technology-glutted world), we face the question, *"How can we too evolve alongside this – to remain apace with it?"* That's an important question that we should all address and answer.

What all businesses must do to remain apace with this change is the following:

- Be purpose-driven. As an organization, have a very clear purpose that your employees are passionate about. Use that purpose to drive the organization to take meaningful actions that have a positive and lasting impact on the world – over and over again throughout the long term.

- Adopt a truly human-centered mindset. This is one that places the human being at the very center of everything you do, including using the means and resources available to you to help a human being achieve their desired outcomes (functional, emotional, social, and transformational) or whatever that outcome may be at a certain point in time.

- Understand, appreciate, and embrace the fact that the problems we'll have to address and solve in the future may bear very little resemblance to the problems our industry has had to solve in the past. This is largely on account of changing societal expectations around what, and how, solutions get purchased, used, consumed, and disposed of. This evolving reality quite often requires fresh new leadership with a fresh new mindset about our industry and its markets, with leaders possibly culled from other, more progressive industries and markets.

- Adopt, institutionalize, and master the human-centered business model innovation process, as prescribed herein.

- Make this process inclusive. Invite your customers and would-be customers into it, letting them help you co-create the future together. Doing this will go a long way toward cultivating a human tribe around your business and its brands. After all, communities are built by talking to people and understanding what they truly care about in life.

- Never, ever lose sight of solving human problems and meeting human needs, at their most foundational levels of aspiration and motivation. In the future, all business success will be rooted in this one thing, no matter what, or how much, technology gets involved. Never let the "shininess" of new technologies blind us from seeing, nor prevent us from solving, the human needs at hand. This *includes* understanding the broader sociological, anthropological, economic, and other cultural influencers that shape these human needs.

- Marry this process, constantly, with your strategic foresight and futuring efforts, ensuring that you can continually impact the future through new human-centered business models that are each relevant to their particular moment in time.

- Solve for all stakeholders – customers, employees, investors, communities, society, and the planet. We're all in this together. Nobody wins until we all win.

- Never let your past successes prevent you from shifting gears to achieve your prospective future successes. Hubris has no place in the future; the future belongs to the humble (and the mildly paranoid).

If businesses follow these nine precepts, and if they use the human-centered business model innovation process as prescribed herein, then they will maximize their chances of achieving long-term success and positive impact for the indefinite and ongoing future. *That* is certainly our aspiration as human business leaders!

So, ask yourself, what does – and should – this look like in our organization? What must our business do to adapt accordingly? Think this through as a leadership team, and then act on the resulting convictions.

Intensifi – outstanding results and a very repeatable process

So, first of all, let's get a confession out of the way. All along in this journey, we've all assumed that Ian, Zoe, Watson (and their team) were all conventional start-up founders. They've certainly operated that way, and they certainly looked that way. However, the truth is, they're not (and, thus, we have our plot twist).

They're actually a corporate team embedded inside of a larger organization. Their business unit – the *New Business Creation* unit – has as its charge uncovering major new opportunities for the organization and, accordingly, chartering new lines of business for it. As such, they have the full support of their corporate leadership, as well as that of countless other stakeholders in and around the organization (which explains where they secured their initial funding). But aside from that, the organization has allowed this team to operate very autonomously, with no unreasonable interference from them, other than to check in with them occasionally to assess their progress. Otherwise, they've operated like any other entrepreneurial start-up would. This also infers that Ian, Zoe, and Watson – and those who've helped them – possess certain dispositions and skills that aid them in this type of ambiguous discovery-oriented work.

We should also note that I (the author) have personally worked in such business units inside large corporate organizations, and I have witnessed first-hand the types of successes they can have when they leverage a process like this one *properly*, as well as the failures they can have when they don't.

So, with that confession out of the way, we can now see that Ian, Zoe, and Watson did in fact launch their new venture, did in fact secure a solid group of initial customers for it (as hoped for, according to their initial go-to-market strategy), did in fact go on to expand into the rest of their targeted market space (leveraging their ever-expanding partner ecosystem), and did in fact ultimately scale up this venture to a level that met their targeted metrics and goals (as set by them and agreed to by their organization). In effect, all seven of their business model's functions turned out to be very well-conceived and very well-defined by using this process.

This isn't to say that the real world didn't hand them some lessons. It did. In particular, they learned in their early days that their customers also wanted *an explicitly defined user community, operated and supported by Intensifi*. This was something that didn't show up in their initial research, mainly because the sample sizes involved were insufficient to detect this latent desire. Nevertheless, they were able to pivot and work this into their business model. It did not fundamentally change their Unique Value Proposition or any other functional elements of their business model. Rather, it simply clarified and expanded on it. Also, there were a few other "real-world lessons" that the market handed them in their initial start-up phase but nothing that they weren't able to handle, on account of having already established such a sound and solid business model in the first place. Ultimately, Intensifi went on to scale up their new venture into quite a large business.

It also wasn't all that long before *competitors* started to arrive in this market with similar competing offerings. But having established upfront that their main Sustainable Competitive Advantage would be a user experience that few others would be willing or able to emulate, Intensifi continued to enjoy strong market leadership in this (new) category – even when some of the entrants were established legacy vendors of wealth-management and similar platforms that had deep pockets. None were able to deliver the user experience that Intensifi had carved out for itself, and therefore, none were able to match Intensifi's brand power in this respect.

Moreover – and perhaps of greater interest here – is the fact that Intensifi's leaders went on to teach this process to dozens of other teams inside its organization, using it as the foundation for a far stronger, and more successful, New Business Creation business unit. They and their corporate leaders ultimately succeeded in institutionalizing the process as *the main process* for this unit and elsewhere in the organization. It was then used to launch several other very successful ventures in a similar manner. And indeed, its consistent use thereafter led to a far higher success rate than the unit had ever experienced before – not to mention unleashing massive new value to its customer base (thereby, also expanding that customer base).

Intensifi's parent organization also successfully integrated its strategic foresight and futuring efforts into this process. Via that combined practice, they were able to address countless fundamental (first principle) user needs around emerging trends and the new needs that those trends spawned, leading to a much more successful overall digital transformation of the organization and its business.

Ironically, one of Intensifi's advisors from academia pointed out to the team that their individual solution enabled an aspiration that actually went back for several years – one known as *Personal Futures*. Personal Futures is a concept rooted in the strategic futuring community, developed in the early 2000s and thereafter driven by professional futurist Dr. Verne Wheelwright. The *aim* of Personal Futures is to, indeed, optimize each area of a person's life by undertaking preemptive life-stage planning, based on different plausible future (personal) scenarios, and then develop proactive personal strategies that are well suited to each of those scenarios. Sound familiar? This is precisely why Intensifi built into its solution the ability to explore different personal future scenarios and undertake different "what if" assessments of various strategies in each scenario. As such, their solution is the very first *real tool* that enables people to carry out what Dr. Wheelwright had originally envisioned in his research of this field. For more on *Personal Futures*, refer to its website at www.personalfutures.net.

Finally, in terms of where Intensifi's parent organization intends to take human-centered business model innovation in the future, it certainly intends to follow the aforementioned nine precepts. Its ultimate goal is to become one of the leading practitioners of this practice anywhere in the world – not for the sake of the process itself but, rather, for the sake of its stakeholders (present and future) and its future business. It's well on its way to achieving that aspiration and the very admirable motivation behind it – namely, to maximize the amount of all-around positive impact it has on the world and everyone in it.

Summary

In this final chapter, we looked back on the journey we've just walked together and saw how we can leverage this human-centered business model innovation process for ongoing success, whether we're start-up founders or corporate venturers. This was an important takeaway, as any such process has to be repeatable so that it can be institutionalized and used indefinitely inside organizations for repeated success in the long run.

We then explored how we can, in fact, institutionalize the process. That included applying certain key principles and undertaking certain key activities, which together let us institutionalize the process in our organization and make it an integral element of how our organization operates, wherever it's appropriate.

We further explored the fact that this process is especially well-suited to Digital Transformation, as it requires us to go back to our first principles and rework our solutions and business models, according to the fundamental human needs involved. Doing this allows organizations to succeed at Digital Transformation after likely failing in the past.

We similarly explored how we can integrate this process with our strategic foresight and futuring efforts, extending it to emerging situations based on evolving trends and events in our environment or out along our horizon. Doing so lets us deliver ever newer human-centered business models relevant to their time.

Finally, we took a look at where human-centered business model innovation is likely to go in the future. That led us to three conclusions – namely, that our future is human, that technology will increasingly aid us in this process, and that human-centered business models will increasingly become the way organizations stand out. We also considered what our own organization must do to remain apace with this evolution.

This brings us to the end of our journey. We now have everything we need to unleash massive new value through innovative – and truly human-centered – business models. I hope you've enjoyed the journey!

In the way of the next steps for yourself, I invite you to look back over this whole book, getting a complete sense of its process and how its steps all combine to carry it out. Pay special attention to the Design Thinking process explored in *Chapters 9* through *Chapter 13*, as well as the complimentary Business Model Synthesis process explored in *Chapter 5*, which is used in *Chapter 14* to complete the

Design Thinking process for the overall business model. Then, work through this same process for yourself – Design Thinking your way through each function of your business model, starting with its Unique Value Proposition and the solution you'll use to support it (you can use any of the tools highlighted in *Chapter 6* for this as well). While doing this, bear in mind all of the insights we shared in *Chapter 8* on centering our business model on humans and making them the "hero of their story." If you apply all of these insights, principles, and activities to your own business model, then you too will come away with far higher chances of success in your own business ambition!

Further reading

- *Back to Human: How Great Leaders Create Connection in the Age of Isolation*, Dan Schawbel, Da Capo Lifelong Books, New York, NY, 2018.

- *It's Your Future… Make it a Good One!*, Verne Wheelwright, PhD, Personal Futures Network, Harlingen, TX, 2012.

Index

P

‹packt›

packtpub.com

Subscribe to our online digital library for full access to over 7,000 books and videos, as well as industry leading tools to help you plan your personal development and advance your career. For more information, please visit our website.

Why subscribe?

- Spend less time learning and more time coding with practical eBooks and Videos from over 4,000 industry professionals
- Improve your learning with Skill Plans built especially for you
- Get a free eBook or video every month
- Fully searchable for easy access to vital information
- Copy and paste, print, and bookmark content

Did you know that Packt offers eBook versions of every book published, with PDF and ePub files available? You can upgrade to the eBook version at packtpub.com and as a print book customer, you are entitled to a discount on the eBook copy. Get in touch with us at customercare@packtpub.com for more details.

At www.packtpub.com, you can also read a collection of free technical articles, sign up for a range of free newsletters, and receive exclusive discounts and offers on Packt books and eBooks.

Other Books You May Enjoy

If you enjoyed this book, you may be interested in these other books by Packt:

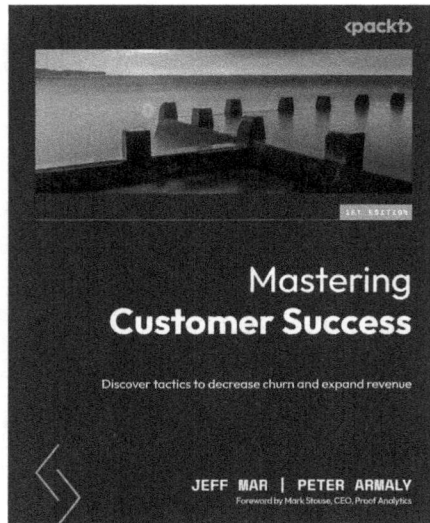

Mastering Customer Success

Jeff Mar, Peter Armaly

ISBN: 978-1-83546-903-3

- Drive higher customer retention and expansion rates with a customer-centric strategy
- Understand the essential role of measurement in achieving service delivery excellence
- Recognize the importance of the human dimension in vendor-customer relationships in the age of AI
- Refine engagement models by incorporating observations of customer behavior
- Discover techniques for creating ideal customer profiles
- Leverage technology to boost business relevance of CSMs
- Identify how to drive successful customer outcomes through collaboration

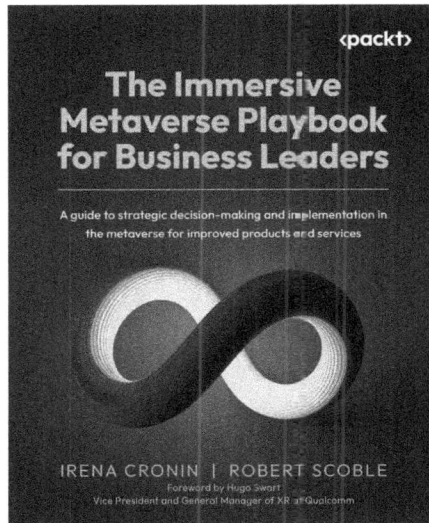

The Immersive Metaverse Playbook for Business Leaders

Irena Cronin, Robert Scoble

ISBN: 978-1-83763-284-8

- Get to grips with the concept of the metaverse, its origin, and its present state
- Understand how AR and VR strategically fit into the metaverse
- Delve into core technologies that power the metaverse
- Dig into use cases that enable finer strategic decision-making
- Understand the benefits and possible dangers of the metaverse
- Plan further ahead by understanding the future of the metaverse

Packt is searching for authors like you

If you're interested in becoming an author for Packt, please visit authors.packtpub.com and apply today. We have worked with thousands of developers and tech professionals, just like you, to help them share their insight with the global tech community. You can make a general application, apply for a specific hot topic that we are recruiting an author for, or submit your own idea.

Share Your Thoughts

Now you've finished *Designing the Human Business*, we'd love to hear your thoughts! Scan the QR code below to go straight to the Amazon review page for this book and share your feedback or leave a review on the site that you purchased it from.

https://packt.link/r/183508494X

Your review is important to us and the tech community and will help us make sure we're delivering excellent quality content.

Download a free PDF copy of this book

Thanks for purchasing this book!

Do you like to read on the go but are unable to carry your print books everywhere?

Is your eBook purchase not compatible with the device of your choice?

Don't worry, now with every Packt book you get a DRM-free PDF version of that book at no cost.

Read anywhere, any place, on any device. Search, copy, and paste code from your favorite technical books directly into your application.

The perks don't stop there, you can get exclusive access to discounts, newsletters, and great free content in your inbox daily

Follow these simple steps to get the benefits:

1. Scan the QR code or visit the link below

https://packt.link/free-ebook/978-1-83508-494-6

2. Submit your proof of purchase
3. That's it! We'll send your free PDF and other benefits to your email directly

www.ingramcontent.com/pod-product-compliance
Lightning Source LLC
Chambersburg PA
CBHW061738210326
41599CB00034B/6720